P9-DNB-102

Oh My Goddess!

ああっ女神さまっ The Fourth Goddess

Oh My Goddess!

ああっ女神さまっ *The Fourth Goddess*

v.12

STORY AND ART BY

Kosuke Fujishima

TRANSLATION BY

Dana Lewis & Toren Smith

LETTERING AND RETOUCH BY

Susie Lee & PC Orz

NEW HANOVER COUNTY
PUBLIC LIBRARY
201 CHESTNUT STREET
WILMINGTON, NC 28401

DARK HORSE COMICS®

PUBLISHER
Mike Richardson

SERIES EDITOR
Rachel Penn

COLLECTION EDITOR
Chris Warner

COLLECTION DESIGNER
Amy Arendts

ART DIRECTOR
Mark Cox

*English-language version produced by Studio Proteus
for Dark Horse Comics, Inc.*

OH MY GODDESS! vol. XII: The Fourth Goddess

© 1999, 2001 by Kosuke Fujishima. All rights reserved. First published in Japan by Kodansha, Ltd., Tokyo. English translation rights arranged through Kodansha Ltd. This English-language edition © 1999, 2001 Studio Proteus and Dark Horse Comics, Inc. All other material © 2001 Dark Horse Comics, Inc. All rights reserved. No portion of this publication may be reproduced, in any form or by any means, without the express written permission of the copyright holders. Names, characters, places, and incidents featured in this publication are either the product of the author's imagination or are used fictitiously. Any resemblance to actual persons (living or dead), events, institutions, or locales, without satiric intent, is coincidental. Dark Horse Comics® and the Dark Horse logo are trademarks of Dark Horse Comics, Inc., registered in various categories and countries. All rights reserved.

This volume collects issues one through eight of the Dark Horse comic book series *Oh My Goddess! Part VII*.

Published by
Dark Horse Comics, Inc.
10956 SE Main Street
Milwaukie, OR 97222

www.darkhorse.com

To find a comics shop in your area, call the Comic Shop
Locator Service toll-free at 1-888-266-4226

First edition: October 2001
ISBN: 1-56971-551-3

3 5 7 9 10 8 6 4 2
Printed in Canada

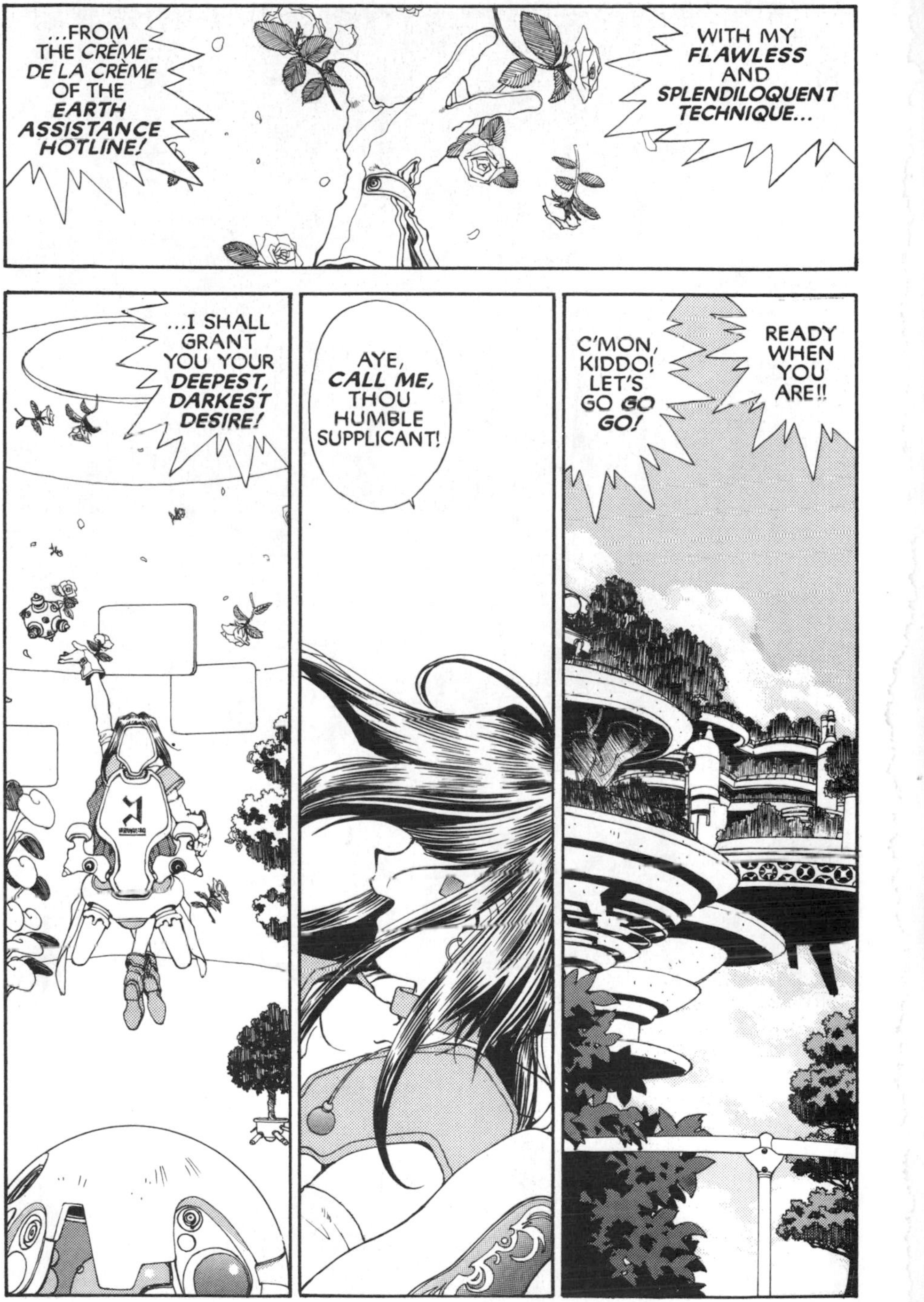
...FROM THE CRÈME DE LA CRÈME OF THE EARTH ASSISTANCE HOTLINE!
WITH MY FLAWLESS AND SPLENDILOQUENT TECHNIQUE...
...I SHALL GRANT YOU YOUR DEEPEST, DARKEST DESIRE!
AYE, CALL ME, THOU HUMBLE SUPPLICANT!
C'MON, KIDDO! LET'S GO GO GO!
READY WHEN YOU ARE!!

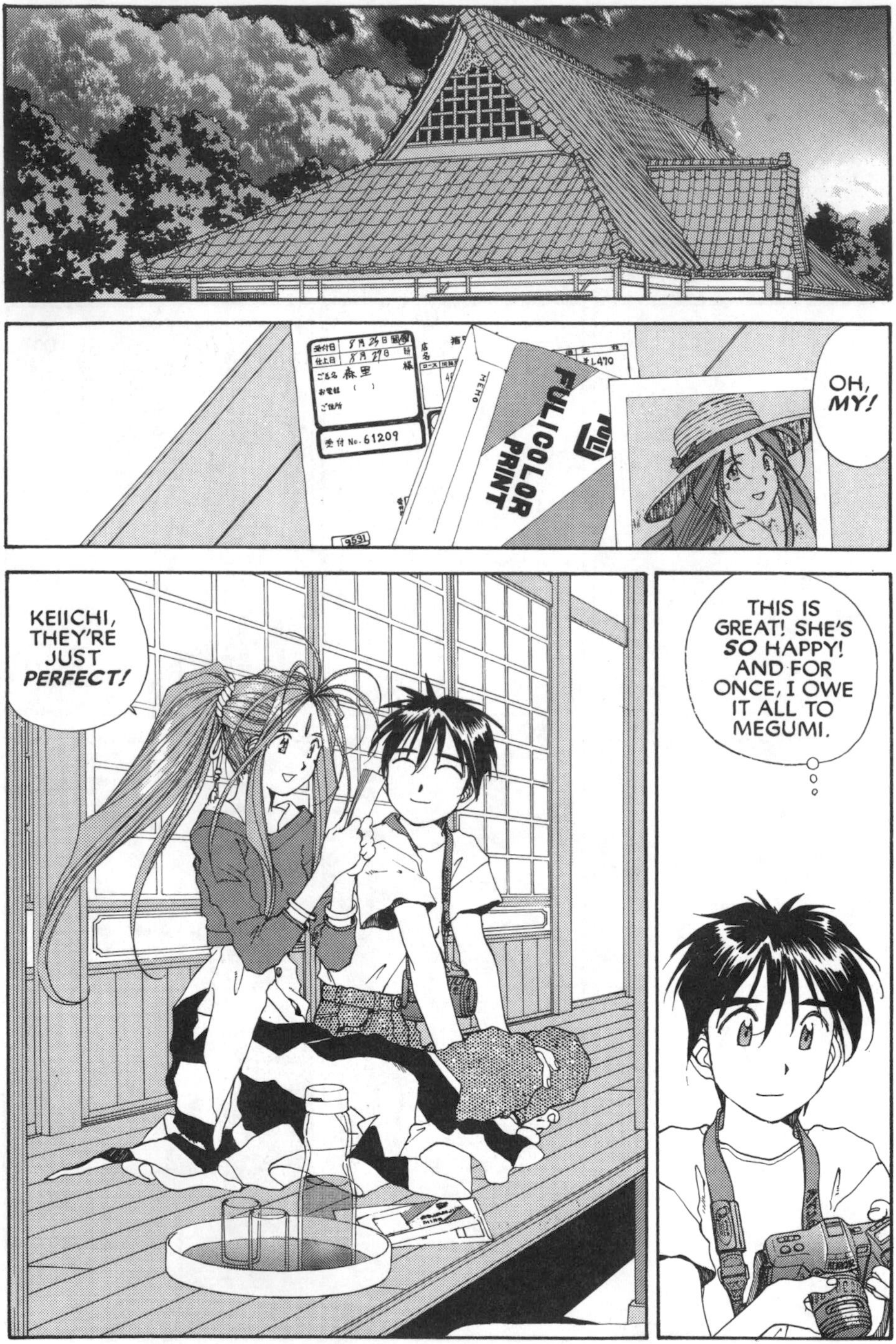
受付No. 61209
FUJICOLOR PRINT
OH, MY!
KEIICHI, THEY'RE JUST PERFECT!
THIS IS GREAT! SHE'S SO HAPPY! AND FOR ONCE, I OWE IT ALL TO MEGUMI.

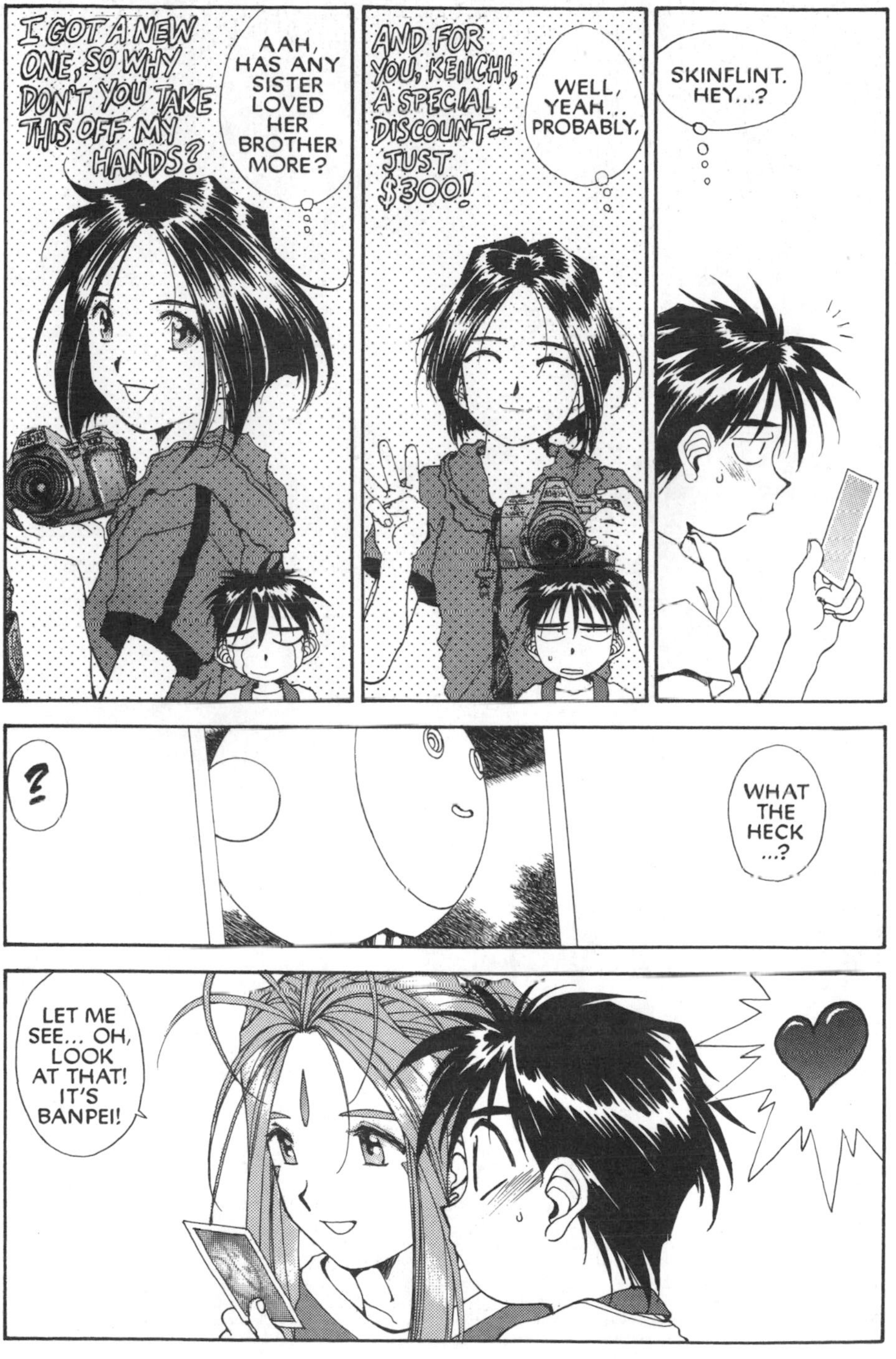
I GOT A NEW ONE, SO WHY DON'T YOU TAKE THIS OFF MY HANDS?
AAH, HAS ANY SISTER LOVED HER BROTHER MORE?
AND FOR YOU, KEIICHI, A SPECIAL DISCOUNT-- JUST $300!
WELL, YEAH... PROBABLY.
SKINFLINT. HEY...?
?
WHAT THE HECK ...?
LET ME SEE... OH, LOOK AT THAT! IT'S BANPEI!

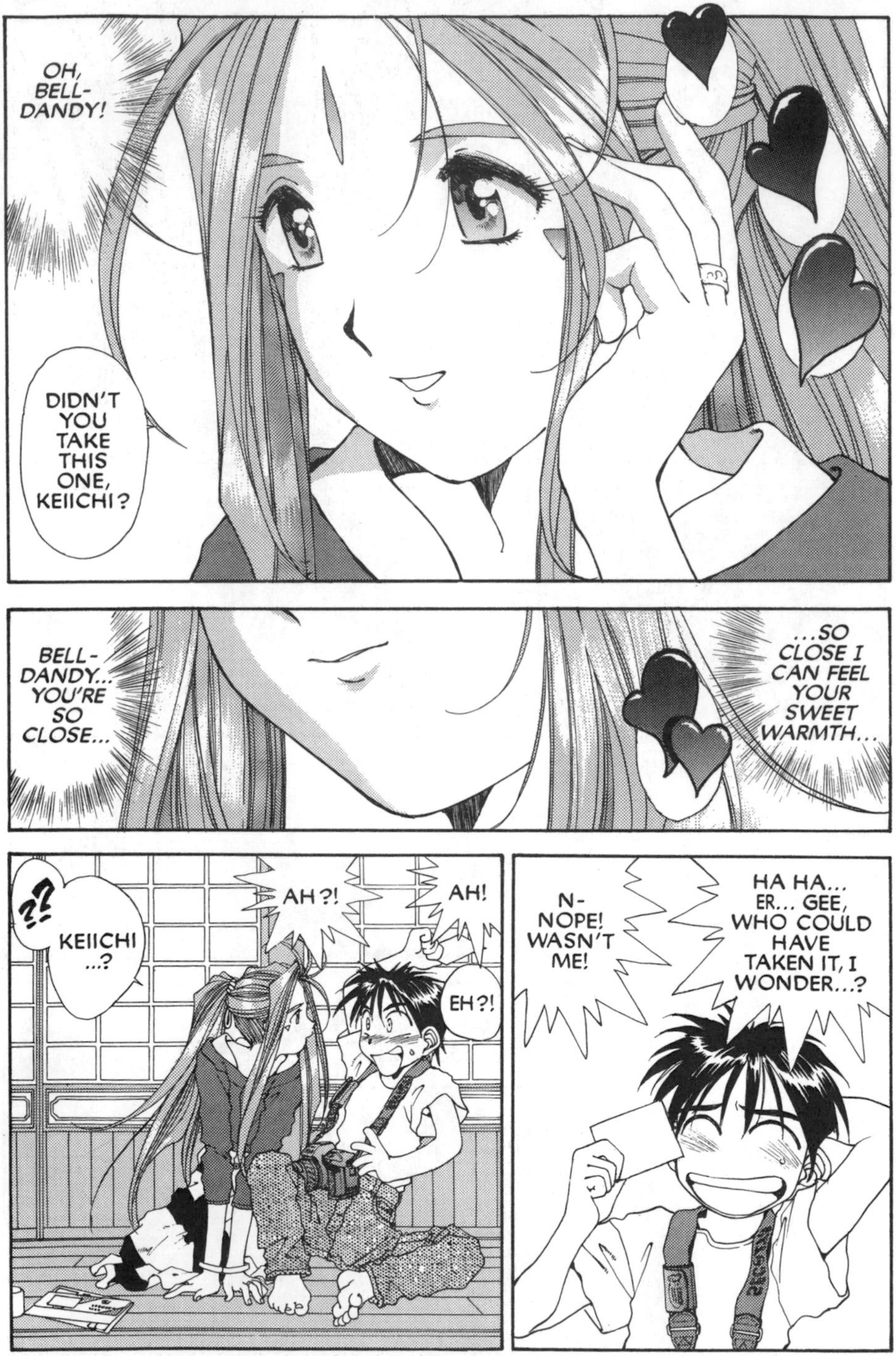
OH, BELL-DANDY!
DIDN'T YOU TAKE THIS ONE, KEIICHI?
BELL-DANDY... YOU'RE SO CLOSE...
...SO CLOSE I CAN FEEL YOUR SWEET WARMTH...
??
KEIICHI ...?
AH?!
AH!
EH?!
N-NOPE! WASN'T ME!
HA HA... ER... GEE, WHO COULD HAVE TAKEN IT, I WONDER...?

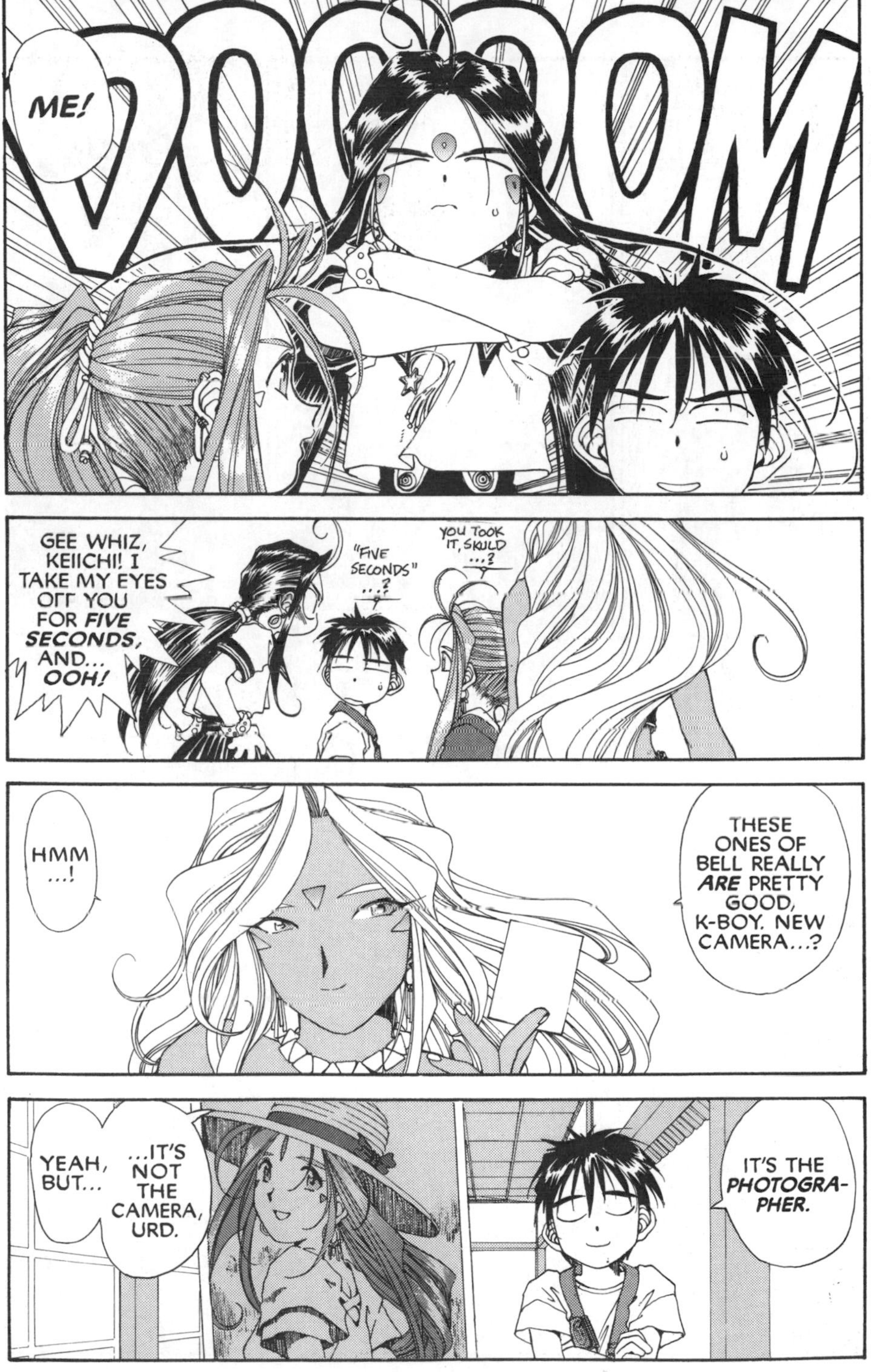
ME!
VOOOOOM
GEE WHIZ, KEIICHI! I TAKE MY EYES OFF YOU FOR FIVE SECONDS, AND... OOH!
"FIVE SECONDS" ...?
YOU TOOK IT, SKULD ...?
HMM ...!
THESE ONES OF BELL REALLY ARE PRETTY GOOD, K-BOY. NEW CAMERA...?
YEAH, BUT...
...IT'S NOT THE CAMERA, URD.
IT'S THE PHOTOGRAPHER.

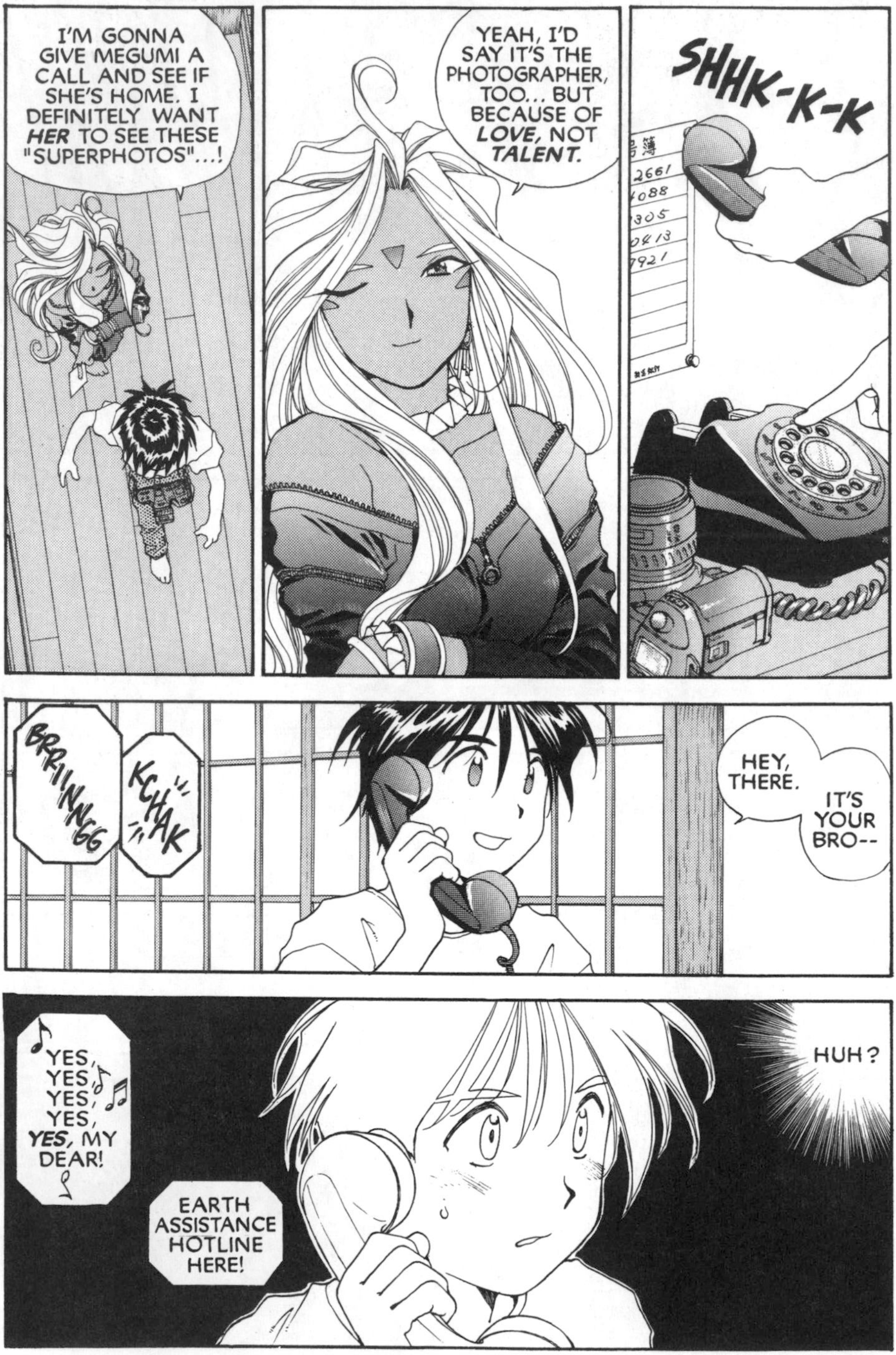
I'M GONNA GIVE MEGUMI A CALL AND SEE IF SHE'S HOME. I DEFINITELY WANT *HER* TO SEE THESE "SUPERPHOTOS"...!
YEAH, I'D SAY IT'S THE PHOTOGRAPHER, TOO... BUT BECAUSE OF *LOVE,* NOT *TALENT.*
SHHK-K-K
BRRIINNGG
KCHAK
HEY, THERE.
IT'S YOUR BRO--
YES, YES, YES, YES, *YES,* MY DEAR!
EARTH ASSISTANCE HOTLINE HERE!
HUH?

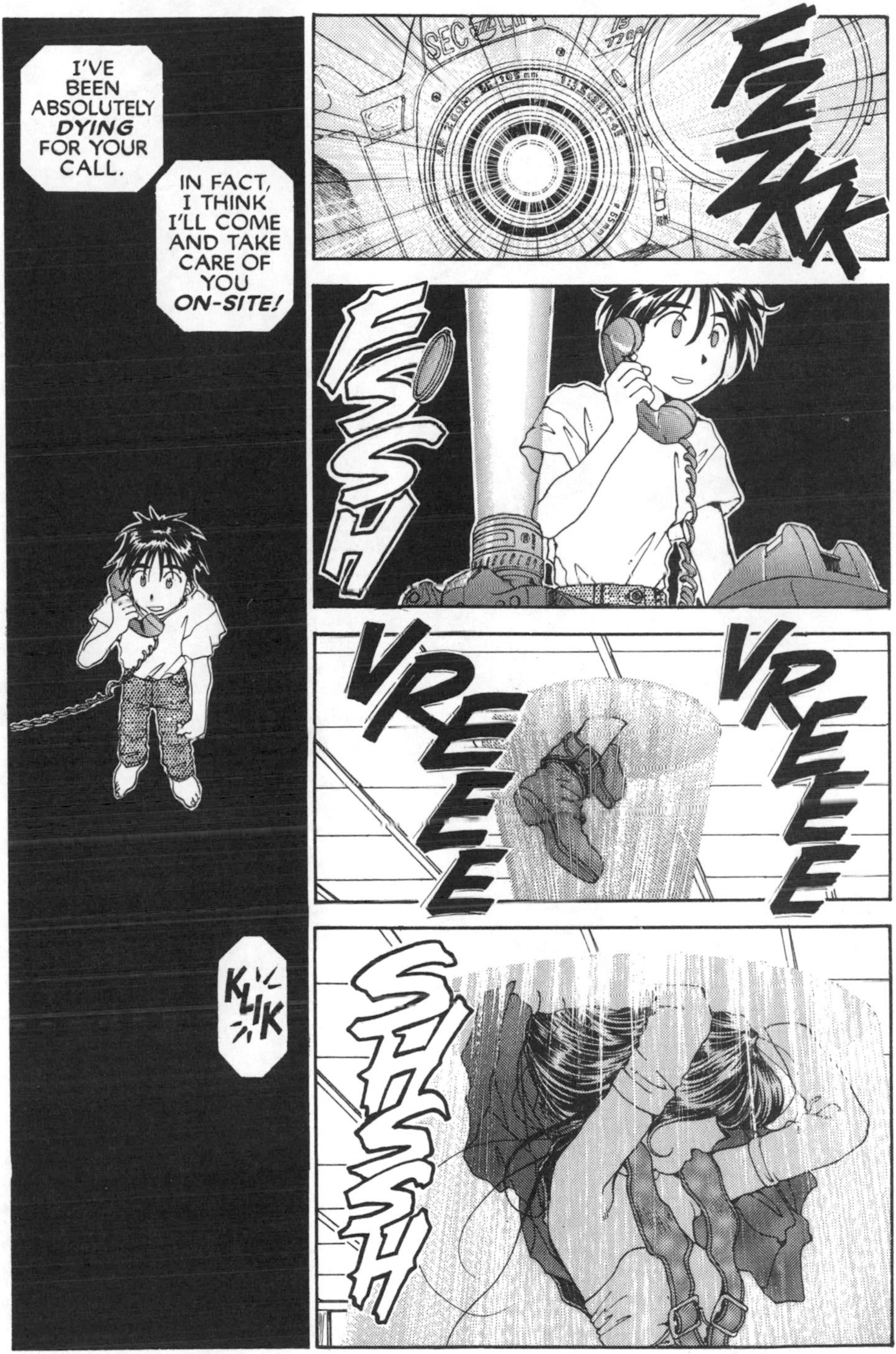
I'VE BEEN ABSOLUTELY DYING FOR YOUR CALL.
IN FACT, I THINK I'LL COME AND TAKE CARE OF YOU ON-SITE!
KLIK
FZZKKK
FSSSH
VREEEE
VREEEE
SHSSSH

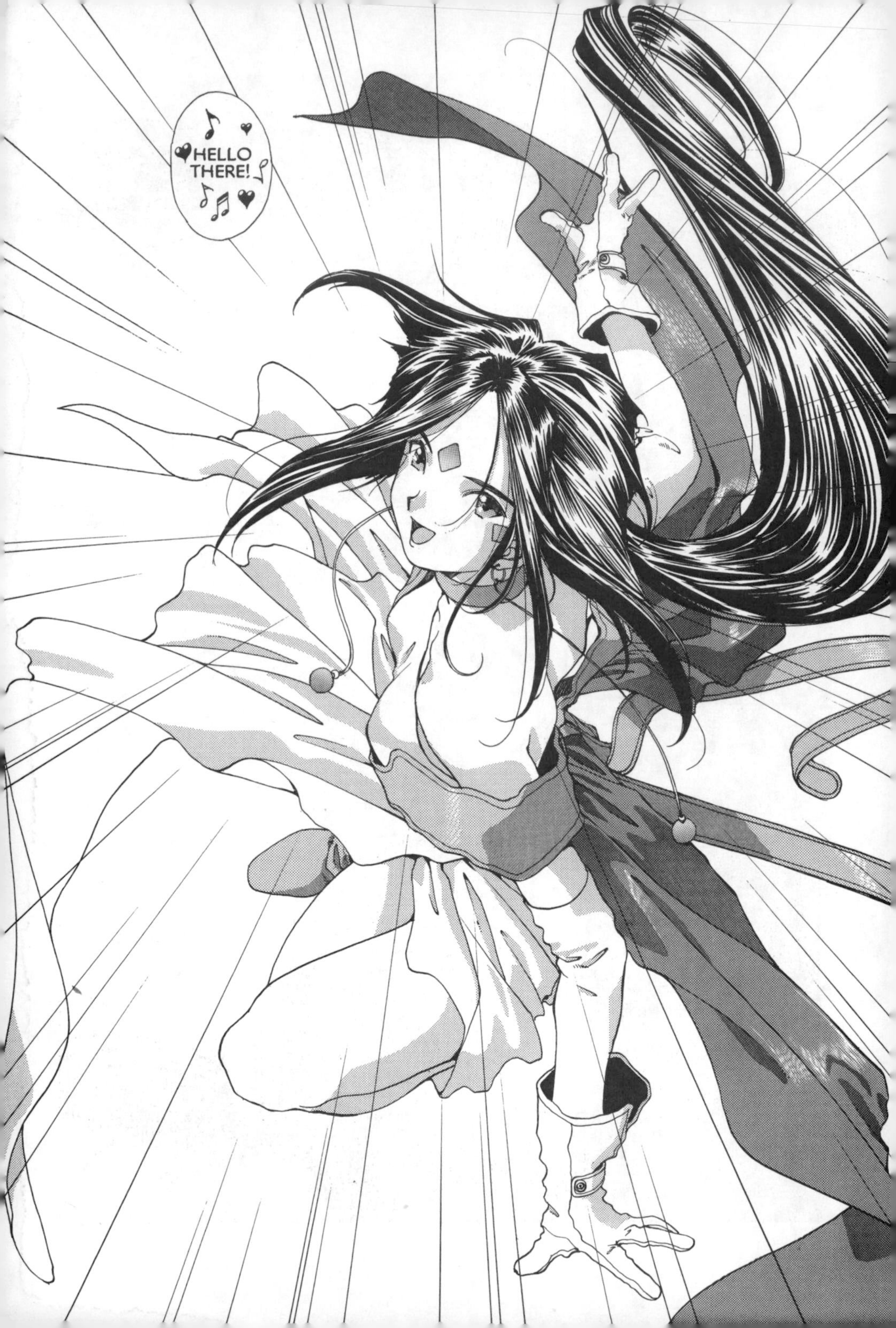
HELLO THERE!

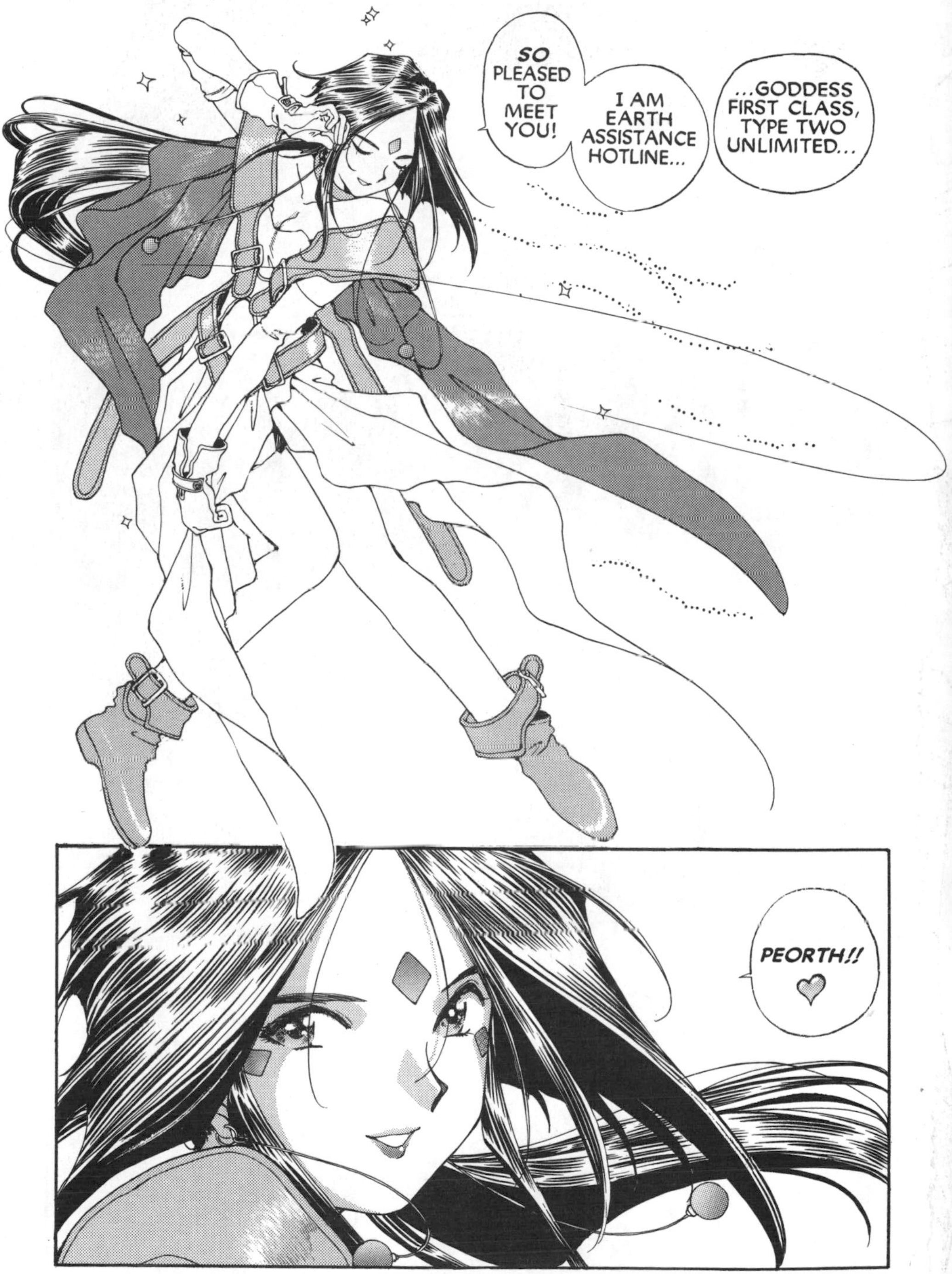
SO PLEASED TO MEET YOU!
I AM EARTH ASSISTANCE HOTLINE...
...GODDESS FIRST CLASS, TYPE TWO UNLIMITED...
PEORTH!! ♥

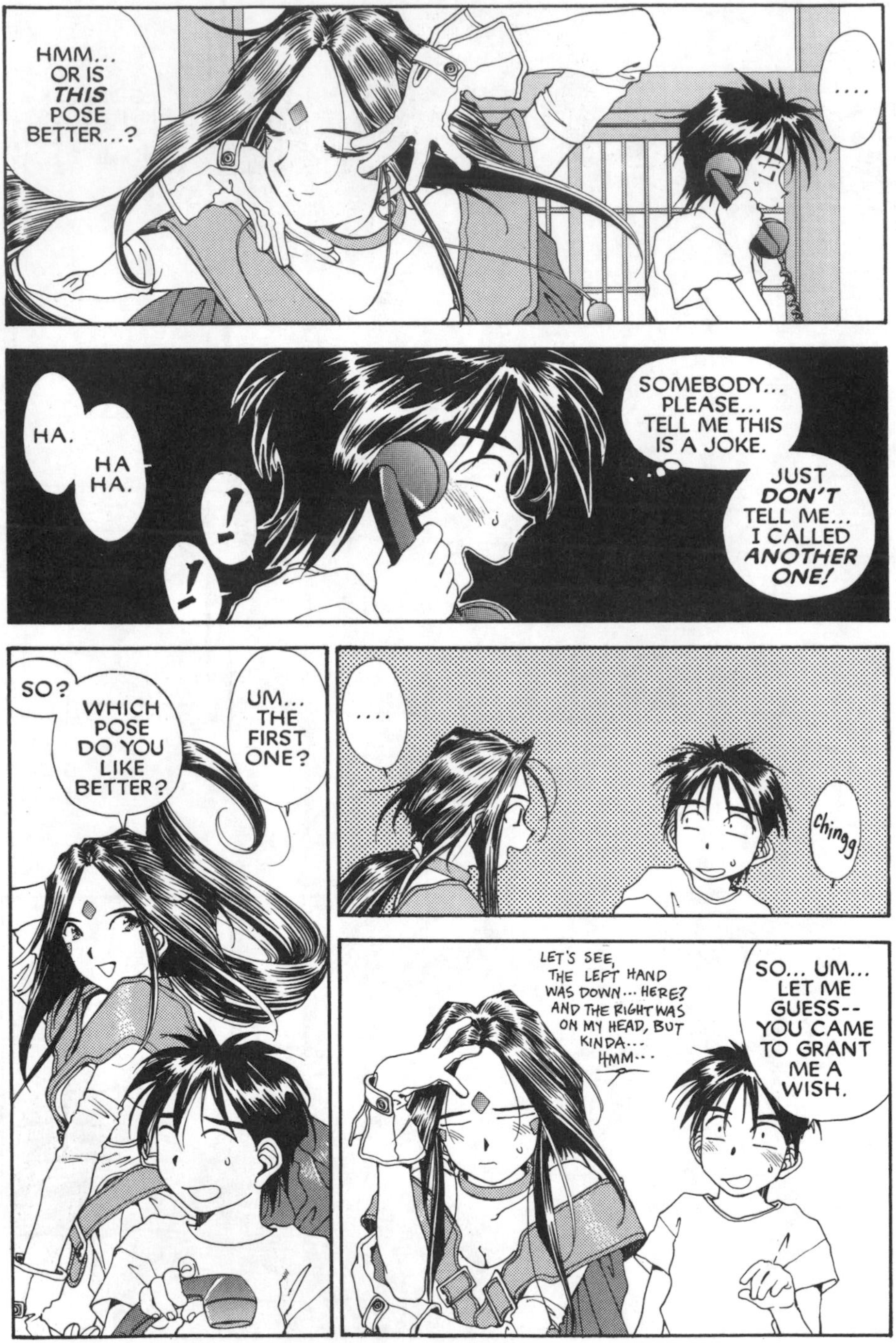
HMM... OR IS *THIS* POSE BETTER...?
....
HA.
HA HA.
!
!
SOMEBODY... PLEASE... TELL ME THIS IS A JOKE.
JUST *DON'T* TELL ME... I CALLED *ANOTHER ONE!*
SO?
WHICH POSE DO YOU LIKE BETTER?
UM... THE FIRST ONE?
....
Chingg
LET'S SEE, THE LEFT HAND WAS DOWN... HERE? AND THE RIGHT WAS ON MY HEAD, BUT KINDA... HMM...
SO... UM... LET ME GUESS-- YOU CAME TO GRANT ME A WISH.

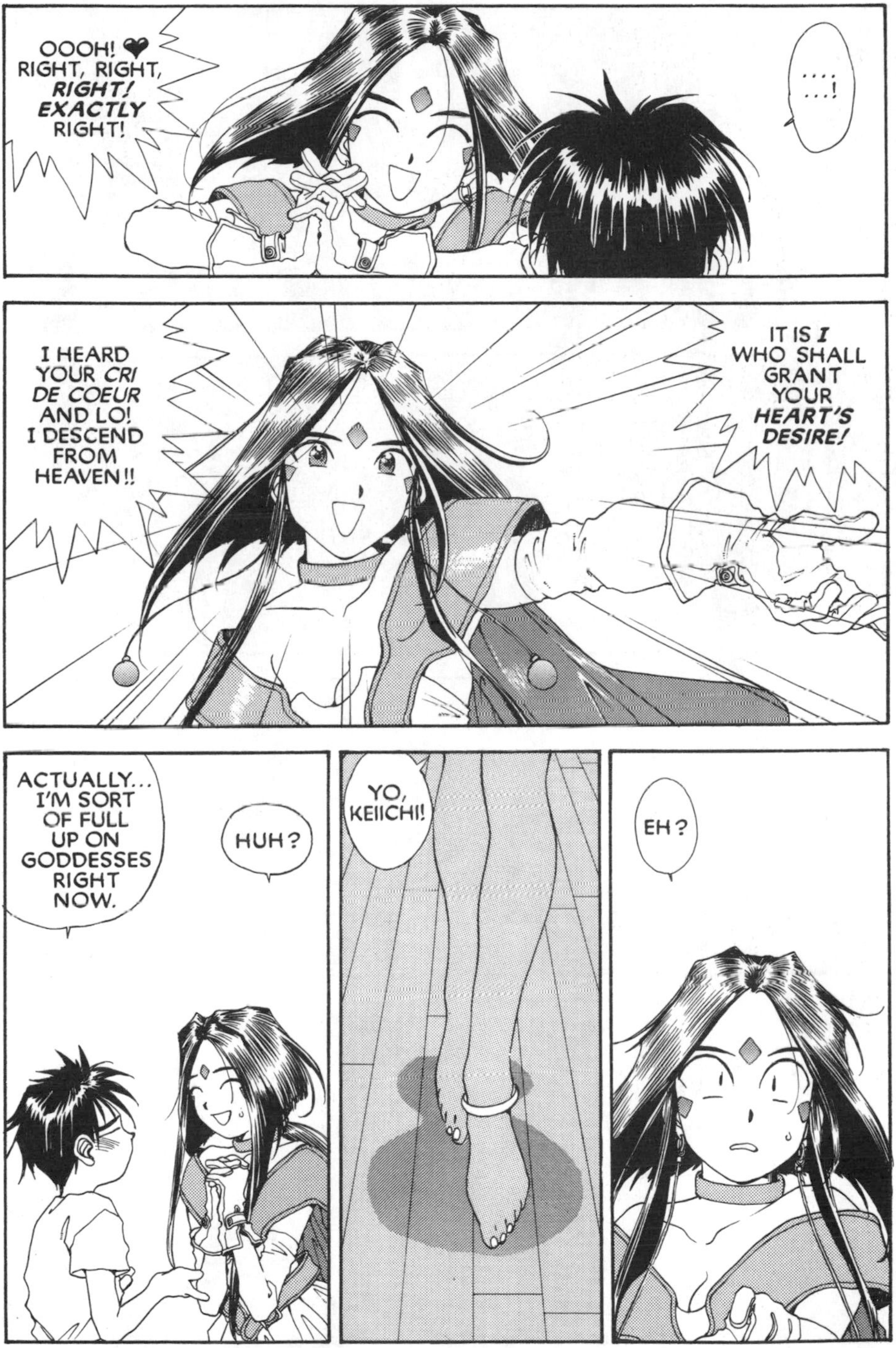
OOOH! ❤ RIGHT, RIGHT, RIGHT! EXACTLY RIGHT!
.....!
I HEARD YOUR CRI DE COEUR AND LO! I DESCEND FROM HEAVEN!!
IT IS I WHO SHALL GRANT YOUR HEART'S DESIRE!
ACTUALLY... I'M SORT OF FULL UP ON GODDESSES RIGHT NOW.
HUH?
YO, KEIICHI!
EH?

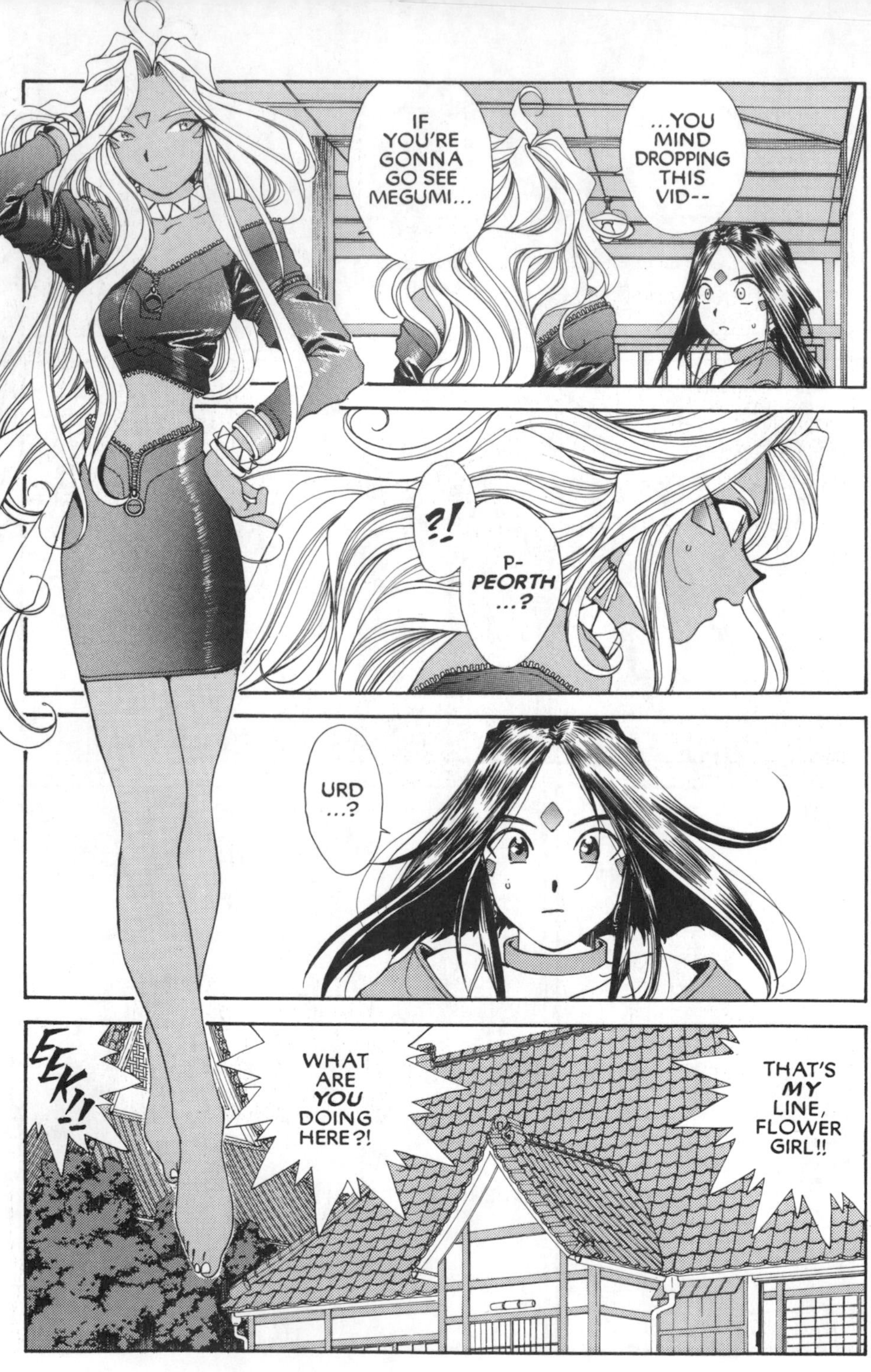
IF YOU'RE GONNA GO SEE MEGUMI...
...YOU MIND DROPPING THIS VID--
?!
P-PEORTH ...?
URD ...?
EEK!!
WHAT ARE YOU DOING HERE?!
THAT'S MY LINE, FLOWER GIRL!!

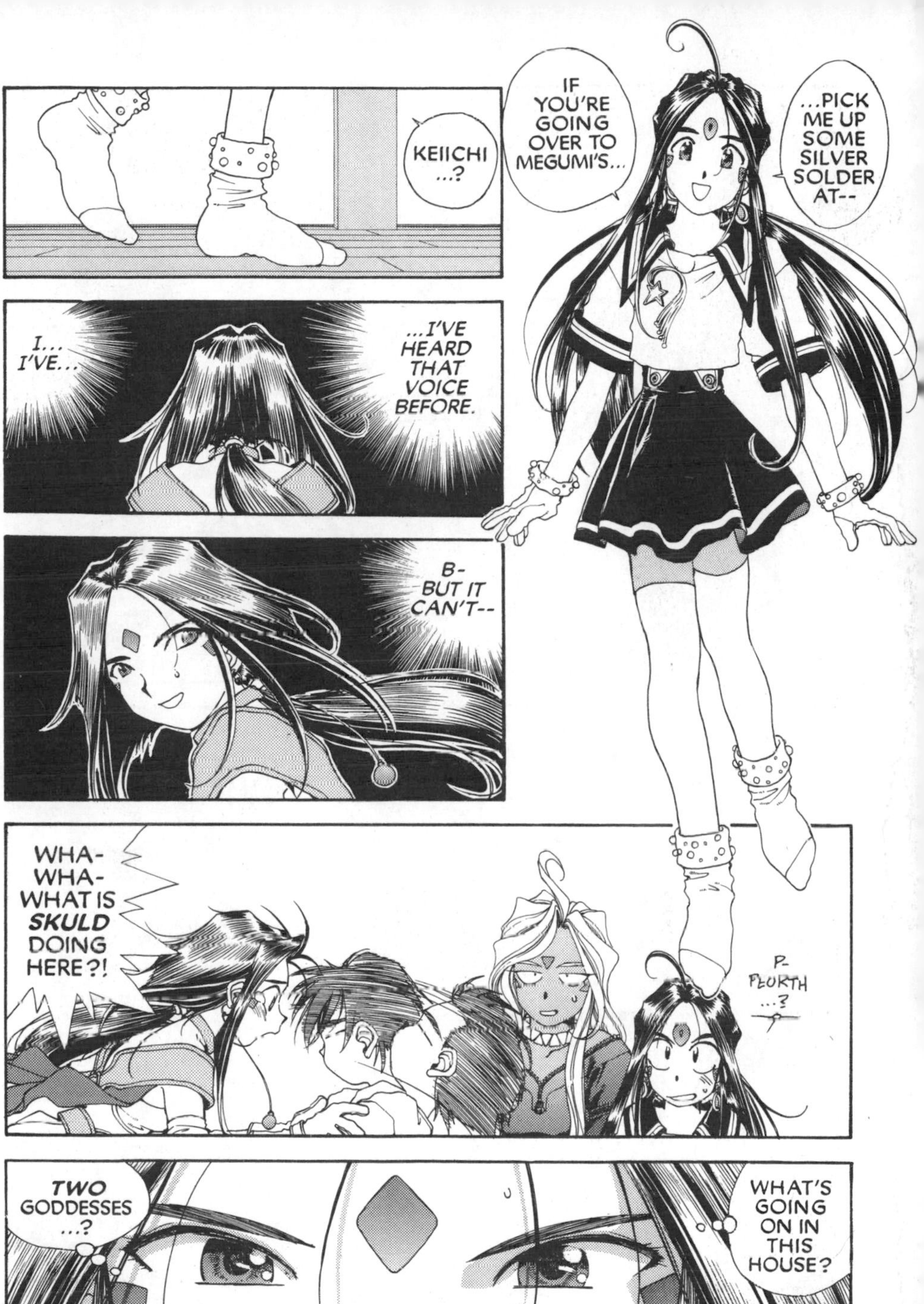
KEIICHI ...?
I... I'VE...
...I'VE HEARD THAT VOICE BEFORE.
B-BUT IT CAN'T--
IF YOU'RE GOING OVER TO MEGUMI'S...
...PICK ME UP SOME SILVER SOLDER AT--
WHA-WHA-WHAT IS SKULD DOING HERE?!
P-PEORTH ...?
TWO GODDESSES ...?
WHAT'S GOING ON IN THIS HOUSE?

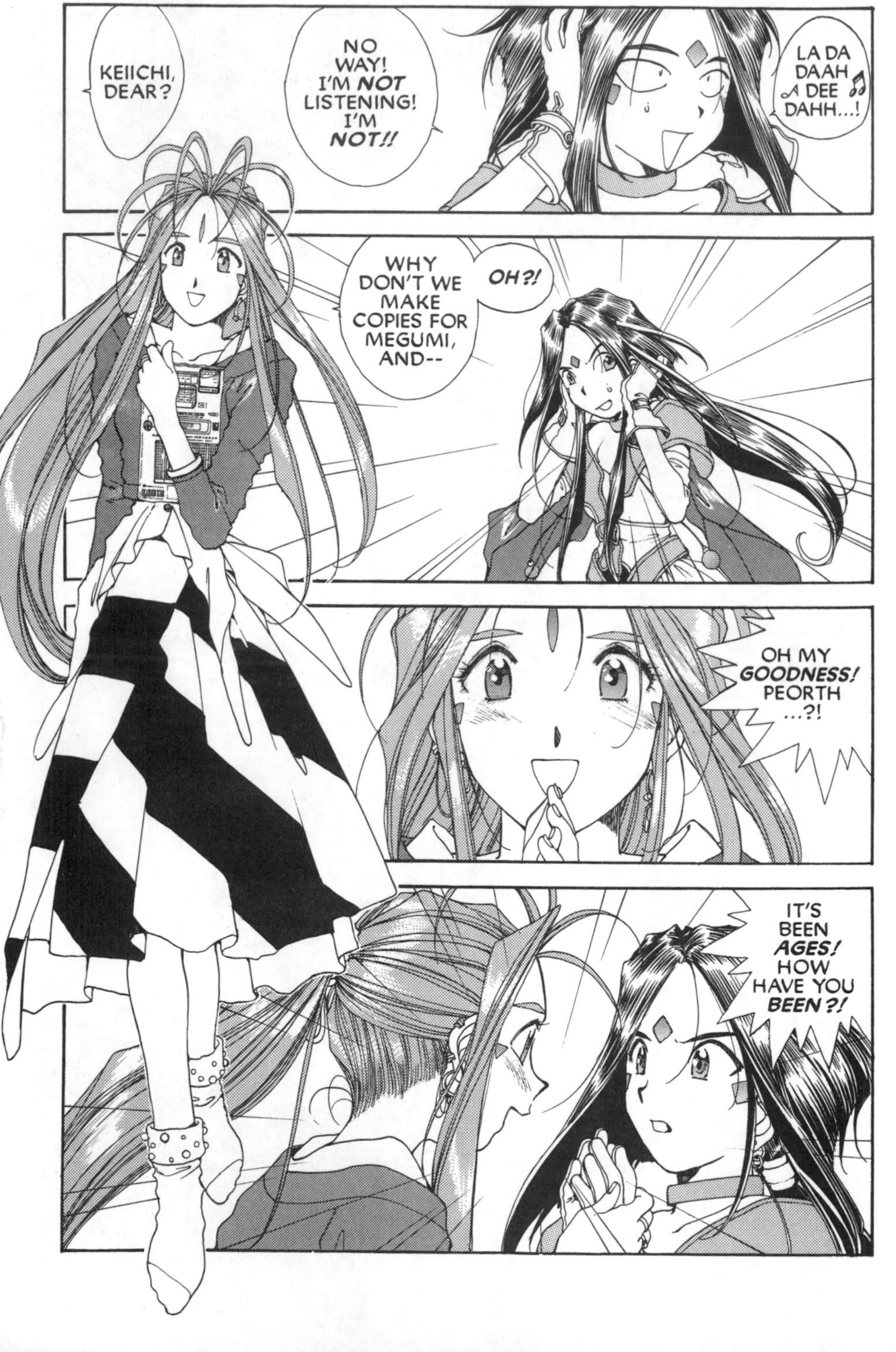
KEIICHI, DEAR?
NO WAY! I'M NOT LISTENING! I'M NOT!!
LA DA DAAH ♫ DEE DAHH...!
WHY DON'T WE MAKE COPIES FOR MEGUMI, AND--
OH?!
OH MY GOODNESS! PEORTH ...?!
IT'S BEEN AGES! HOW HAVE YOU BEEN?!

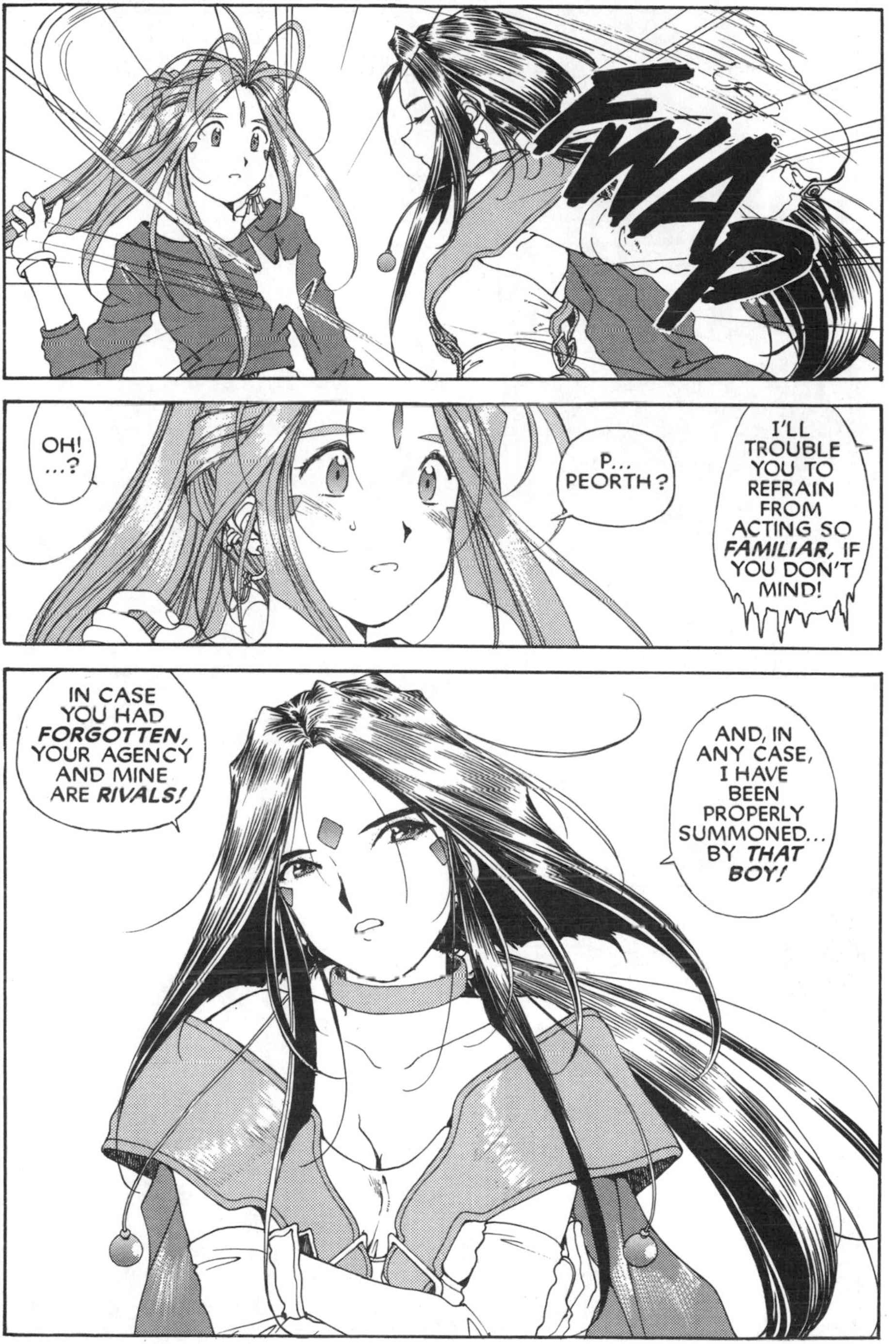
FWAP
OH! ...?
P... PEORTH?
I'LL TROUBLE YOU TO REFRAIN FROM ACTING SO *FAMILIAR,* IF YOU DON'T MIND!
IN CASE YOU HAD *FORGOTTEN,* YOUR AGENCY AND MINE ARE *RIVALS!*
AND, IN ANY CASE, I HAVE BEEN PROPERLY SUMMONED... BY *THAT BOY!*

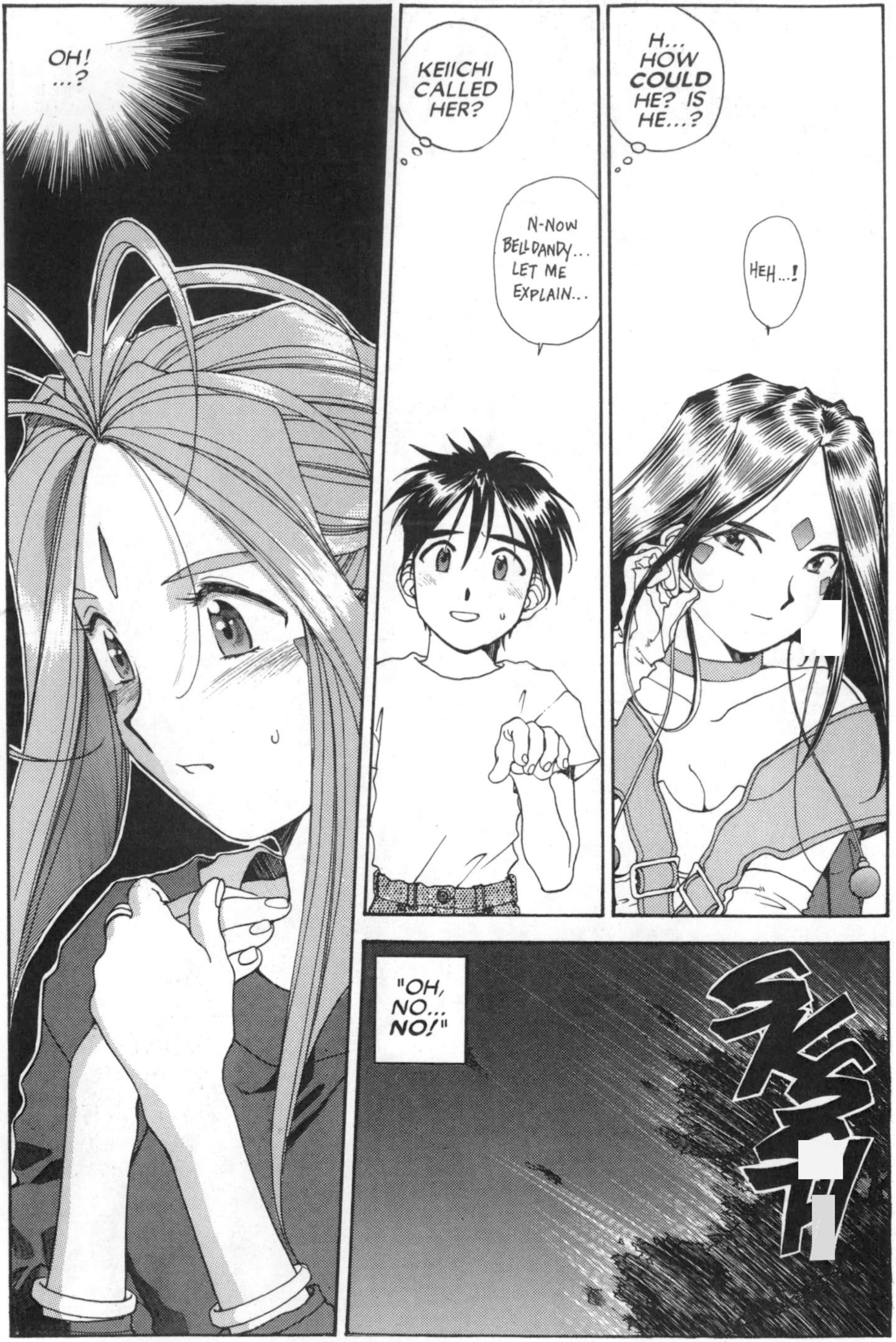
OH! ...?
KEIICHI CALLED HER?
N-NOW BELLDANDY... LET ME EXPLAIN...
H... HOW COULD HE? IS HE...?
HEH...!
"OH, NO... NO!"

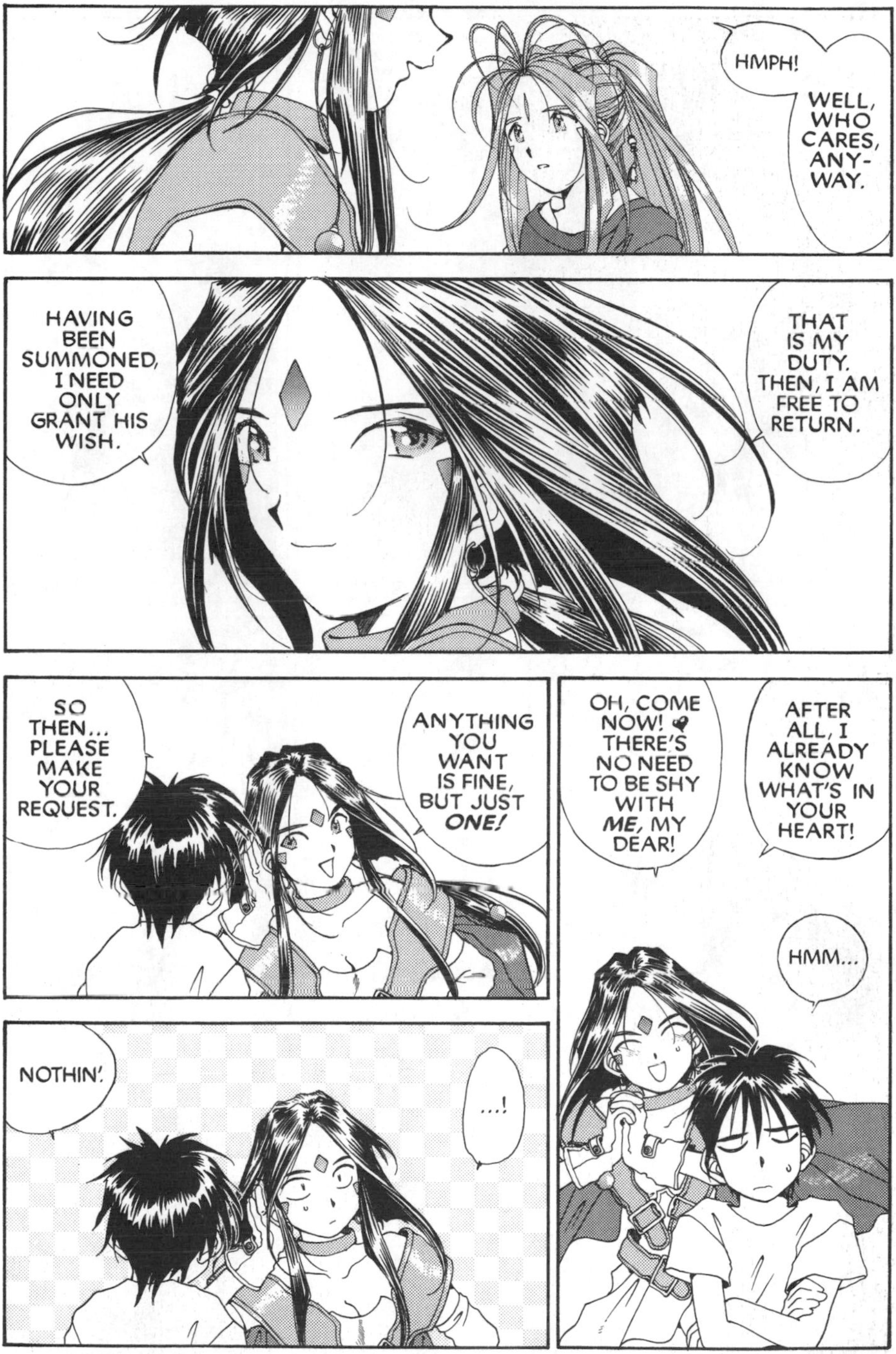
HMPH!
WELL, WHO CARES, ANYWAY.
HAVING BEEN SUMMONED, I NEED ONLY GRANT HIS WISH.
THAT IS MY DUTY. THEN, I AM FREE TO RETURN.
SO THEN... PLEASE MAKE YOUR REQUEST.
ANYTHING YOU WANT IS FINE, BUT JUST ONE!
NOTHIN'.
...!
OH, COME NOW! ♥ THERE'S NO NEED TO BE SHY WITH ME, MY DEAR!
AFTER ALL, I ALREADY KNOW WHAT'S IN YOUR HEART!
HMM...

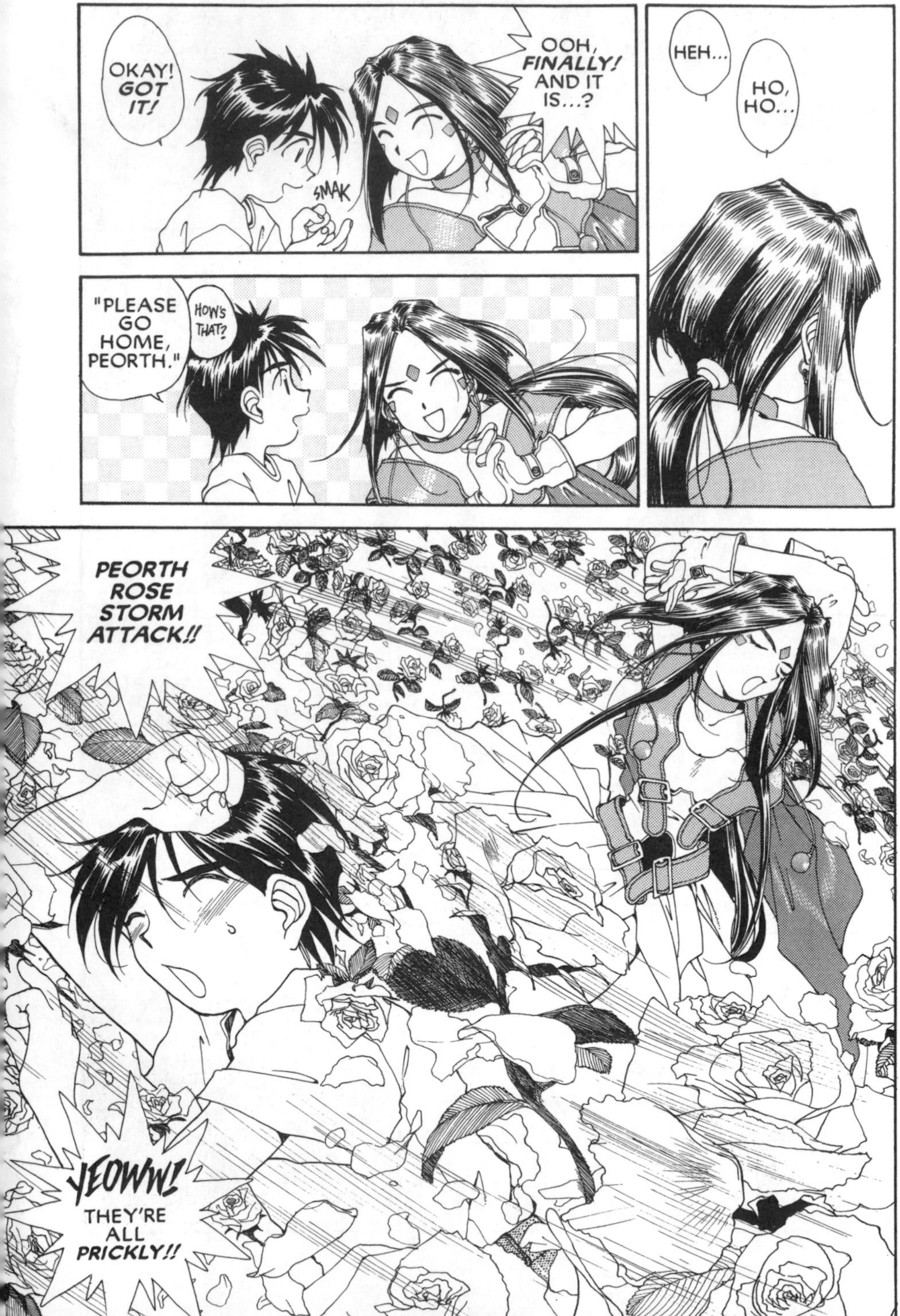
OKAY! GOT IT!
SMAK
OOH, FINALLY! AND IT IS...?
HEH...
HO, HO...
"PLEASE GO HOME, PEORTH."
HOW'S THAT?
PEORTH ROSE STORM ATTACK!!
YEOWW! THEY'RE ALL PRICKLY!!

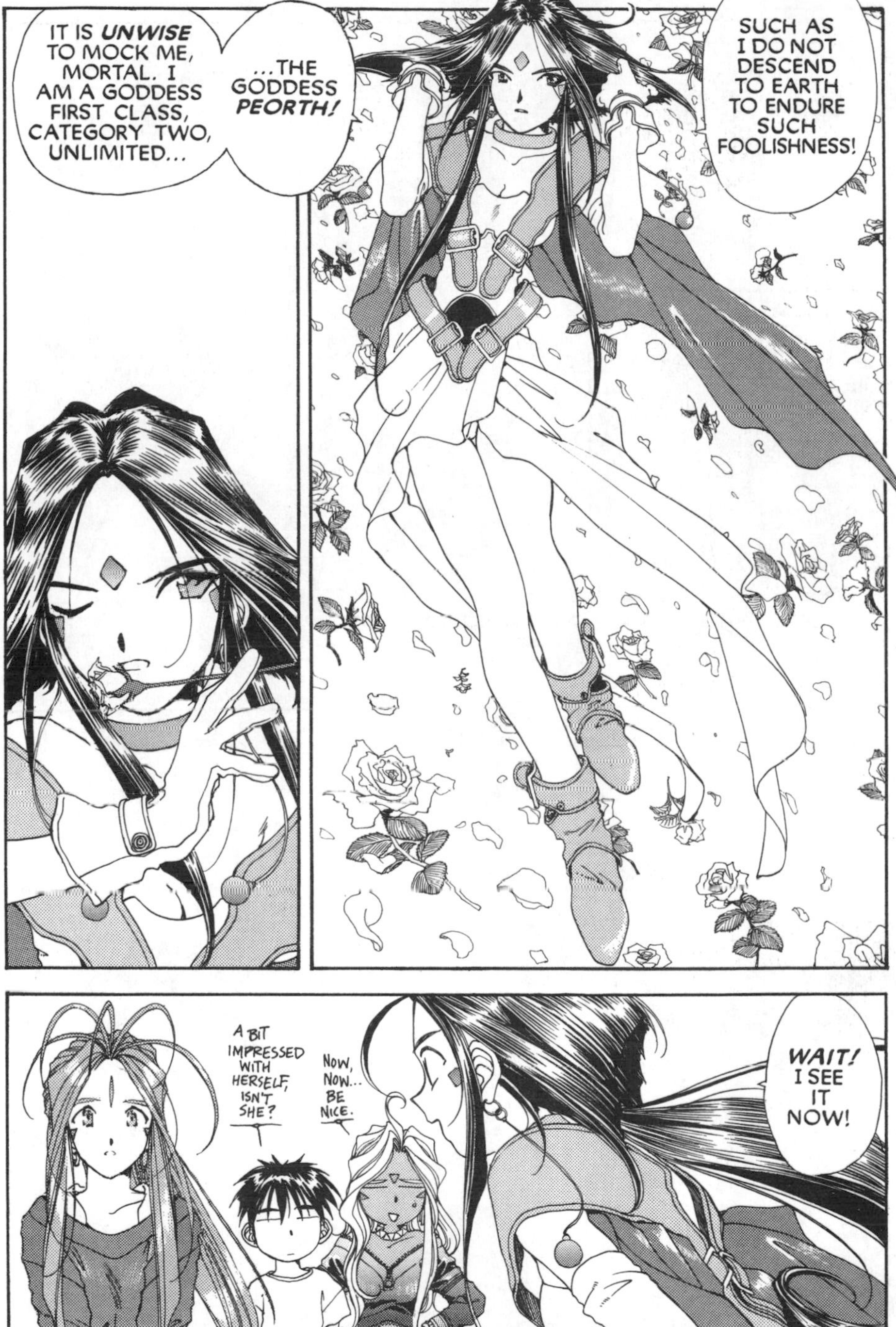
IT IS UNWISE TO MOCK ME, MORTAL. I AM A GODDESS FIRST CLASS, CATEGORY TWO, UNLIMITED...
...THE GODDESS PEORTH!
SUCH AS I DO NOT DESCEND TO EARTH TO ENDURE SUCH FOOLISHNESS!
A BIT IMPRESSED WITH HERSELF, ISN'T SHE?
NOW, NOW... BE NICE.
WAIT! I SEE IT NOW!

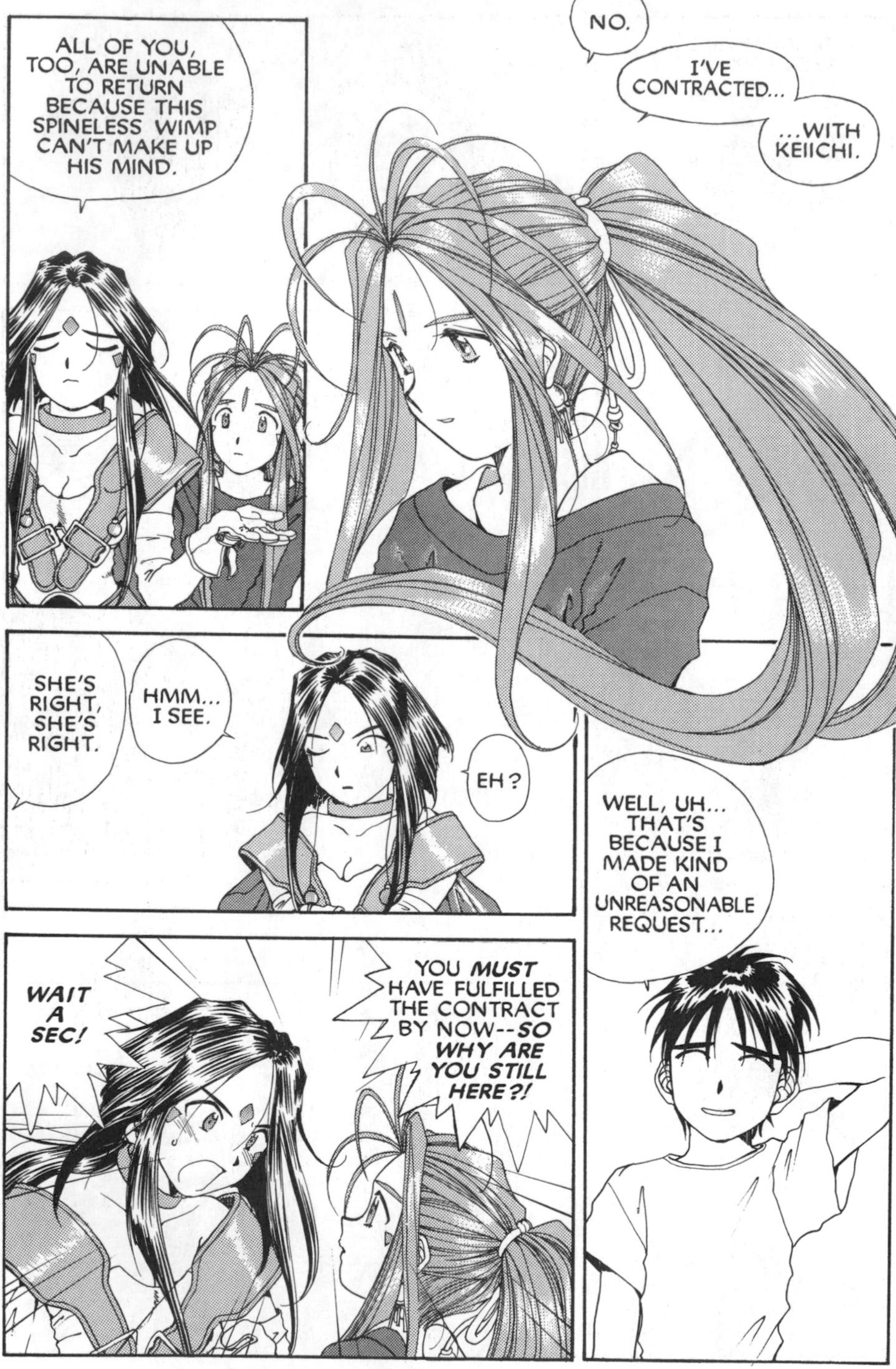
ALL OF YOU, TOO, ARE UNABLE TO RETURN BECAUSE THIS SPINELESS WIMP CAN'T MAKE UP HIS MIND.
NO.
I'VE CONTRACTED...
...WITH KEIICHI.
SHE'S RIGHT, SHE'S RIGHT.
HMM... I SEE.
EH?
WAIT A SEC!
YOU MUST HAVE FULFILLED THE CONTRACT BY NOW--SO WHY ARE YOU STILL HERE?!
WELL, UH... THAT'S BECAUSE I MADE KIND OF AN UNREASONABLE REQUEST...

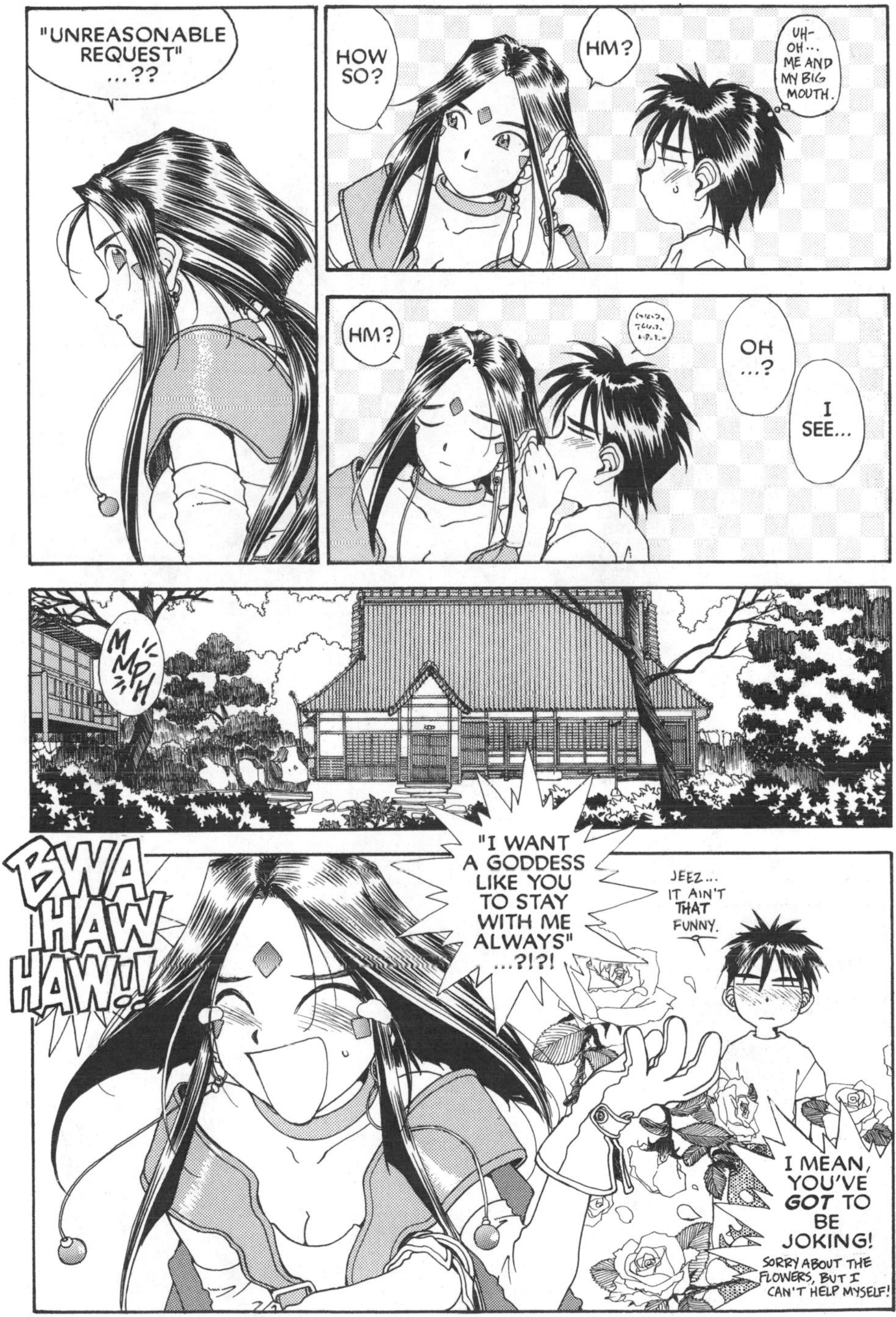
"UNREASONABLE REQUEST" ...??
HOW SO?
HM?
UH-OH... ME AND MY BIG MOUTH.
HM?
OH ...?
I SEE...
MMPH
BWA HAW HAW HAW!!
"I WANT A GODDESS LIKE YOU TO STAY WITH ME ALWAYS" ...?!?!
JEEZ... IT AIN'T THAT FUNNY.
I MEAN, YOU'VE GOT TO BE JOKING!
SORRY ABOUT THE FLOWERS, BUT I CAN'T HELP MYSELF!

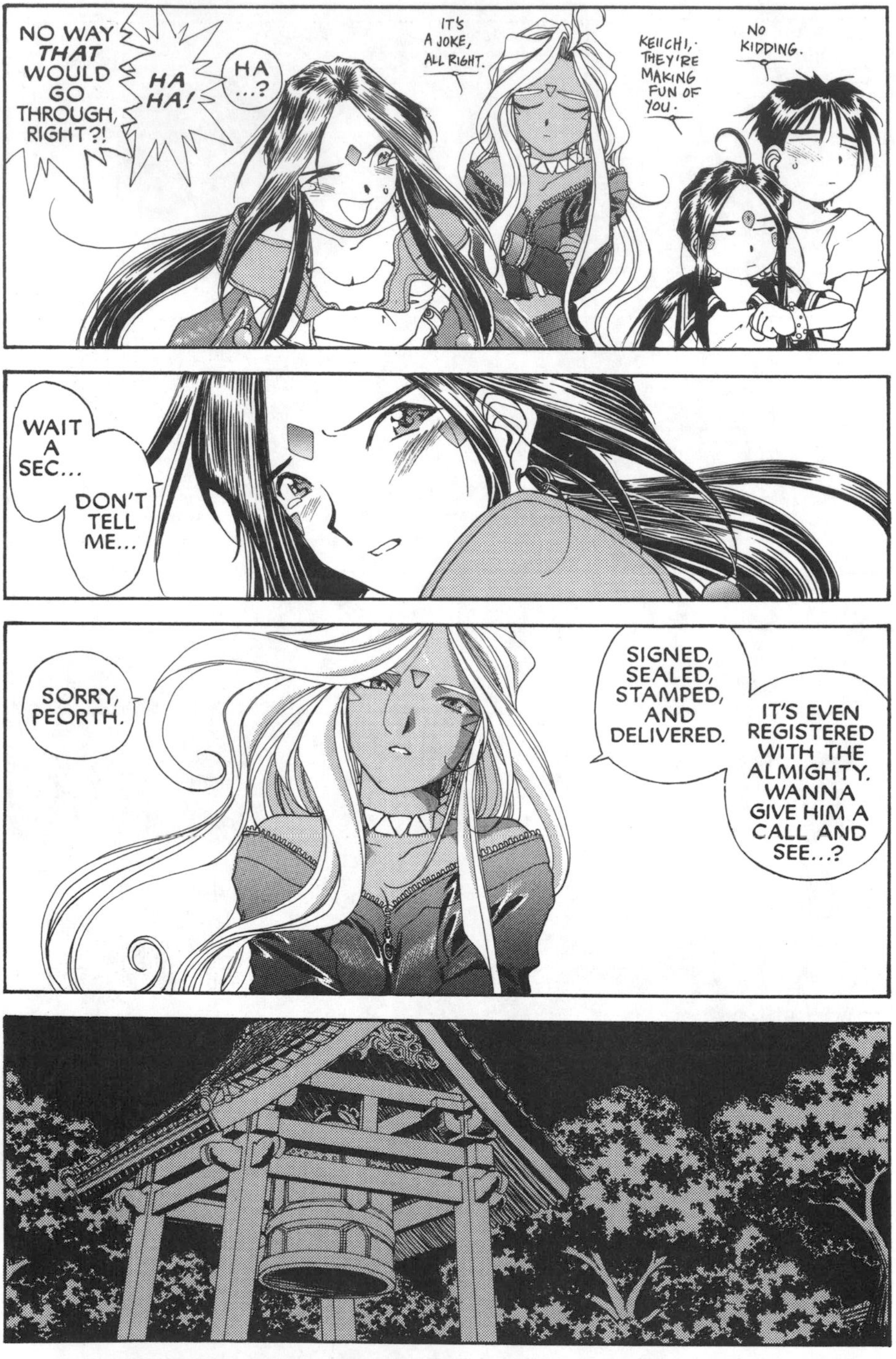
NO WAY THAT WOULD GO THROUGH, RIGHT?!
HA HA!
HA ...?
IT'S A JOKE, ALL RIGHT.
KEIICHI, THEY'RE MAKING FUN OF YOU.
NO KIDDING.
WAIT A SEC...
DON'T TELL ME...
SORRY, PEORTH.
SIGNED, SEALED, STAMPED, AND DELIVERED.
IT'S EVEN REGISTERED WITH THE ALMIGHTY. WANNA GIVE HIM A CALL AND SEE...?

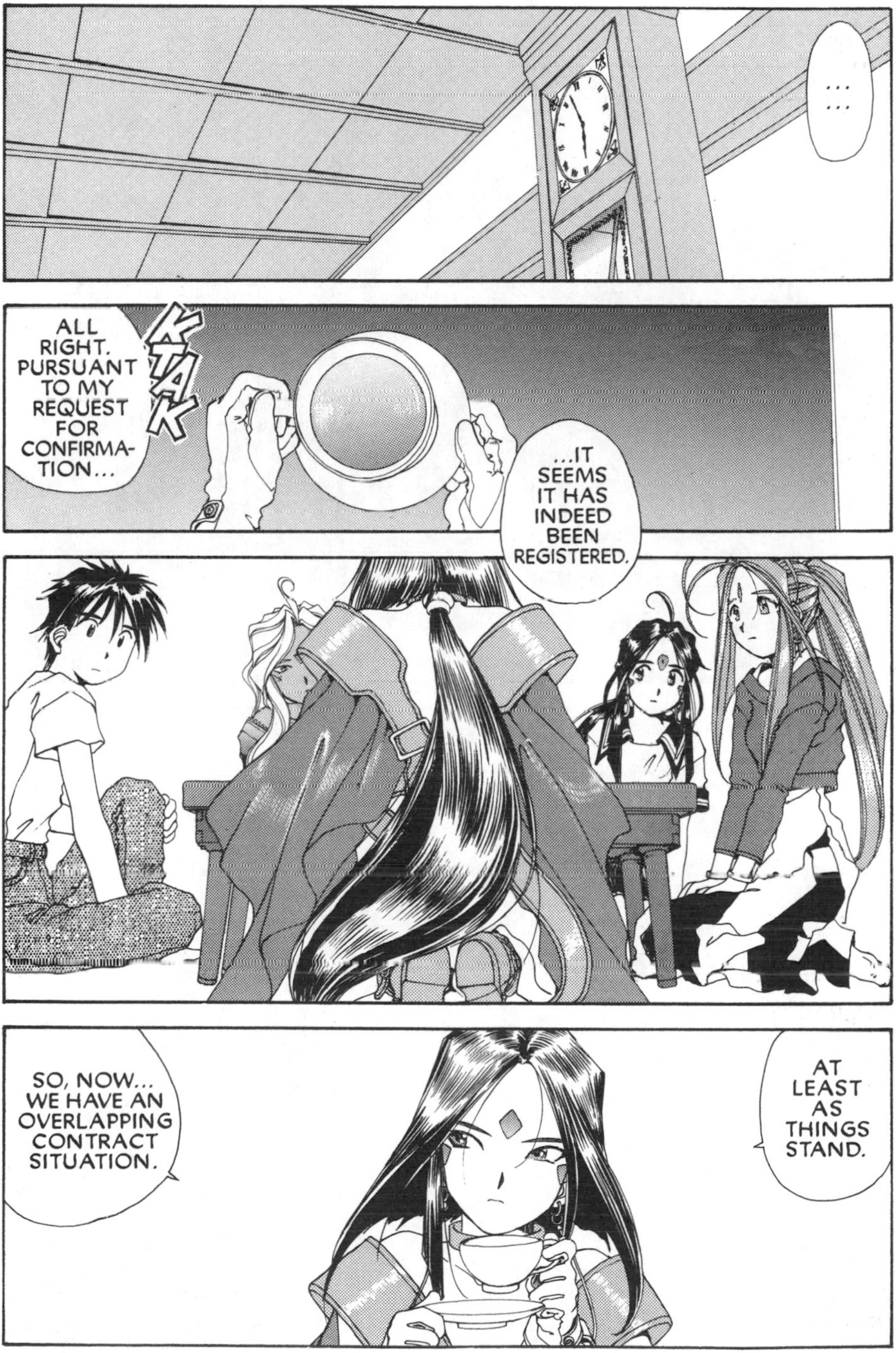
. . .
. . .
ALL RIGHT. PURSUANT TO MY REQUEST FOR CONFIRMATION...
KTAK
...IT SEEMS IT HAS INDEED BEEN REGISTERED.
SO, NOW... WE HAVE AN OVERLAPPING CONTRACT SITUATION.
AT LEAST AS THINGS STAND.

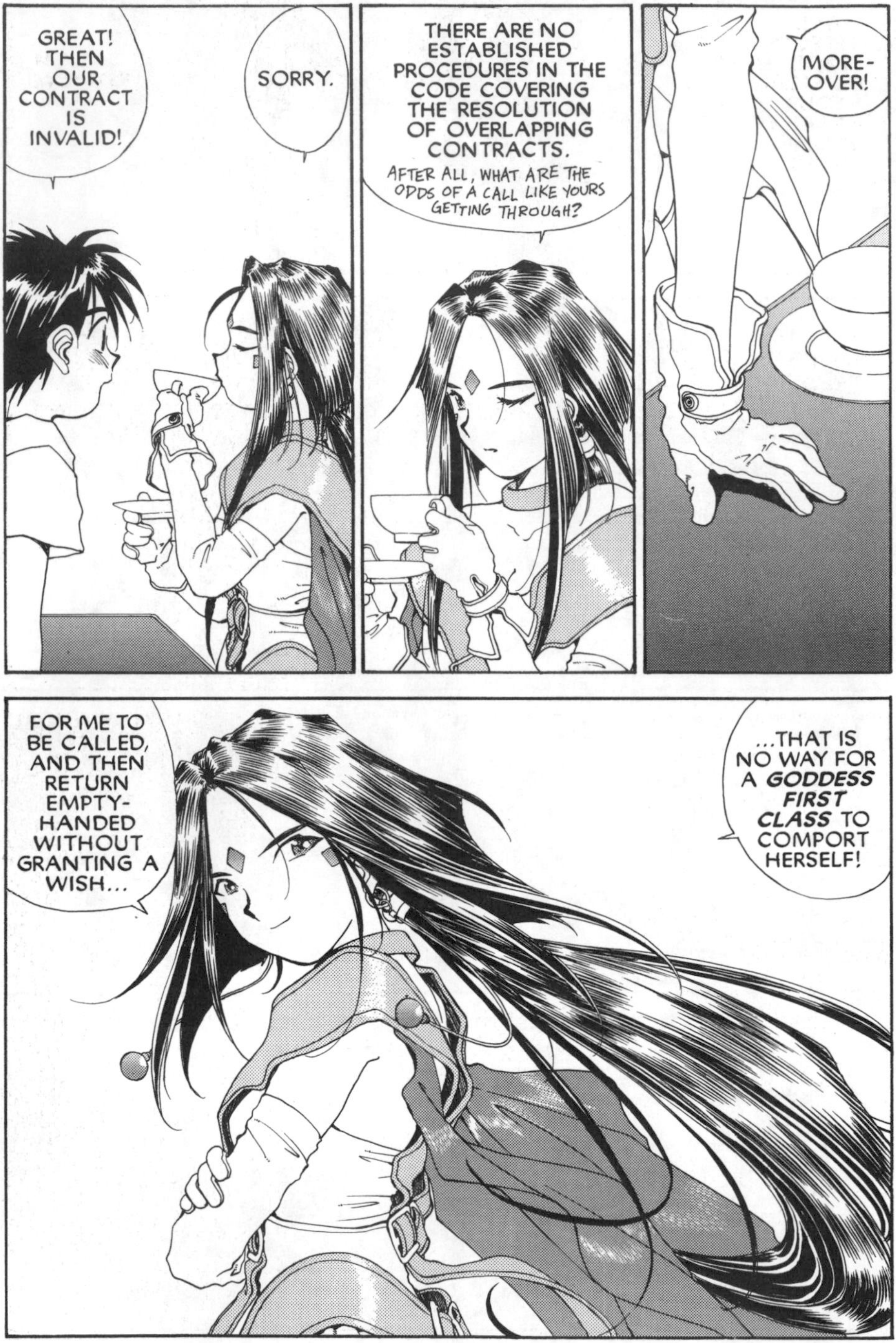
GREAT! THEN OUR CONTRACT IS INVALID!
SORRY.
THERE ARE NO ESTABLISHED PROCEDURES IN THE CODE COVERING THE RESOLUTION OF OVERLAPPING CONTRACTS.
AFTER ALL, WHAT ARE THE ODDS OF A CALL LIKE YOURS GETTING THROUGH?
MORE-OVER!
FOR ME TO BE CALLED, AND THEN RETURN EMPTY-HANDED WITHOUT GRANTING A WISH...
...THAT IS NO WAY FOR A *GODDESS FIRST CLASS* TO COMPORT HERSELF!

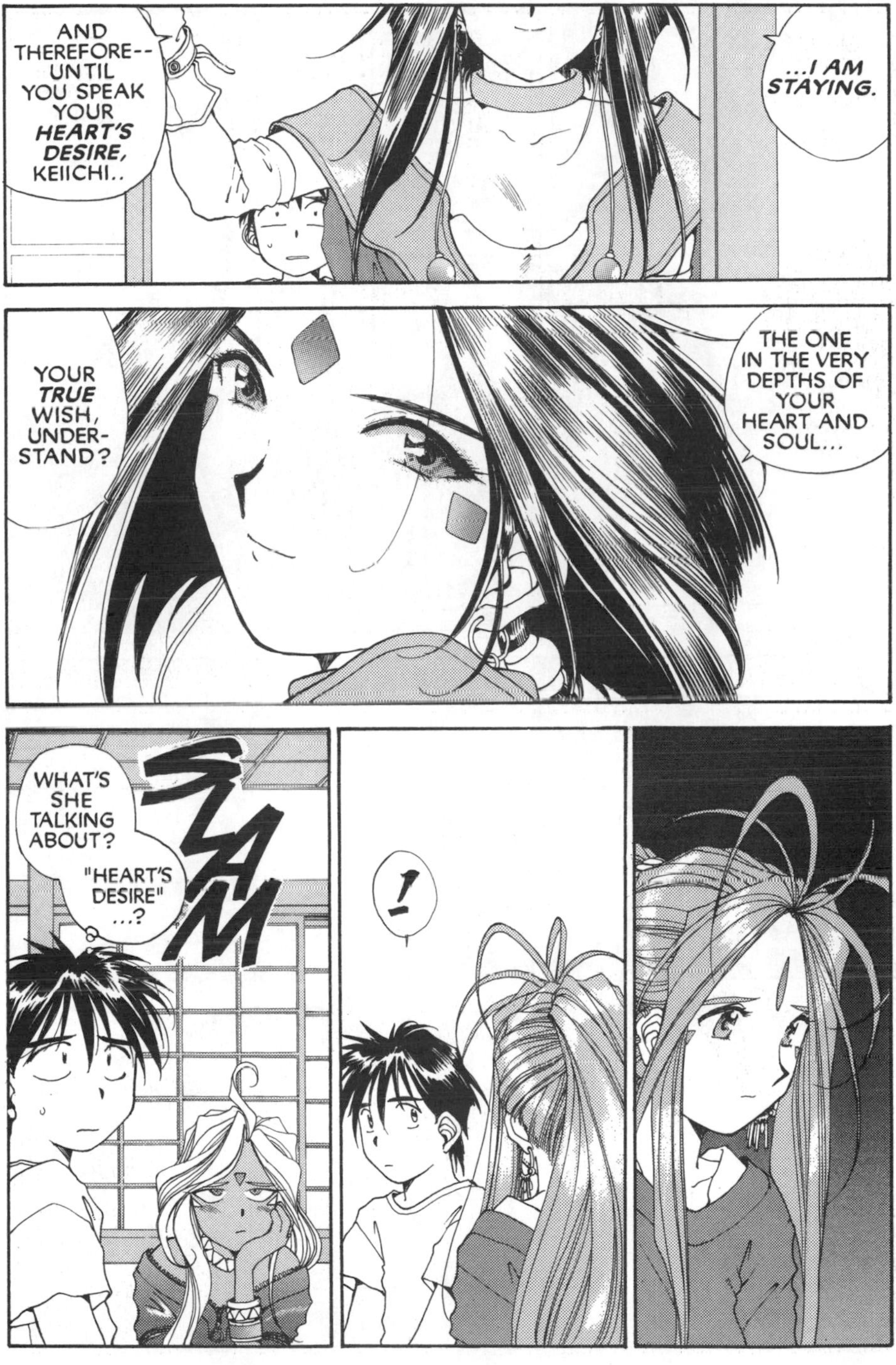

AND THEREFORE-- UNTIL YOU SPEAK YOUR ***HEART'S DESIRE,*** KEIICHI..
...*I AM STAYING.*
YOUR ***TRUE*** WISH, UNDER-STAND?
THE ONE IN THE VERY DEPTHS OF YOUR HEART AND SOUL...
WHAT'S SHE TALKING ABOUT?
"HEART'S DESIRE" ...?
SLAM
!

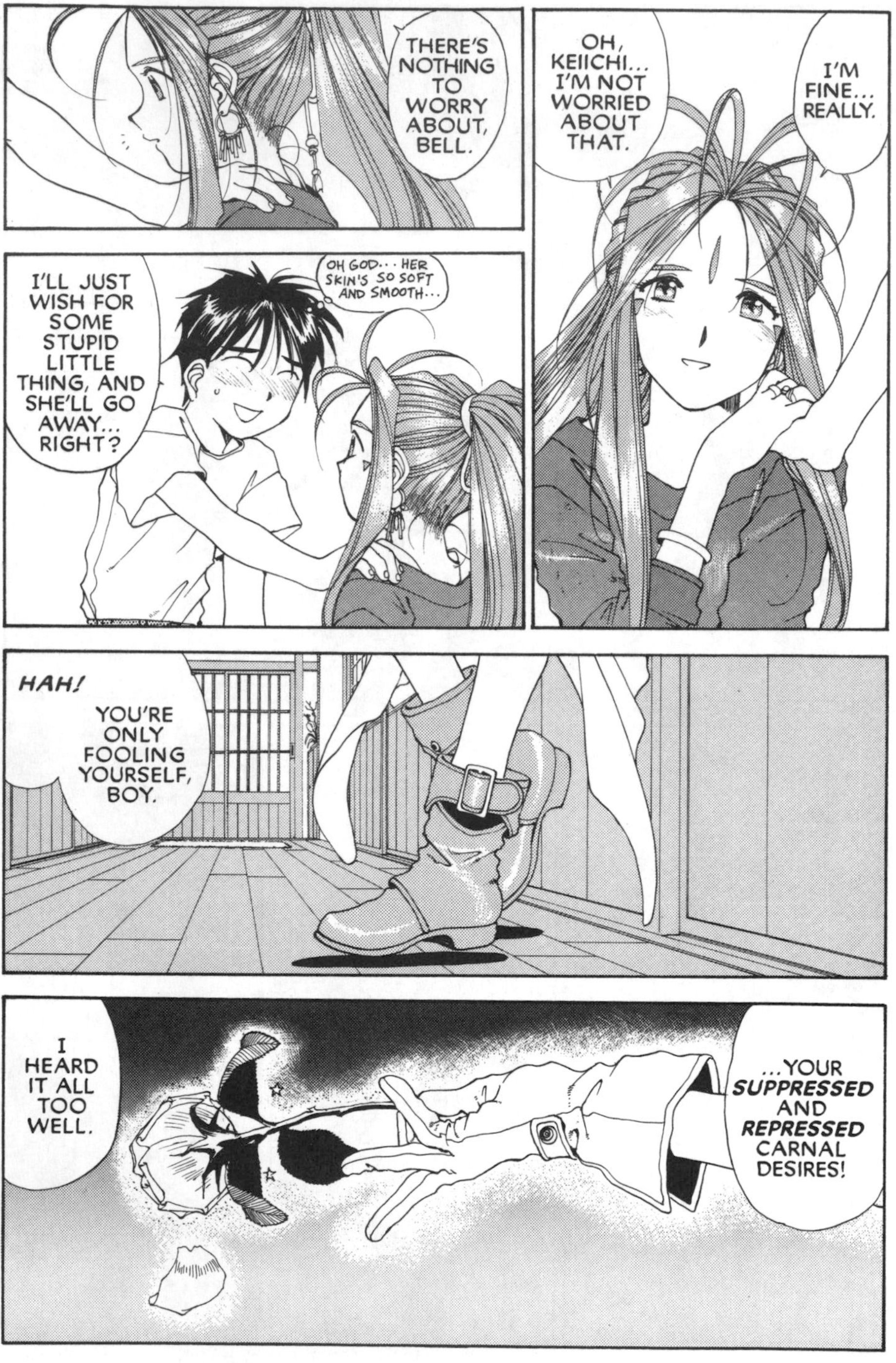
THERE'S NOTHING TO WORRY ABOUT, BELL.
I'LL JUST WISH FOR SOME STUPID LITTLE THING, AND SHE'LL GO AWAY... RIGHT?
OH GOD... HER SKIN'S SO SOFT AND SMOOTH...
OH, KEIICHI... I'M NOT WORRIED ABOUT THAT.
I'M FINE... REALLY.
HAH!
YOU'RE ONLY FOOLING YOURSELF, BOY.
I HEARD IT ALL TOO WELL.
...YOUR SUPPRESSED AND REPRESSED CARNAL DESIRES!

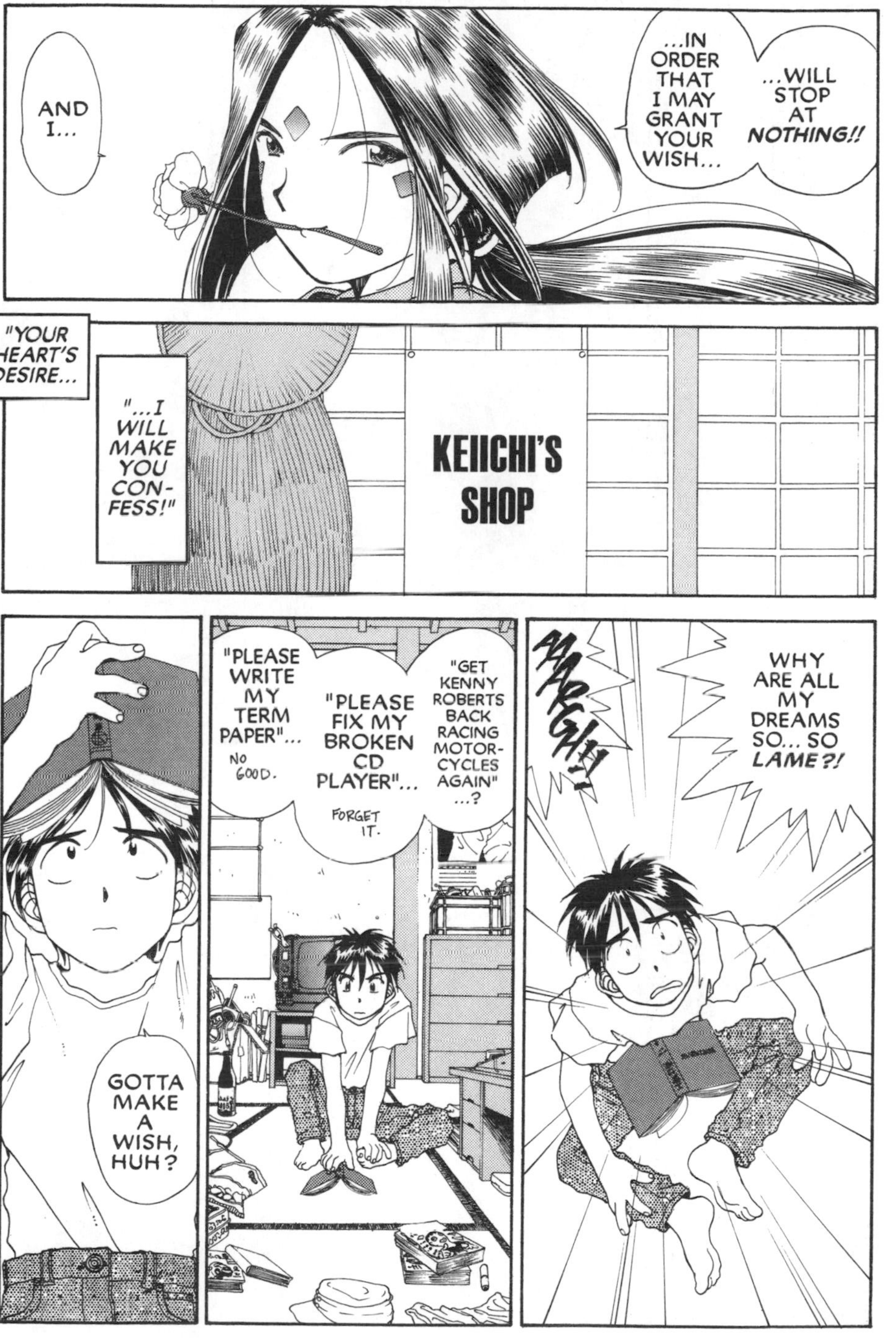
AND I...
...IN ORDER THAT I MAY GRANT YOUR WISH...
...WILL STOP AT NOTHING!!
"YOUR HEART'S DESIRE...
"...I WILL MAKE YOU CON-FESS!"
KEIICHI'S SHOP
GOTTA MAKE A WISH, HUH?
"PLEASE WRITE MY TERM PAPER"...
NO GOOD.
"PLEASE FIX MY BROKEN CD PLAYER"...
FORGET IT.
"GET KENNY ROBERTS BACK RACING MOTOR-CYCLES AGAIN" ...?
AAARGH!!
WHY ARE ALL MY DREAMS SO... SO LAME?!

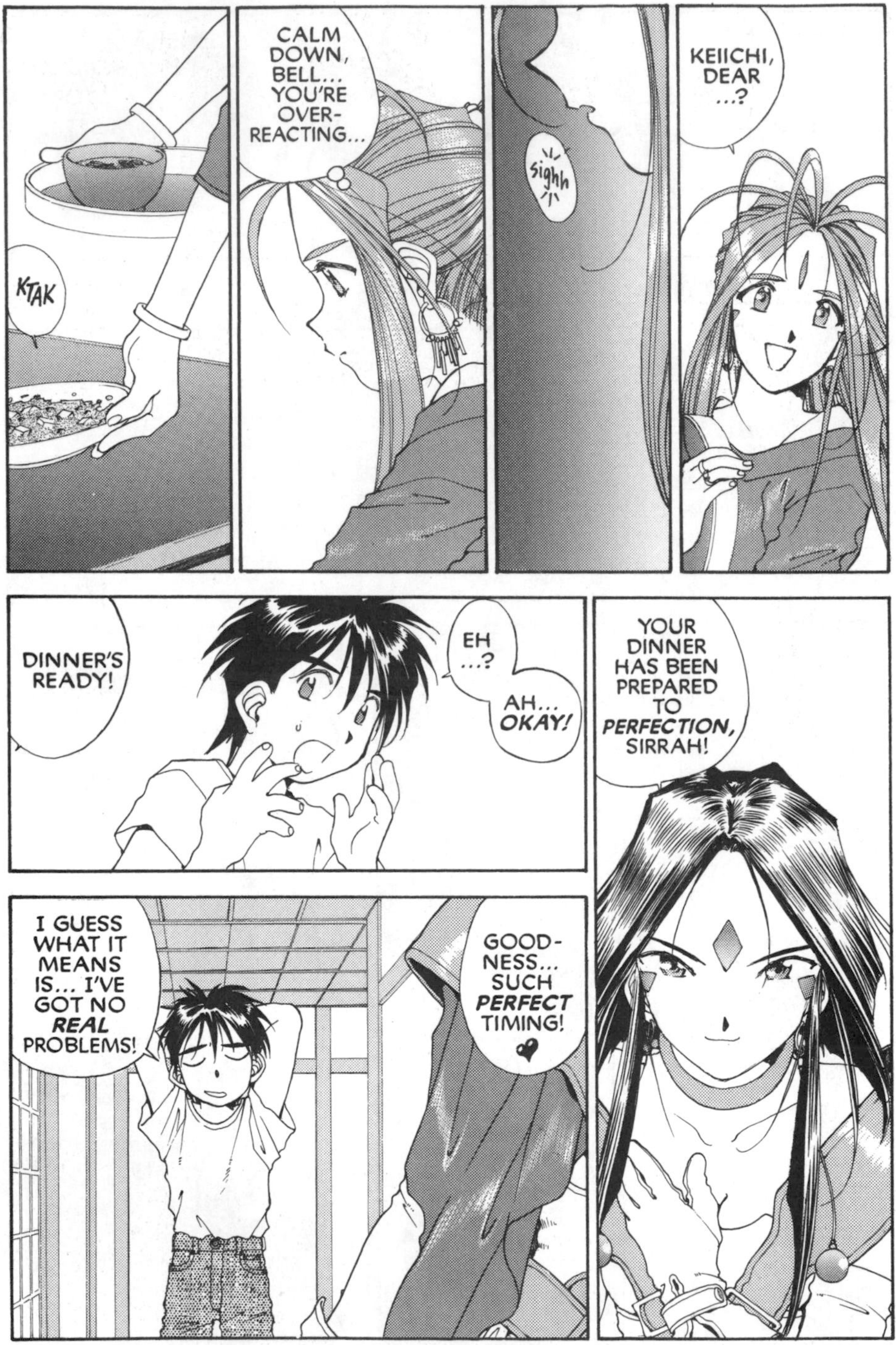
KTAK
CALM DOWN, BELL... YOU'RE OVER-REACTING...
sighh
KEIICHI, DEAR ...?
DINNER'S READY!
EH ...?
AH... OKAY!
YOUR DINNER HAS BEEN PREPARED TO PERFECTION, SIRRAH!
I GUESS WHAT IT MEANS IS... I'VE GOT NO REAL PROBLEMS!
GOODNESS... SUCH PERFECT TIMING!

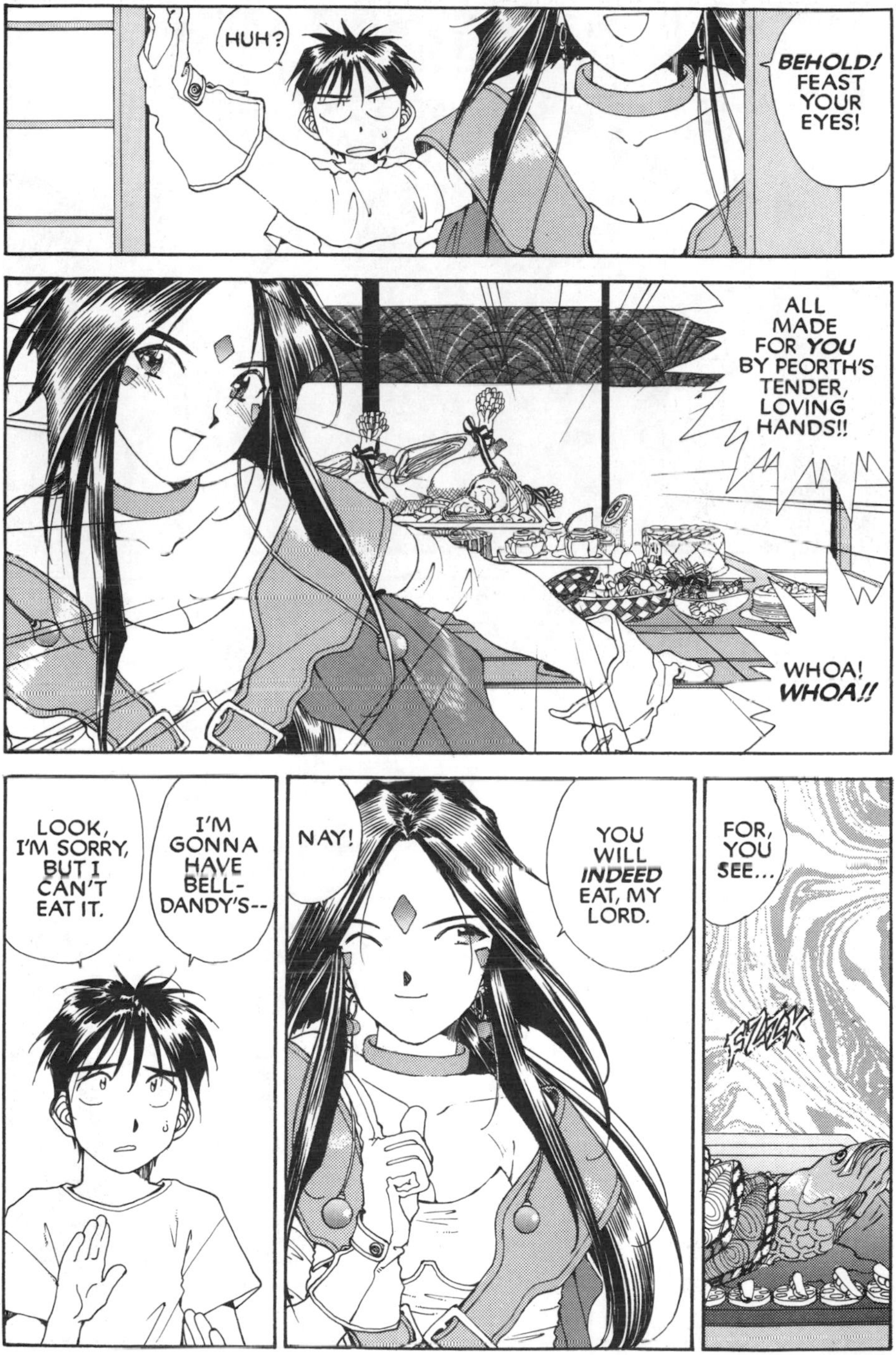
HUH?
BEHOLD! FEAST YOUR EYES!
ALL MADE FOR YOU BY PEORTH'S TENDER, LOVING HANDS!!
WHOA! WHOA!!
LOOK, I'M SORRY, BUT I CAN'T EAT IT.
I'M GONNA HAVE BELL-DANDY'S--
NAY!
YOU WILL INDEED EAT, MY LORD.
FOR, YOU SEE...

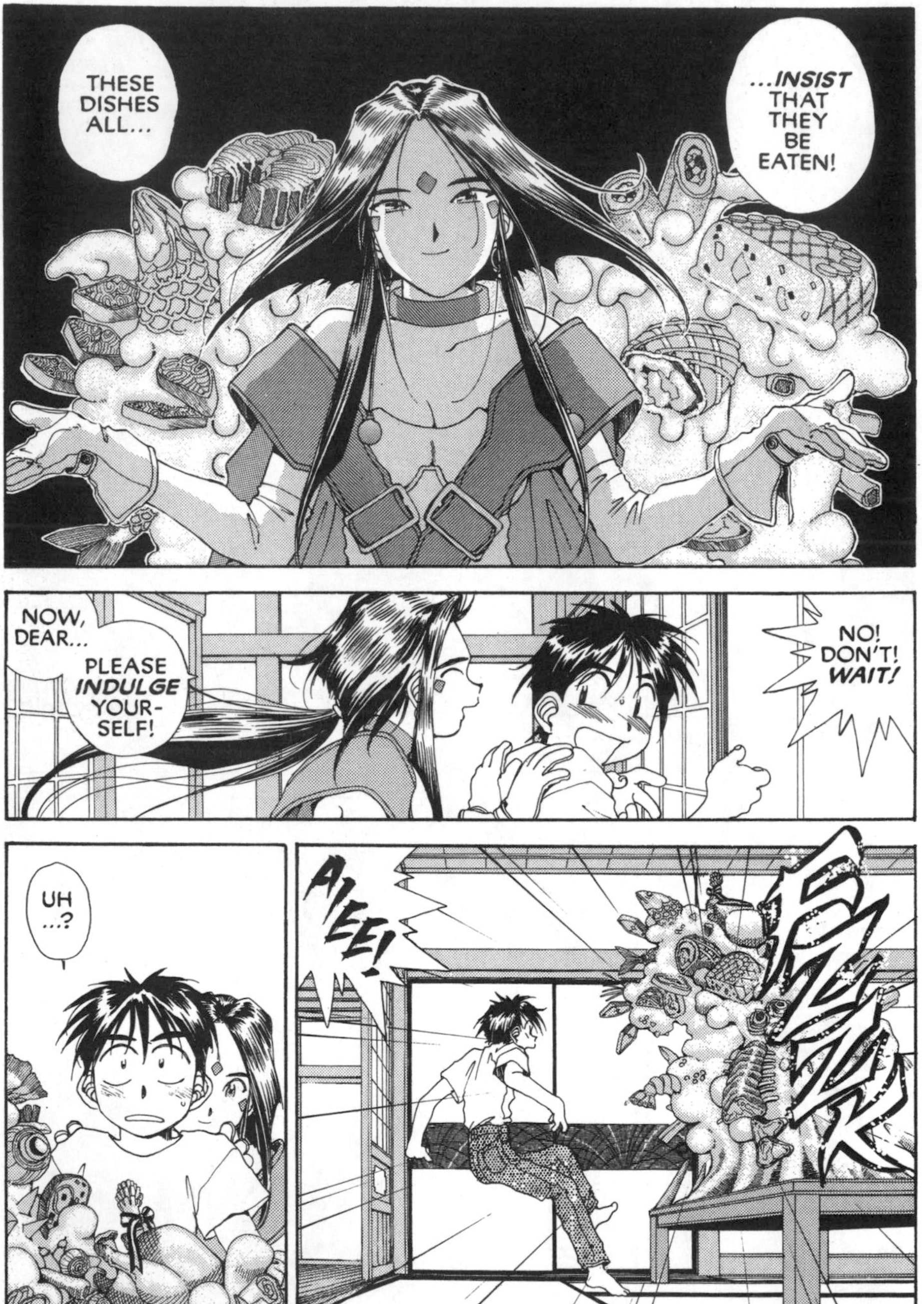
THESE DISHES ALL...
...*INSIST* THAT THEY BE EATEN!
NOW, DEAR...
PLEASE *INDULGE* YOURSELF!
NO! DON'T! *WAIT!*
UH ...?
AIEE!

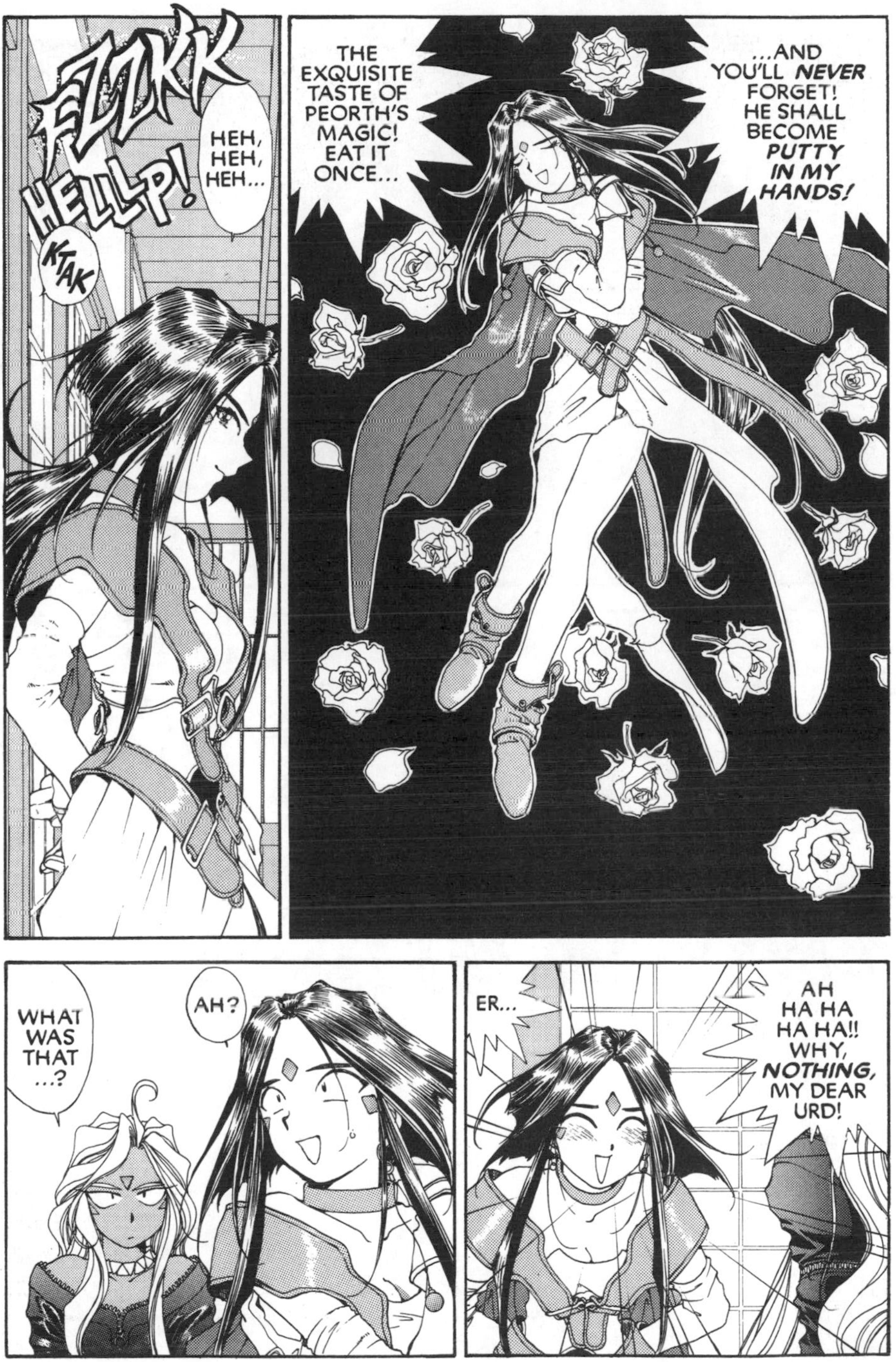
FZZKK
HELLLP!
KYAK
HEH, HEH, HEH...
THE EXQUISITE TASTE OF PEORTH'S MAGIC! EAT IT ONCE...
...AND YOU'LL *NEVER* FORGET! HE SHALL BECOME *PUTTY IN MY HANDS!*
WHAT WAS THAT ...?
AH?
ER...
AH HA HA HA HA!! WHY, *NOTHING,* MY DEAR URD!

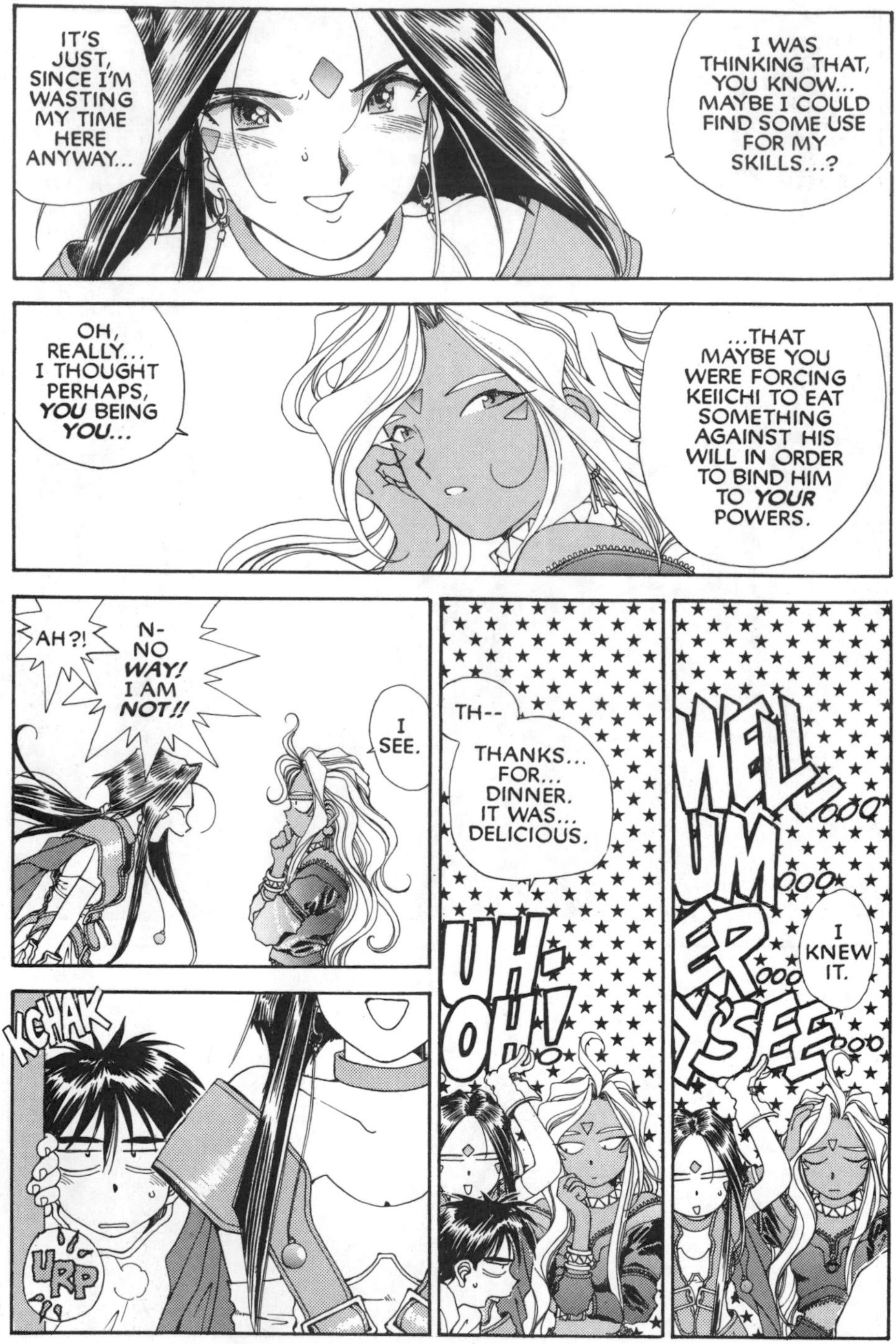
IT'S JUST, SINCE I'M WASTING MY TIME HERE ANYWAY...
I WAS THINKING THAT, YOU KNOW... MAYBE I COULD FIND SOME USE FOR MY SKILLS...?
OH, REALLY... I THOUGHT PERHAPS, *YOU* BEING *YOU*...
...THAT MAYBE YOU WERE FORCING KEIICHI TO EAT SOMETHING AGAINST HIS WILL IN ORDER TO BIND HIM TO *YOUR* POWERS.
AH?!
N-NO *WAY!* I AM *NOT!!*
I SEE.
KCHAK
URP
TH--
THANKS... FOR... DINNER. IT WAS... DELICIOUS.
UH-OH!
WELLooo
UMooo
ERooo
Y'SEEooo
I KNEW IT.

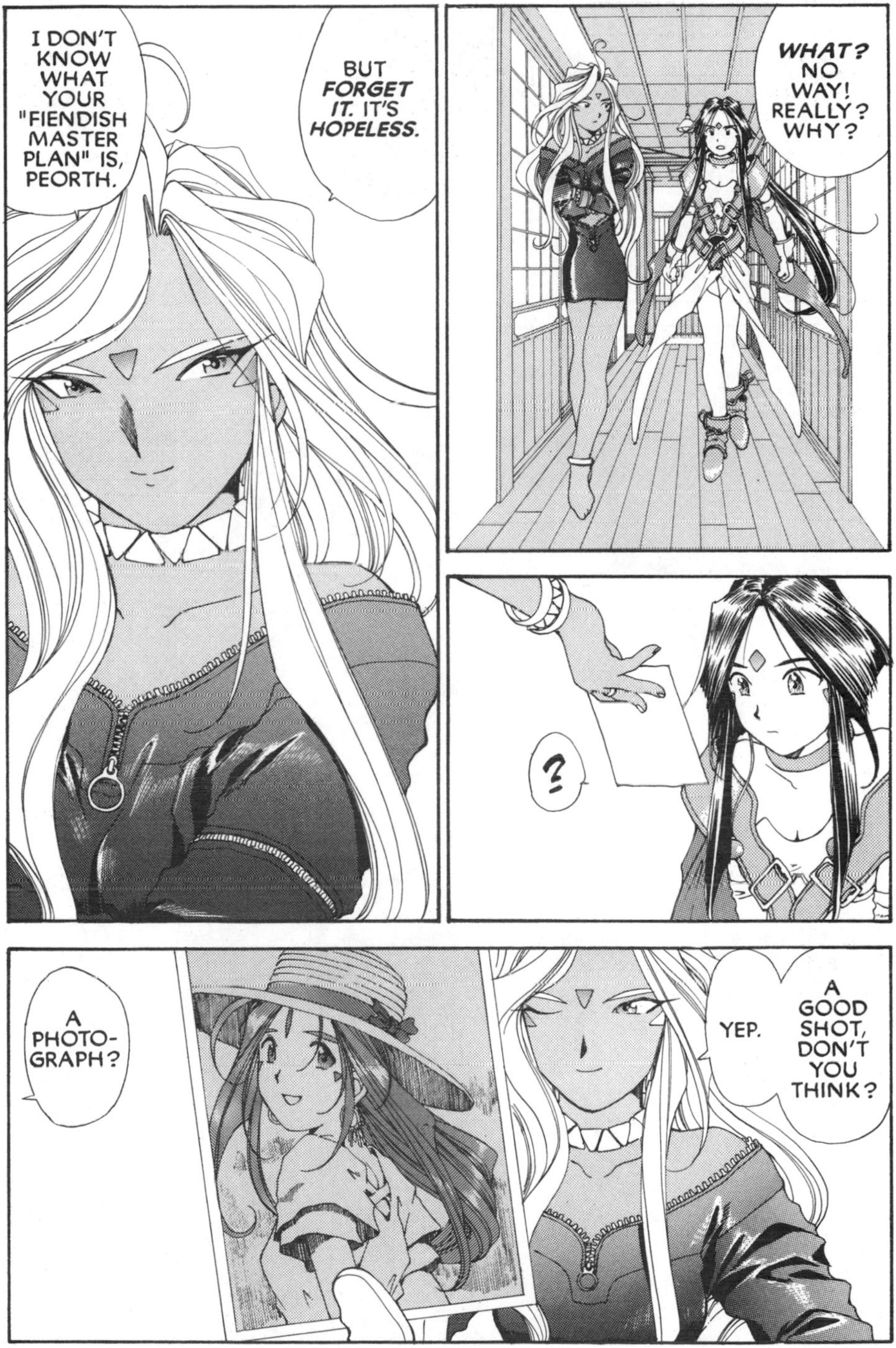
I DON'T KNOW WHAT YOUR "FIENDISH MASTER PLAN" IS, PEORTH.
BUT *FORGET IT.* IT'S *HOPELESS.*
WHAT? NO WAY! REALLY? WHY?
?
A PHOTO-GRAPH?
YEP.
A GOOD SHOT, DON'T YOU THINK?

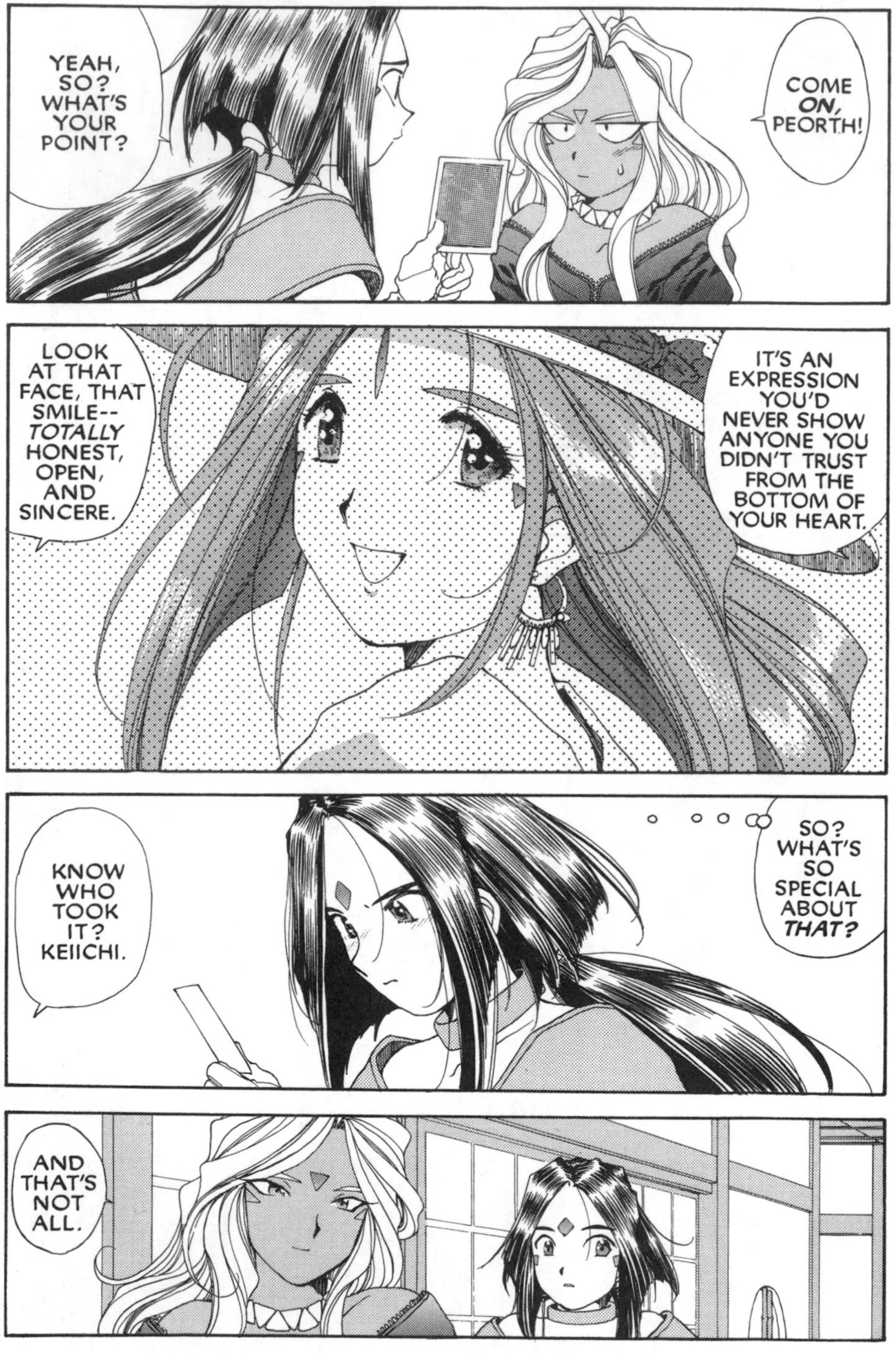
YEAH, SO? WHAT'S YOUR POINT?
COME ON, PEORTH!
LOOK AT THAT FACE, THAT SMILE-- TOTALLY HONEST, OPEN, AND SINCERE.
IT'S AN EXPRESSION YOU'D NEVER SHOW ANYONE YOU DIDN'T TRUST FROM THE BOTTOM OF YOUR HEART.
KNOW WHO TOOK IT? KEIICHI.
SO? WHAT'S SO SPECIAL ABOUT THAT?
AND THAT'S NOT ALL.

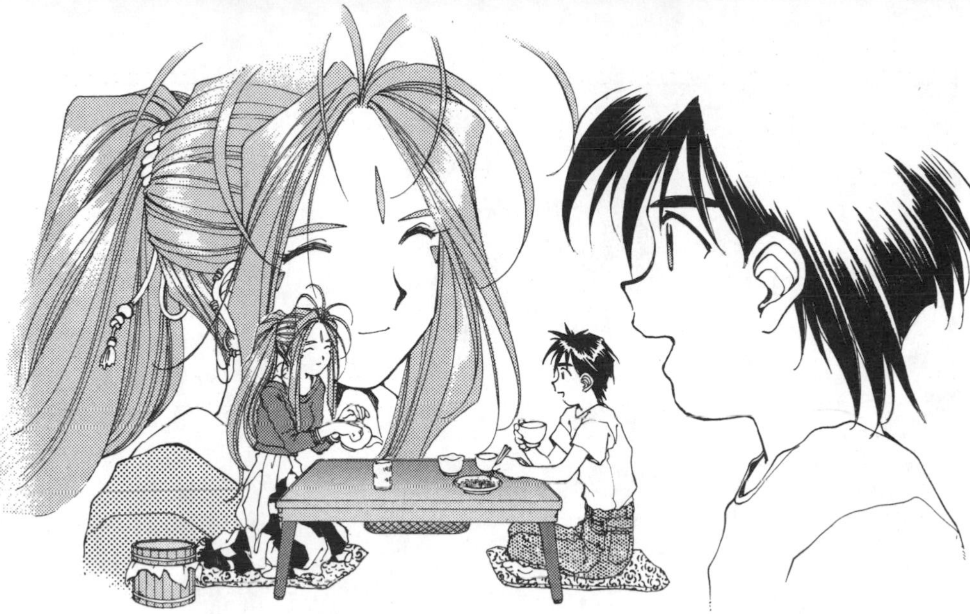

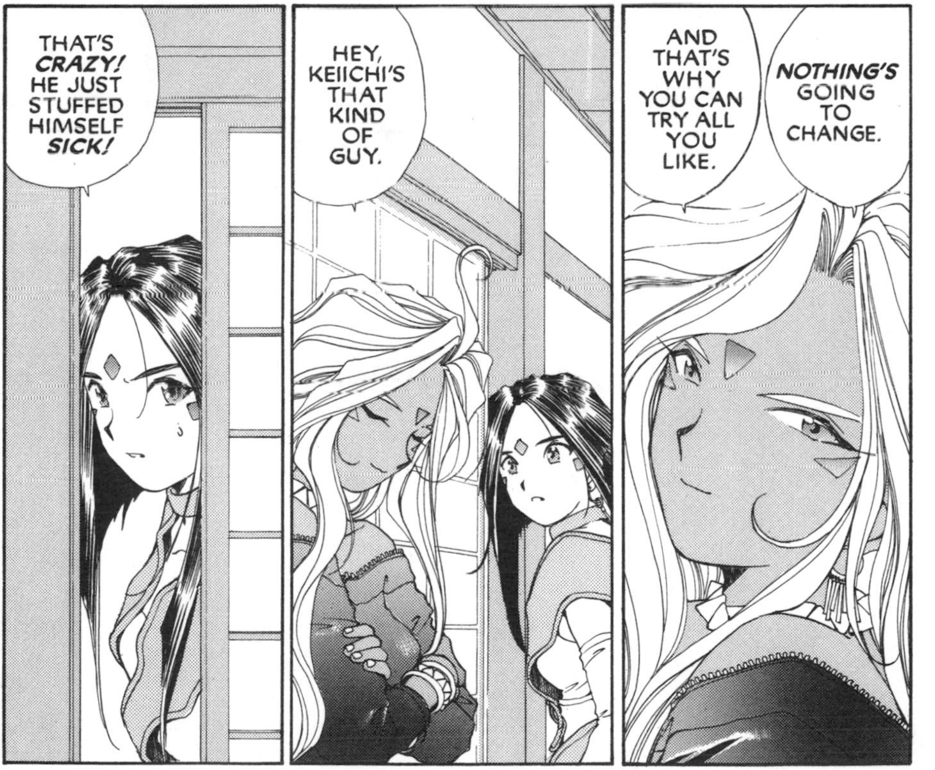

THAT'S CRAZY! HE JUST STUFFED HIMSELF SICK!
HEY, KEIICHI'S THAT KIND OF GUY.
AND THAT'S WHY YOU CAN TRY ALL YOU LIKE.
NOTHING'S GOING TO CHANGE.

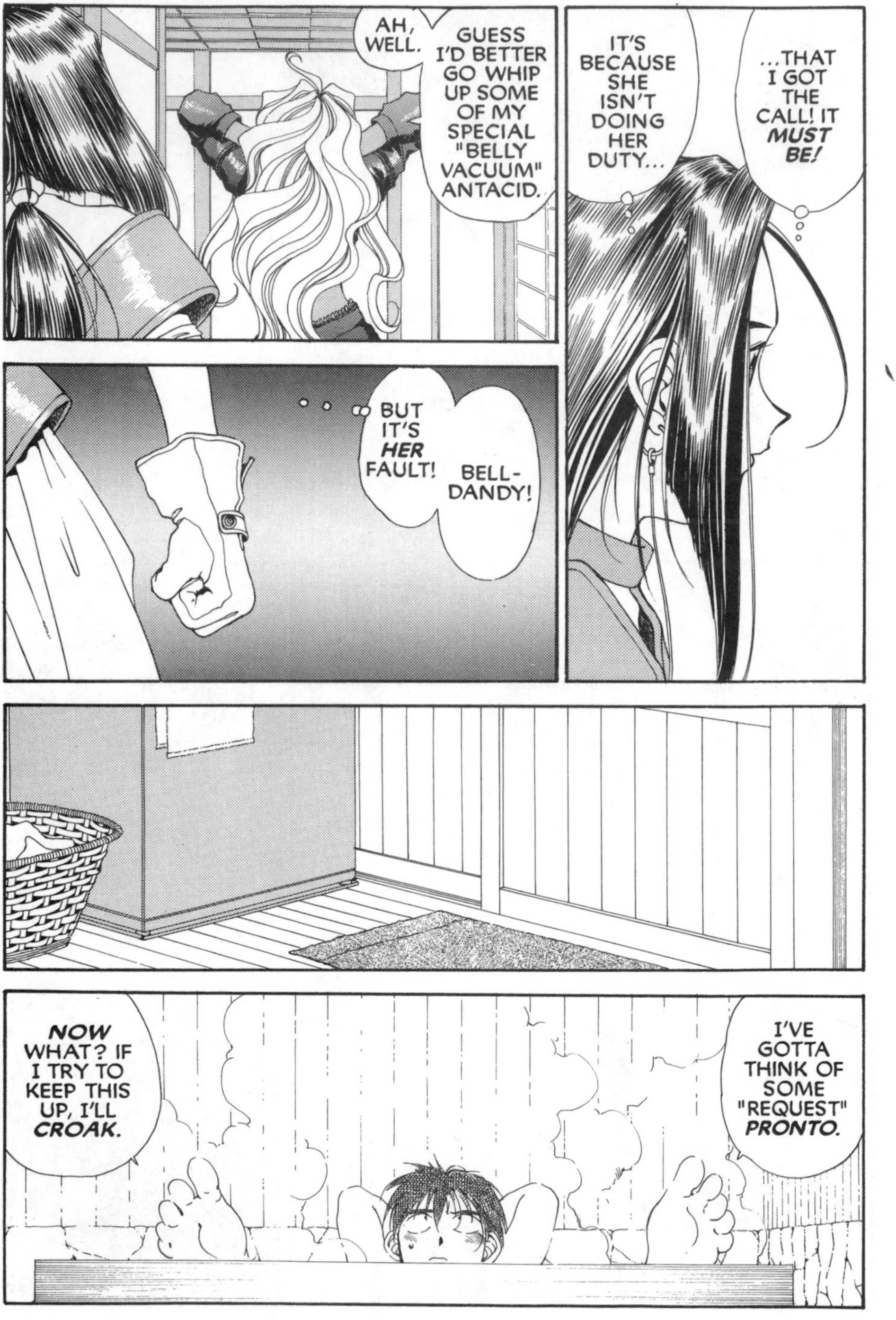
AH, WELL.
GUESS I'D BETTER GO WHIP UP SOME OF MY SPECIAL "BELLY VACUUM" ANTACID.
IT'S BECAUSE SHE ISN'T DOING HER DUTY...
...THAT I GOT THE CALL! IT *MUST BE!*
BUT IT'S *HER* FAULT!
BELL-DANDY!
NOW WHAT? IF I TRY TO KEEP THIS UP, I'LL *CROAK.*
I'VE GOTTA THINK OF SOME "REQUEST" *PRONTO.*

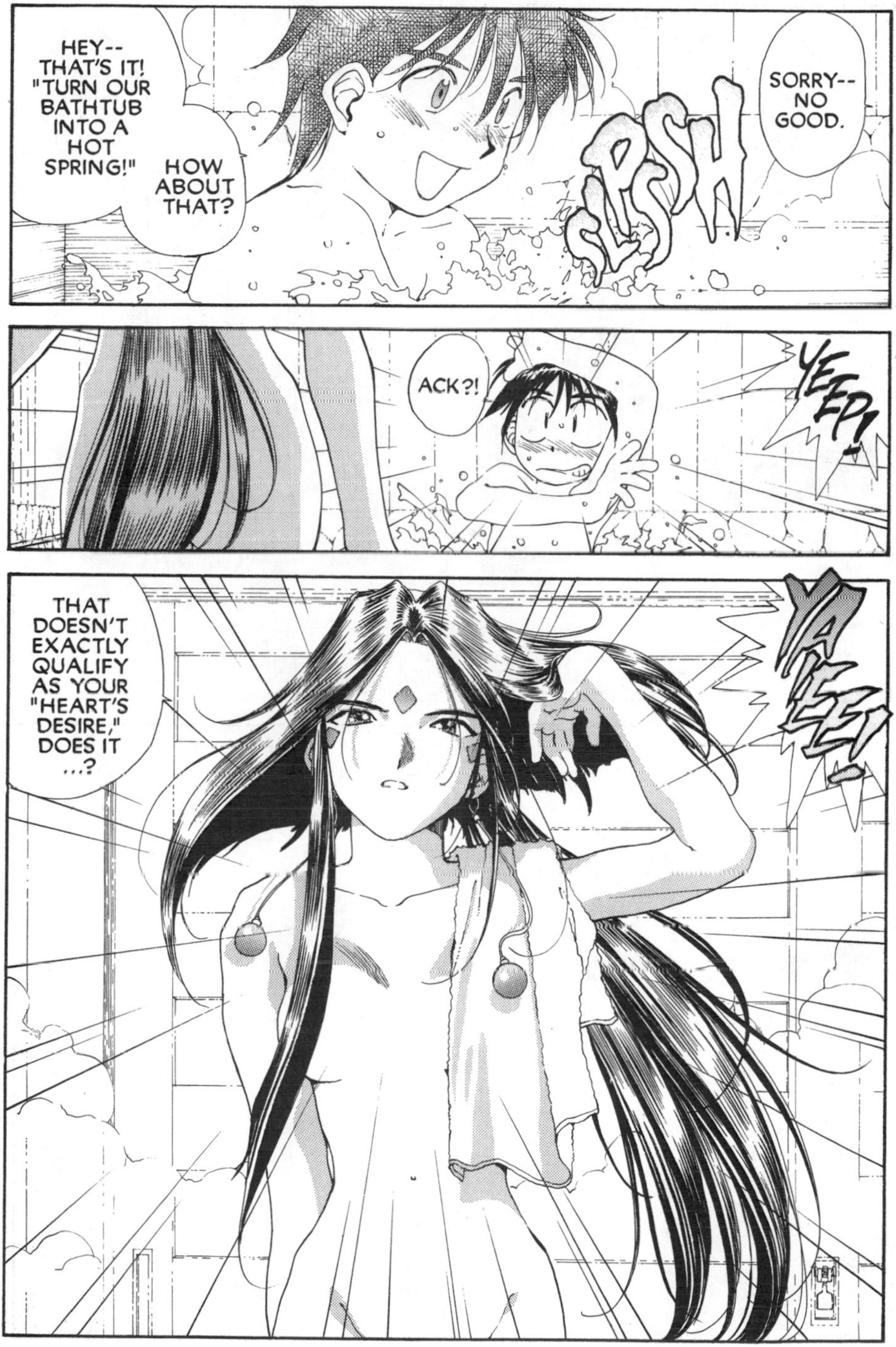
HEY-- THAT'S IT! "TURN OUR BATHTUB INTO A HOT SPRING!"
HOW ABOUT THAT?
SPLSH
SORRY-- NO GOOD.
ACK?!
YEEP!
THAT DOESN'T EXACTLY QUALIFY AS YOUR "HEART'S DESIRE," DOES IT ...?
YAEEE!

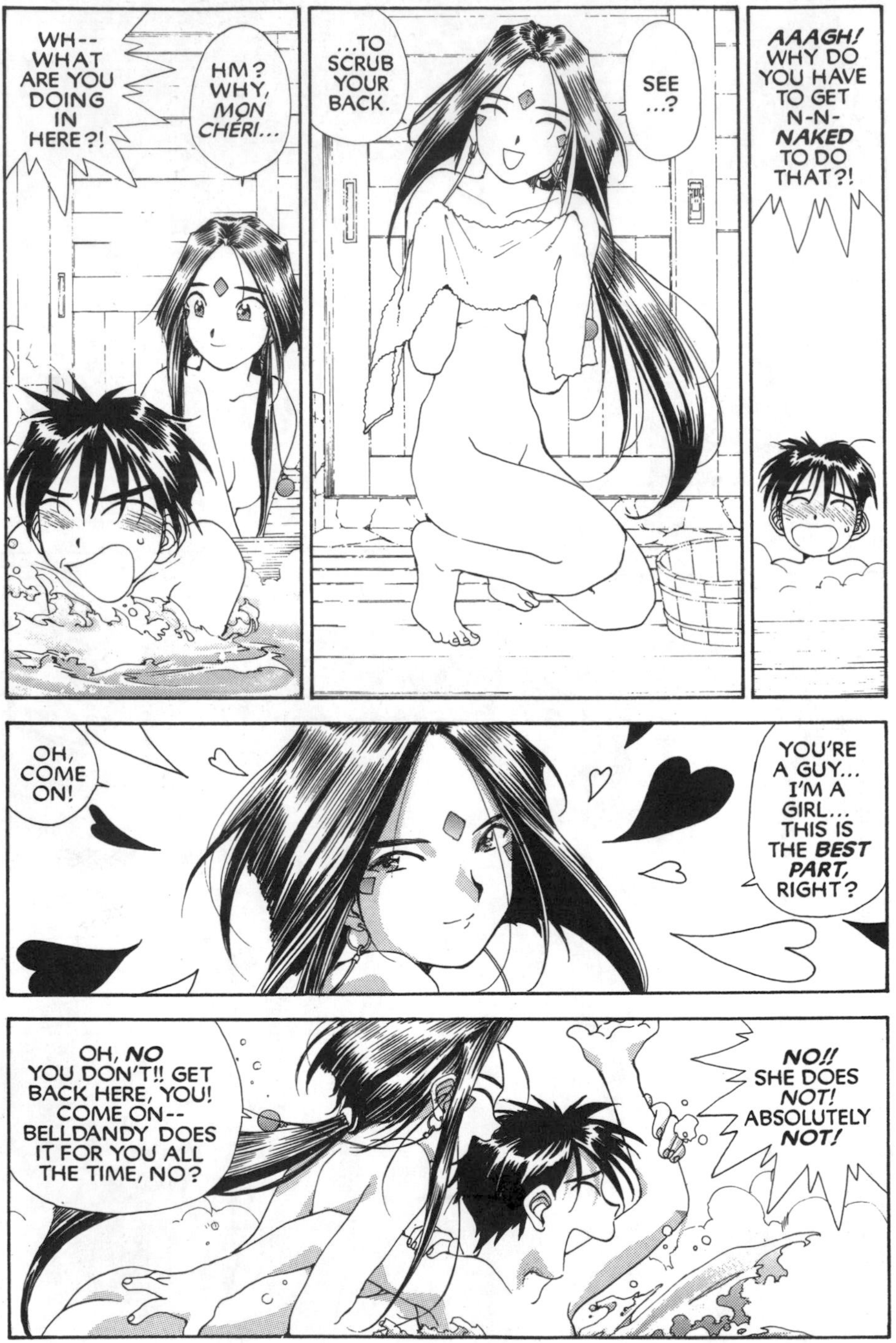
WH-- WHAT ARE YOU DOING IN HERE?!
HM? WHY, *MON CHÉRI*...
...TO SCRUB YOUR BACK.
SEE ...?
AAAGH! WHY DO YOU HAVE TO GET N-N-***NAKED*** TO DO THAT?!
OH, COME ON!
YOU'RE A GUY... I'M A GIRL... THIS IS THE ***BEST PART,*** RIGHT?
OH, ***NO*** YOU DON'T!! GET BACK HERE, YOU! COME ON-- BELLDANDY DOES IT FOR YOU ALL THE TIME, NO?
NO!! SHE DOES ***NOT!*** ABSOLUTELY ***NOT!***

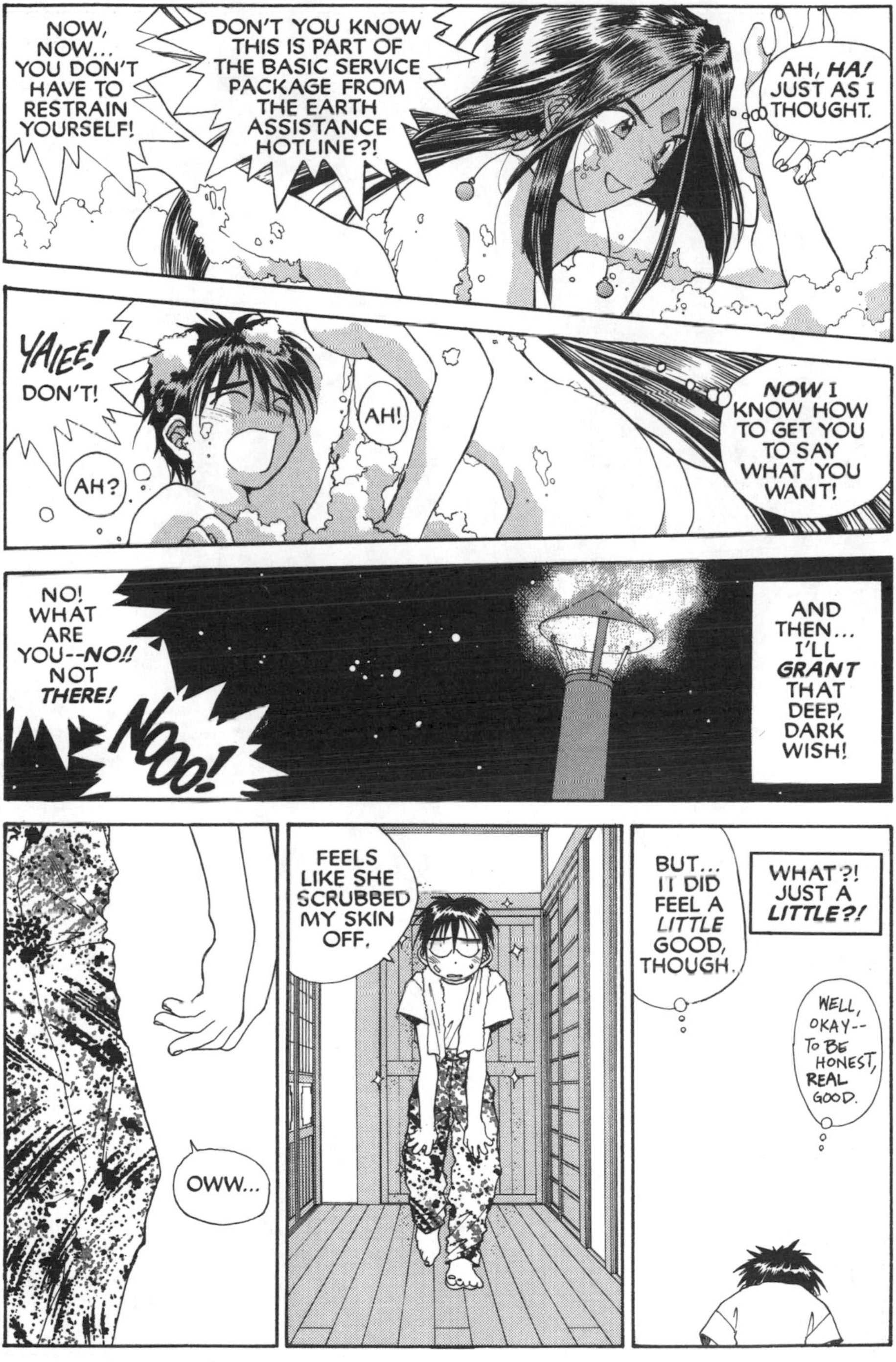
NOW, NOW... YOU DON'T HAVE TO RESTRAIN YOURSELF!
DON'T YOU KNOW THIS IS PART OF THE BASIC SERVICE PACKAGE FROM THE EARTH ASSISTANCE HOTLINE?!
AH, HA! JUST AS I THOUGHT.
YAIEE! DON'T!
AH?
AH!
NOW I KNOW HOW TO GET YOU TO SAY WHAT YOU WANT!
NO! WHAT ARE YOU--NO!! NOT THERE!
NOOO!
AND THEN... I'LL GRANT THAT DEEP, DARK WISH!
OWW...
FEELS LIKE SHE SCRUBBED MY SKIN OFF.
BUT... IT DID FEEL A LITTLE GOOD, THOUGH.
WHAT?! JUST A LITTLE?!
WELL, OKAY-- TO BE HONEST, REAL GOOD.

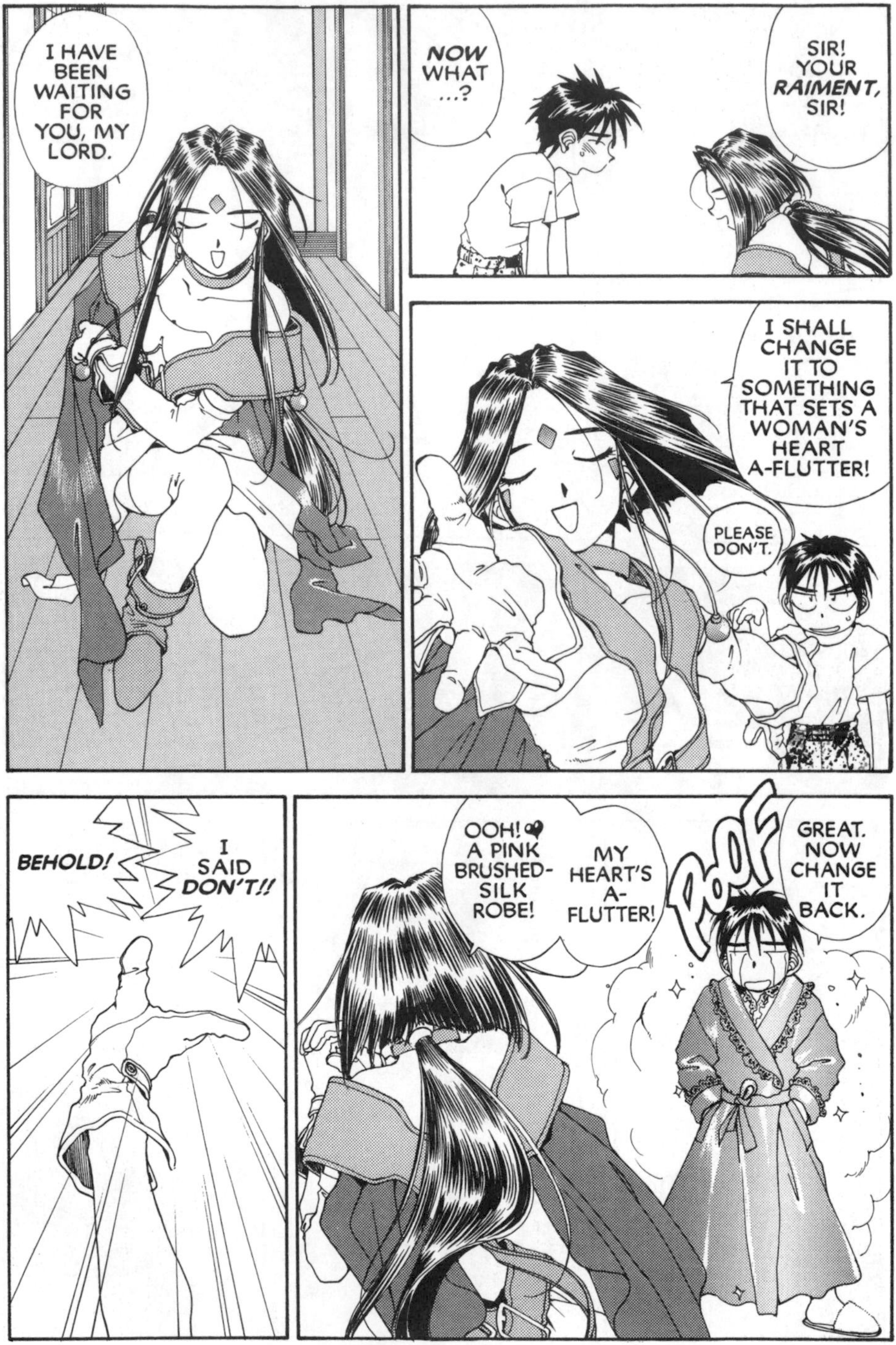

I HAVE BEEN WAITING FOR YOU, MY LORD.
NOW WHAT ...?
SIR! YOUR RAIMENT, SIR!
I SHALL CHANGE IT TO SOMETHING THAT SETS A WOMAN'S HEART A-FLUTTER!
PLEASE DON'T.
BEHOLD!
I SAID DON'T!!
OOH! A PINK BRUSHED-SILK ROBE!
MY HEART'S A-FLUTTER!
POOF
GREAT. NOW CHANGE IT BACK.

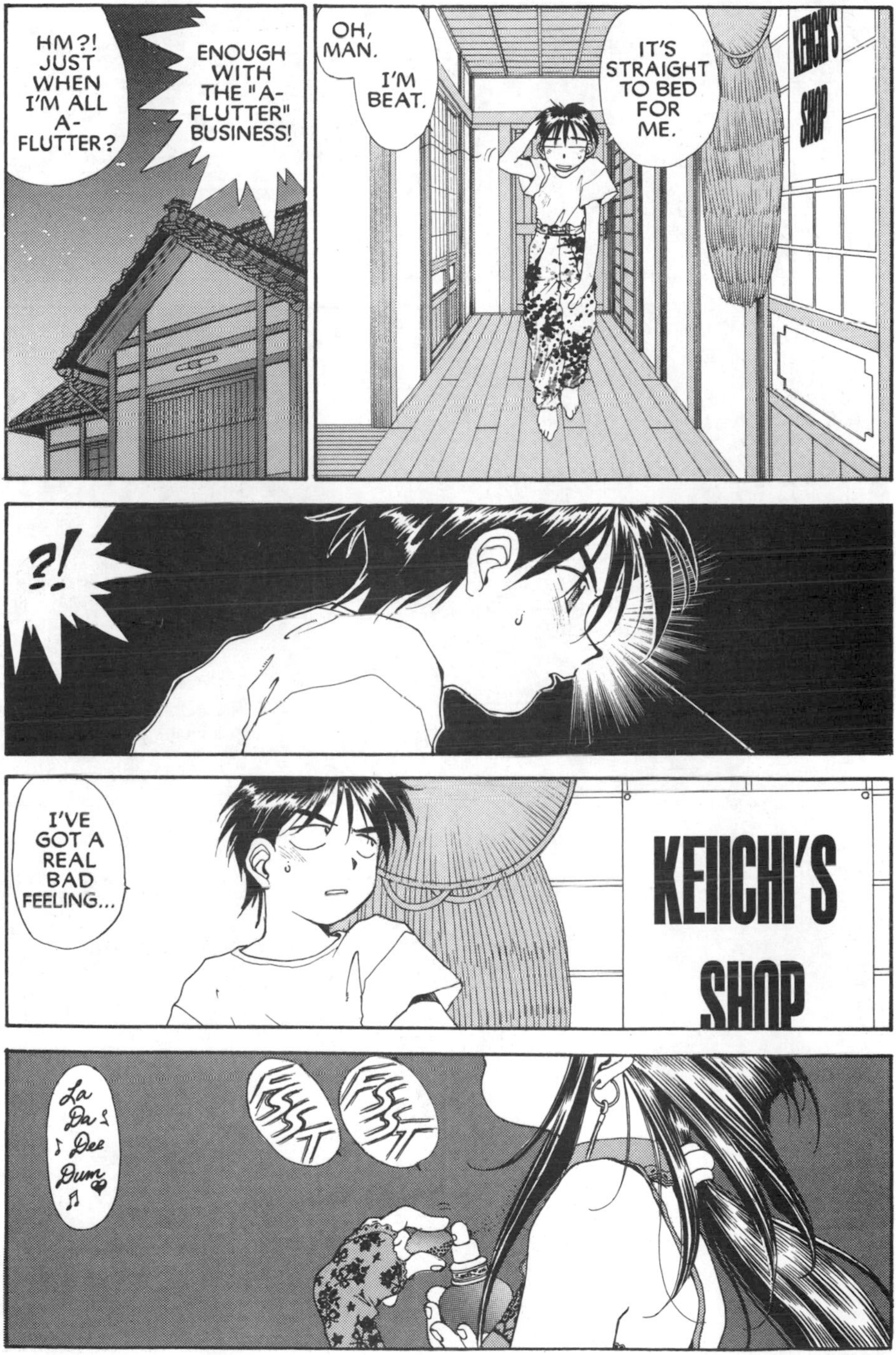
HM?! JUST WHEN I'M ALL A-FLUTTER?
ENOUGH WITH THE "A-FLUTTER" BUSINESS!
OH, MAN.
I'M BEAT.
IT'S STRAIGHT TO BED FOR ME.
KEIICHI'S SHOP
?!
I'VE GOT A REAL BAD FEELING...
KEIICHI'S SHOP
La Da Dee Dum
FSSST
FSSST

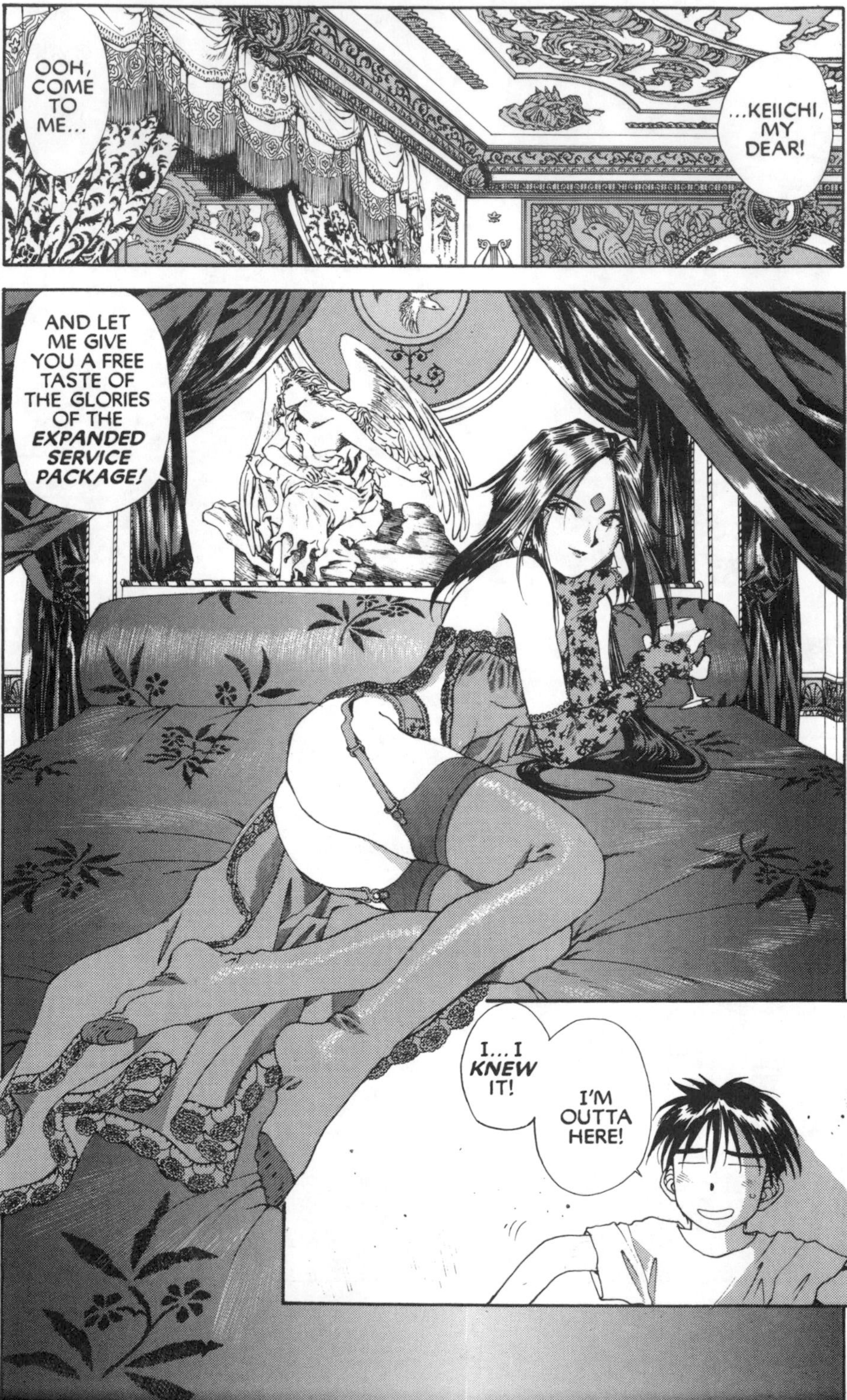
OOH, COME TO ME...
...KEIICHI, MY DEAR!
AND LET ME GIVE YOU A FREE TASTE OF THE GLORIES OF THE ***EXPANDED SERVICE PACKAGE!***
I... I ***KNEW*** IT!
I'M OUTTA HERE!

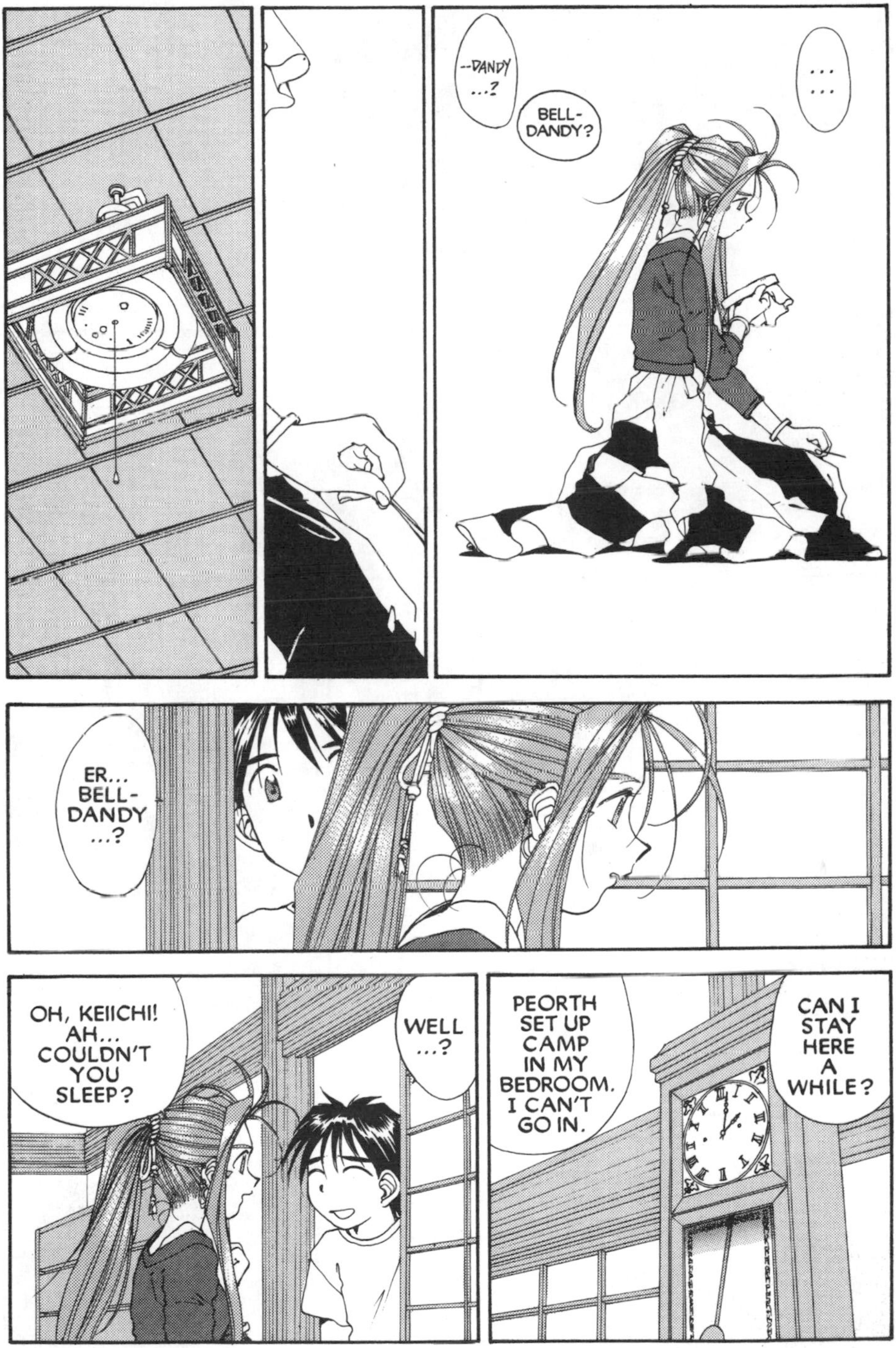
--DANDY ...?
BELL-DANDY?
... ...
ER... BELL-DANDY ...?
OH, KEIICHI! AH... COULDN'T YOU SLEEP?
WELL ...?
PEORTH SET UP CAMP IN MY BEDROOM. I CAN'T GO IN.
CAN I STAY HERE A WHILE?

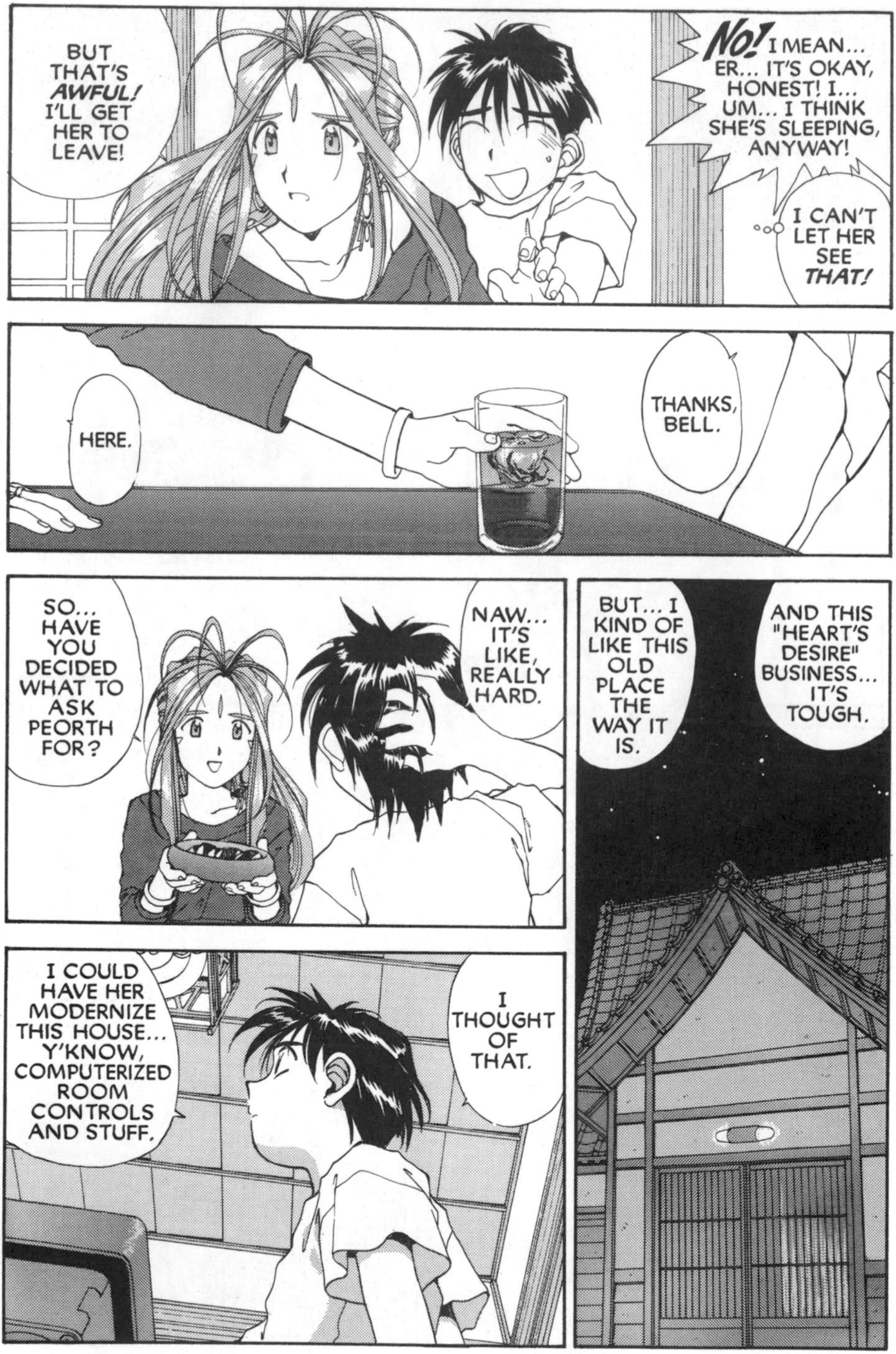
BUT THAT'S *AWFUL!* I'LL GET HER TO LEAVE!
NO! I MEAN... ER... IT'S OKAY, HONEST! I... UM... I THINK SHE'S SLEEPING, ANYWAY!
I CAN'T LET HER SEE *THAT!*
HERE.
THANKS, BELL.
SO... HAVE YOU DECIDED WHAT TO ASK PEORTH FOR?
NAW... IT'S LIKE, REALLY HARD.
I COULD HAVE HER MODERNIZE THIS HOUSE... Y'KNOW, COMPUTERIZED ROOM CONTROLS AND STUFF.
I THOUGHT OF THAT.
BUT... I KIND OF LIKE THIS OLD PLACE THE WAY IT IS.
AND THIS "HEART'S DESIRE" BUSINESS... IT'S TOUGH.

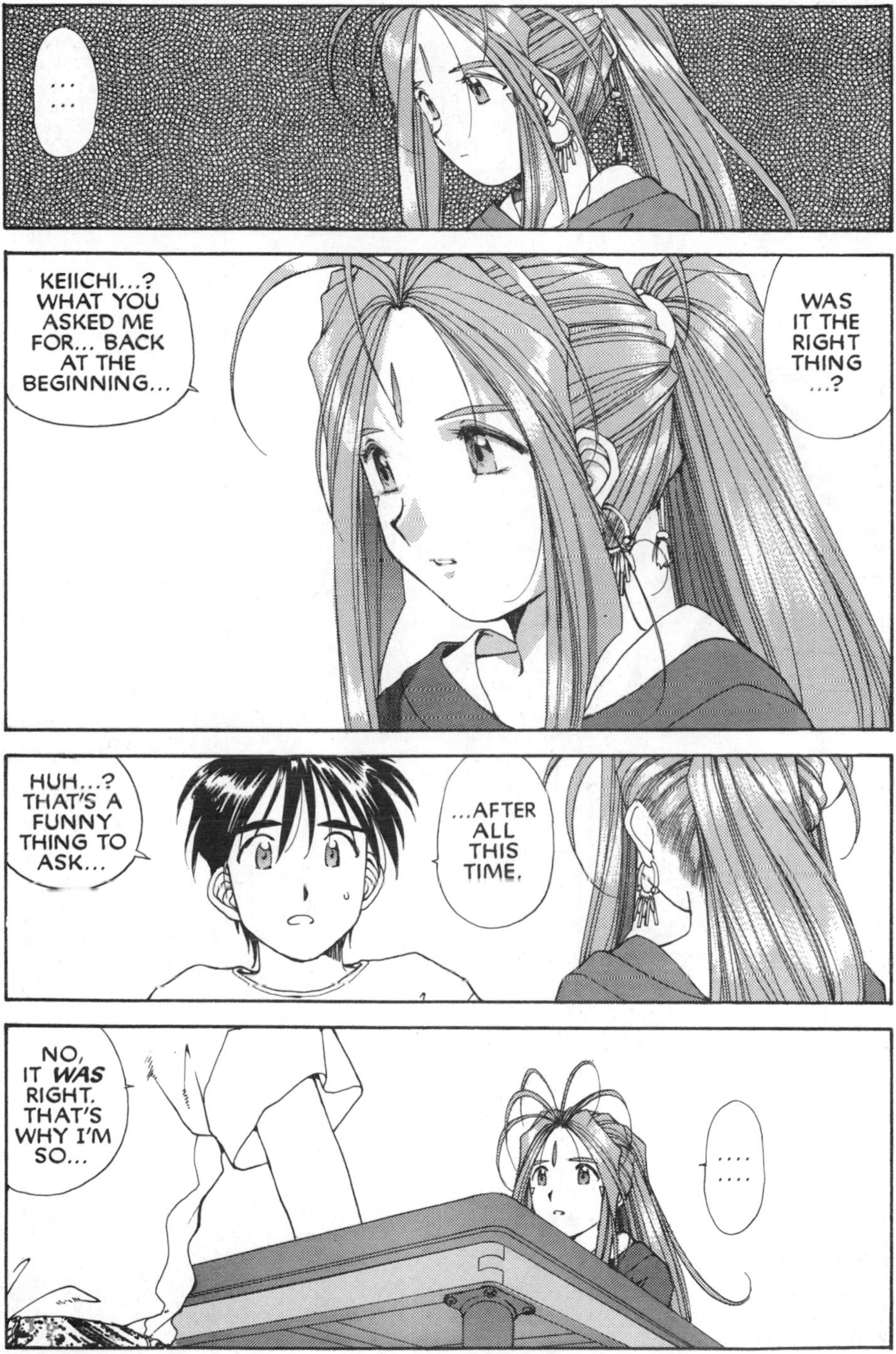
......
KEIICHI...? WHAT YOU ASKED ME FOR... BACK AT THE BEGINNING...
WAS IT THE RIGHT THING ...?
HUH...? THAT'S A FUNNY THING TO ASK...
...AFTER ALL THIS TIME.
NO, IT ***WAS*** RIGHT. THAT'S WHY I'M SO...
....

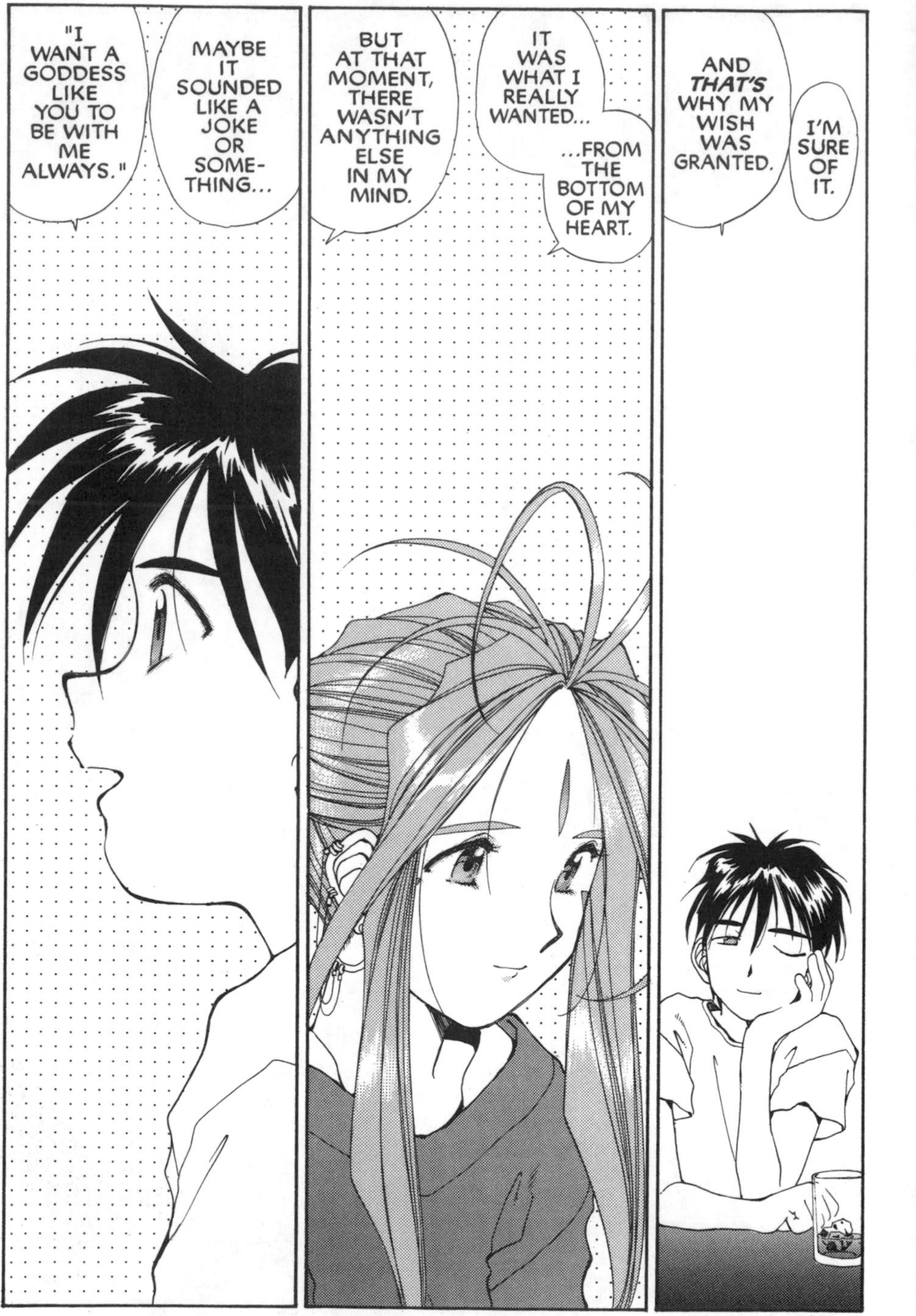
"I WANT A GODDESS LIKE YOU TO BE WITH ME ALWAYS."
MAYBE IT SOUNDED LIKE A JOKE OR SOME-THING...
BUT AT THAT MOMENT, THERE WASN'T ANYTHING ELSE IN MY MIND.
IT WAS WHAT I REALLY WANTED...
...FROM THE BOTTOM OF MY HEART.
AND *THAT'S* WHY MY WISH WAS GRANTED.
I'M SURE OF IT.

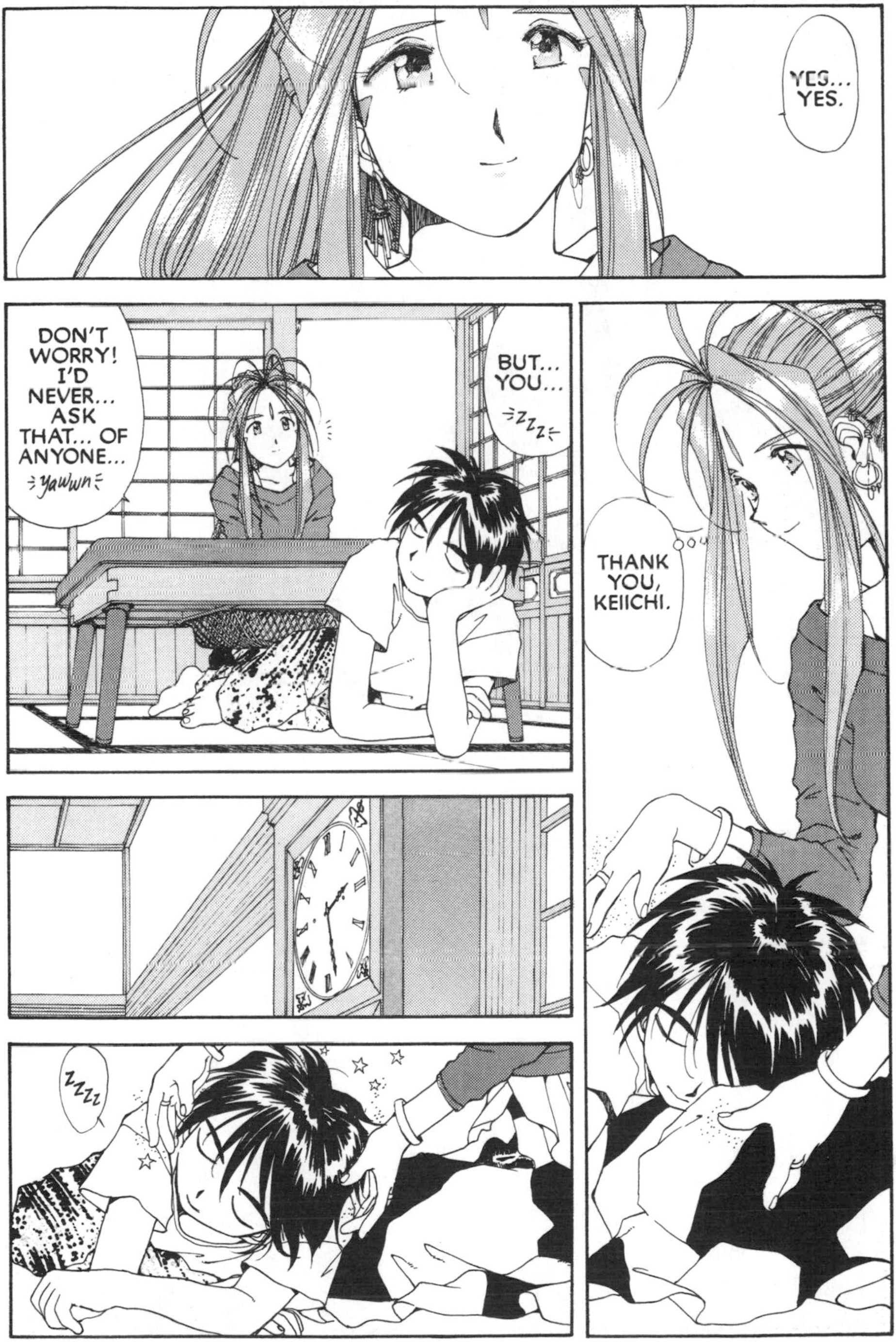
YES... YES.
DON'T WORRY! I'D NEVER... ASK THAT... OF ANYONE...
YAWWN
BUT... YOU...
ZZZ
ZZZZ
THANK YOU, KEIICHI.

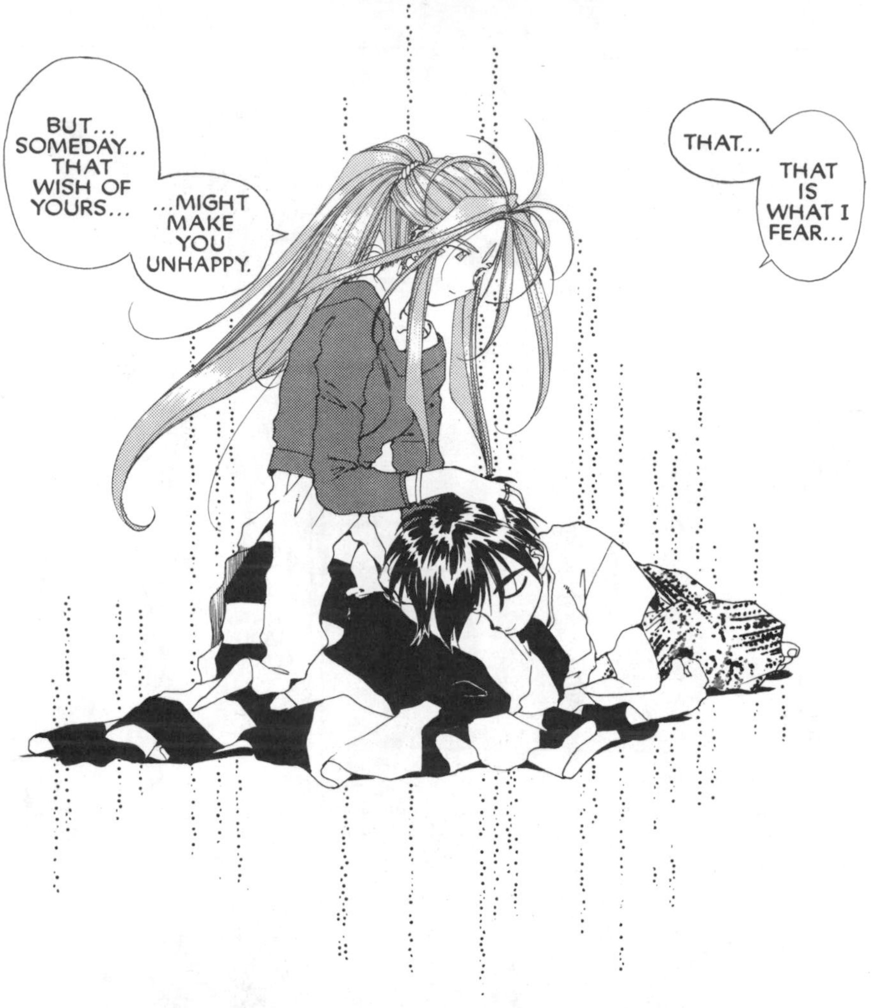
BUT... SOMEDAY... THAT WISH OF YOURS...
...MIGHT MAKE YOU UNHAPPY.
THAT...
THAT IS WHAT I FEAR...

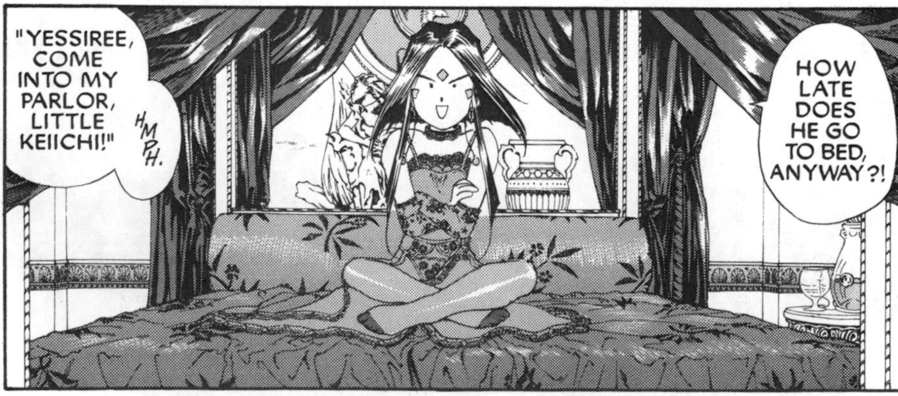
"YESSIREE, COME INTO MY PARLOR, LITTLE KEIICHI!"
HMPH.
HOW LATE DOES HE GO TO BED, ANYWAY?!

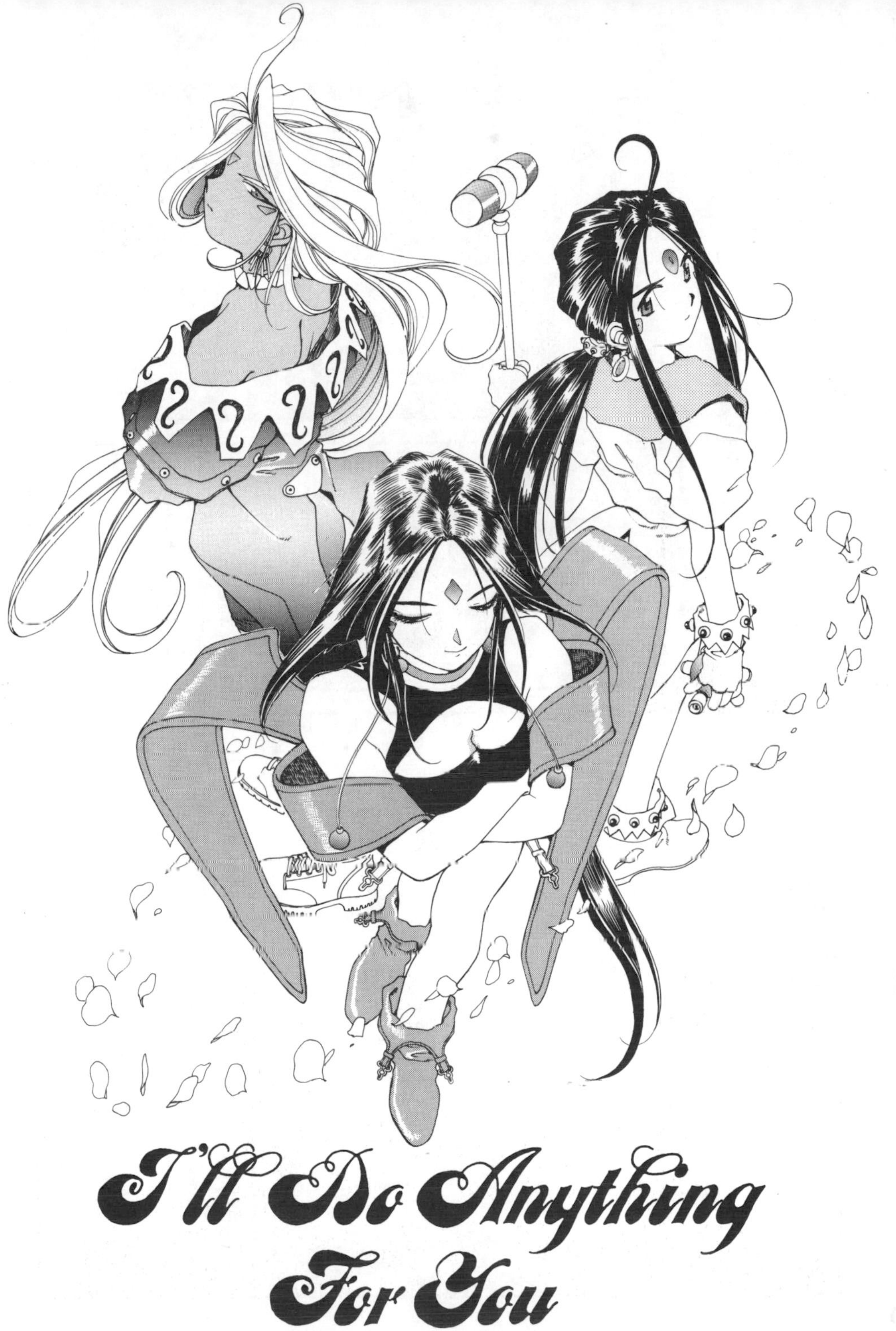

I'll Do Anything For You

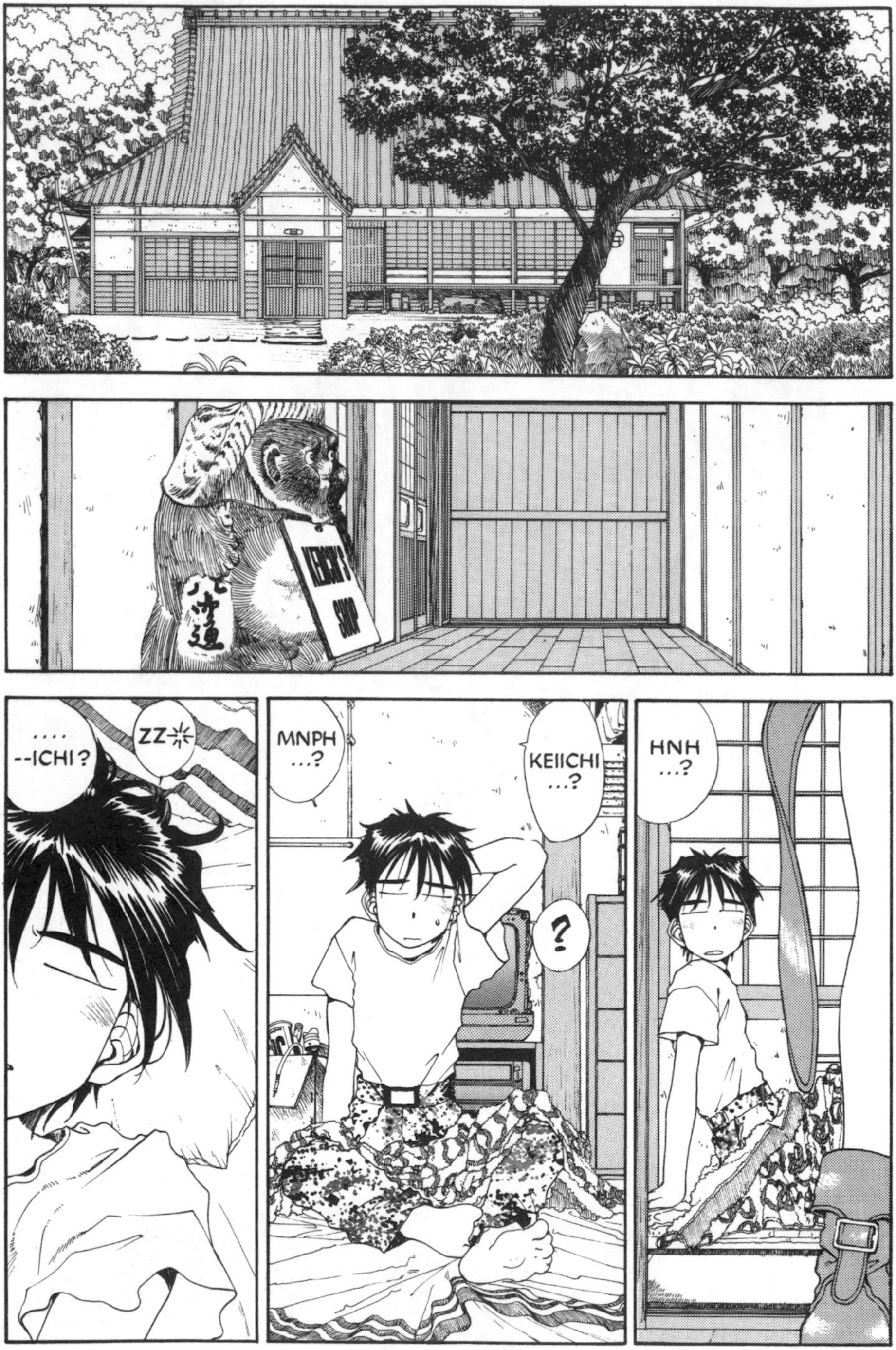
KEIICHI'S SHOP
....
--ICHI?
ZZ
MNPH
...?
KEIICHI
...?
?
HNH
...?

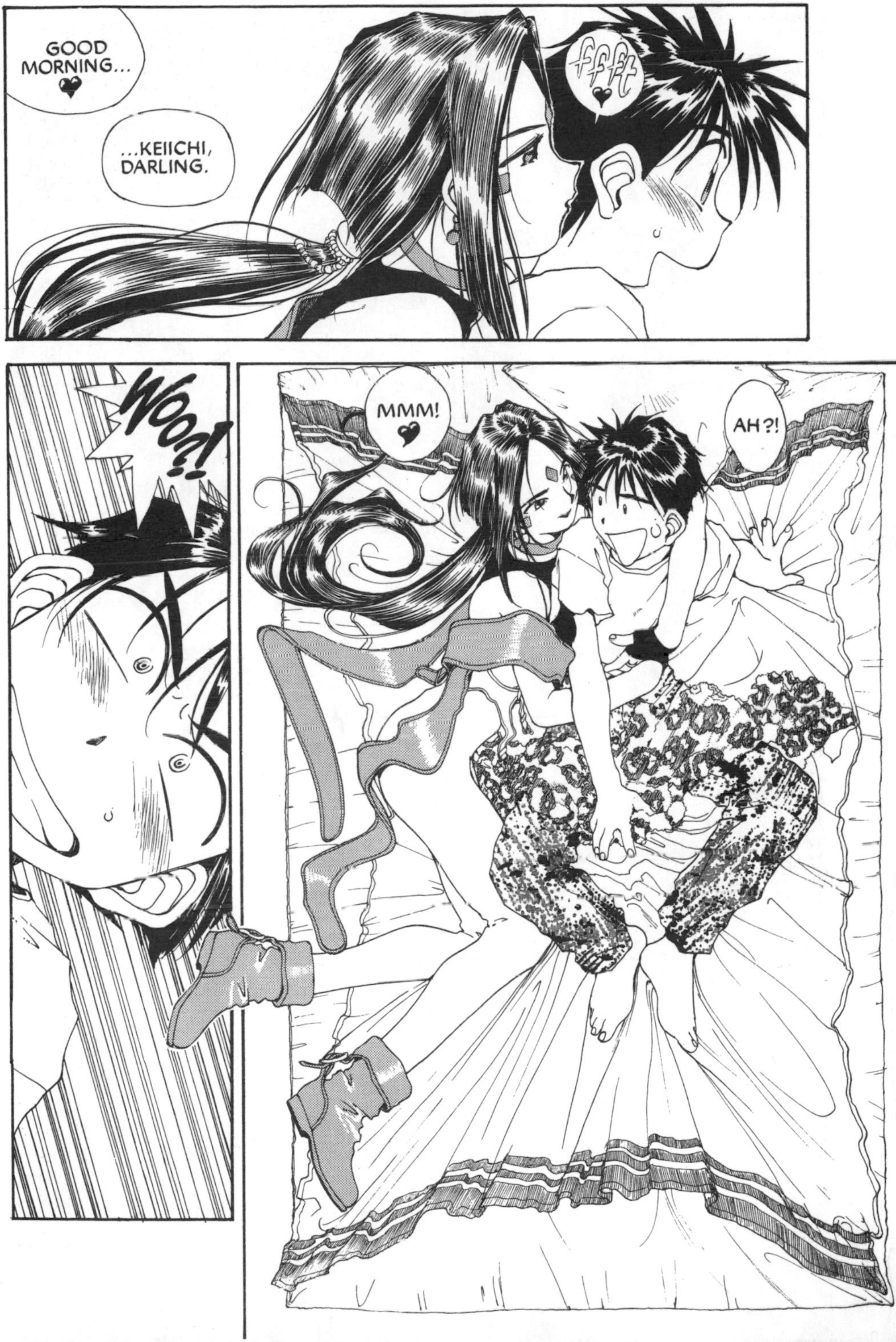
GOOD MORNING... ♥
...KEIICHI, DARLING.
ffft ♥
WOO?!
MMM! ♥
AH?!

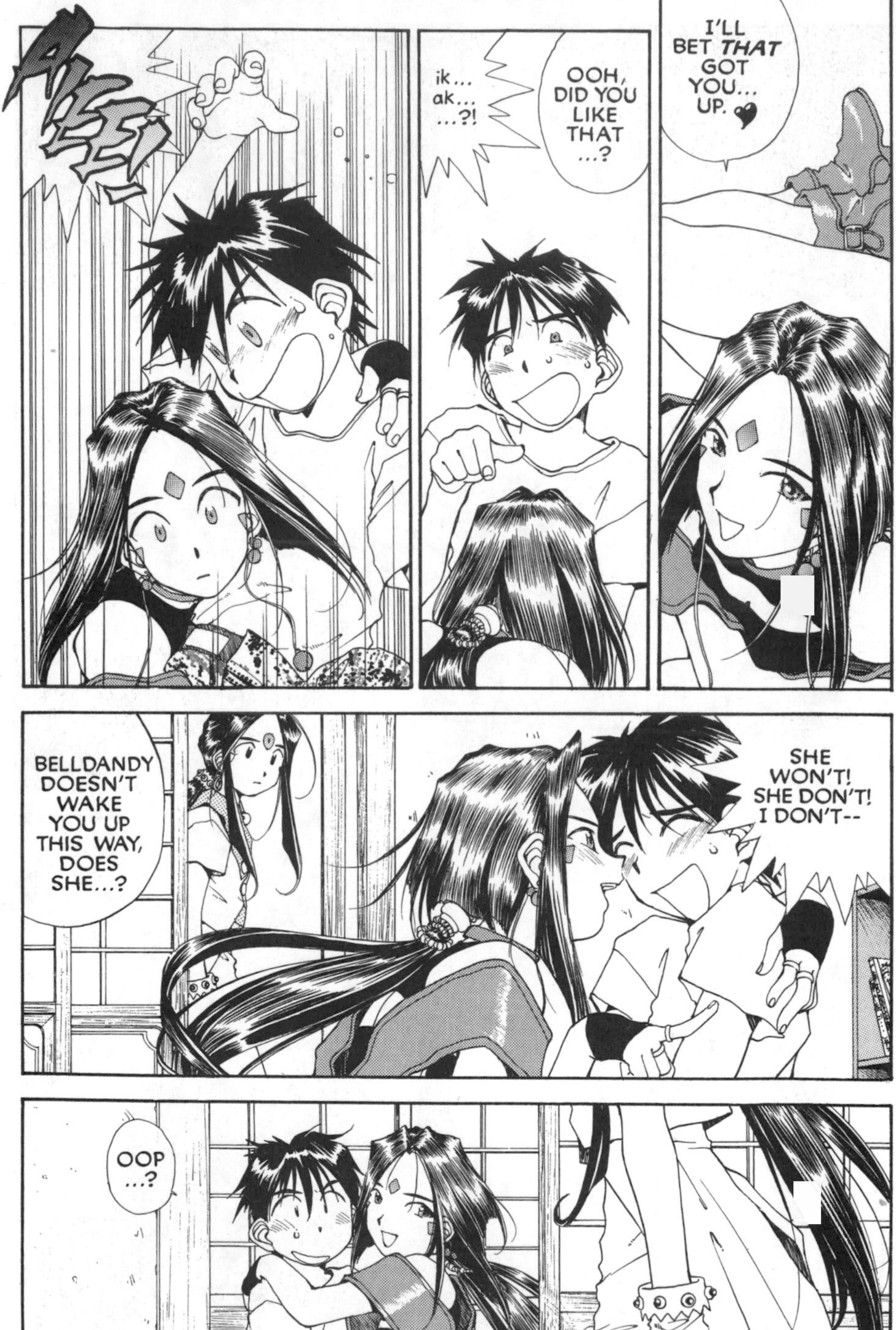
AIEEE
ik... ak... ...?!
OOH, DID YOU LIKE THAT ...?
I'LL BET *THAT* GOT YOU... UP.
BELLDANDY DOESN'T WAKE YOU UP THIS WAY, DOES SHE...?
SHE WON'T! SHE DON'T! I DON'T--
OOP ...?

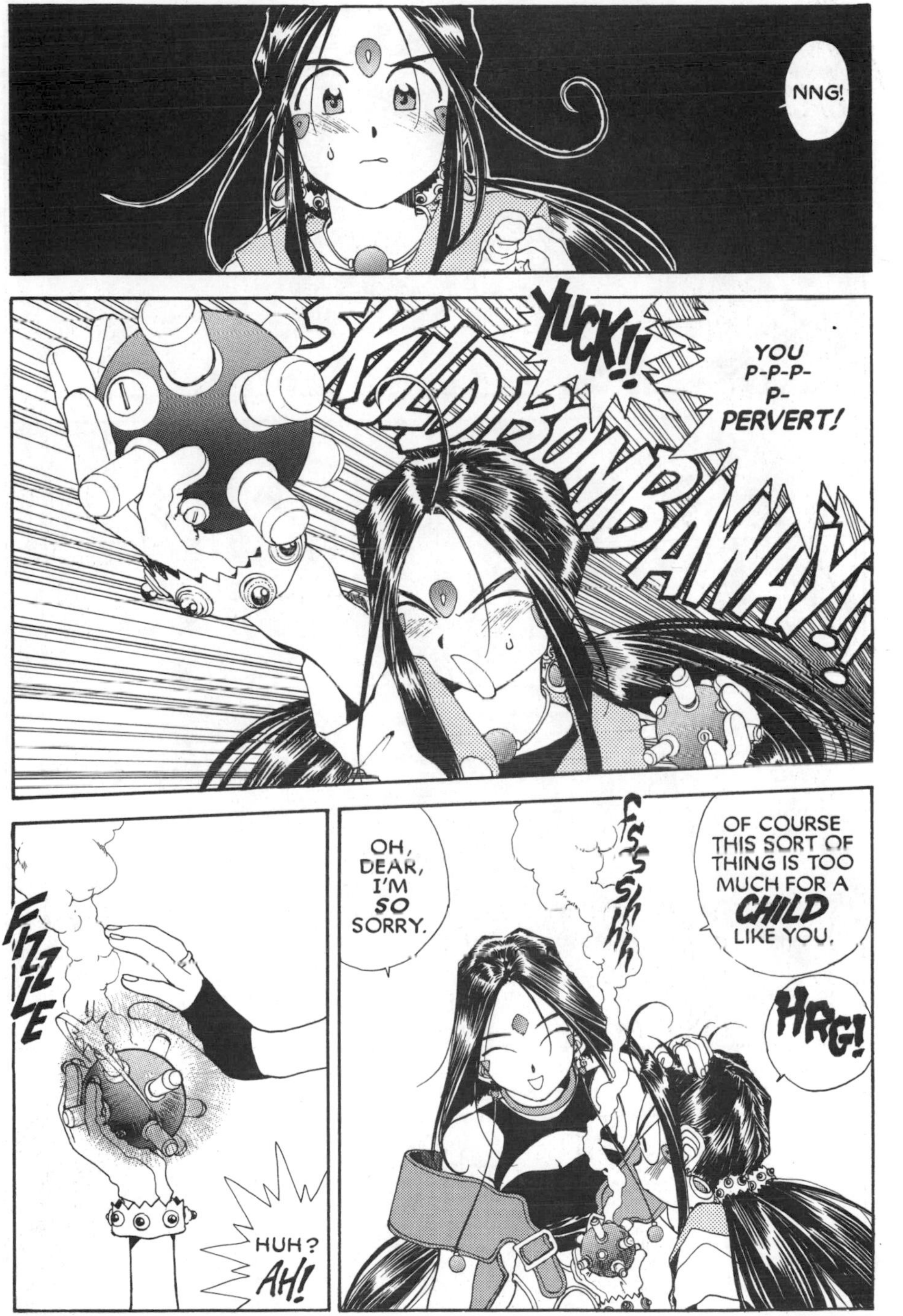
NNG!
YUCK!!
SKULD BOMB AWAY!!
YOU P-P-P-P-PERVERT!
FIZZLE
HUH? AH!
OH, DEAR, I'M SO SORRY.
FSSSHHH
OF COURSE THIS SORT OF THING IS TOO MUCH FOR A CHILD LIKE YOU.
HRG!

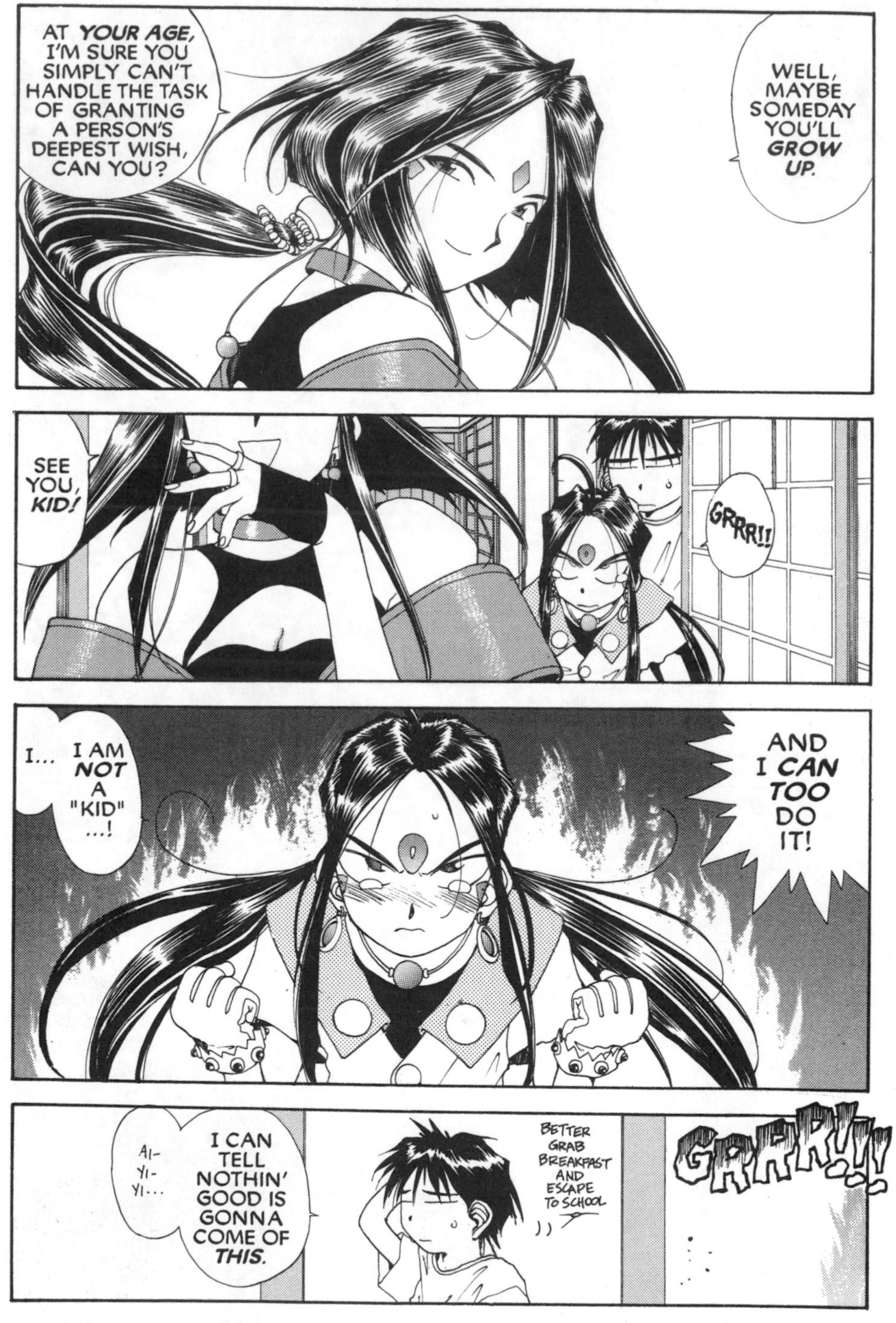
AT YOUR AGE, I'M SURE YOU SIMPLY CAN'T HANDLE THE TASK OF GRANTING A PERSON'S DEEPEST WISH, CAN YOU?
WELL, MAYBE SOMEDAY YOU'LL GROW UP.
SEE YOU, KID!
GRRR!!
I... I AM NOT A "KID" ...!
AND I CAN TOO DO IT!
AI-YI-YI...
I CAN TELL NOTHIN' GOOD IS GONNA COME OF THIS.
BETTER GRAB BREAKFAST AND ESCAPE TO SCHOOL
GRRR!!

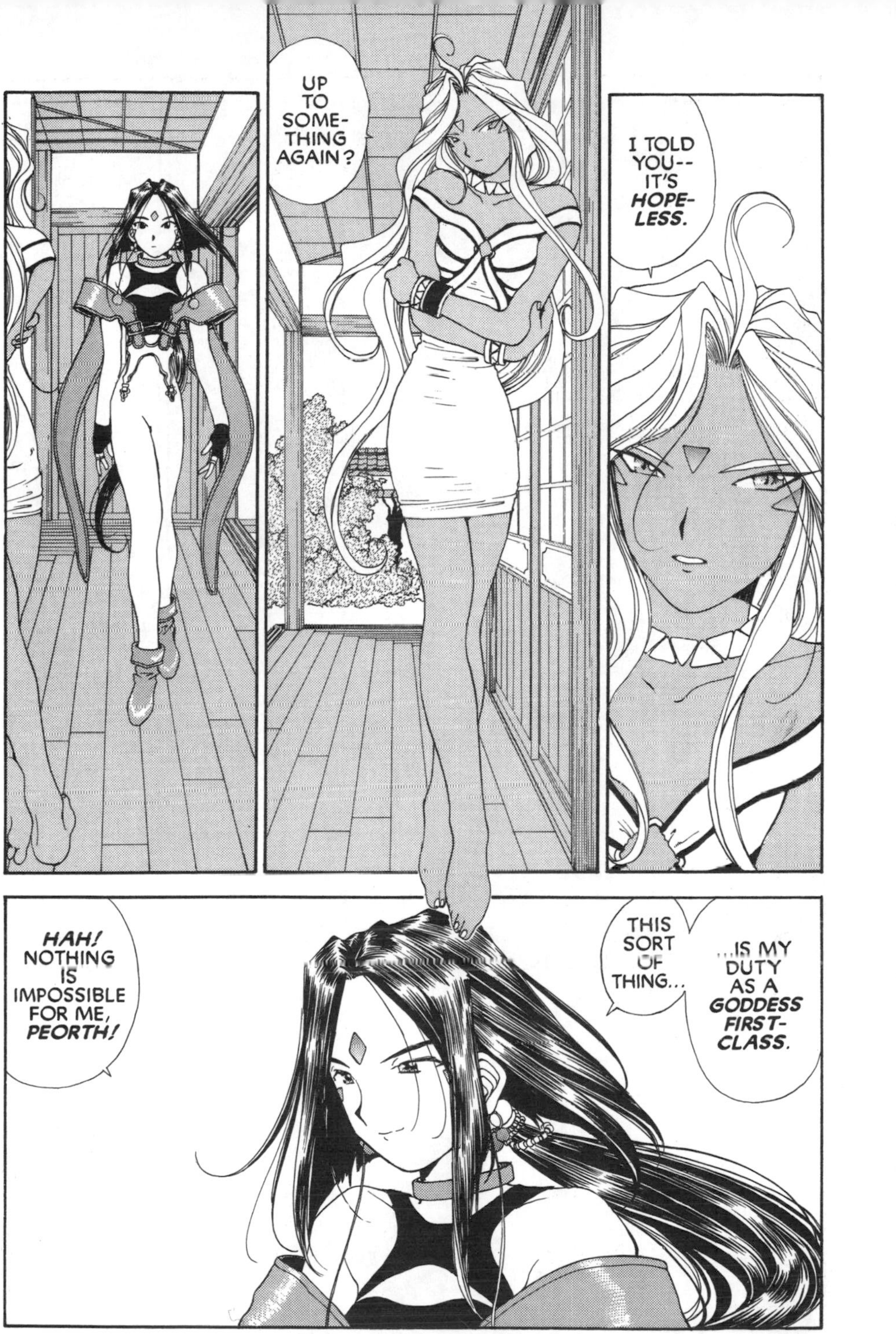
UP TO SOMETHING AGAIN?
I TOLD YOU-- IT'S *HOPELESS.*
HAH! NOTHING IS IMPOSSIBLE FOR ME, ***PEORTH!***
THIS SORT OF THING...
...IS MY DUTY AS A ***GODDESS FIRST-CLASS.***

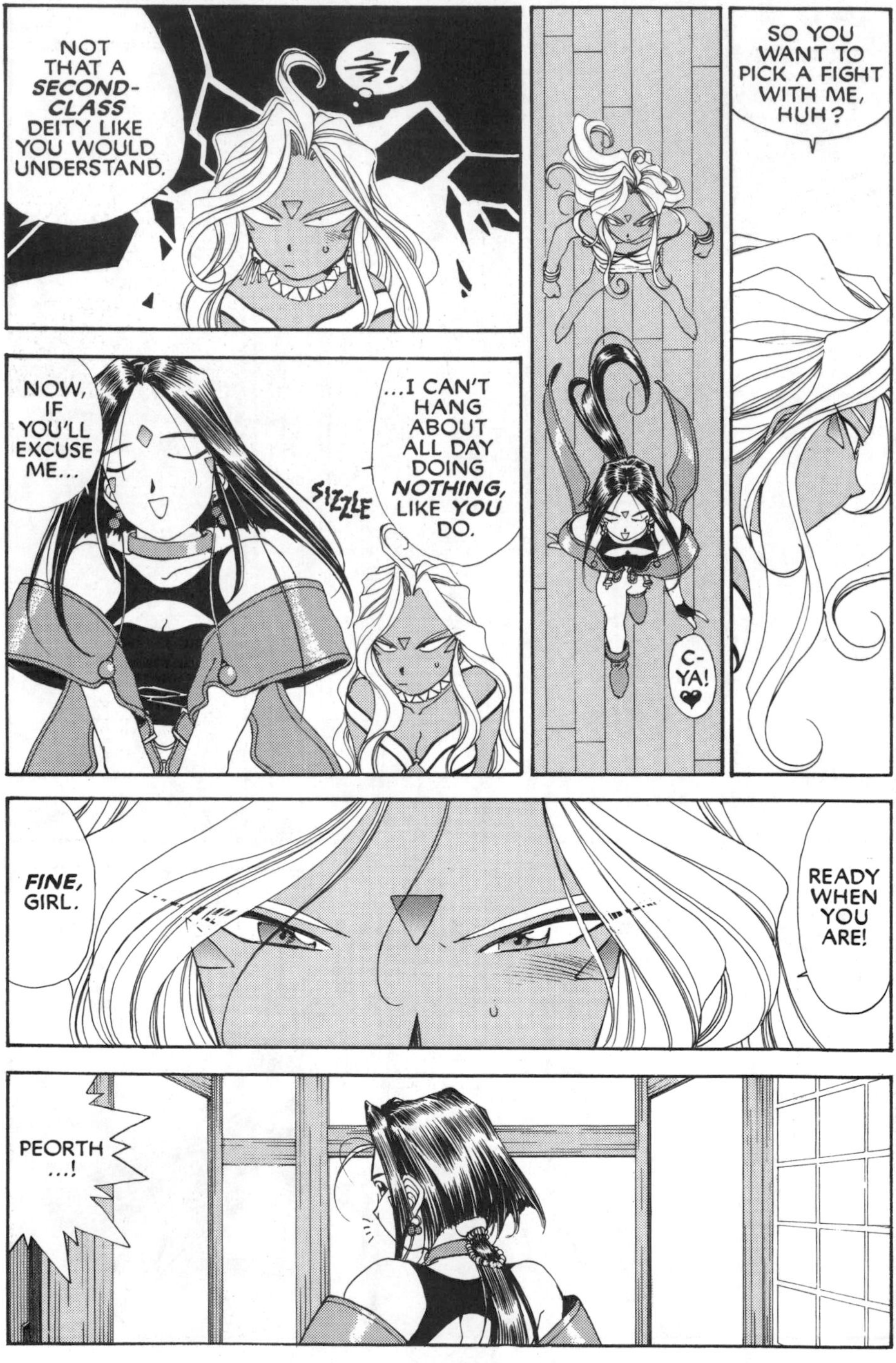
NOT THAT A SECOND-CLASS DEITY LIKE YOU WOULD UNDERSTAND.
NOW, IF YOU'LL EXCUSE ME...
SIZZLE
...I CAN'T HANG ABOUT ALL DAY DOING NOTHING, LIKE YOU DO.
C-YA! ♥
SO YOU WANT TO PICK A FIGHT WITH ME, HUH?
FINE, GIRL.
READY WHEN YOU ARE!
PEORTH ...!

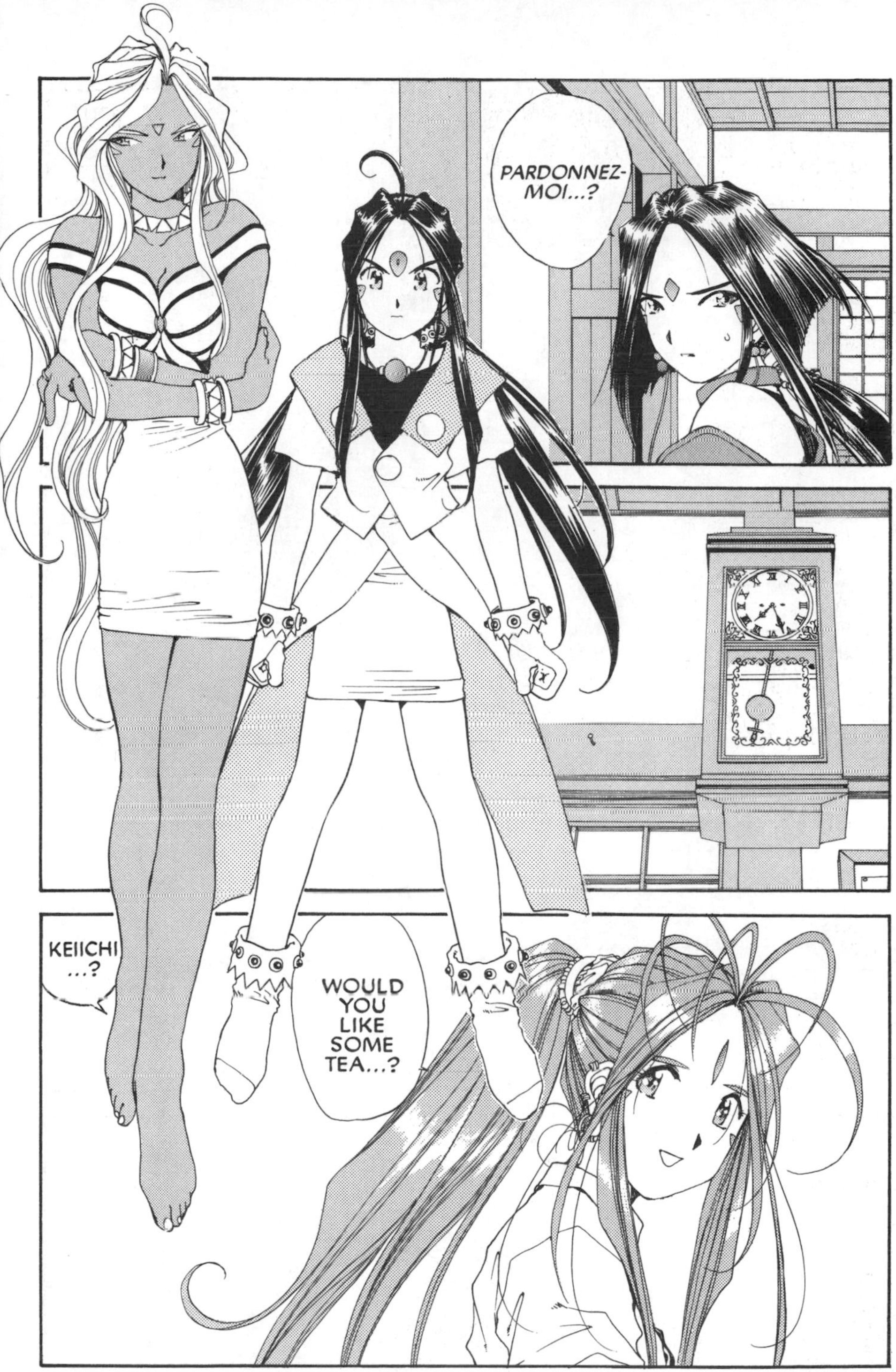
PARDONNEZ-MOI...?
KEIICHI ...?
WOULD YOU LIKE SOME TEA...?

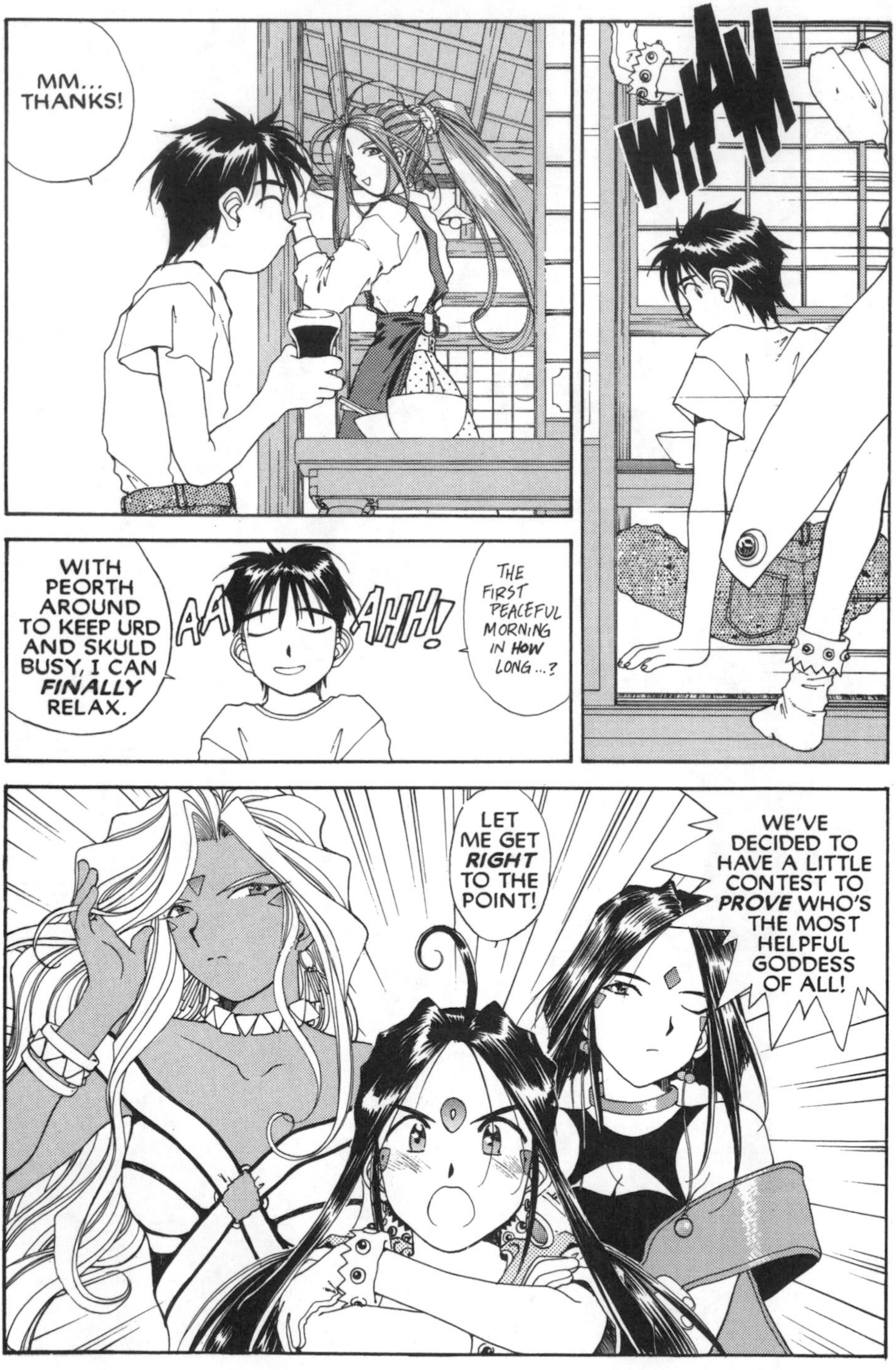
MM... THANKS!
WITH PEORTH AROUND TO KEEP URD AND SKULD BUSY, I CAN FINALLY RELAX.
AAAHH!
THE FIRST PEACEFUL MORNING IN HOW LONG...?
WHAM
LET ME GET RIGHT TO THE POINT!
WE'VE DECIDED TO HAVE A LITTLE CONTEST TO PROVE WHO'S THE MOST HELPFUL GODDESS OF ALL!

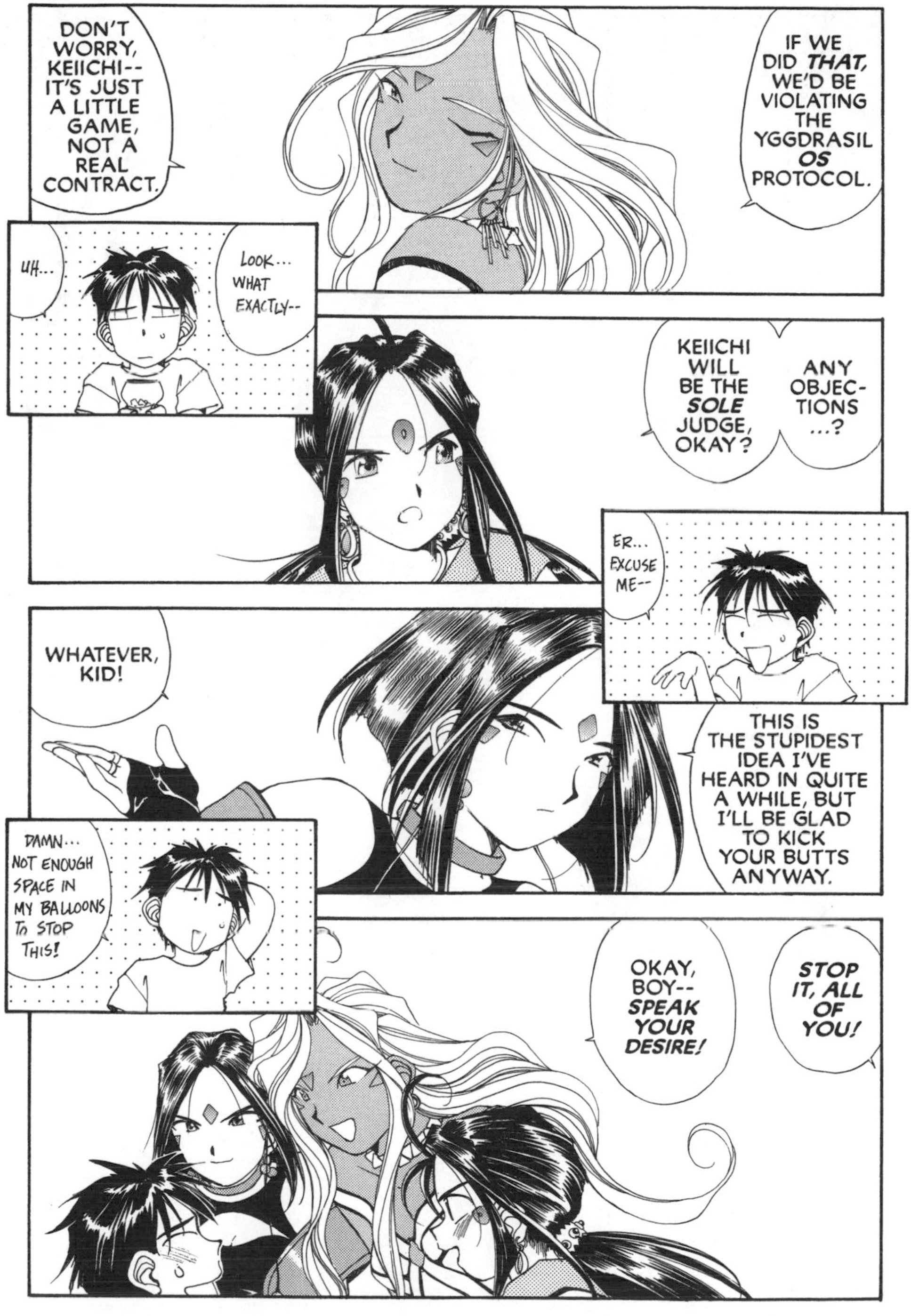

DON'T WORRY, KEIICHI-- IT'S JUST A LITTLE GAME, NOT A REAL CONTRACT.
IF WE DID *THAT,* WE'D BE VIOLATING THE YGGDRASIL *OS* PROTOCOL.
UH...
LOOK... WHAT EXACTLY--
KEIICHI WILL BE THE *SOLE* JUDGE, OKAY?
ANY OBJECTIONS ...?
ER... EXCUSE ME--
WHATEVER, KID!
THIS IS THE STUPIDEST IDEA I'VE HEARD IN QUITE A WHILE, BUT I'LL BE GLAD TO KICK YOUR BUTTS ANYWAY.
DAMN... NOT ENOUGH SPACE IN MY BALLOONS TO STOP THIS!
OKAY, BOY-- *SPEAK YOUR DESIRE!*
STOP IT, ALL OF YOU!

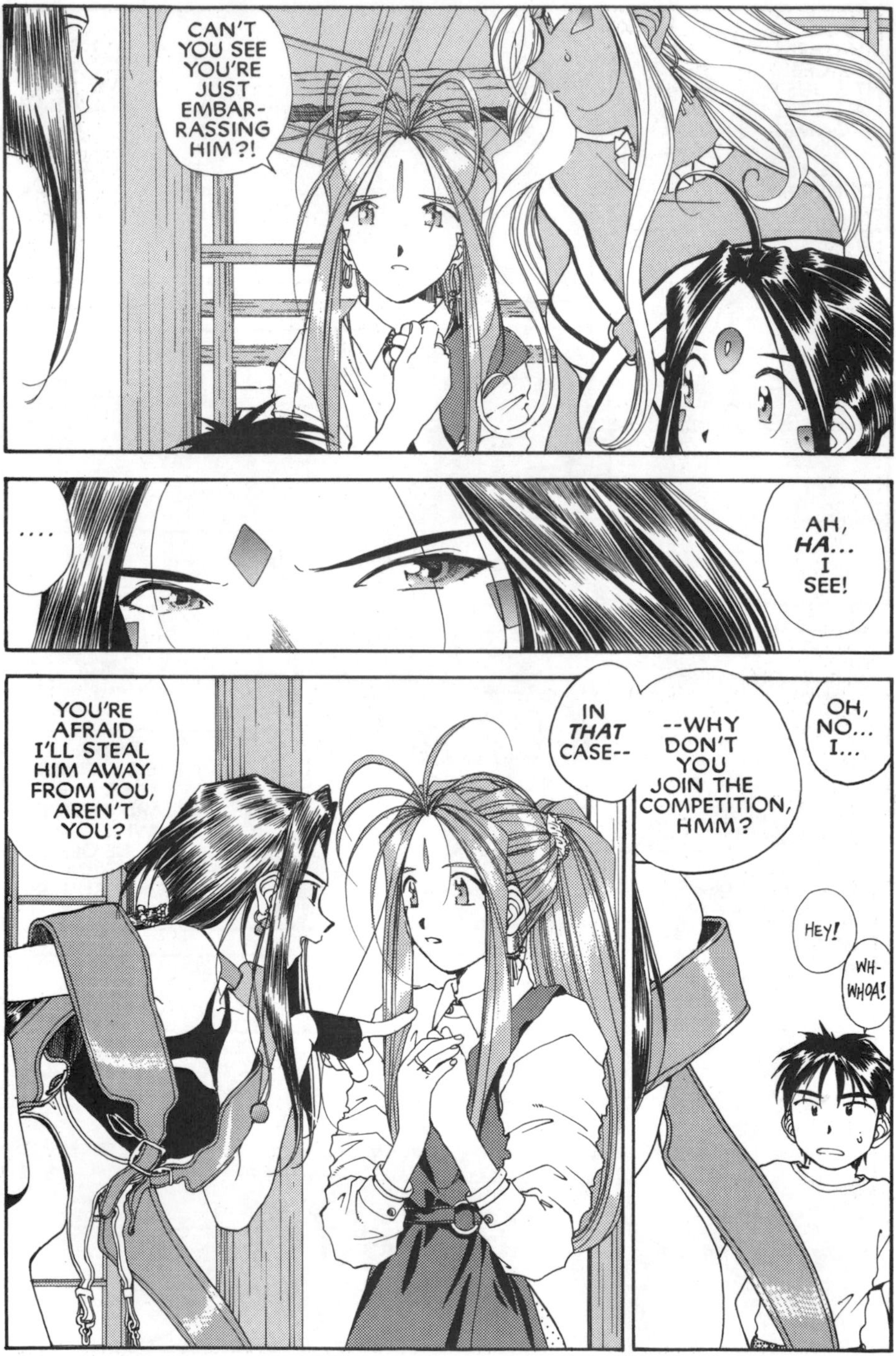
CAN'T YOU SEE YOU'RE JUST EMBAR-RASSING HIM?!
....
AH, *HA*... I SEE!
YOU'RE AFRAID I'LL STEAL HIM AWAY FROM YOU, AREN'T YOU?
IN *THAT* CASE--
--WHY DON'T YOU JOIN THE COMPETITION, HMM?
OH, NO... I...
HEY!
WH-WHOA!

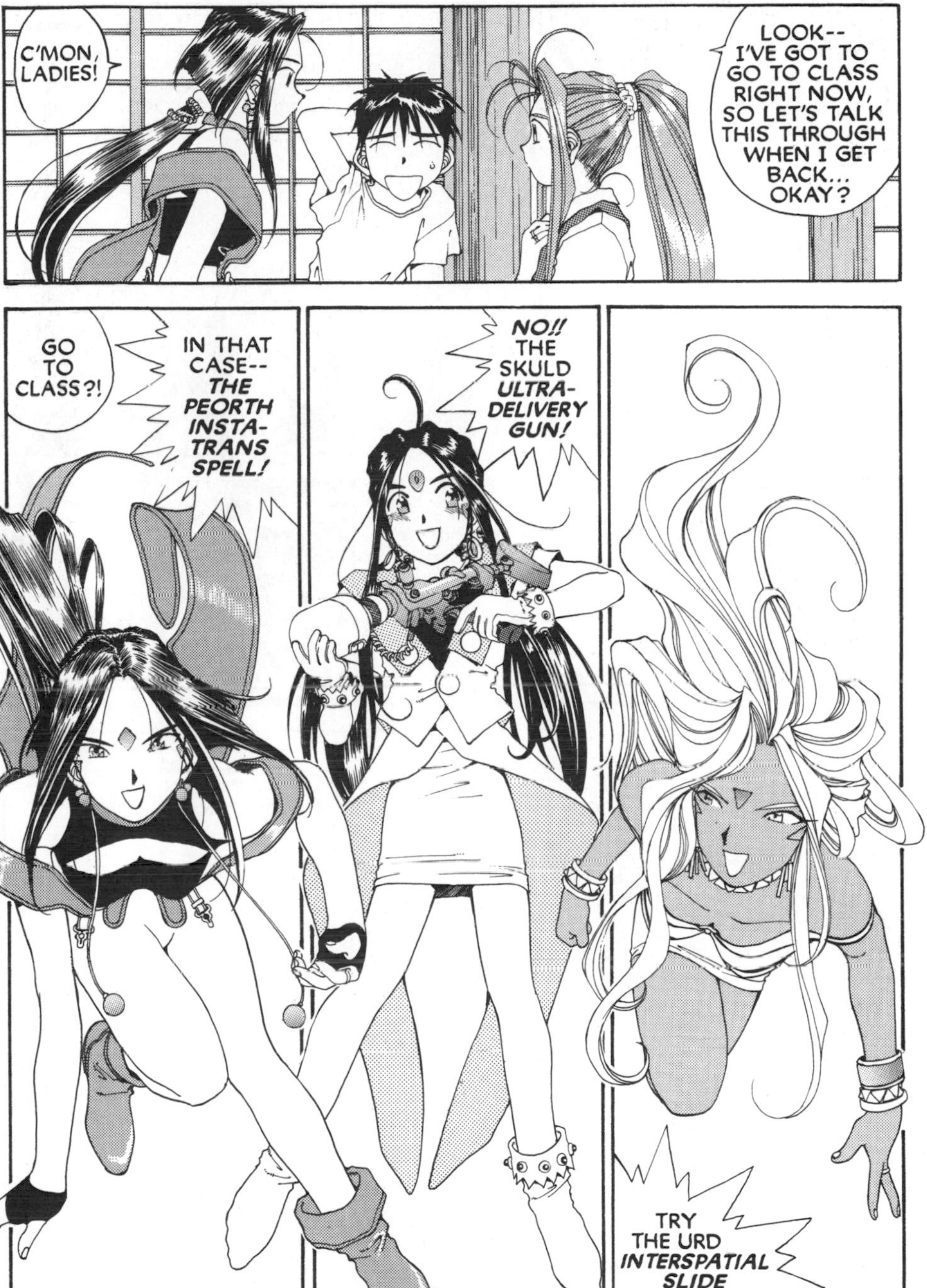
C'MON, LADIES!
LOOK-- I'VE GOT TO GO TO CLASS RIGHT NOW, SO LET'S TALK THIS THROUGH WHEN I GET BACK... OKAY?
GO TO CLASS?!
IN THAT CASE-- *THE PEORTH INSTA-TRANS SPELL!*
NO!! THE SKULD *ULTRA-DELIVERY GUN!*
TRY THE URD *INTERSPATIAL SLIDE TECHNIQUE!*

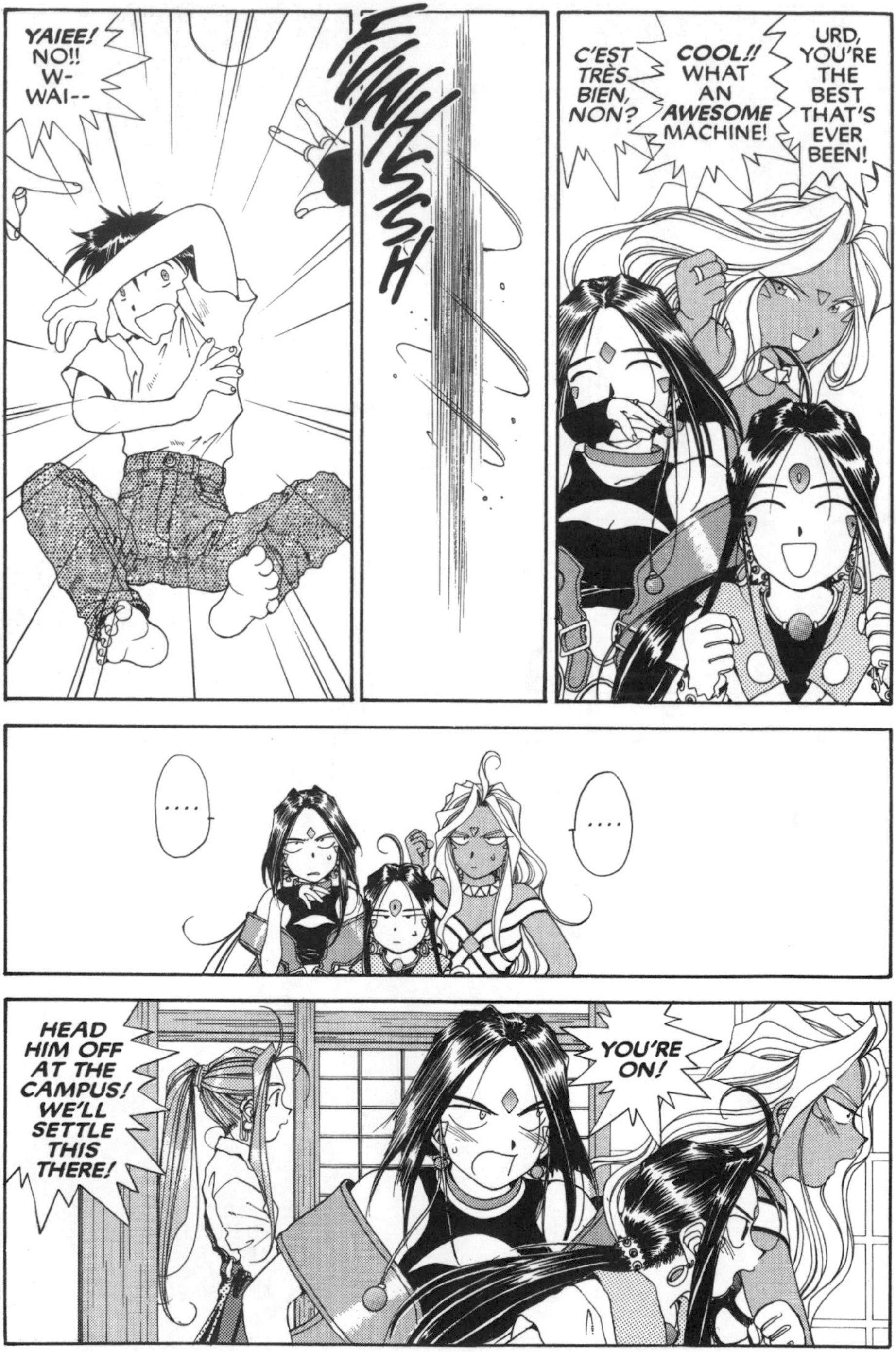
YAIEE! NO!! W-WAI--
FWHSSSH
C'EST TRÈS BIEN, NON?
COOL!! WHAT AN AWESOME MACHINE!
URD, YOU'RE THE BEST THAT'S EVER BEEN!
....
....
HEAD HIM OFF AT THE CAMPUS! WE'LL SETTLE THIS THERE!
YOU'RE ON!

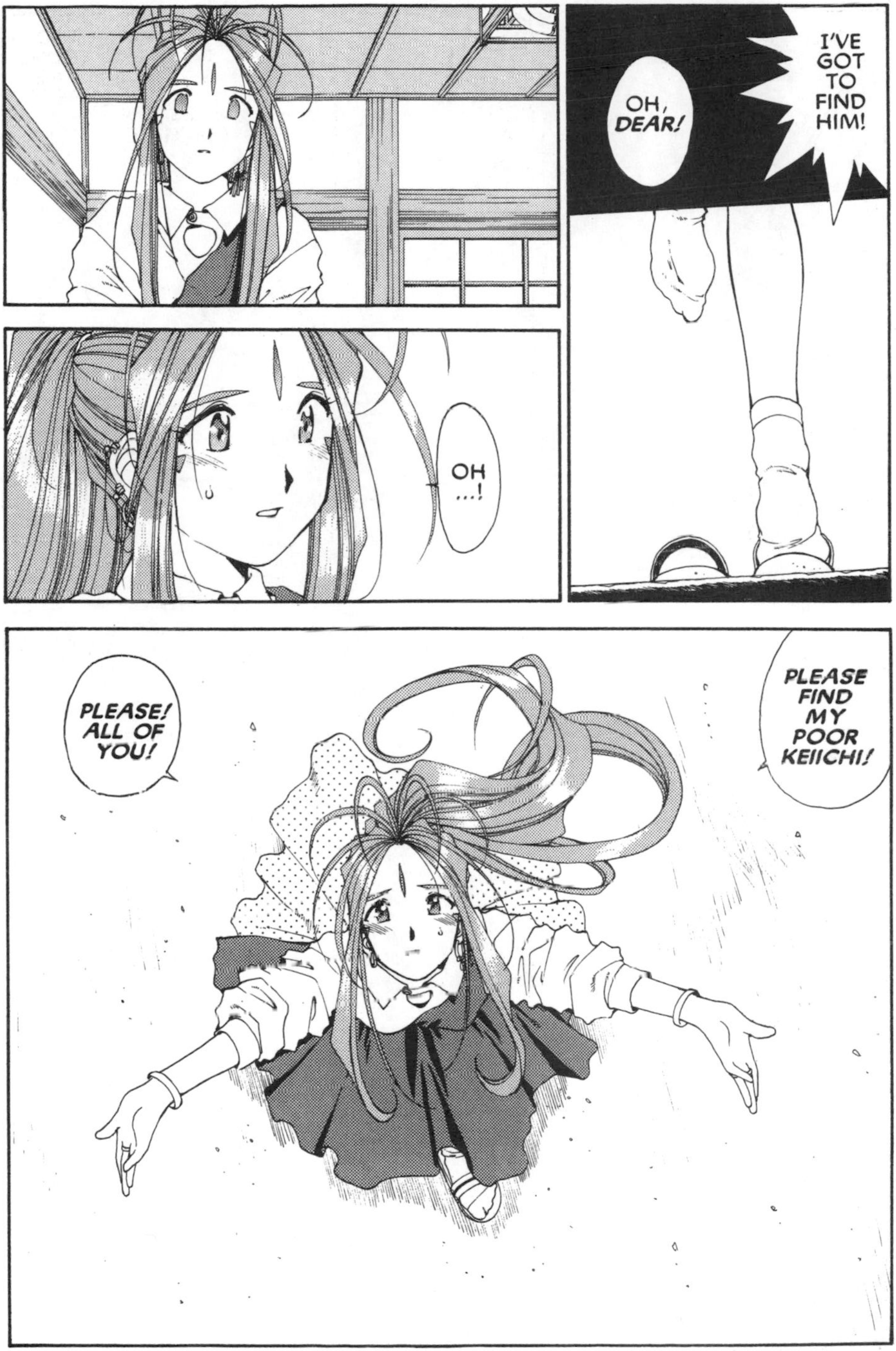
OH ...!
OH, DEAR!
I'VE GOT TO FIND HIM!
PLEASE! ALL OF YOU!
PLEASE FIND MY POOR KEIICHI!

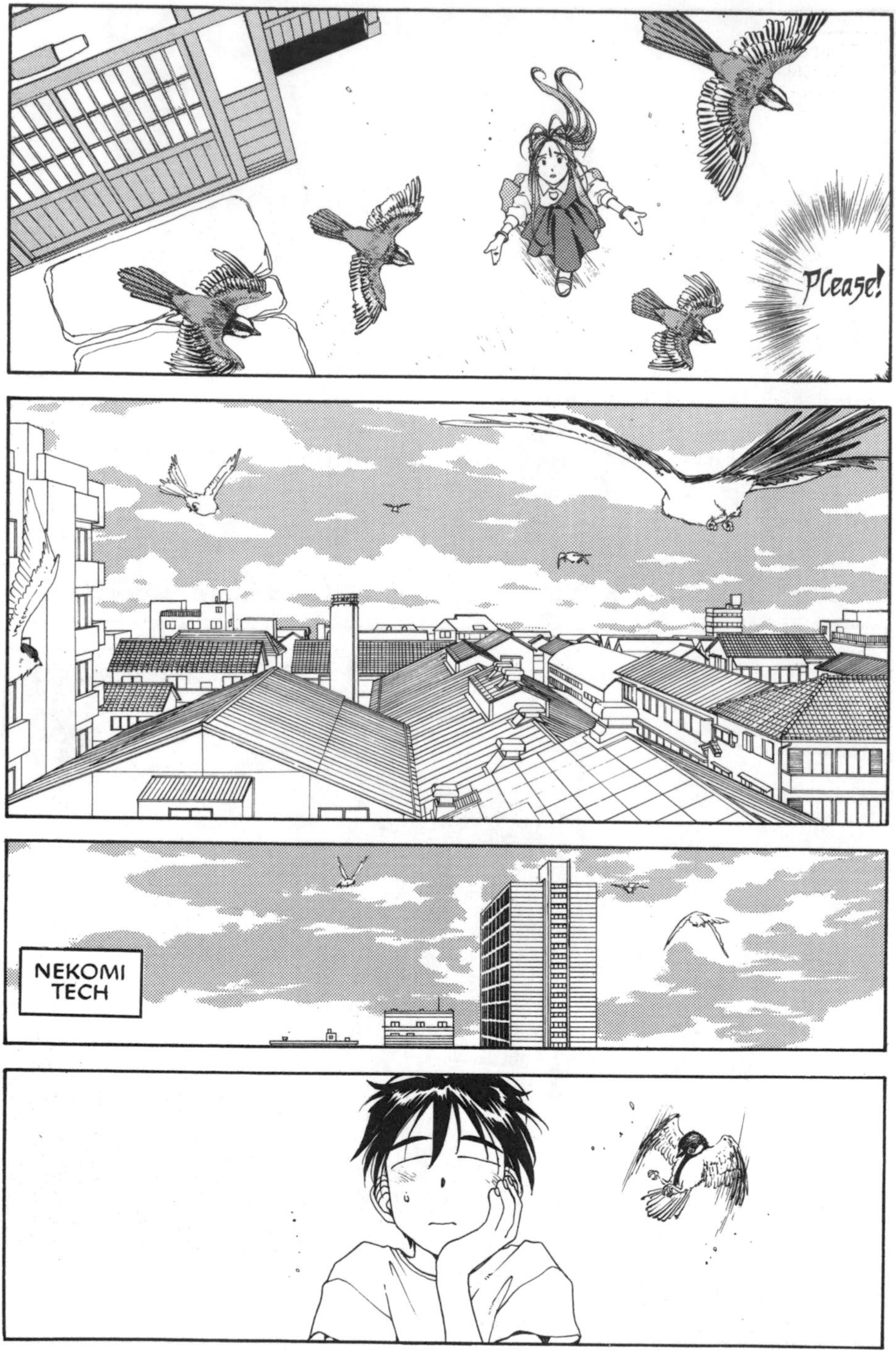
Please!
NEKOMI TECH

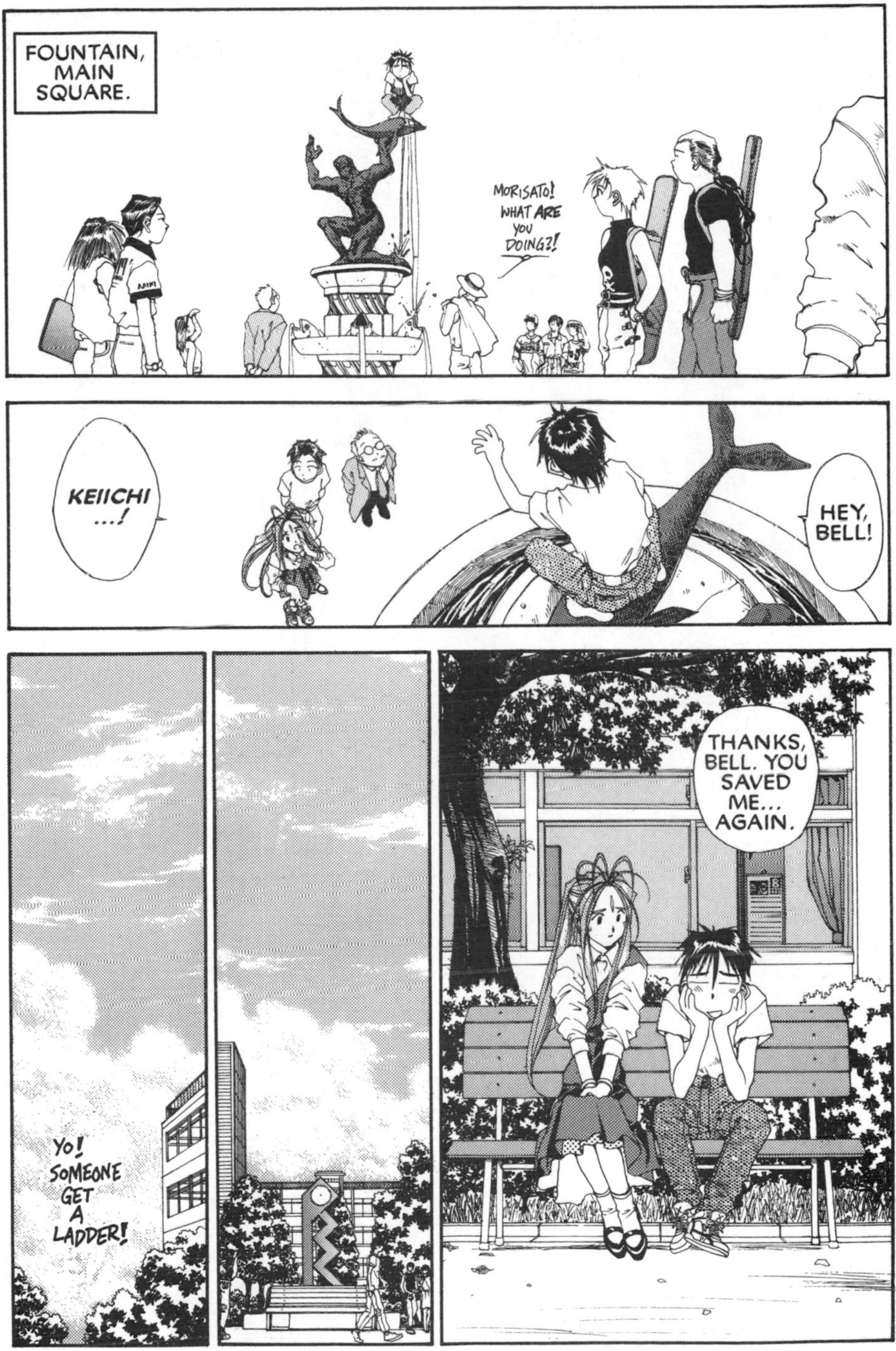
FOUNTAIN, MAIN SQUARE.
MORISATO! WHAT ARE YOU DOING?!
KEIICHI ...!
HEY, BELL!
YO! SOMEONE GET A LADDER!
THANKS, BELL. YOU SAVED ME... AGAIN.

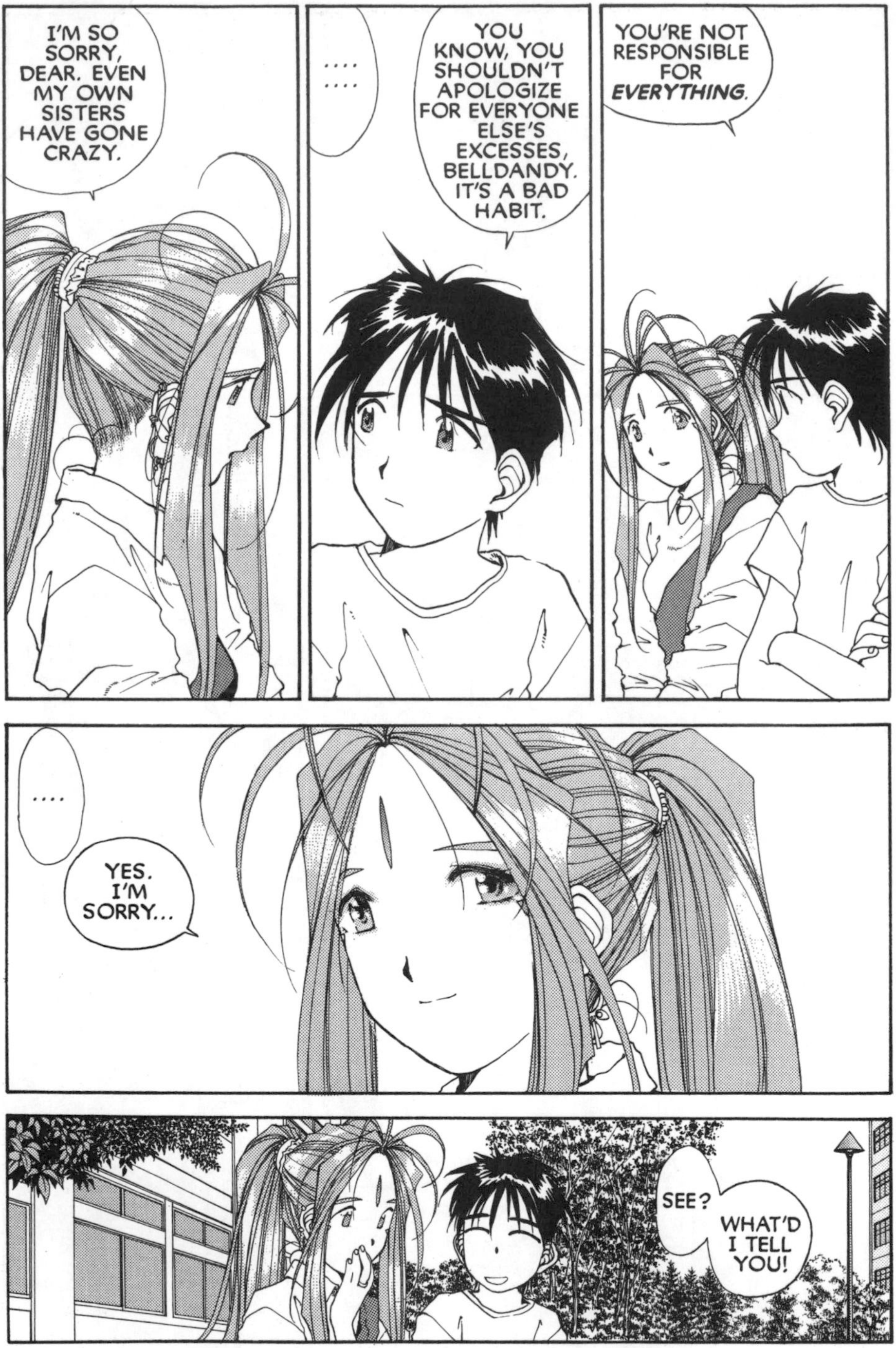
I'M SO SORRY, DEAR. EVEN MY OWN SISTERS HAVE GONE CRAZY.
....
....
YOU KNOW, YOU SHOULDN'T APOLOGIZE FOR EVERYONE ELSE'S EXCESSES, BELLDANDY. IT'S A BAD HABIT.
YOU'RE NOT RESPONSIBLE FOR *EVERYTHING*.
....
YES. I'M SORRY...
SEE?
WHAT'D I TELL YOU!

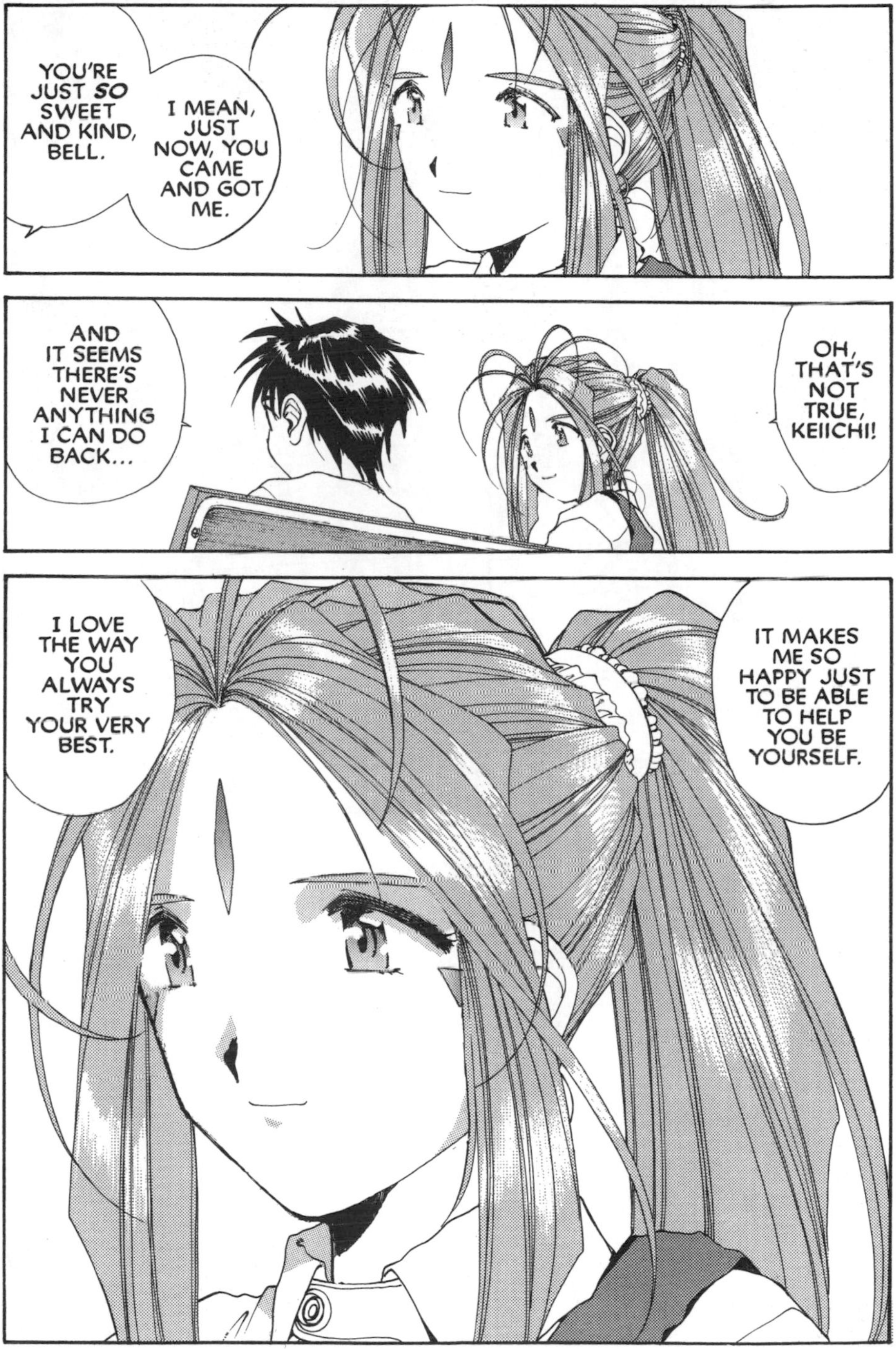
YOU'RE JUST SO SWEET AND KIND, BELL.
I MEAN, JUST NOW, YOU CAME AND GOT ME.
AND IT SEEMS THERE'S NEVER ANYTHING I CAN DO BACK...
OH, THAT'S NOT TRUE, KEIICHI!
I LOVE THE WAY YOU ALWAYS TRY YOUR VERY BEST.
IT MAKES ME SO HAPPY JUST TO BE ABLE TO HELP YOU BE YOURSELF.

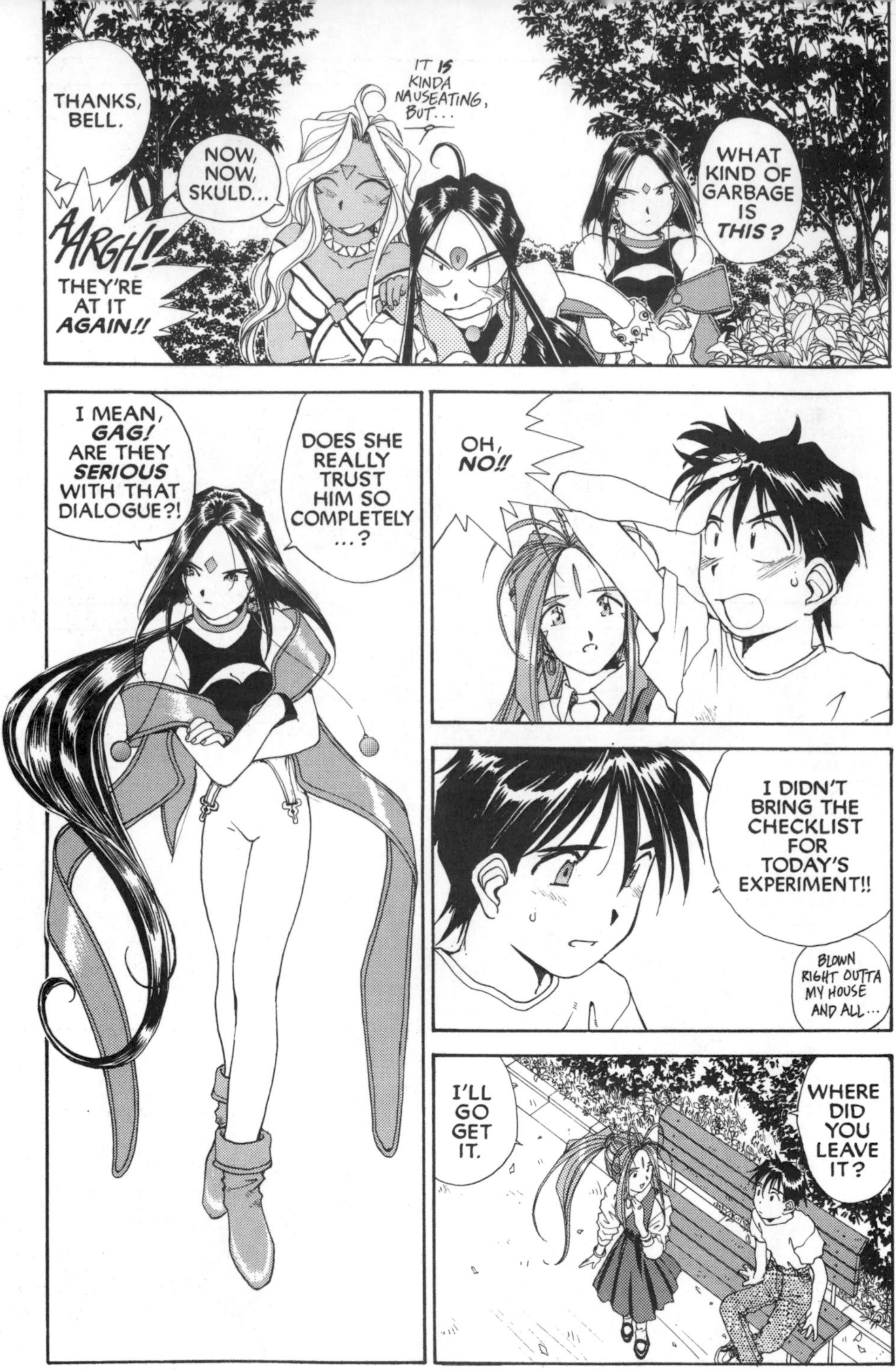
THANKS, BELL.
IT IS KINDA NAUSEATING, BUT...
NOW, NOW, SKULD...
WHAT KIND OF GARBAGE IS THIS?
AARGH!! THEY'RE AT IT AGAIN!!
I MEAN, GAG! ARE THEY SERIOUS WITH THAT DIALOGUE?!
DOES SHE REALLY TRUST HIM SO COMPLETELY ...?
OH, NO!!
I DIDN'T BRING THE CHECKLIST FOR TODAY'S EXPERIMENT!!
BLOWN RIGHT OUTTA MY HOUSE AND ALL...
I'LL GO GET IT.
WHERE DID YOU LEAVE IT?

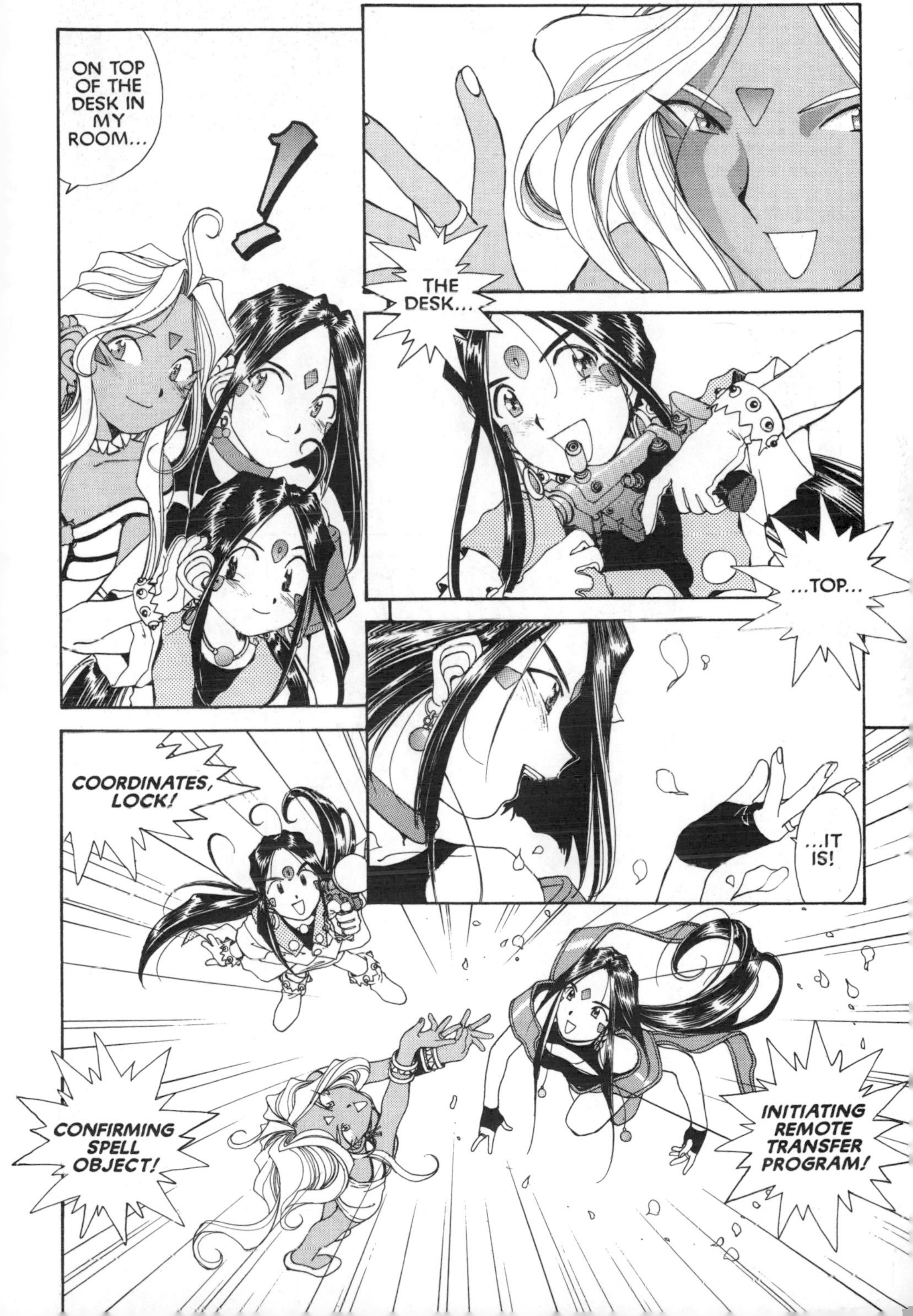

ON TOP OF THE DESK IN MY ROOM...
THE DESK...
...TOP...
...IT IS!
COORDINATES, LOCK!
CONFIRMING SPELL OBJECT!
INITIATING REMOTE TRANSFER PROGRAM!

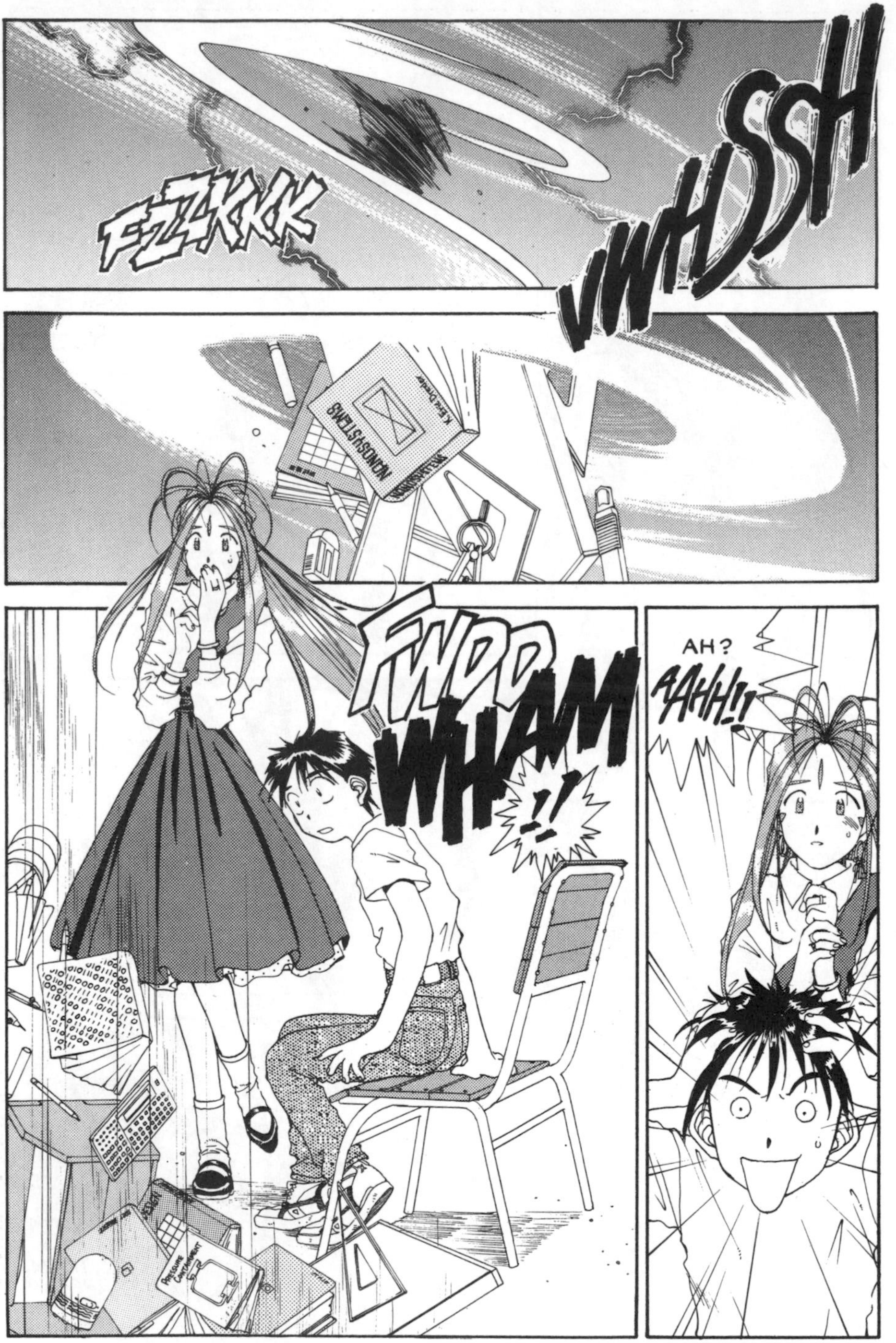
FZZKKK
VWHSSH
FWDD
WHAM
!!
AH?
AAHH!!
PRESSURE CONTAINMENT

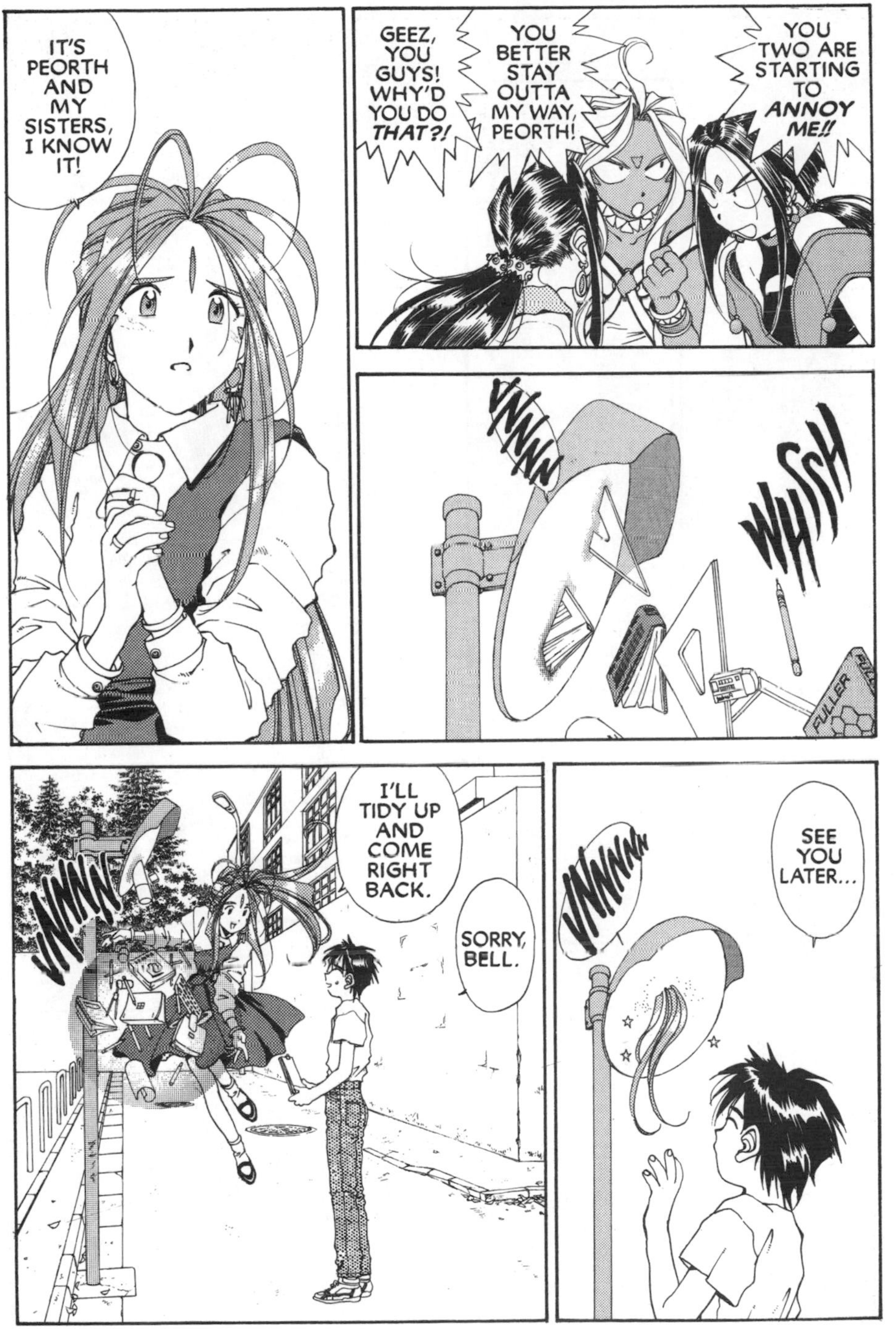
IT'S PEORTH AND MY SISTERS, I KNOW IT!
GEEZ, YOU GUYS! WHY'D YOU DO *THAT?!*
YOU BETTER STAY OUTTA MY WAY, PEORTH!
YOU TWO ARE STARTING TO *ANNOY ME!!*
VNNNN
WHUSH
FULLER
VNNNN
I'LL TIDY UP AND COME RIGHT BACK.
SORRY, BELL.
VNNNNNN
SEE YOU LATER...

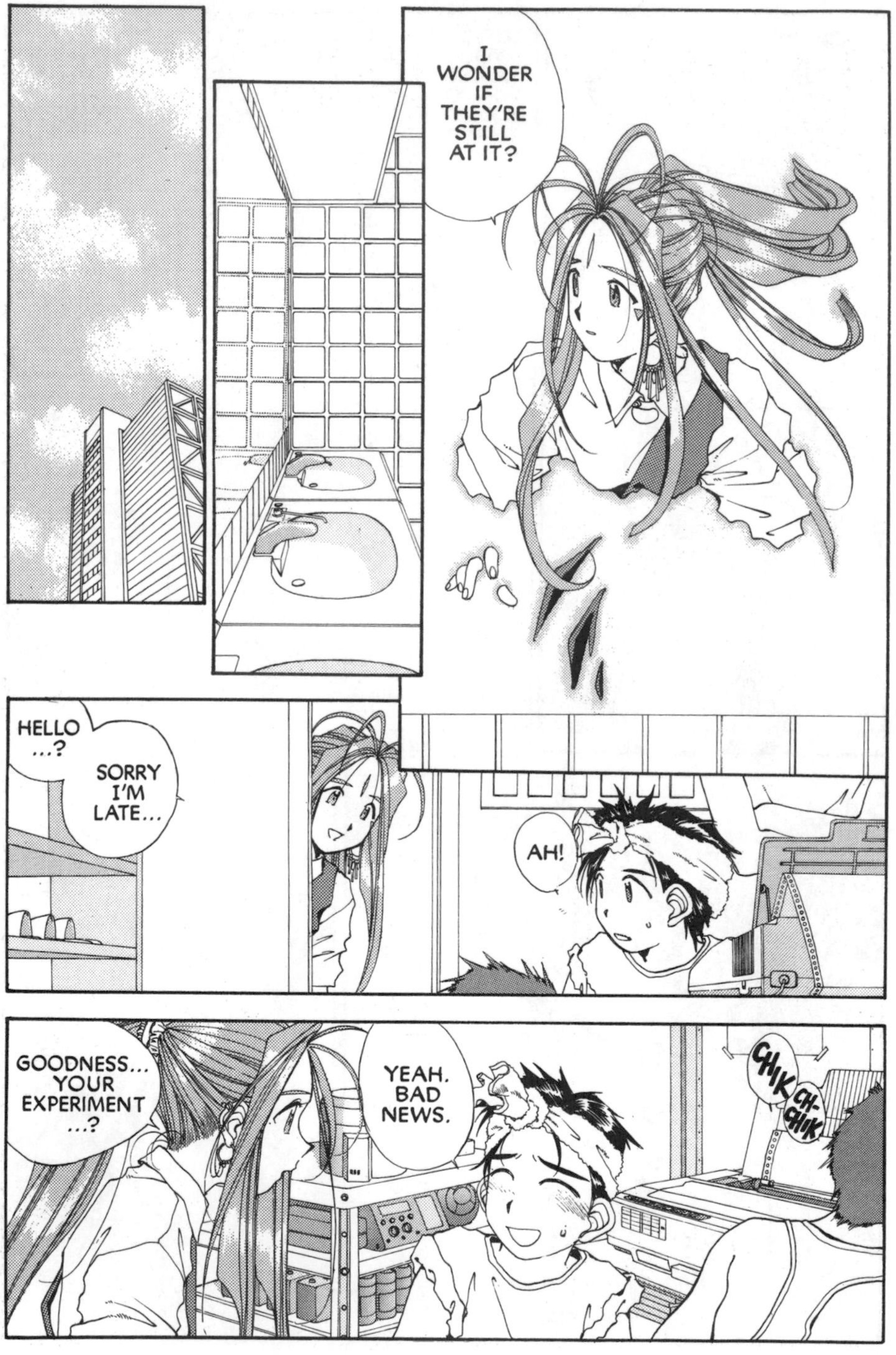
I WONDER IF THEY'RE STILL AT IT?
HELLO ...?
SORRY I'M LATE...
AH!
GOODNESS... YOUR EXPERIMENT ...?
YEAH. BAD NEWS.
CHIK
CH-CHIK

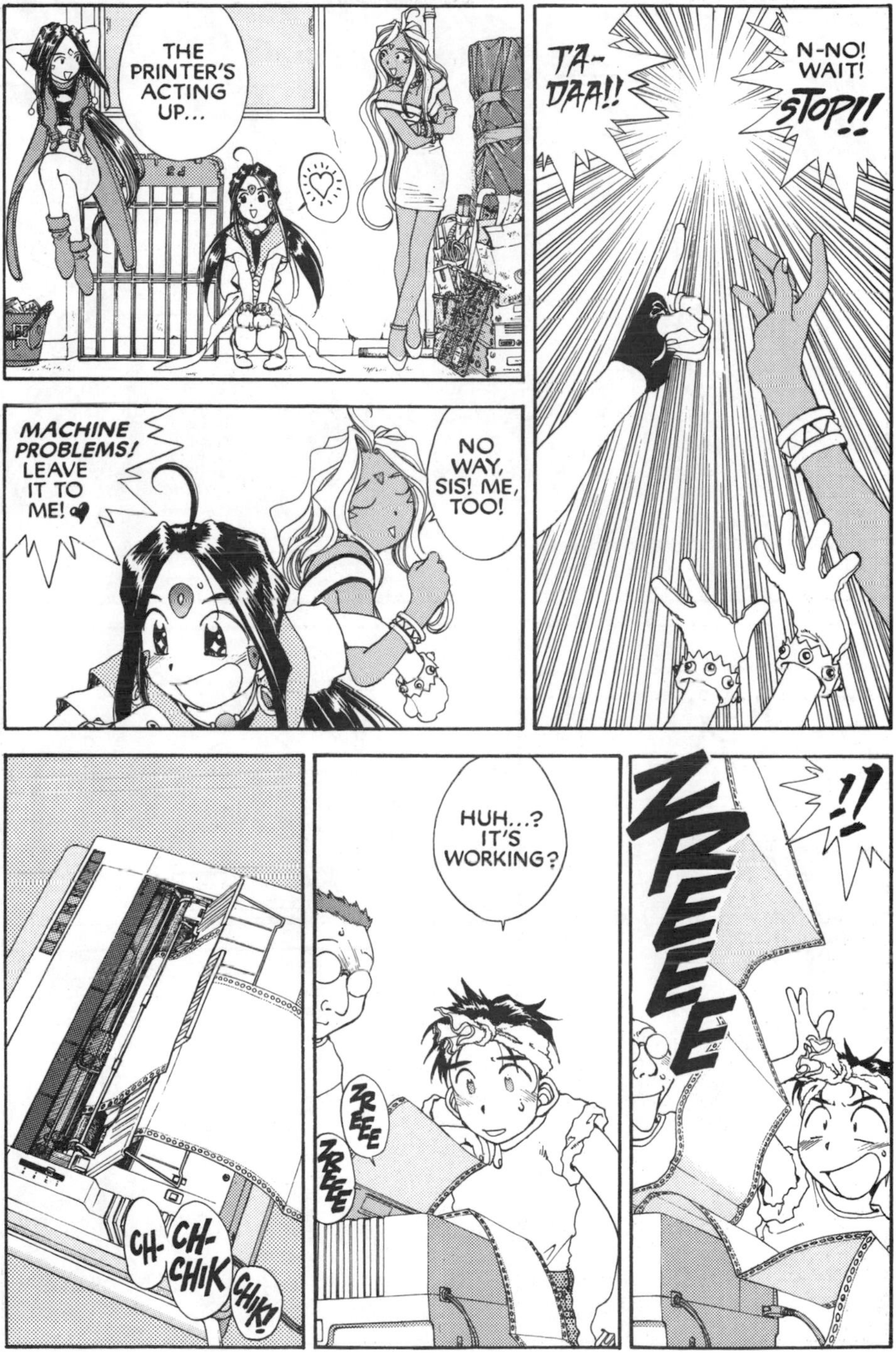
THE PRINTER'S ACTING UP...
MACHINE PROBLEMS! LEAVE IT TO ME!
NO WAY, SIS! ME, TOO!
TA-DAA!!
N-NO! WAIT! STOP!!
CH-
CH-CHIK
CHIK!
HUH...? IT'S WORKING?
ZREEE
ZREEE
ZREEEE
!!

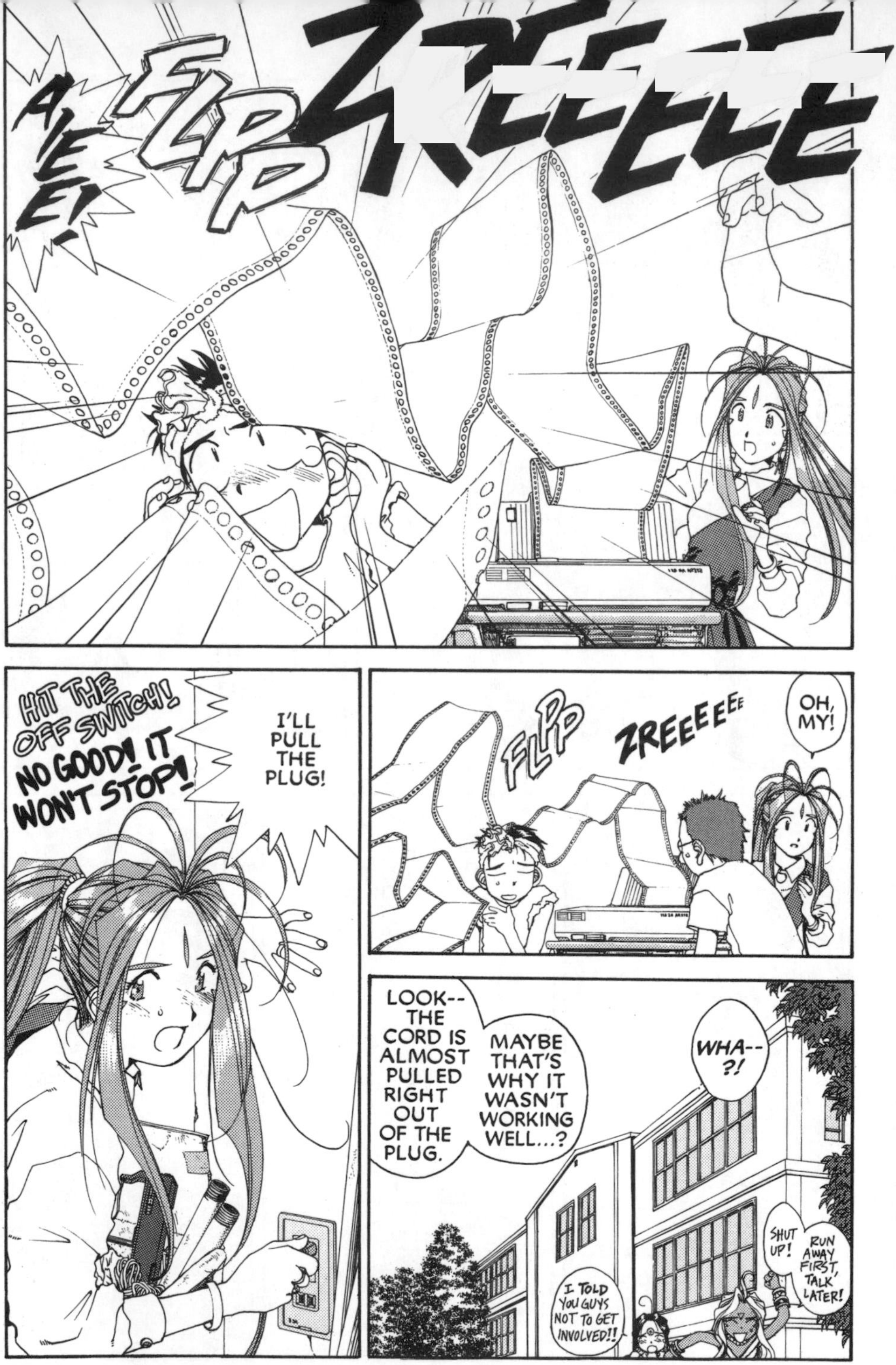
AIEEE!
FLIP
ZREEEEE
HIT THE OFF SWITCH!
NO GOOD! IT WON'T STOP!
I'LL PULL THE PLUG!
FLIP
ZREEEEEE
OH, MY!
LOOK-- THE CORD IS ALMOST PULLED RIGHT OUT OF THE PLUG.
MAYBE THAT'S WHY IT WASN'T WORKING WELL...?
WHA--?!
I TOLD YOU GUYS NOT TO GET INVOLVED!!
SHUT UP!
RUN AWAY FIRST, TALK LATER!

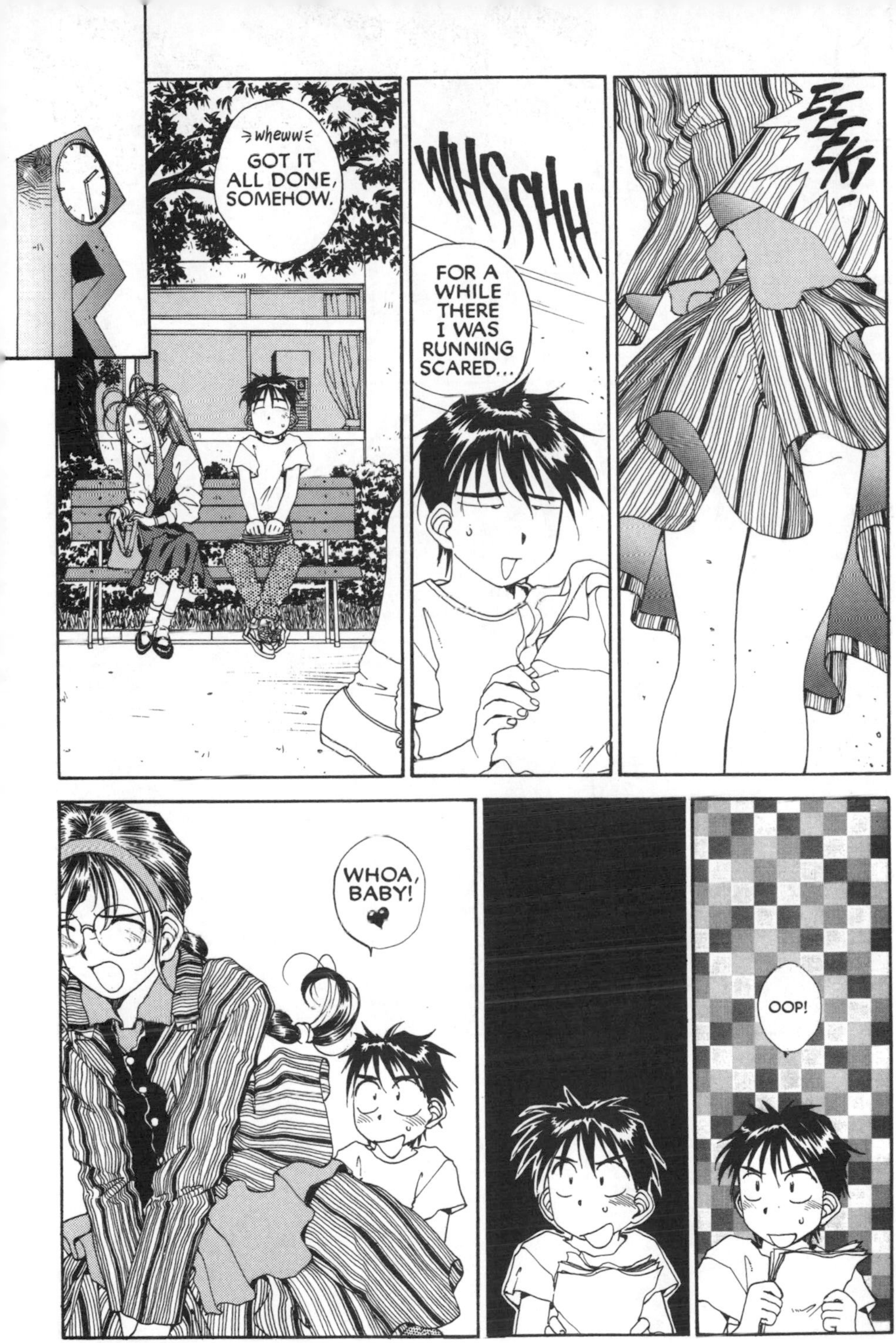

wheww
GOT IT ALL DONE, SOMEHOW.
WHSSHH
FOR A WHILE THERE I WAS RUNNING SCARED...
EEEEK!
WHOA, BABY!
OOP!

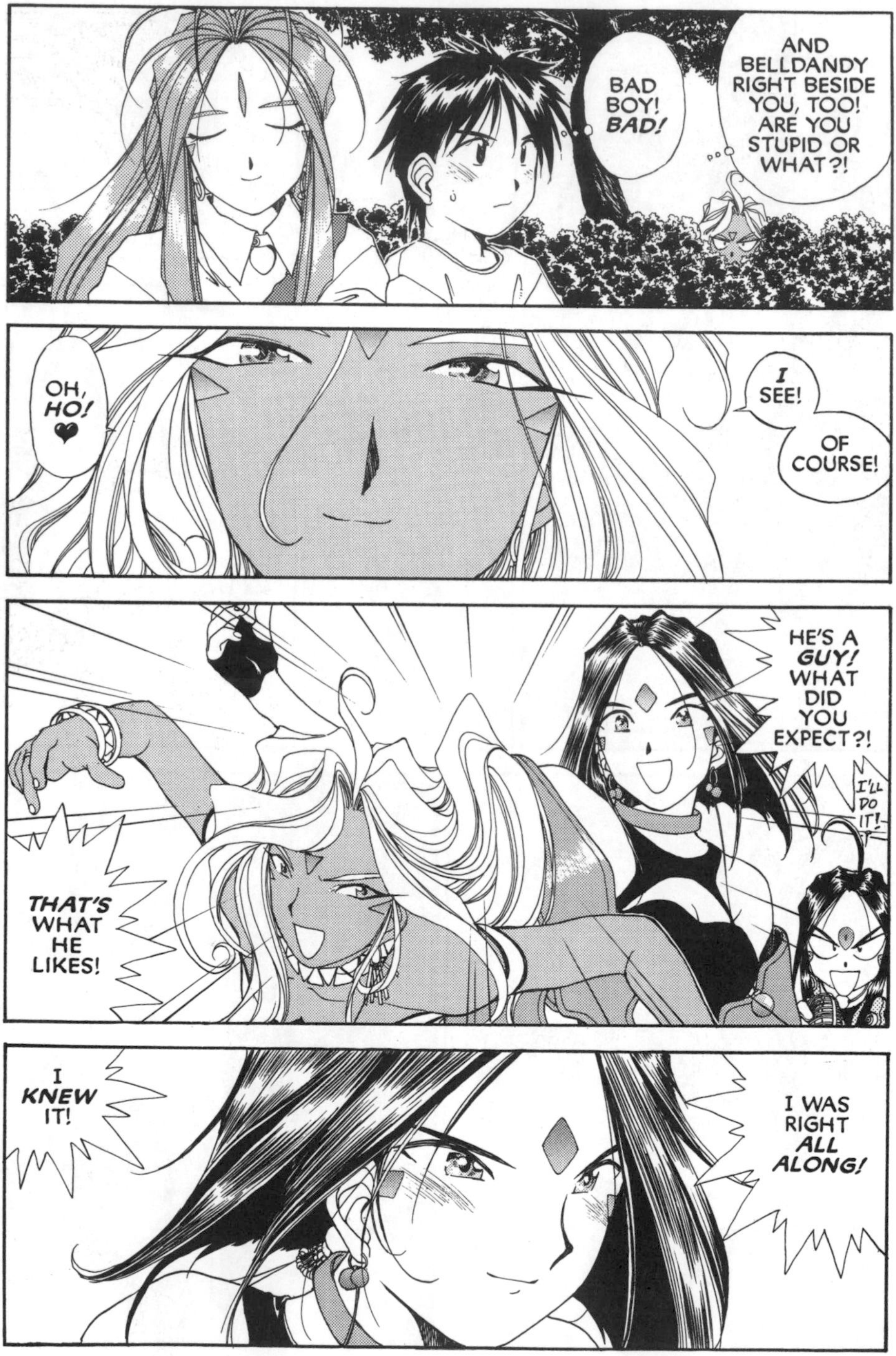
BAD BOY! BAD!
AND BELLDANDY RIGHT BESIDE YOU, TOO! ARE YOU STUPID OR WHAT?!
OH, HO! ❤
I SEE!
OF COURSE!
THAT'S WHAT HE LIKES!
HE'S A GUY! WHAT DID YOU EXPECT?!
I'LL DO IT!
I KNEW IT!
I WAS RIGHT ALL ALONG!

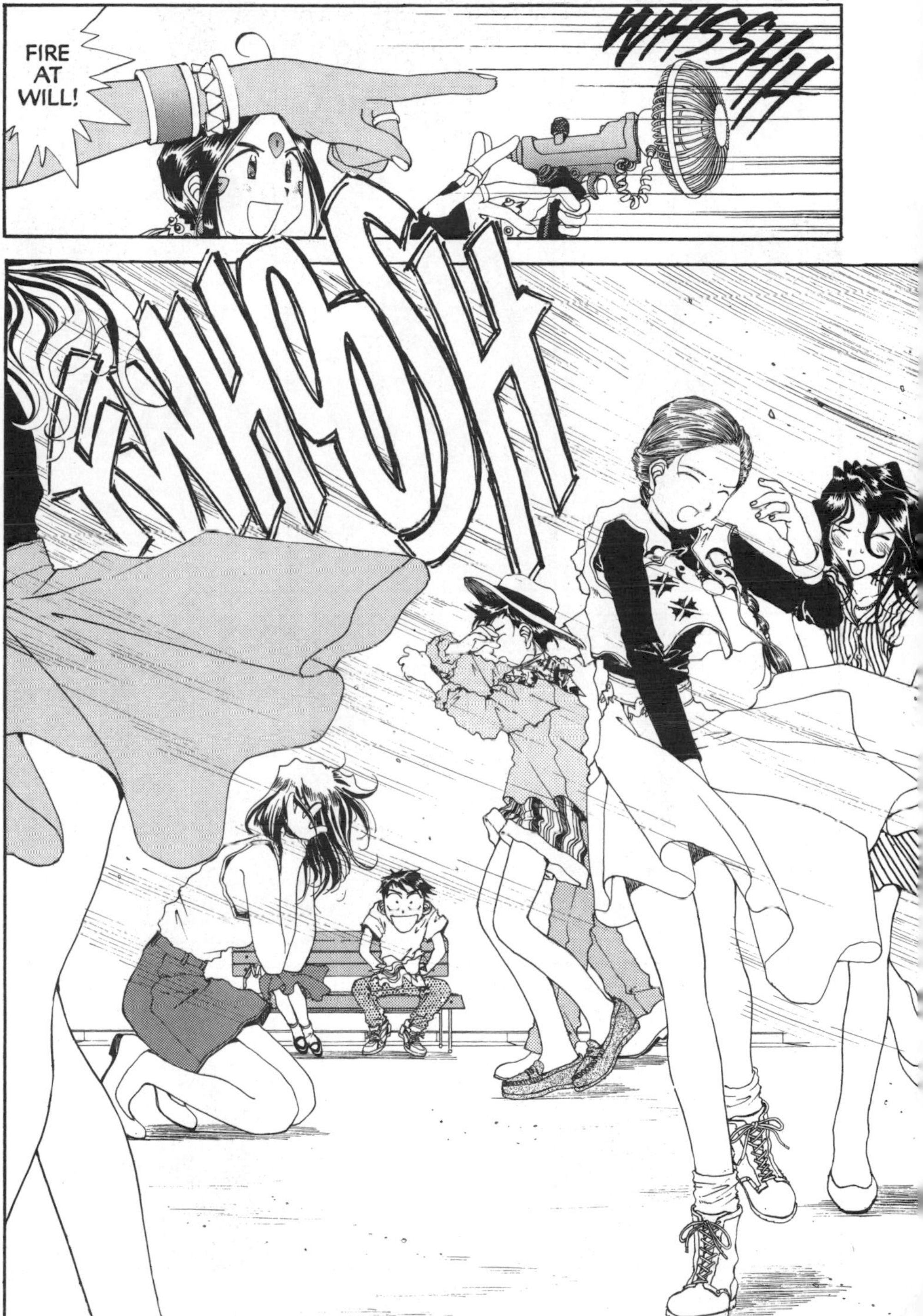
FIRE AT WILL!
WHSSHH
WHOOSH

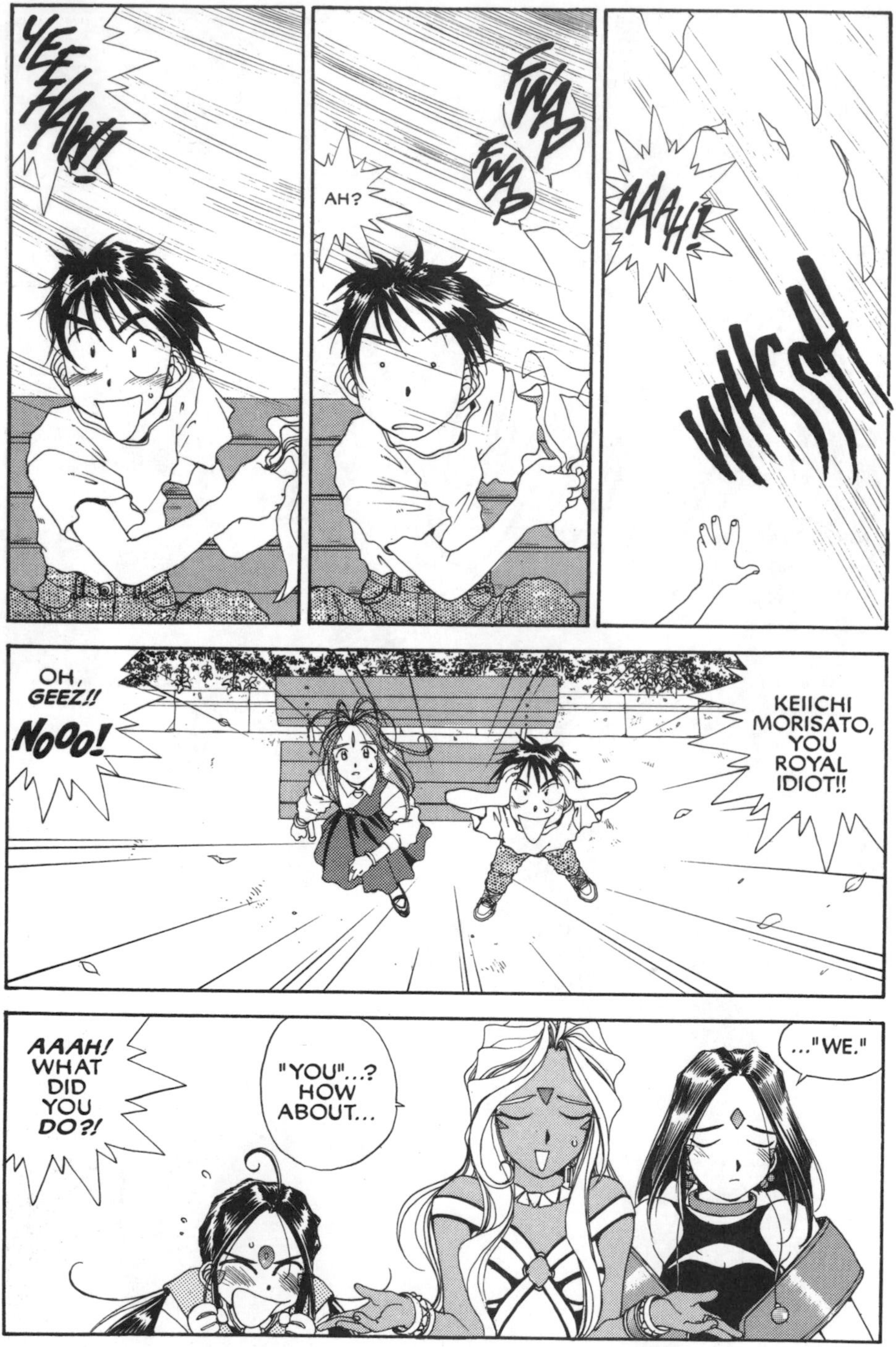
YEEHAW!!
AH?
FWAP
FWAP
AAAH!
WHSH
OH, GEEZ!!
NOOO!
KEIICHI MORISATO, YOU ROYAL IDIOT!!
AAAH! WHAT DID YOU DO?!
"YOU"...? HOW ABOUT...
..."WE."

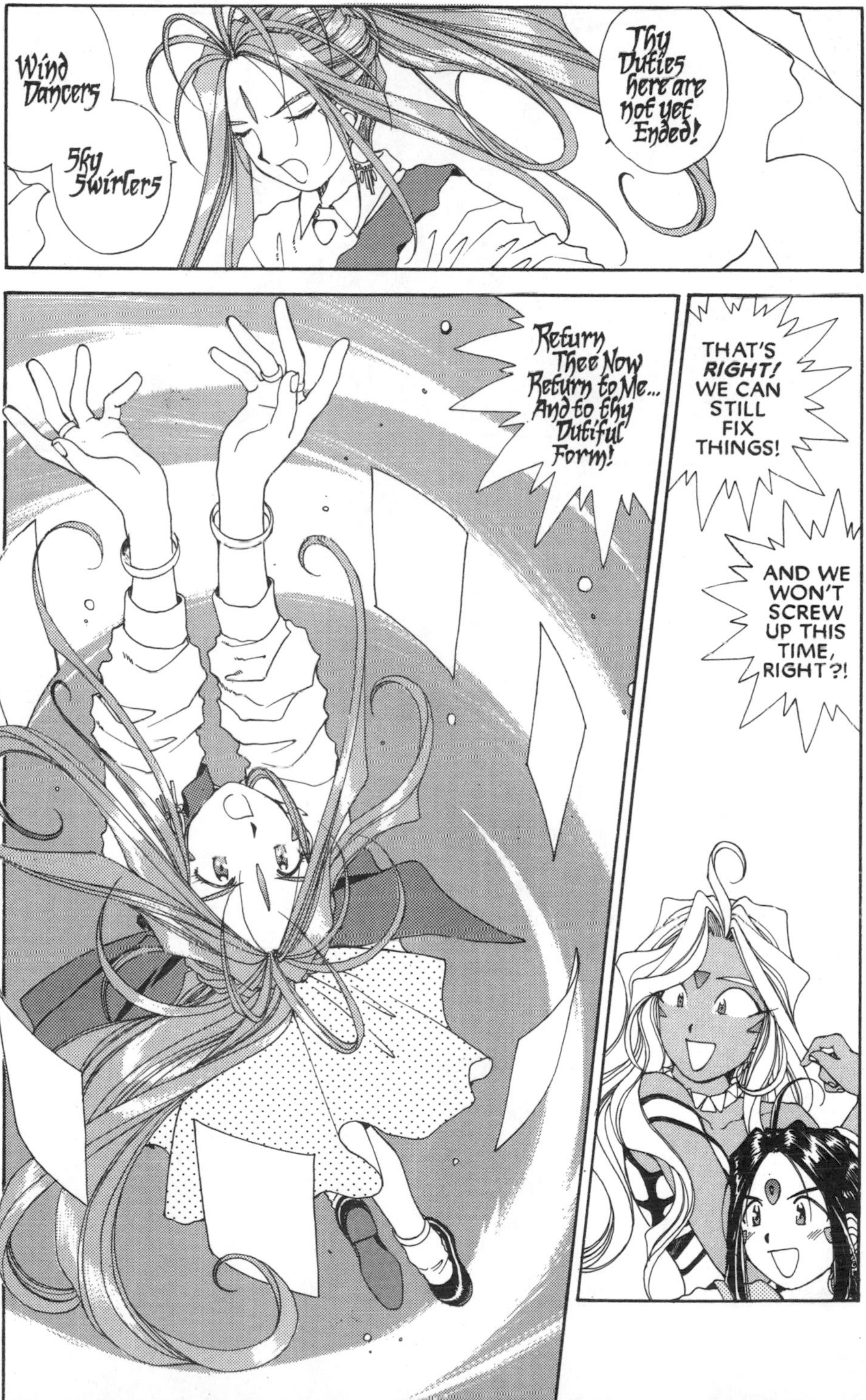

Wind Dancers
Sky Swirlers
Thy Duties here are not yet Ended!
Return Thee Now Return to Me... And to thy Dutiful Form!
THAT'S *RIGHT!* WE CAN STILL FIX THINGS!
AND WE WON'T SCREW UP THIS TIME, RIGHT?!

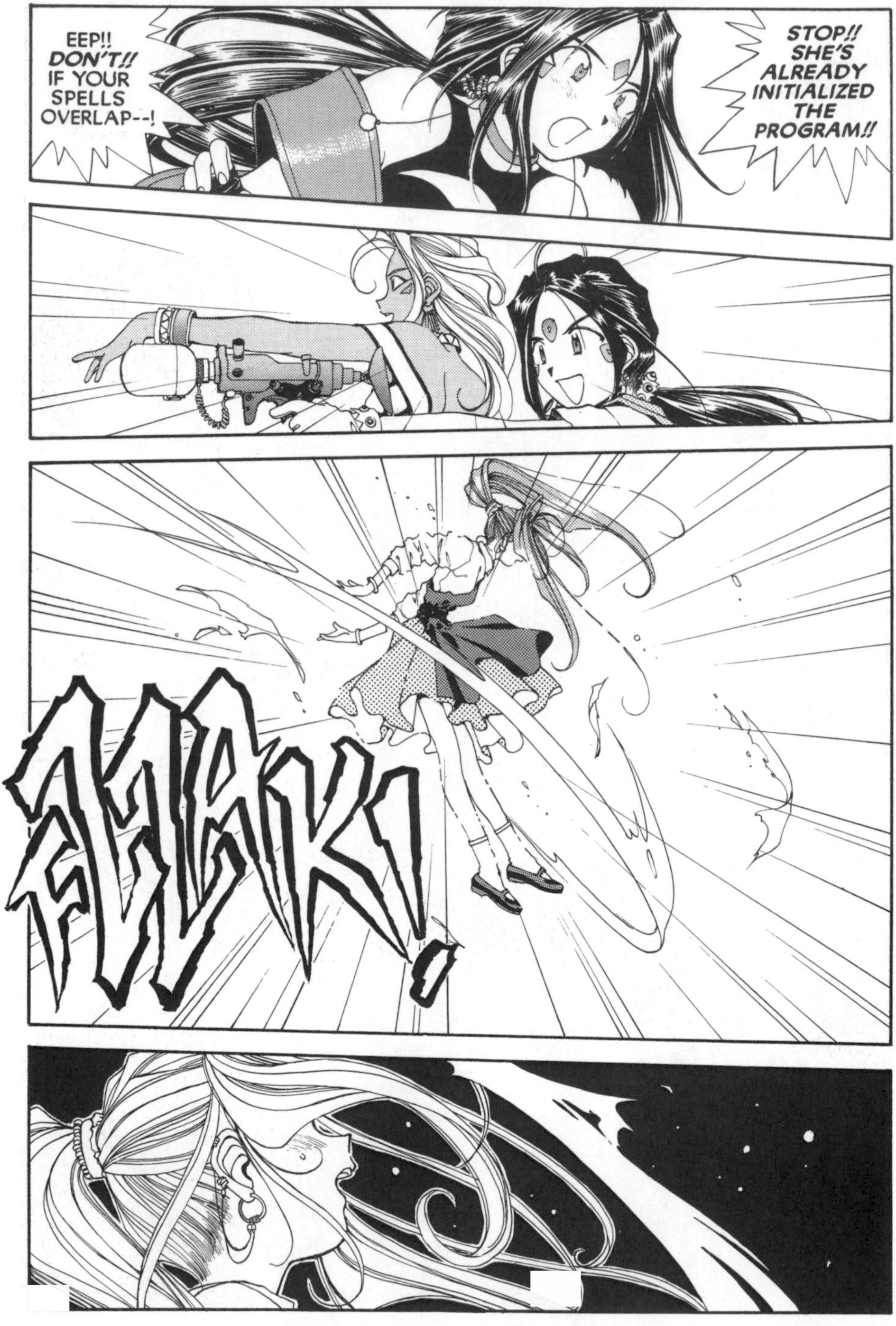
EEP!! DON'T!! IF YOUR SPELLS OVERLAP--!
STOP!! SHE'S ALREADY INITIALIZED THE PROGRAM!!
FLAAK!

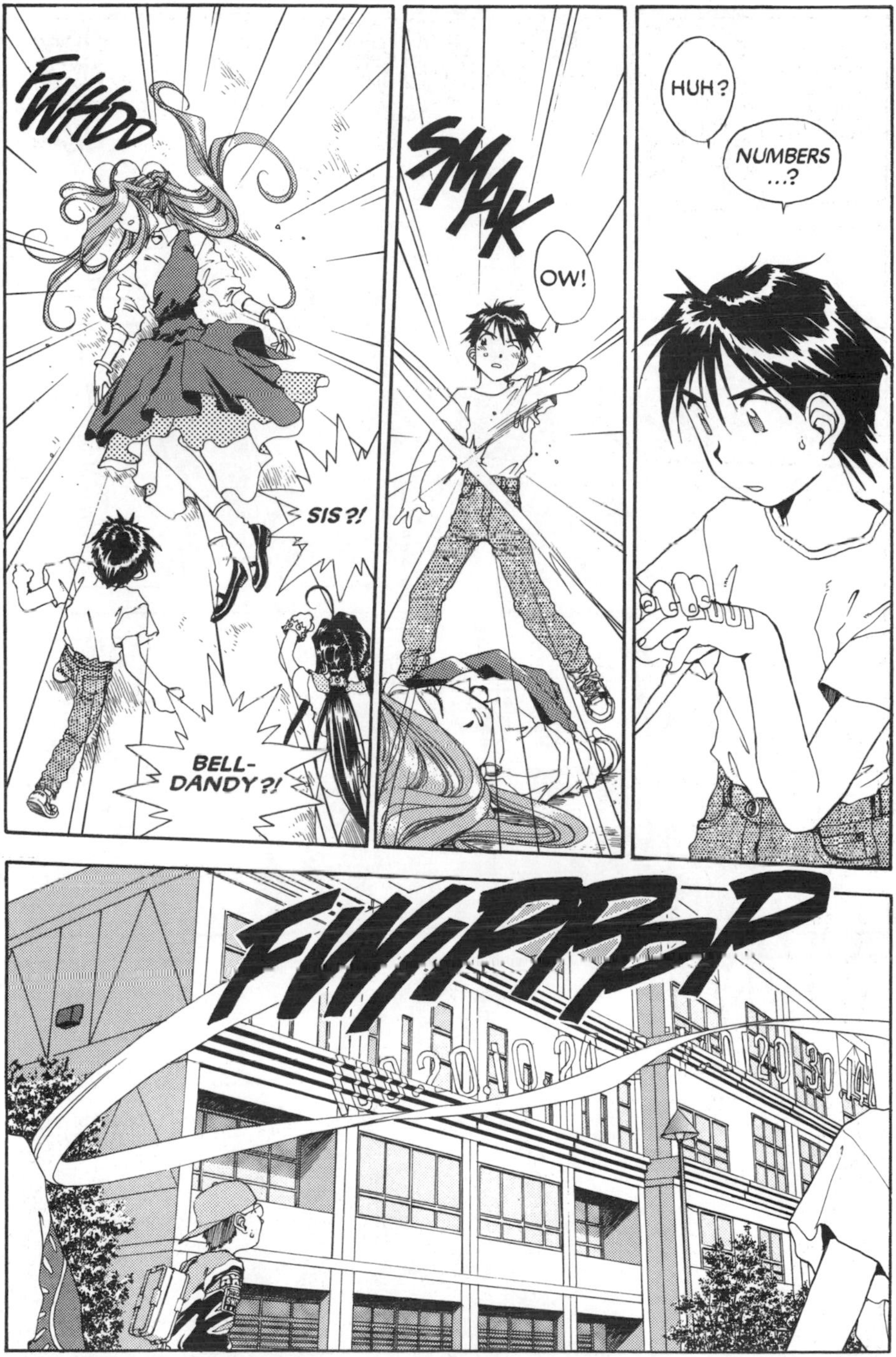
FWHOO
SIS?!
BELL-DANDY?!
SMAK
OW!
HUH?
NUMBERS ...?
FWIPPBP

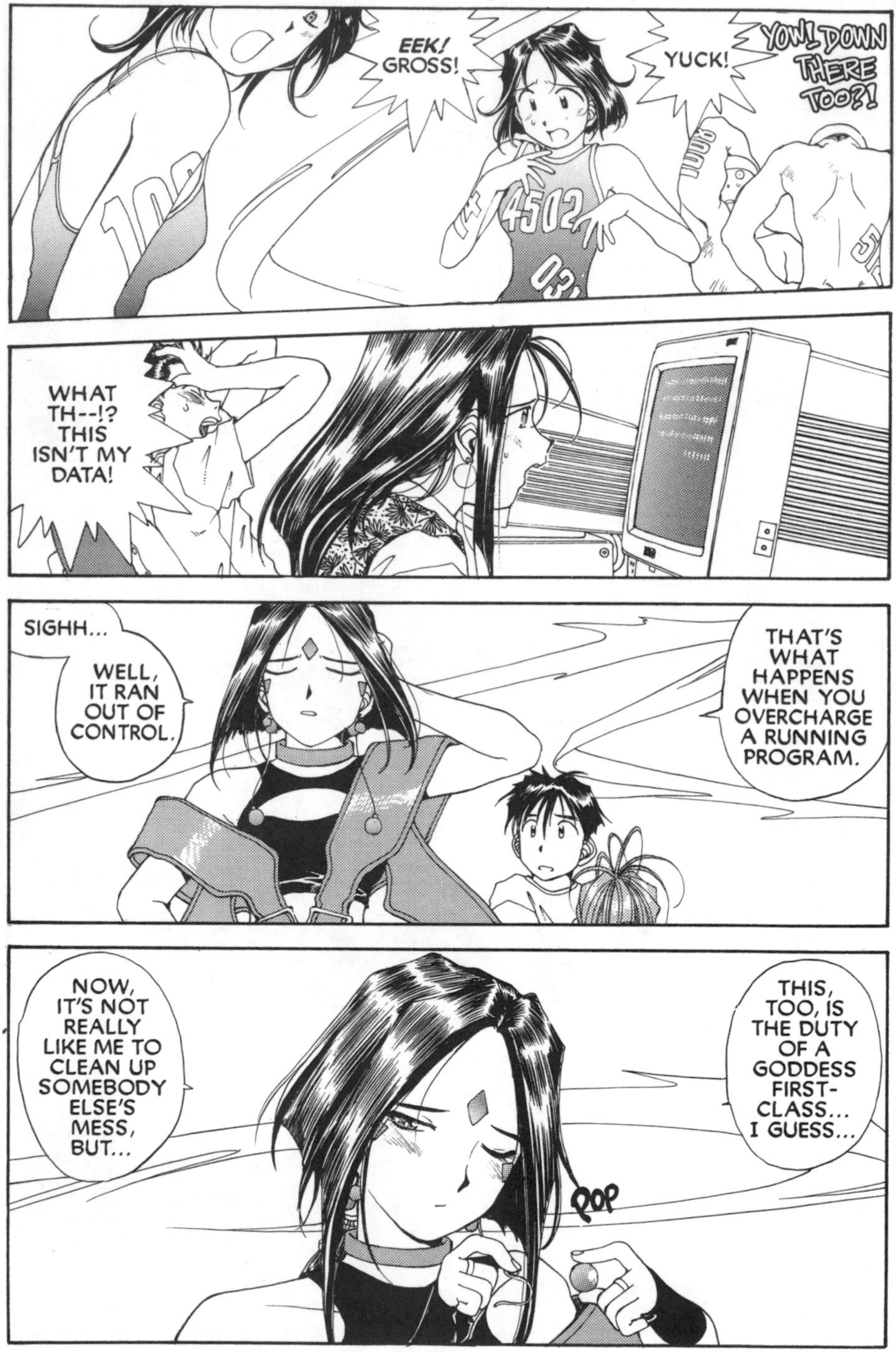
EEK! GROSS!
YUCK!
YOW! DOWN THERE TOO?!
WHAT TH--!? THIS ISN'T MY DATA!
SIGHH...
WELL, IT RAN OUT OF CONTROL.
THAT'S WHAT HAPPENS WHEN YOU OVERCHARGE A RUNNING PROGRAM.
NOW, IT'S NOT REALLY LIKE ME TO CLEAN UP SOMEBODY ELSE'S MESS, BUT...
THIS, TOO, IS THE DUTY OF A GODDESS FIRST-CLASS... I GUESS...
POP

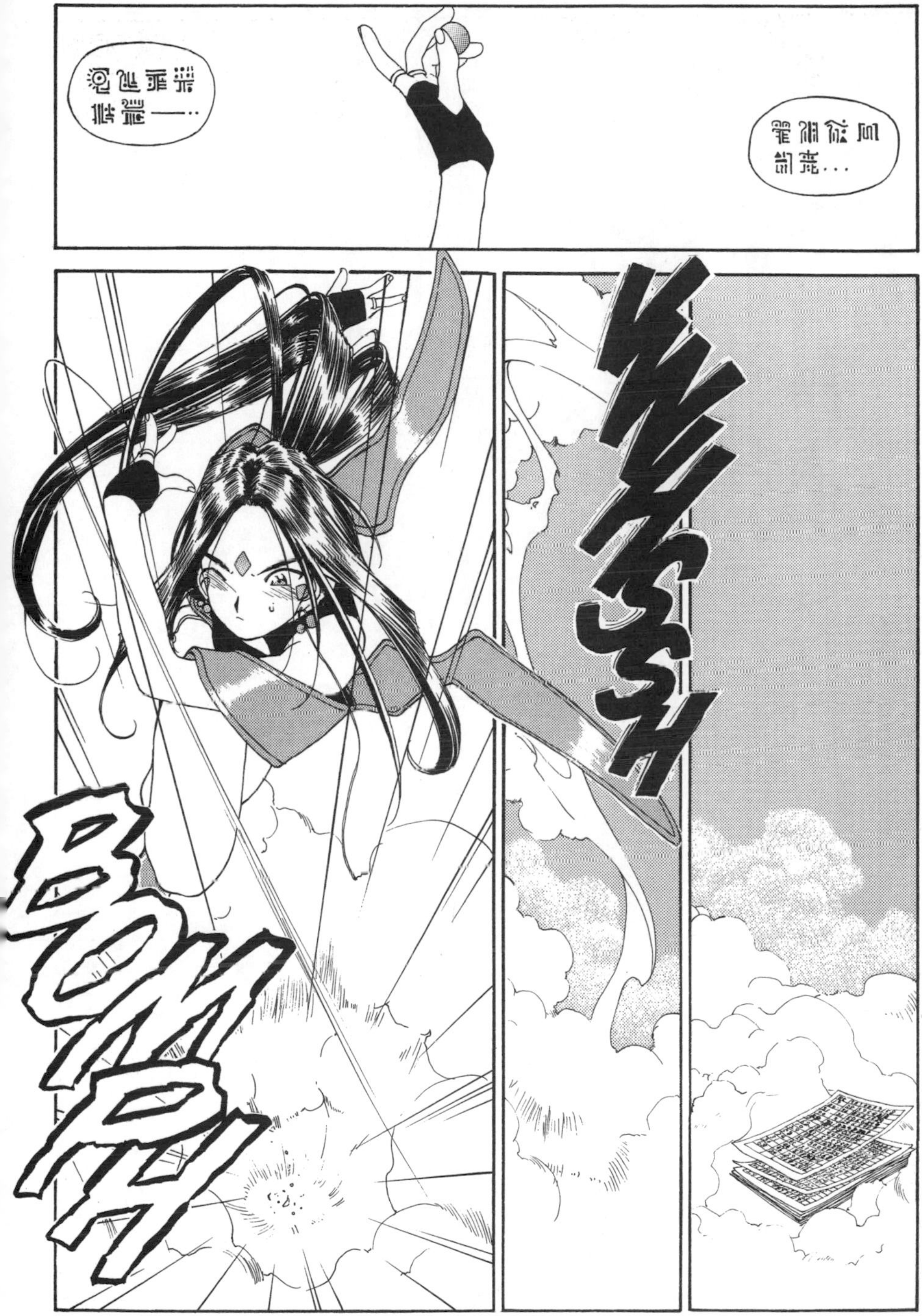
BOMPH

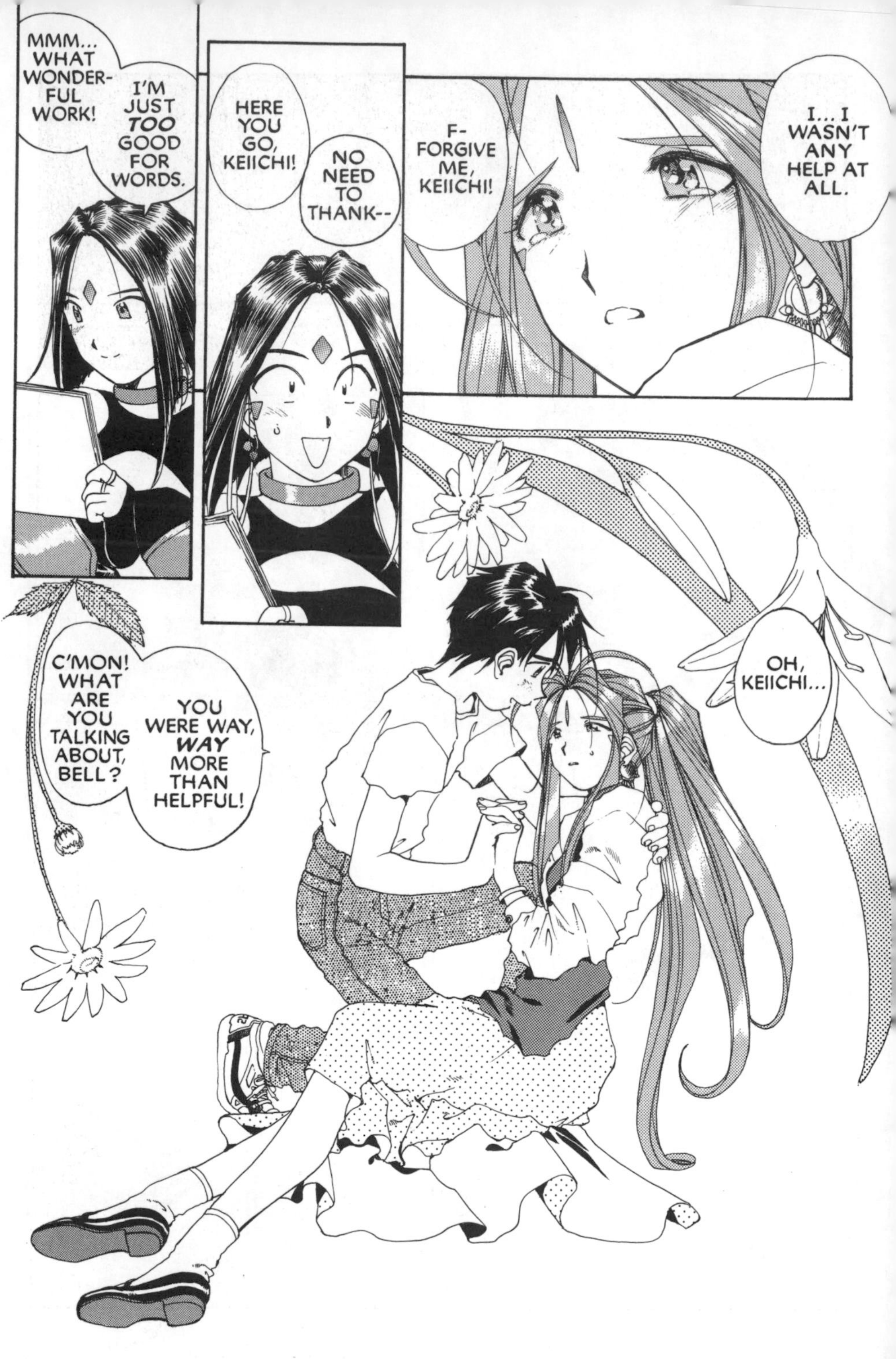
MMM... WHAT WONDERFUL WORK!
I'M JUST *TOO* GOOD FOR WORDS.
HERE YOU GO, KEIICHI!
NO NEED TO THANK--
F-FORGIVE ME, KEIICHI!
I... I WASN'T ANY HELP AT ALL.
C'MON! WHAT ARE YOU TALKING ABOUT, BELL?
YOU WERE WAY, *WAY* MORE THAN HELPFUL!
OH, KEIICHI...

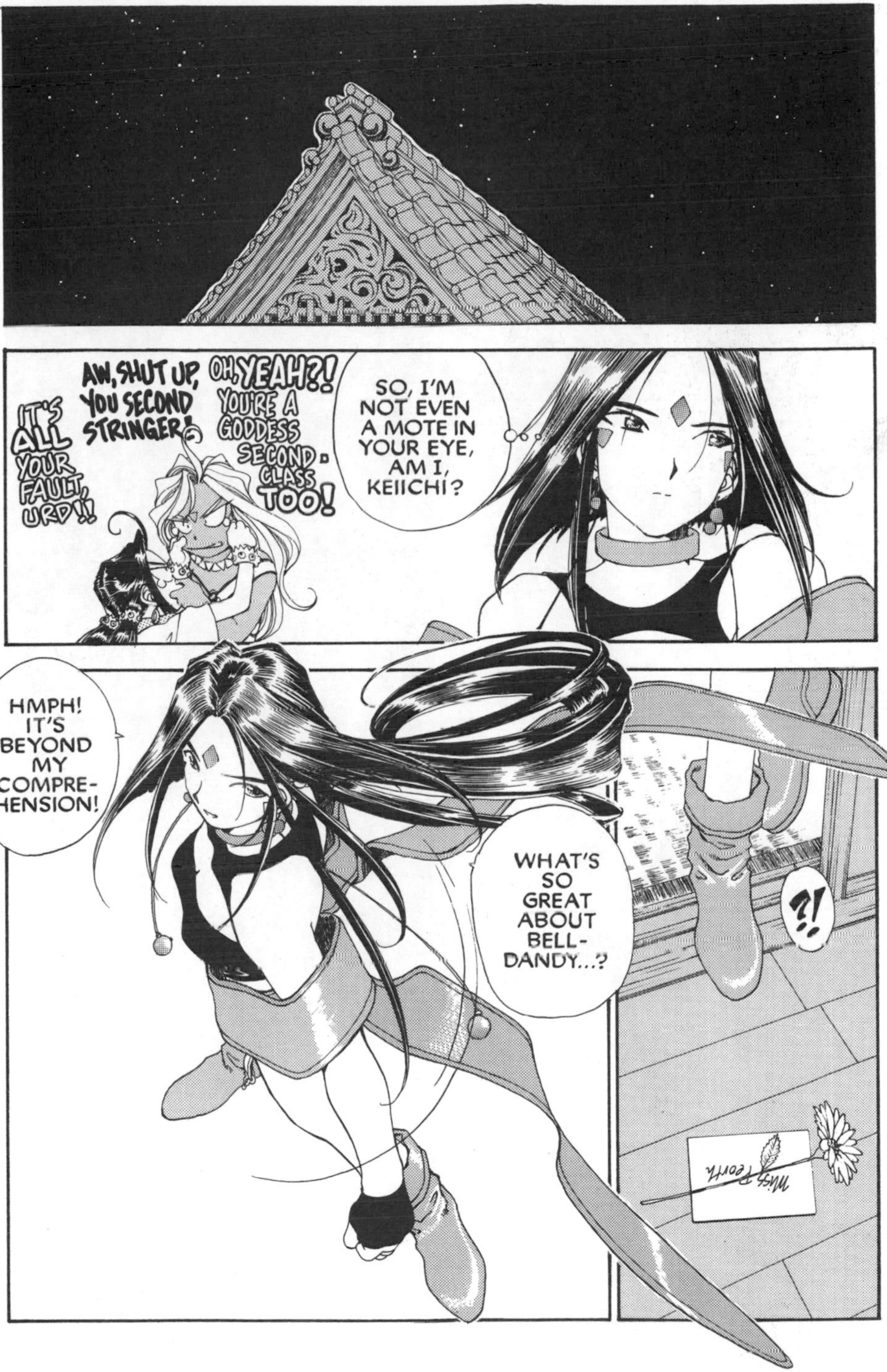

IT'S ALL YOUR FAULT, URD!!
AW, SHUT UP, YOU SECOND STRINGER!
OH, YEAH?! YOU'RE A GODDESS SECOND CLASS TOO!
SO, I'M NOT EVEN A MOTE IN YOUR EYE, AM I, KEIICHI?
HMPH! IT'S BEYOND MY COMPREHENSION!
WHAT'S SO GREAT ABOUT BELL-DANDY...?
?!
Miss Peorth.

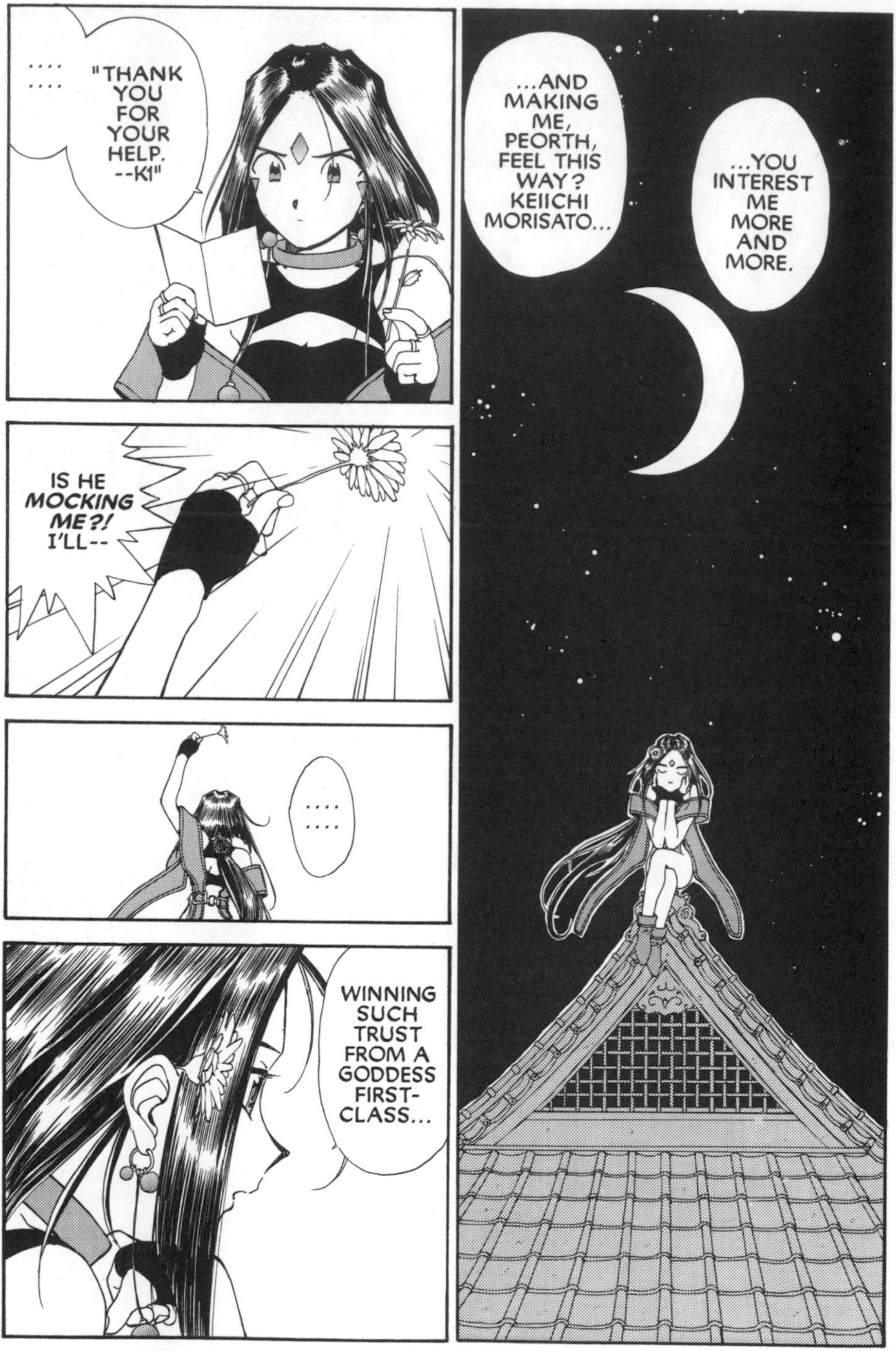
....
....
"THANK YOU FOR YOUR HELP. --K1"
IS HE *MOCKING ME?!* I'LL--
....
....
WINNING SUCH TRUST FROM A GODDESS FIRST-CLASS...
...AND MAKING ME, PEORTH, FEEL THIS WAY? KEIICHI MORISATO...
...YOU INTEREST ME MORE AND MORE.

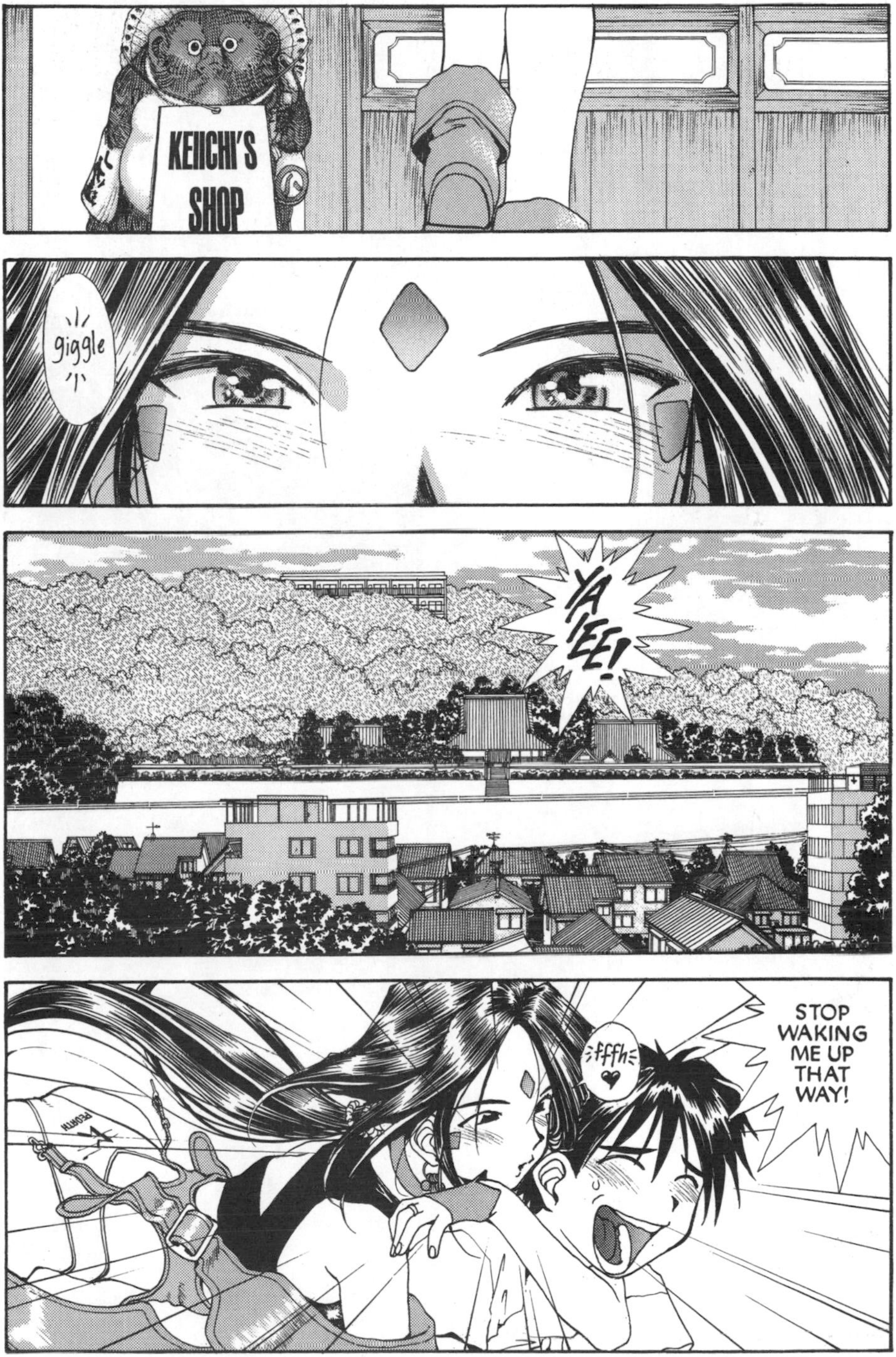
KEIICHI'S SHOP
giggle
YAIEE!
fffh
STOP WAKING ME UP THAT WAY!

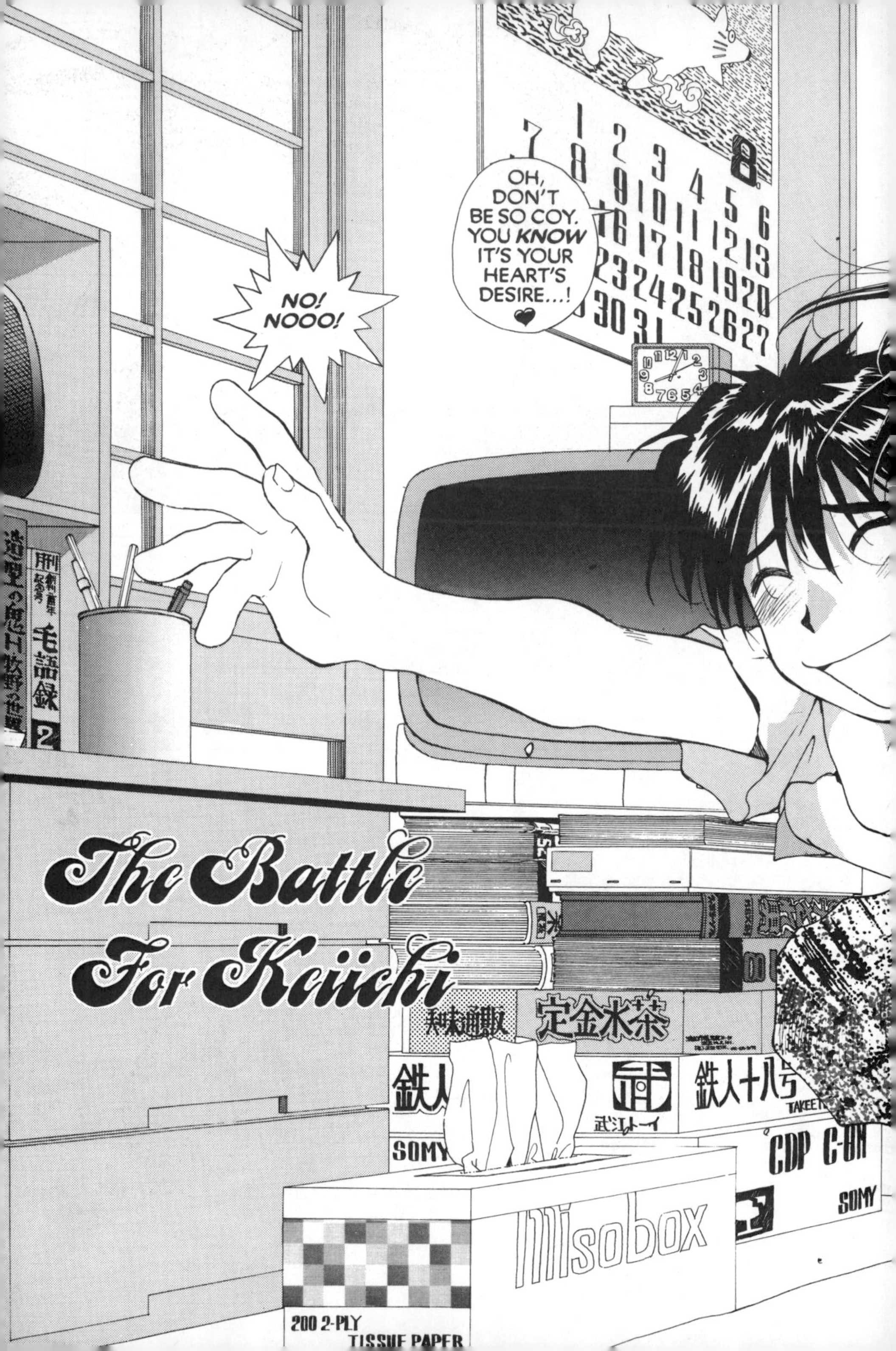
NO! NOOO!
OH, DON'T BE SO COY. YOU *KNOW* IT'S YOUR HEART'S DESIRE...! ❤
The Battle For Keiichi
定金水茶
鉄人
鉄人十八号
SOMY
CDP C-UH
SOMY
Misobox
200 2-PLY TISSUE PAPER

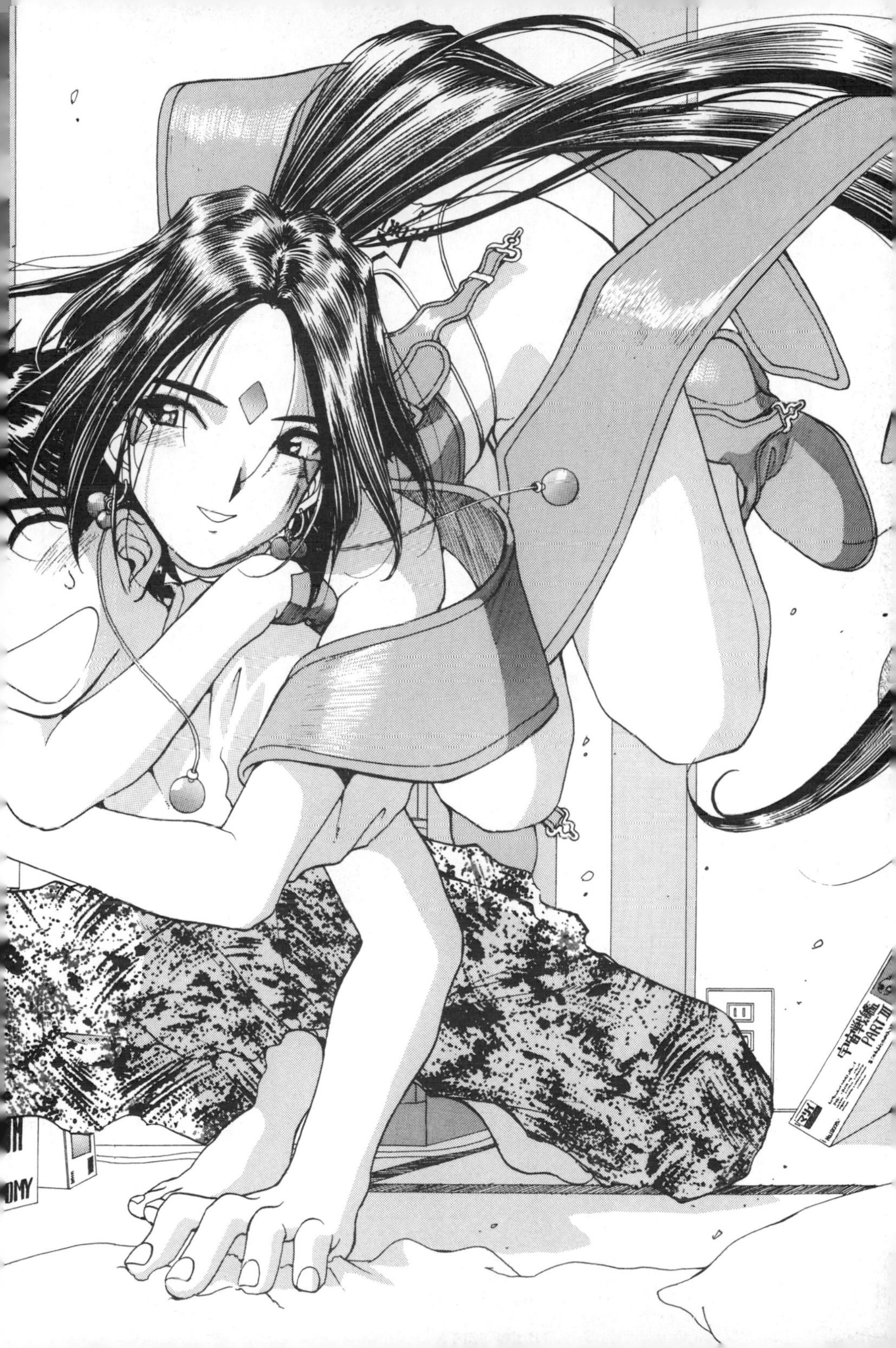
PART III

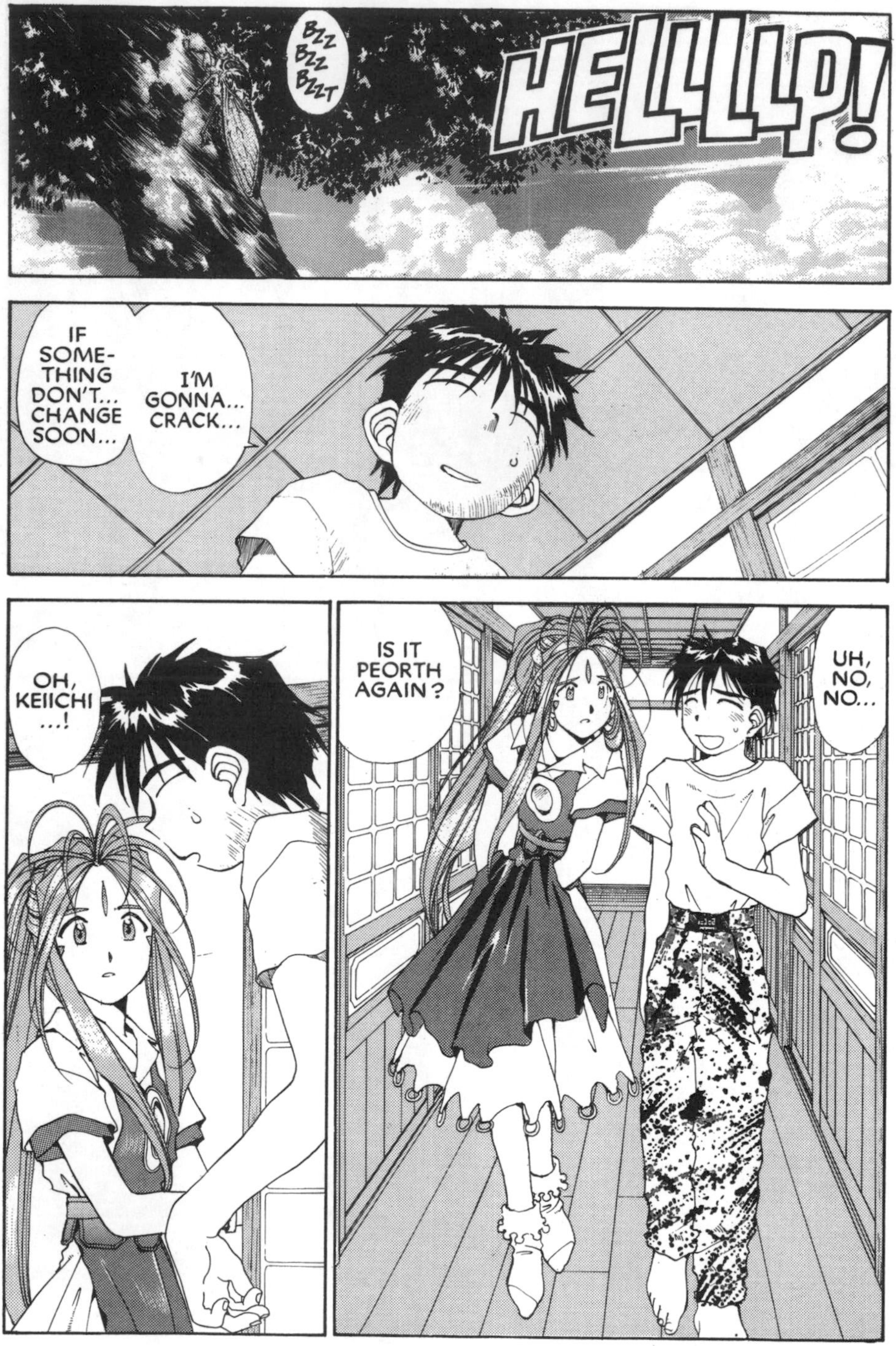
BZZ BZZ BZZT
HELLLLP!
IF SOME-THING DON'T... CHANGE SOON...
I'M GONNA... CRACK...
OH, KEIICHI ...!
IS IT PEORTH AGAIN?
UH, NO, NO...

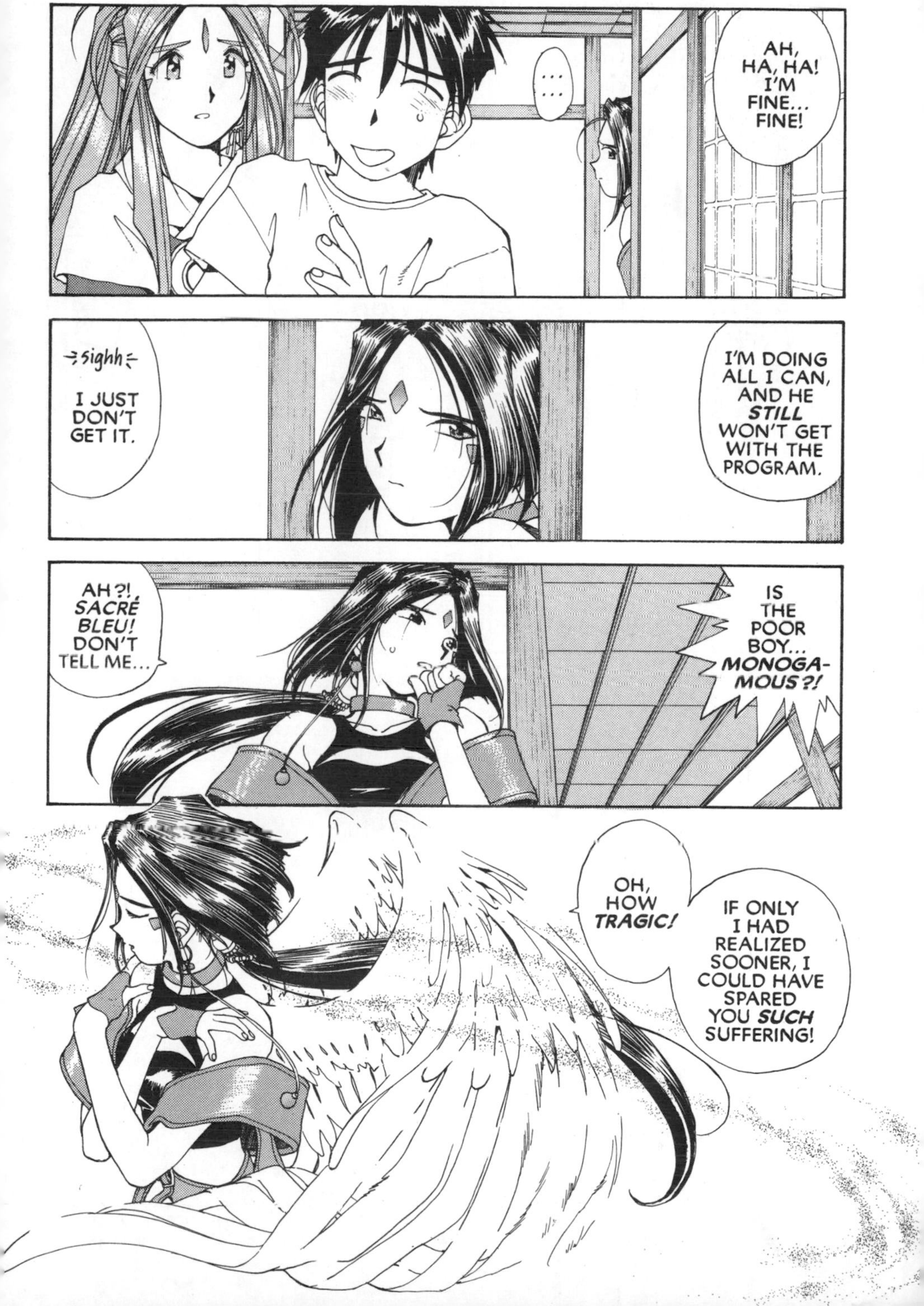
. . .
. . .
AH, HA, HA! I'M FINE... FINE!
≑sighh≑
I JUST DON'T GET IT.
I'M DOING ALL I CAN, AND HE *STILL* WON'T GET WITH THE PROGRAM.
AH?! *SACRÉ BLEU!* DON'T TELL ME...
IS THE POOR BOY... *MONOGAMOUS?!*
OH, HOW *TRAGIC!*
IF ONLY I HAD REALIZED SOONER, I COULD HAVE SPARED YOU *SUCH* SUFFERING!

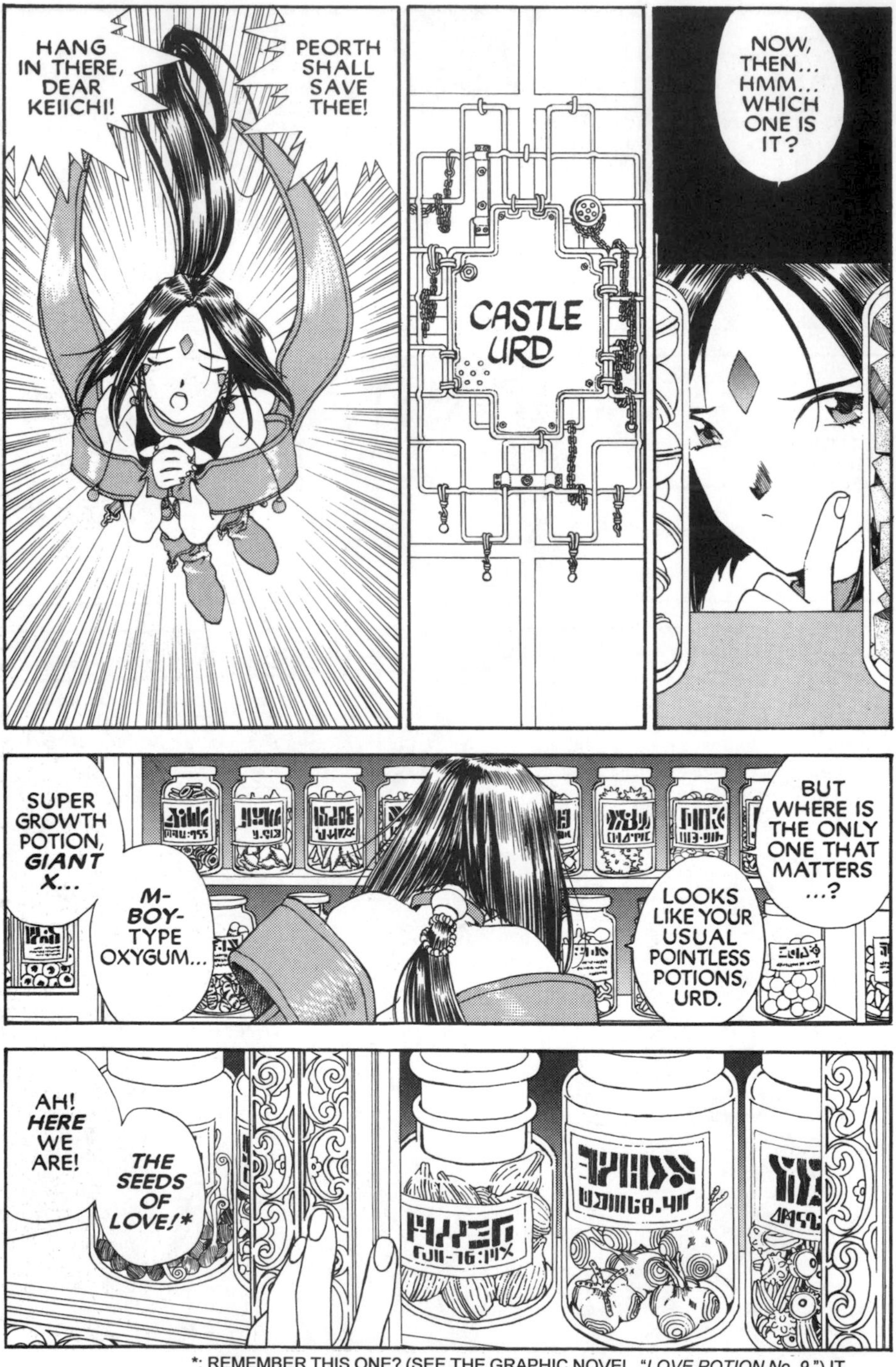
HANG IN THERE, DEAR KEIICHI!
PEORTH SHALL SAVE THEE!
CASTLE URD
NOW, THEN... HMM... WHICH ONE IS IT?
SUPER GROWTH POTION, *GIANT X*...
M-BOY-TYPE OXYGUM...
LOOKS LIKE YOUR USUAL POINTLESS POTIONS, URD.
BUT WHERE IS THE ONLY ONE THAT MATTERS ...?
AH! *HERE* WE ARE!
*THE SEEDS OF LOVE!**

*: REMEMBER THIS ONE? (SEE THE GRAPHIC NOVEL, "*LOVE POTION No. 9.*") IT MAKES WHOEVER TAKES IT FALL IN LOVE WITH THE FIRST PERSON THEY SEE. --Ed.

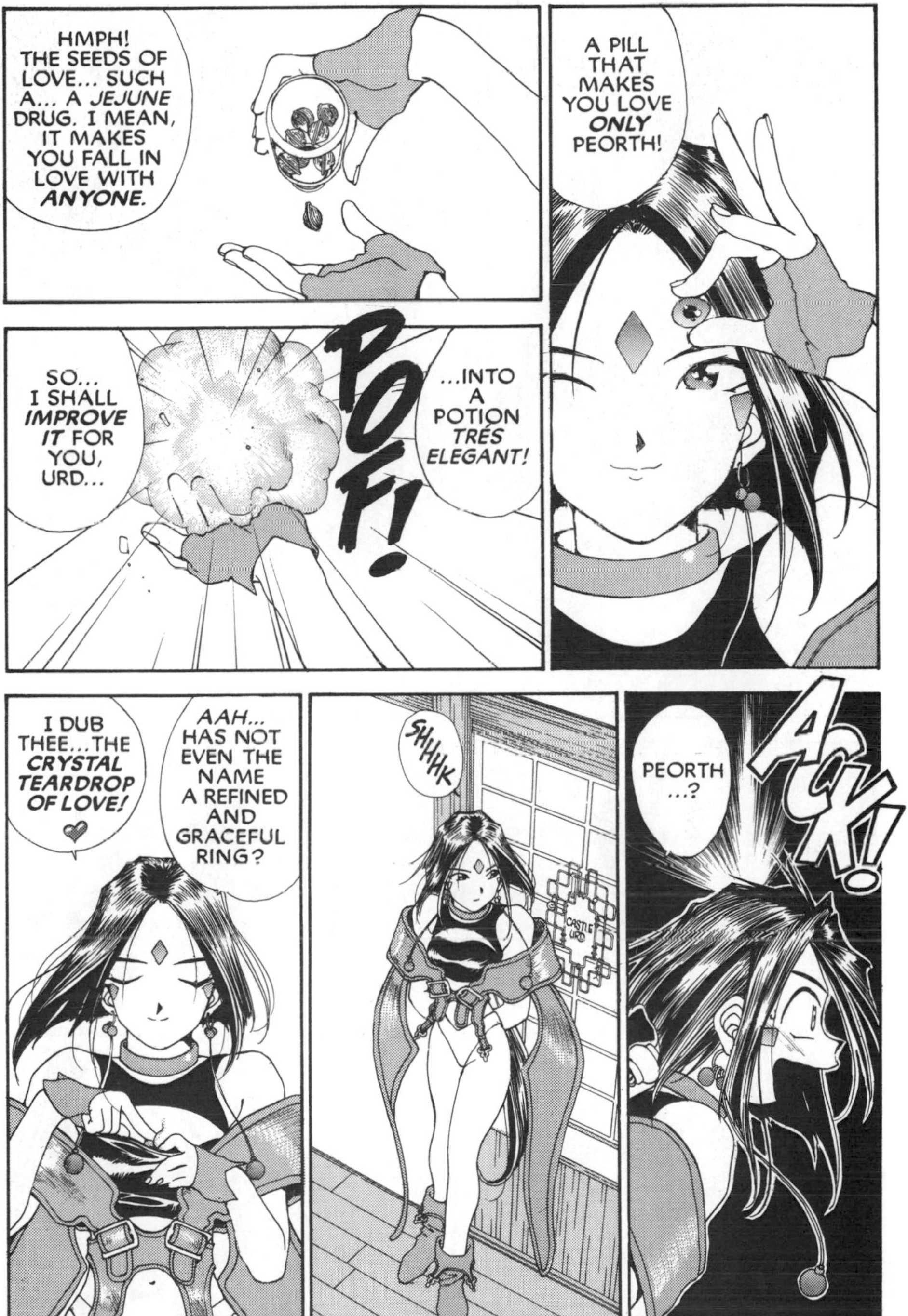
HMPH! THE SEEDS OF LOVE... SUCH A... A *JEJUNE* DRUG. I MEAN, IT MAKES YOU FALL IN LOVE WITH ***ANYONE.***
SO... I SHALL ***IMPROVE IT*** FOR YOU, URD...
POF!
...INTO A POTION *TRÉS* ELEGANT!
A PILL THAT MAKES YOU LOVE ***ONLY*** PEORTH!
I DUB THEE...THE ***CRYSTAL TEARDROP OF LOVE!*** ♥
AAH... HAS NOT EVEN THE NAME A REFINED AND GRACEFUL RING?
SHHHK
CASTLE URD
PEORTH ...?
ACK!

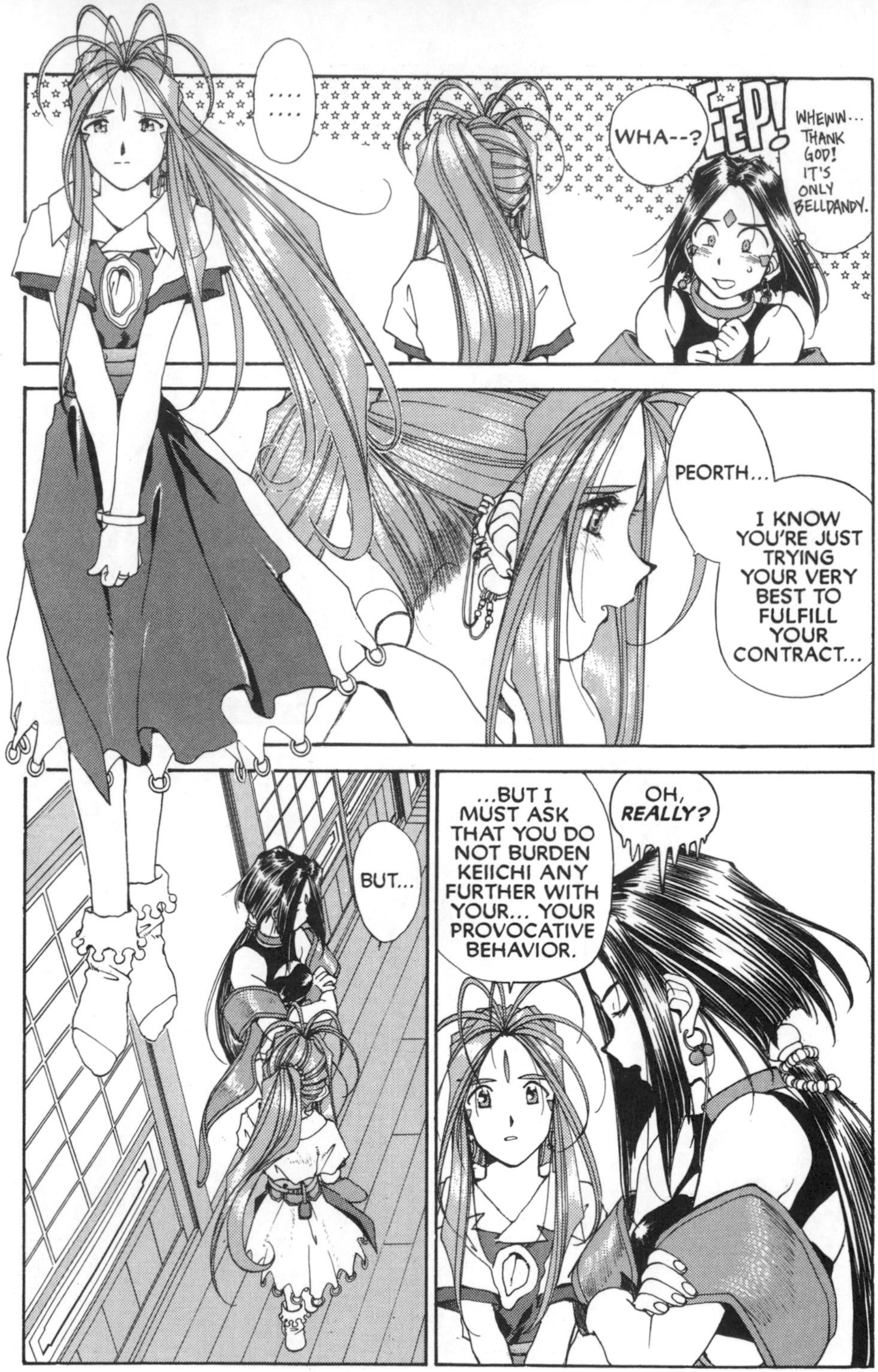

....
....
WHA--?
EEP!
WHEWW... THANK GOD! IT'S ONLY BELLDANDY.
PEORTH...
I KNOW YOU'RE JUST TRYING YOUR VERY BEST TO FULFILL YOUR CONTRACT...
BUT...
...BUT I MUST ASK THAT YOU DO NOT BURDEN KEIICHI ANY FURTHER WITH YOUR... YOUR PROVOCATIVE BEHAVIOR.
OH, *REALLY?*

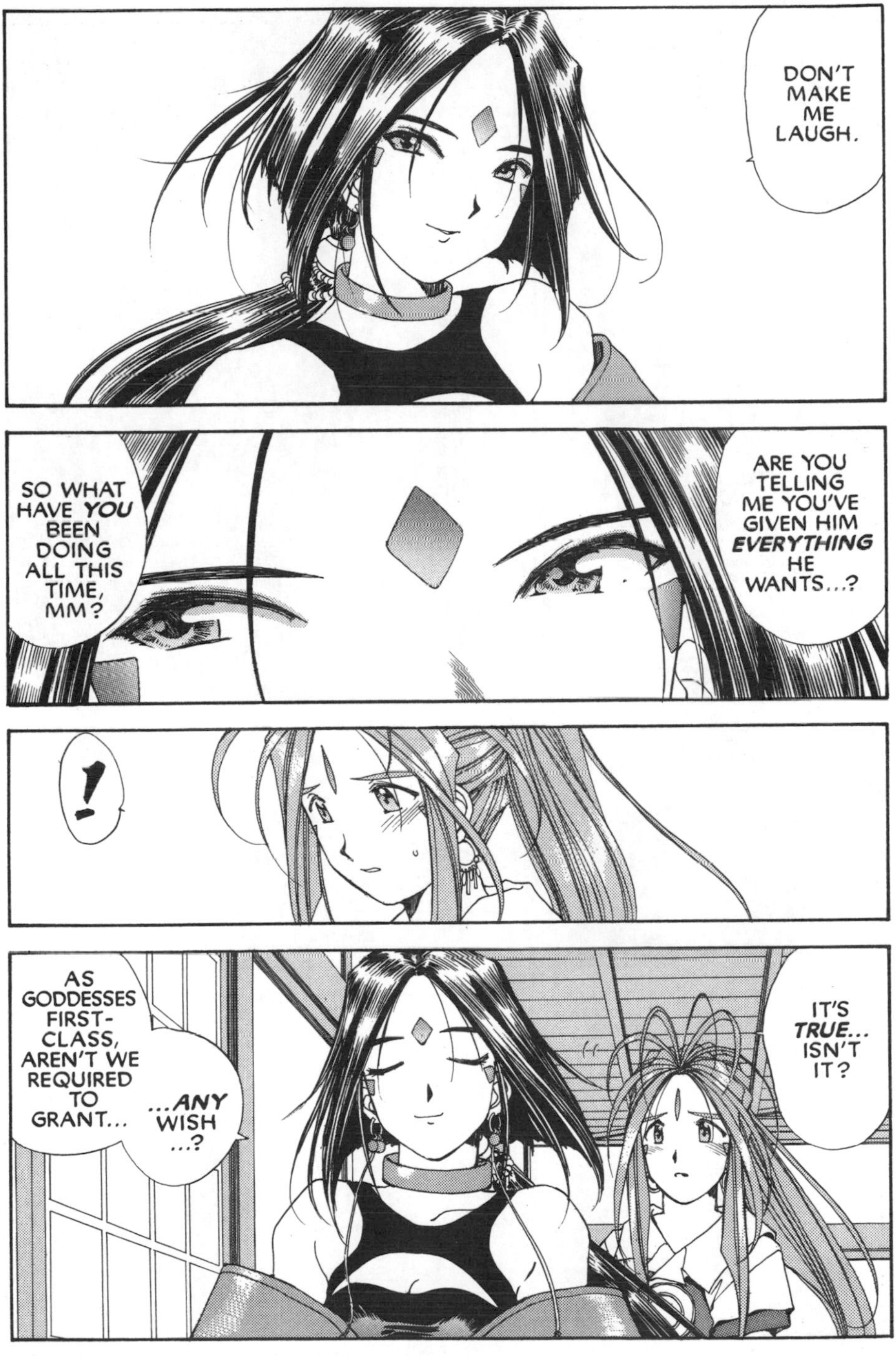
DON'T MAKE ME LAUGH.
SO WHAT HAVE *YOU* BEEN DOING ALL THIS TIME, MM?
ARE YOU TELLING ME YOU'VE GIVEN HIM *EVERYTHING* HE WANTS...?
!
AS GODDESSES FIRST-CLASS, AREN'T WE REQUIRED TO GRANT...
...*ANY* WISH ...?
IT'S *TRUE*... ISN'T IT?

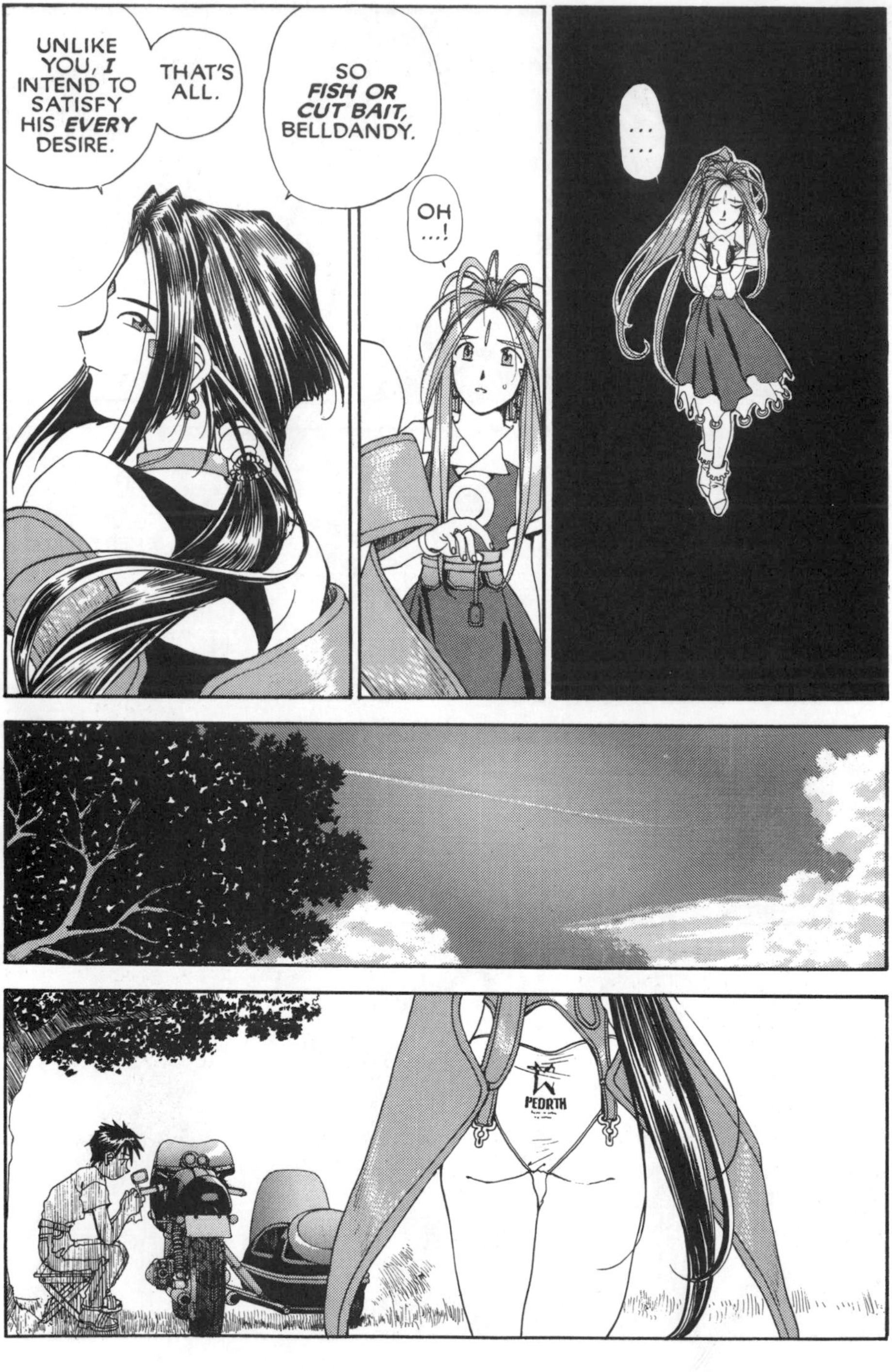
UNLIKE YOU, I INTEND TO SATISFY HIS EVERY DESIRE.
THAT'S ALL.
SO FISH OR CUT BAIT, BELLDANDY.
OH ...!
... ...

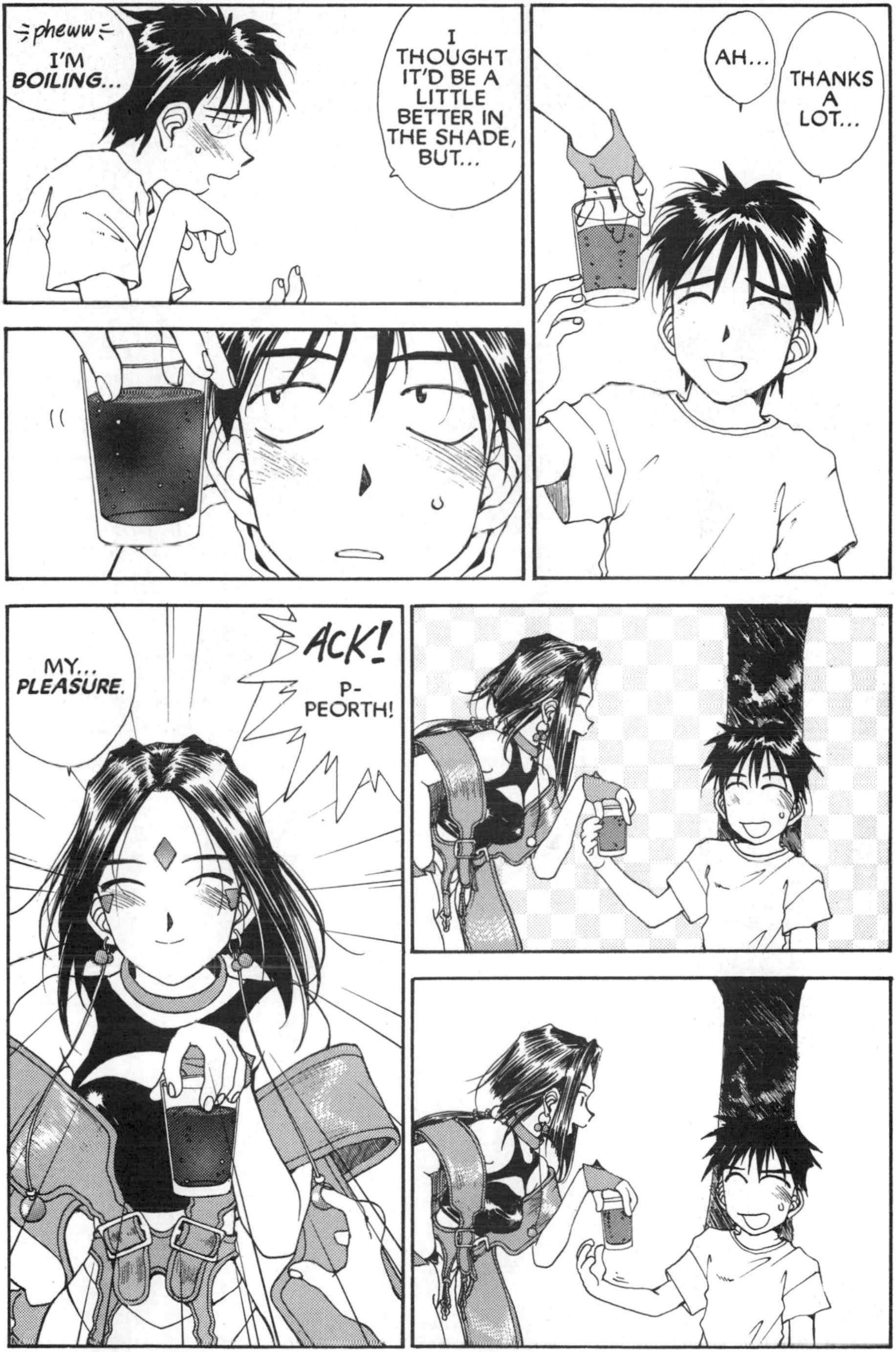

pheww
I'M BOILING...
I THOUGHT IT'D BE A LITTLE BETTER IN THE SHADE, BUT...
AH...
THANKS A LOT...
MY... PLEASURE.
ACK!
P-PEORTH!

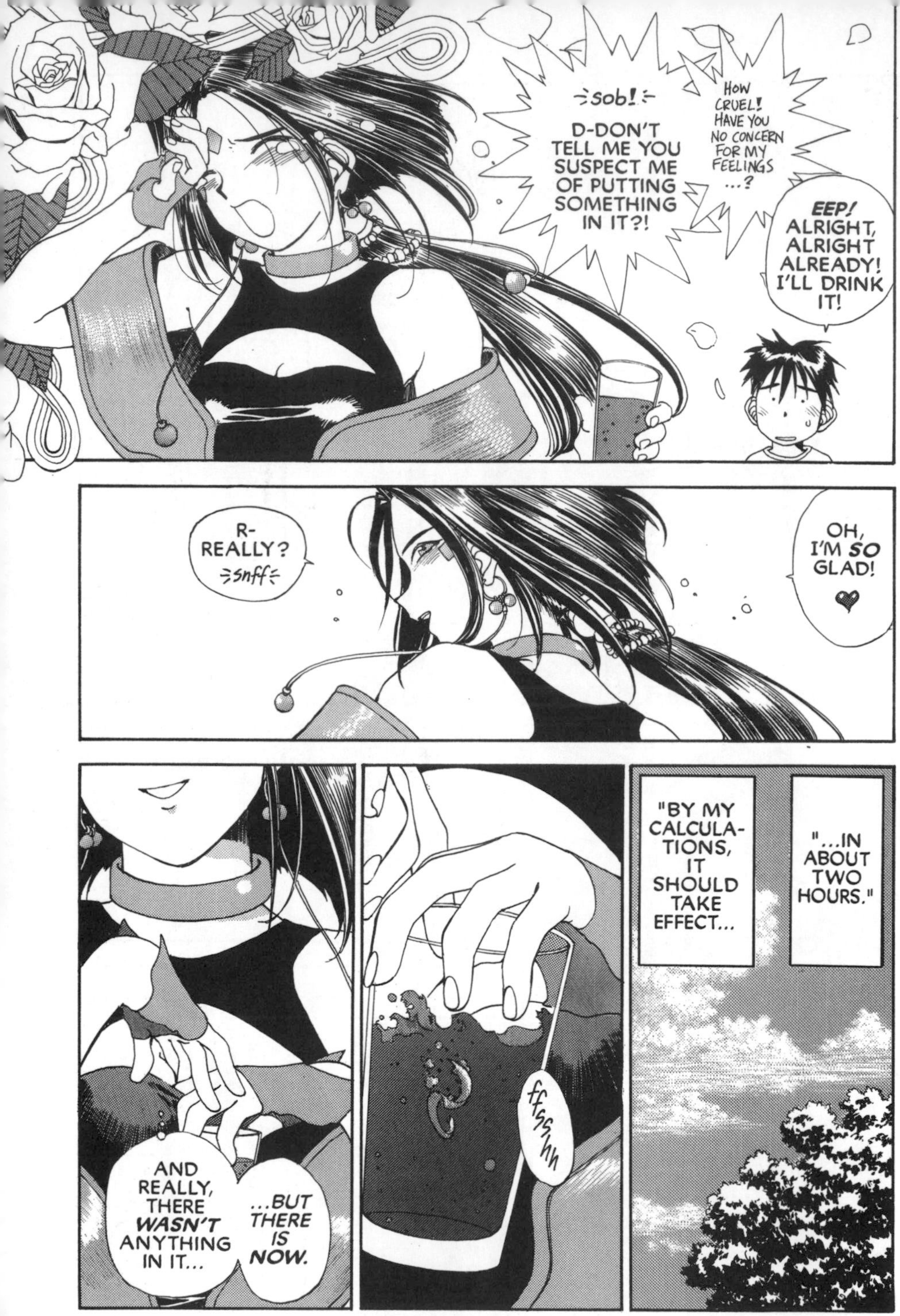
sob!
D-DON'T TELL ME YOU SUSPECT ME OF PUTTING SOMETHING IN IT?!
HOW CRUEL! HAVE YOU NO CONCERN FOR MY FEELINGS ...?
EEP! ALRIGHT, ALRIGHT ALREADY! I'LL DRINK IT!
R-REALLY? snff
OH, I'M SO GLAD!
AND REALLY, THERE WASN'T ANYTHING IN IT...
...BUT THERE IS NOW.
ffsshh
"BY MY CALCULATIONS, IT SHOULD TAKE EFFECT...
"...IN ABOUT TWO HOURS."

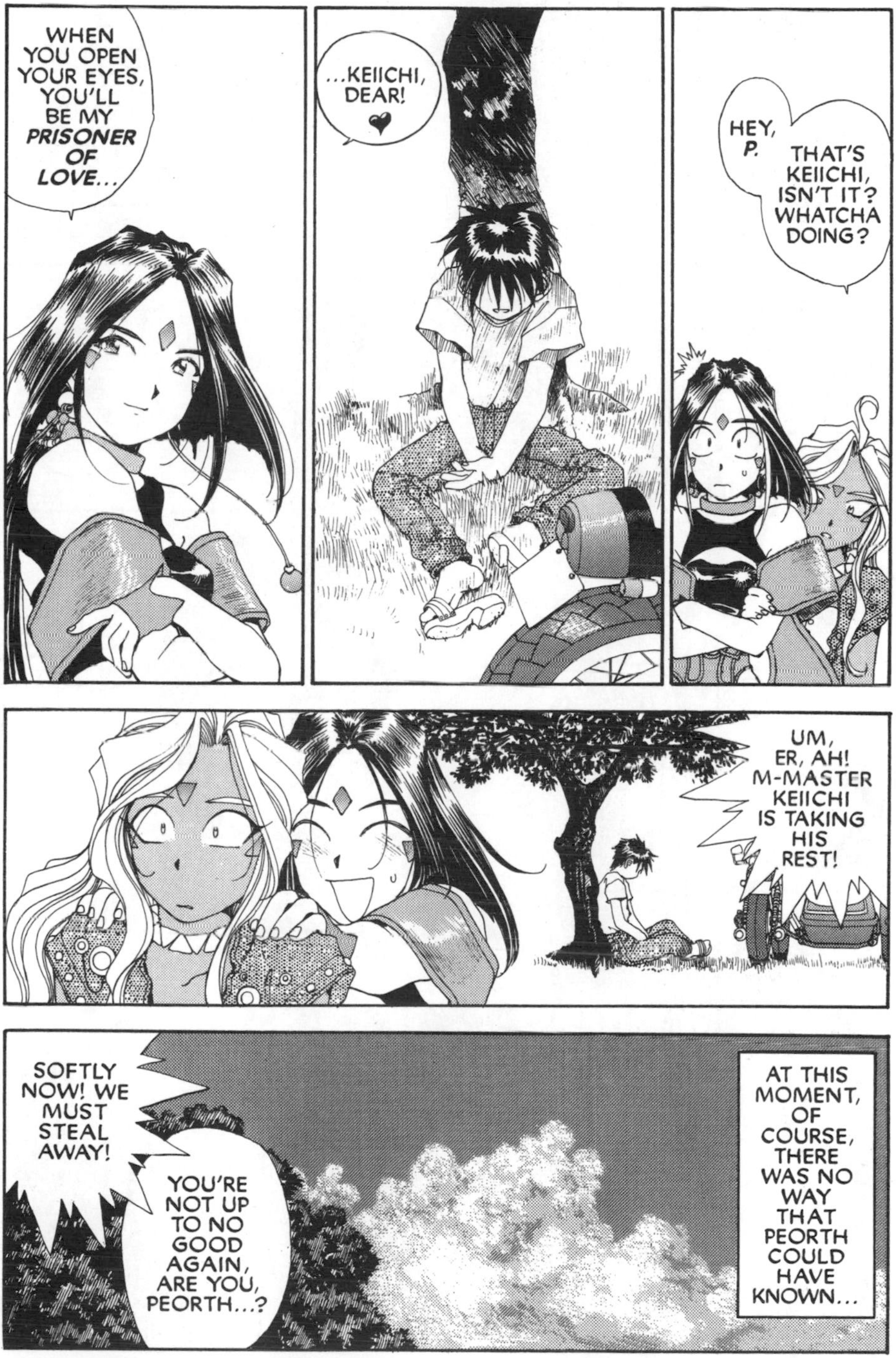
WHEN YOU OPEN YOUR EYES, YOU'LL BE MY *PRISONER OF LOVE*...
...KEIICHI, DEAR! ♥
HEY, *P.*
THAT'S KEIICHI, ISN'T IT? WHATCHA DOING?
UM, ER, AH! M-MASTER KEIICHI IS TAKING HIS REST!
SOFTLY NOW! WE MUST STEAL AWAY!
YOU'RE NOT UP TO NO GOOD AGAIN, ARE YOU, PEORTH...?
AT THIS MOMENT, OF COURSE, THERE WAS NO WAY THAT PEORTH COULD HAVE KNOWN...

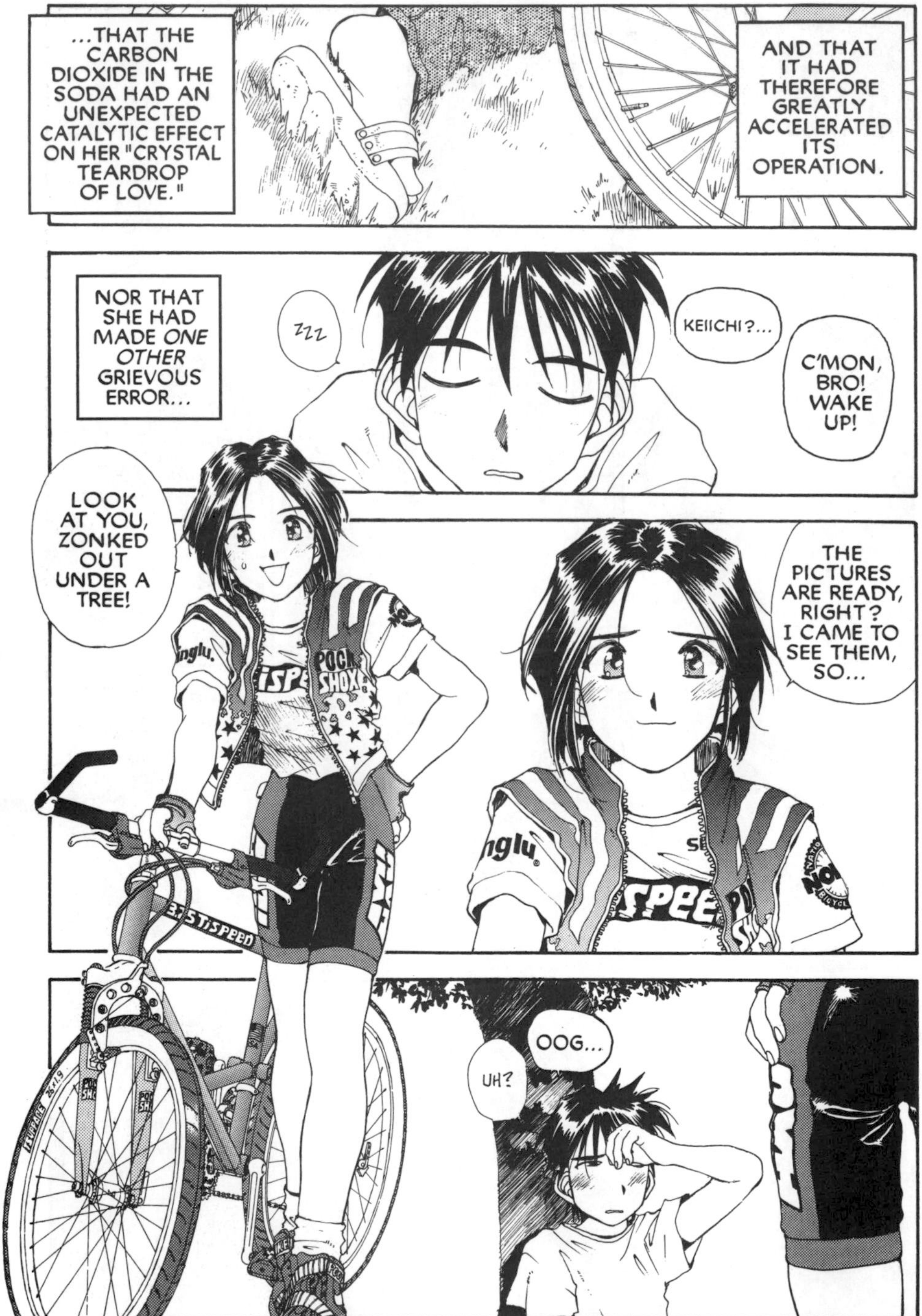
...THAT THE CARBON DIOXIDE IN THE SODA HAD AN UNEXPECTED CATALYTIC EFFECT ON HER "CRYSTAL TEARDROP OF LOVE."
AND THAT IT HAD THEREFORE GREATLY ACCELERATED ITS OPERATION.
NOR THAT SHE HAD MADE *ONE OTHER* GRIEVOUS ERROR...
ZZZ
KEIICHI?...
C'MON, BRO! WAKE UP!
LOOK AT YOU, ZONKED OUT UNDER A TREE!
THE PICTURES ARE READY, RIGHT? I CAME TO SEE THEM, SO...
UH?
OOG...

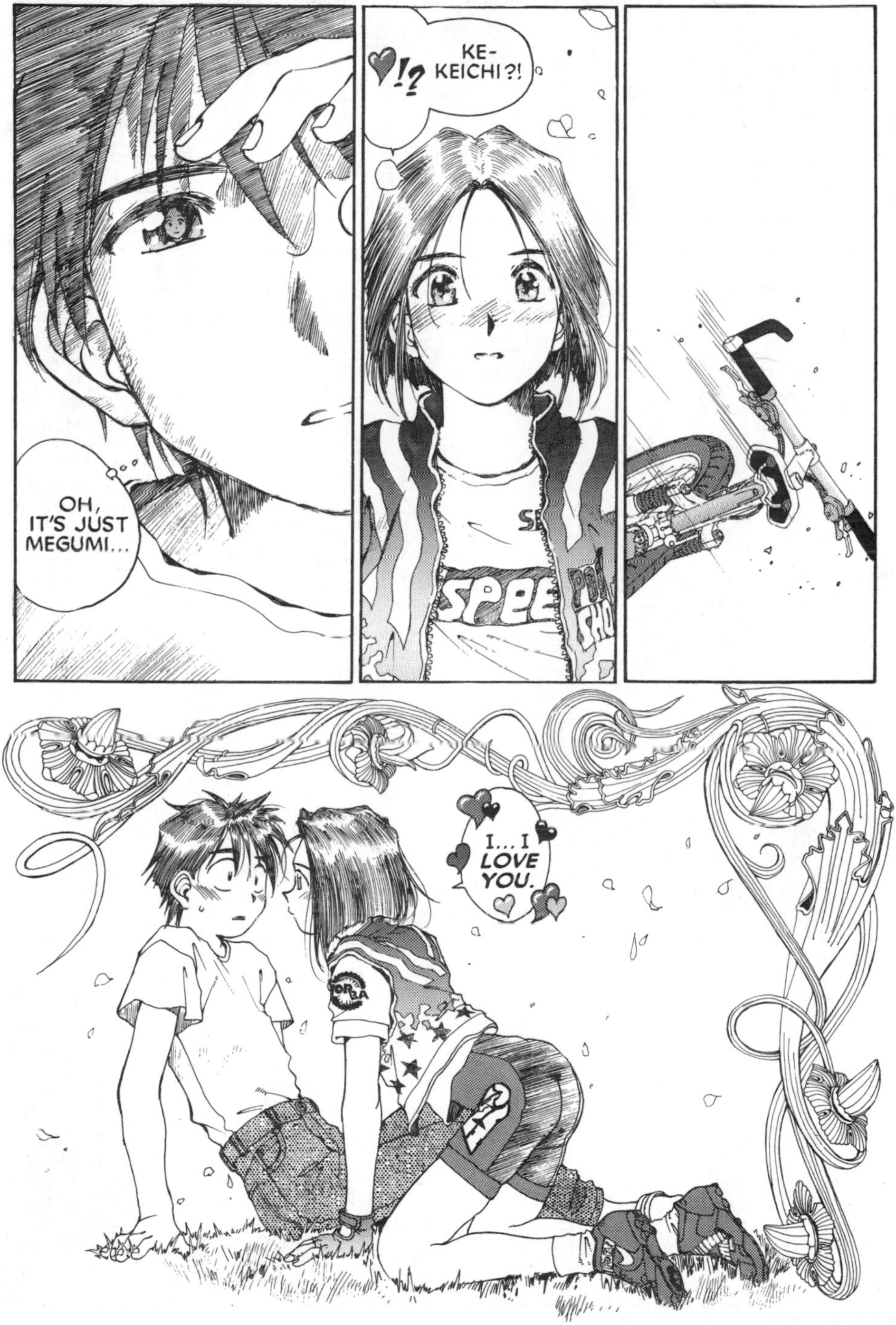
OH, IT'S JUST MEGUMI...
!?
KE-KEICHI?!
I... I LOVE YOU.

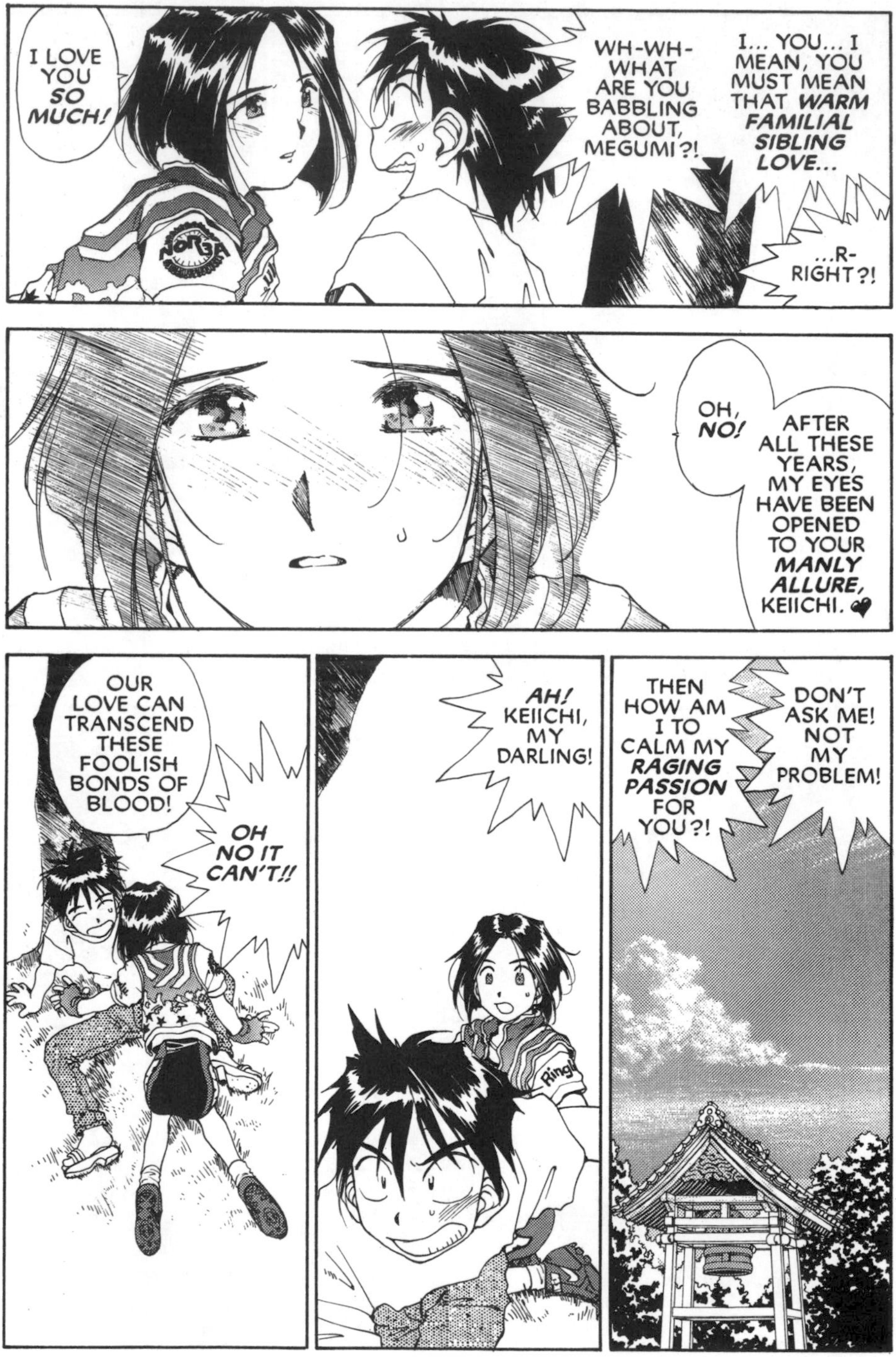
I LOVE YOU SO MUCH!
WH-WH-WHAT ARE YOU BABBLING ABOUT, MEGUMI?!
I... YOU... I MEAN, YOU MUST MEAN THAT WARM FAMILIAL SIBLING LOVE...
...R-RIGHT?!
OH, NO!
AFTER ALL THESE YEARS, MY EYES HAVE BEEN OPENED TO YOUR MANLY ALLURE, KEIICHI.
OUR LOVE CAN TRANSCEND THESE FOOLISH BONDS OF BLOOD!
OH NO IT CAN'T!!
AH! KEIICHI, MY DARLING!
THEN HOW AM I TO CALM MY RAGING PASSION FOR YOU?!
DON'T ASK ME! NOT MY PROBLEM!

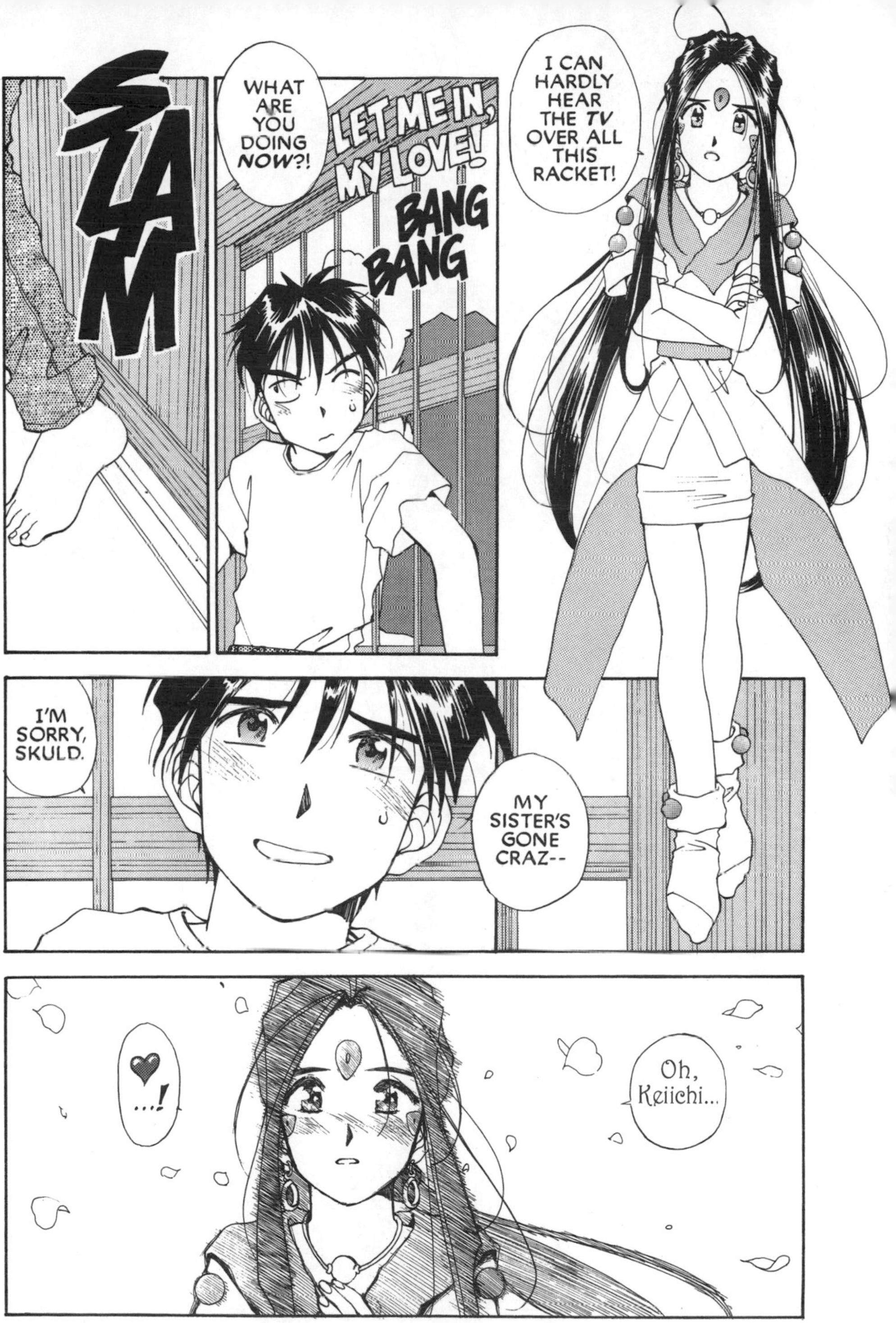
SLAM
WHAT ARE YOU DOING *NOW*?!
LET ME IN, MY LOVE!
BANG BANG
I'M SORRY, SKULD.
MY SISTER'S GONE CRAZ--
I CAN HARDLY HEAR THE *TV* OVER ALL THIS RACKET!
♥ ...!
Oh, Keiichi...

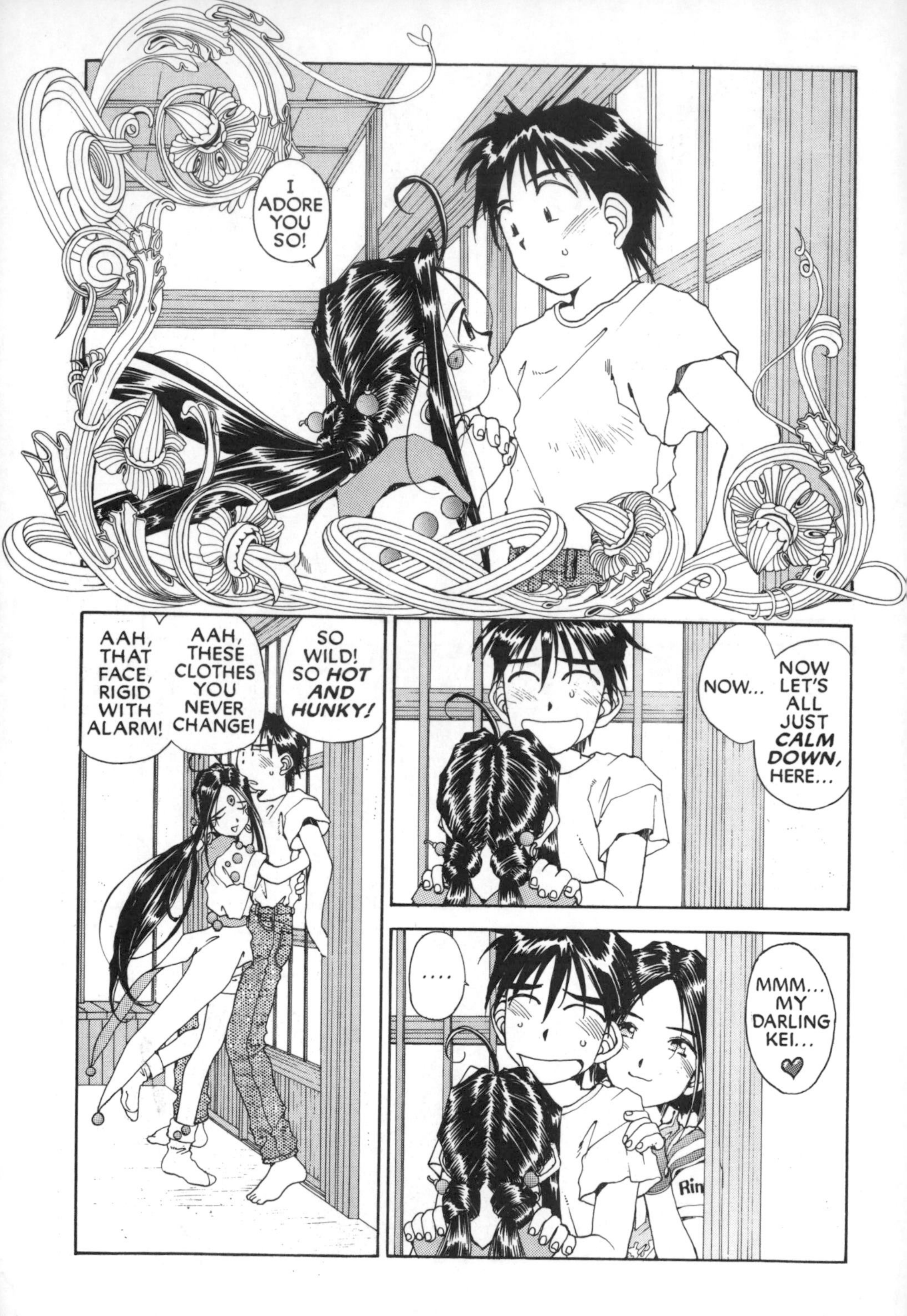

I ADORE YOU SO!
AAH, THAT FACE, RIGID WITH ALARM!
AAH, THESE CLOTHES YOU NEVER CHANGE!
SO WILD! SO ***HOT AND HUNKY!***
NOW...
NOW LET'S ALL JUST ***CALM DOWN,*** HERE...
....
MMM... MY DARLING KEI... ♥

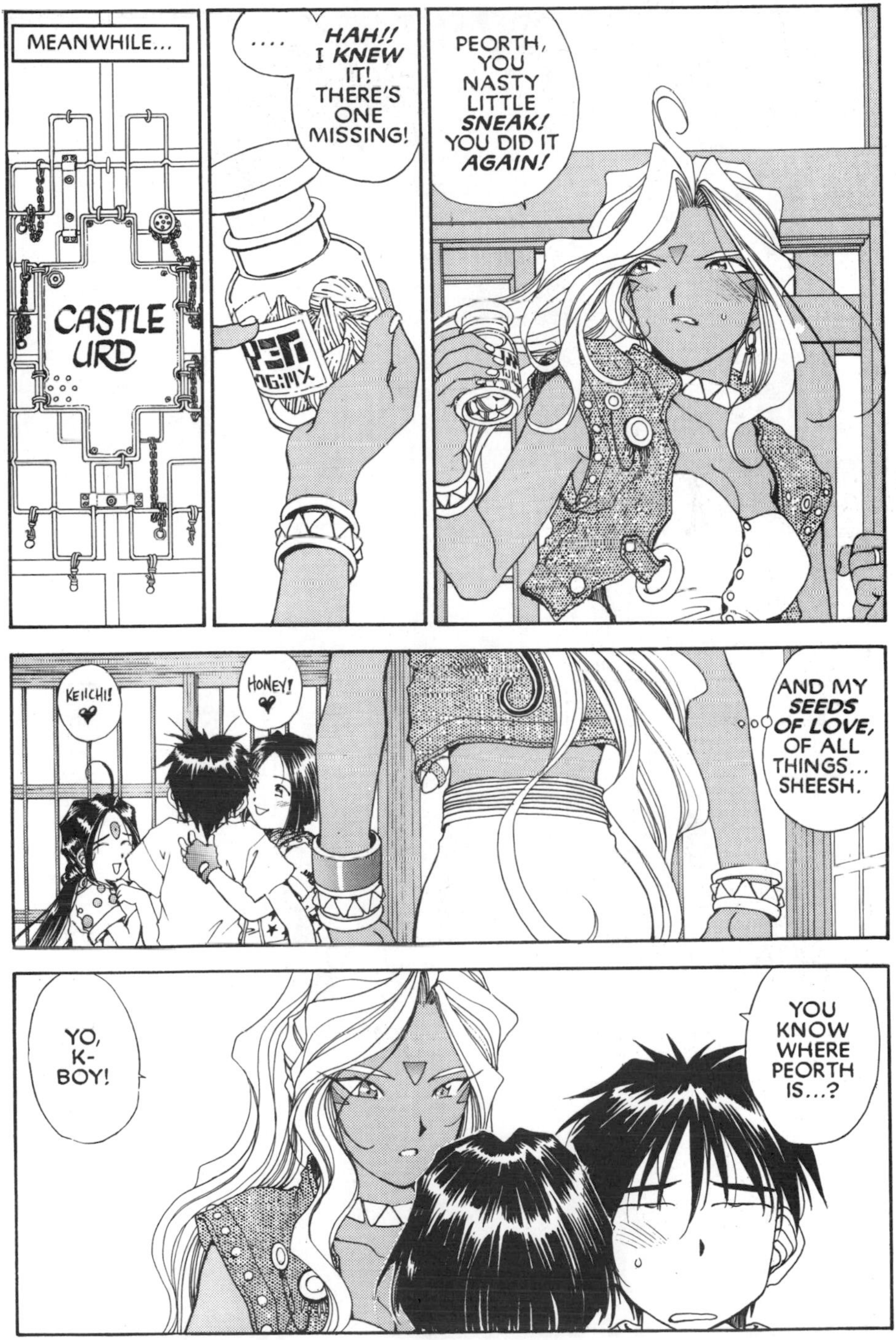
MEANWHILE...
CASTLE URD
.... HAH!! I KNEW IT! THERE'S ONE MISSING!
PEORTH, YOU NASTY LITTLE SNEAK! YOU DID IT AGAIN!
KEIICHI! ♥
HONEY! ♥
AND MY SEEDS OF LOVE, OF ALL THINGS... SHEESH.
YO, K-BOY!
YOU KNOW WHERE PEORTH IS...?

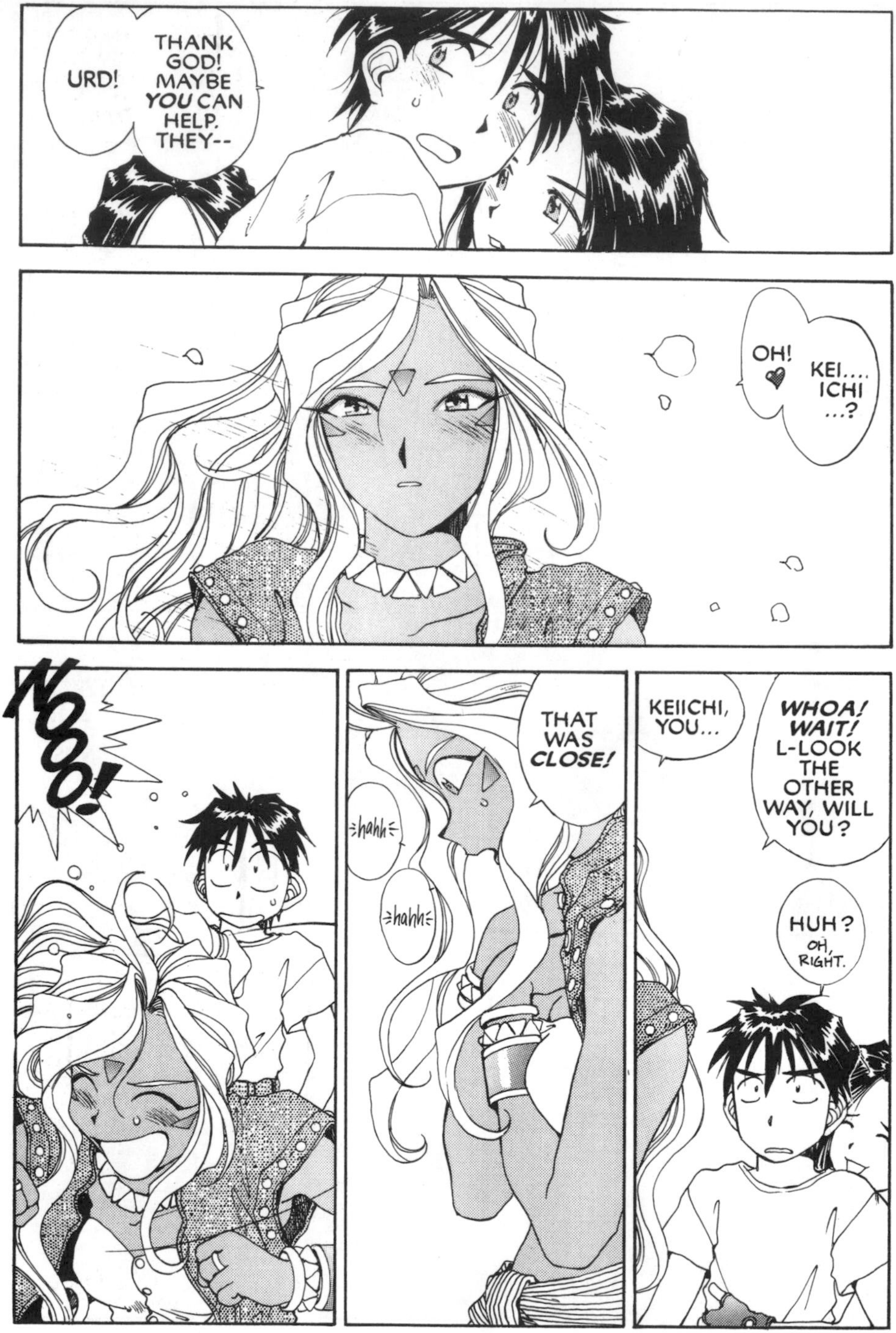
URD!
THANK GOD! MAYBE *YOU* CAN HELP. THEY--
OH! ♥
KEI.... ICHI ...?
NOOO!
THAT WAS *CLOSE!*
hahh
hahh
KEIICHI, YOU...
WHOA! WAIT! L-LOOK THE OTHER WAY, WILL YOU?
HUH? OH, RIGHT.

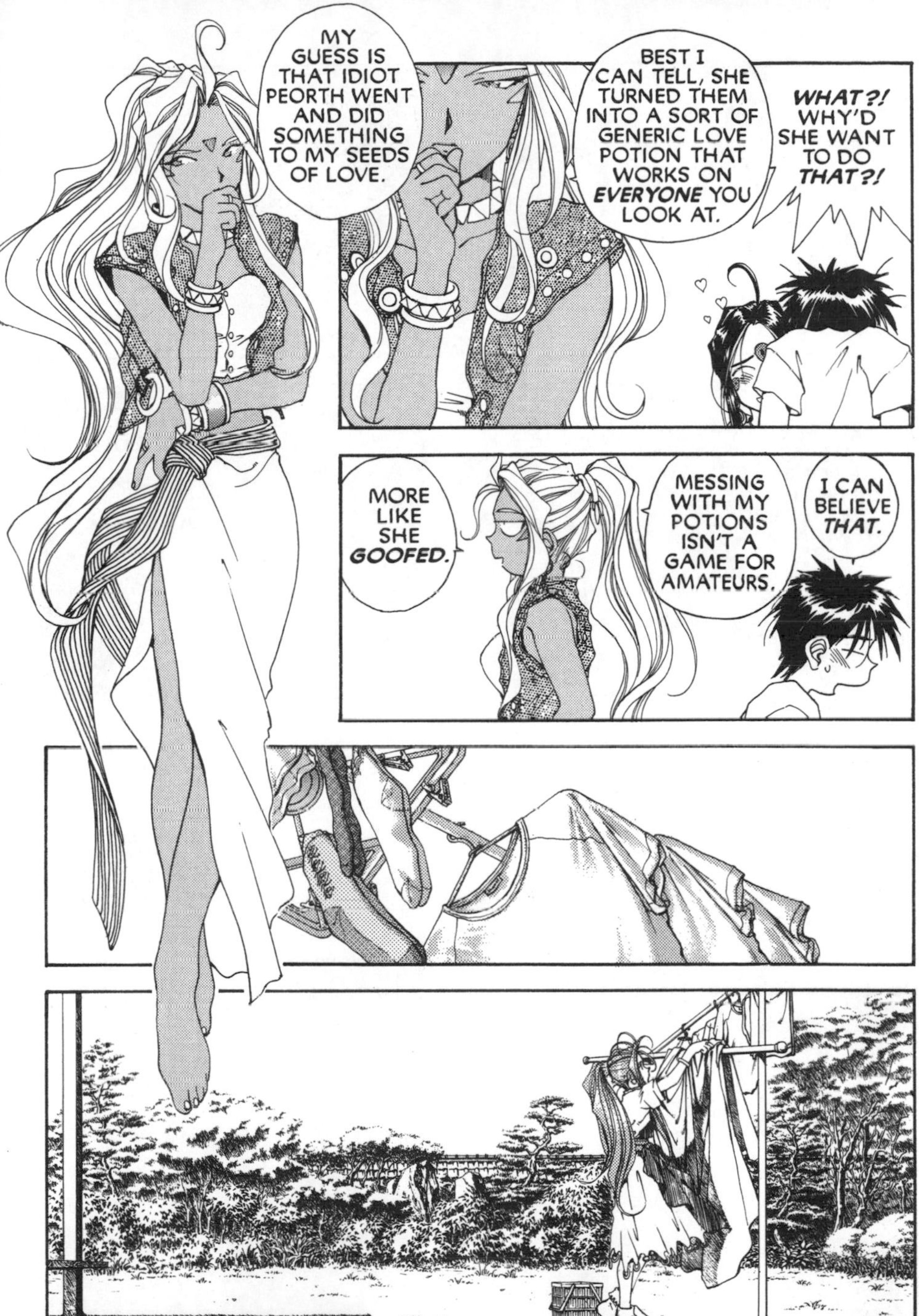
MY GUESS IS THAT IDIOT PEORTH WENT AND DID SOMETHING TO MY SEEDS OF LOVE.
BEST I CAN TELL, SHE TURNED THEM INTO A SORT OF GENERIC LOVE POTION THAT WORKS ON *EVERYONE* YOU LOOK AT.
WHAT?! WHY'D SHE WANT TO DO *THAT?!*
MORE LIKE SHE *GOOFED.*
MESSING WITH MY POTIONS ISN'T A GAME FOR AMATEURS.
I CAN BELIEVE *THAT.*

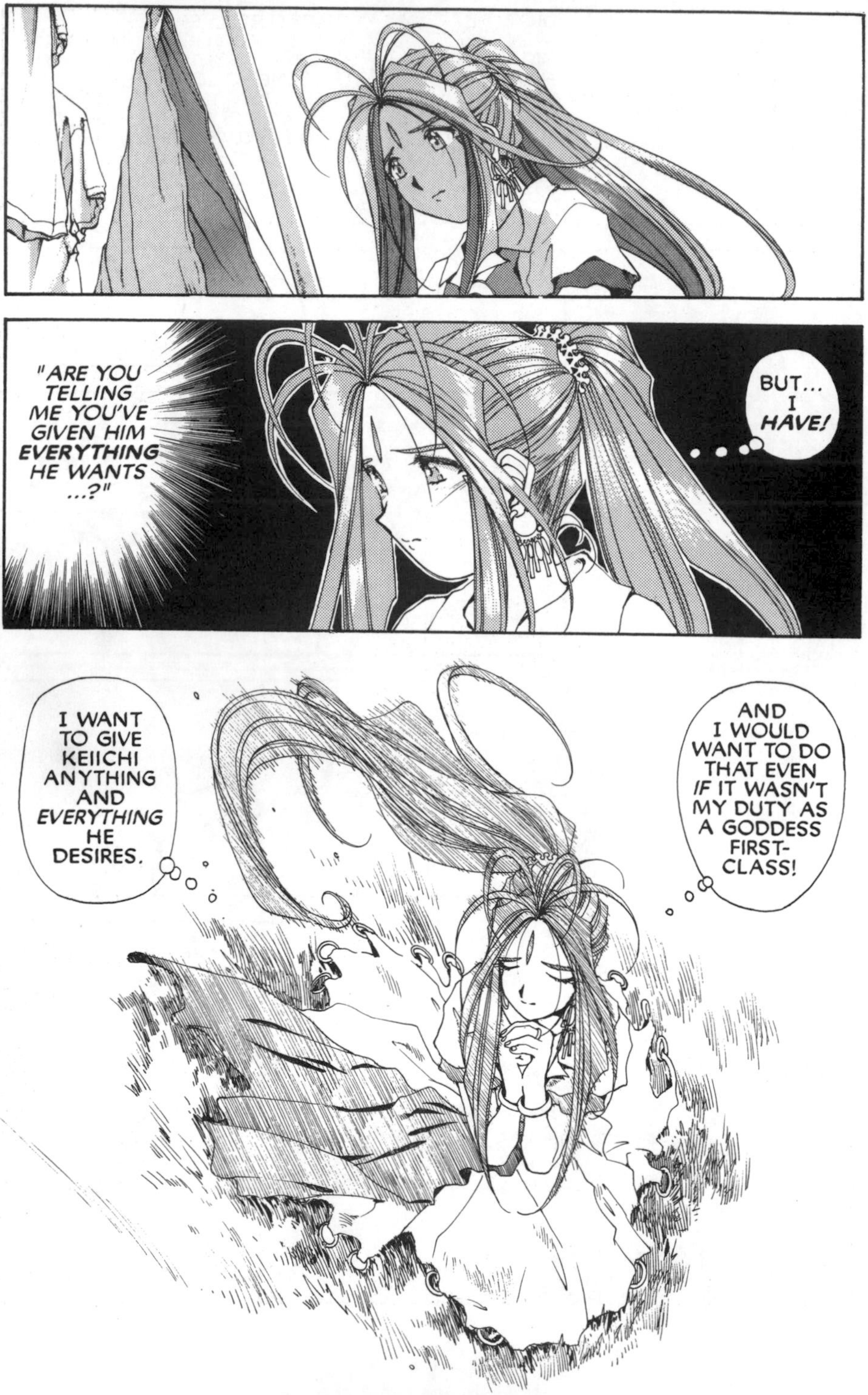
"ARE YOU TELLING ME YOU'VE GIVEN HIM *EVERYTHING* HE WANTS ...?"
BUT... I *HAVE!*
I WANT TO GIVE KEIICHI ANYTHING AND *EVERYTHING* HE DESIRES.
AND I WOULD WANT TO DO THAT EVEN *IF* IT WASN'T MY DUTY AS A GODDESS FIRST-CLASS!

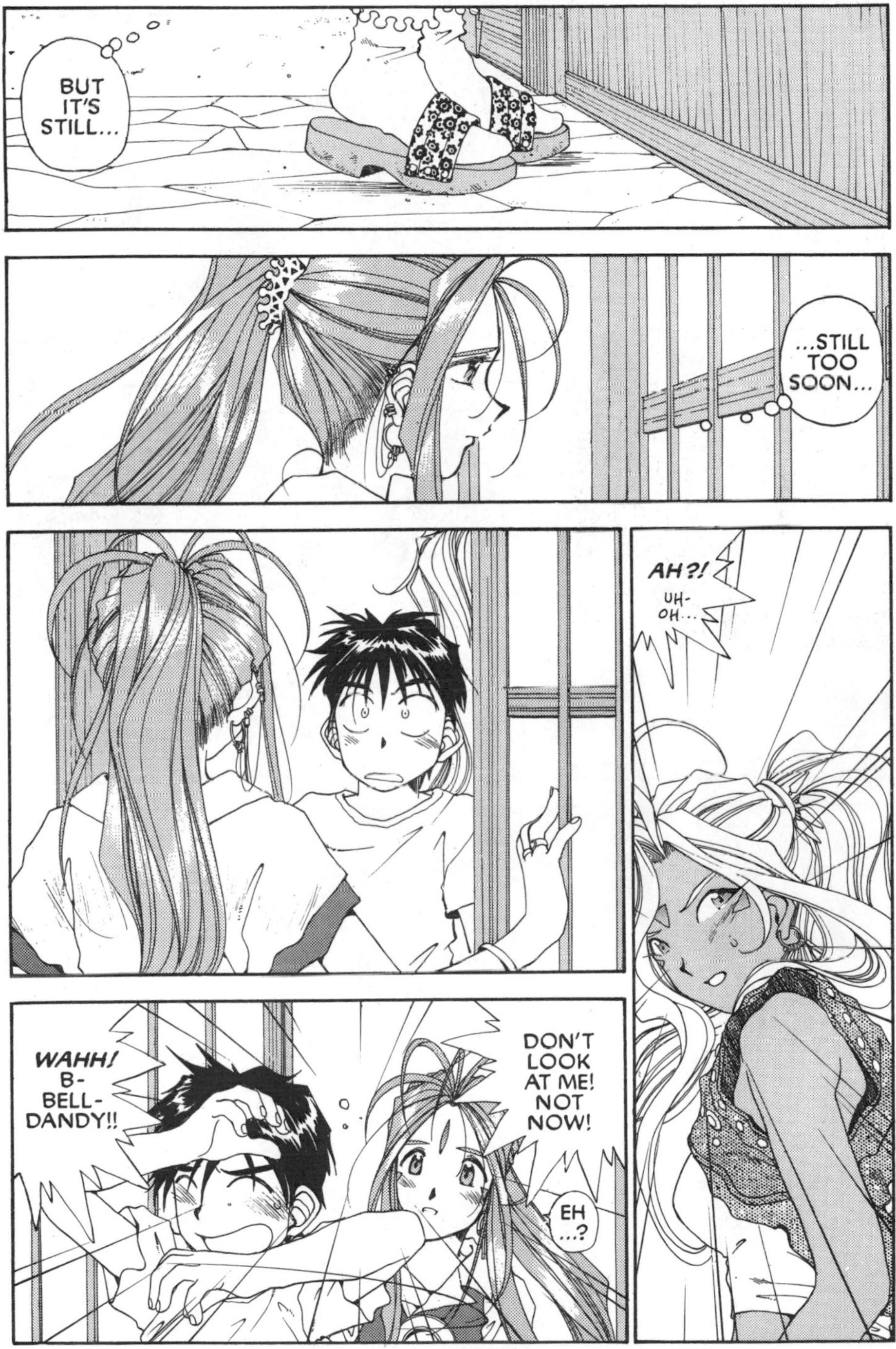
BUT IT'S STILL...
...STILL TOO SOON...
WAHH! B-BELL-DANDY!!
DON'T LOOK AT ME! NOT NOW!
EH ...?
AH?!
UH-OH...

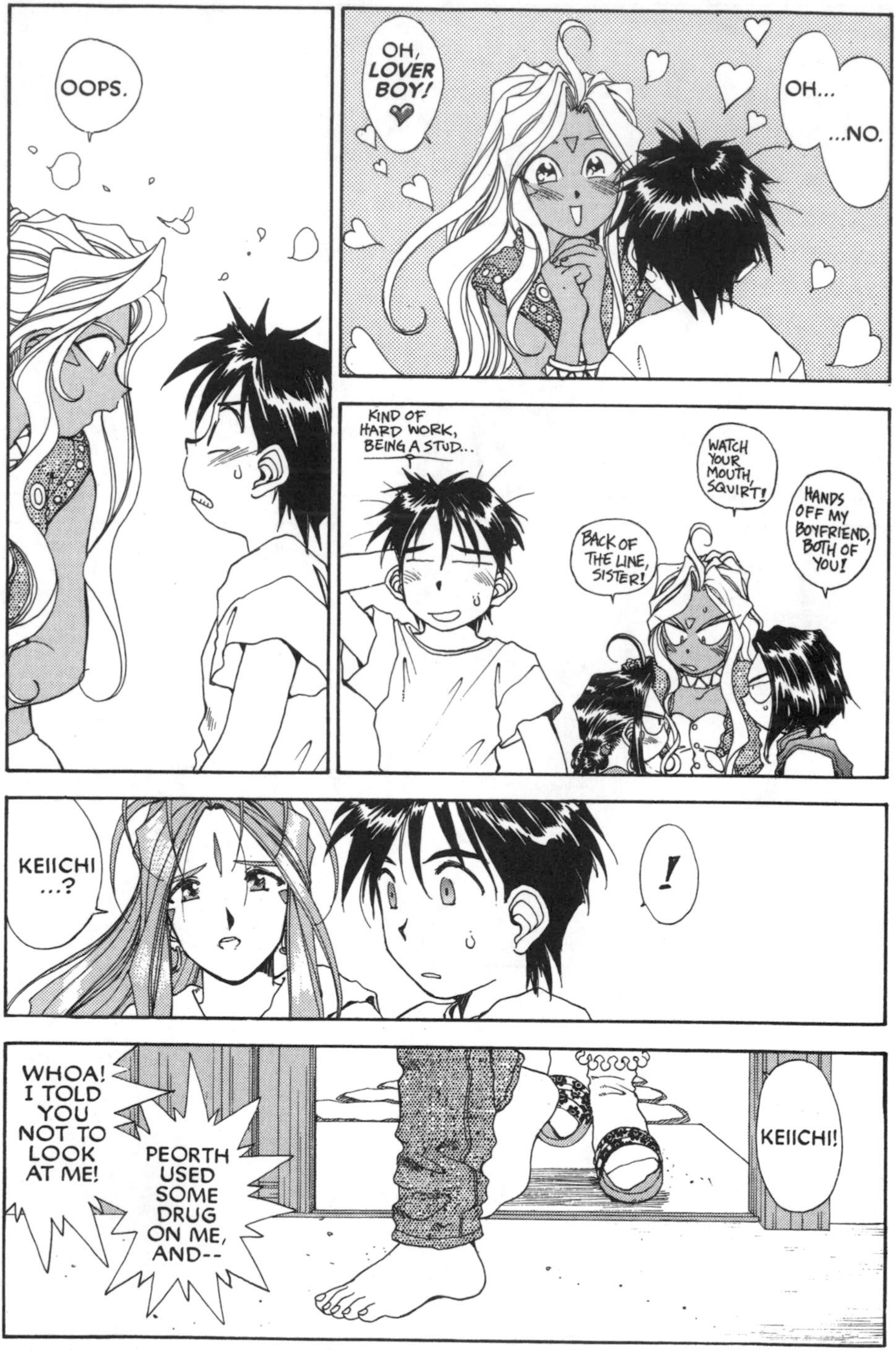
OOPS.
OH, LOVER BOY! ♥
OH... ...NO.
KIND OF HARD WORK, BEING A STUD...
WATCH YOUR MOUTH, SQUIRT!
BACK OF THE LINE, SISTER!
HANDS OFF MY BOYFRIEND, BOTH OF YOU!
KEIICHI ...?
!
WHOA! I TOLD YOU NOT TO LOOK AT ME!
PEORTH USED SOME DRUG ON ME, AND--
KEIICHI!

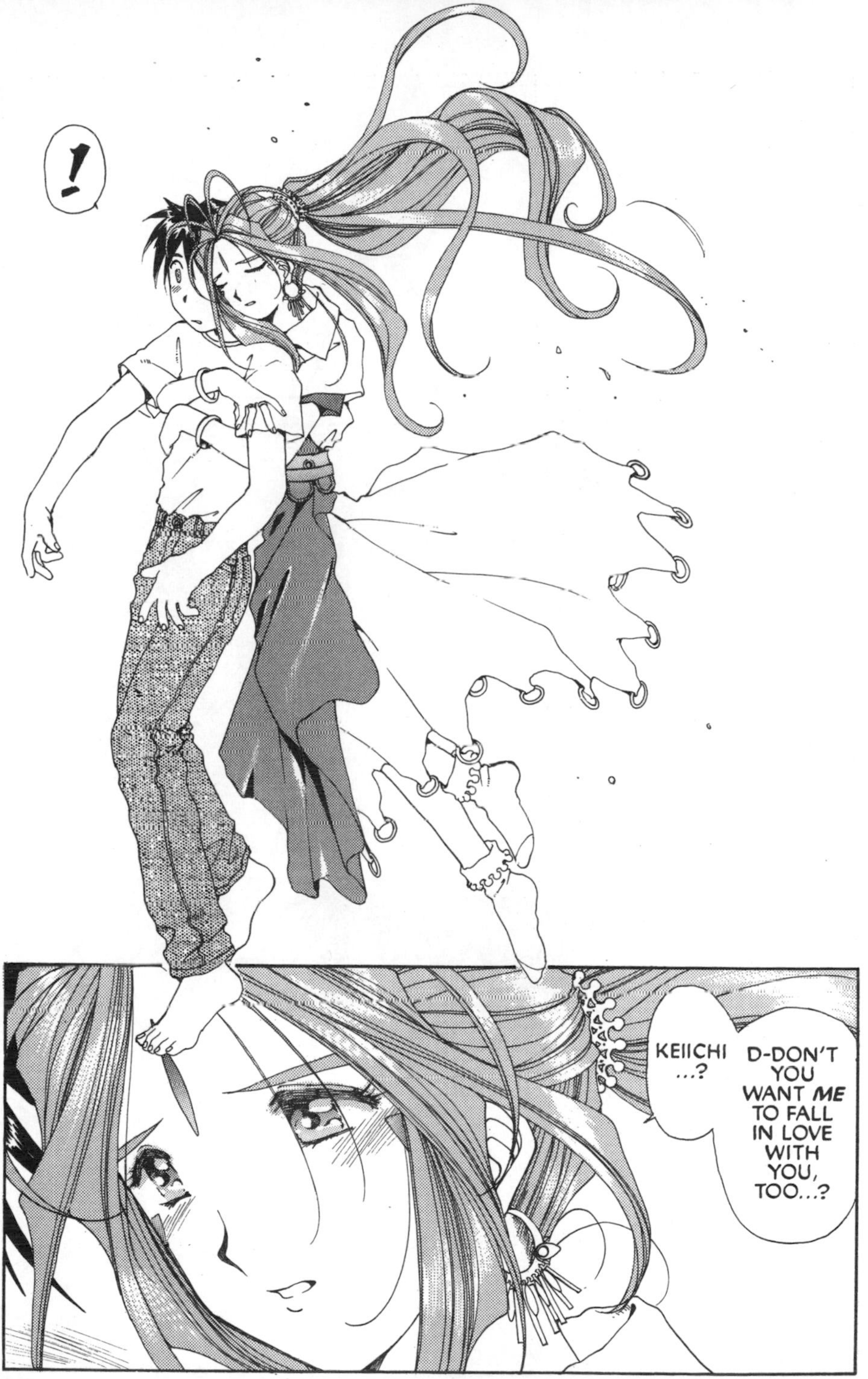
!
KEIICHI ...?
D-DON'T YOU WANT *ME* TO FALL IN LOVE WITH YOU, TOO...?

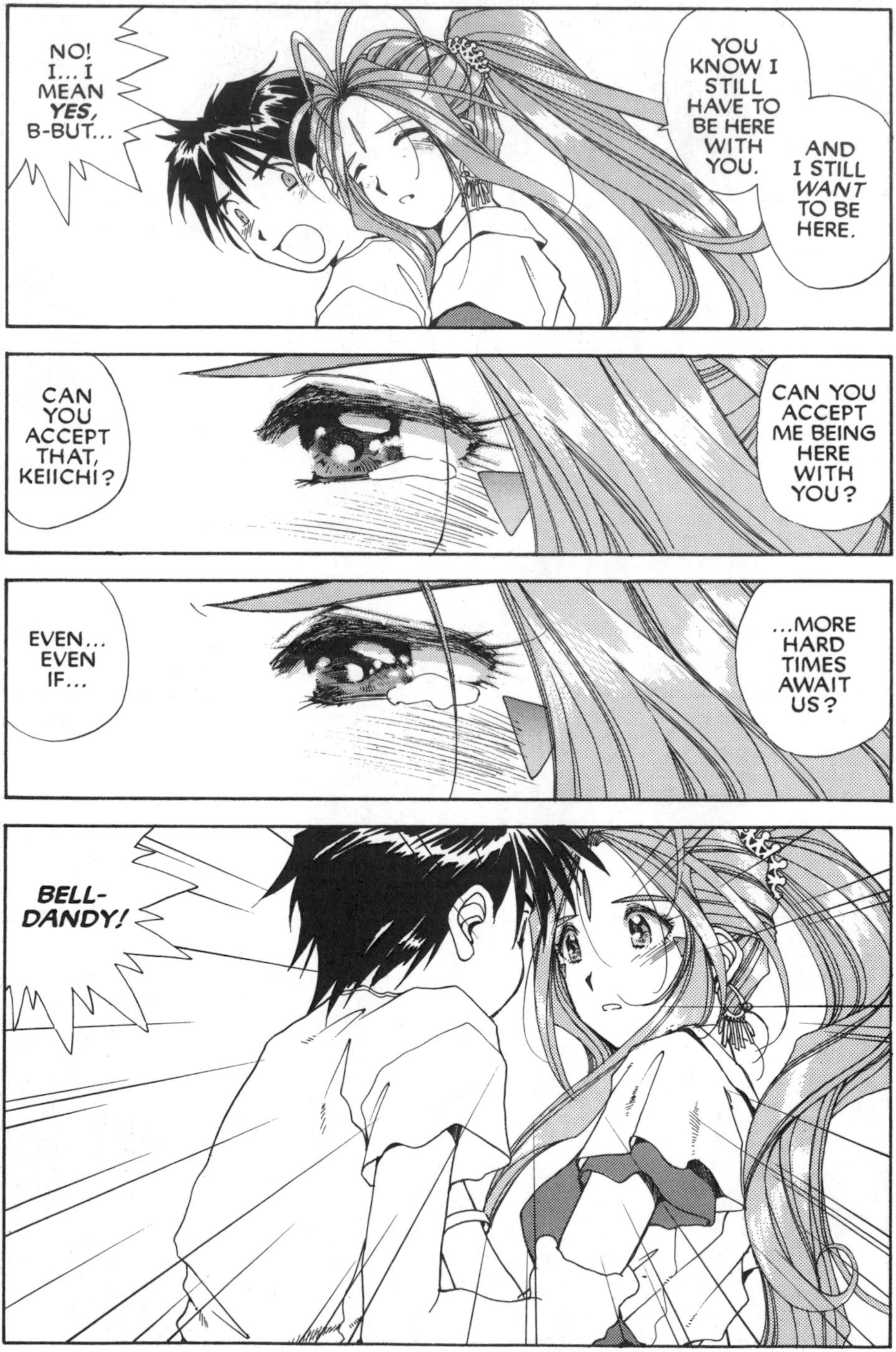
NO! I... I MEAN *YES,* B-BUT...
YOU KNOW I STILL HAVE TO BE HERE WITH YOU.
AND I STILL *WANT* TO BE HERE.
CAN YOU ACCEPT THAT, KEIICHI?
CAN YOU ACCEPT ME BEING HERE WITH YOU?
EVEN... EVEN IF...
...MORE HARD TIMES AWAIT US?
BELL-DANDY!

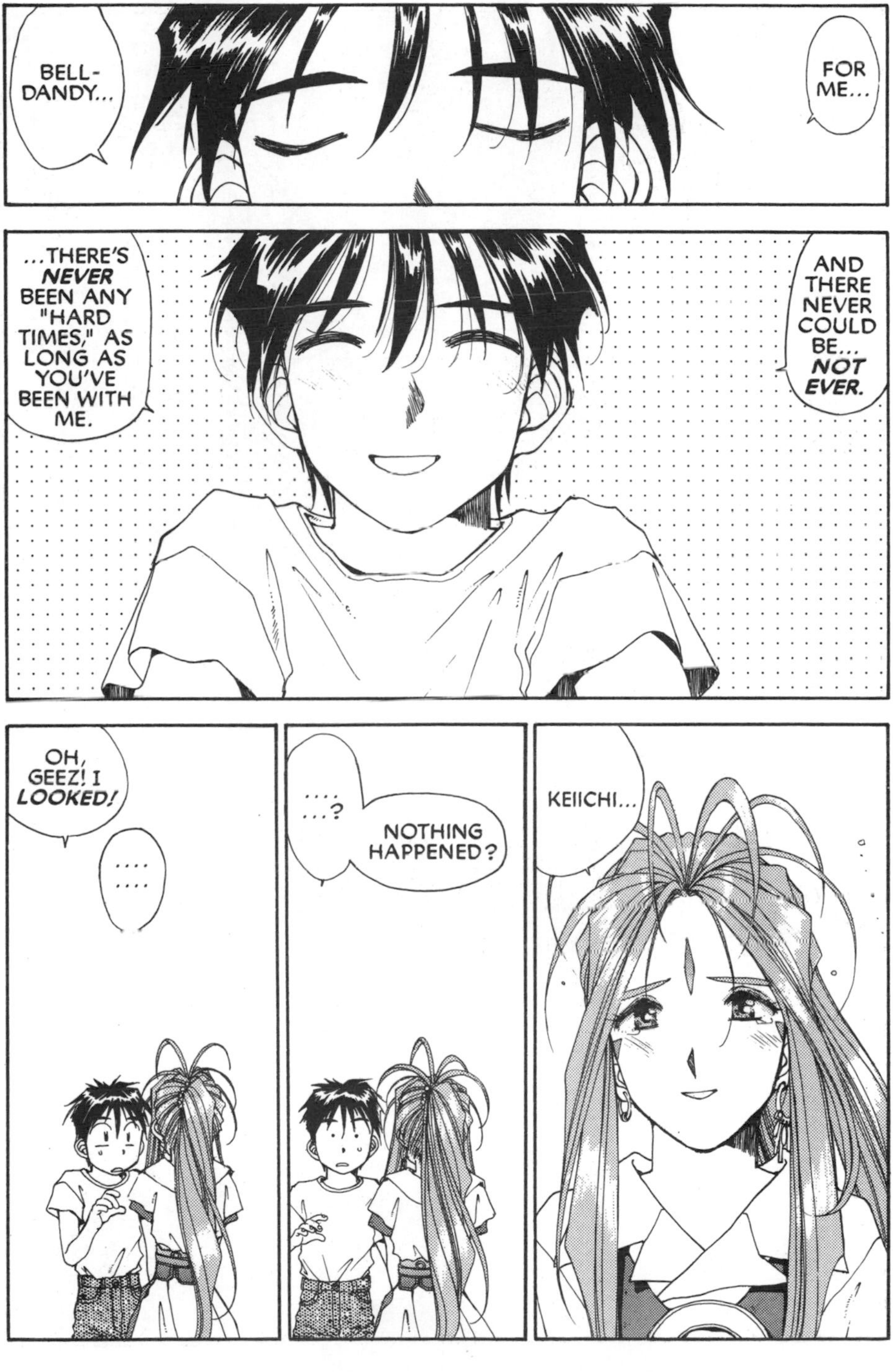
BELL-DANDY...
FOR ME...
...THERE'S NEVER BEEN ANY "HARD TIMES," AS LONG AS YOU'VE BEEN WITH ME.
AND THERE NEVER COULD BE... NOT EVER.
OH, GEEZ! I LOOKED!
....
....?
NOTHING HAPPENED?
KEIICHI...

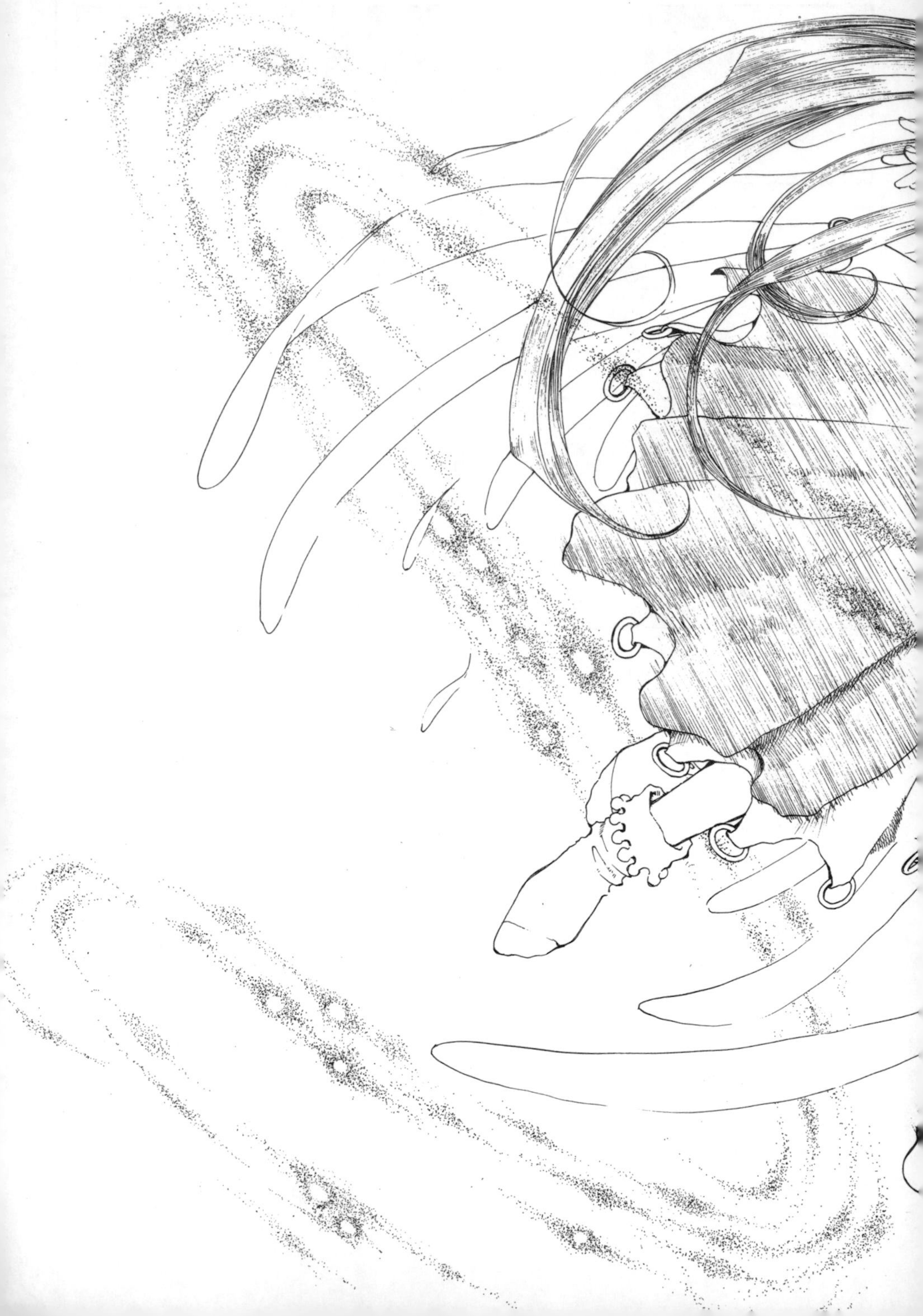

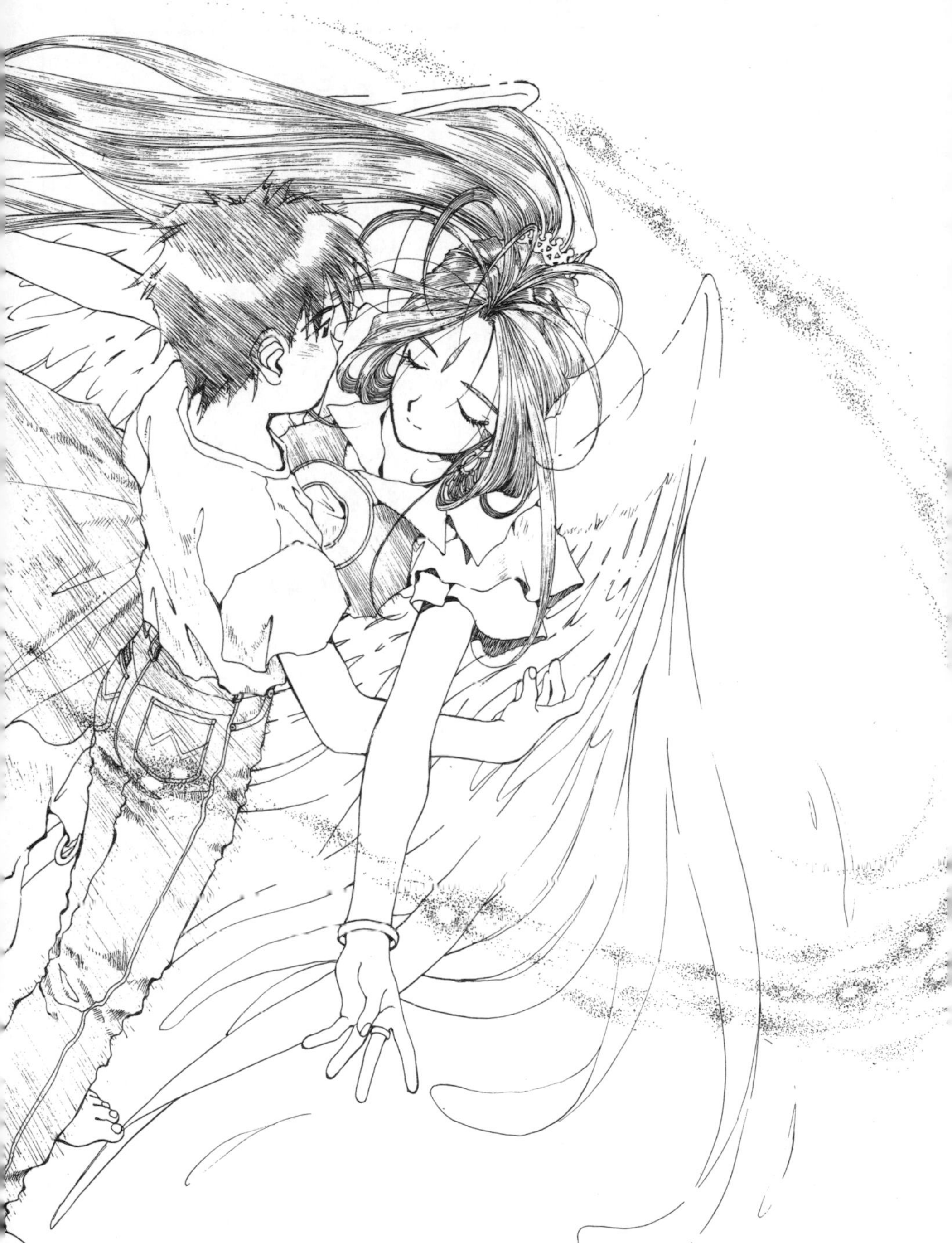

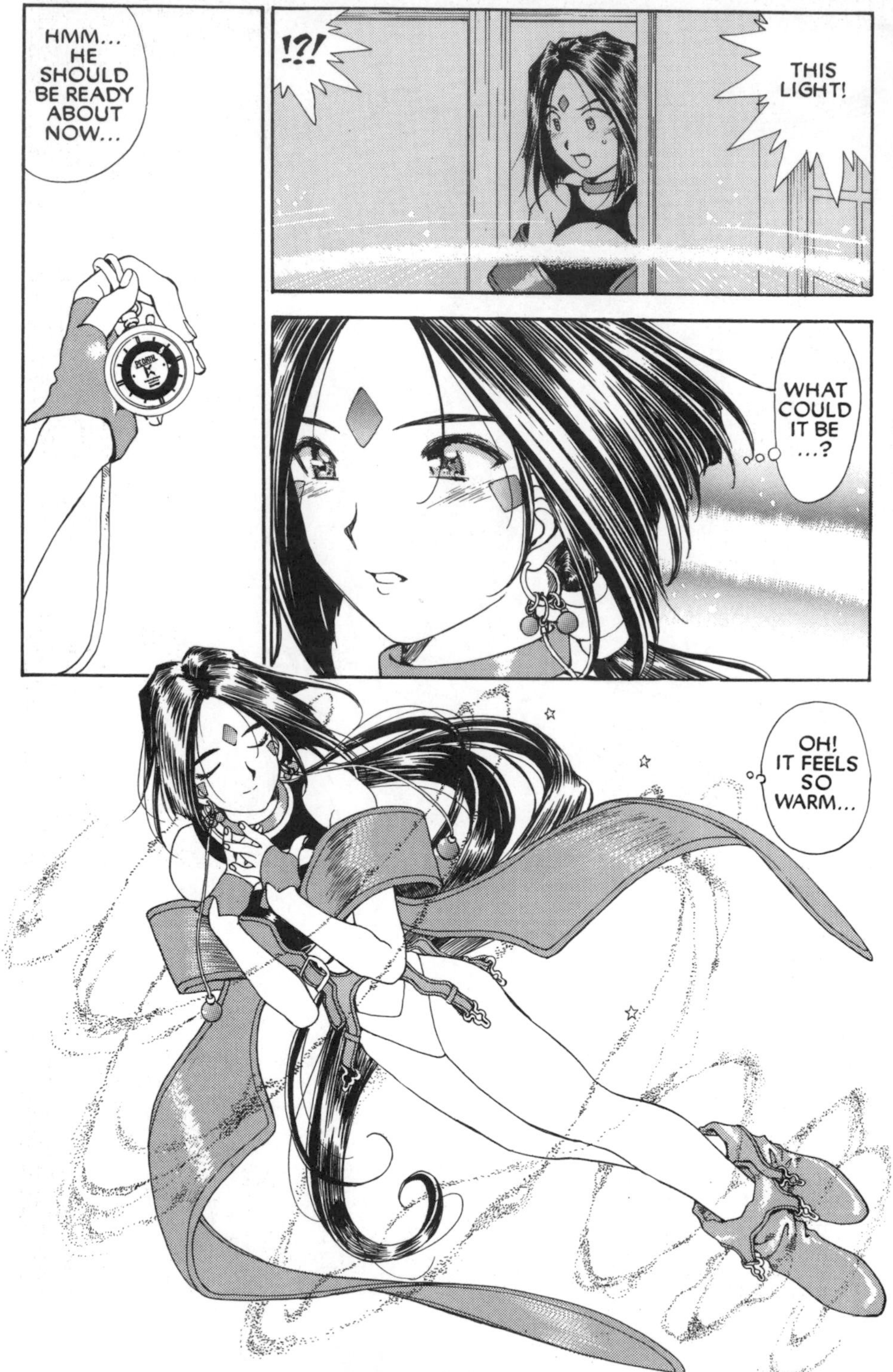
HMM... HE SHOULD BE READY ABOUT NOW...
!?!
THIS LIGHT!
WHAT COULD IT BE ...?
OH! IT FEELS SO WARM...

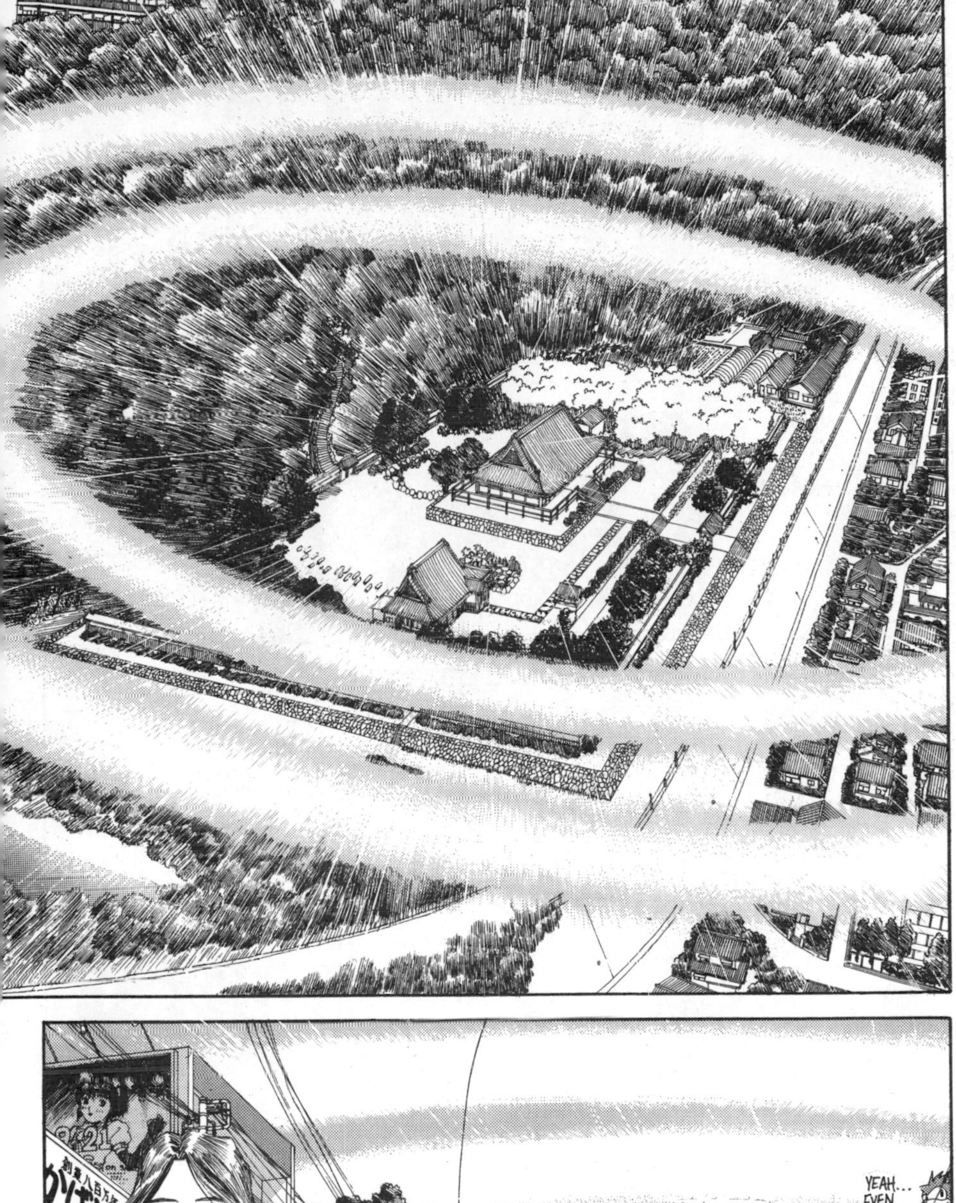

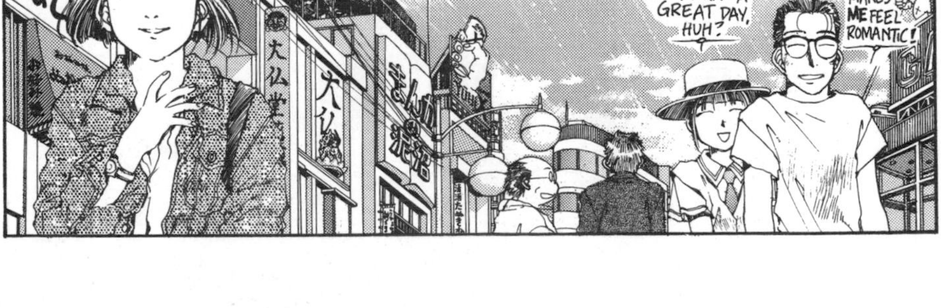
WOW, WHAT A GREAT DAY, HUH?
YEAH... EVEN MAKES ME FEEL ROMANTIC!

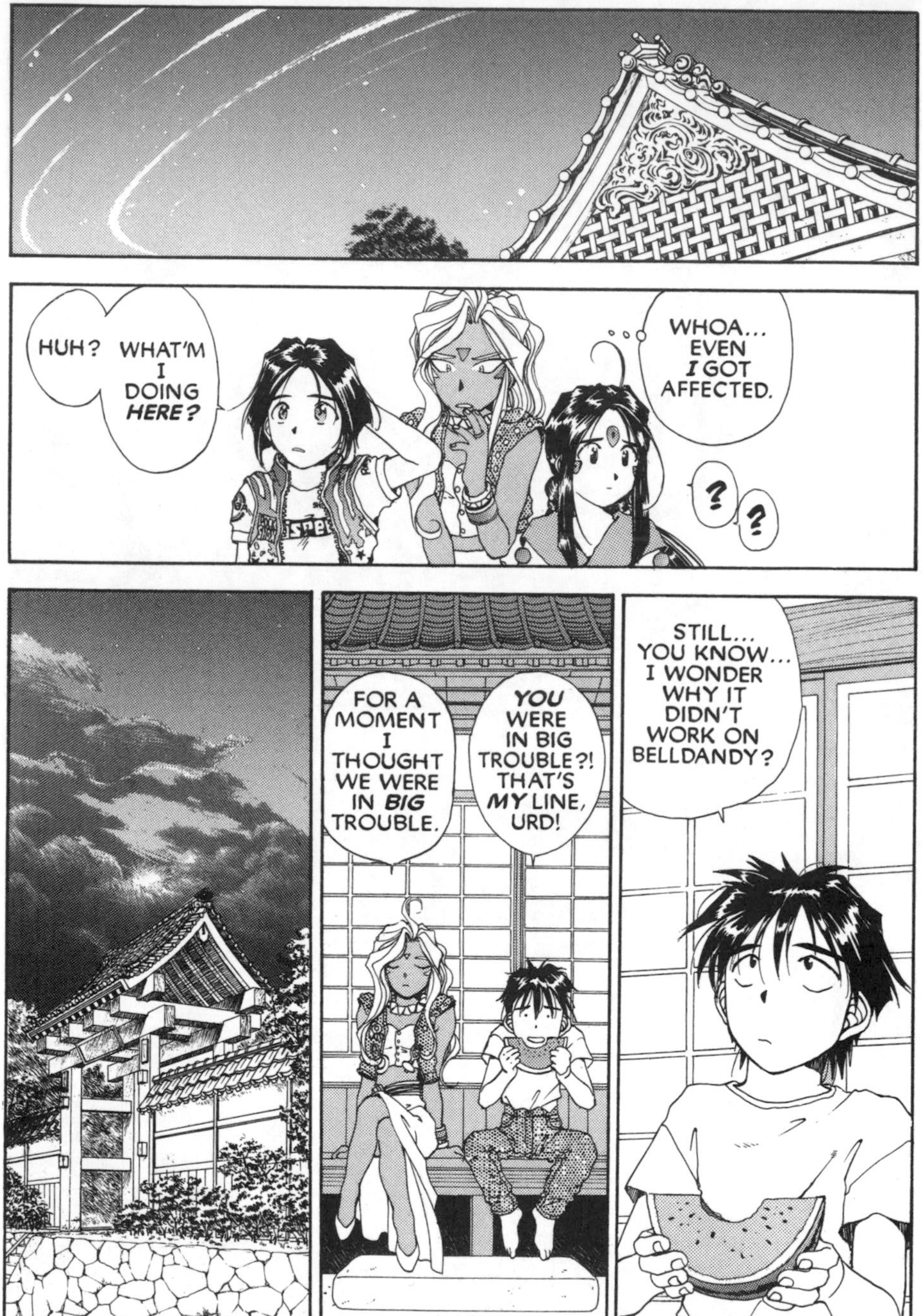
HUH? WHAT'M I DOING *HERE?*
WHOA... EVEN *I* GOT AFFECTED.
?
?
FOR A MOMENT I THOUGHT WE WERE IN *BIG* TROUBLE.
YOU WERE IN BIG TROUBLE?! THAT'S *MY* LINE, URD!
STILL... YOU KNOW... I WONDER WHY IT DIDN'T WORK ON BELLDANDY?

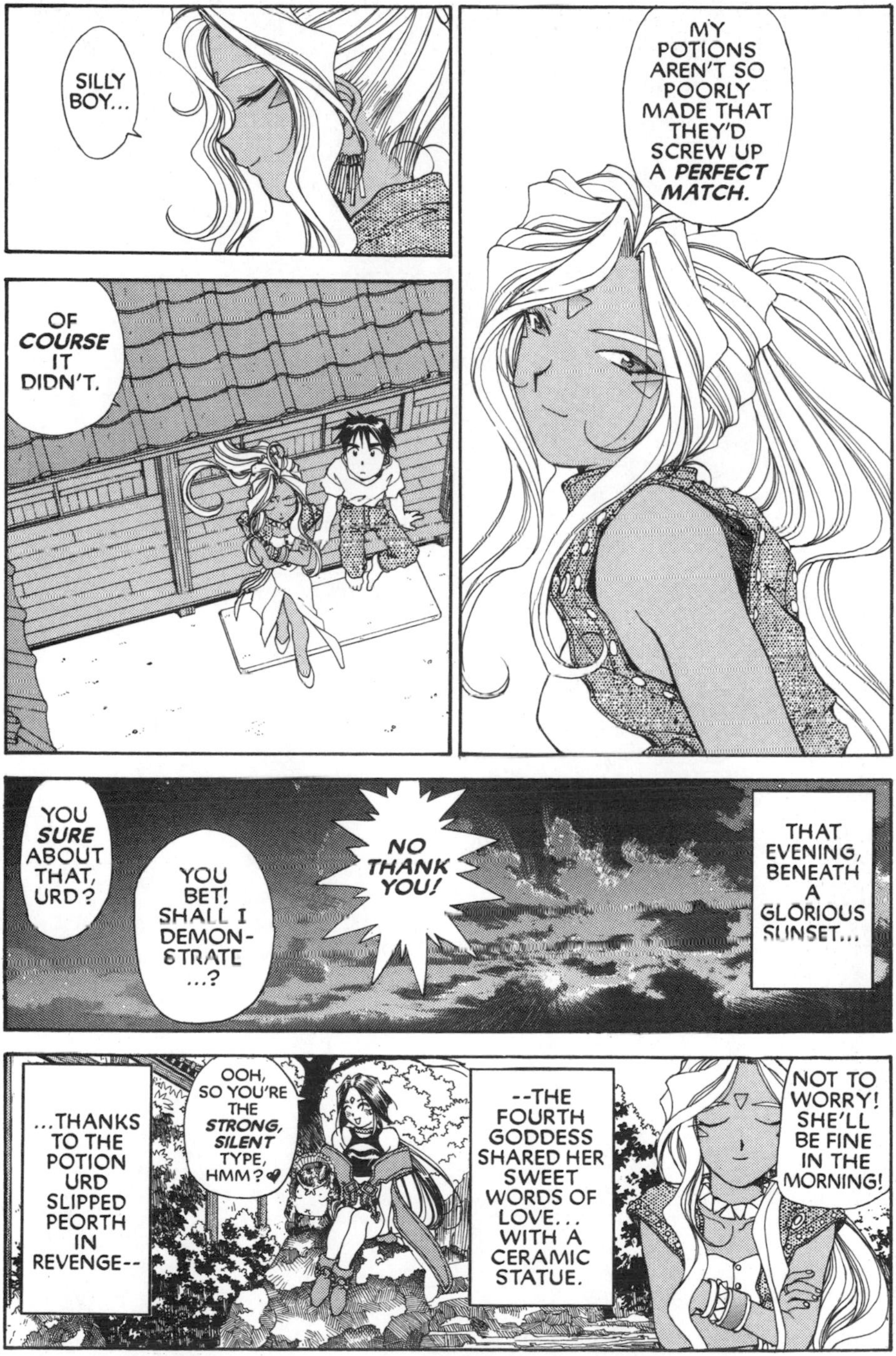
SILLY BOY...
OF COURSE IT DIDN'T.
MY POTIONS AREN'T SO POORLY MADE THAT THEY'D SCREW UP A PERFECT MATCH.
YOU SURE ABOUT THAT, URD?
YOU BET! SHALL I DEMON-STRATE ...?
NO THANK YOU!
THAT EVENING, BENEATH A GLORIOUS SUNSET...
...THANKS TO THE POTION URD SLIPPED PEORTH IN REVENGE--
OOH, SO YOU'RE THE STRONG, SILENT TYPE, HMM?♥
--THE FOURTH GODDESS SHARED HER SWEET WORDS OF LOVE... WITH A CERAMIC STATUE.
NOT TO WORRY! SHE'LL BE FINE IN THE MORNING!

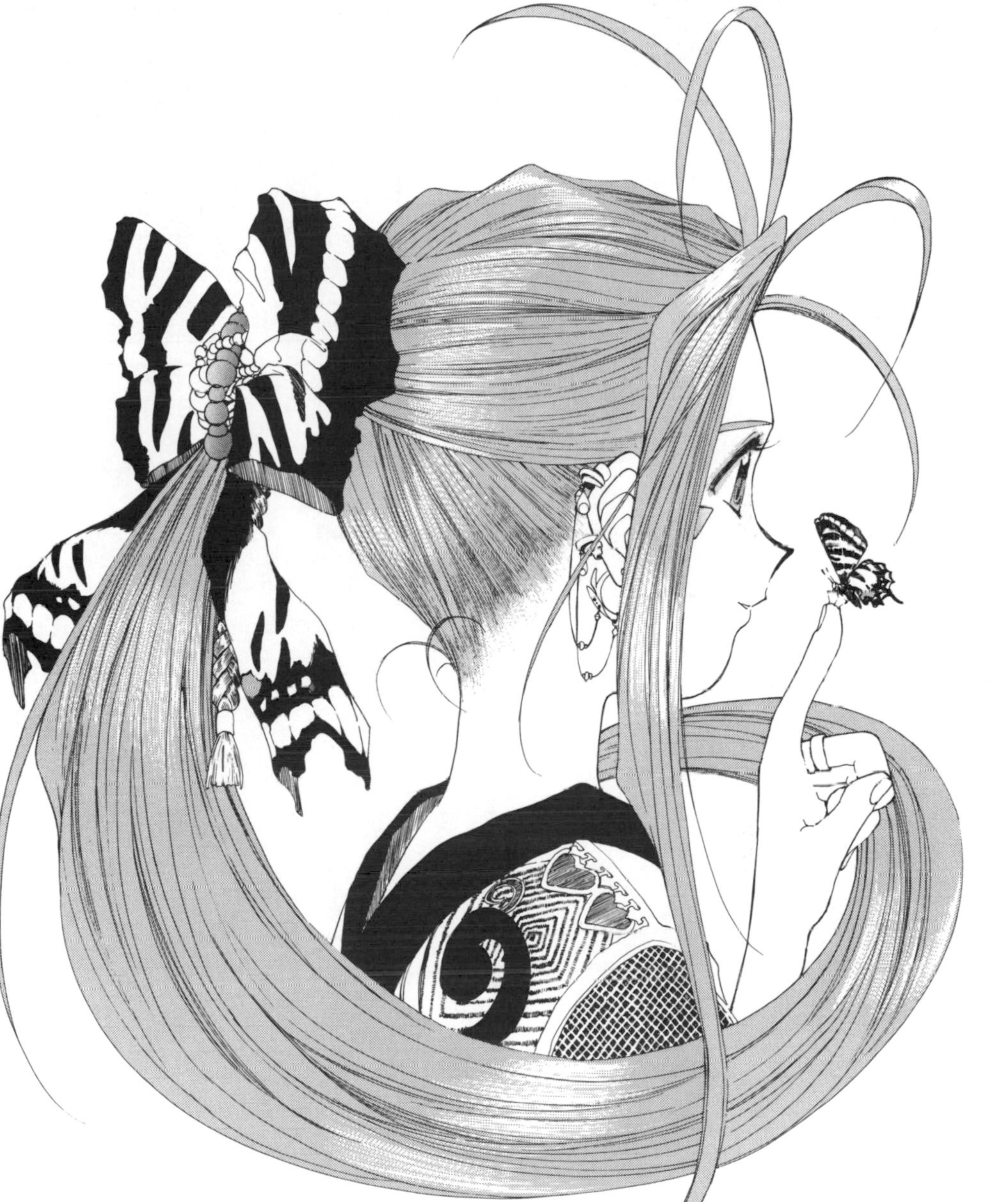

The Dating Game

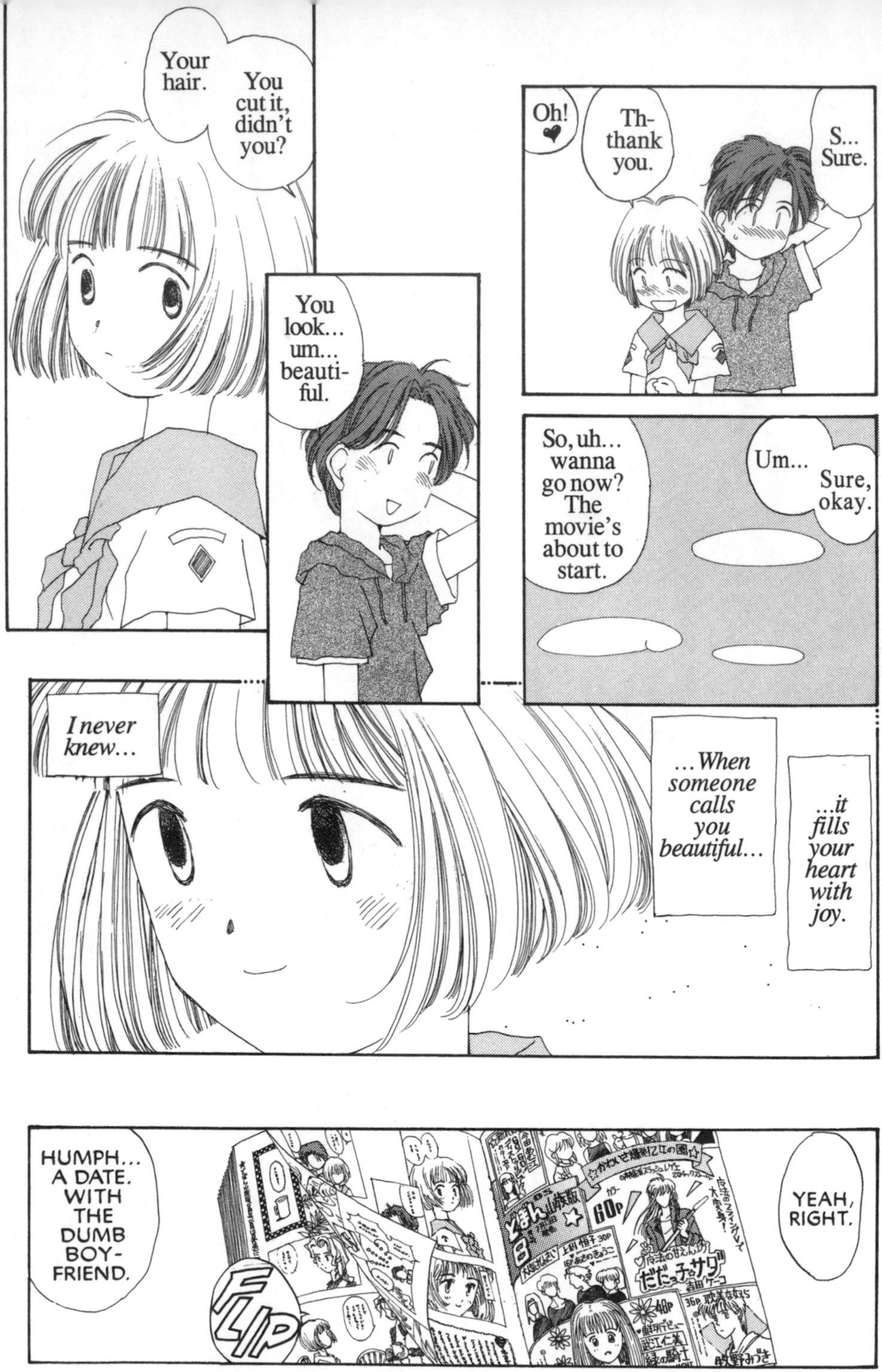
Your hair.
You cut it, didn't you?
You look... um... beautiful.
Oh! ❤
Th-thank you.
S... Sure.
So, uh... wanna go now? The movie's about to start.
Um...
Sure, okay.
I never knew...
...When someone calls you beautiful...
...it fills your heart with joy.
HUMPH... A DATE. WITH THE DUMB BOY-FRIEND.
FLIP
YEAH, RIGHT.

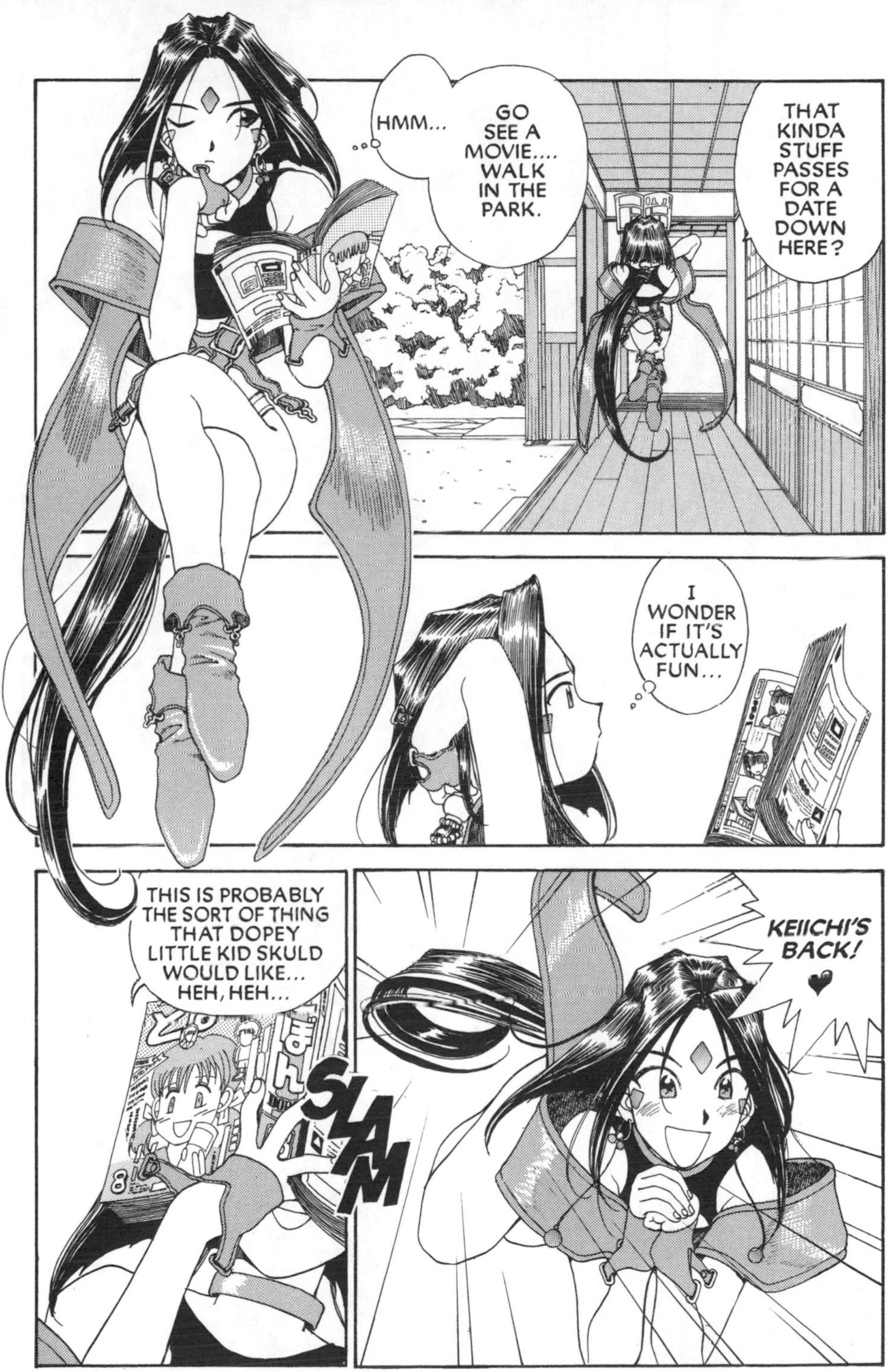
HMM...
GO SEE A MOVIE.... WALK IN THE PARK.
THAT KINDA STUFF PASSES FOR A DATE DOWN HERE?
I WONDER IF IT'S ACTUALLY FUN...
THIS IS PROBABLY THE SORT OF THING THAT DOPEY LITTLE KID SKULD WOULD LIKE... HEH, HEH...
SLAM
KEIICHI'S BACK!

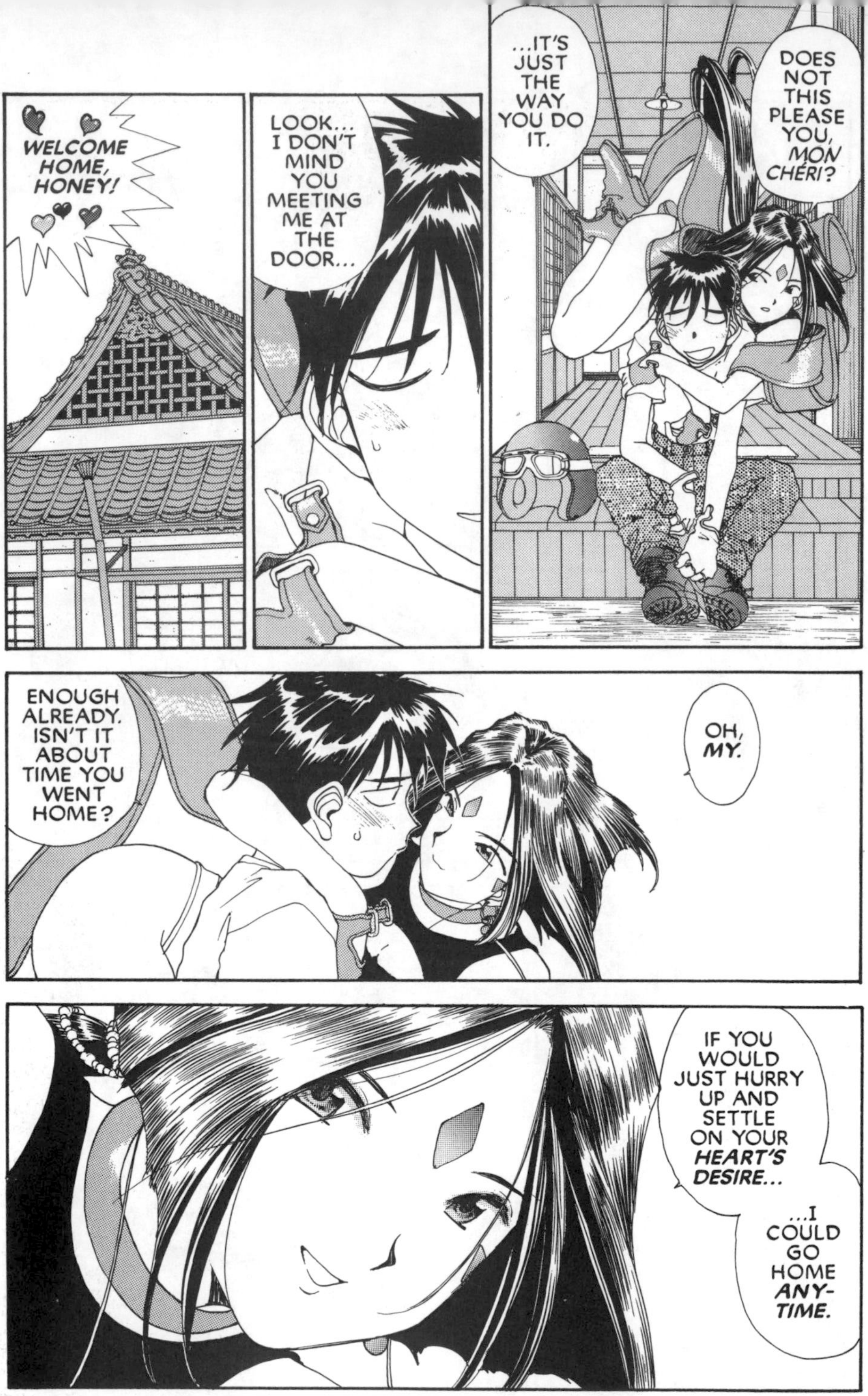
WELCOME HOME, HONEY!
LOOK... I DON'T MIND YOU MEETING ME AT THE DOOR...
...IT'S JUST THE WAY YOU DO IT.
DOES NOT THIS PLEASE YOU, MON CHÉRI?
ENOUGH ALREADY. ISN'T IT ABOUT TIME YOU WENT HOME?
OH, MY.
IF YOU WOULD JUST HURRY UP AND SETTLE ON YOUR HEART'S DESIRE...
...I COULD GO HOME ANY-TIME.

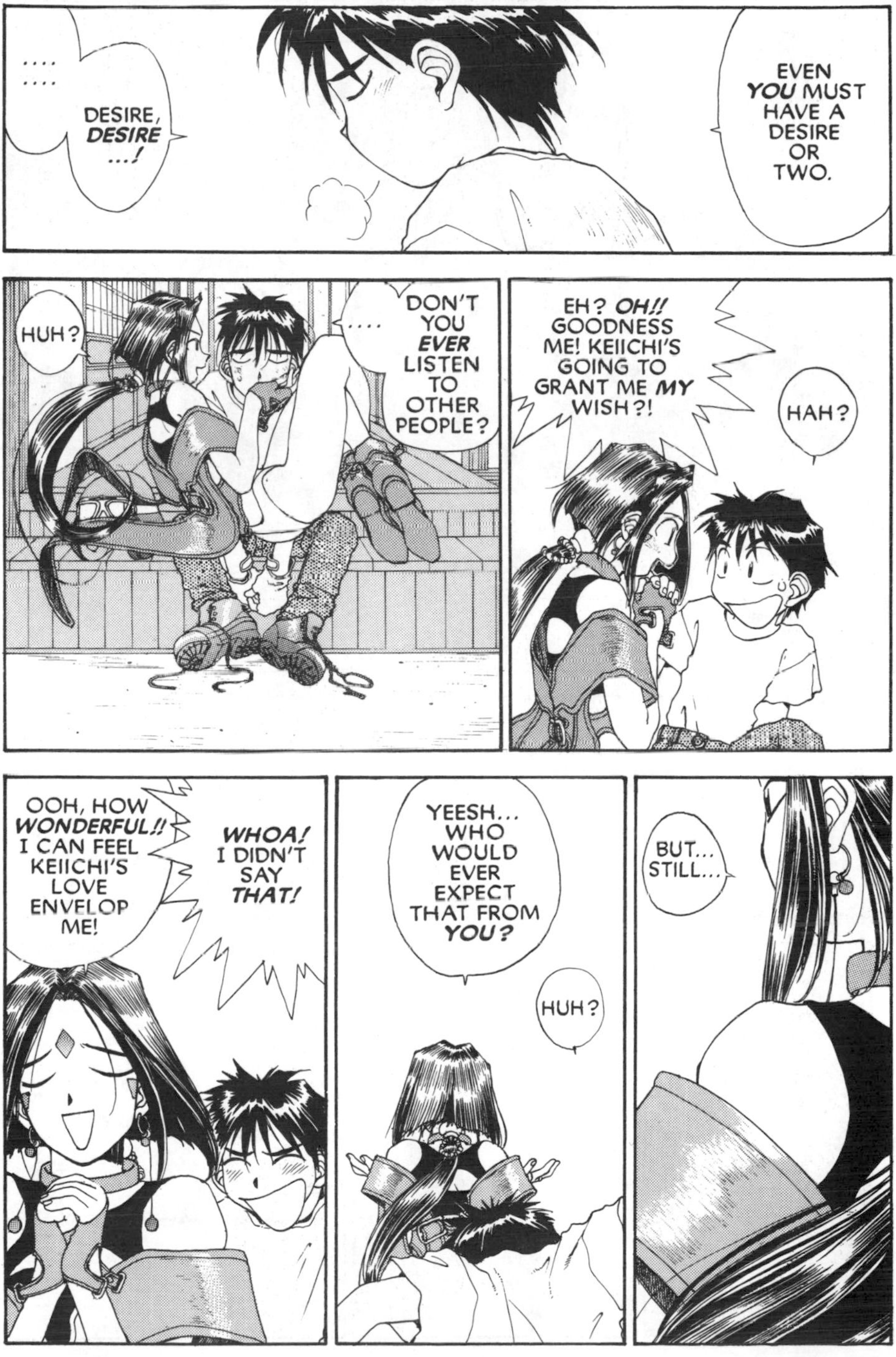
....
....
DESIRE, DESIRE ...!
EVEN YOU MUST HAVE A DESIRE OR TWO.
HUH?
....
DON'T YOU EVER LISTEN TO OTHER PEOPLE?
EH? OH!! GOODNESS ME! KEIICHI'S GOING TO GRANT ME MY WISH?!
HAH?
OOH, HOW WONDERFUL!! I CAN FEEL KEIICHI'S LOVE ENVELOP ME!
WHOA! I DIDN'T SAY THAT!
YEESH... WHO WOULD EVER EXPECT THAT FROM YOU?
HUH?
BUT... STILL...

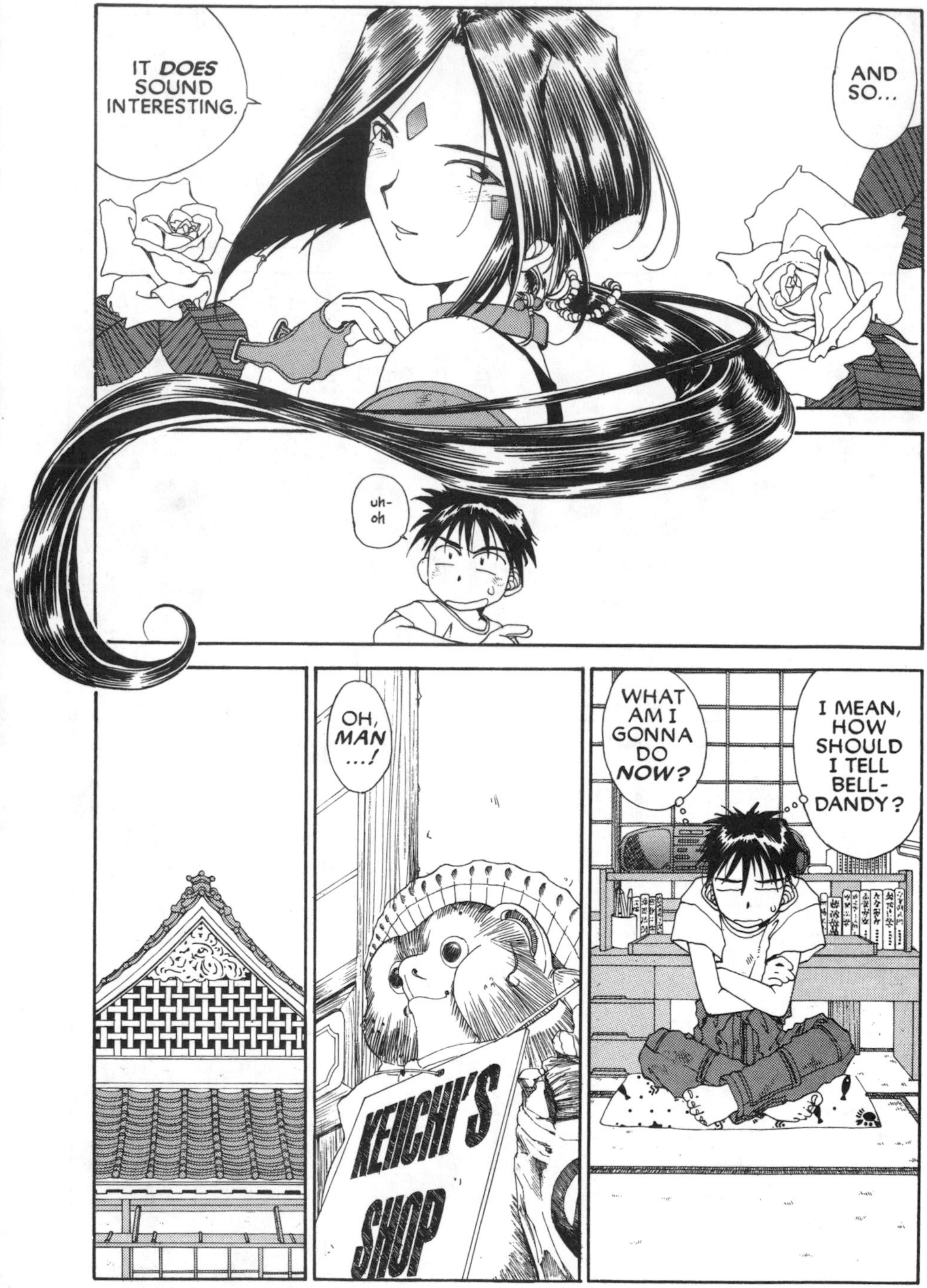
IT DOES SOUND INTERESTING.
AND SO...
uh-oh
OH, MAN ...!
KEIICHI'S SHOP
WHAT AM I GONNA DO NOW?
I MEAN, HOW SHOULD I TELL BELL-DANDY?

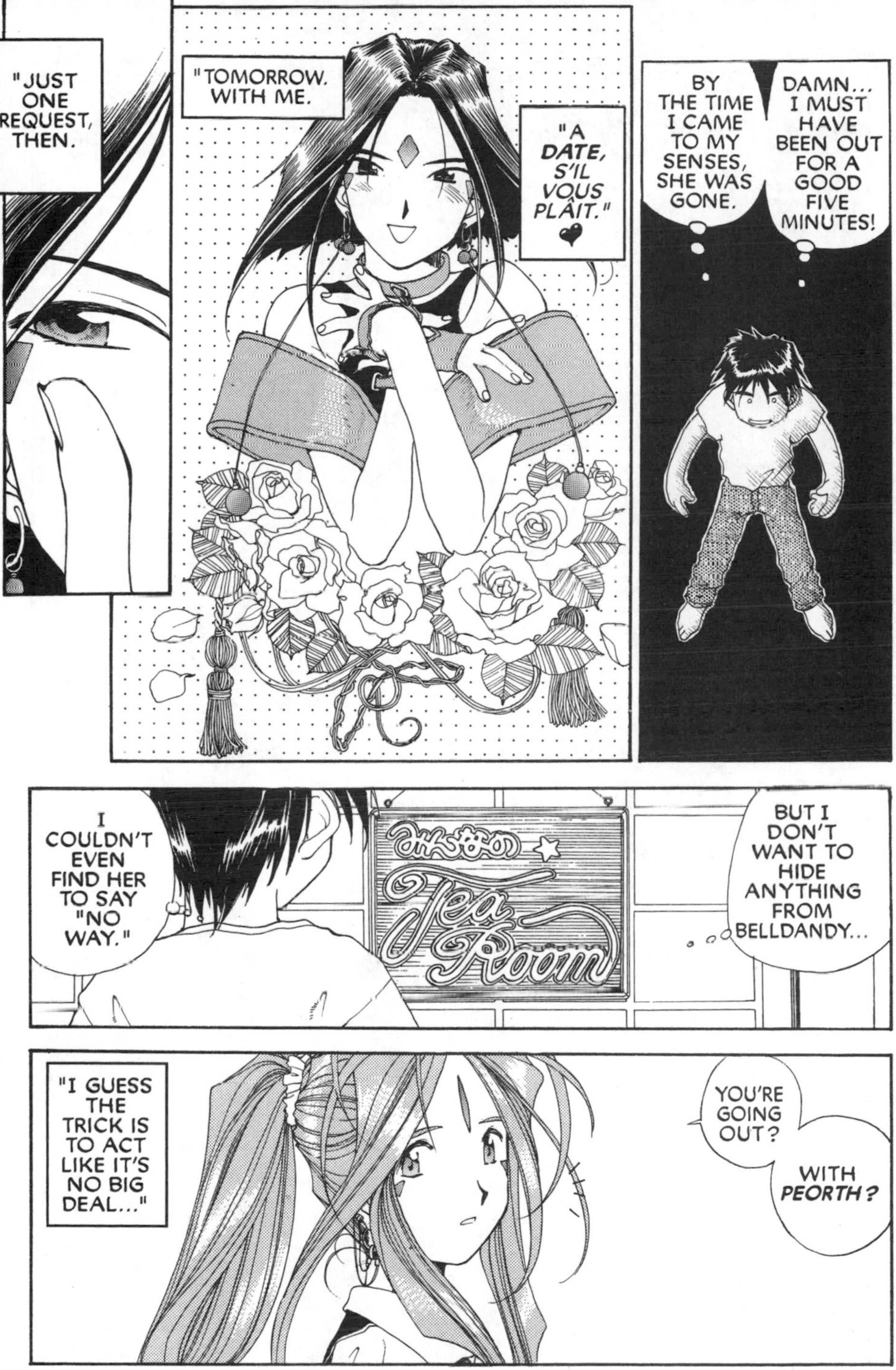
"JUST ONE REQUEST, THEN.
"TOMORROW. WITH ME.
"A *DATE, S'IL VOUS PLAÎT.*" ❤
BY THE TIME I CAME TO MY SENSES, SHE WAS GONE.
DAMN... I MUST HAVE BEEN OUT FOR A GOOD FIVE MINUTES!
I COULDN'T EVEN FIND HER TO SAY "NO WAY."
みんなの ★ Tea Room
BUT I DON'T WANT TO HIDE ANYTHING FROM BELLDANDY...
"I GUESS THE TRICK IS TO ACT LIKE IT'S NO BIG DEAL..."
YOU'RE GOING OUT?
WITH *PEORTH?*

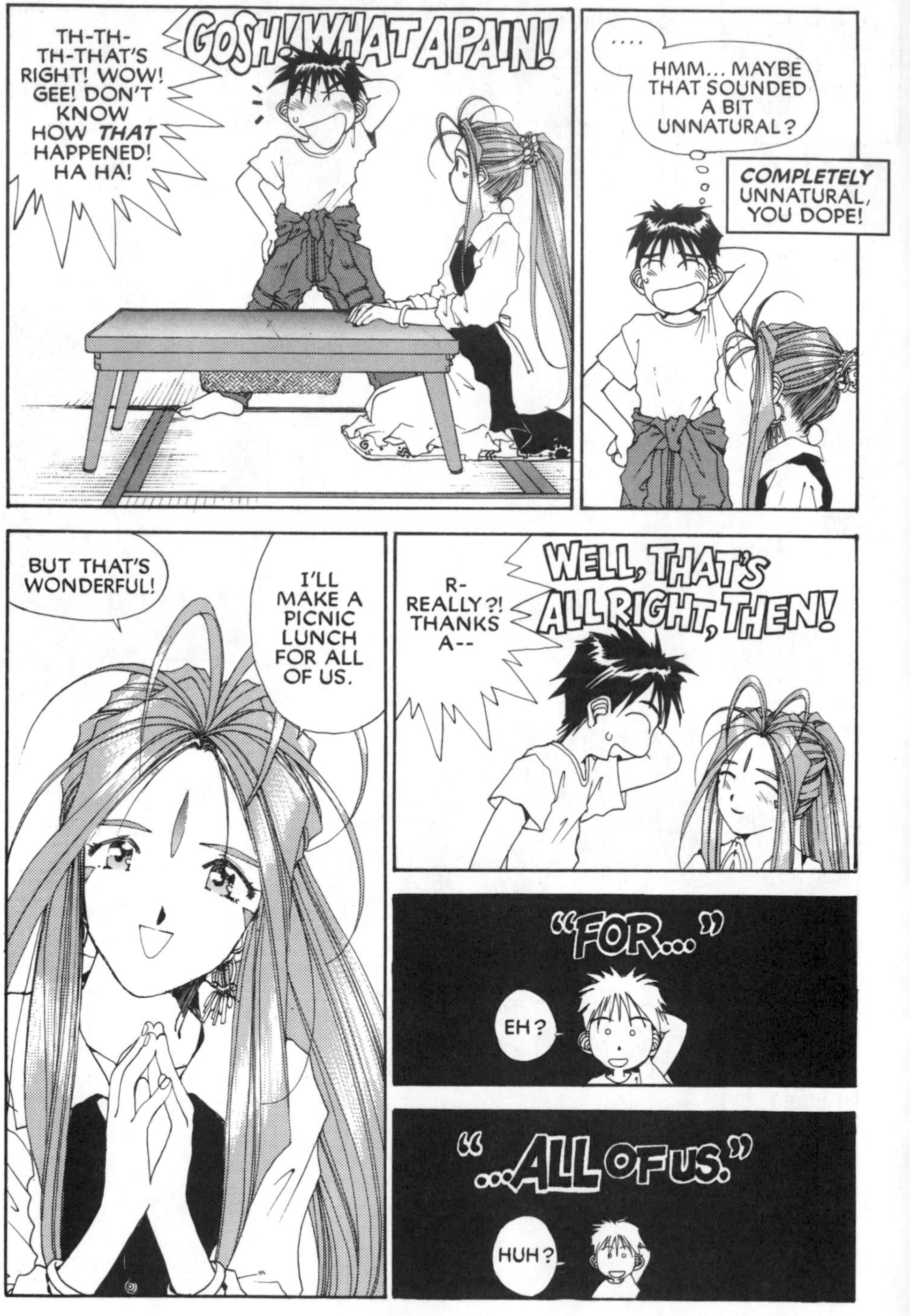
TH-TH-TH-THAT'S RIGHT! WOW! GEE! DON'T KNOW HOW *THAT* HAPPENED! HA HA!
GOSH! WHAT A PAIN!
. . . . .
HMM... MAYBE THAT SOUNDED A BIT UNNATURAL?
COMPLETELY UNNATURAL, YOU DOPE!
BUT THAT'S WONDERFUL!
I'LL MAKE A PICNIC LUNCH FOR ALL OF US.
R-REALLY?! THANKS A--
WELL, THAT'S ALL RIGHT, THEN!
"FOR..."
EH?
"...ALL OF US."
HUH?

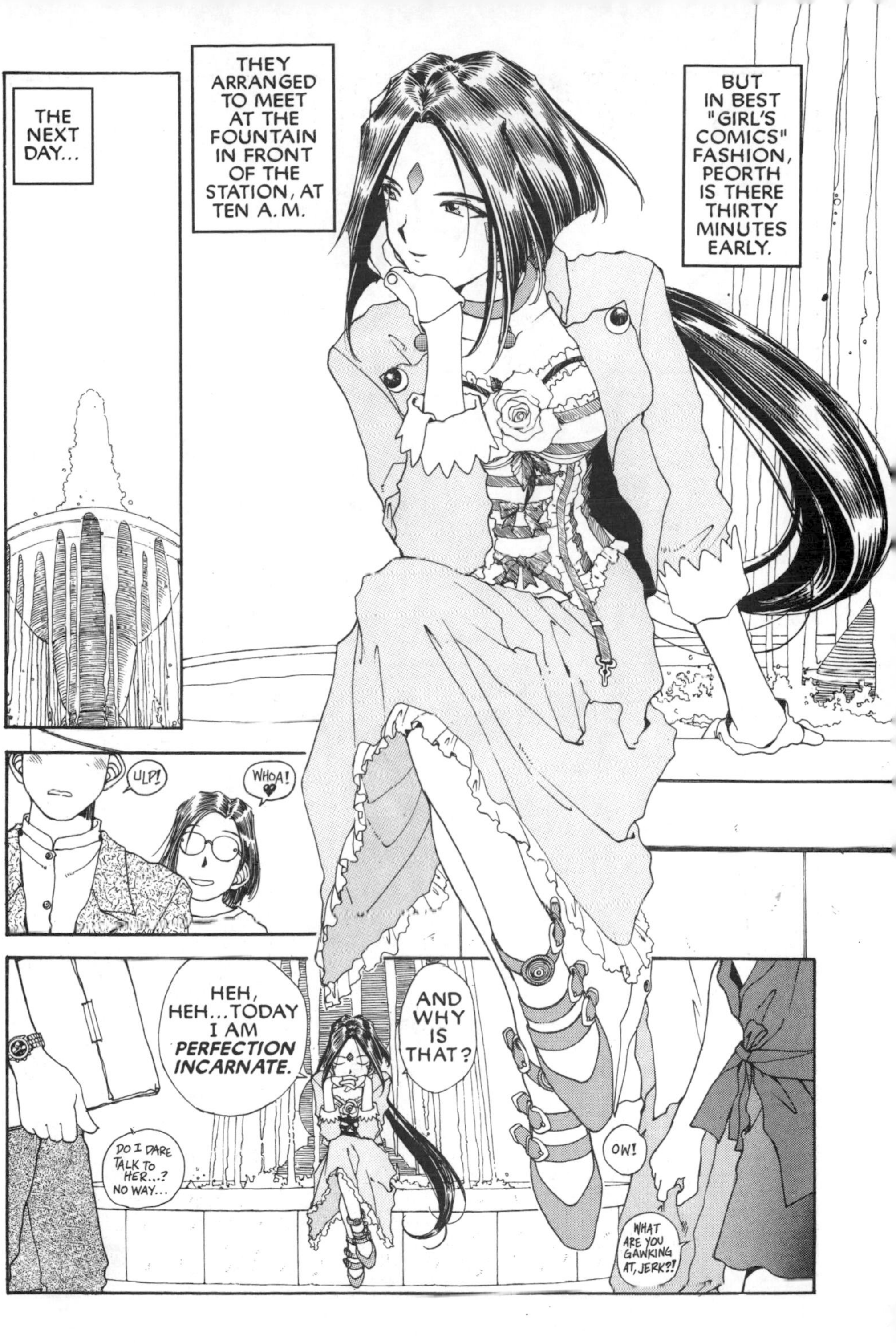
THE NEXT DAY...
THEY ARRANGED TO MEET AT THE FOUNTAIN IN FRONT OF THE STATION, AT TEN A.M.
BUT IN BEST "GIRL'S COMICS" FASHION, PEORTH IS THERE THIRTY MINUTES EARLY.
ULP!
WHOA!
HEH, HEH...TODAY I AM *PERFECTION INCARNATE.*
DO I DARE TALK TO HER...? NO WAY...
AND WHY IS THAT?
OW!
WHAT ARE YOU GAWKING AT, JERK?!

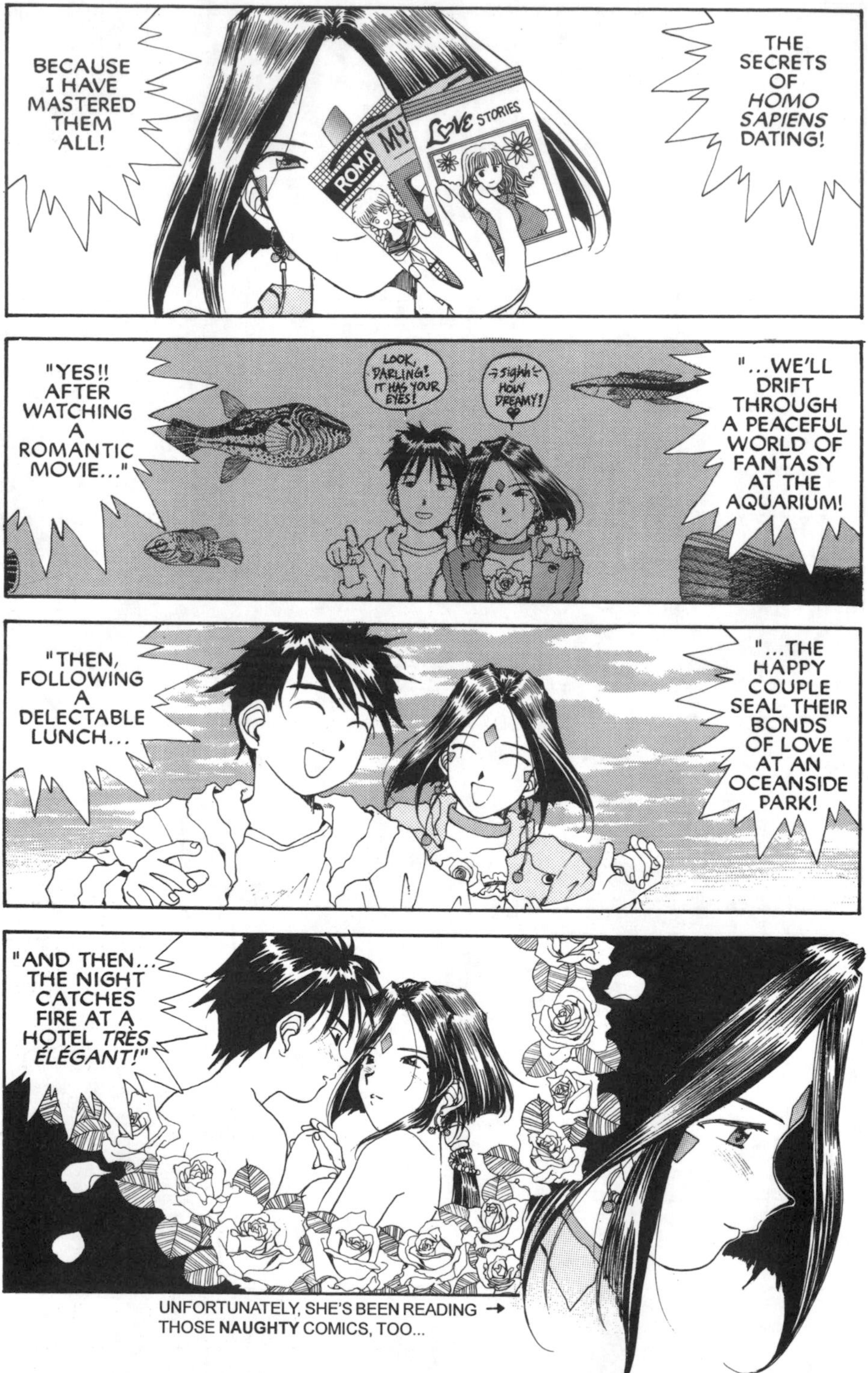
BECAUSE I HAVE MASTERED THEM ALL!
THE SECRETS OF *HOMO SAPIENS* DATING!
ROMA
MY
LOVE STORIES
"YES!! AFTER WATCHING A ROMANTIC MOVIE..."
LOOK, DARLING! IT HAS YOUR EYES!
sigh HOW DREAMY!
"...WE'LL DRIFT THROUGH A PEACEFUL WORLD OF FANTASY AT THE AQUARIUM!
"THEN, FOLLOWING A DELECTABLE LUNCH...
"...THE HAPPY COUPLE SEAL THEIR BONDS OF LOVE AT AN OCEANSIDE PARK!
"AND THEN... THE NIGHT CATCHES FIRE AT A HOTEL *TRÈS ÉLÉGANT!*"

UNFORTUNATELY, SHE'S BEEN READING →
THOSE **NAUGHTY** COMICS, TOO...

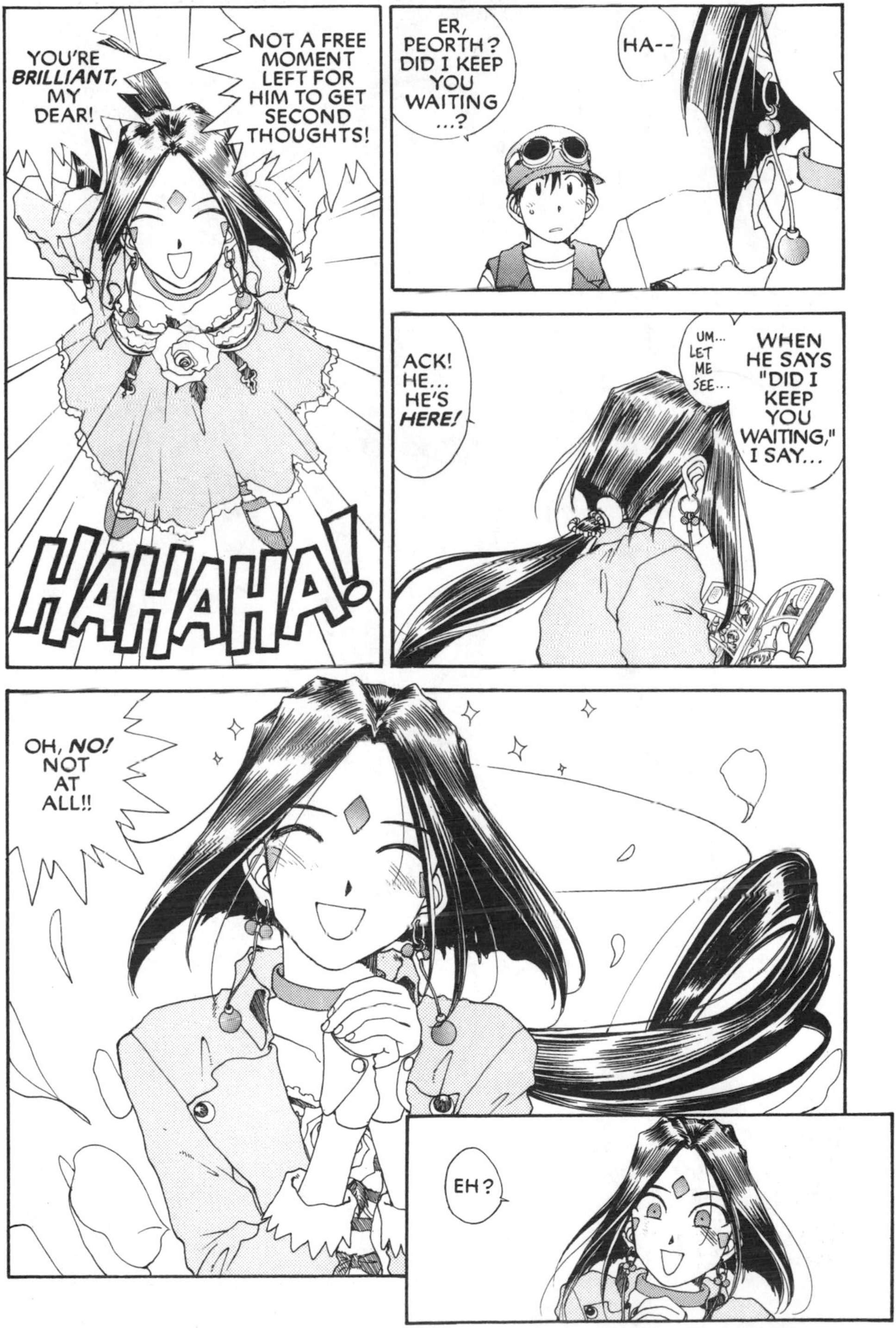
YOU'RE *BRILLIANT,* MY DEAR!
NOT A FREE MOMENT LEFT FOR HIM TO GET SECOND THOUGHTS!
HAHAHA!
ER, PEORTH? DID I KEEP YOU WAITING ...?
HA--
ACK! HE... HE'S *HERE!*
UM... LET ME SEE...
WHEN HE SAYS "DID I KEEP YOU WAITING," I SAY...
OH, *NO!* NOT AT ALL!!
EH?

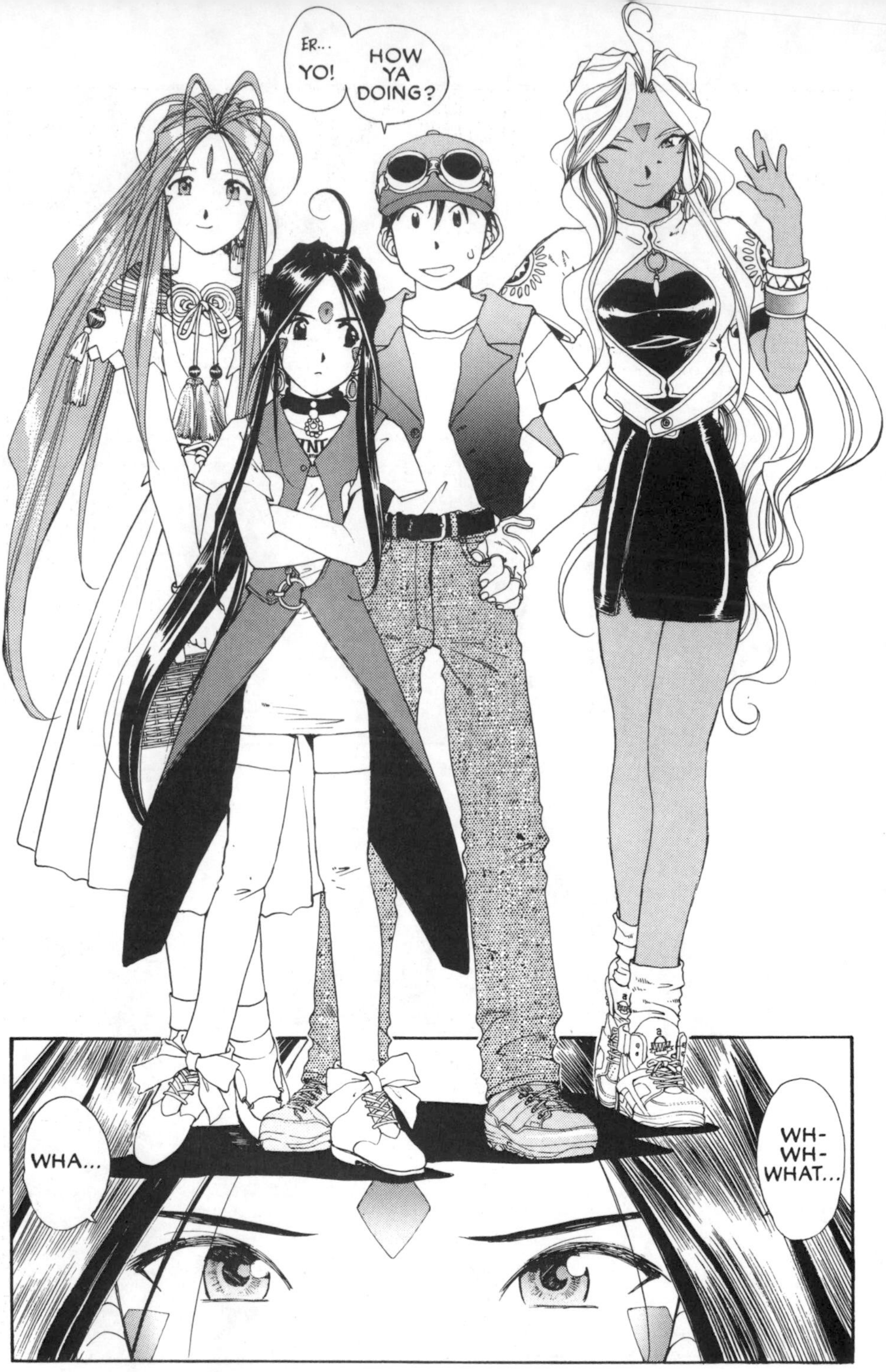
ER... YO! HOW YA DOING?
WHA...
WH- WH- WHAT...

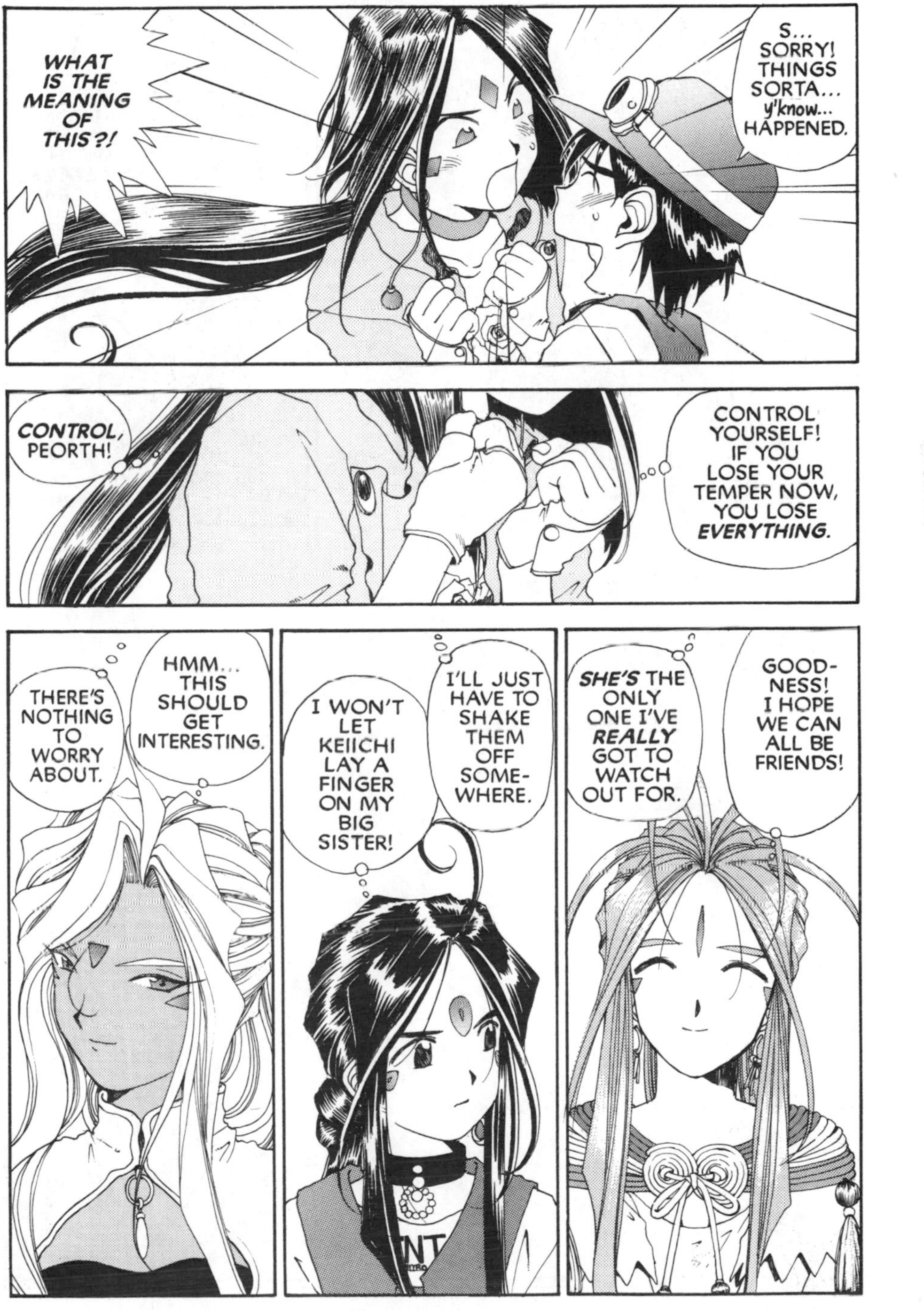
WHAT IS THE MEANING OF THIS?!
S... SORRY! THINGS SORTA... y'know... HAPPENED.
CONTROL, PEORTH!
CONTROL YOURSELF! IF YOU LOSE YOUR TEMPER NOW, YOU LOSE EVERYTHING.
THERE'S NOTHING TO WORRY ABOUT.
HMM... THIS SHOULD GET INTERESTING.
I WON'T LET KEIICHI LAY A FINGER ON MY BIG SISTER!
I'LL JUST HAVE TO SHAKE THEM OFF SOME-WHERE.
SHE'S THE ONLY ONE I'VE REALLY GOT TO WATCH OUT FOR.
GOOD-NESS! I HOPE WE CAN ALL BE FRIENDS!

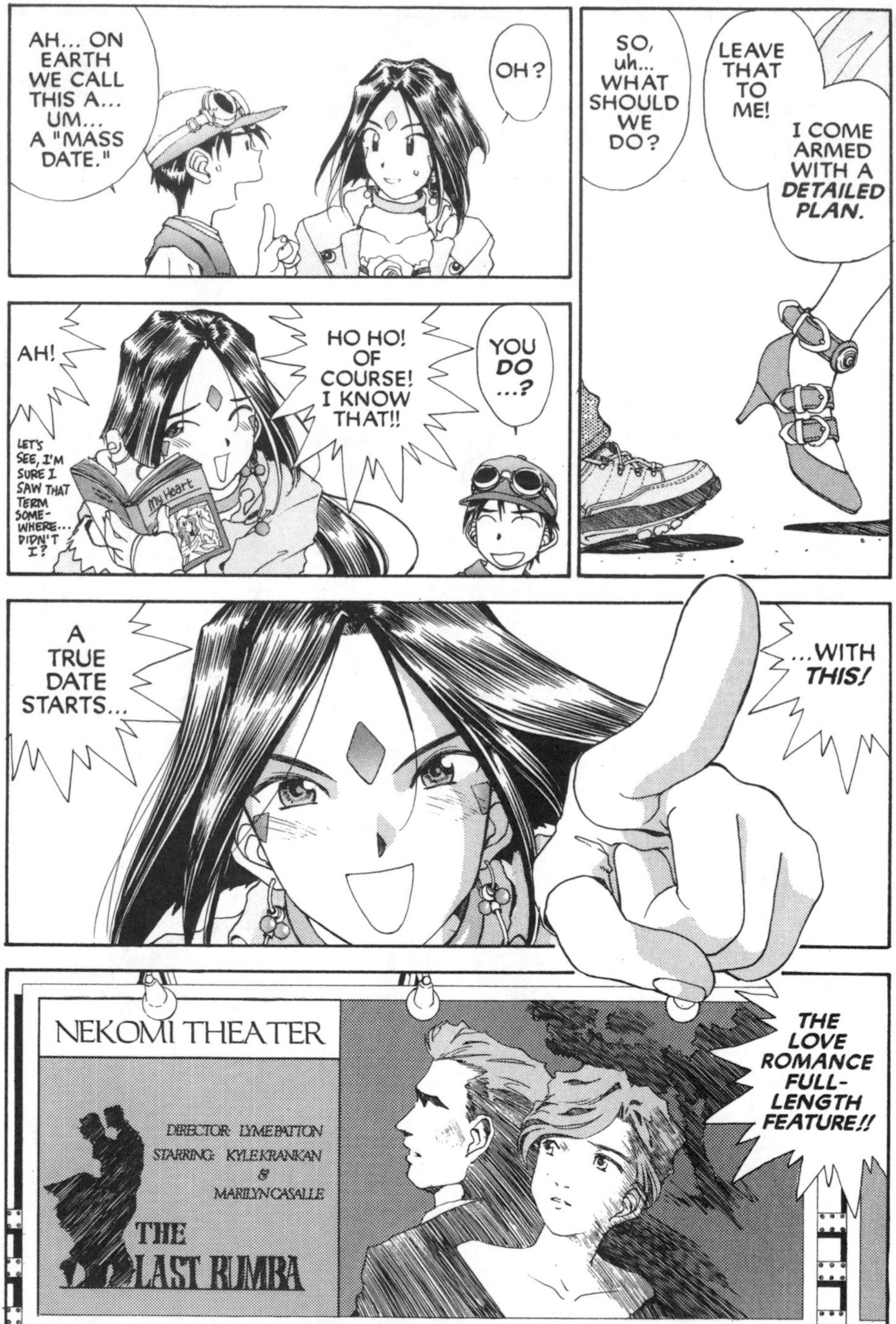
AH... ON EARTH WE CALL THIS A... UM... A "MASS DATE."
OH?
SO, uh... WHAT SHOULD WE DO?
LEAVE THAT TO ME!
I COME ARMED WITH A DETAILED PLAN.
AH!
LET'S SEE, I'M SURE I SAW THAT TERM SOME-WHERE... DIDN'T I?
My Heart
HO HO! OF COURSE! I KNOW THAT!!
YOU DO ...?
A TRUE DATE STARTS...
...WITH THIS!
NEKOMI THEATER
DIRECTOR: LYME BATTON
STARRING: KYLE KRANKAN & MARILYN CASALLE
THE LAST RUMBA
THE LOVE ROMANCE FULL-LENGTH FEATURE!!

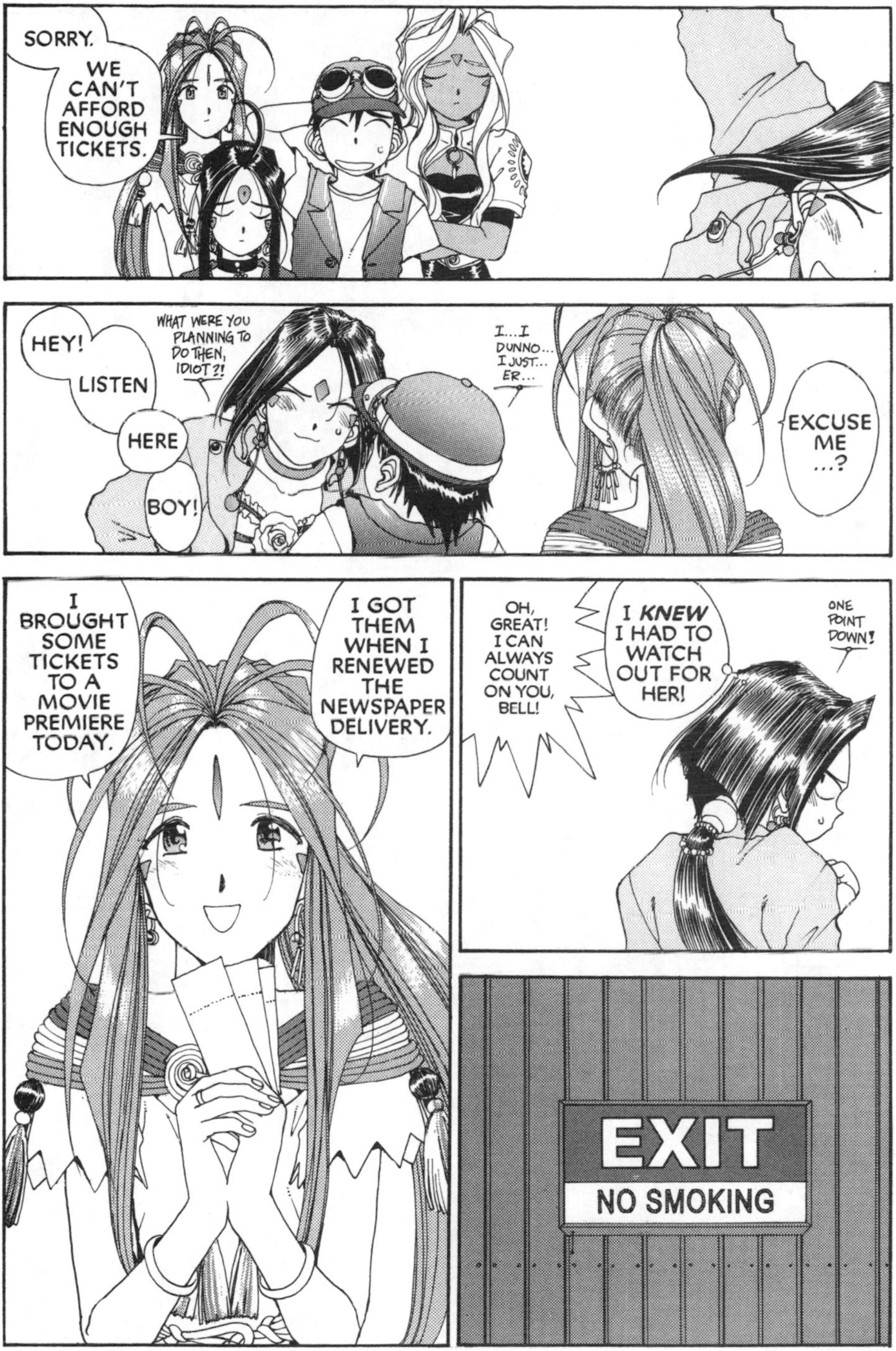
SORRY.
WE CAN'T AFFORD ENOUGH TICKETS.
HEY!
LISTEN
HERE
BOY!
WHAT WERE YOU PLANNING TO DO THEN, IDIOT?!
I...I DUNNO... I JUST... ER...
EXCUSE ME ...?
I BROUGHT SOME TICKETS TO A MOVIE PREMIERE TODAY.
I GOT THEM WHEN I RENEWED THE NEWSPAPER DELIVERY.
OH, GREAT! I CAN ALWAYS COUNT ON YOU, BELL!
I *KNEW* I HAD TO WATCH OUT FOR HER!
ONE POINT DOWN!
EXIT
NO SMOKING

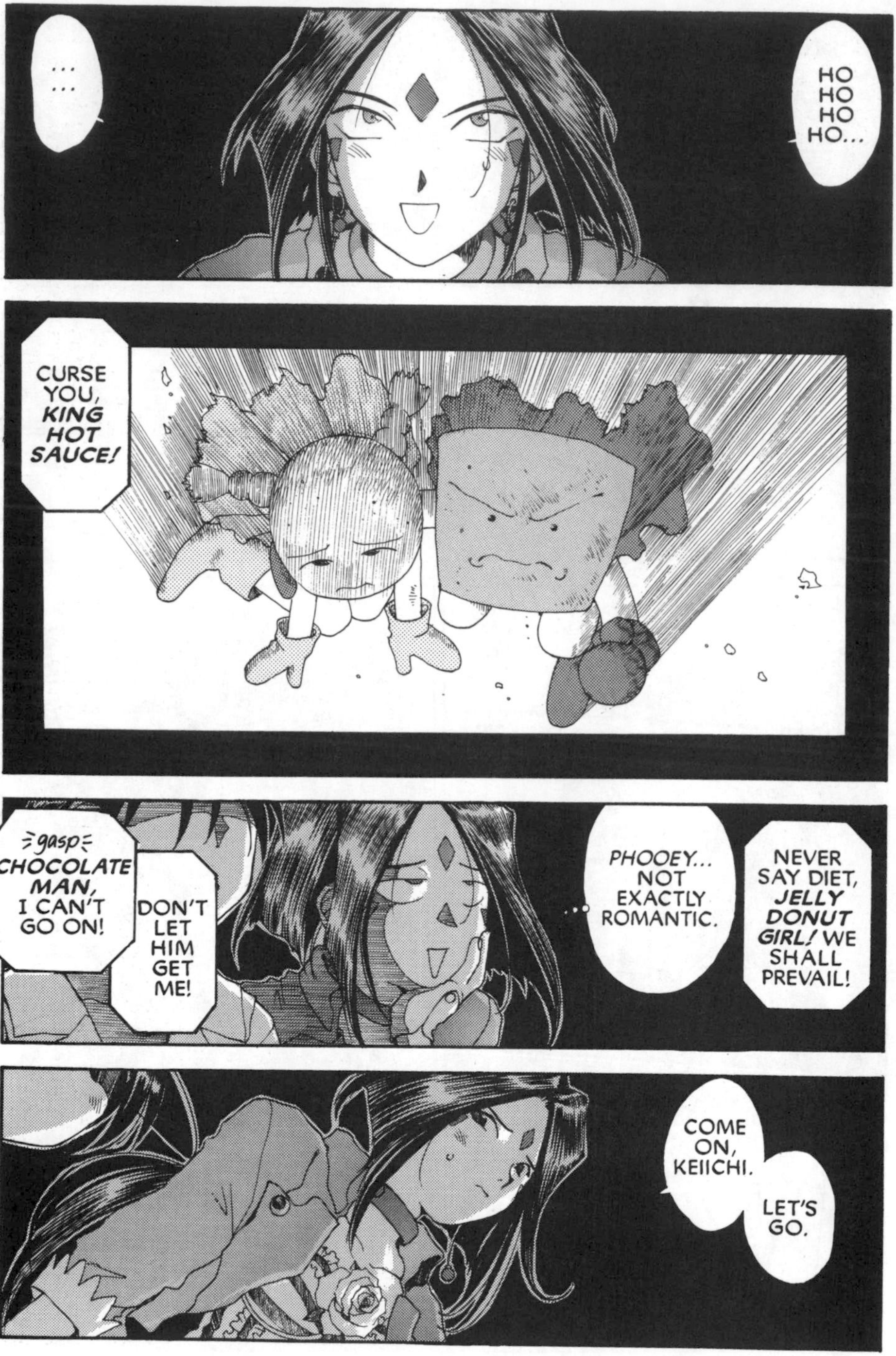
. . .
. . .
HO HO HO HO...
CURSE YOU, ***KING HOT SAUCE!***
gasp CHOCOLATE MAN, I CAN'T GO ON!
DON'T LET HIM GET ME!
PHOOEY... NOT EXACTLY ROMANTIC.
NEVER SAY DIET, ***JELLY DONUT GIRL!*** WE SHALL PREVAIL!
COME ON, KEIICHI.
LET'S GO.

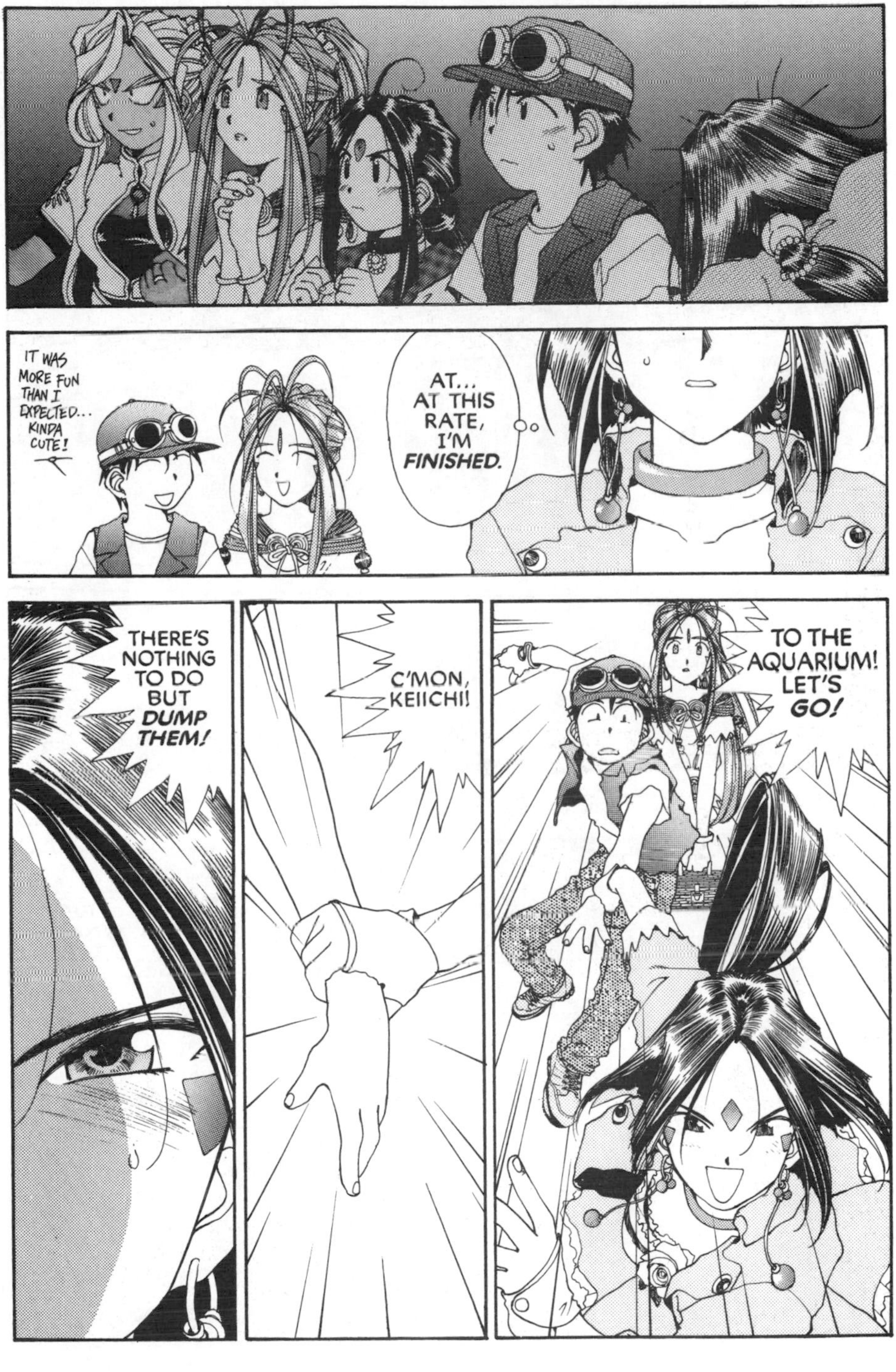
IT WAS MORE FUN THAN I EXPECTED... KINDA CUTE!
AT... AT THIS RATE, I'M *FINISHED.*
THERE'S NOTHING TO DO BUT *DUMP THEM!*
C'MON, KEIICHI!
TO THE AQUARIUM! LET'S *GO!*

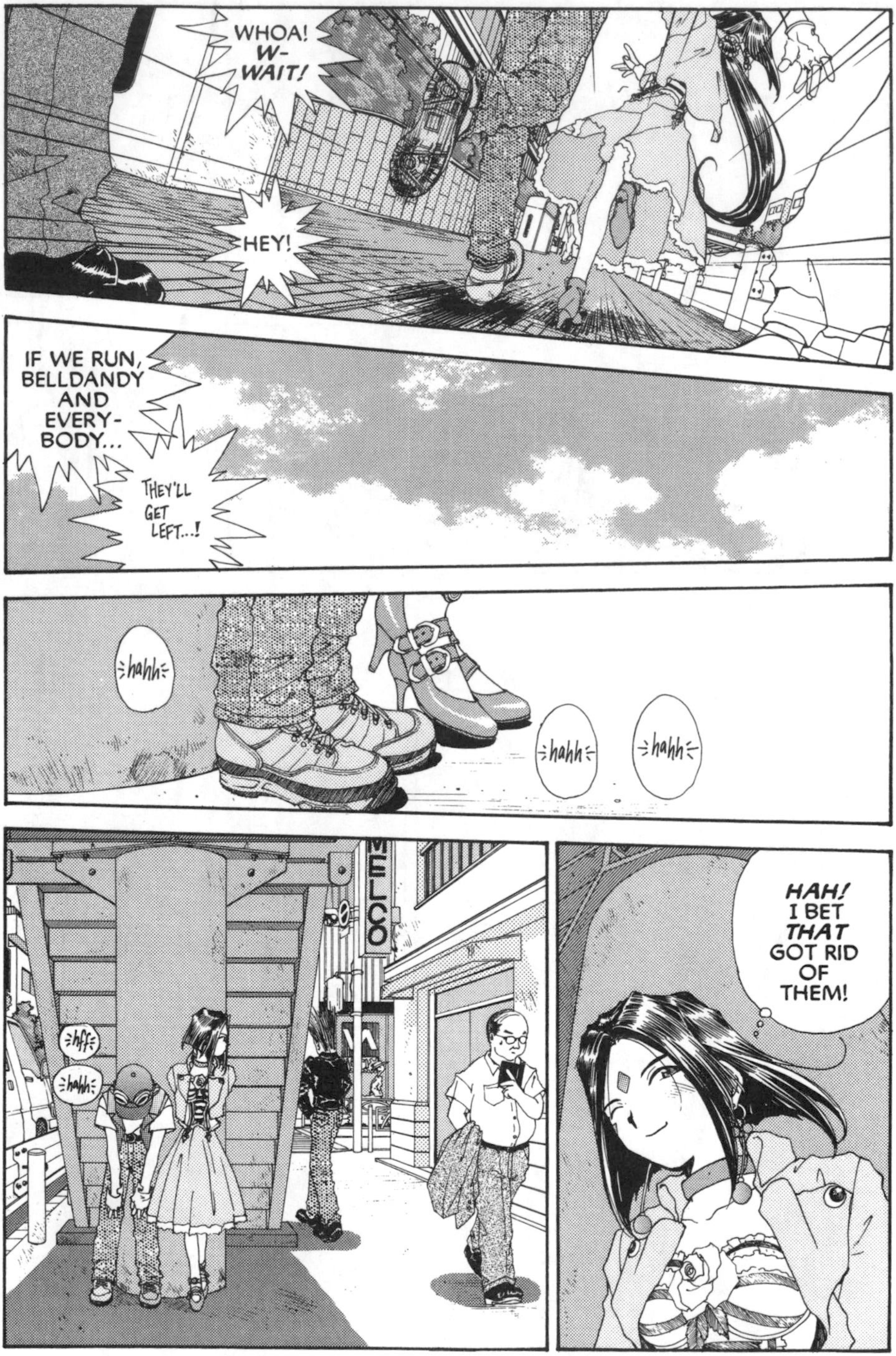
WHOA! W-WAIT!
HEY!
IF WE RUN, BELLDANDY AND EVERY-BODY...
THEY'LL GET LEFT...!
hahh
hahh
hahh
MELCO
hff
hahh
HAH! I BET THAT GOT RID OF THEM!

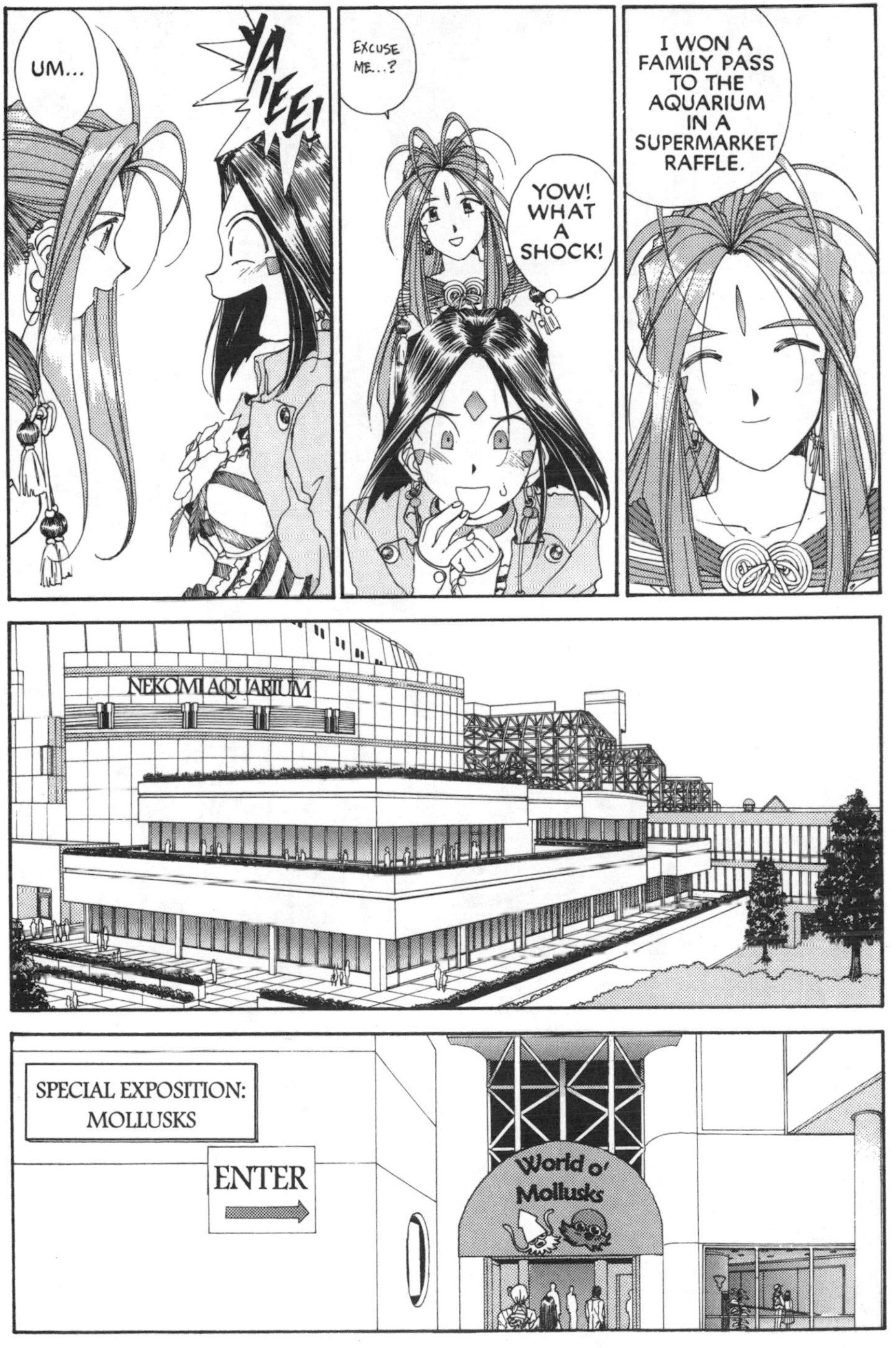
UM...
YAIEE!
EXCUSE ME...?
YOW! WHAT A SHOCK!
I WON A FAMILY PASS TO THE AQUARIUM IN A SUPERMARKET RAFFLE.
NEKOMI AQUARIUM
SPECIAL EXPOSITION: MOLLUSKS
ENTER
World o' Mollusks

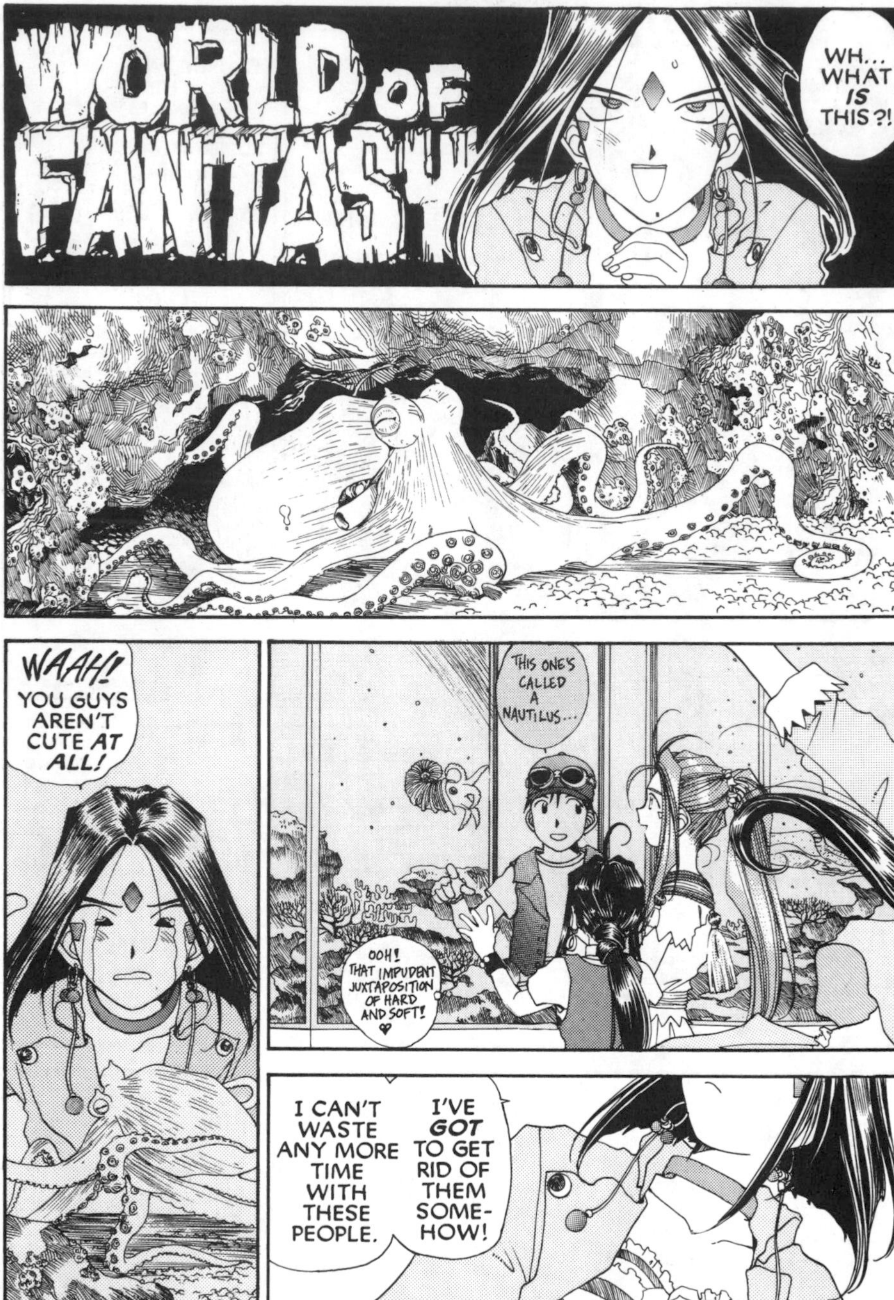
WORLD OF FANTASY
WH... WHAT IS THIS?!
WAAH! YOU GUYS AREN'T CUTE AT ALL!
THIS ONE'S CALLED A NAUTILUS...
OOH! THAT IMPUDENT JUXTAPOSITION OF HARD AND SOFT!
I CAN'T WASTE ANY MORE TIME WITH THESE PEOPLE.
I'VE GOT TO GET RID OF THEM SOME-HOW!

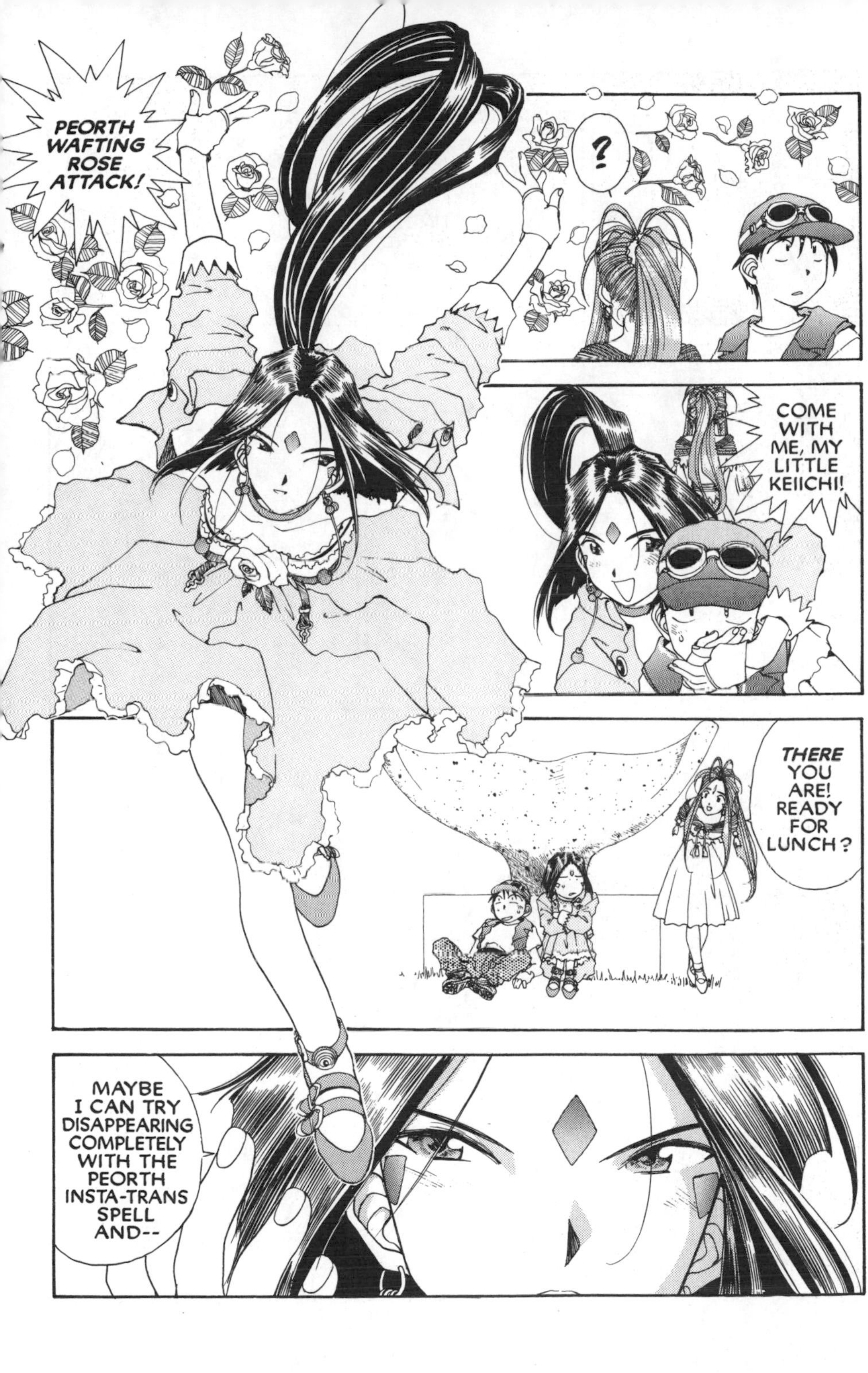
PEORTH WAFTING ROSE ATTACK!
?
COME WITH ME, MY LITTLE KEIICHI!
THERE YOU ARE! READY FOR LUNCH?
MAYBE I CAN TRY DISAPPEARING COMPLETELY WITH THE PEORTH INSTA-TRANS SPELL AND--

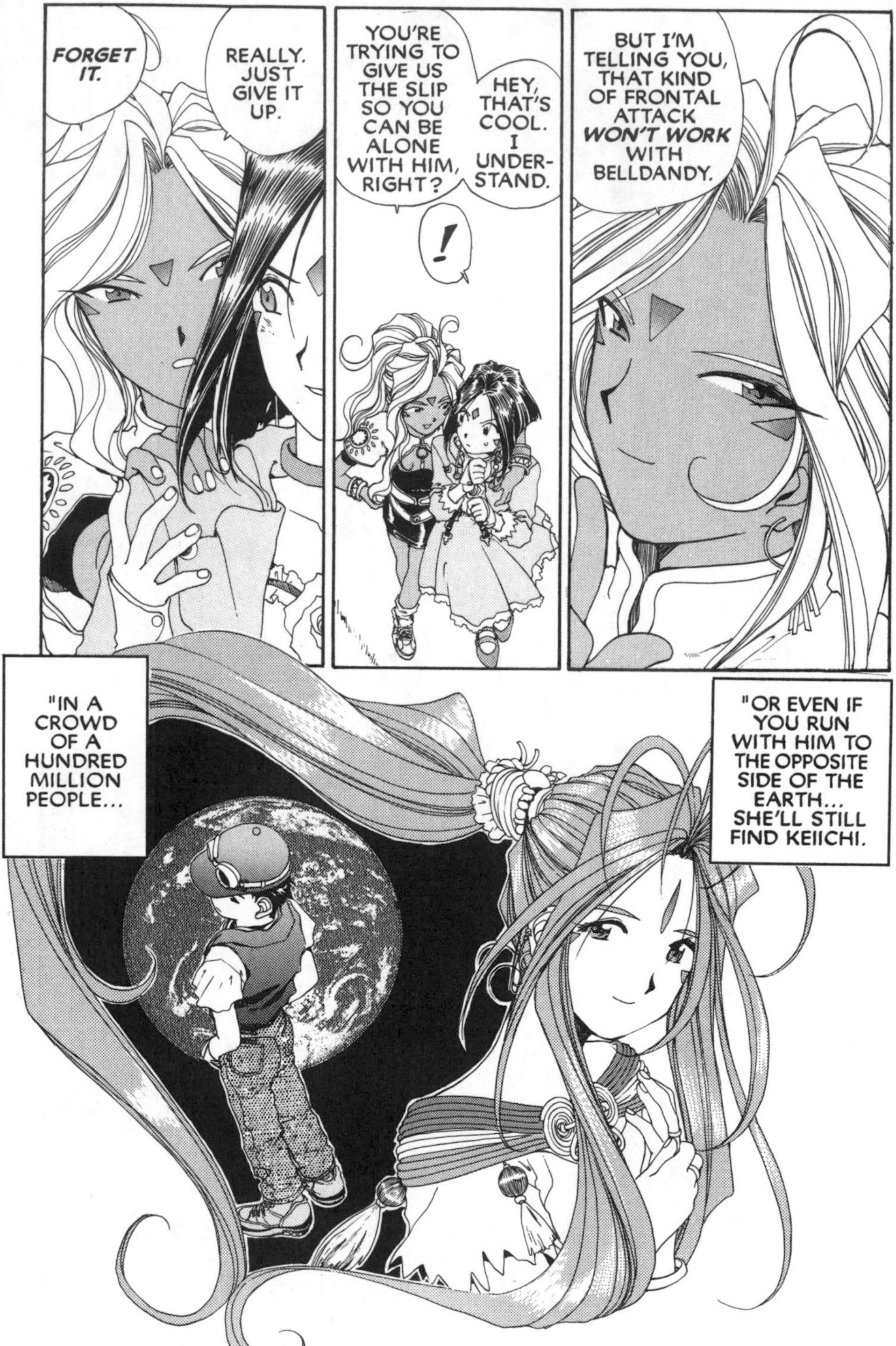

FORGET IT.
REALLY. JUST GIVE IT UP.
YOU'RE TRYING TO GIVE US THE SLIP SO YOU CAN BE ALONE WITH HIM, RIGHT?
HEY, THAT'S COOL. I UNDERSTAND.
!
BUT I'M TELLING YOU, THAT KIND OF FRONTAL ATTACK WON'T WORK WITH BELLDANDY.
"IN A CROWD OF A HUNDRED MILLION PEOPLE...
"OR EVEN IF YOU RUN WITH HIM TO THE OPPOSITE SIDE OF THE EARTH... SHE'LL STILL FIND KEIICHI.

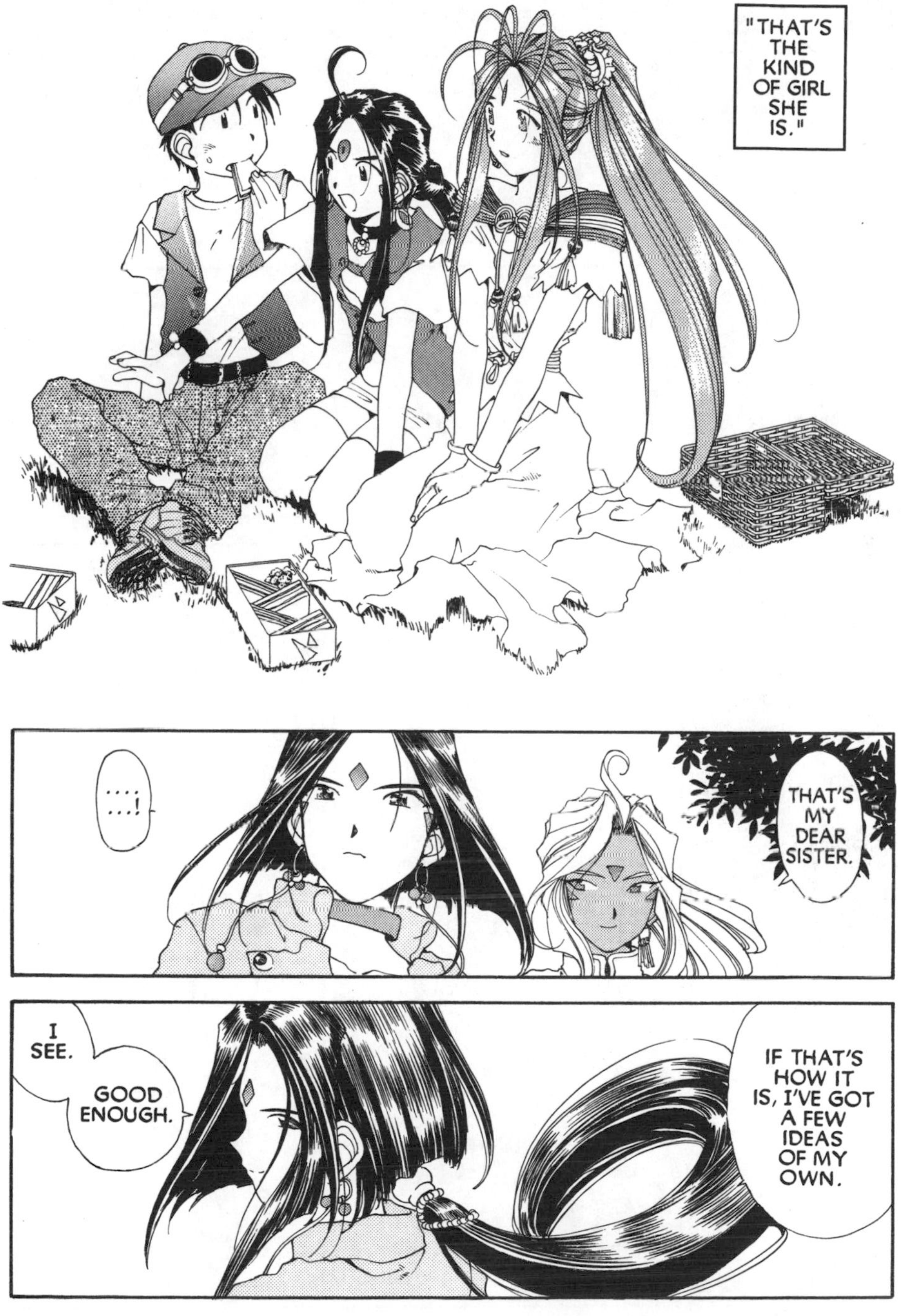
"THAT'S THE KIND OF GIRL SHE IS."
........!
THAT'S MY DEAR SISTER.
I SEE.
GOOD ENOUGH.
IF THAT'S HOW IT IS, I'VE GOT A FEW IDEAS OF MY OWN.

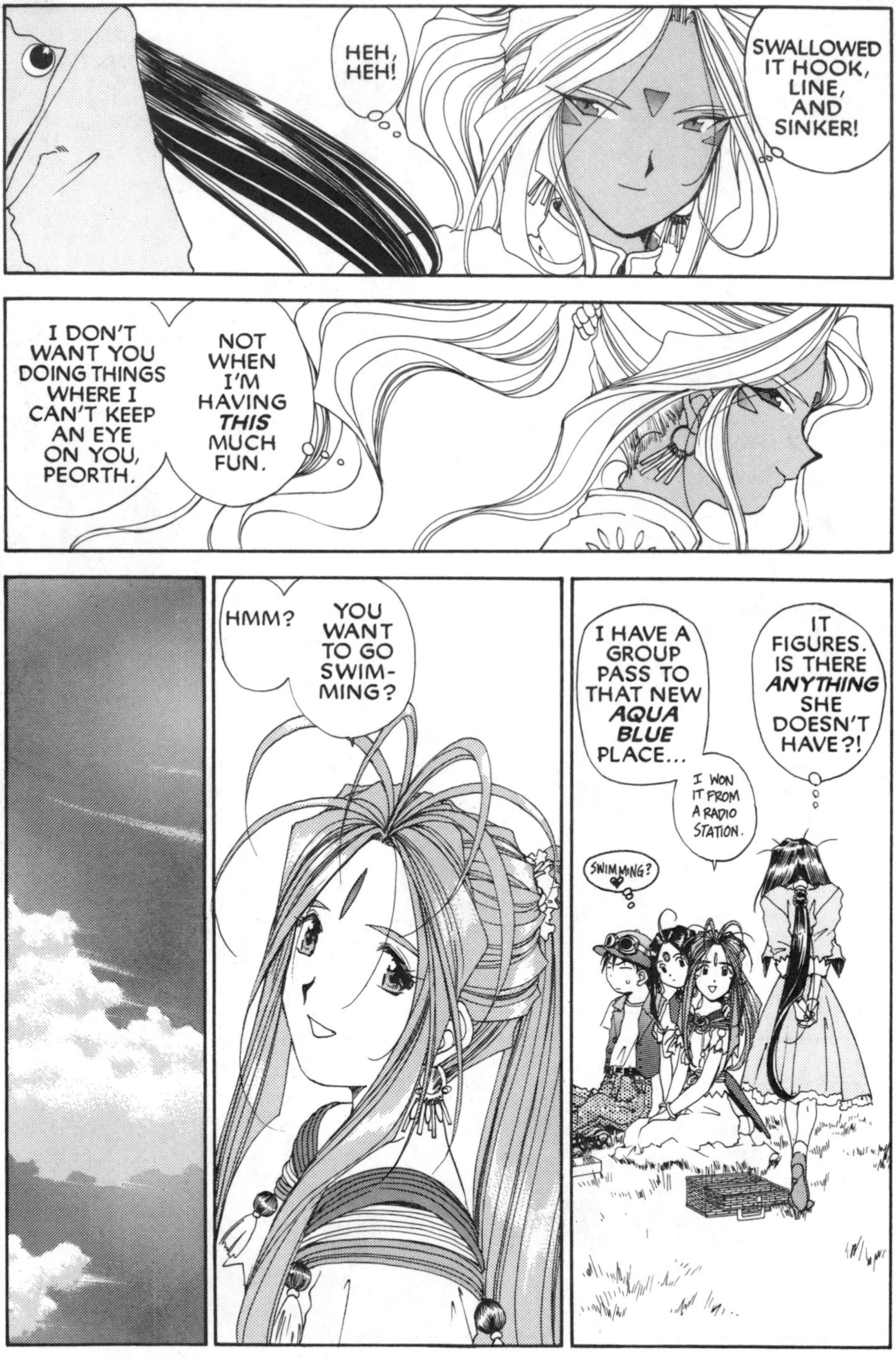
HEH, HEH!
SWALLOWED IT HOOK, LINE, AND SINKER!
I DON'T WANT YOU DOING THINGS WHERE I CAN'T KEEP AN EYE ON YOU, PEORTH.
NOT WHEN I'M HAVING ***THIS*** MUCH FUN.
HMM?
YOU WANT TO GO SWIM-MING?
I HAVE A GROUP PASS TO THAT NEW ***AQUA BLUE*** PLACE...
I WON IT FROM A RADIO STATION.
SWIMMING?
IT FIGURES. IS THERE ***ANYTHING*** SHE DOESN'T HAVE?!

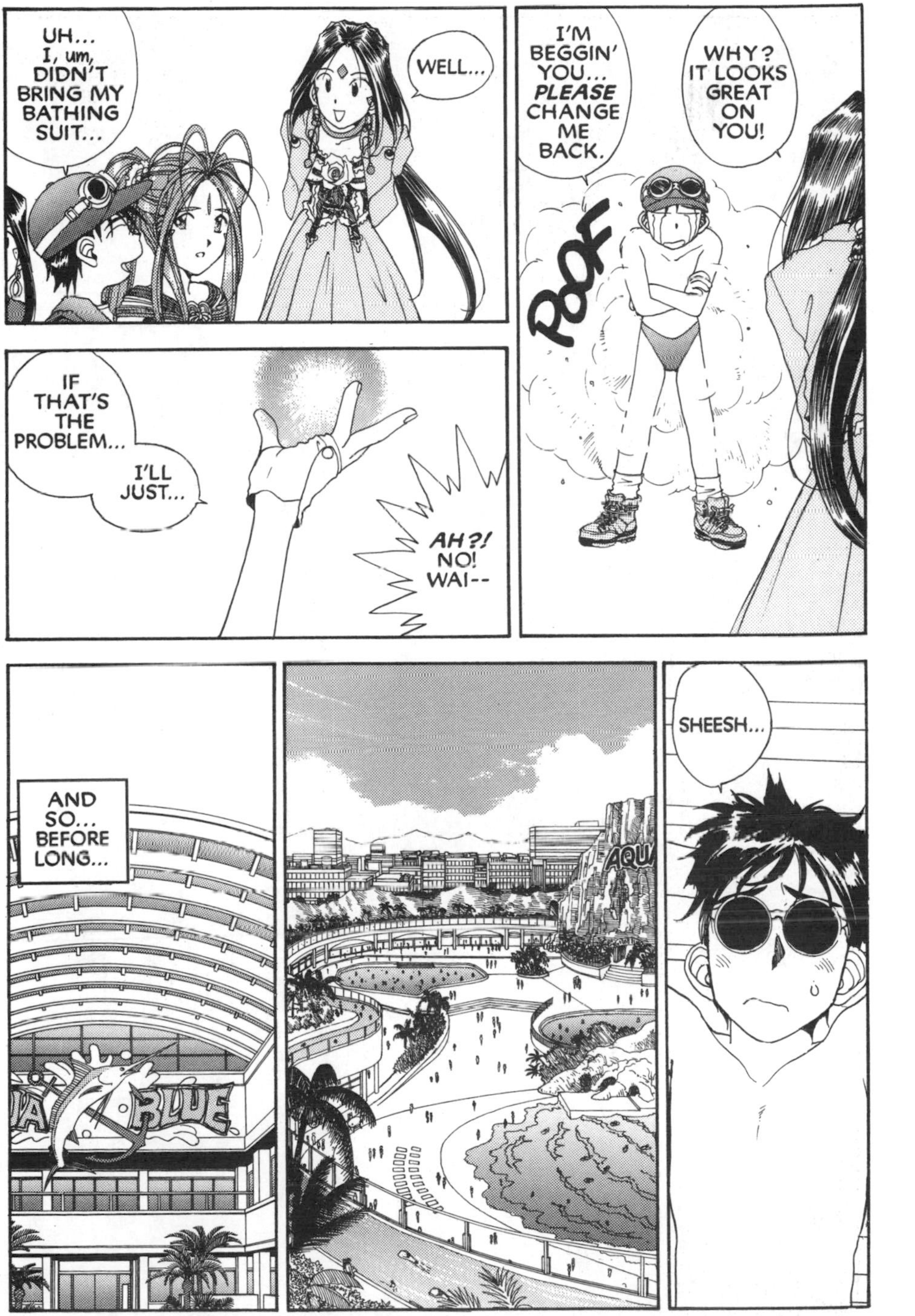
UH... I, um, DIDN'T BRING MY BATHING SUIT...
WELL...
IF THAT'S THE PROBLEM...
I'LL JUST...
AH?! NO! WAI--
ROOF
I'M BEGGIN' YOU... *PLEASE* CHANGE ME BACK.
WHY? IT LOOKS GREAT ON YOU!
AND SO... BEFORE LONG...
BLUE
SHEESH...

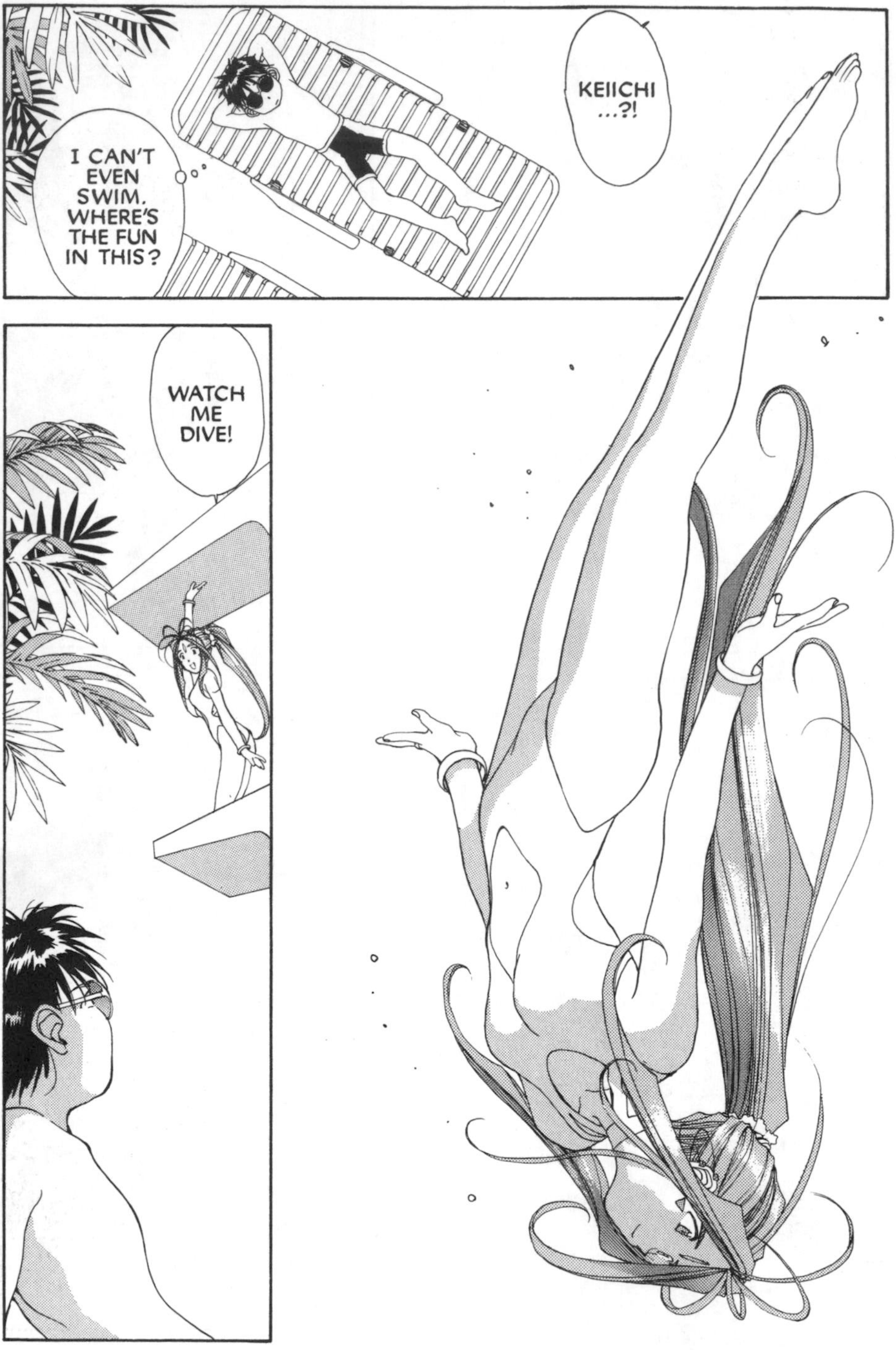
I CAN'T EVEN SWIM. WHERE'S THE FUN IN THIS?
KEIICHI ...?!
WATCH ME DIVE!

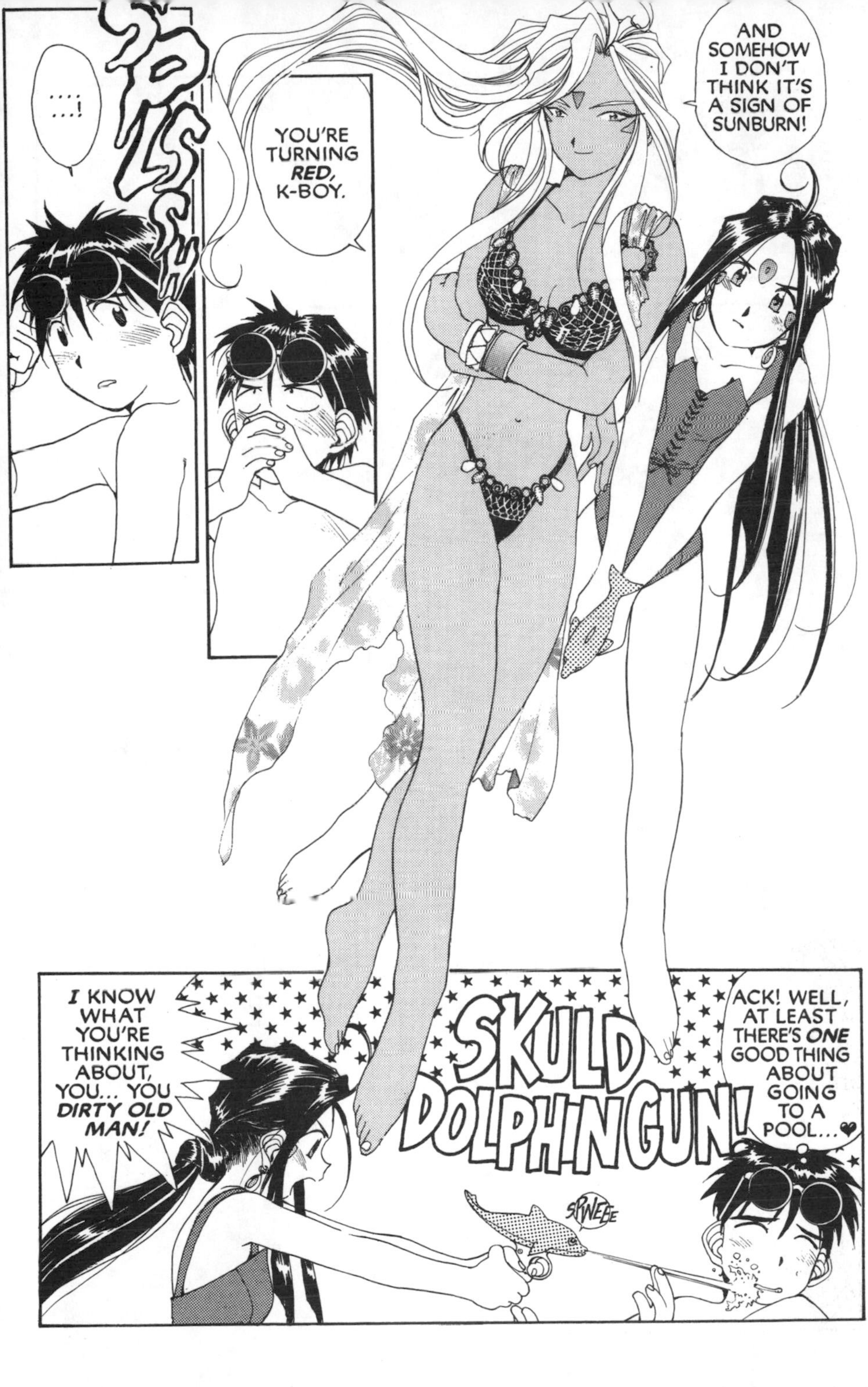
....!
....!
PLSSH
YOU'RE TURNING *RED*, K-BOY.
AND SOMEHOW I DON'T THINK IT'S A SIGN OF SUNBURN!
I KNOW WHAT YOU'RE THINKING ABOUT, YOU... YOU *DIRTY OLD MAN!*
SKULD DOLPHIN GUN!
SPWEEE
ACK! WELL, AT LEAST THERE'S *ONE* GOOD THING ABOUT GOING TO A POOL...♥

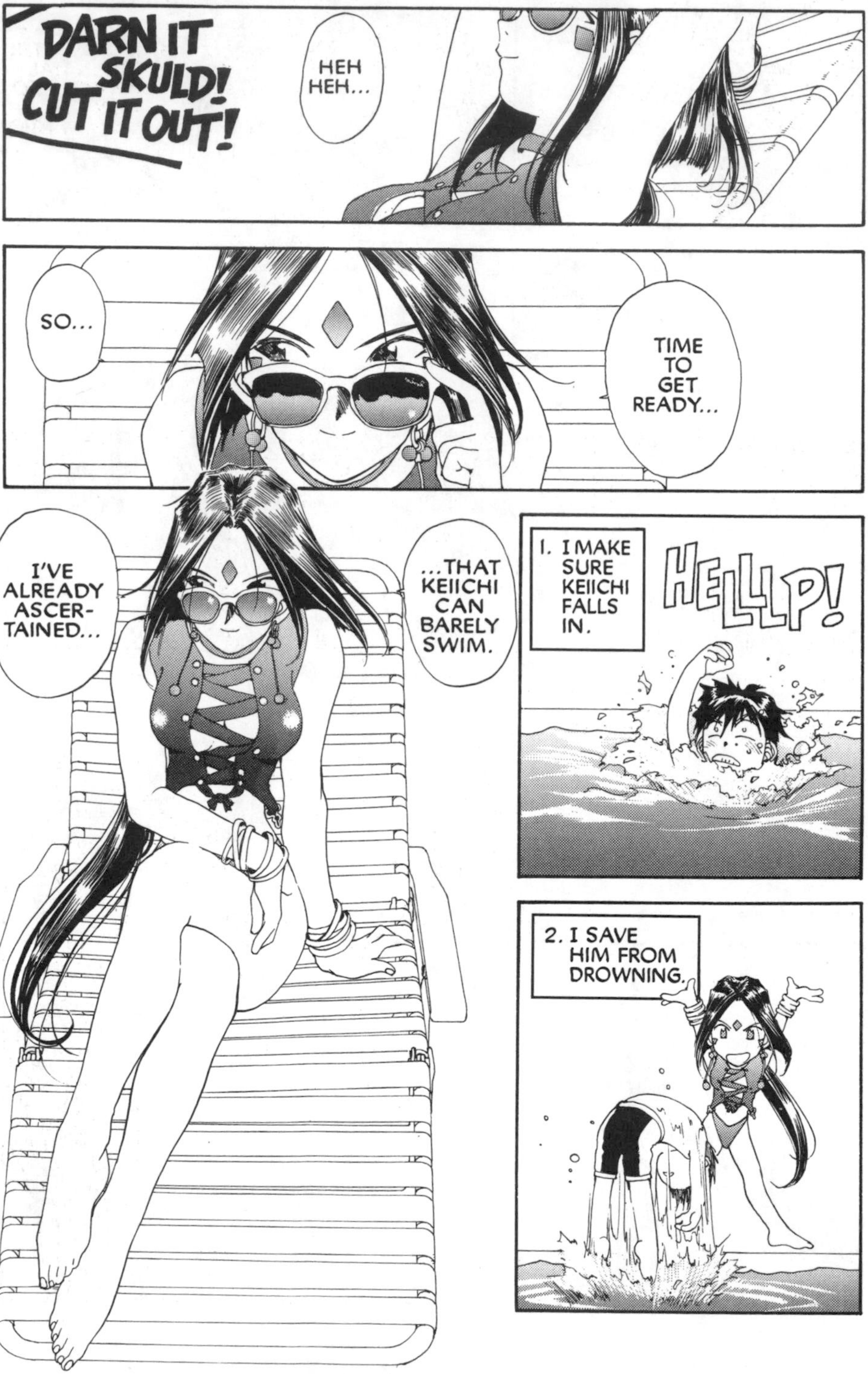
DARN IT SKULD! CUT IT OUT!
HEH HEH...
SO...
TIME TO GET READY...
I'VE ALREADY ASCER-TAINED...
...THAT KEIICHI CAN BARELY SWIM.
1. I MAKE SURE KEIICHI FALLS IN.
HELLLP!
2. I SAVE HIM FROM DROWNING.

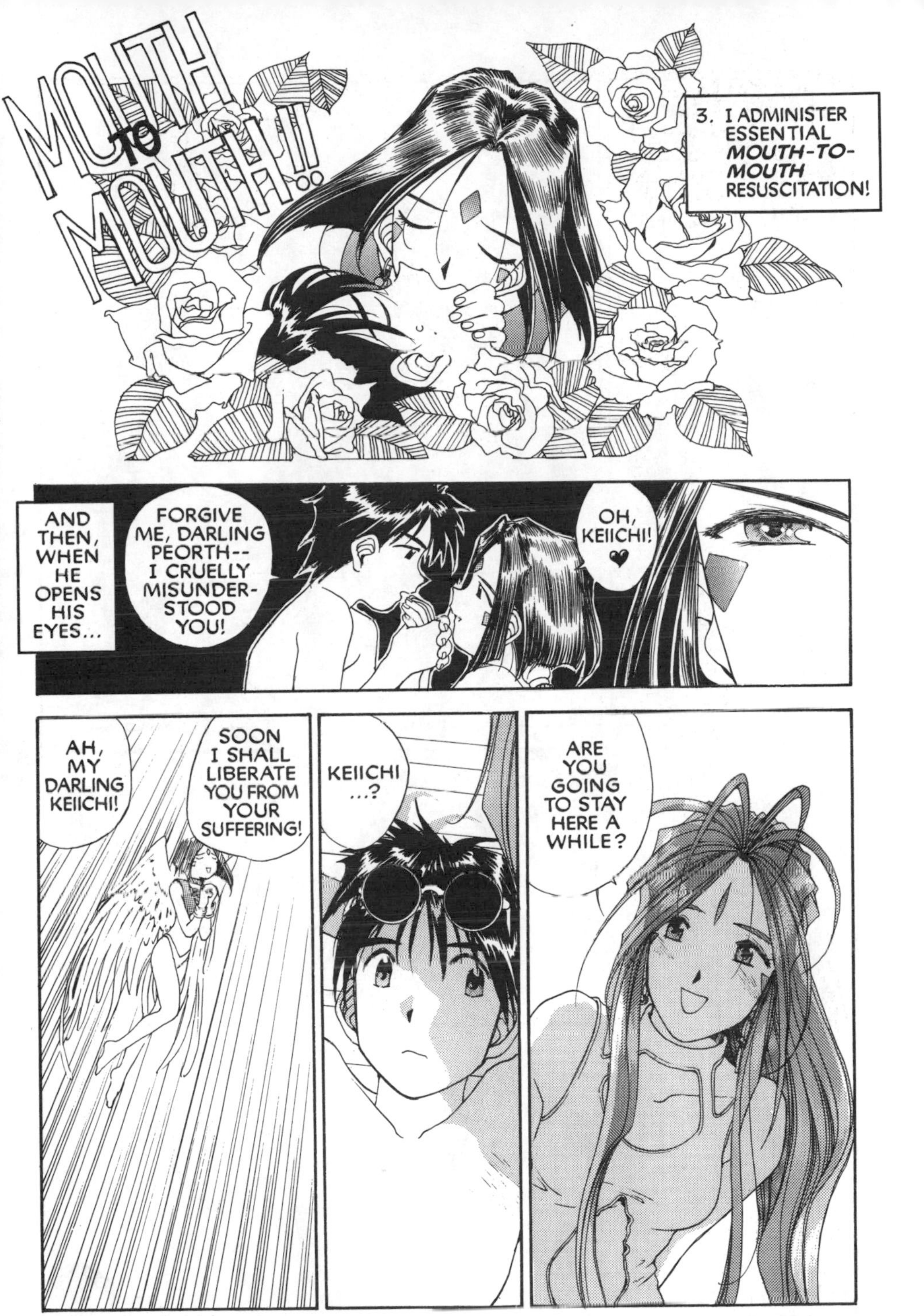
MOUTH TO MOUTH!!
3. I ADMINISTER ESSENTIAL MOUTH-TO-MOUTH RESUSCITATION!
AND THEN, WHEN HE OPENS HIS EYES...
FORGIVE ME, DARLING PEORTH-- I CRUELLY MISUNDERSTOOD YOU!
OH, KEIICHI! ♥
AH, MY DARLING KEIICHI!
SOON I SHALL LIBERATE YOU FROM YOUR SUFFERING!
KEIICHI ...?
ARE YOU GOING TO STAY HERE A WHILE?

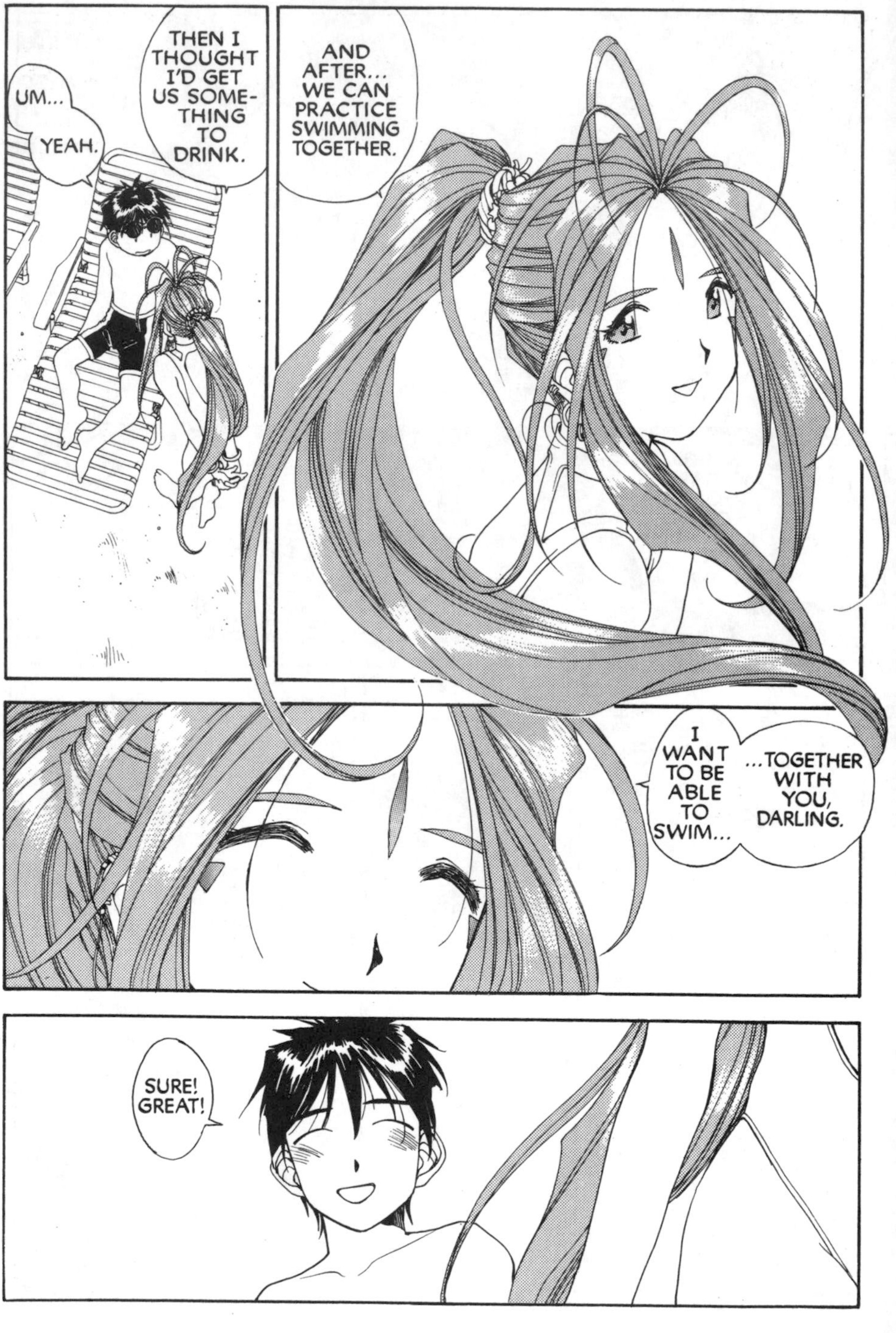
THEN I THOUGHT I'D GET US SOME-THING TO DRINK.
UM...
YEAH.
AND AFTER... WE CAN PRACTICE SWIMMING TOGETHER.
I WANT TO BE ABLE TO SWIM...
...TOGETHER WITH YOU, DARLING.
SURE! GREAT!

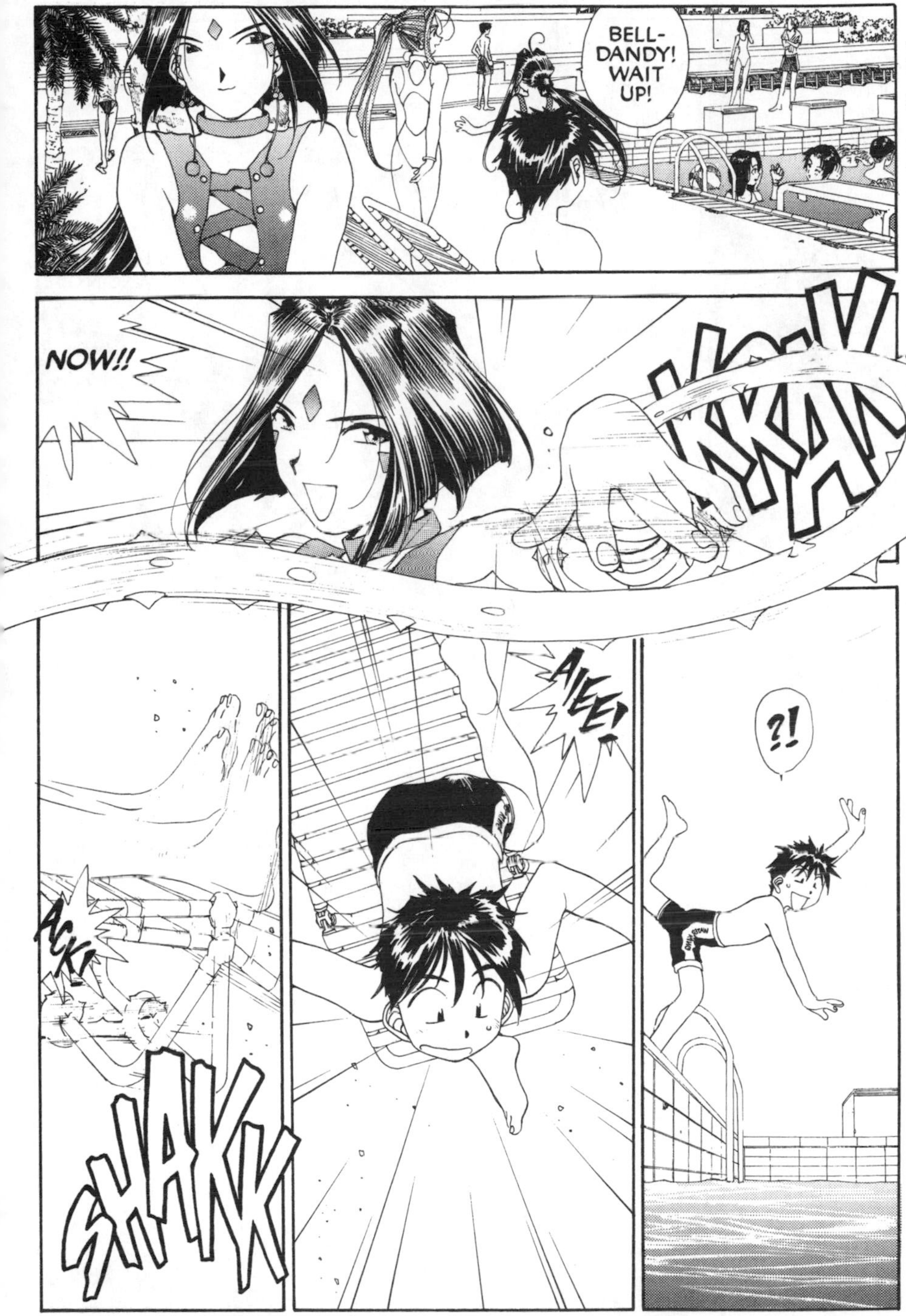
BELL-DANDY! WAIT UP!
NOW!!
KKAK
ACK!
SHAKK
AIEEE!
?!

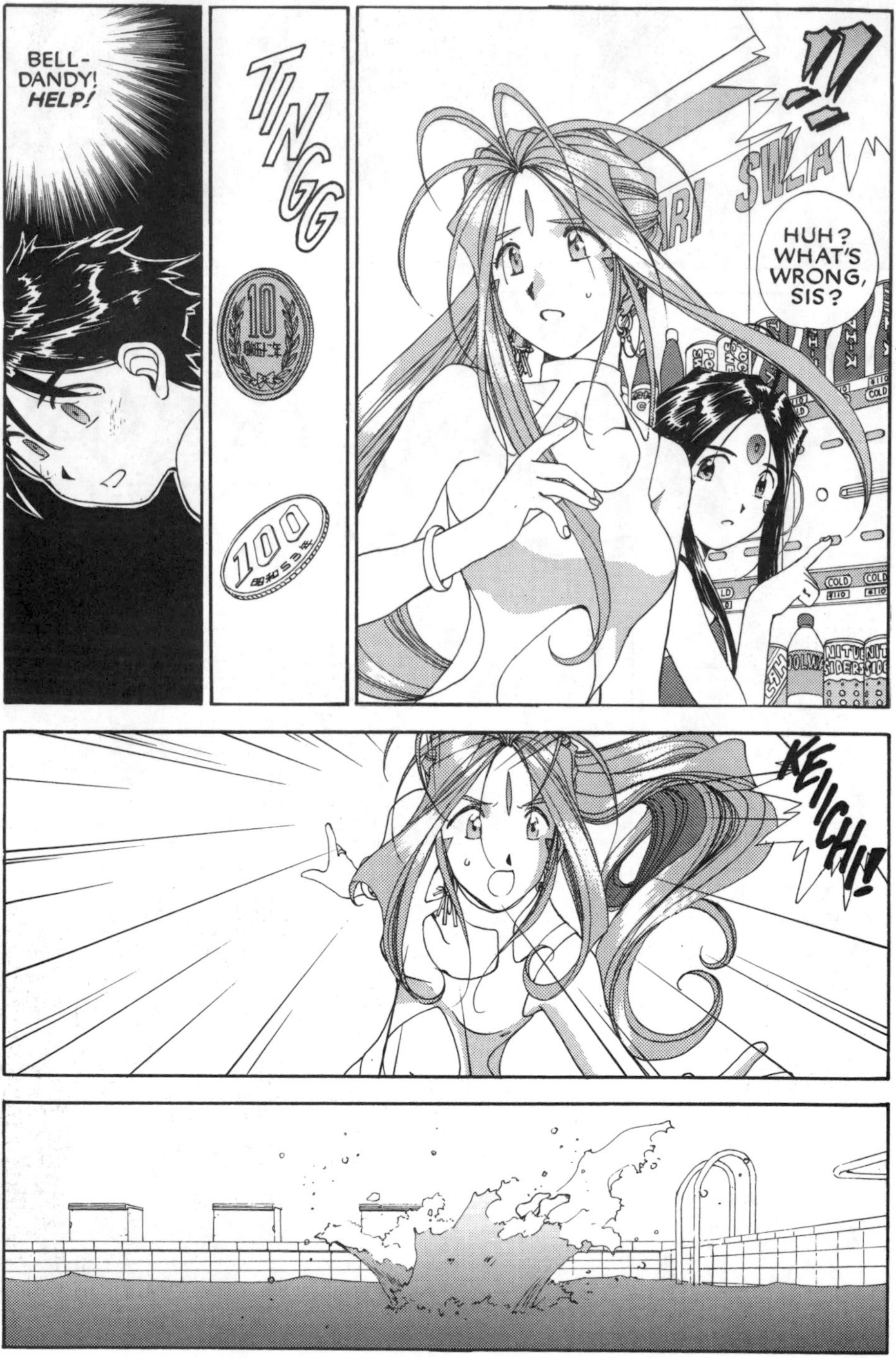
BELL-DANDY! *HELP!*
TINGG
!!
HUH? WHAT'S WRONG, SIS?
KEIICHI!

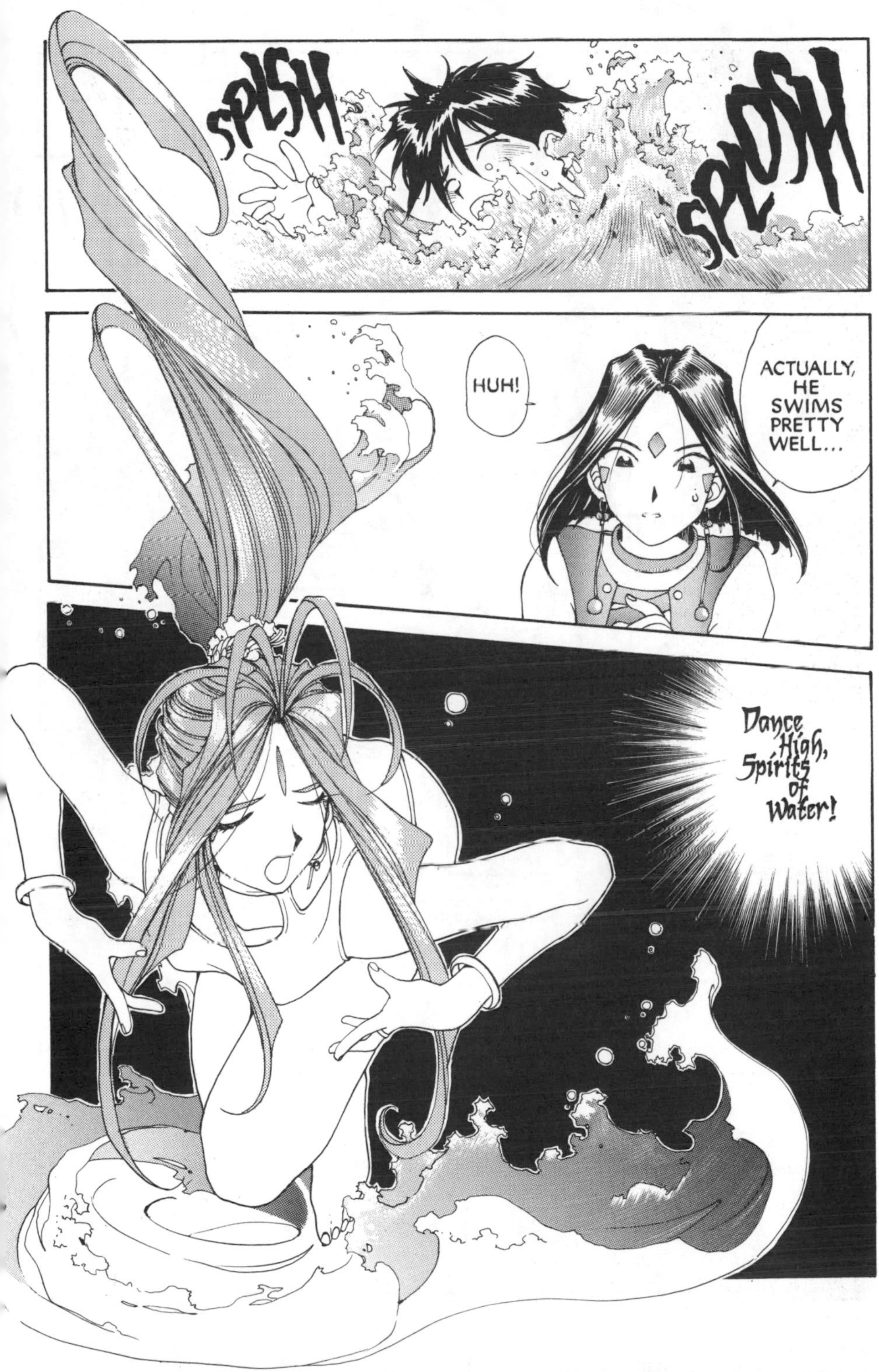
SPLSH
SPLOSH
HUH!
ACTUALLY, HE SWIMS PRETTY WELL...
Dance High, Spirits of Water!

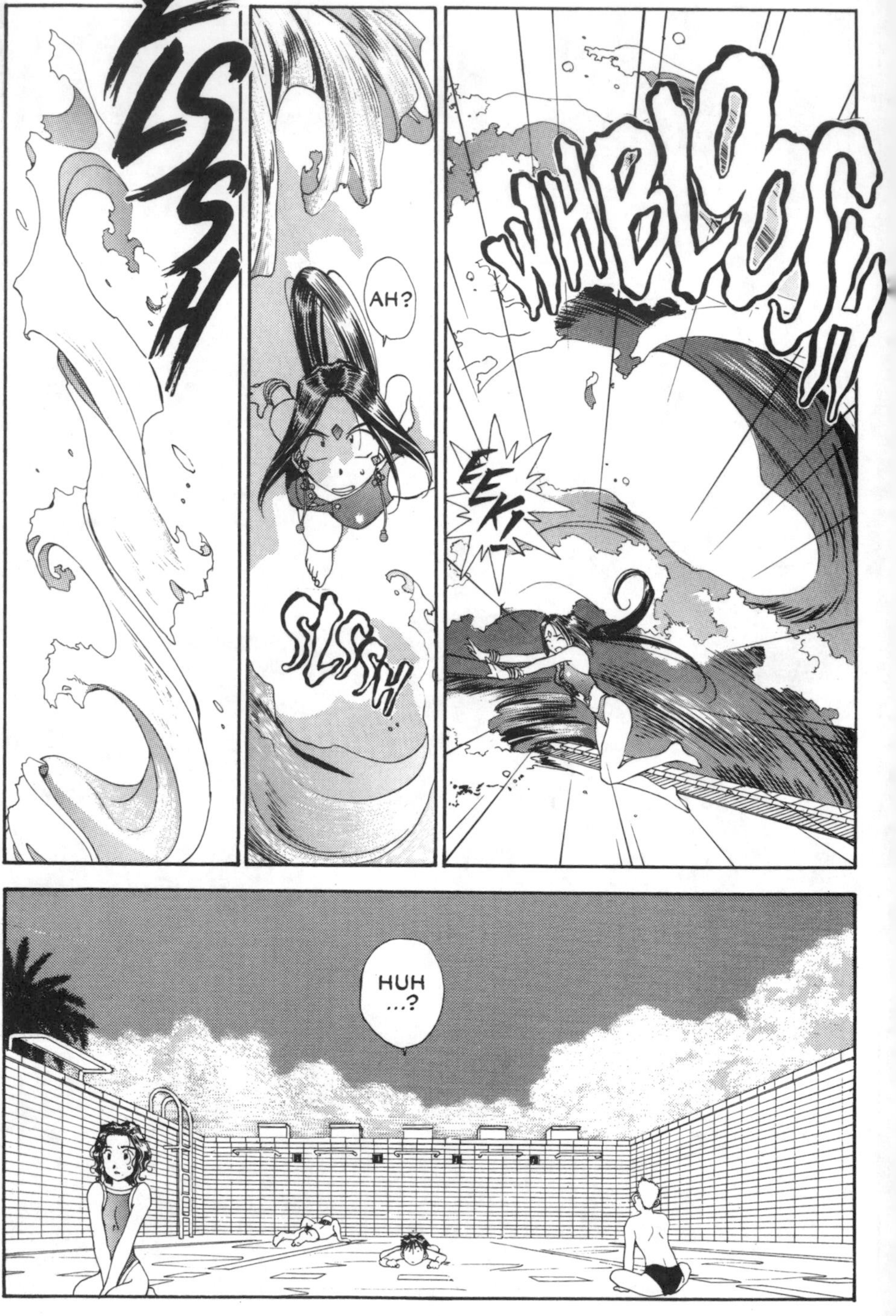
FLSSH
AH?
SLSSH
WHBLOOSH
EEK!
HUH ...?

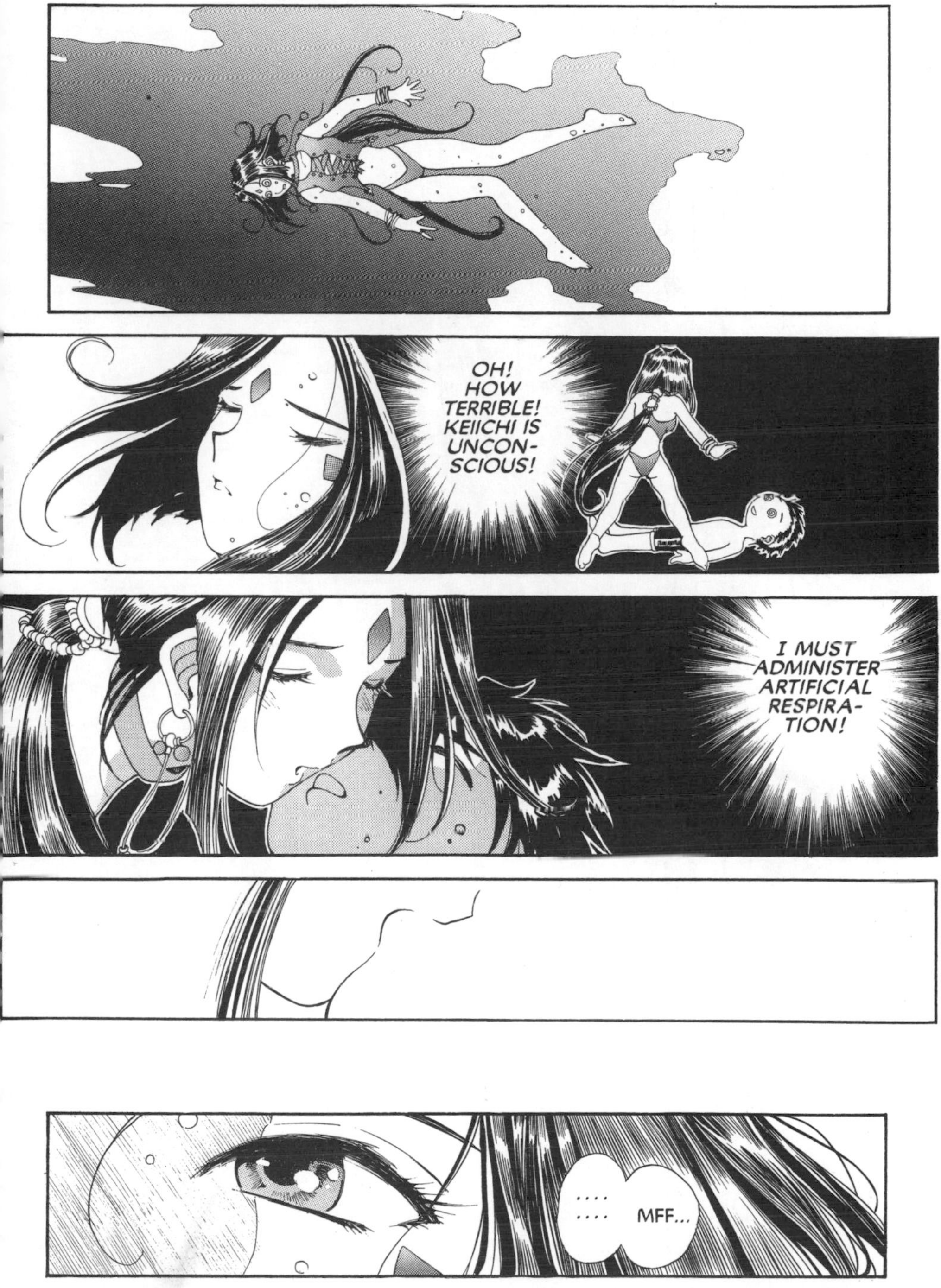
OH! HOW TERRIBLE! KEIICHI IS UNCONSCIOUS!
I MUST ADMINISTER ARTIFICIAL RESPIRATION!
....
....
MFF...

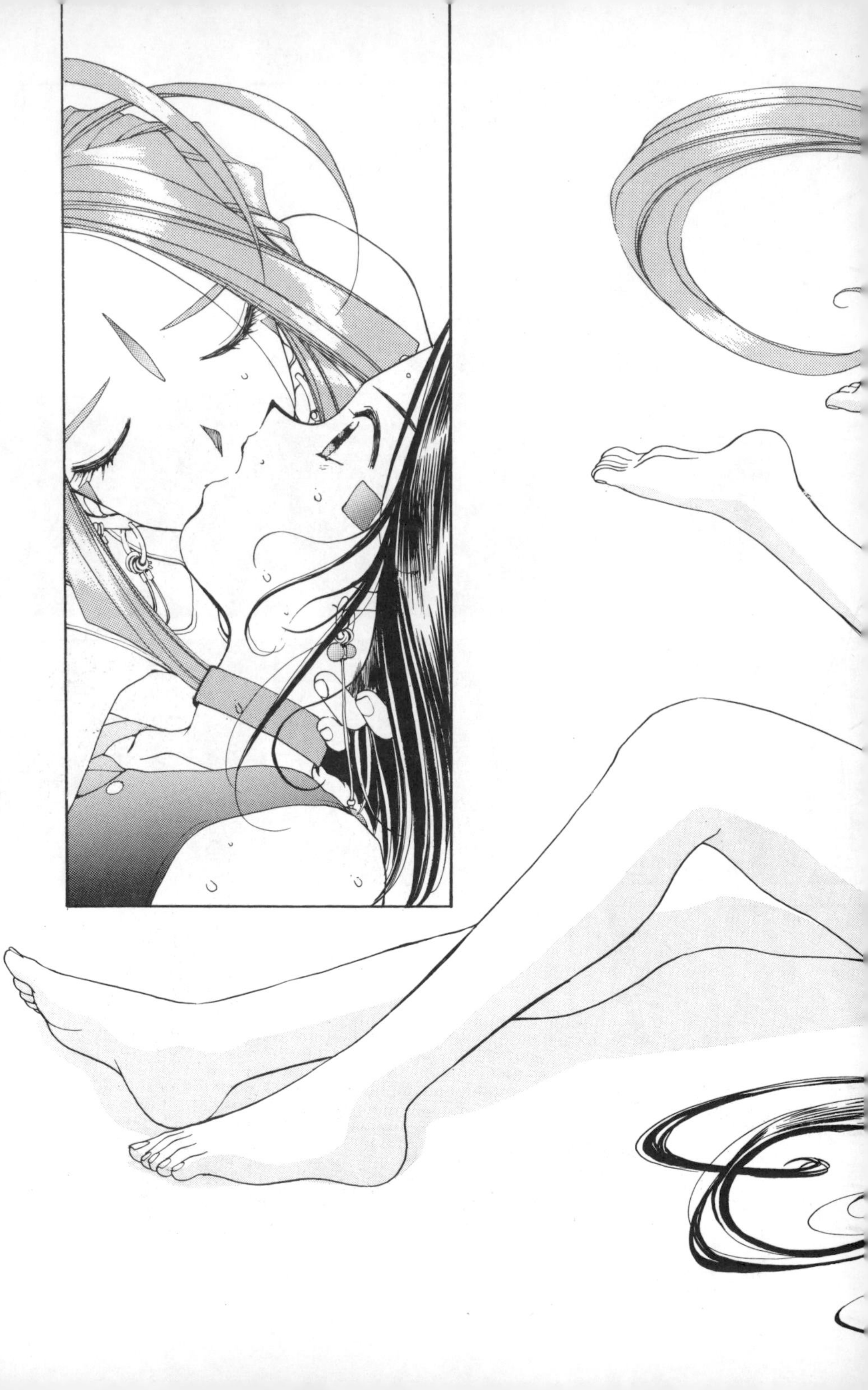

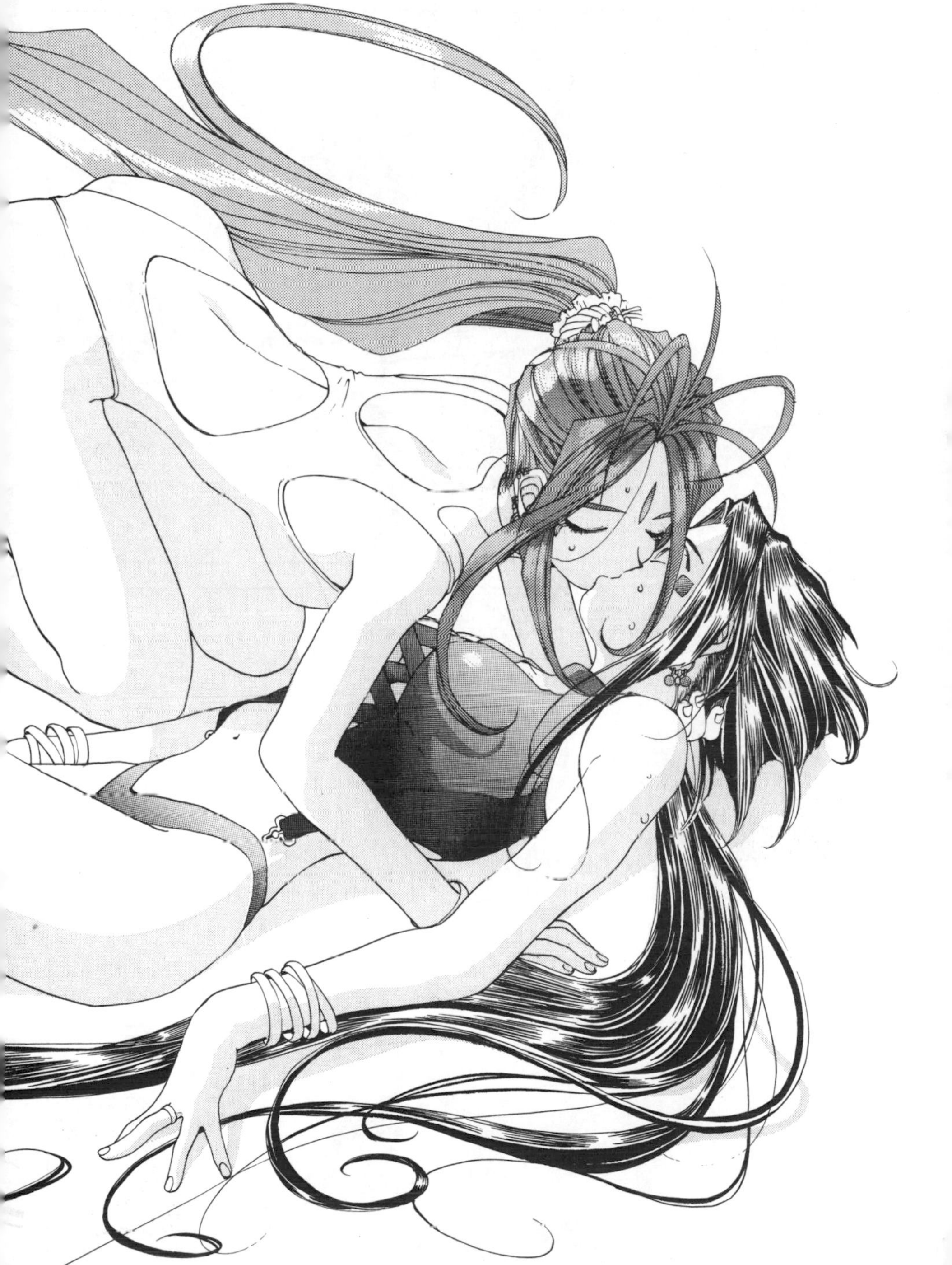

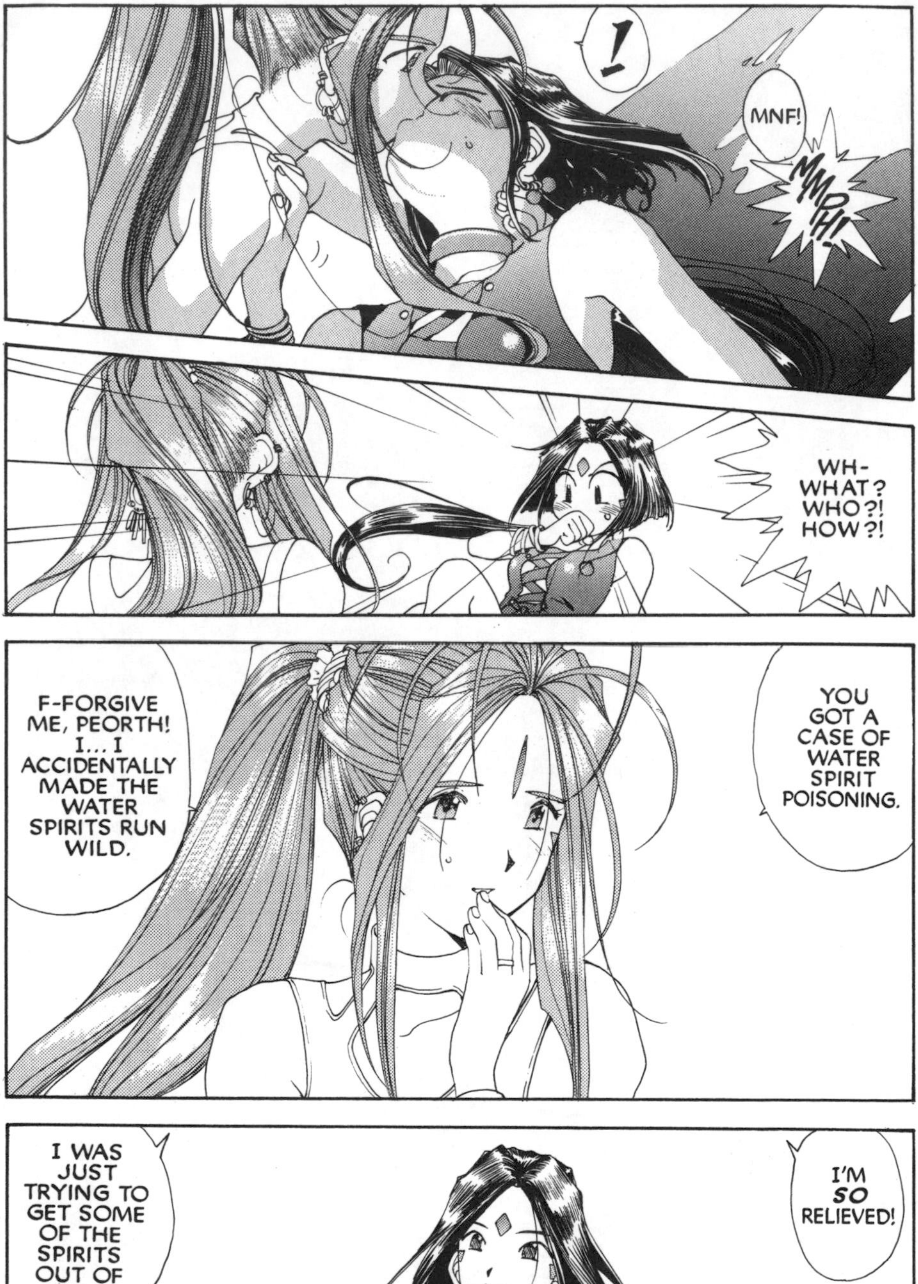
!
MNF!
MMPH!
WH- WHAT? WHO?! HOW?!
F-FORGIVE ME, PEORTH! I... I ACCIDENTALLY MADE THE WATER SPIRITS RUN WILD.
YOU GOT A CASE OF WATER SPIRIT POISONING.
I WAS JUST TRYING TO GET SOME OF THE SPIRITS OUT OF YOUR BODY.
I'M *SO* RELIEVED!

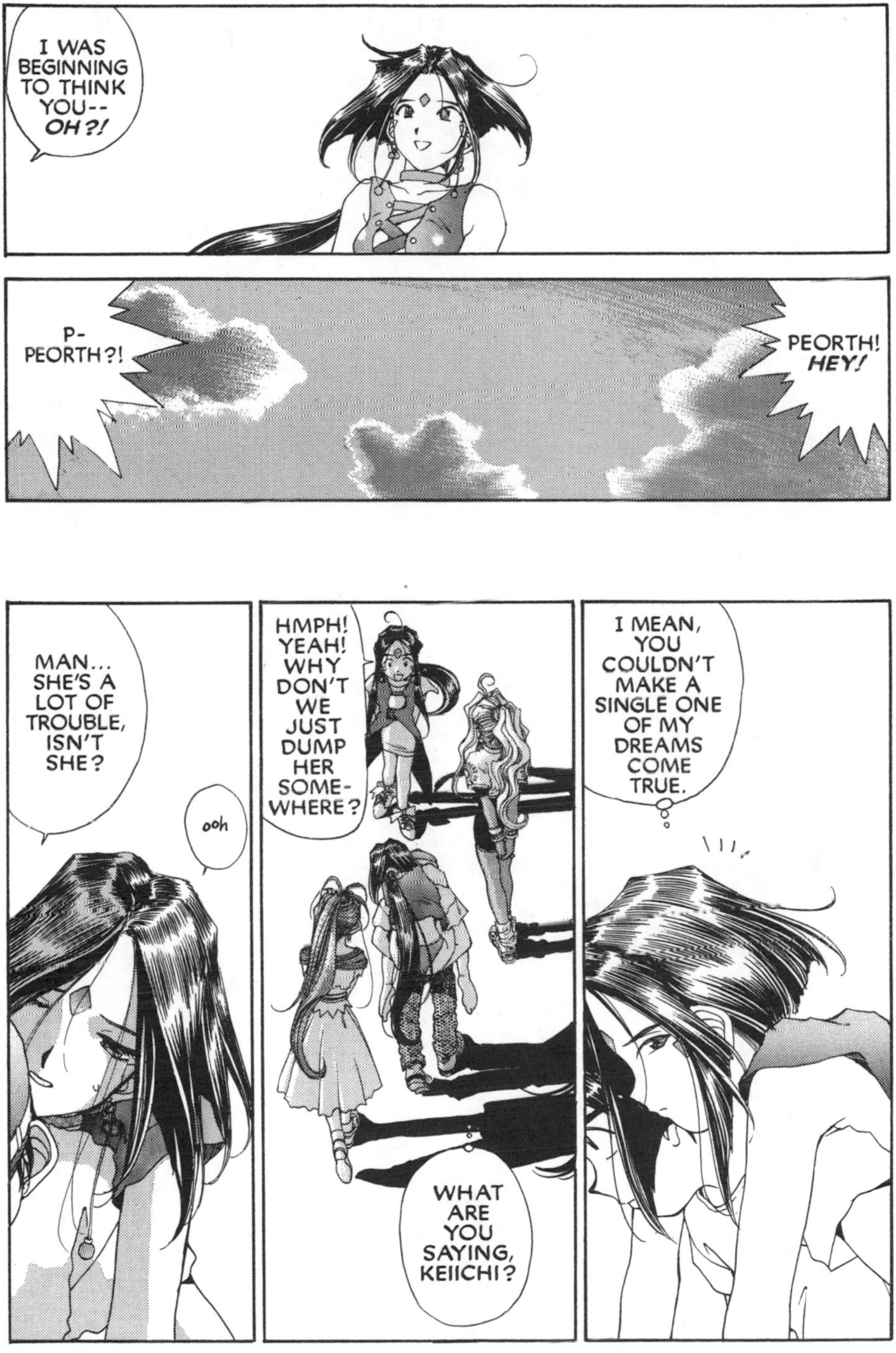
I WAS BEGINNING TO THINK YOU-- OH?!
P- PEORTH?!
PEORTH! HEY!
MAN... SHE'S A LOT OF TROUBLE, ISN'T SHE?
ooh
HMPH! YEAH! WHY DON'T WE JUST DUMP HER SOME-WHERE?
WHAT ARE YOU SAYING, KEIICHI?
I MEAN, YOU COULDN'T MAKE A SINGLE ONE OF MY DREAMS COME TRUE.

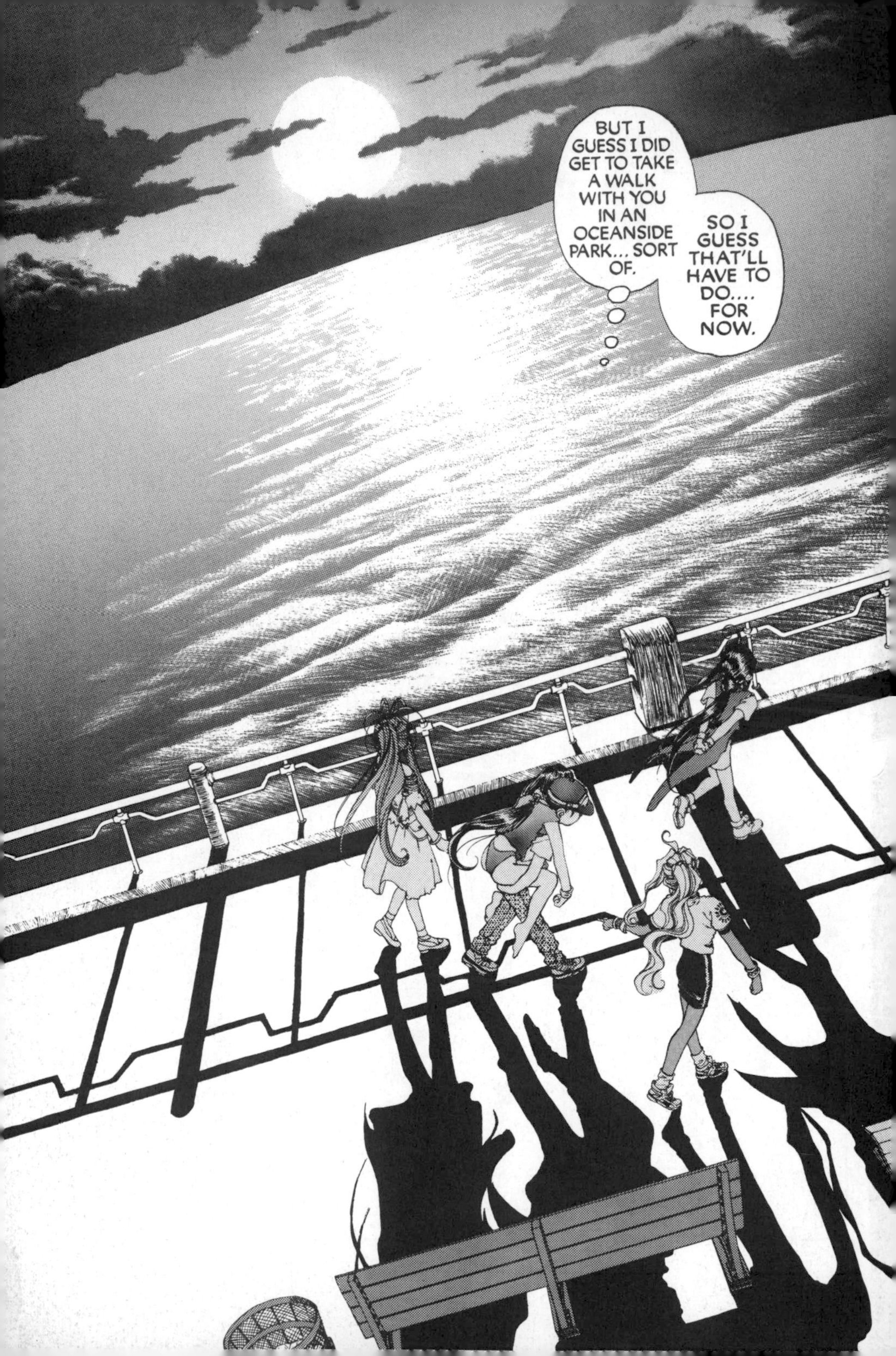
BUT I GUESS I DID GET TO TAKE A WALK WITH YOU IN AN OCEANSIDE PARK... SORT OF.
SO I GUESS THAT'LL HAVE TO DO.... FOR NOW.

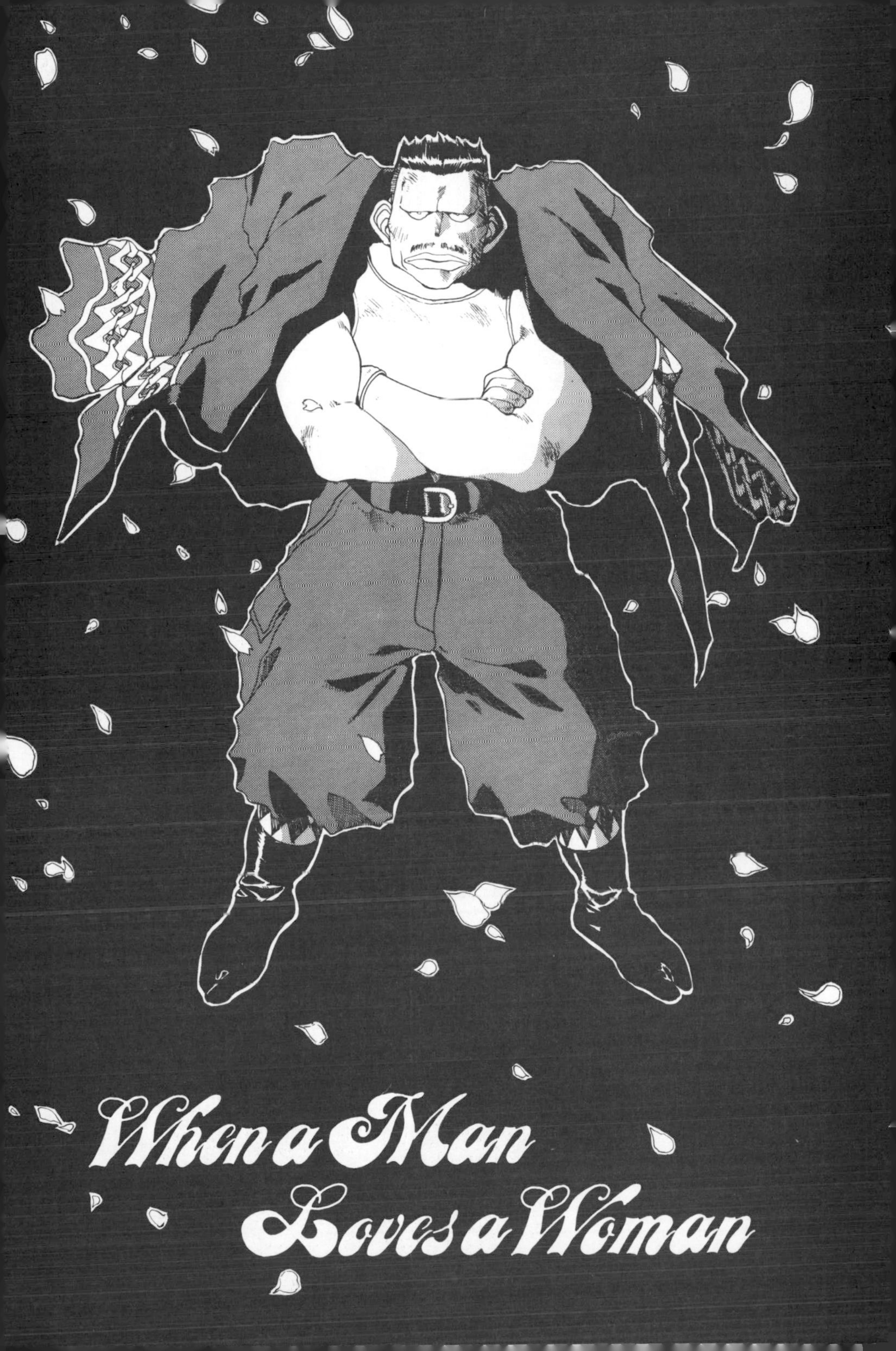
When a Man
Loves a Woman

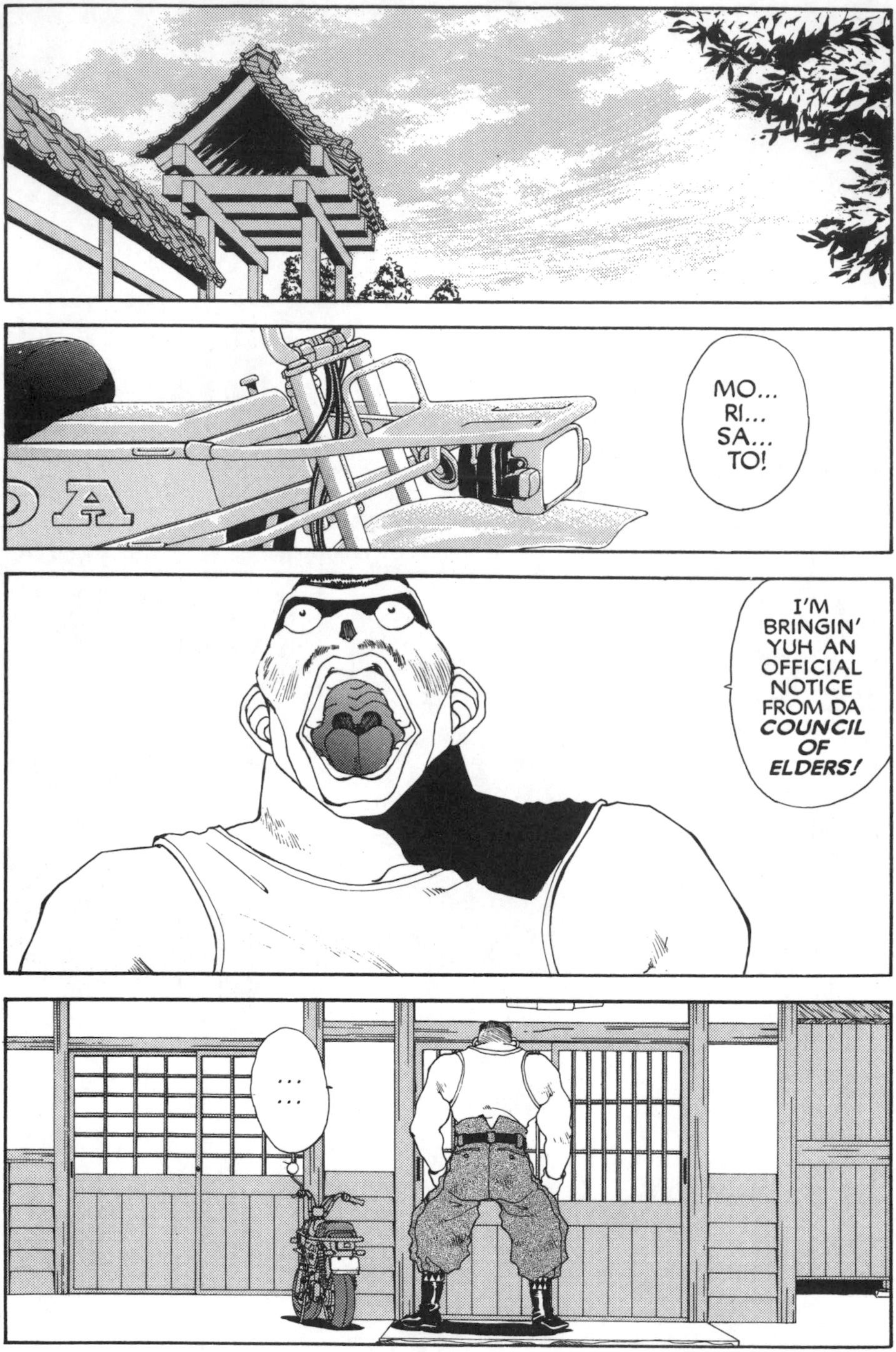
DA
MO... RI... SA... TO!
I'M BRINGIN' YUH AN OFFICIAL NOTICE FROM DA COUNCIL OF ELDERS!
... ...

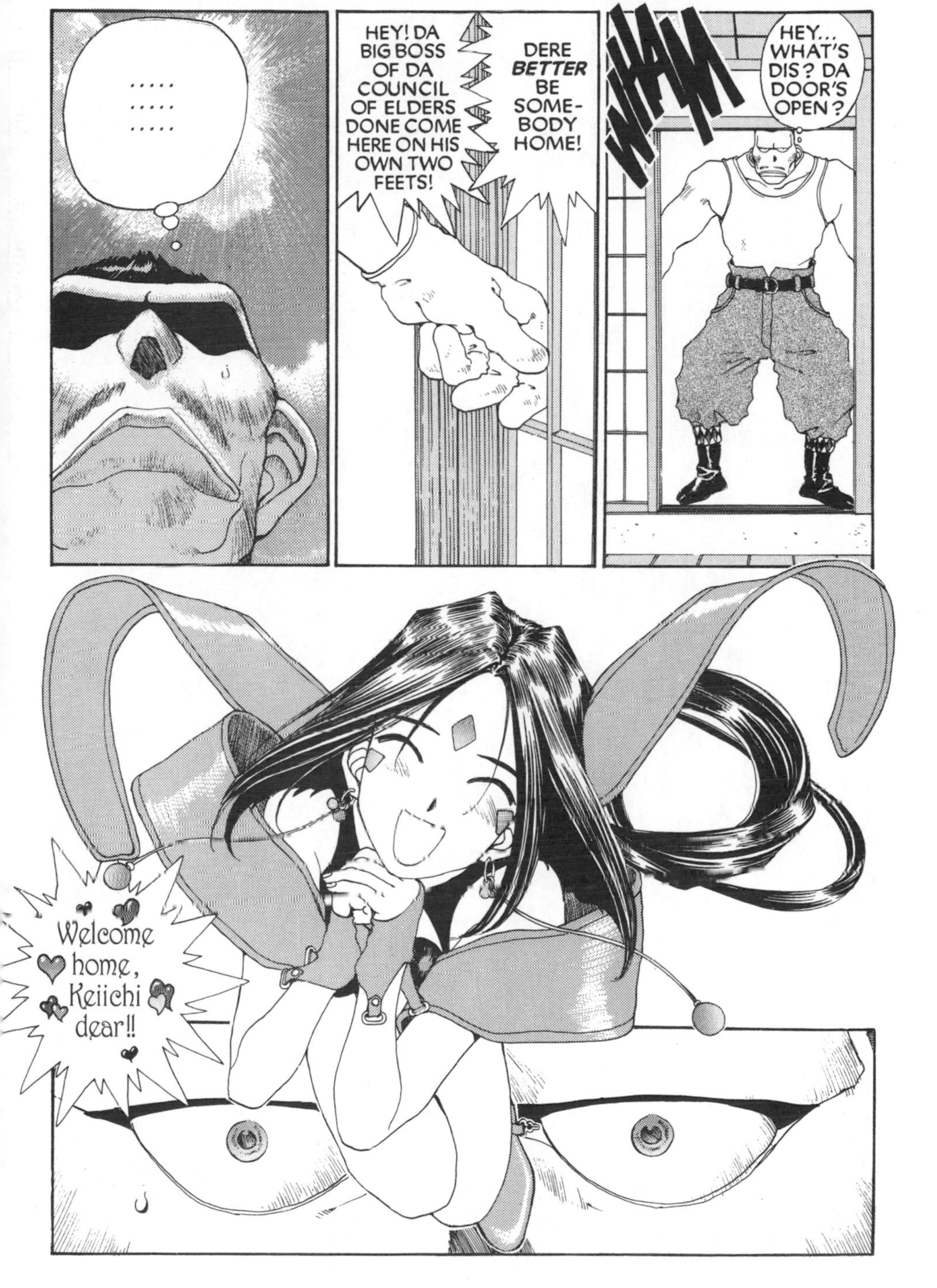
.....
.....
.....
HEY! DA BIG BOSS OF DA COUNCIL OF ELDERS DONE COME HERE ON HIS OWN TWO FEETS!
DERE BETTER BE SOMEBODY HOME!
WHAM
HEY... WHAT'S DIS? DA DOOR'S OPEN?
Welcome home, Keiichi dear!!

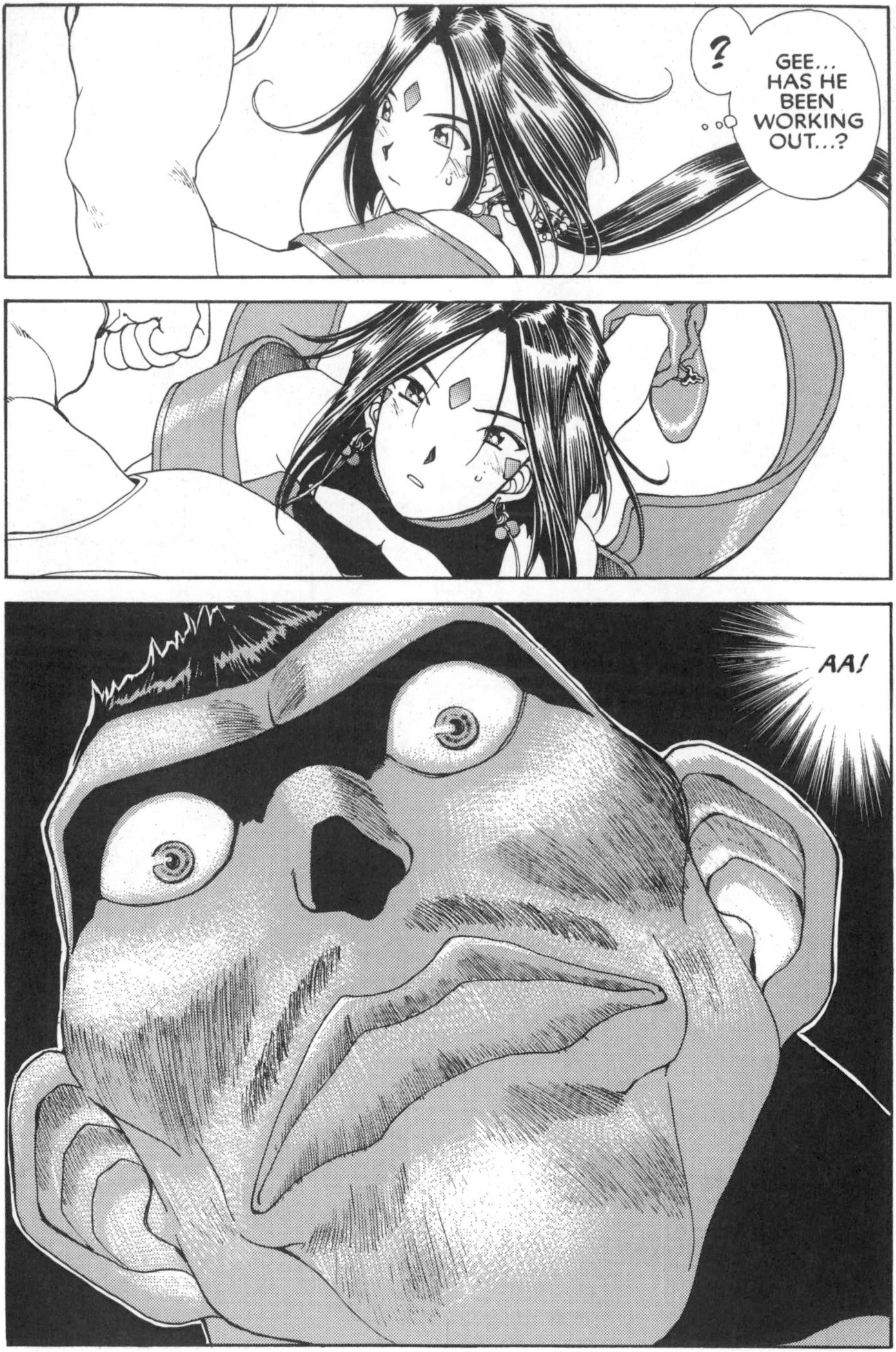
?
GEE... HAS HE BEEN WORKING OUT...?
AA!

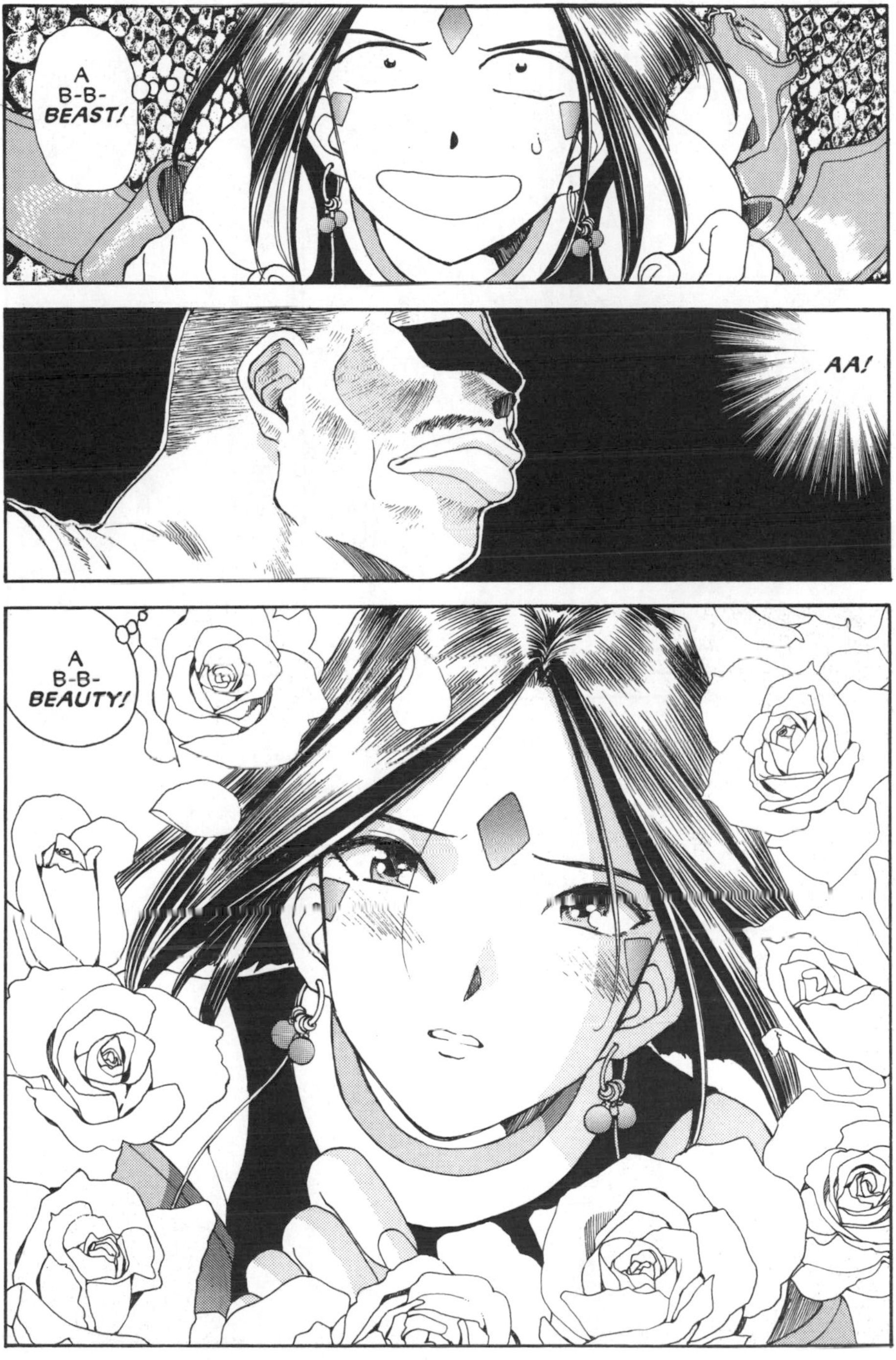
A B-B- BEAST!
AA!
A B-B- BEAUTY!

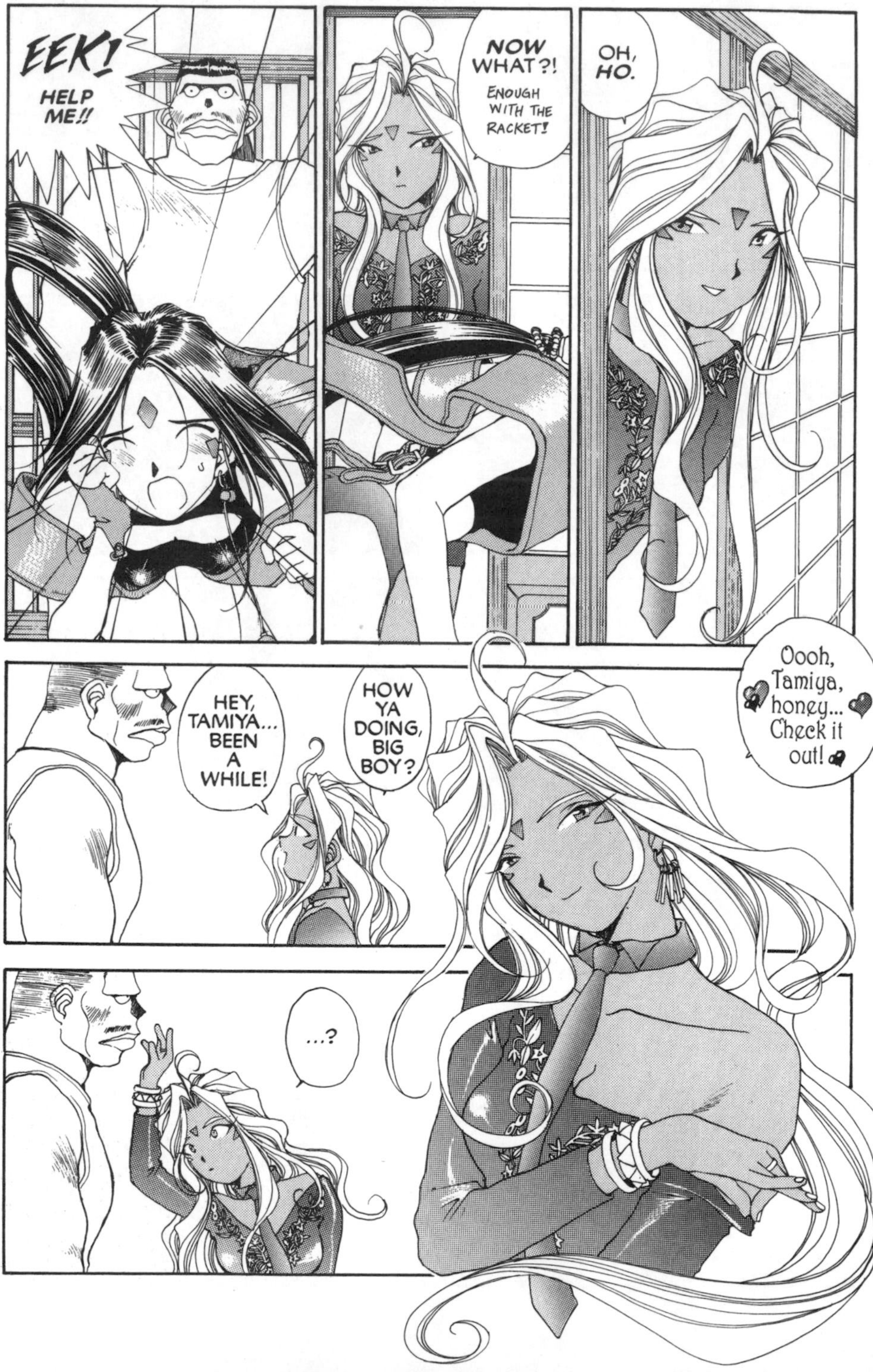
EEK!
HELP ME!!
NOW WHAT?! ENOUGH WITH THE RACKET!
OH, HO.
HEY, TAMIYA... BEEN A WHILE!
HOW YA DOING, BIG BOY?
Oooh, Tamiya, honey... Check it out!
...?

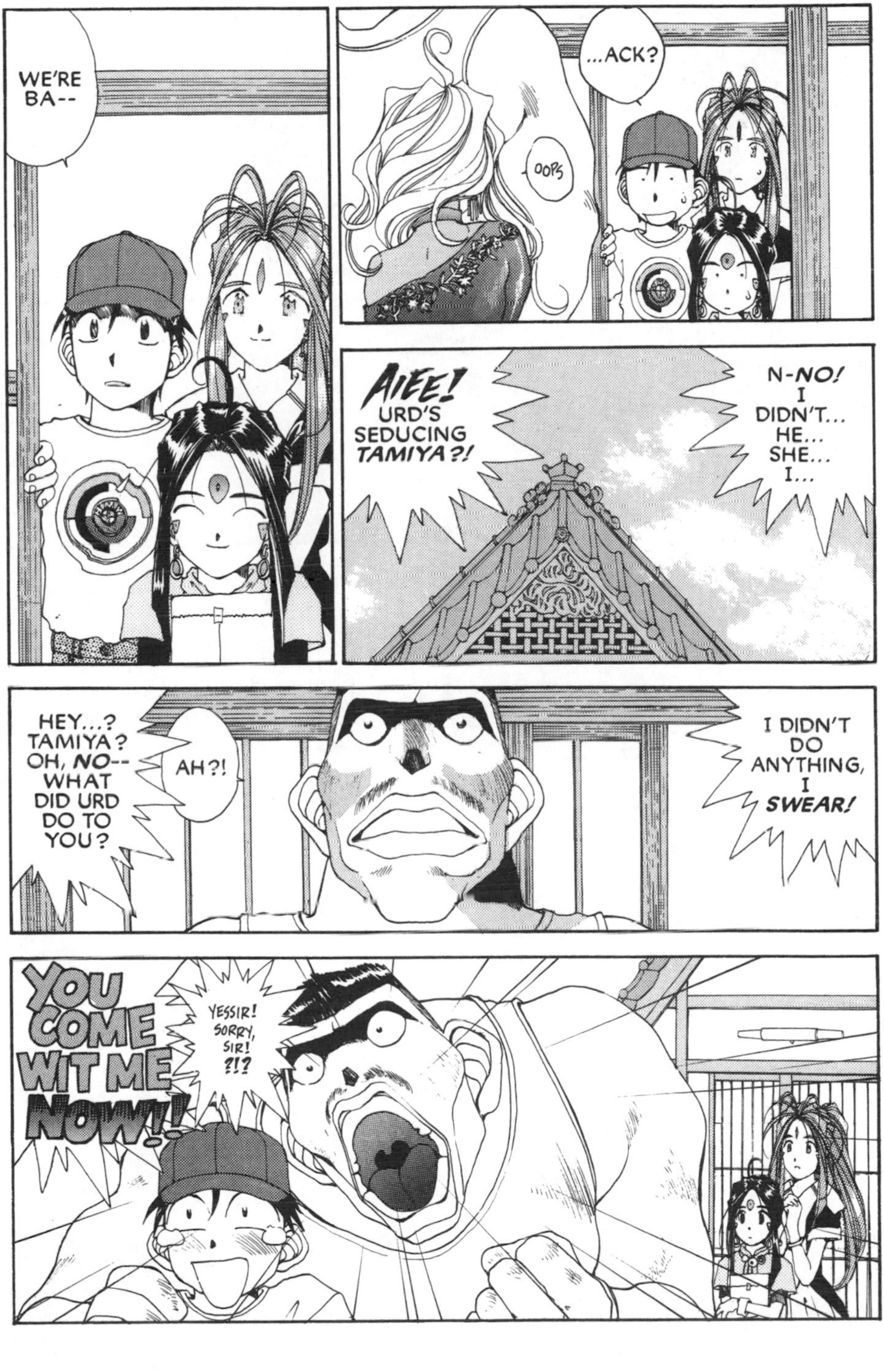
WE'RE BA--
...ACK?
OOPS
AIEE! URD'S SEDUCING TAMIYA?!
N-NO! I DIDN'T... HE... SHE... I...
HEY...? TAMIYA? OH, NO-- WHAT DID URD DO TO YOU?
AH?!
I DIDN'T DO ANYTHING, I SWEAR!
YOU COME WIT ME NOW!!
YESSIR! SORRY, SIR! ?!?

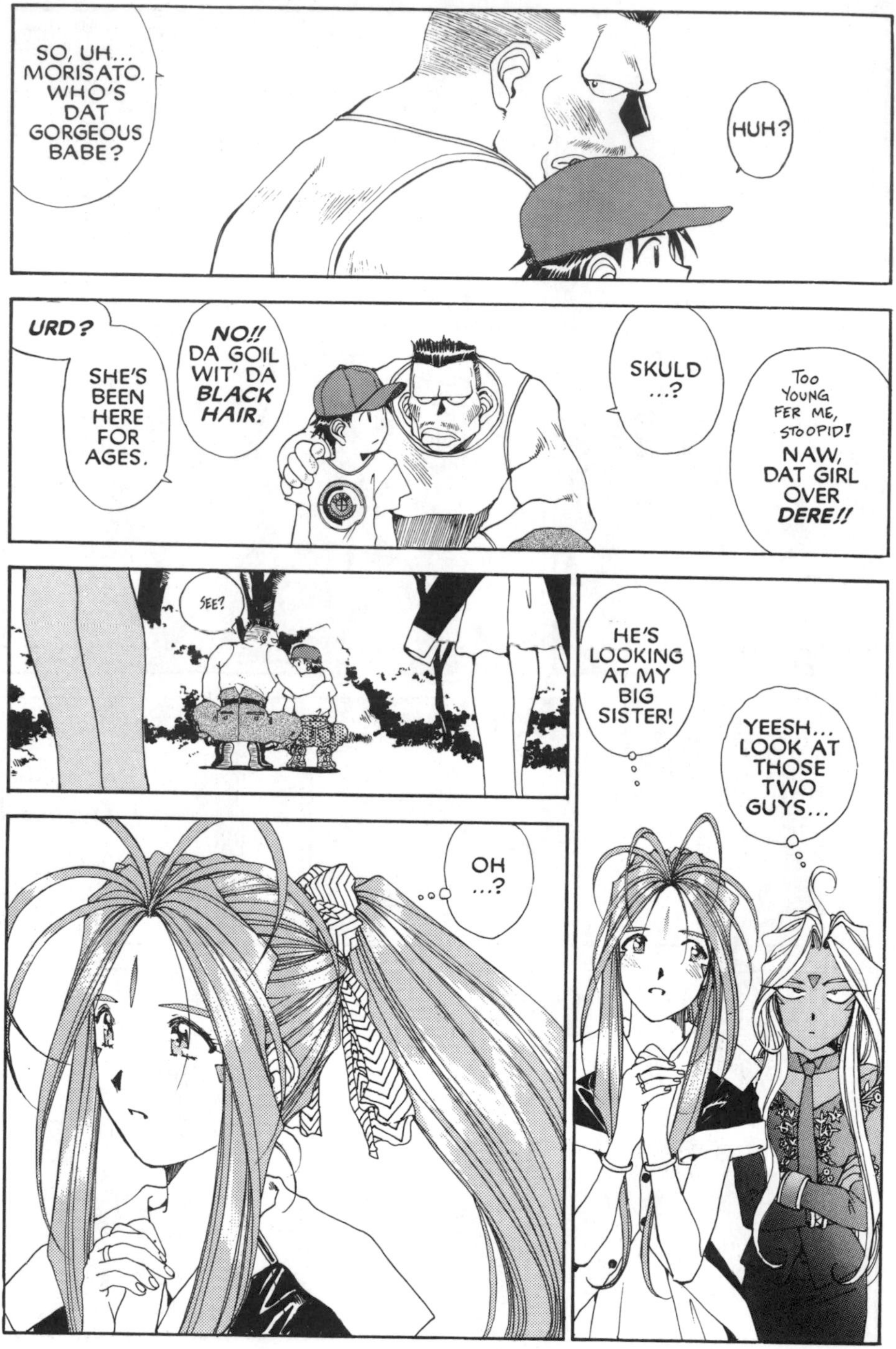
SO, UH... MORISATO. WHO'S DAT GORGEOUS BABE?
HUH?
URD? SHE'S BEEN HERE FOR AGES.
NO!! DA GOIL WIT' DA BLACK HAIR.
SKULD ...?
TOO YOUNG FER ME, STOOPID! NAW, DAT GIRL OVER DERE!!
SEE?
OH ...?
HE'S LOOKING AT MY BIG SISTER!
YEESH... LOOK AT THOSE TWO GUYS...

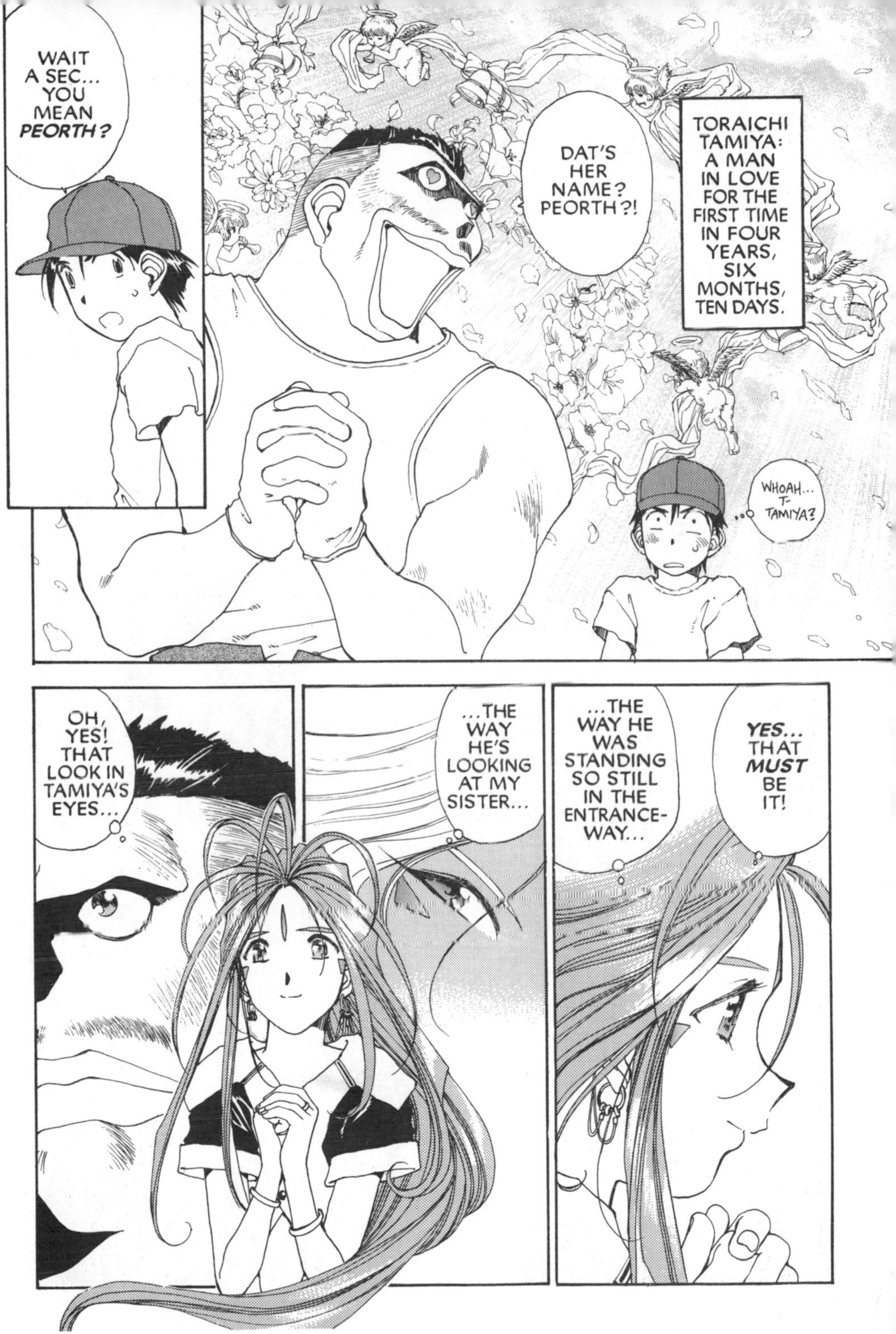
WAIT A SEC... YOU MEAN PEORTH?
DAT'S HER NAME? PEORTH?!
TORAICHI TAMIYA: A MAN IN LOVE FOR THE FIRST TIME IN FOUR YEARS, SIX MONTHS, TEN DAYS.
WHOAH... T-TAMIYA?
OH, YES! THAT LOOK IN TAMIYA'S EYES...
...THE WAY HE'S LOOKING AT MY SISTER...
...THE WAY HE WAS STANDING SO STILL IN THE ENTRANCE-WAY...
YES... THAT MUST BE IT!

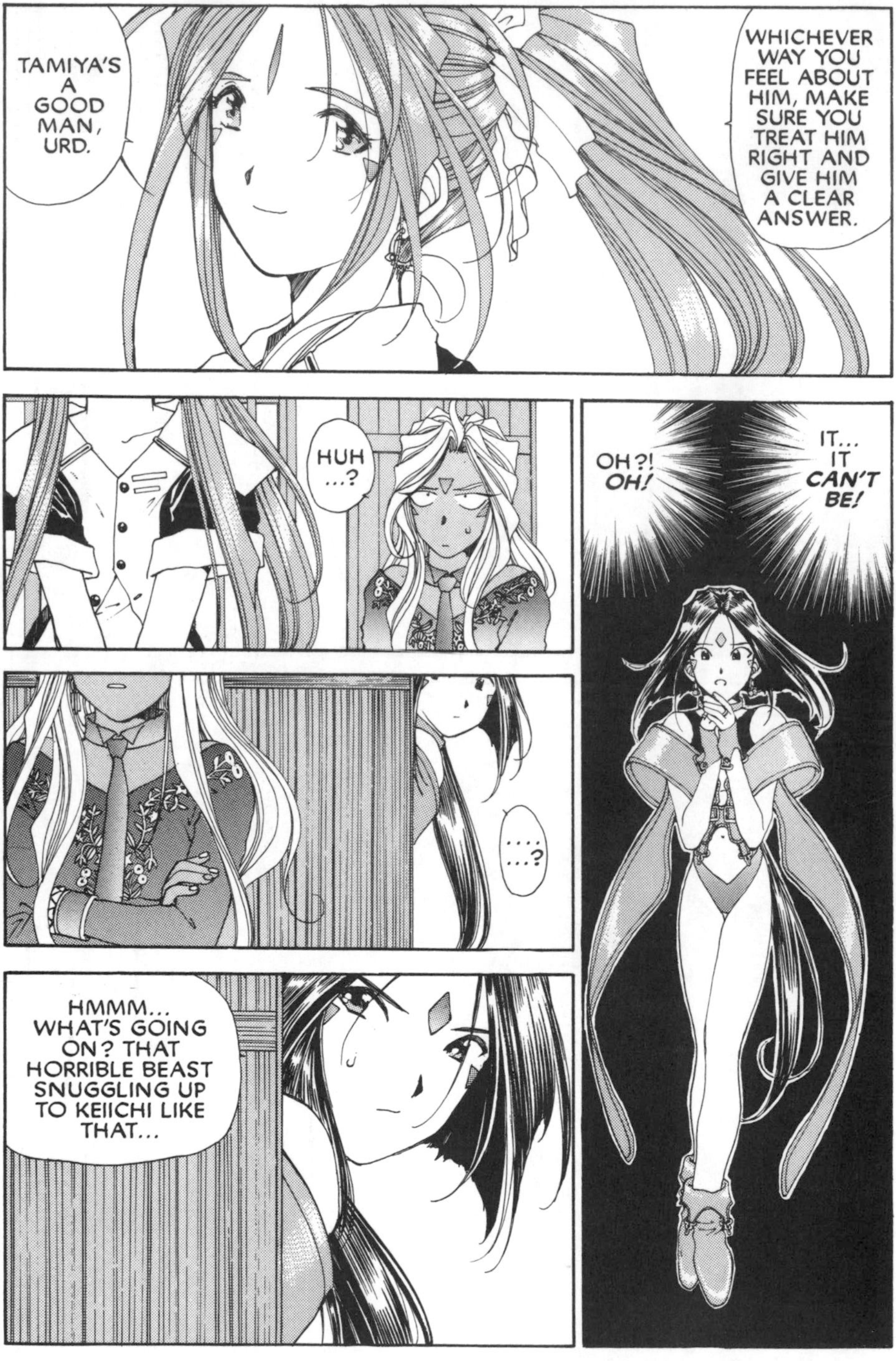
TAMIYA'S A GOOD MAN, URD.
WHICHEVER WAY YOU FEEL ABOUT HIM, MAKE SURE YOU TREAT HIM RIGHT AND GIVE HIM A CLEAR ANSWER.
HUH ...?
....?
HMMM... WHAT'S GOING ON? THAT HORRIBLE BEAST SNUGGLING UP TO KEIICHI LIKE THAT...
OH?! *OH!*
IT... IT *CAN'T BE!*

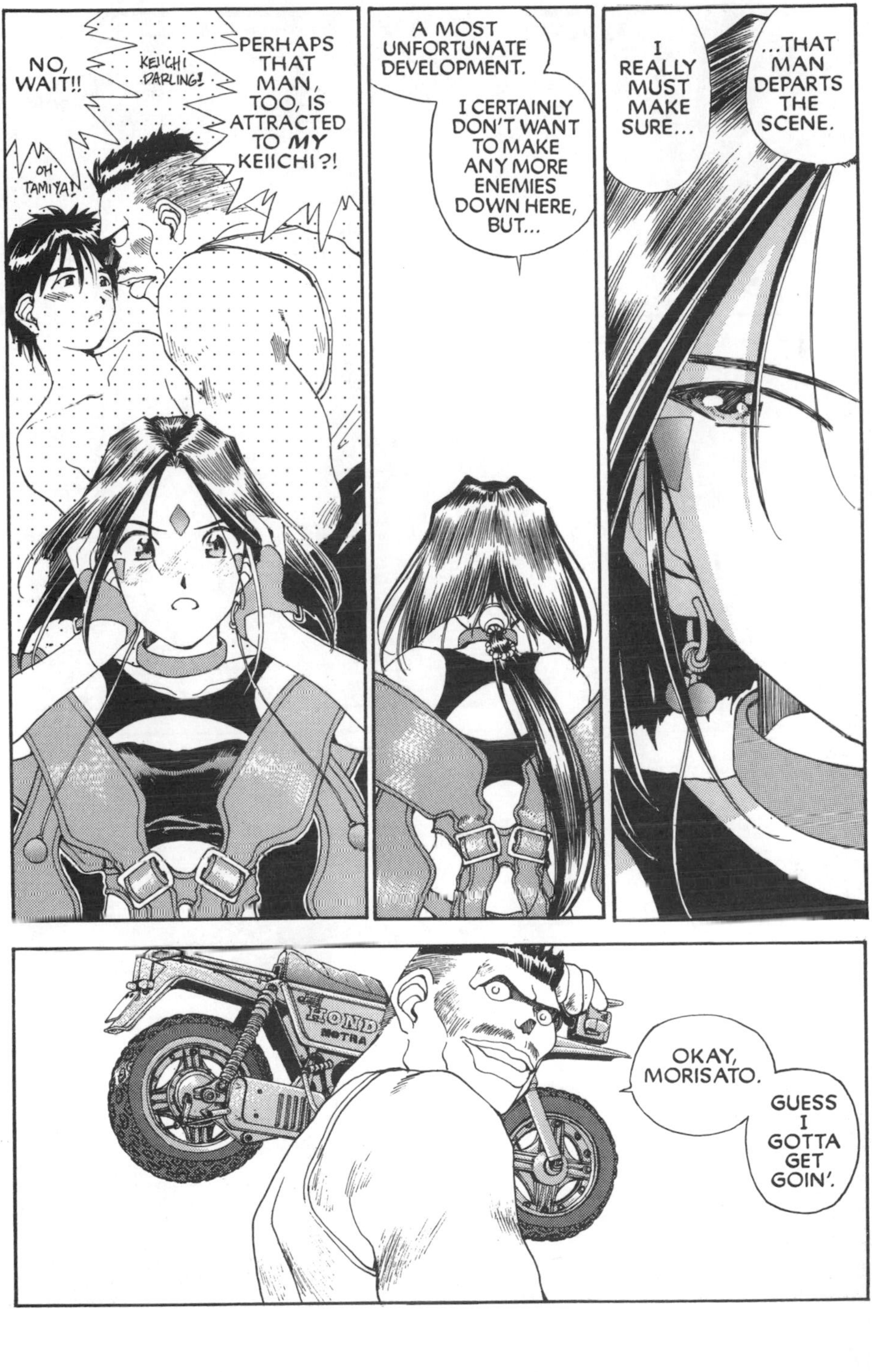
NO, WAIT!!
OH TAMIYA!
KEIICHI DARLING!
PERHAPS THAT MAN, TOO, IS ATTRACTED TO MY KEIICHI?!
A MOST UNFORTUNATE DEVELOPMENT.
I CERTAINLY DON'T WANT TO MAKE ANY MORE ENEMIES DOWN HERE, BUT...
I REALLY MUST MAKE SURE...
...THAT MAN DEPARTS THE SCENE.
HOND
MOTRA
OKAY, MORISATO.
GUESS I GOTTA GET GOIN'.

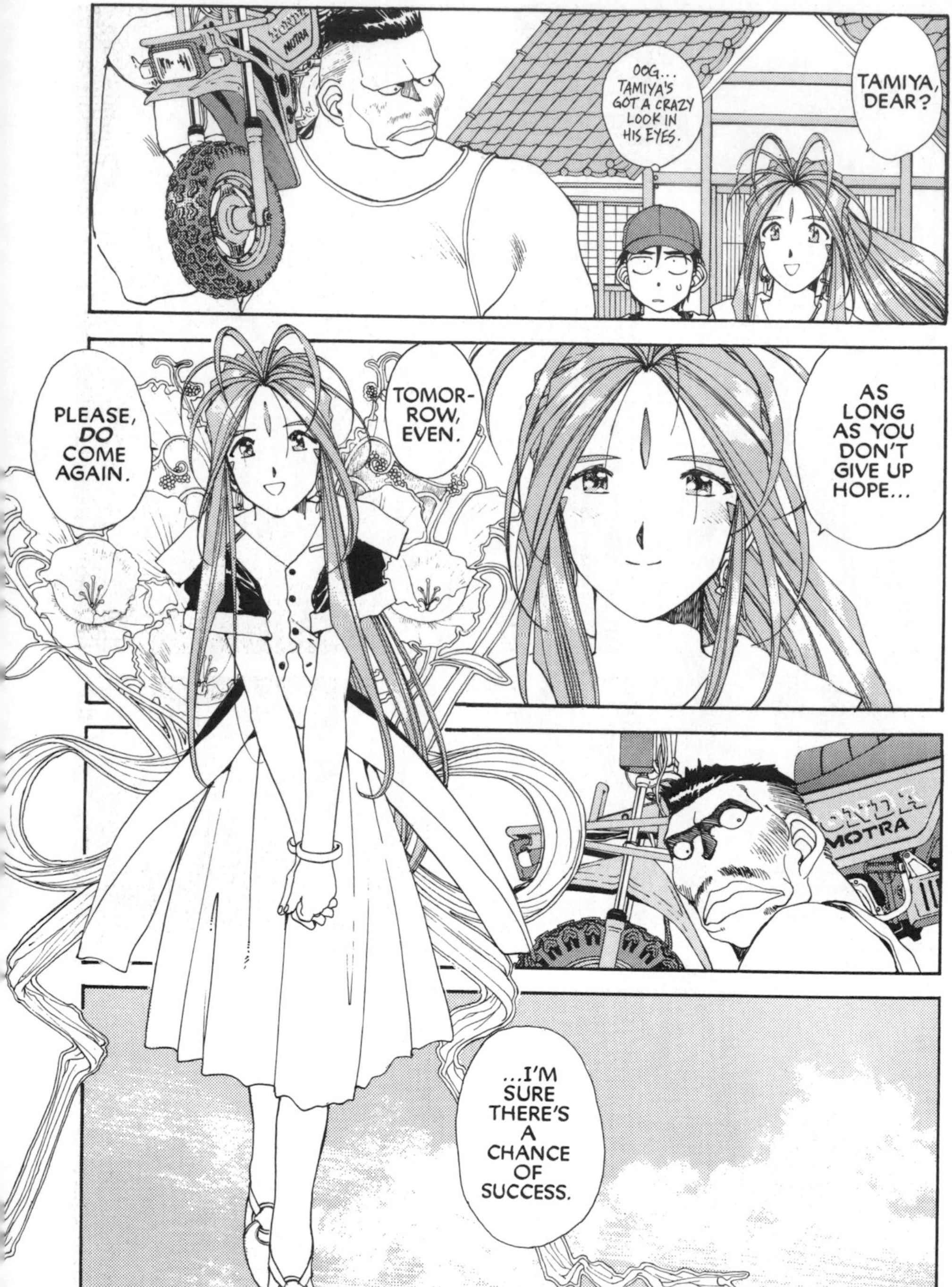
OOG... TAMIYA'S GOT A CRAZY LOOK IN HIS EYES.
TAMIYA, DEAR?
PLEASE, ***DO*** COME AGAIN.
TOMOR-ROW, EVEN.
AS LONG AS YOU DON'T GIVE UP HOPE...
...I'M SURE THERE'S A CHANCE OF SUCCESS.

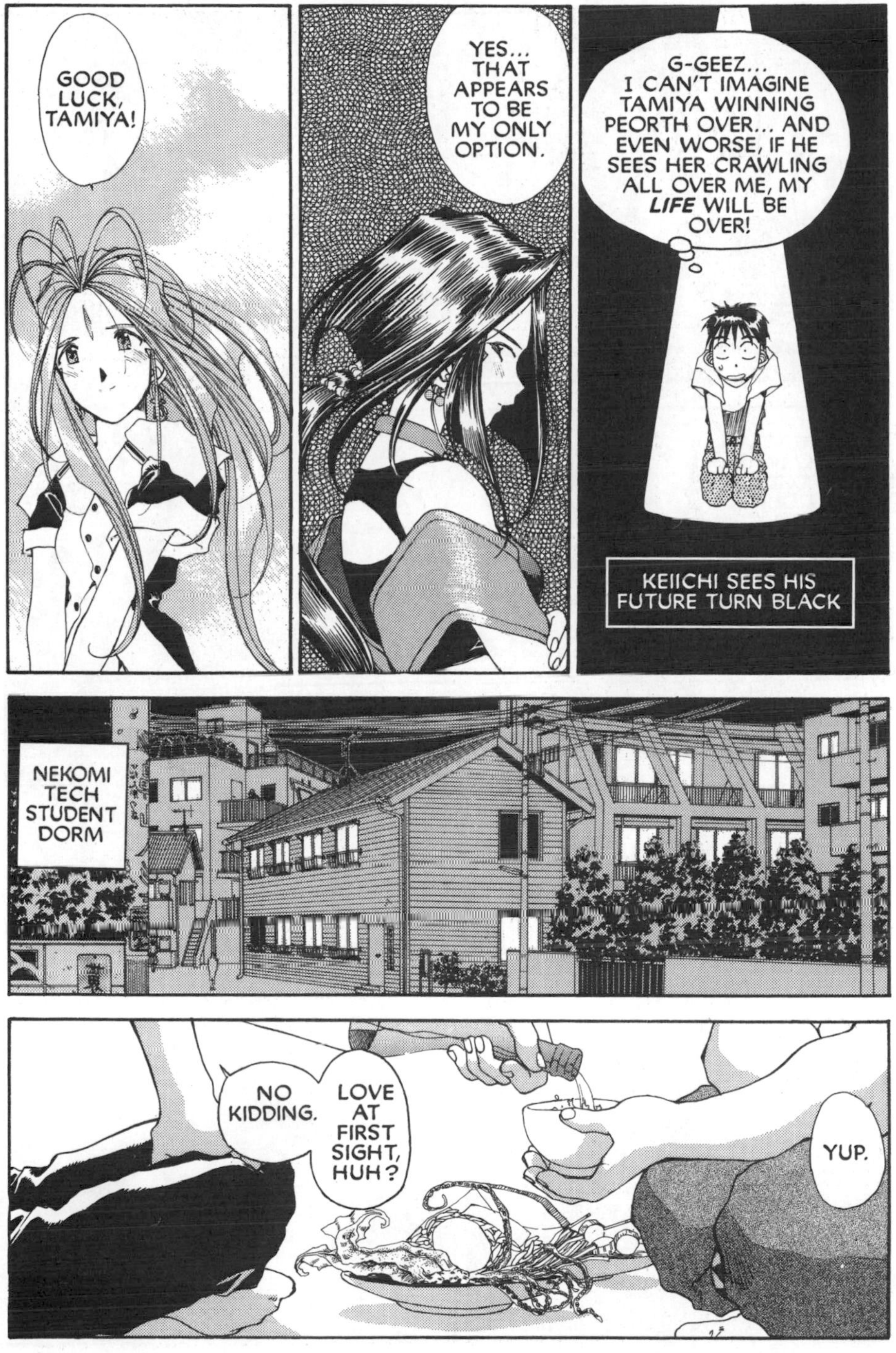
GOOD LUCK, TAMIYA!
YES... THAT APPEARS TO BE MY ONLY OPTION.
G-GEEZ... I CAN'T IMAGINE TAMIYA WINNING PEORTH OVER... AND EVEN WORSE, IF HE SEES HER CRAWLING ALL OVER ME, MY LIFE WILL BE OVER!
KEIICHI SEES HIS FUTURE TURN BLACK
NEKOMI TECH STUDENT DORM
NO KIDDING.
LOVE AT FIRST SIGHT, HUH?
YUP.

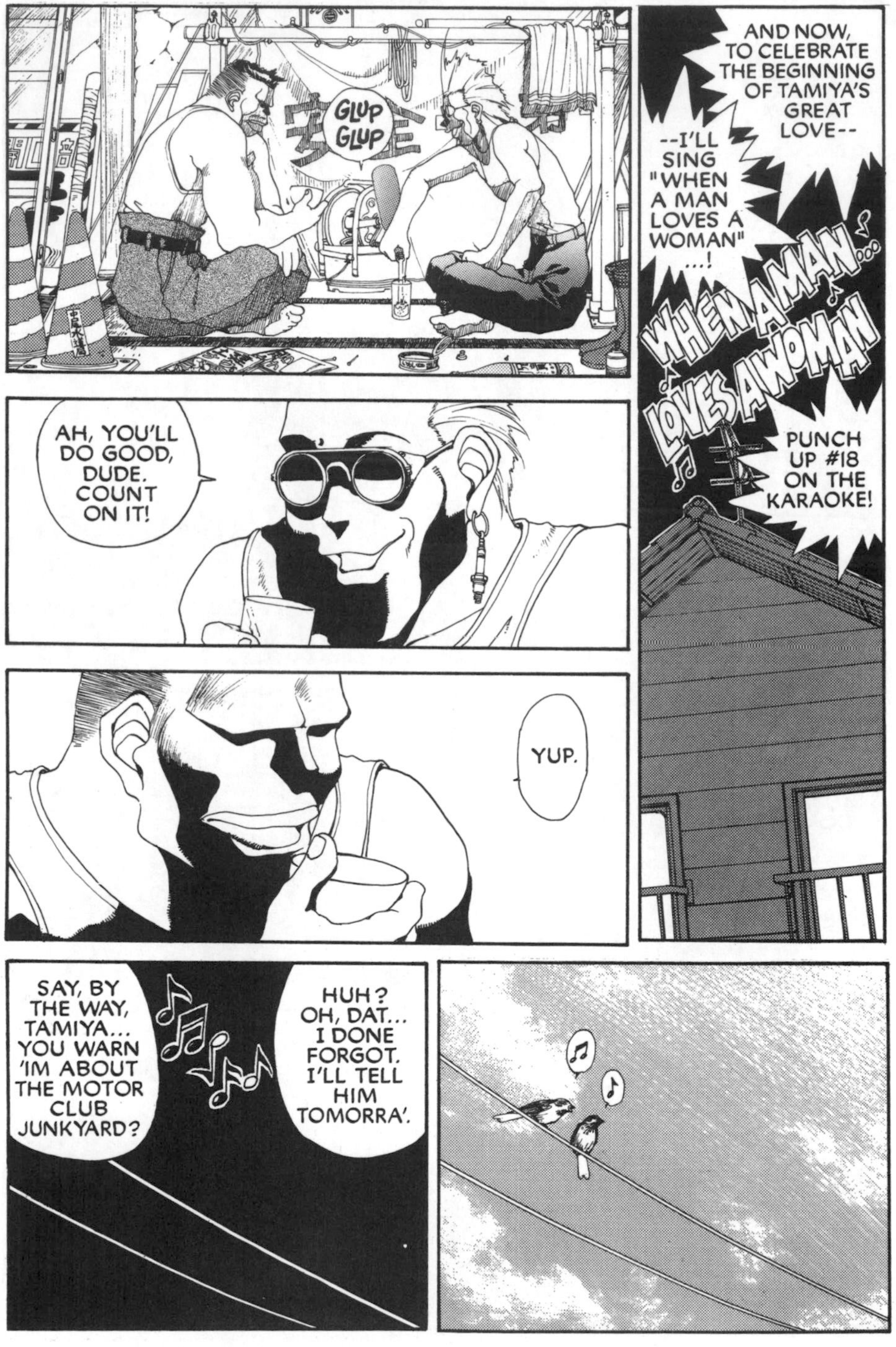
GLUP GLUP
AH, YOU'LL DO GOOD, DUDE. COUNT ON IT!
YUP.
AND NOW, TO CELEBRATE THE BEGINNING OF TAMIYA'S GREAT LOVE--
--I'LL SING "WHEN A MAN LOVES A WOMAN" ...!
WHEN A MAN... LOVES A WOMAN
PUNCH UP #18 ON THE KARAOKE!
SAY, BY THE WAY, TAMIYA... YOU WARN 'IM ABOUT THE MOTOR CLUB JUNKYARD?
HUH? OH, DAT... I DONE FORGOT. I'LL TELL HIM TOMORRA'.

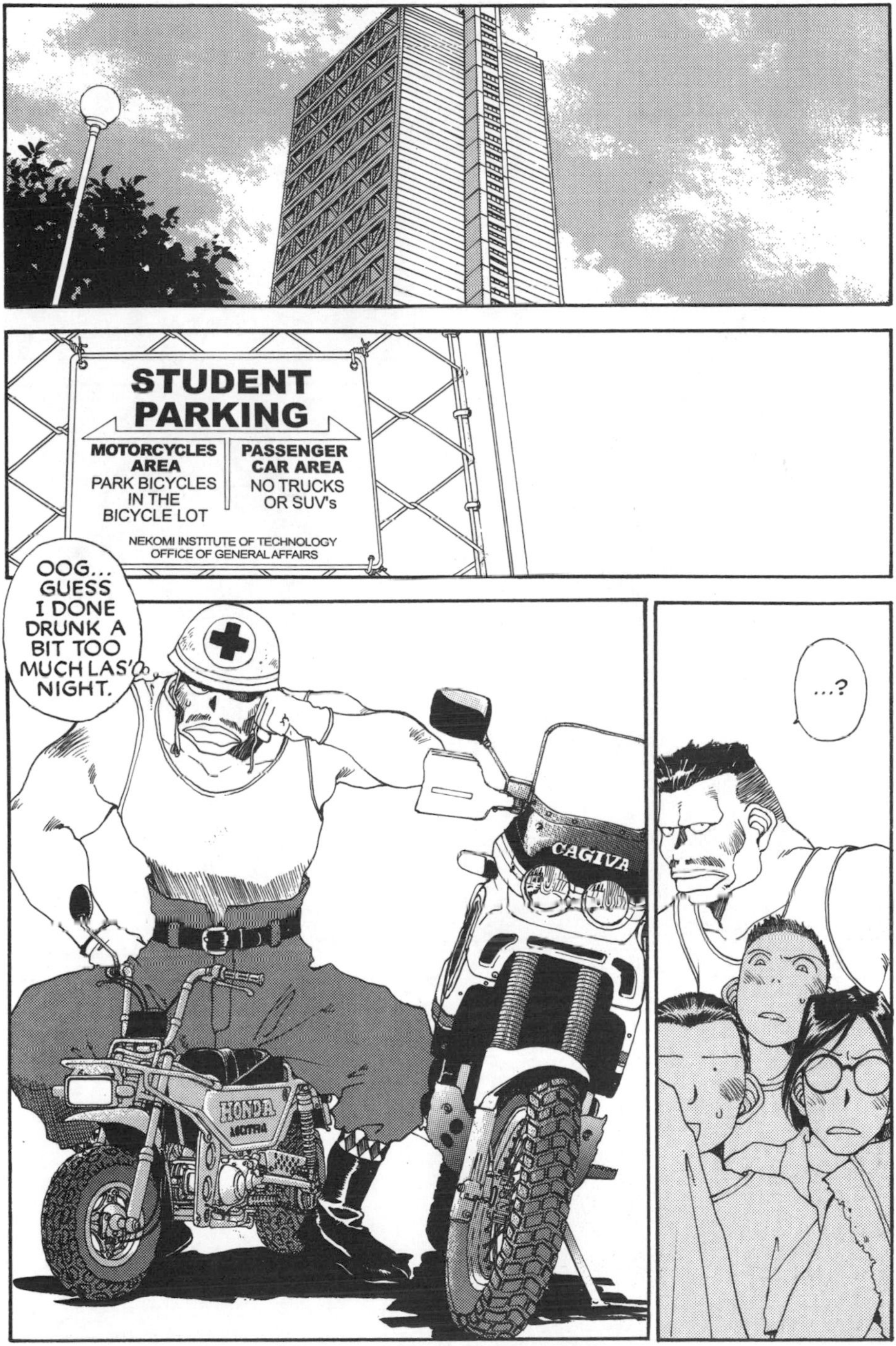
STUDENT PARKING
MOTORCYCLES AREA
PARK BICYCLES IN THE BICYCLE LOT
PASSENGER CAR AREA
NO TRUCKS OR SUV's
NEKOMI INSTITUTE OF TECHNOLOGY
OFFICE OF GENERAL AFFAIRS
OOG... GUESS I DONE DRUNK A BIT TOO MUCH LAS' NIGHT.
CAGIVA
HONDA
...?

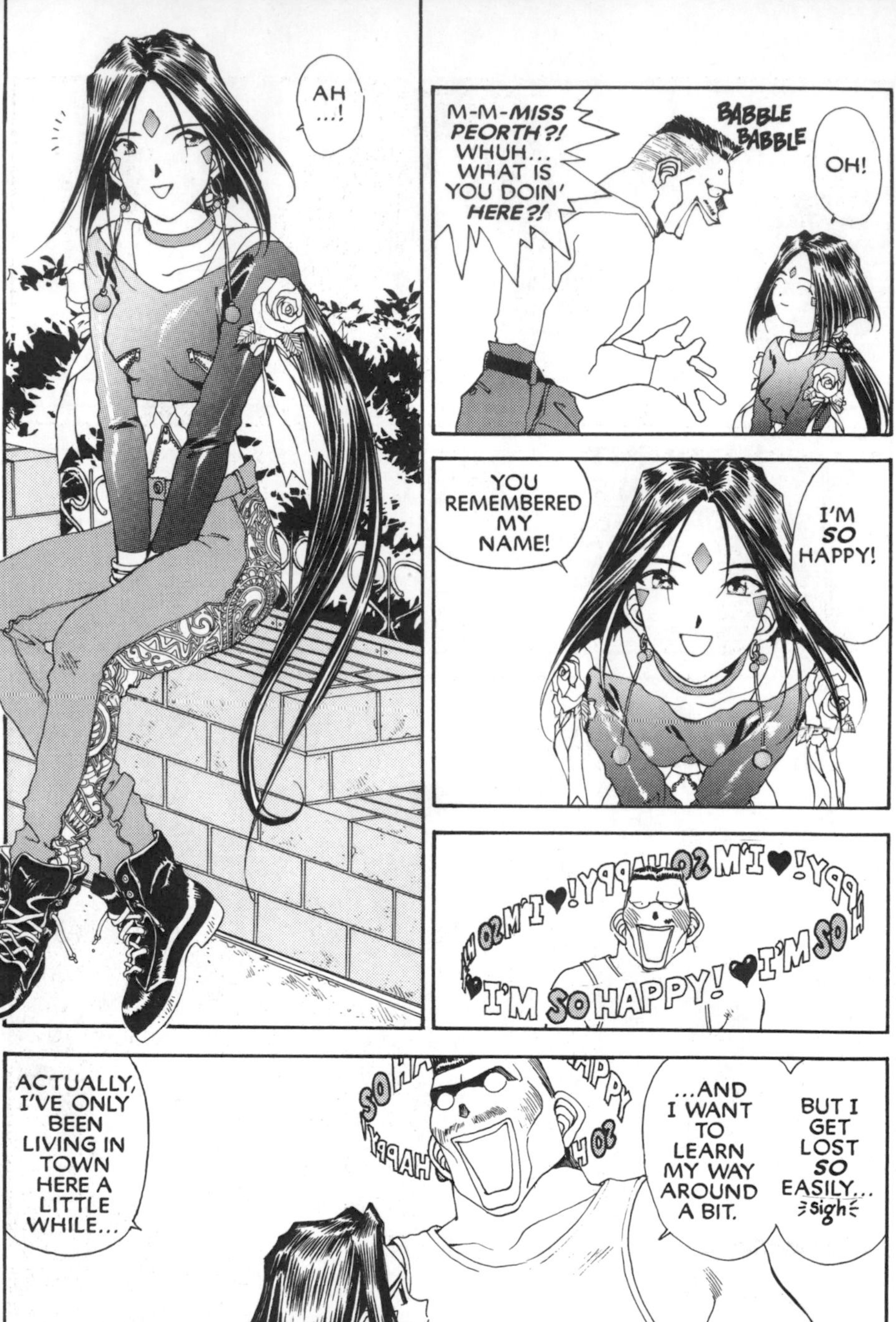
AH ...!
M-M-MISS PEORTH?! WHUH... WHAT IS YOU DOIN' HERE?!
BABBLE BABBLE
OH!
YOU REMEMBERED MY NAME!
I'M SO HAPPY!
I'M SO HAPPY! ♥ I'M SO HAPPY! ♥ I'M SO HAPPY!
ACTUALLY, I'VE ONLY BEEN LIVING IN TOWN HERE A LITTLE WHILE...
...AND I WANT TO LEARN MY WAY AROUND A BIT.
BUT I GET LOST SO EASILY... sigh

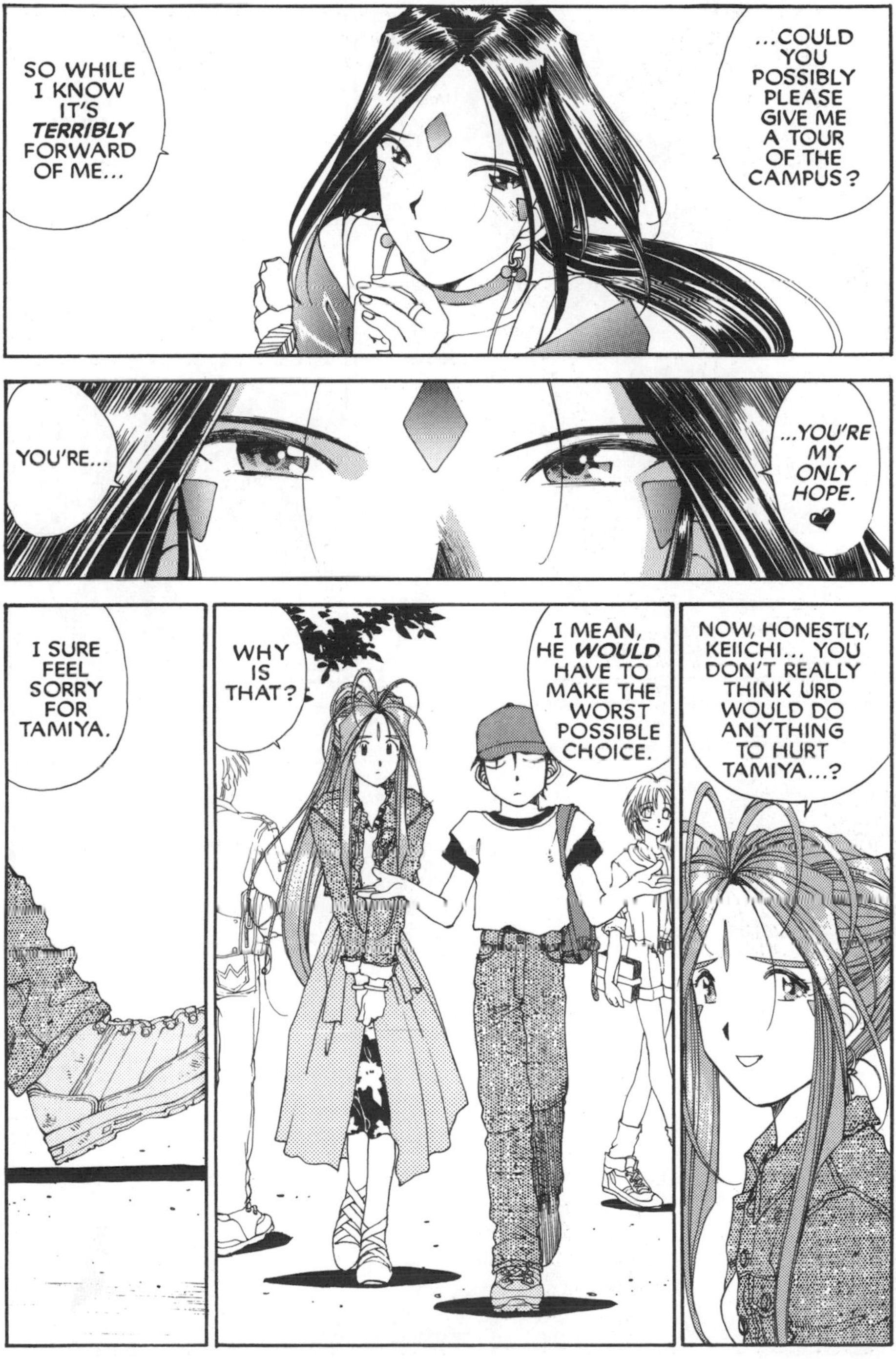
SO WHILE I KNOW IT'S *TERRIBLY* FORWARD OF ME...
...COULD YOU POSSIBLY PLEASE GIVE ME A TOUR OF THE CAMPUS?
YOU'RE...
...*YOU'RE MY ONLY HOPE.* ❤
I SURE FEEL SORRY FOR TAMIYA.
WHY IS THAT?
I MEAN, HE *WOULD* HAVE TO MAKE THE WORST POSSIBLE CHOICE.
NOW, HONESTLY, KEIICHI... YOU DON'T REALLY THINK URD WOULD DO ANYTHING TO HURT TAMIYA...?

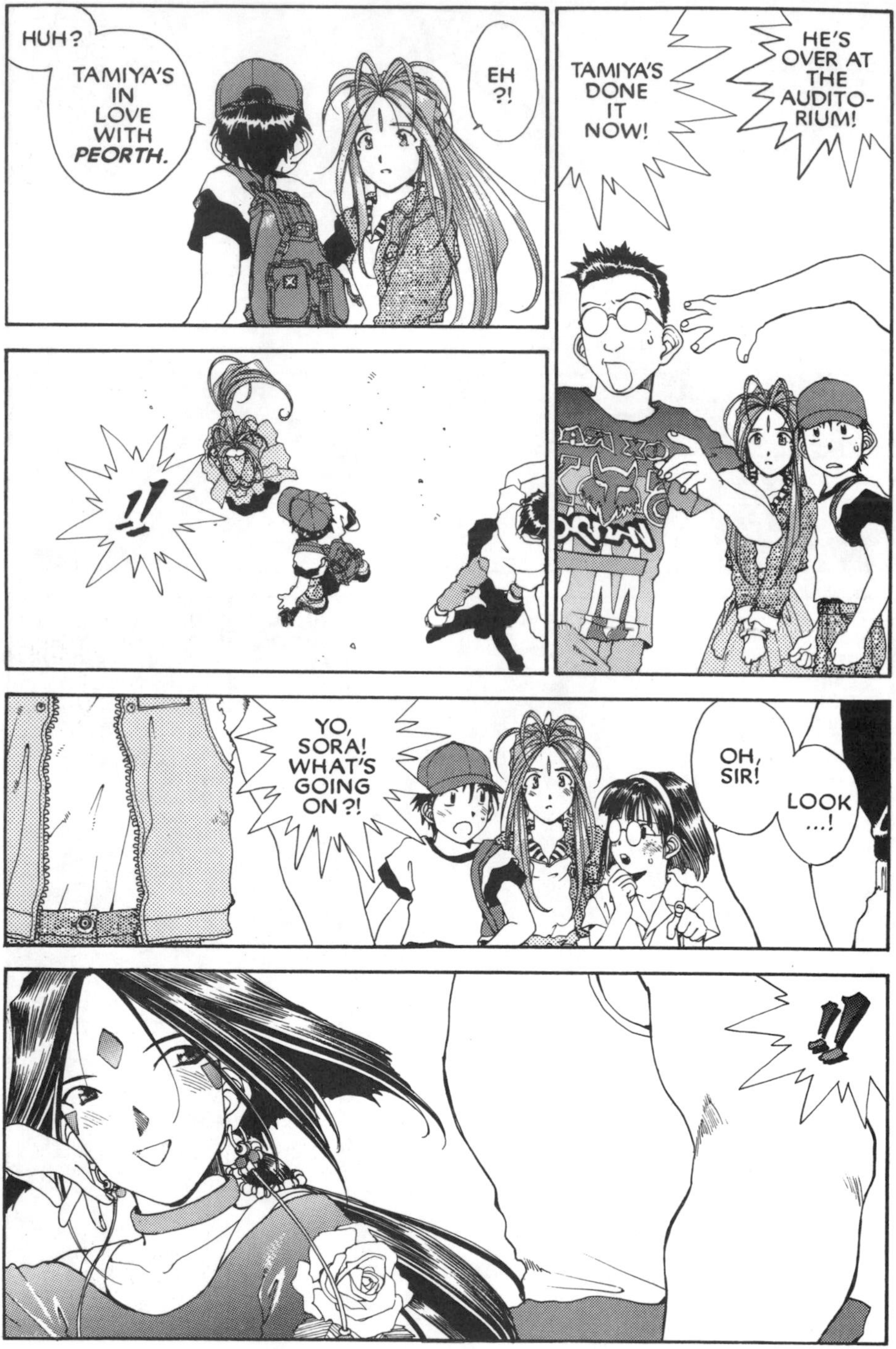
HUH?
TAMIYA'S IN LOVE WITH PEORTH.
EH ?!
TAMIYA'S DONE IT NOW!
HE'S OVER AT THE AUDITO-RIUM!
!!
YO, SORA! WHAT'S GOING ON ?!
OH, SIR!
LOOK ...!
!!

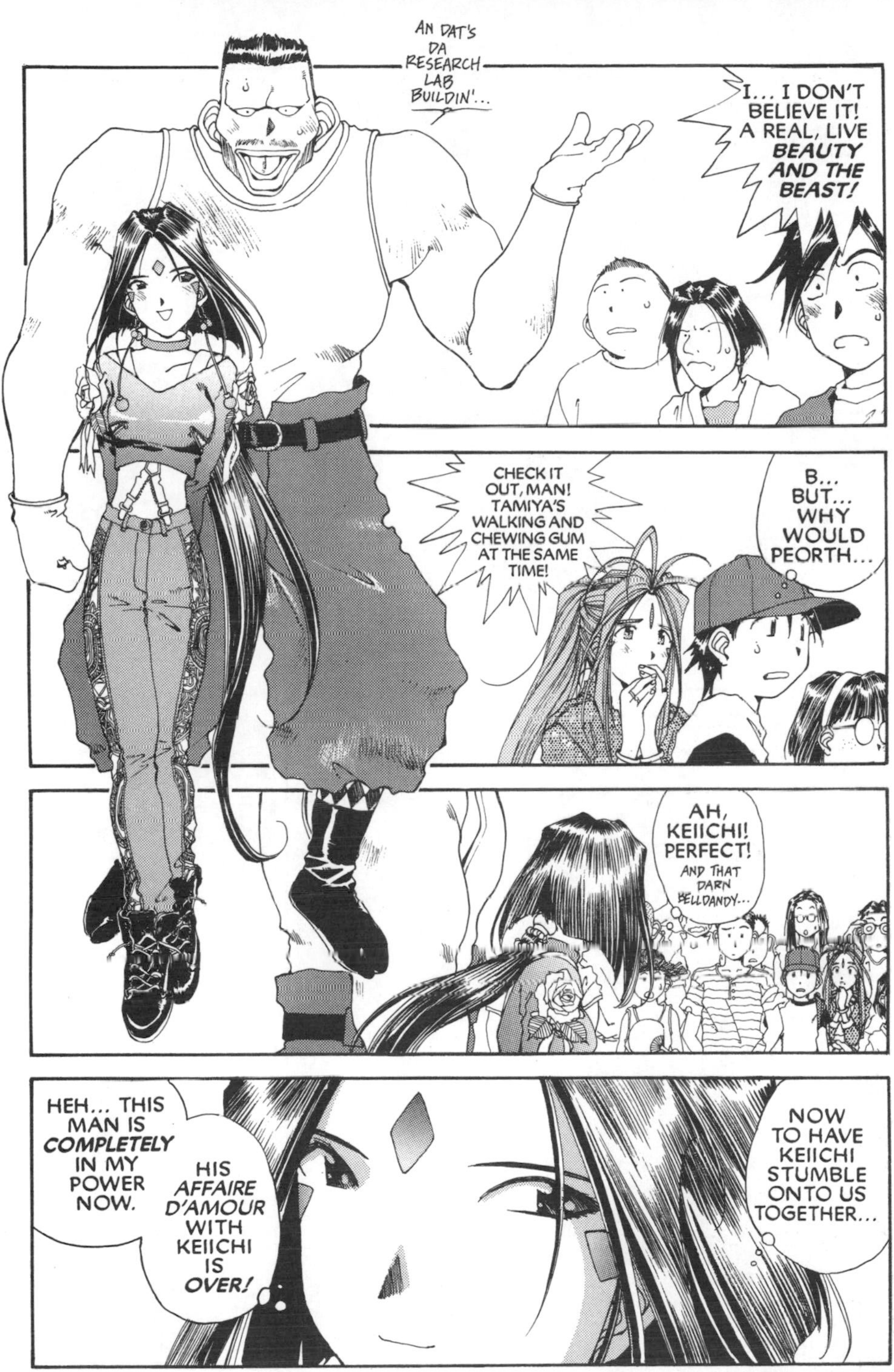
AN DAT'S DA RESEARCH LAB BUILDIN'...
I... I DON'T BELIEVE IT! A REAL, LIVE *BEAUTY AND THE BEAST!*
CHECK IT OUT, MAN! TAMIYA'S WALKING AND CHEWING GUM AT THE SAME TIME!
B... BUT... WHY WOULD PEORTH...
AH, KEIICHI! PERFECT!
AND THAT DARN BELLDANDY...
HEH... THIS MAN IS *COMPLETELY* IN MY POWER NOW.
HIS *AFFAIRE D'AMOUR* WITH KEIICHI IS *OVER!*
NOW TO HAVE KEIICHI STUMBLE ONTO US TOGETHER...

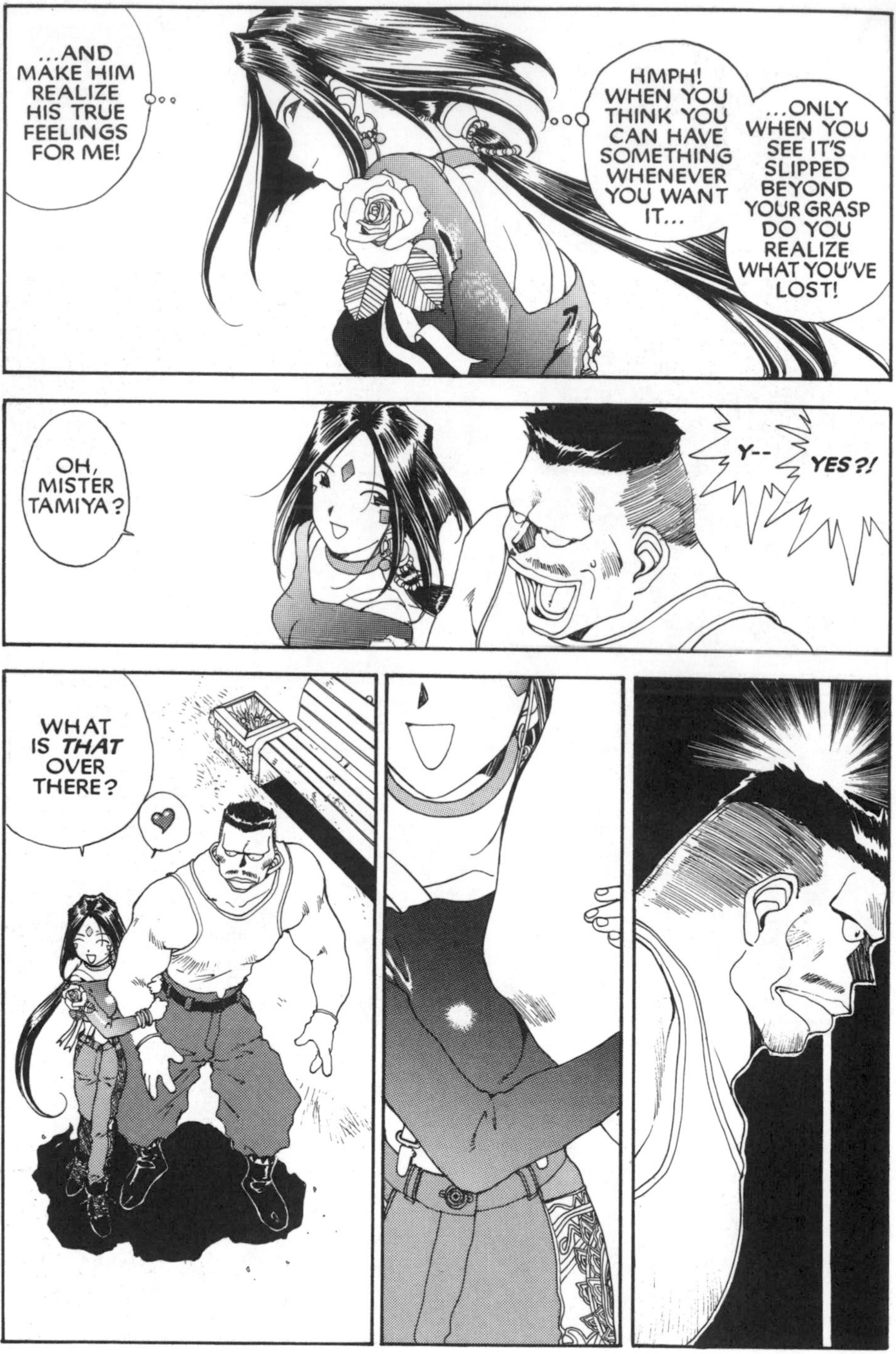
...AND MAKE HIM REALIZE HIS TRUE FEELINGS FOR ME!
HMPH! WHEN YOU THINK YOU CAN HAVE SOMETHING WHENEVER YOU WANT IT...
...ONLY WHEN YOU SEE IT'S SLIPPED BEYOND YOUR GRASP DO YOU REALIZE WHAT YOU'VE LOST!
OH, MISTER TAMIYA?
Y--
YES?!
WHAT IS *THAT* OVER THERE?
♥

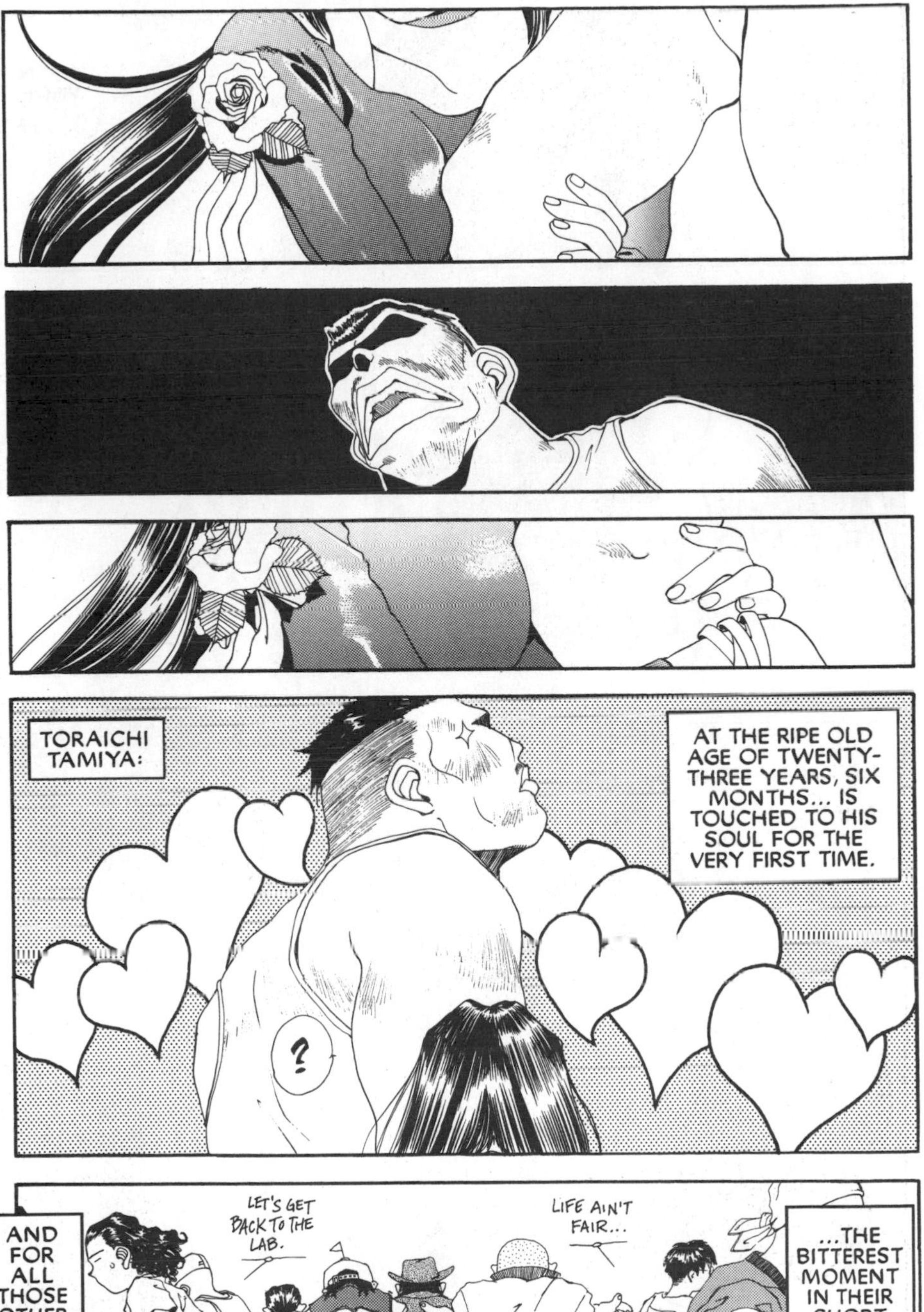
TORAICHI TAMIYA:
AT THE RIPE OLD AGE OF TWENTY-THREE YEARS, SIX MONTHS... IS TOUCHED TO HIS SOUL FOR THE VERY FIRST TIME.
?
AND FOR ALL THOSE OTHER GUYS...
LET'S GET BACK TO THE LAB.
LIFE AIN'T FAIR...
...THE BITTEREST MOMENT IN THEIR SHORT LIVES.

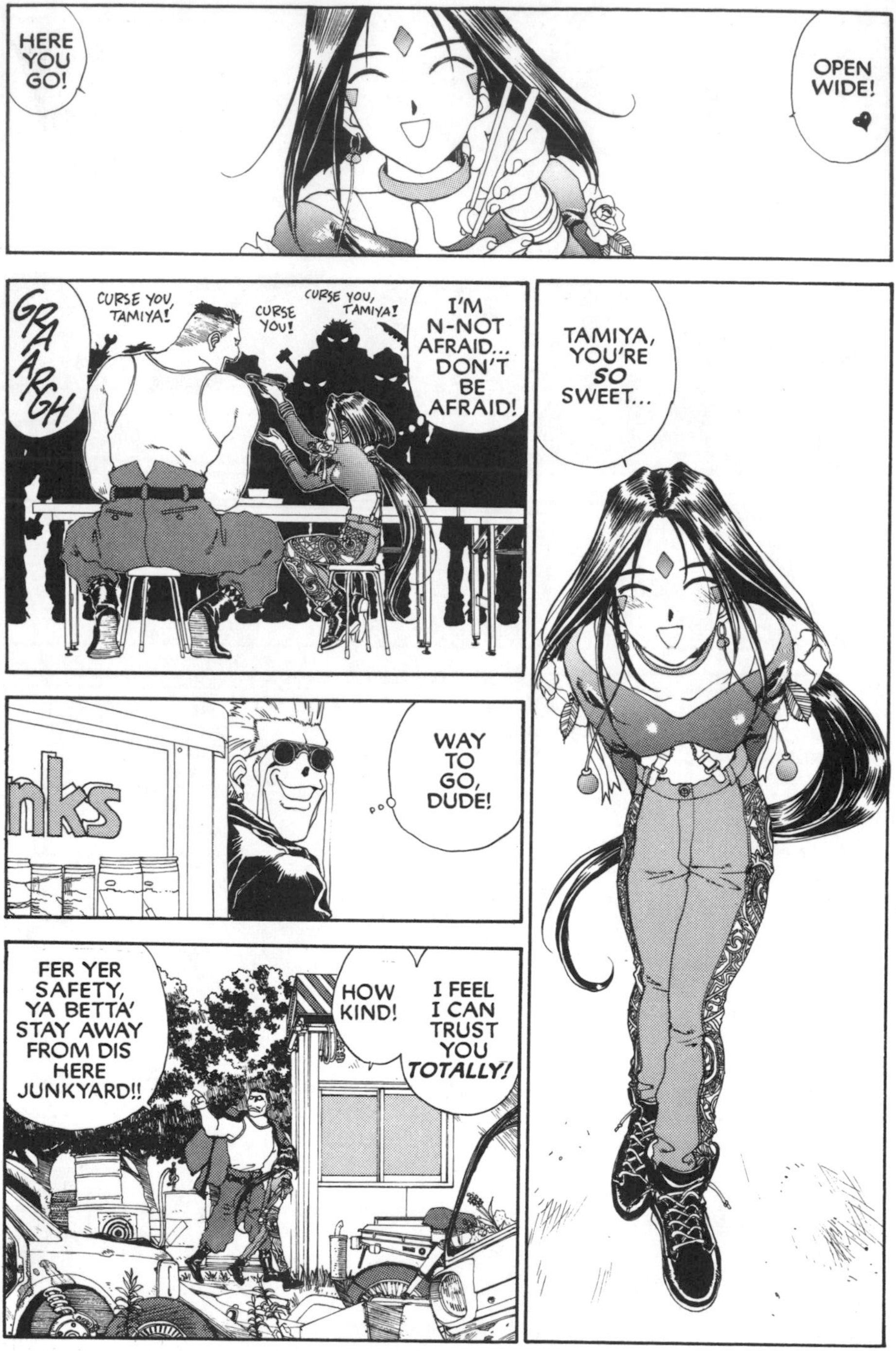
HERE YOU GO!
OPEN WIDE! ♥
GRAAARGH
CURSE YOU, TAMIYA!
CURSE YOU!
CURSE YOU, TAMIYA!
I'M N-NOT AFRAID... DON'T BE AFRAID!
WAY TO GO, DUDE!
FER YER SAFETY, YA BETTA' STAY AWAY FROM DIS HERE JUNKYARD!!
HOW KIND!
I FEEL I CAN TRUST YOU *TOTALLY!*
TAMIYA, YOU'RE *SO* SWEET...

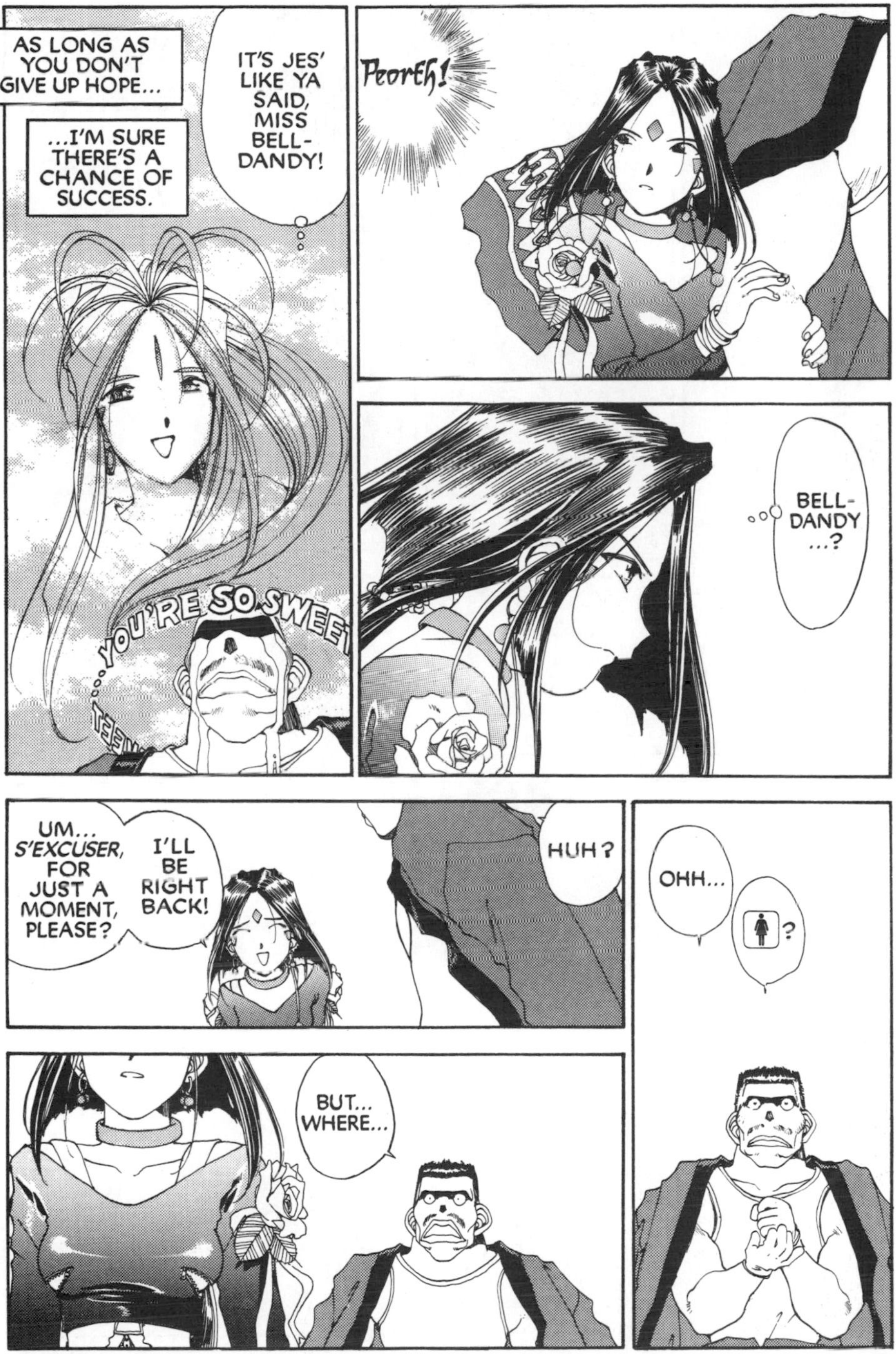
AS LONG AS YOU DON'T GIVE UP HOPE...
...I'M SURE THERE'S A CHANCE OF SUCCESS.
IT'S JES' LIKE YA SAID, MISS BELL-DANDY!
YOU'RE SO SWEET
Peorth!
BELL-DANDY ...?
UM... S'EXCUSER, FOR JUST A MOMENT, PLEASE?
I'LL BE RIGHT BACK!
HUH?
BUT... WHERE...
OHH...
?

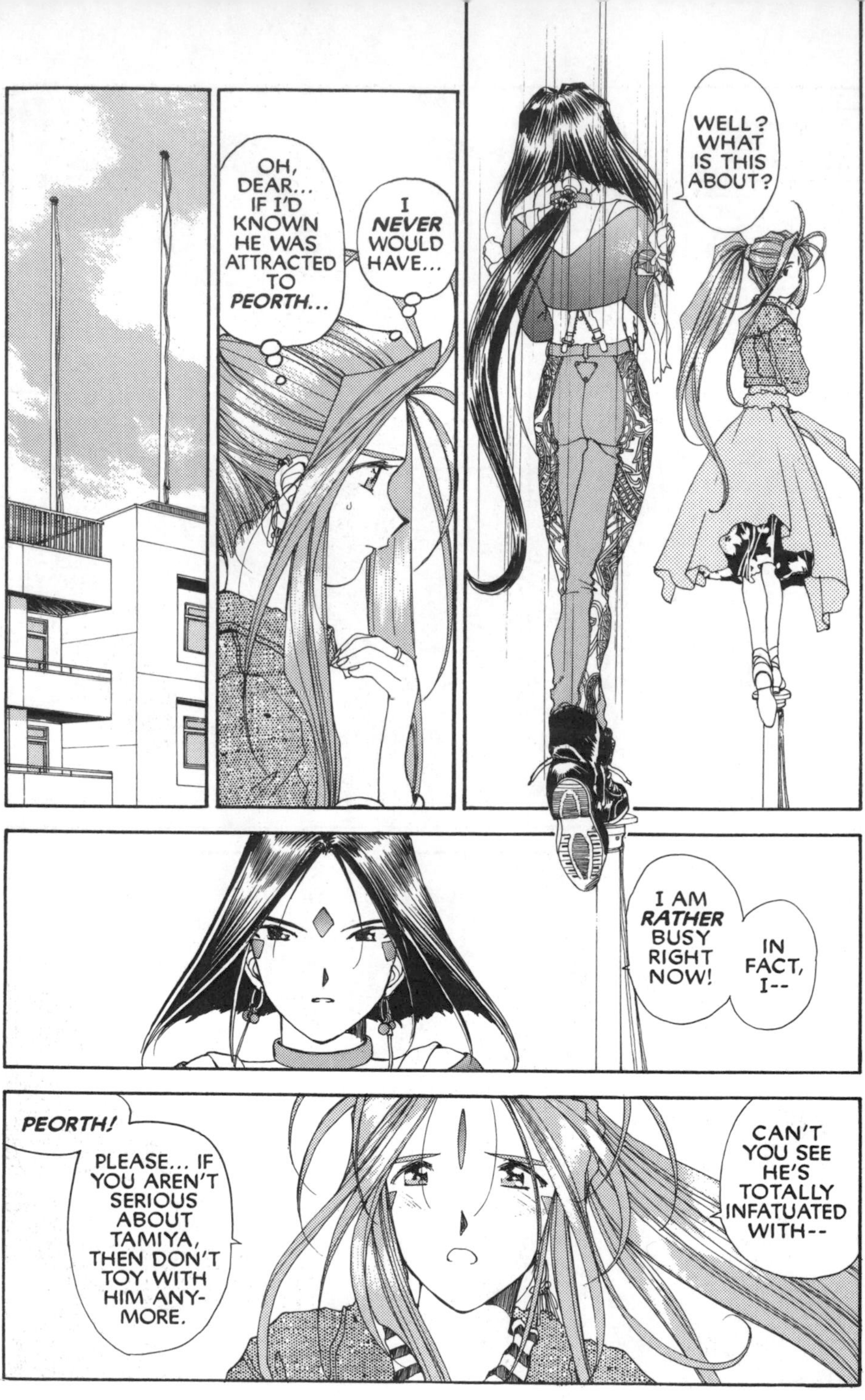
OH, DEAR... IF I'D KNOWN HE WAS ATTRACTED TO *PEORTH...*
I *NEVER* WOULD HAVE...
WELL? WHAT IS THIS ABOUT?
I AM *RATHER* BUSY RIGHT NOW!
IN FACT, I--
PEORTH!
PLEASE... IF YOU AREN'T SERIOUS ABOUT TAMIYA, THEN DON'T TOY WITH HIM ANY-MORE.
CAN'T YOU SEE HE'S TOTALLY INFATUATED WITH--

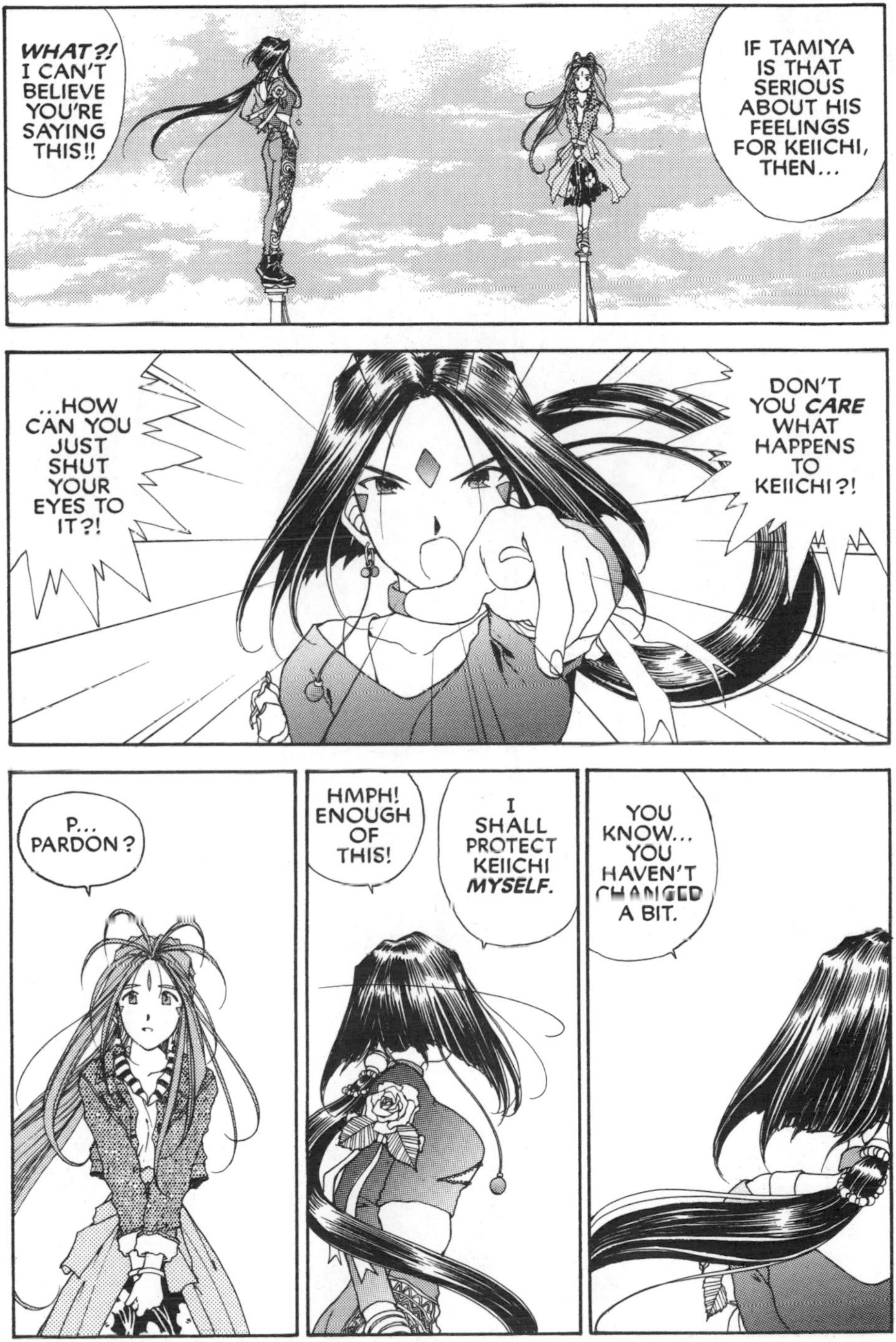
WHAT?! I CAN'T BELIEVE YOU'RE SAYING THIS!!
IF TAMIYA IS THAT SERIOUS ABOUT HIS FEELINGS FOR KEIICHI, THEN...
...HOW CAN YOU JUST SHUT YOUR EYES TO IT?!
DON'T YOU CARE WHAT HAPPENS TO KEIICHI?!
P... PARDON?
HMPH! ENOUGH OF THIS!
I SHALL PROTECT KEIICHI MYSELF.
YOU KNOW... YOU HAVEN'T CHANGED A BIT.

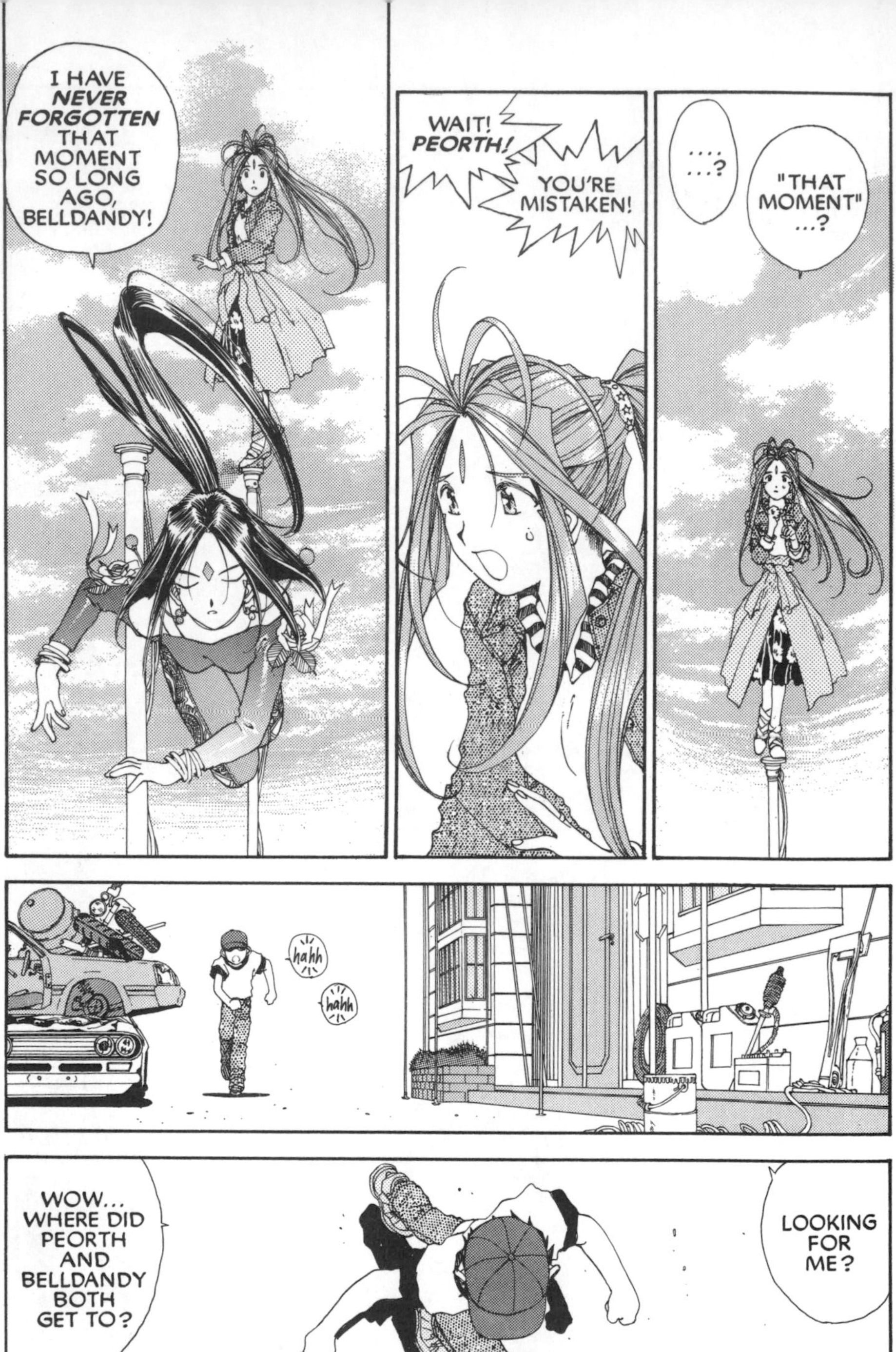
I HAVE NEVER FORGOTTEN THAT MOMENT SO LONG AGO, BELLDANDY!
WAIT! PEORTH!
YOU'RE MISTAKEN!
...., ...?
"THAT MOMENT" ...?
hahh
hahh
WOW... WHERE DID PEORTH AND BELLDANDY BOTH GET TO?
LOOKING FOR ME?

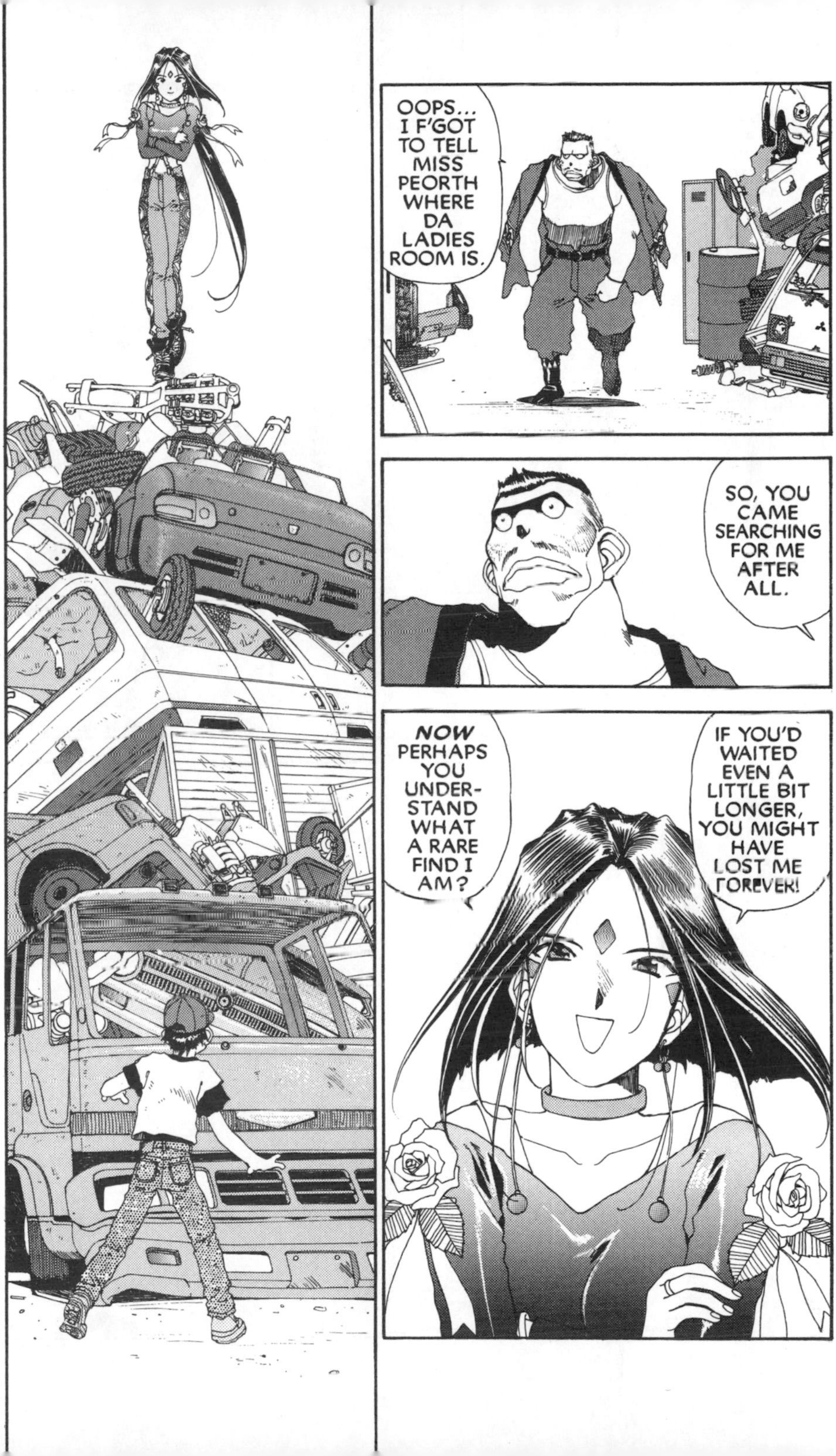

OOPS... I F'GOT TO TELL MISS PEORTH WHERE DA LADIES ROOM IS.
SO, YOU CAME SEARCHING FOR ME AFTER ALL.
NOW PERHAPS YOU UNDER-STAND WHAT A RARE FIND I AM?
IF YOU'D WAITED EVEN A LITTLE BIT LONGER, YOU MIGHT HAVE LOST ME FOREVER!

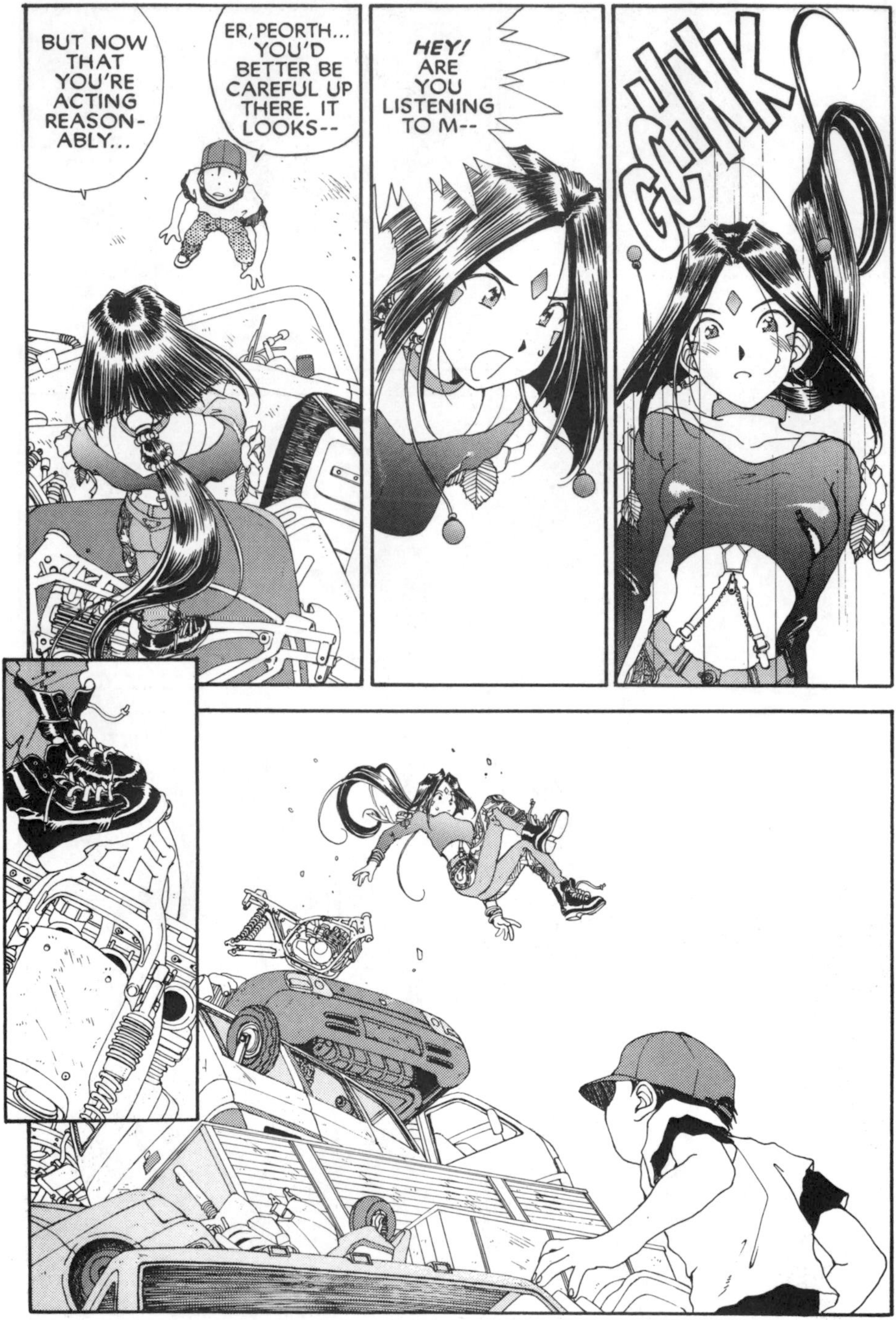
BUT NOW THAT YOU'RE ACTING REASON-ABLY...
ER, PEORTH... YOU'D BETTER BE CAREFUL UP THERE. IT LOOKS--
HEY! ARE YOU LISTENING TO M--
GGINK

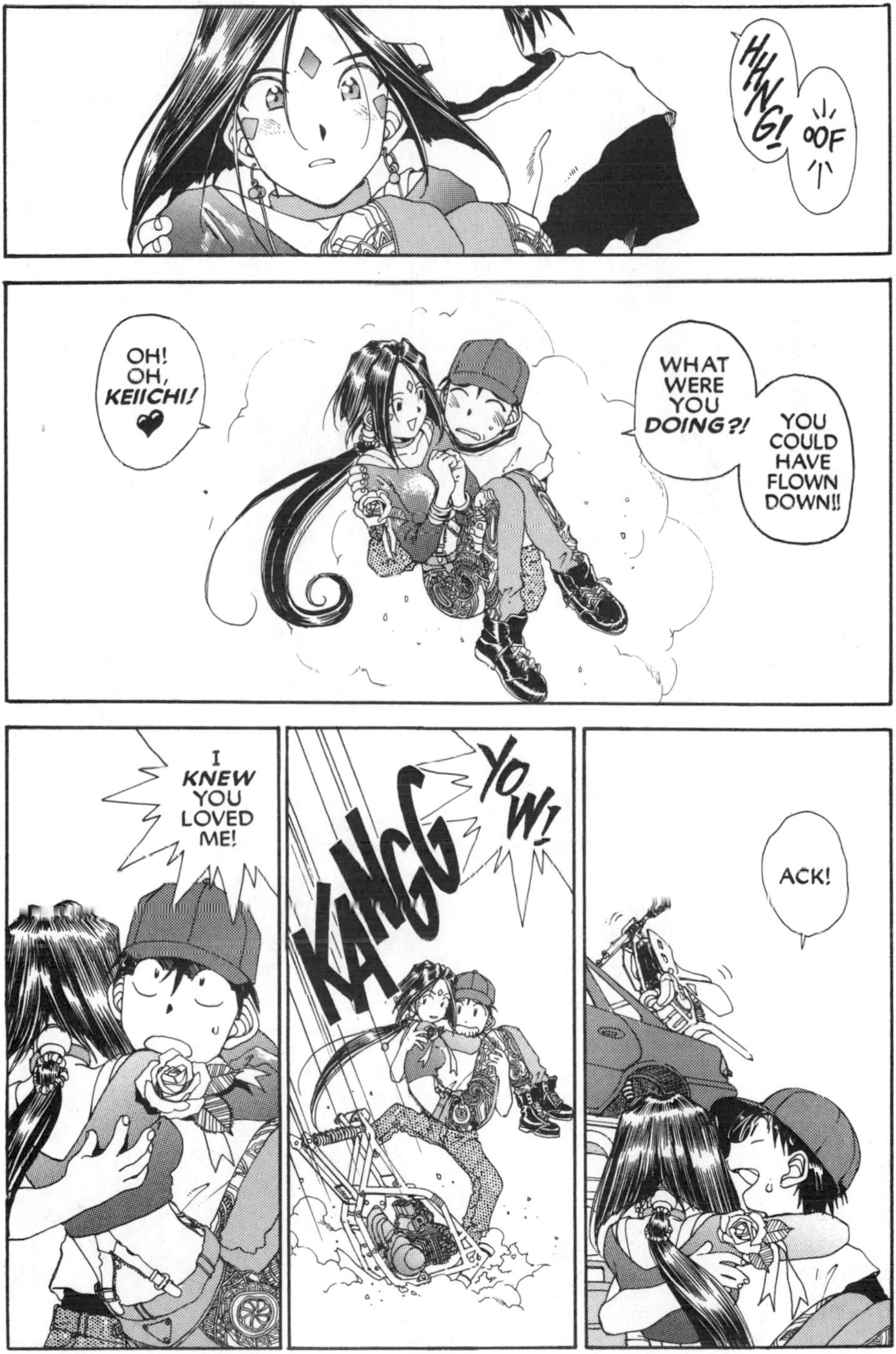
HHNG!
OOF
OH! OH, KEIICHI!
WHAT WERE YOU DOING?!
YOU COULD HAVE FLOWN DOWN!!
I KNEW YOU LOVED ME!
KANGG
YOW!
ACK!

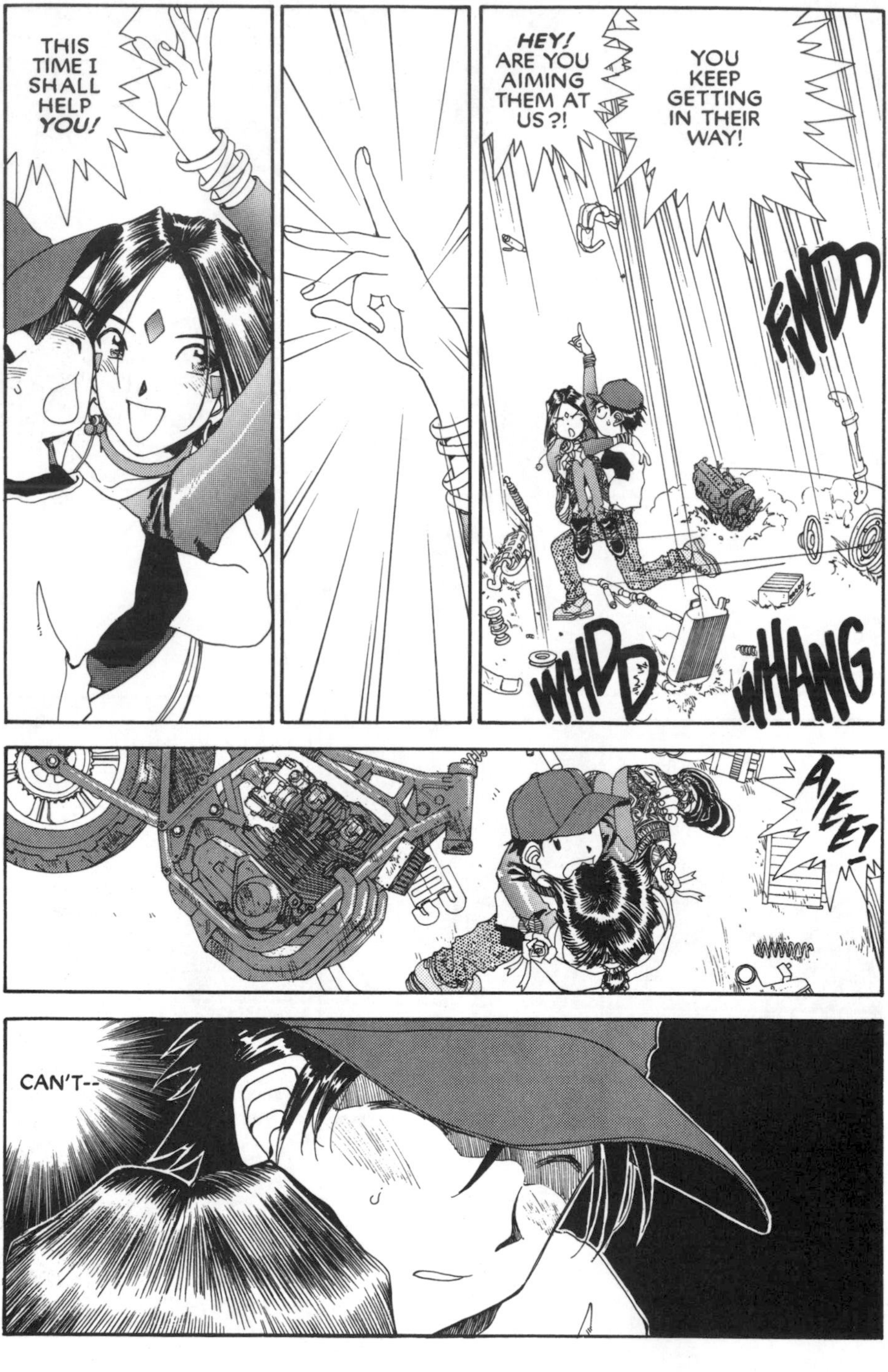
THIS TIME I SHALL HELP *YOU!*
HEY! ARE YOU AIMING THEM AT US?!
YOU KEEP GETTING IN THEIR WAY!
FWDD
WHDD
WHANG
AIEEE!
CAN'T--

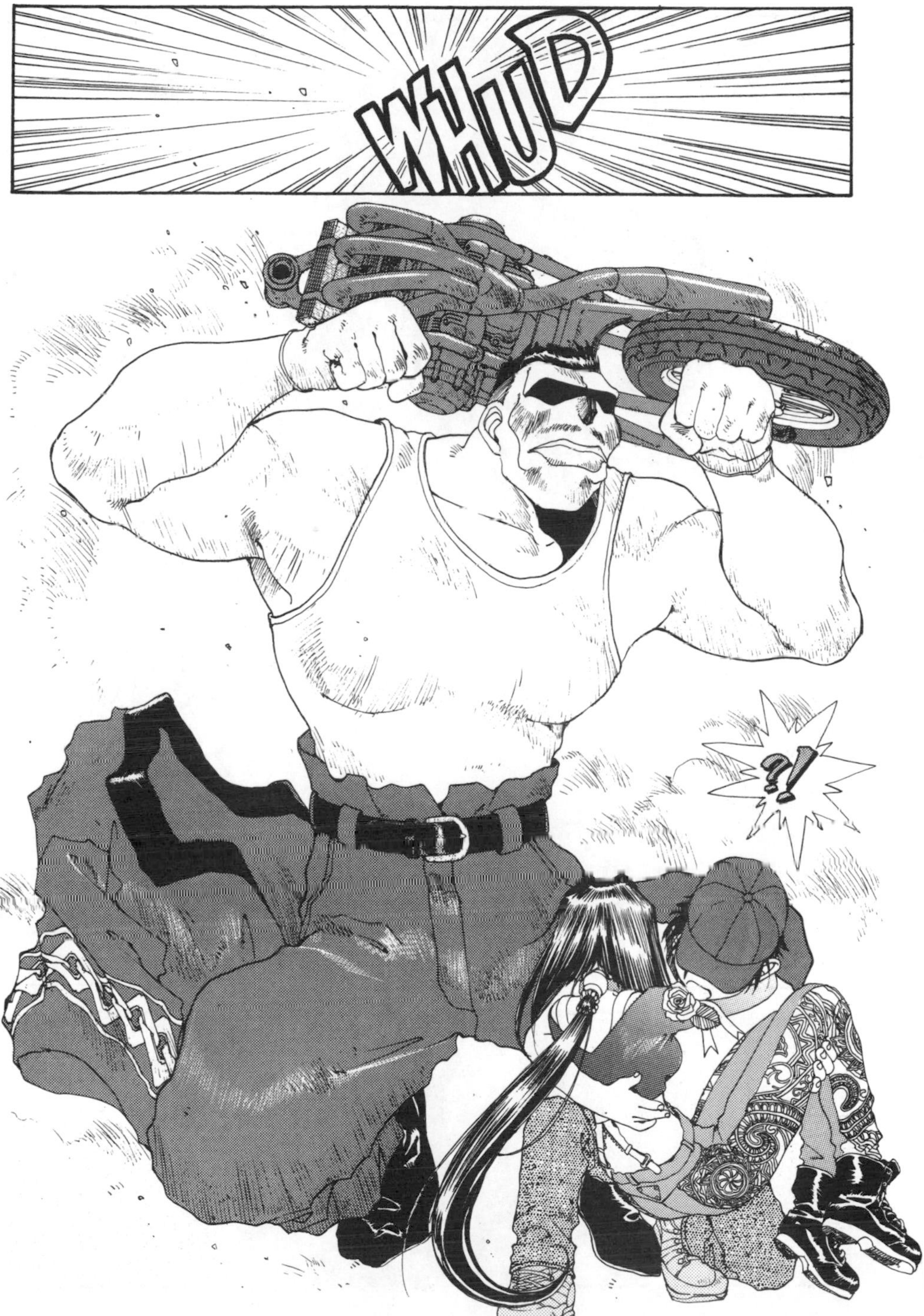
WHUD
?!

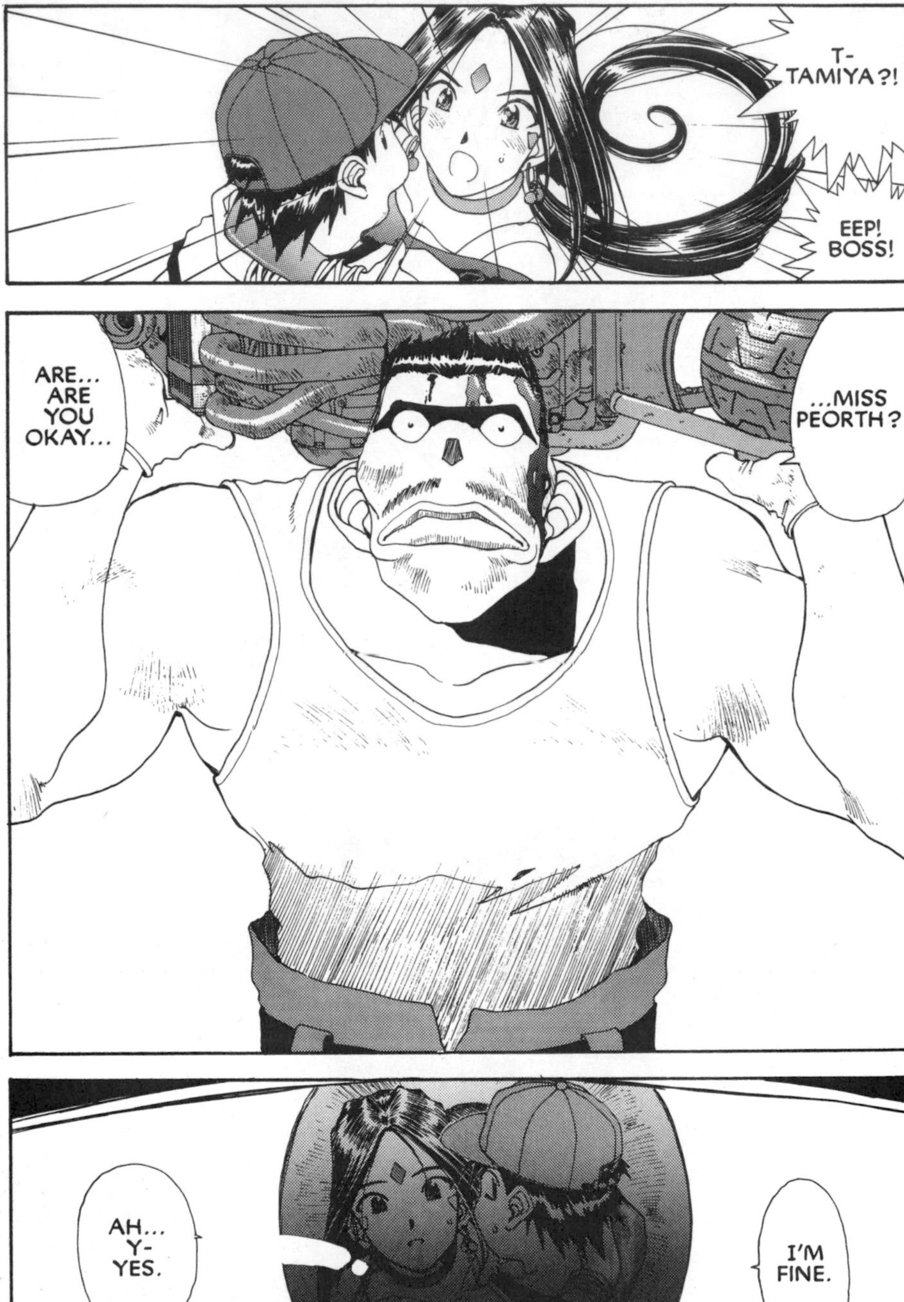
T-TAMIYA?!
EEP! BOSS!
ARE... ARE YOU OKAY...
...MISS PEORTH?
AH... Y-YES.
I'M FINE.

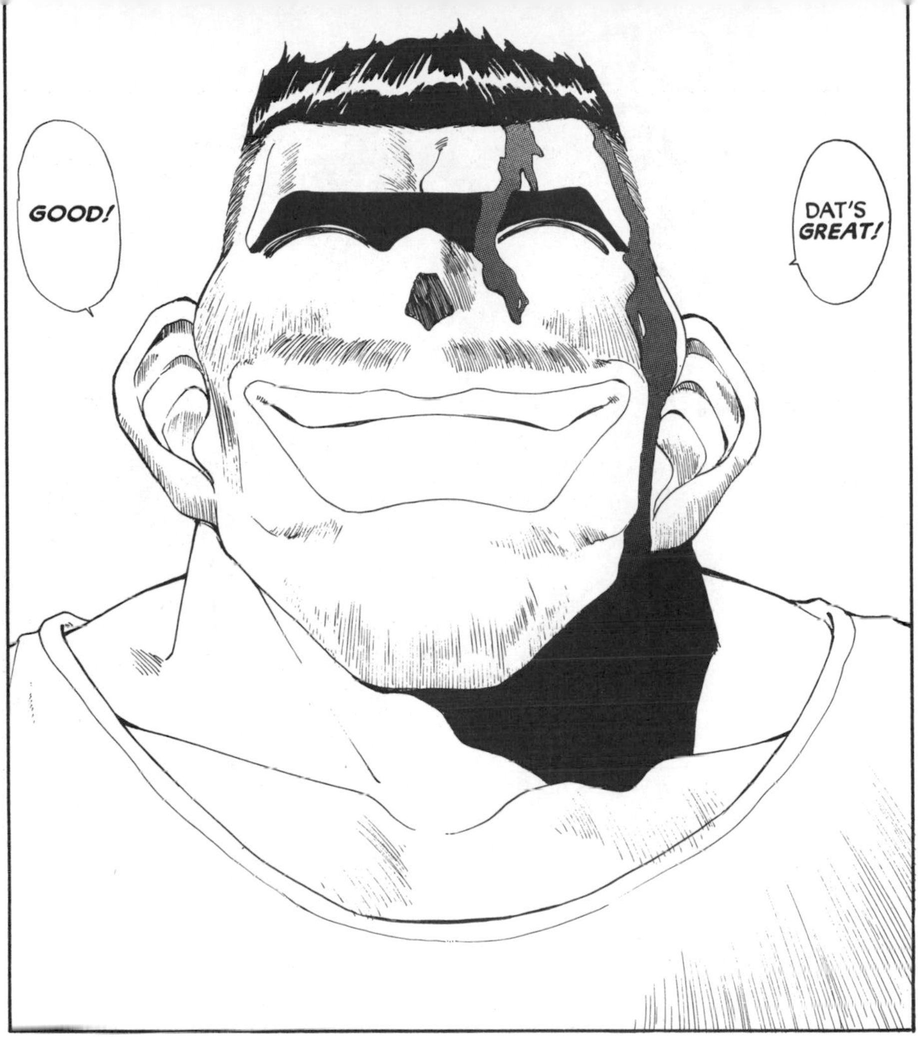
GOOD!
DAT'S *GREAT!*
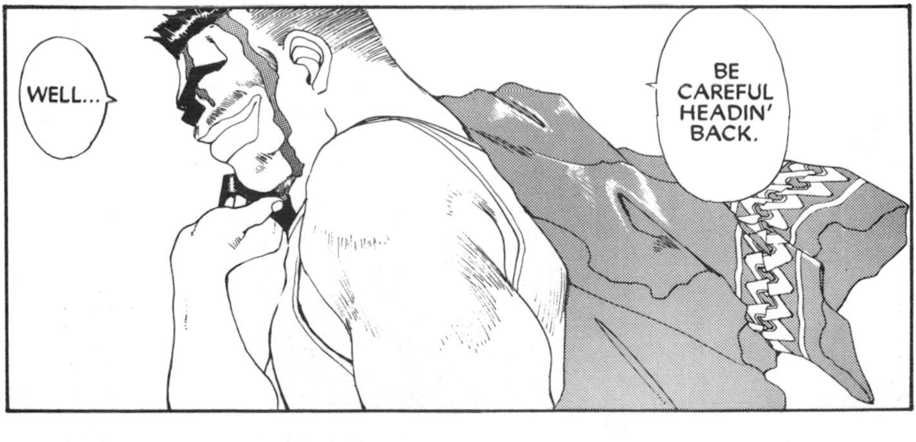
WELL...
BE CAREFUL HEADIN' BACK.

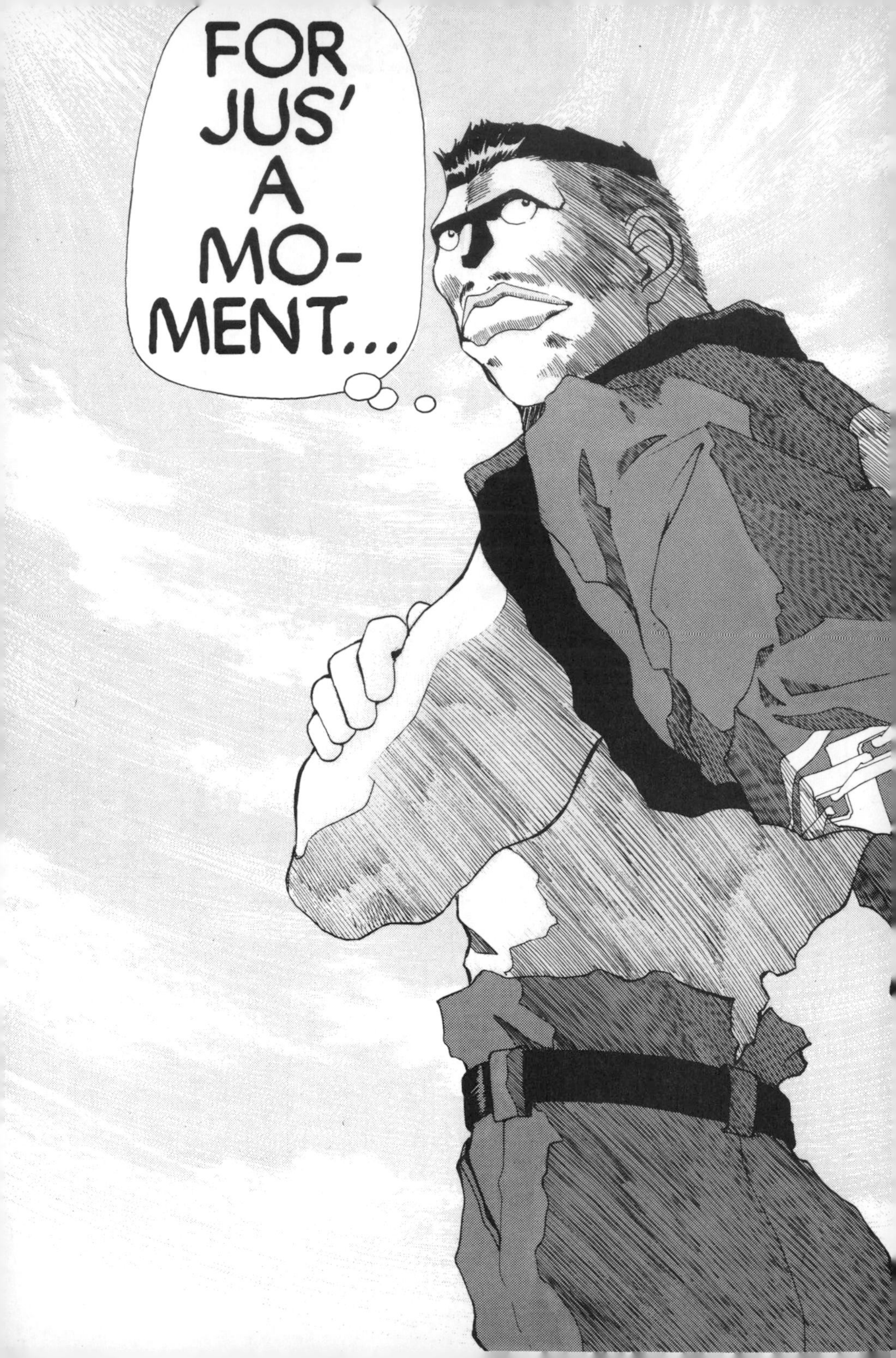
FOR JUS' A MO-MENT...

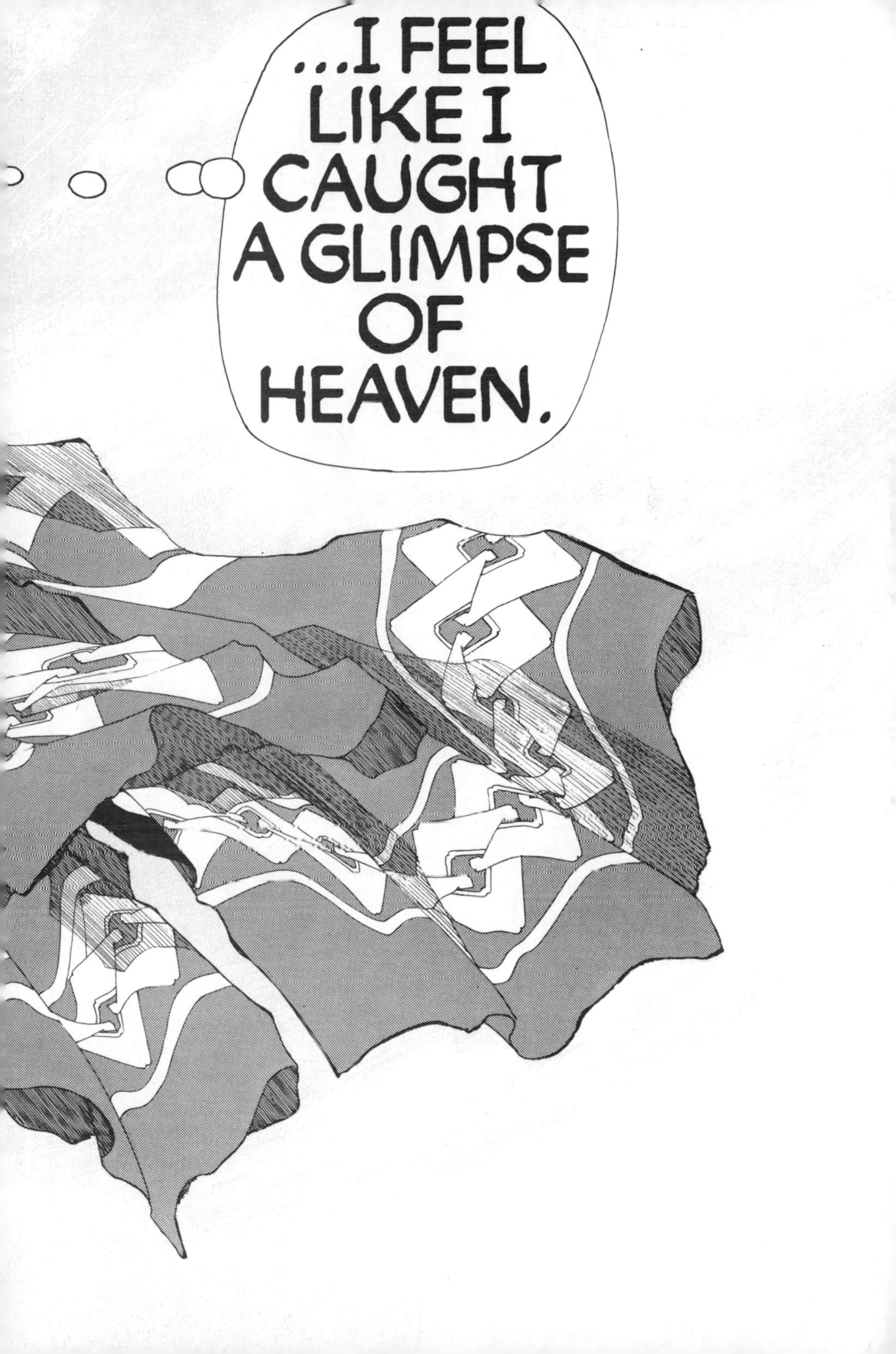
...I FEEL LIKE I CAUGHT A GLIMPSE OF HEAVEN.

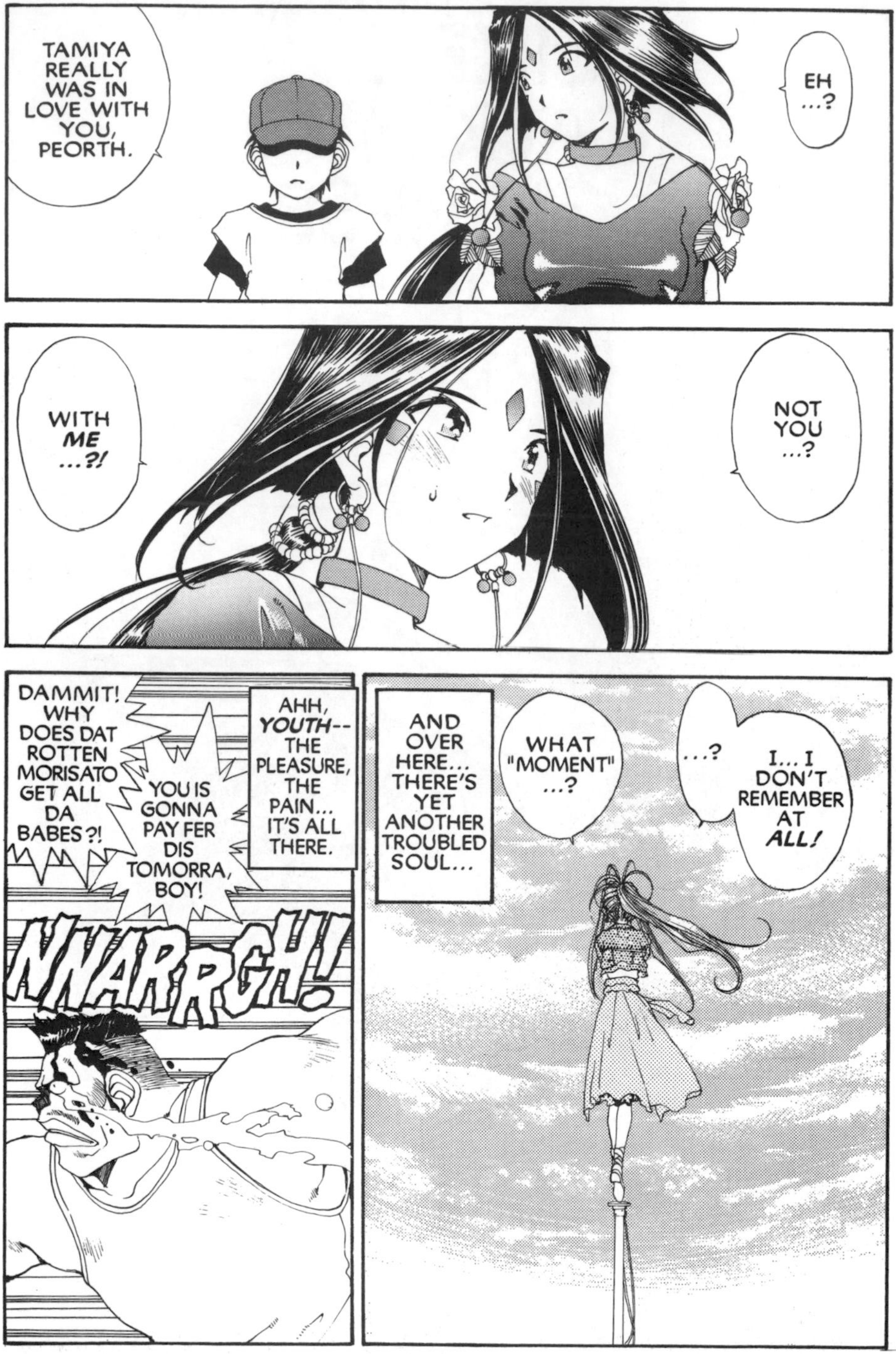
TAMIYA REALLY WAS IN LOVE WITH YOU, PEORTH.
EH ...?
WITH *ME* ...?!
NOT YOU ...?
DAMMIT! WHY DOES DAT ROTTEN MORISATO GET ALL DA BABES?!
YOU IS GONNA PAY FER DIS TOMORRA, BOY!
AHH, *YOUTH*-- THE PLEASURE, THE PAIN... IT'S ALL THERE.
NNARRGH!
AND OVER HERE... THERE'S YET ANOTHER TROUBLED SOUL...
WHAT "MOMENT" ...?
...?
I... I DON'T REMEMBER AT *ALL!*

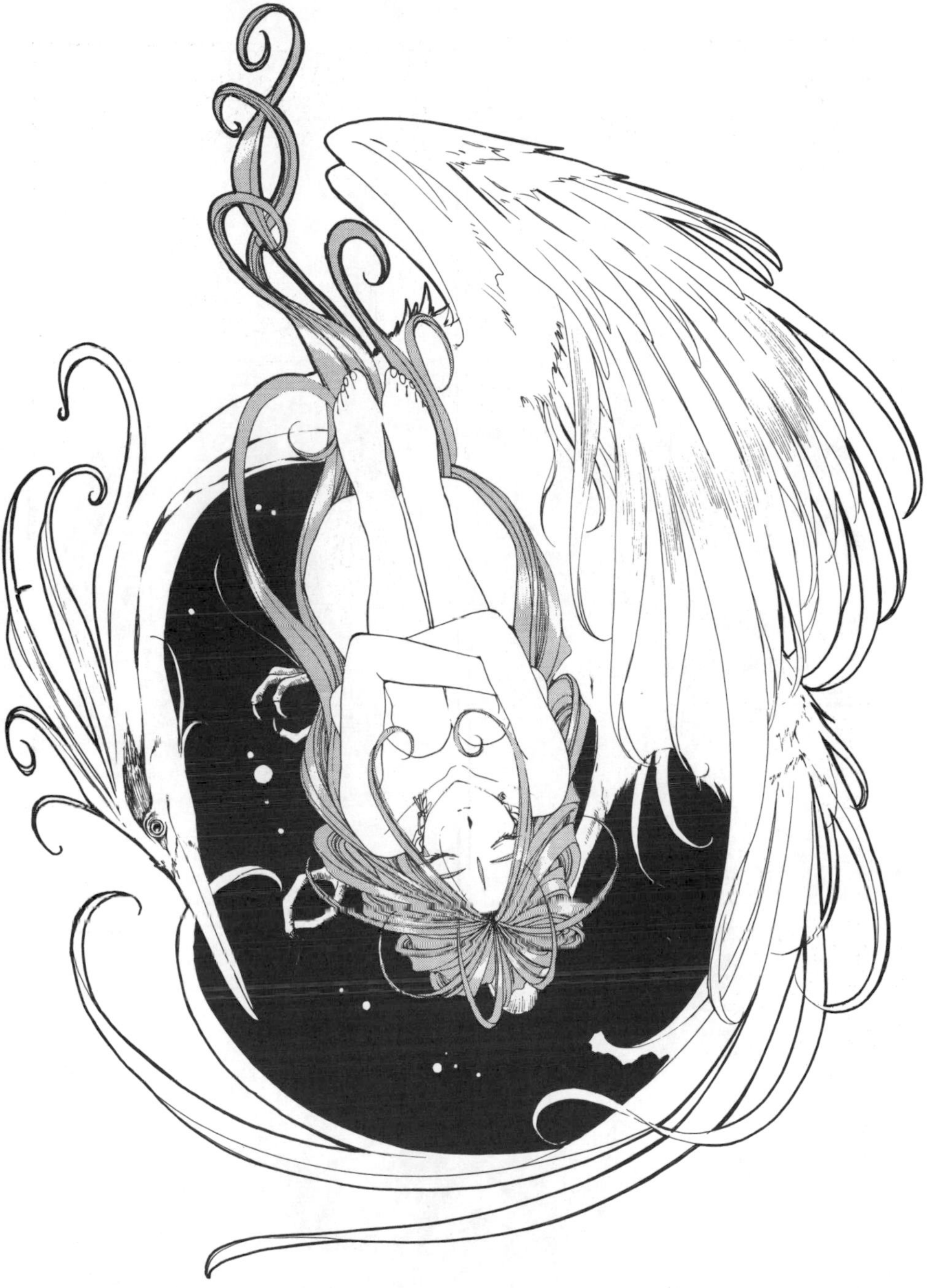

A Goddess Never Forgets

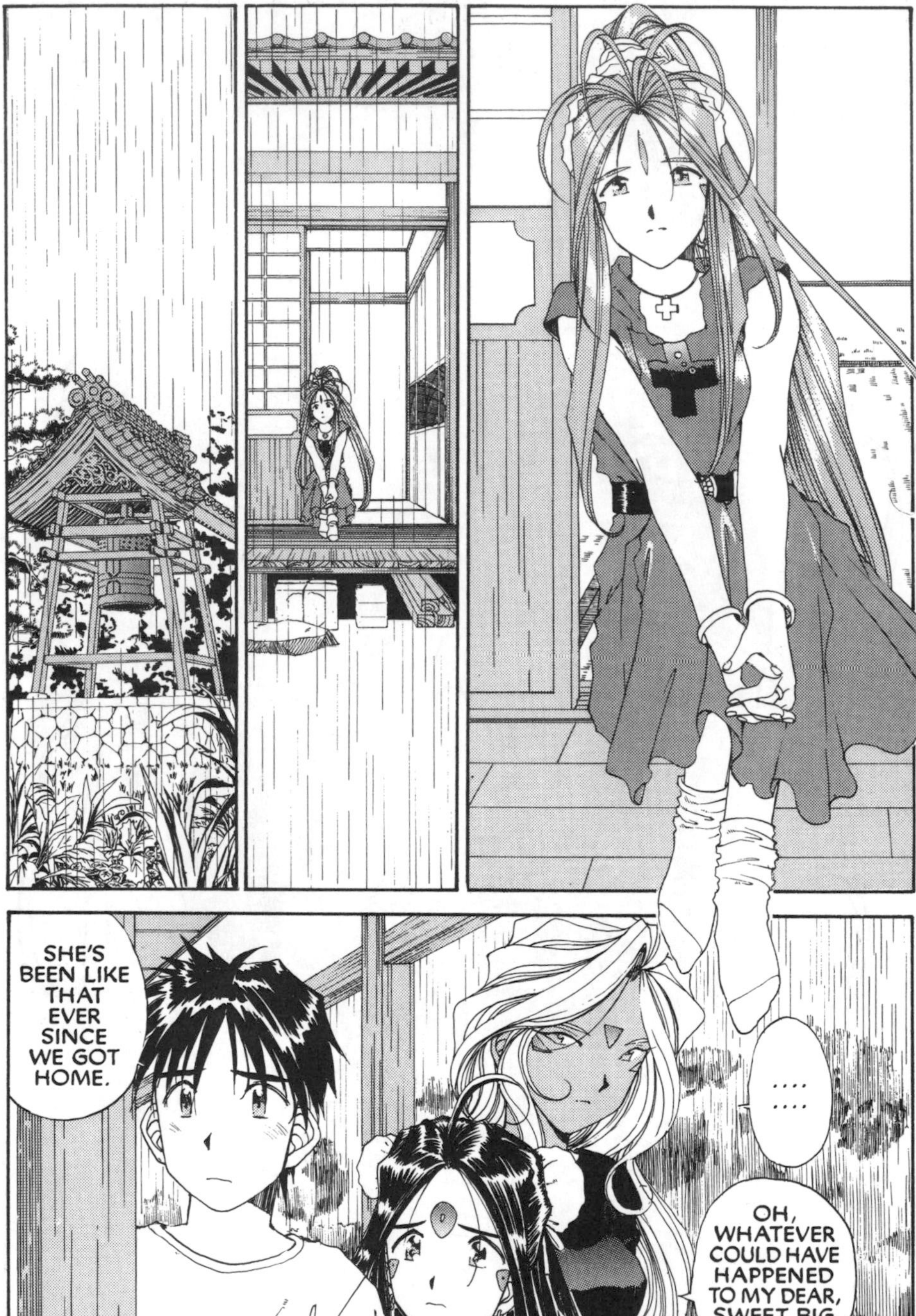
SHE'S BEEN LIKE THAT EVER SINCE WE GOT HOME.
....
OH, WHATEVER COULD HAVE HAPPENED TO MY DEAR, SWEET BIG SISTER?!

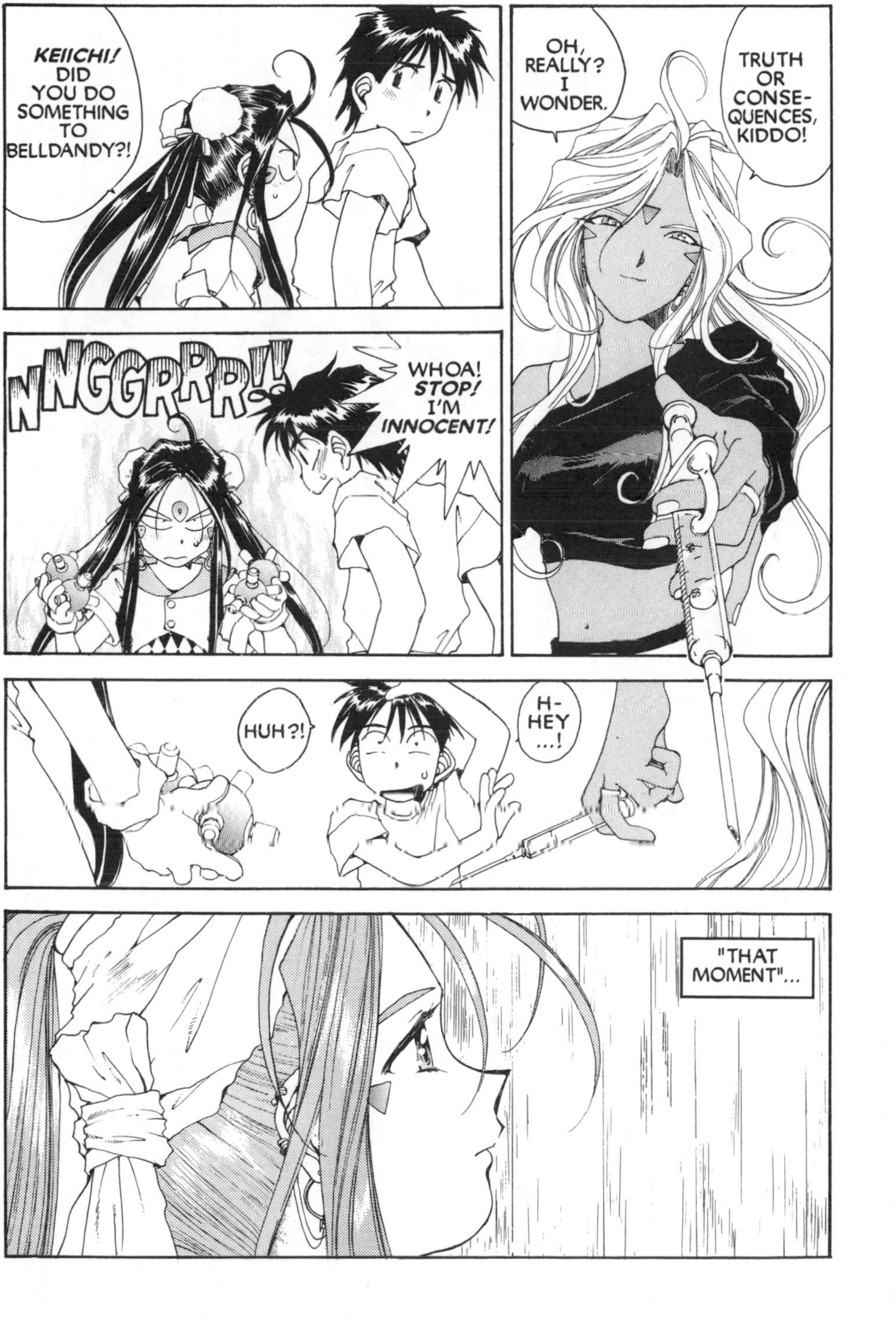
KEIICHI! DID YOU DO SOMETHING TO BELLDANDY?!
NNGGRRRR!!
WHOA! STOP! I'M INNOCENT!
OH, REALLY? I WONDER.
TRUTH OR CONSE-QUENCES, KIDDO!
HUH?!
H-HEY ...!
"THAT MOMENT"...

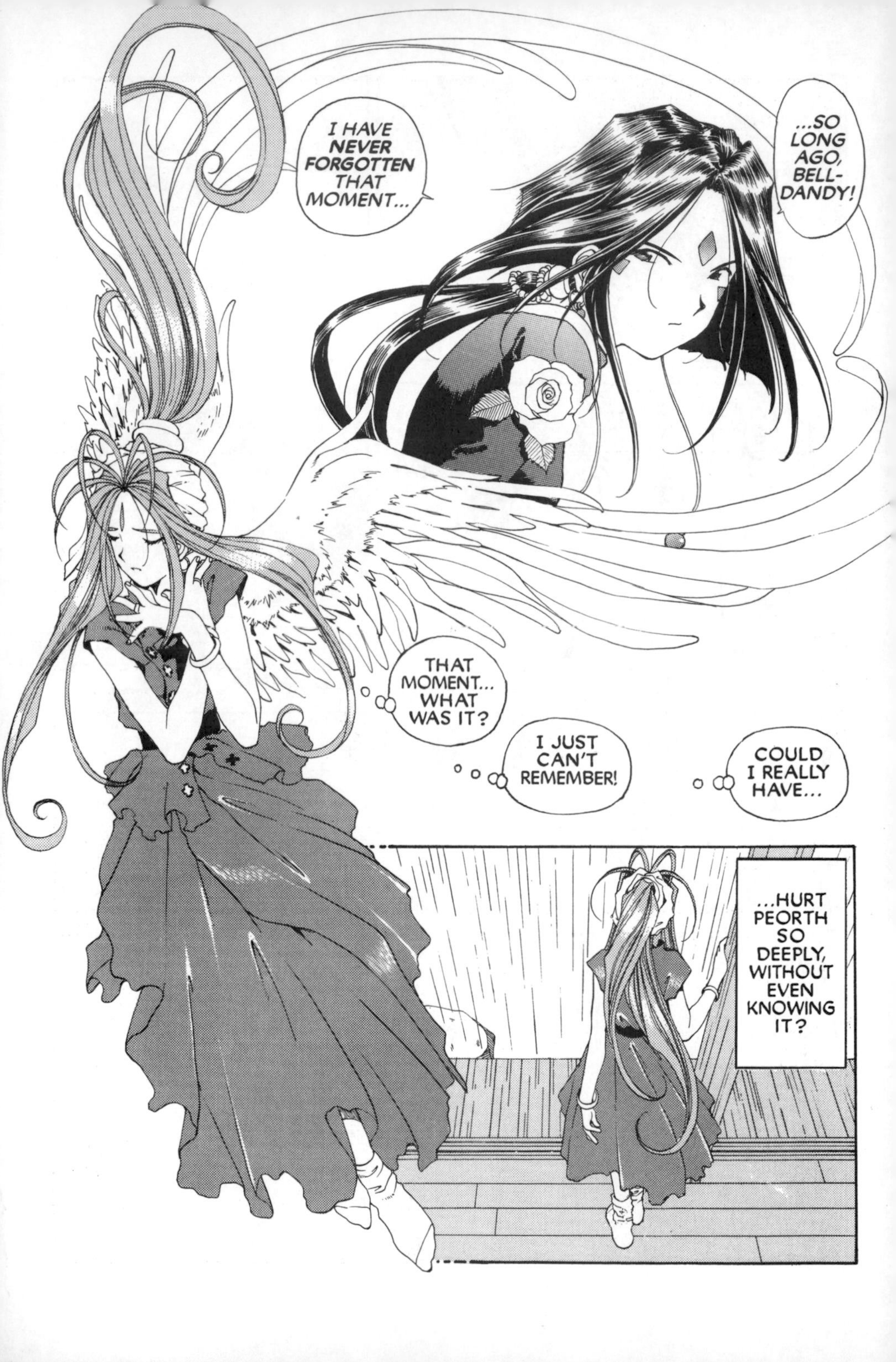
I HAVE NEVER FORGOTTEN THAT MOMENT...
...SO LONG AGO, BELL-DANDY!
THAT MOMENT... WHAT WAS IT?
I JUST CAN'T REMEMBER!
COULD I REALLY HAVE...
...HURT PEORTH SO DEEPLY, WITHOUT EVEN KNOWING IT?

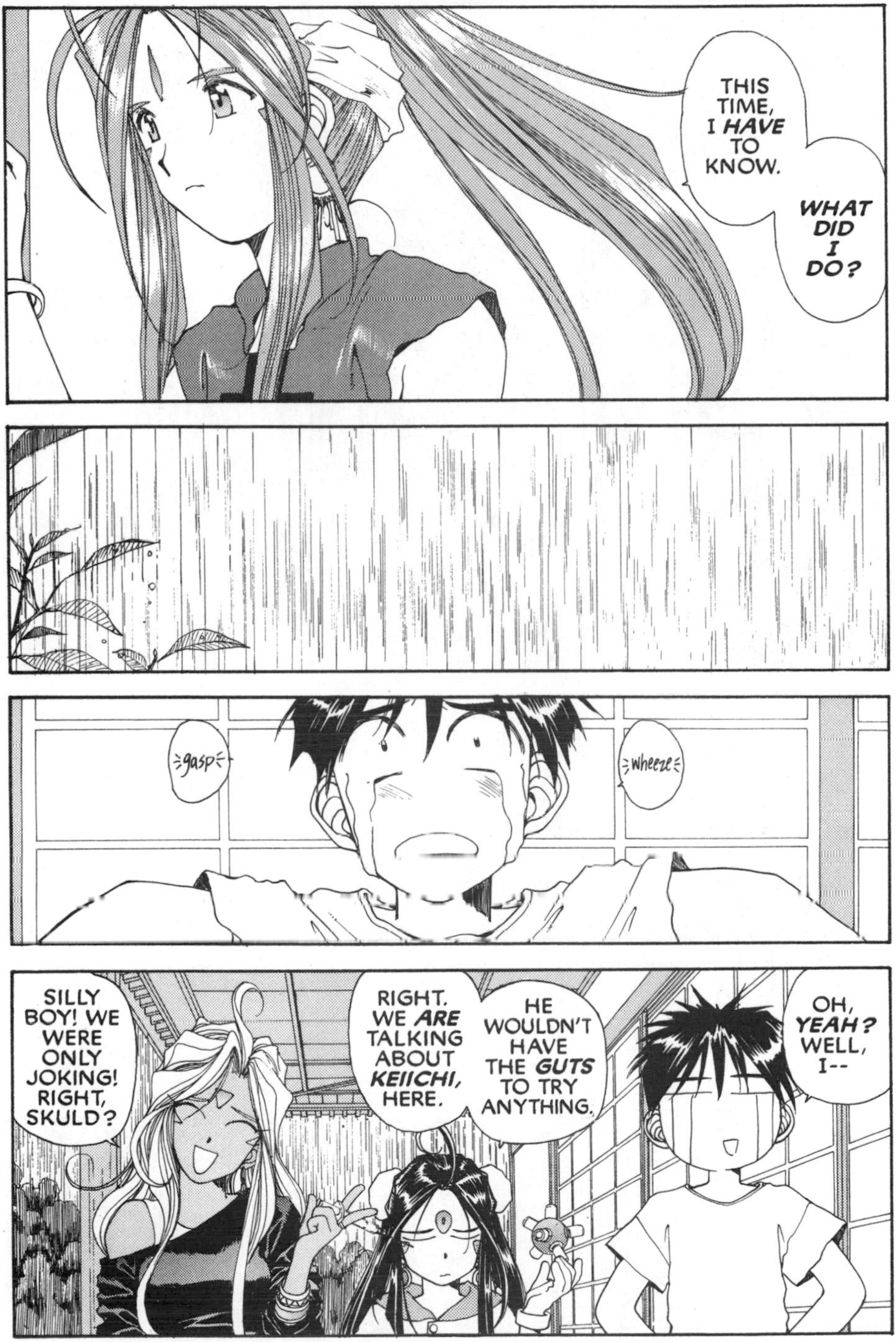
THIS TIME, I HAVE TO KNOW.
WHAT DID I DO?
gasp
wheeze
SILLY BOY! WE WERE ONLY JOKING! RIGHT, SKULD?
RIGHT. WE ARE TALKING ABOUT KEIICHI, HERE.
HE WOULDN'T HAVE THE GUTS TO TRY ANYTHING.
OH, YEAH? WELL, I--

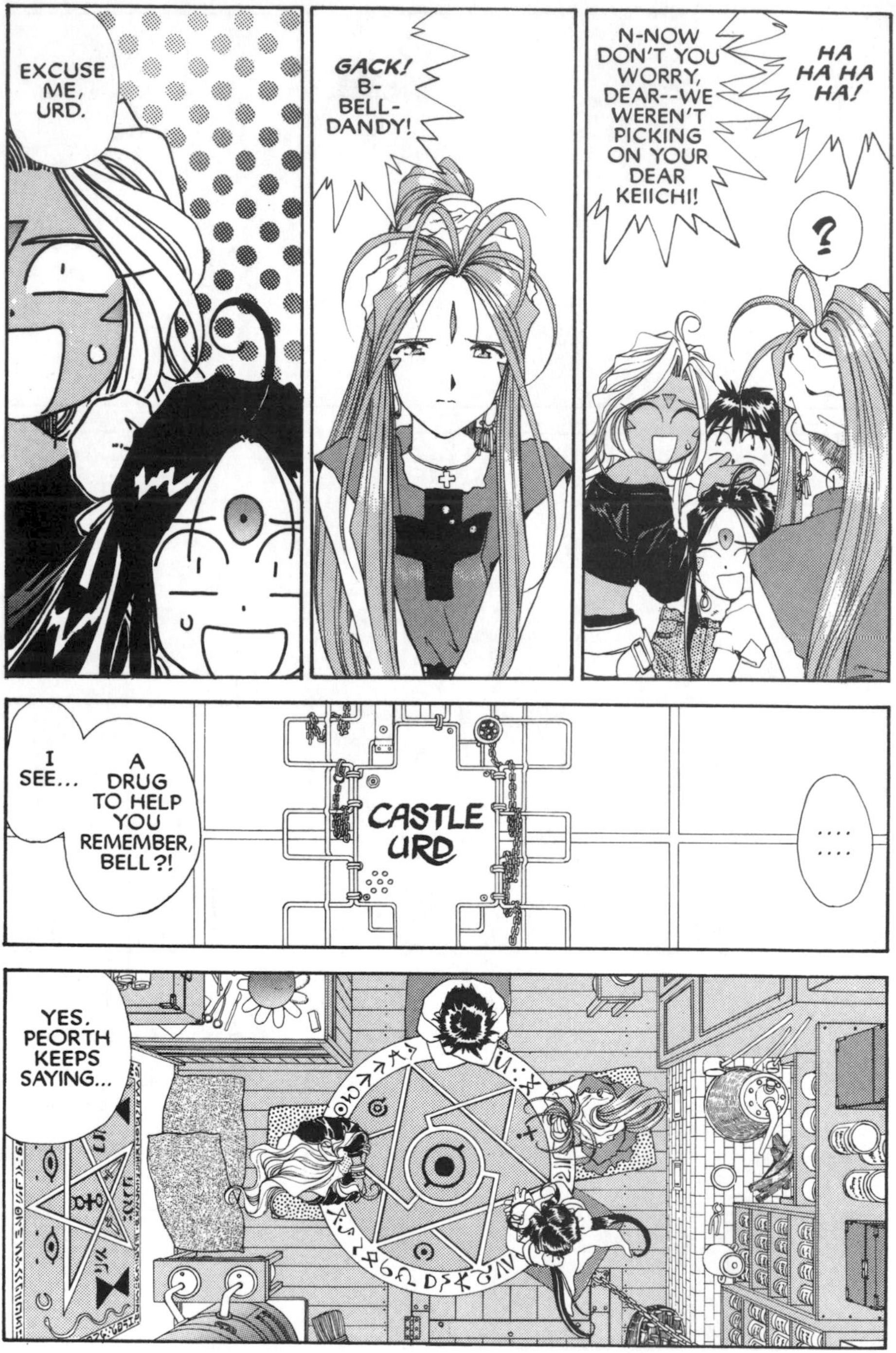
EXCUSE ME, URD.
GACK! B-BELLDANDY!
N-NOW DON'T YOU WORRY, DEAR--WE WEREN'T PICKING ON YOUR DEAR KEIICHI!
HA HA HA HA!
?
I SEE...
A DRUG TO HELP YOU REMEMBER, BELL?!
CASTLE URD
....
YES. PEORTH KEEPS SAYING...

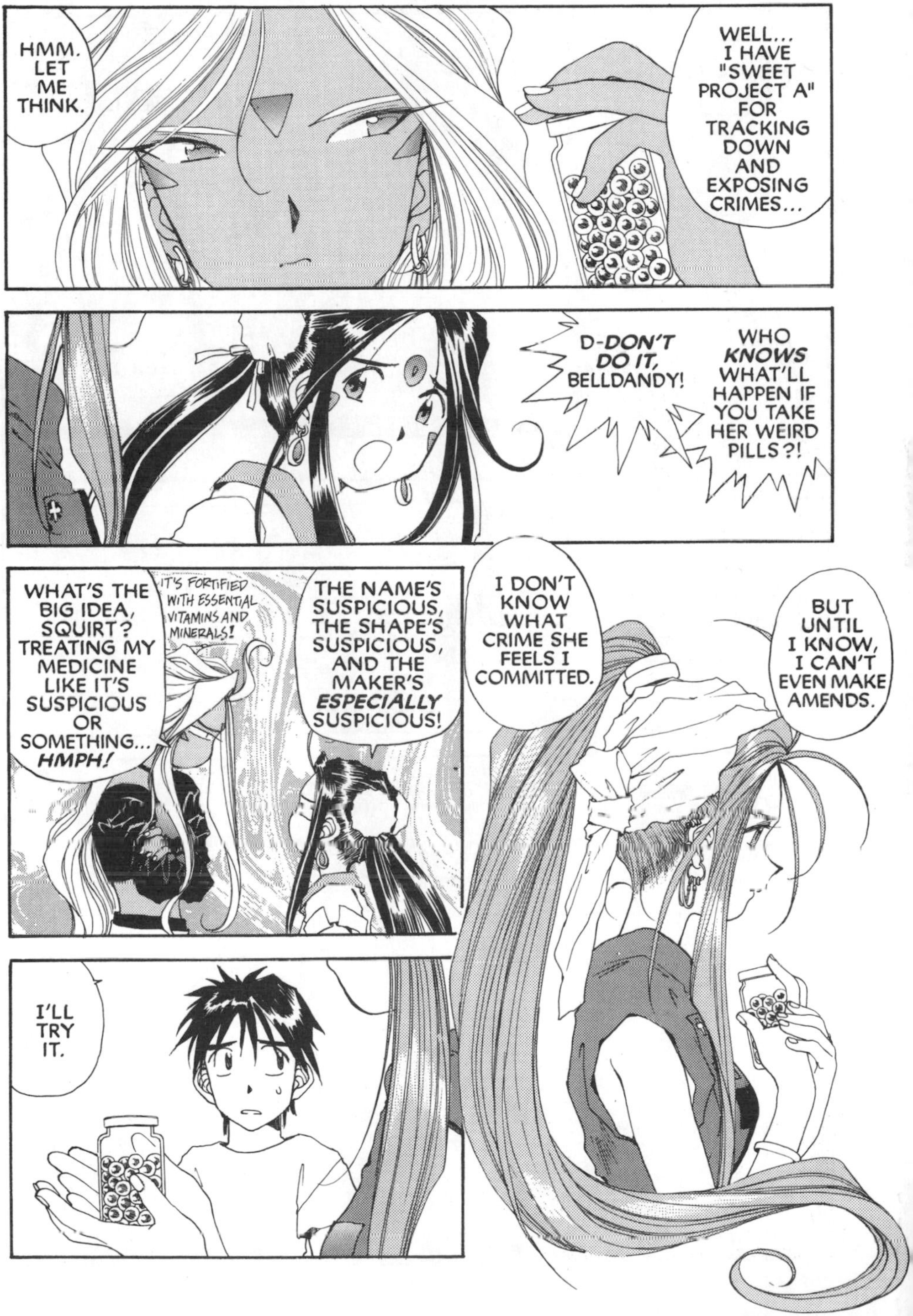
HMM. LET ME THINK.
WELL... I HAVE "SWEET PROJECT A" FOR TRACKING DOWN AND EXPOSING CRIMES...
D-*DON'T DO IT*, BELLDANDY!
WHO *KNOWS* WHAT'LL HAPPEN IF YOU TAKE HER WEIRD PILLS?!
WHAT'S THE BIG IDEA, SQUIRT? TREATING MY MEDICINE LIKE IT'S SUSPICIOUS OR SOMETHING... *HMPH!*
IT'S FORTIFIED WITH ESSENTIAL VITAMINS AND MINERALS!
THE NAME'S SUSPICIOUS, THE SHAPE'S SUSPICIOUS, AND THE MAKER'S *ESPECIALLY* SUSPICIOUS!
I DON'T KNOW WHAT CRIME SHE FEELS I COMMITTED.
BUT UNTIL I KNOW, I CAN'T EVEN MAKE AMENDS.
I'LL TRY IT.

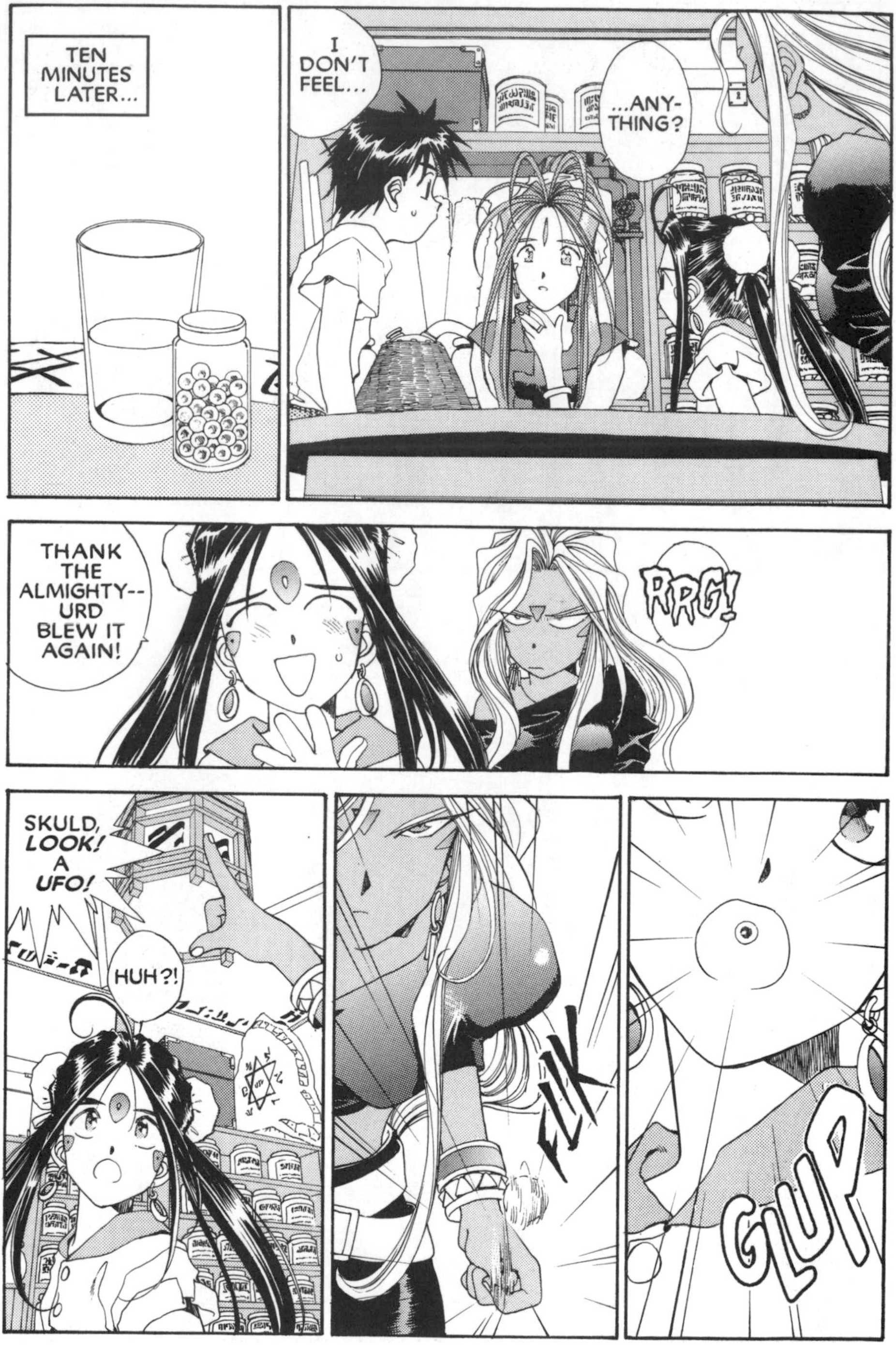

TEN MINUTES LATER...
I DON'T FEEL...
...ANY-THING?
THANK THE ALMIGHTY-- URD BLEW IT AGAIN!
RRG!
SKULD, LOOK! A UFO!
HUH?!
FLIK
GLUP

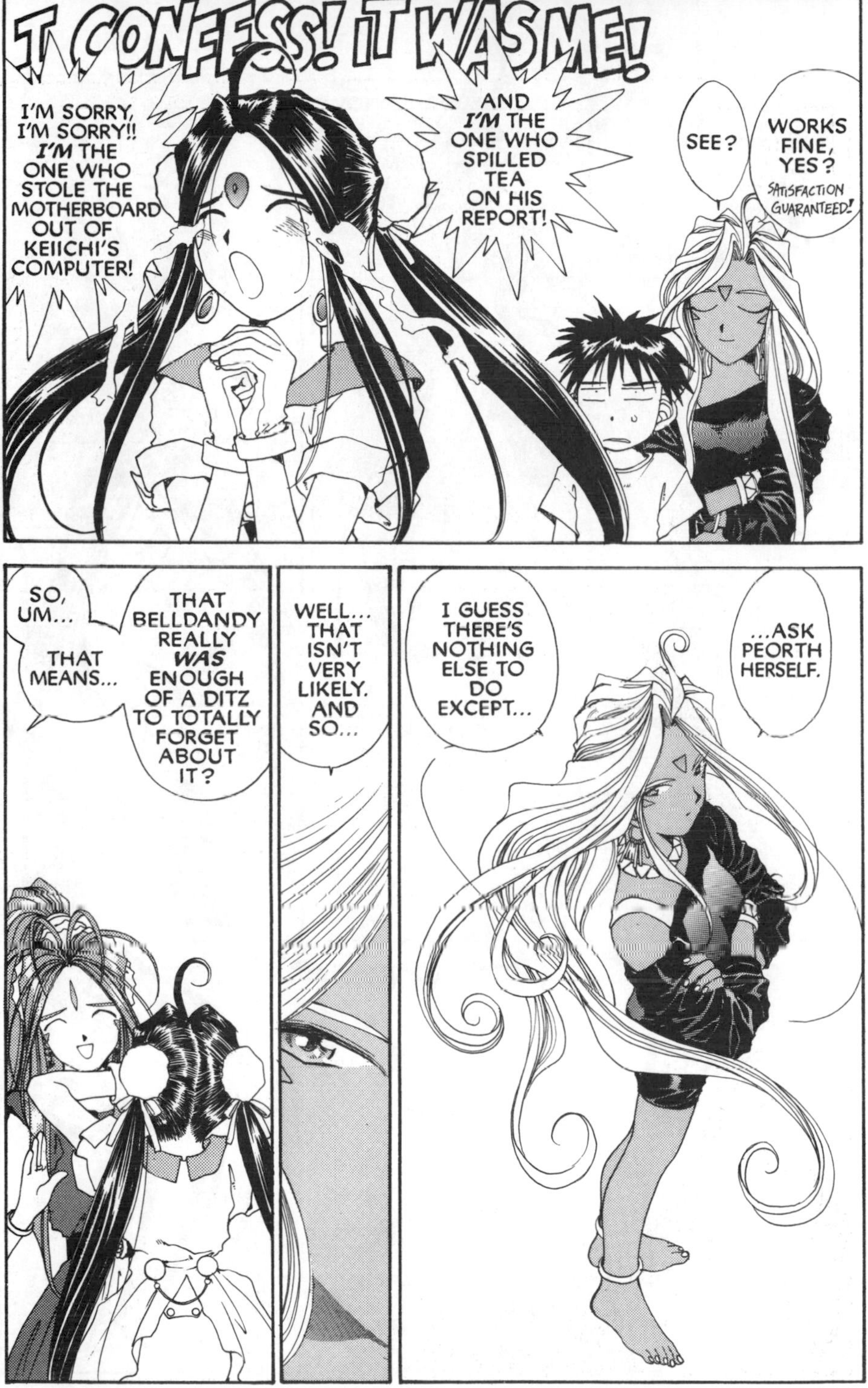
I CONFESS! IT WAS ME!
I'M SORRY, I'M SORRY!! I'M THE ONE WHO STOLE THE MOTHERBOARD OUT OF KEIICHI'S COMPUTER!
AND I'M THE ONE WHO SPILLED TEA ON HIS REPORT!
SEE?
WORKS FINE, YES?
SATISFACTION GUARANTEED!
SO, UM...
THAT MEANS...
THAT BELLDANDY REALLY WAS ENOUGH OF A DITZ TO TOTALLY FORGET ABOUT IT?
WELL... THAT ISN'T VERY LIKELY. AND SO...
I GUESS THERE'S NOTHING ELSE TO DO EXCEPT...
...ASK PEORTH HERSELF.

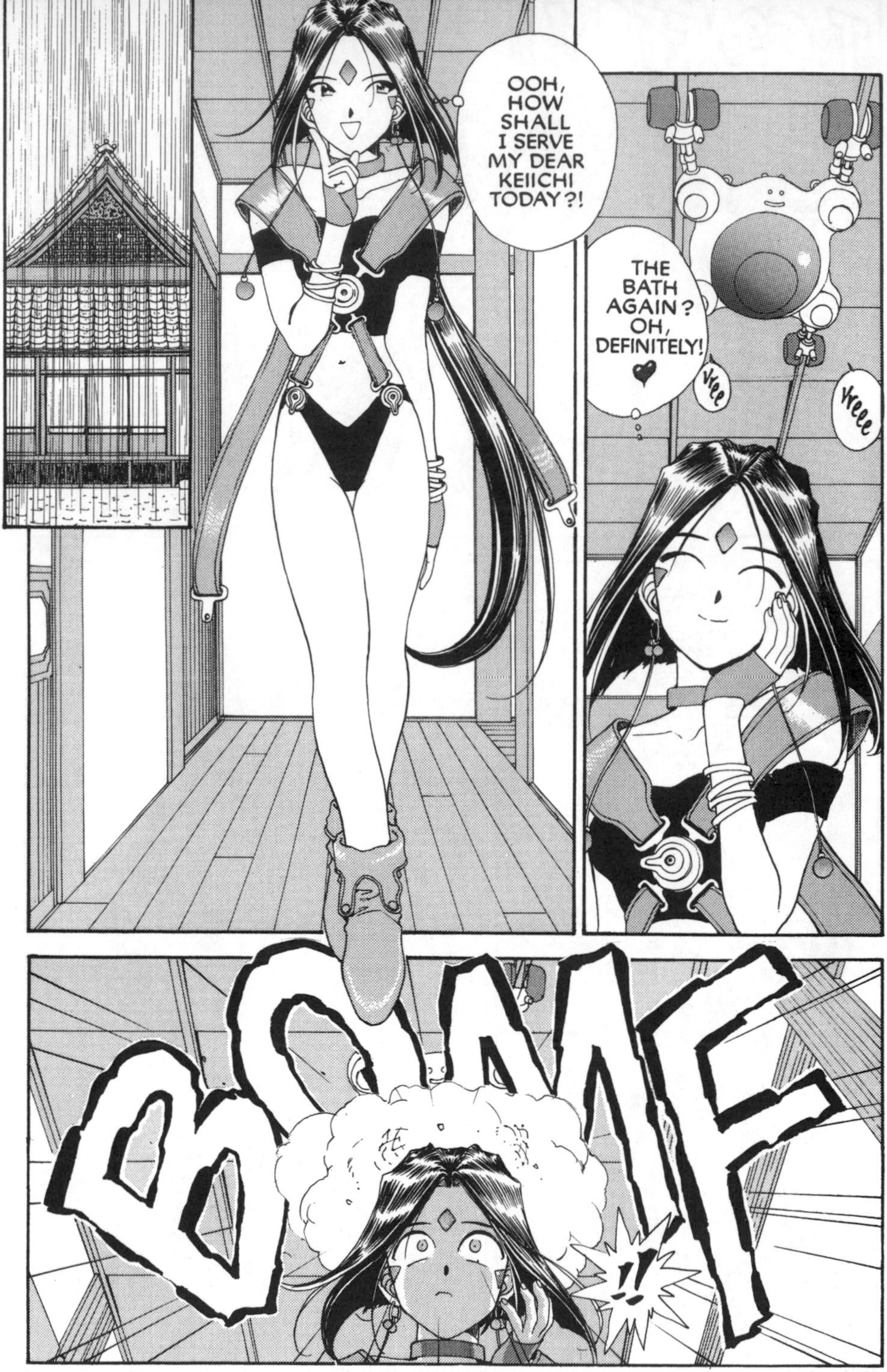
OOH, HOW SHALL I SERVE MY DEAR KEIICHI TODAY?!
THE BATH AGAIN? OH, DEFINITELY! ♥
vree
vreee
BOMF
!!

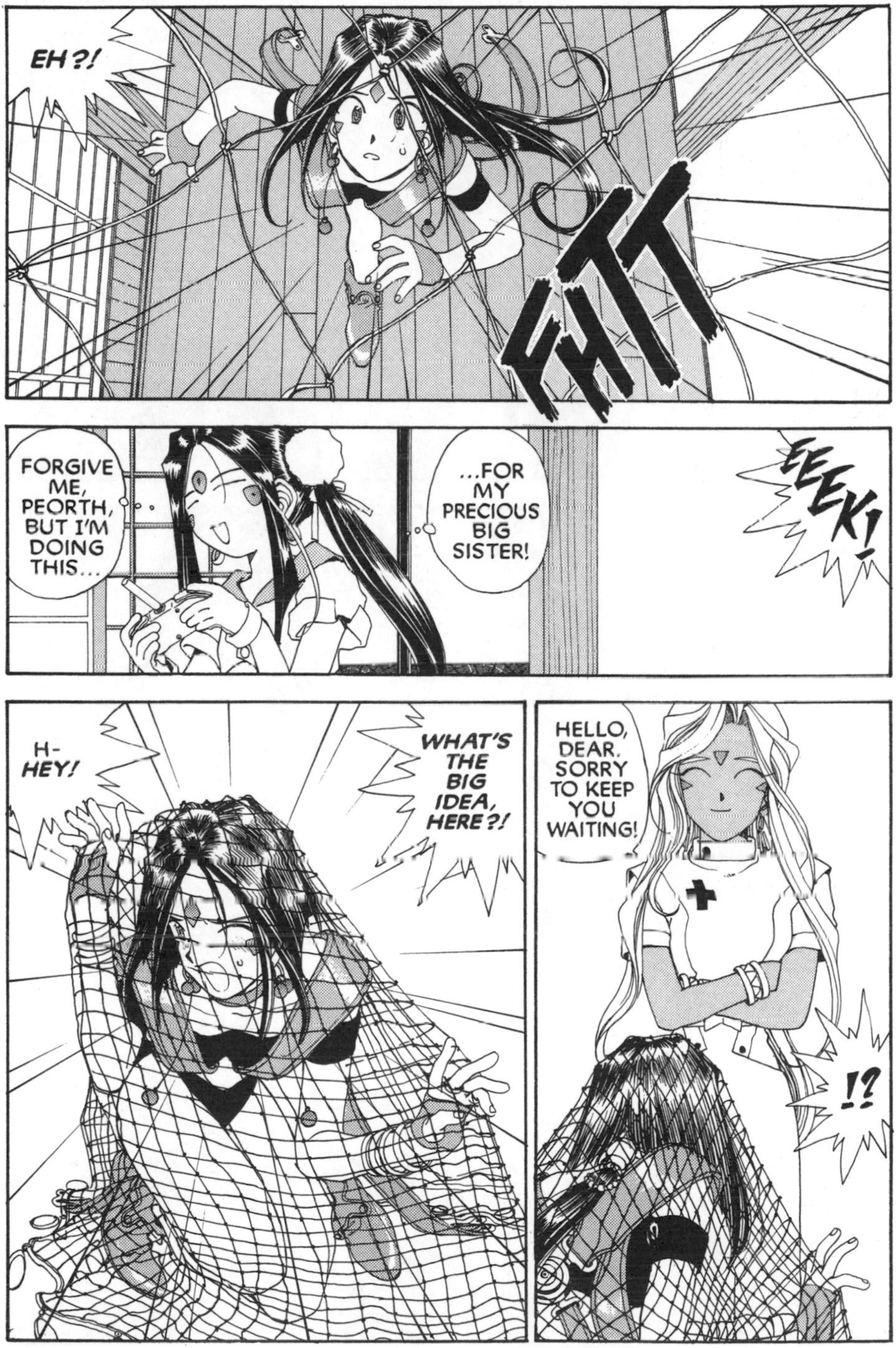
EH?!
FHTT
FORGIVE ME, PEORTH, BUT I'M DOING THIS...
...FOR MY PRECIOUS BIG SISTER!
EEEEK!
H- HEY!
WHAT'S THE BIG IDEA, HERE?!
HELLO, DEAR. SORRY TO KEEP YOU WAITING!
!?

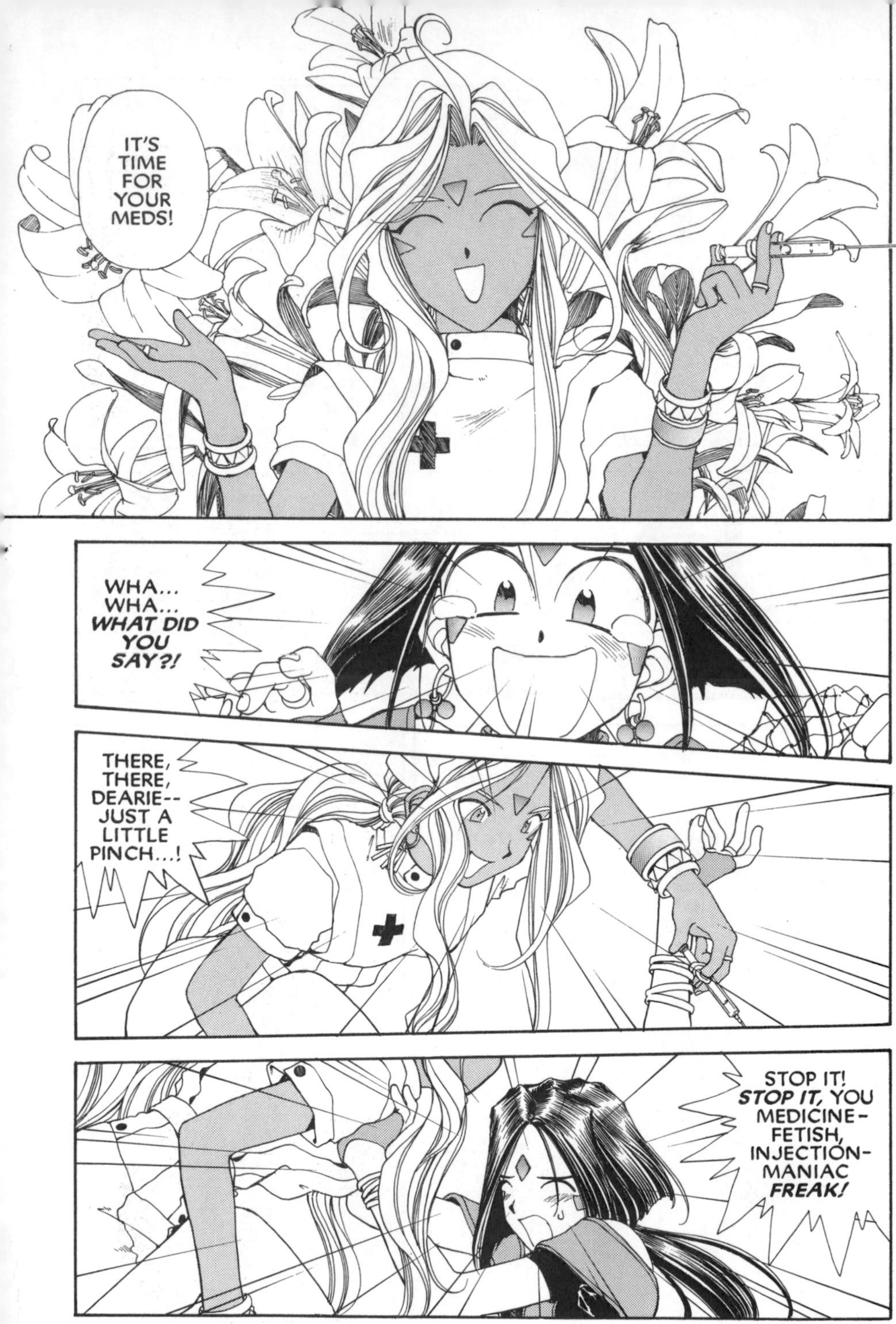
IT'S TIME FOR YOUR MEDS!
WHA... WHA... WHAT DID YOU SAY?!
THERE, THERE, DEARIE-- JUST A LITTLE PINCH...!
STOP IT! STOP IT, YOU MEDICINE-FETISH, INJECTION-MANIAC FREAK!

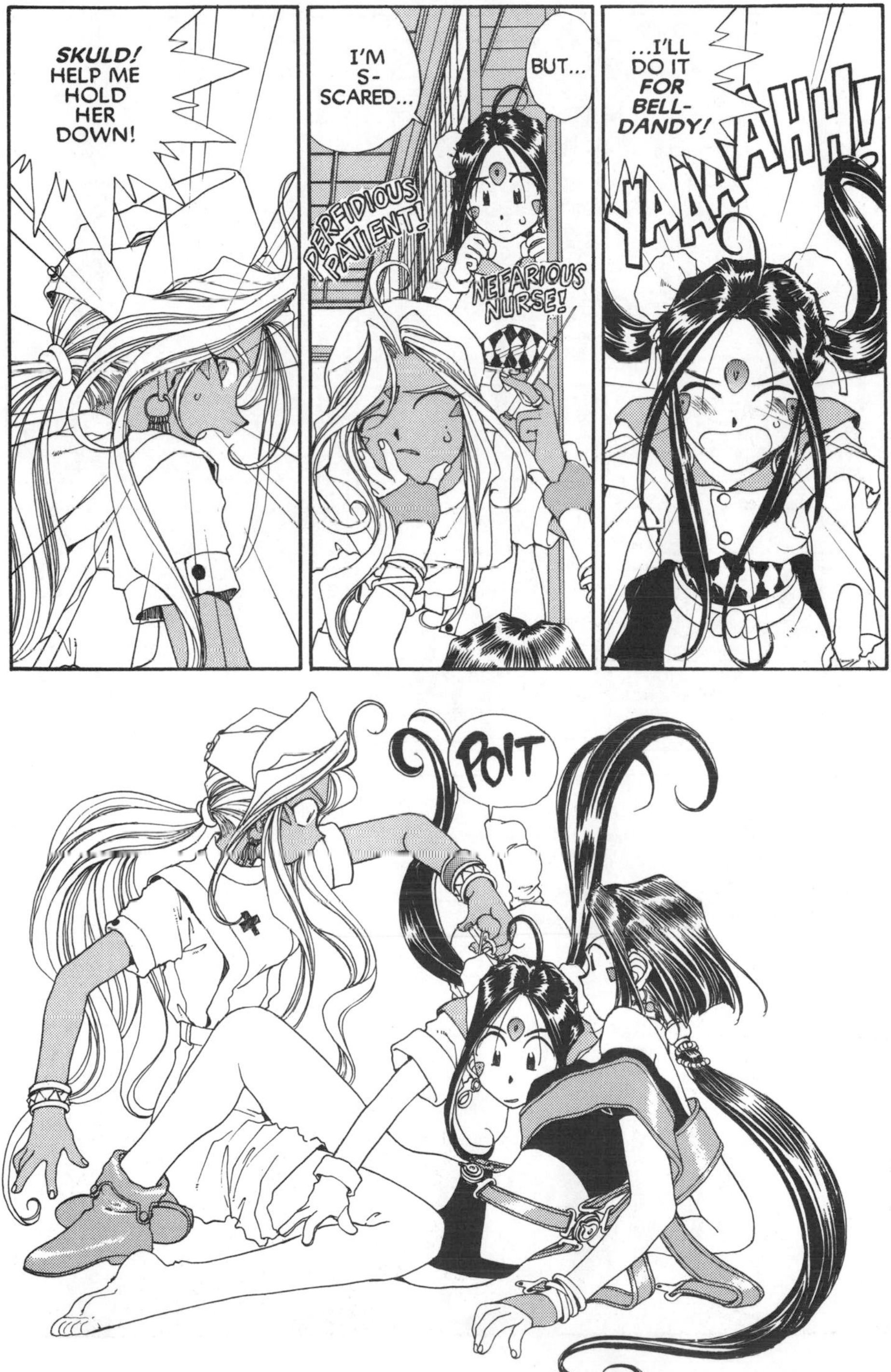
SKULD! HELP ME HOLD HER DOWN!
I'M S-SCARED...
BUT...
PERFIDIOUS PATIENT!
NEFARIOUS NURSE!
...I'LL DO IT FOR BELL-DANDY!
YAAAAHH!
POIT

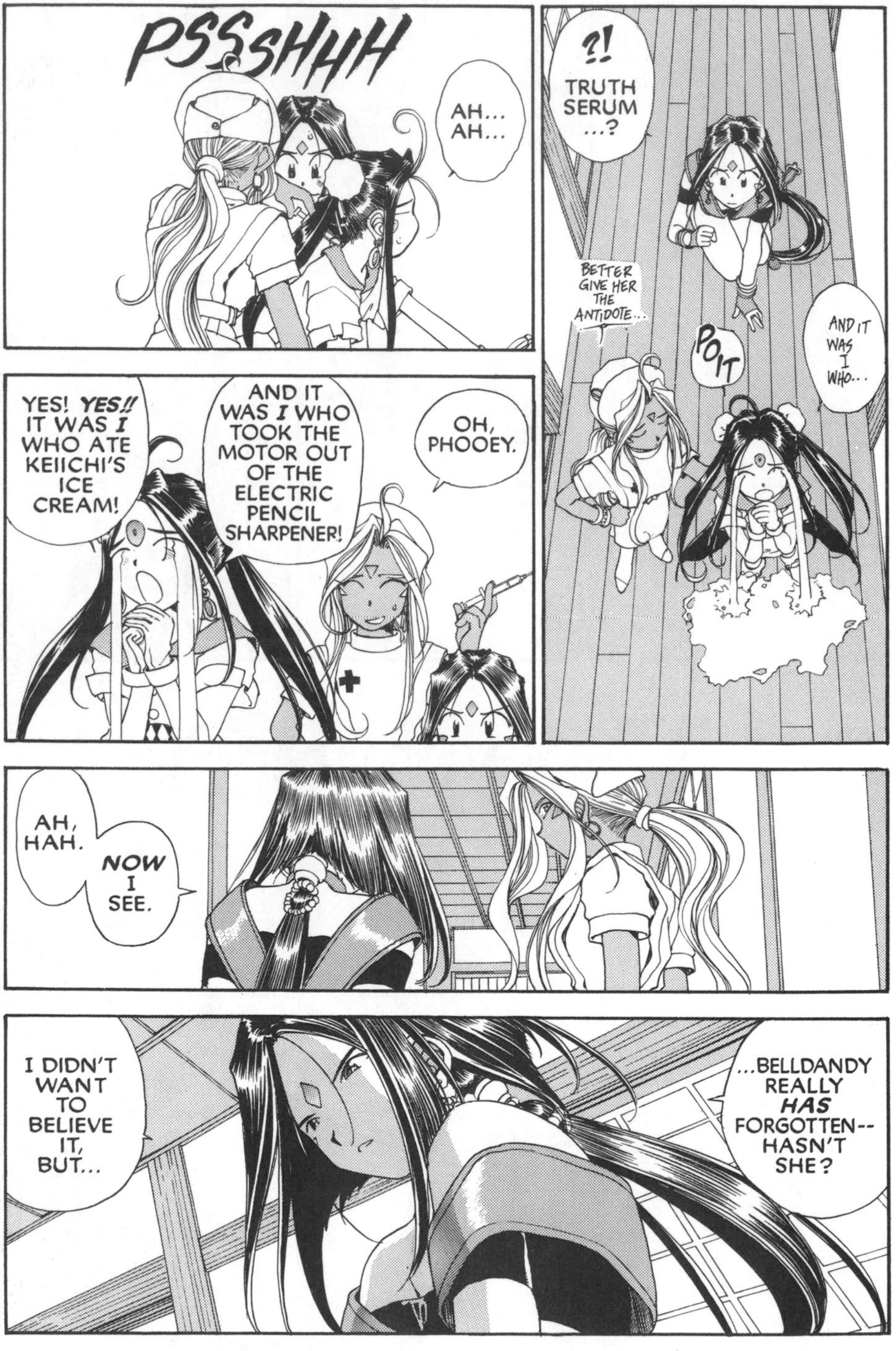
PSSSHHH
AH... AH...
YES! YES!! IT WAS I WHO ATE KEIICHI'S ICE CREAM!
AND IT WAS I WHO TOOK THE MOTOR OUT OF THE ELECTRIC PENCIL SHARPENER!
OH, PHOOEY.
?! TRUTH SERUM ...?
BETTER GIVE HER THE ANTIDOTE...
POIT
AND IT WAS I WHO...
AH, HAH.
NOW I SEE.
I DIDN'T WANT TO BELIEVE IT, BUT...
...BELLDANDY REALLY HAS FORGOTTEN-- HASN'T SHE?

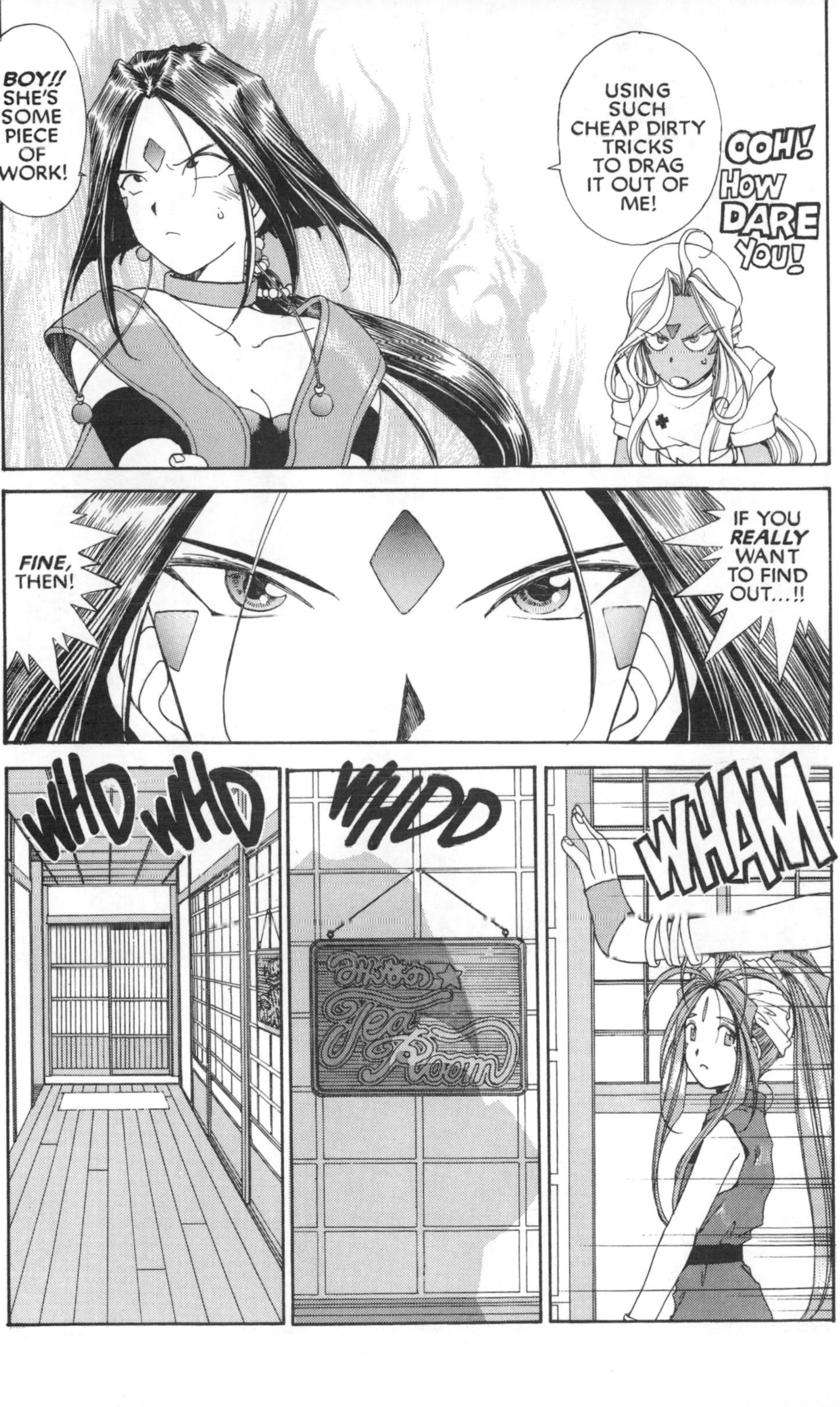
BOY!! SHE'S SOME PIECE OF WORK!
USING SUCH CHEAP DIRTY TRICKS TO DRAG IT OUT OF ME!
OOH! How DARE YOU!
FINE, THEN!
IF YOU REALLY WANT TO FIND OUT...!!
WHD WHD
WHDD
WHAM

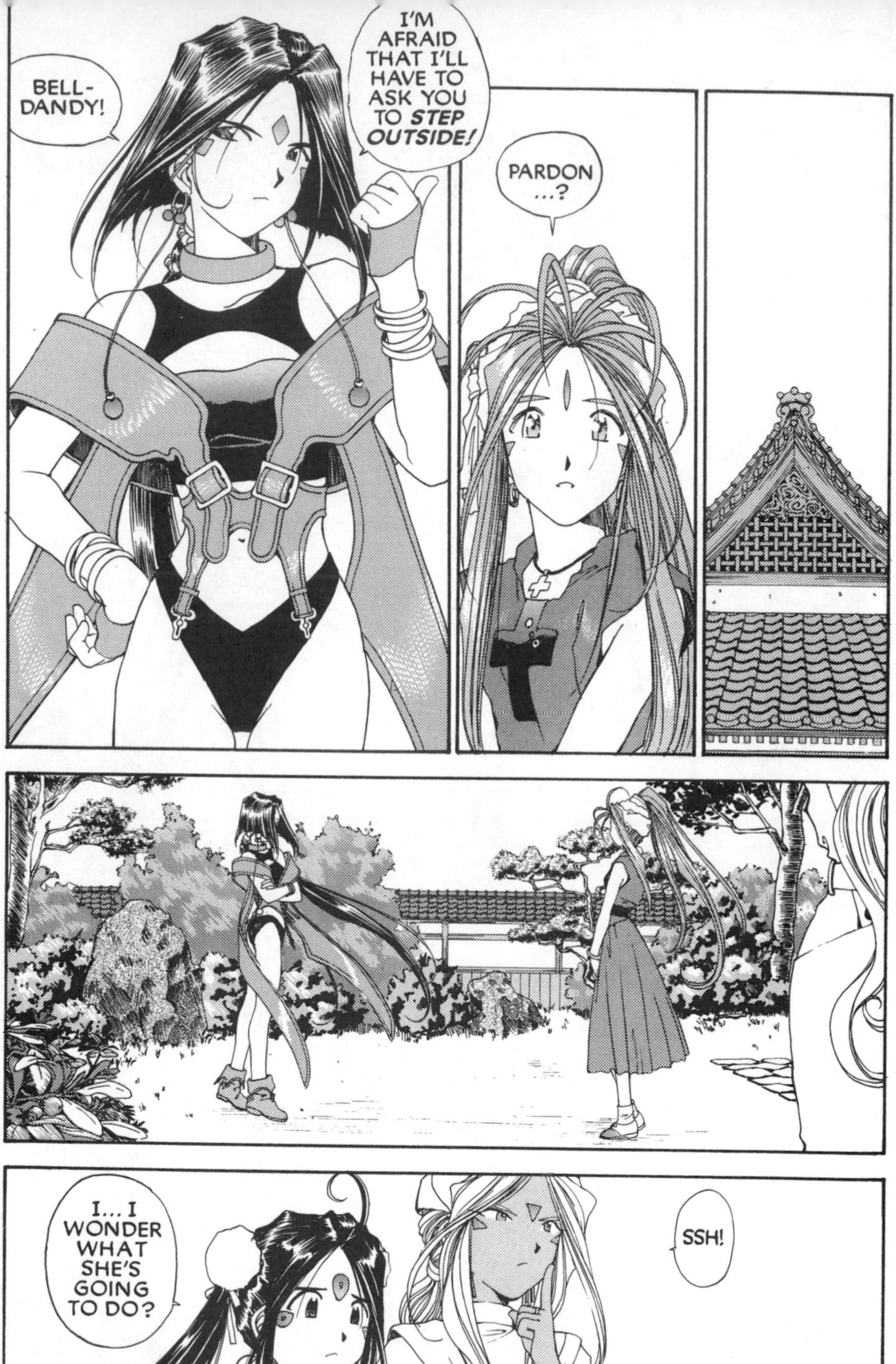
BELL-DANDY!
I'M AFRAID THAT I'LL HAVE TO ASK YOU TO STEP OUTSIDE!
PARDON ...?
I... I WONDER WHAT SHE'S GOING TO DO?
SSH!

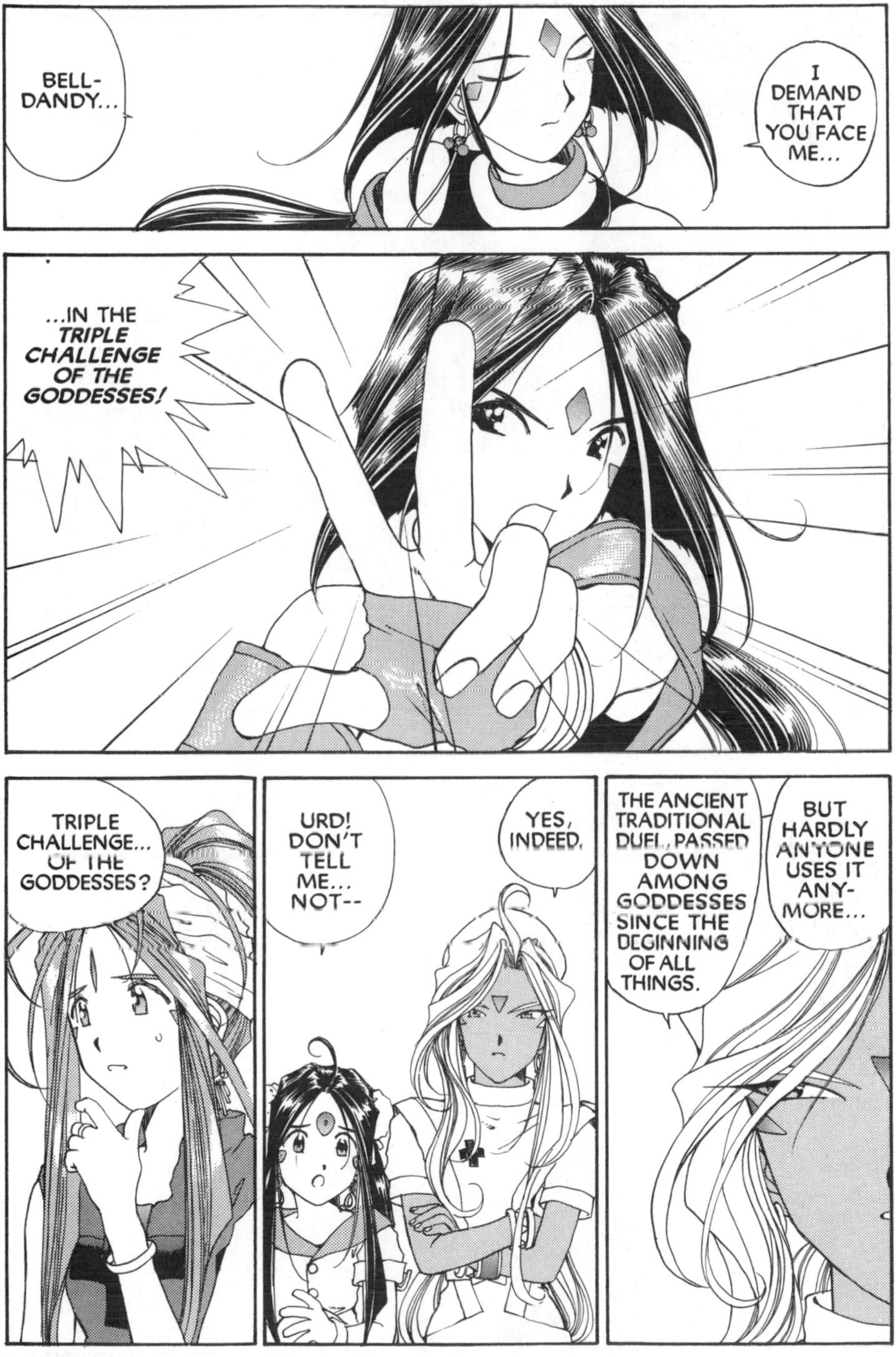
BELL-DANDY...
I DEMAND THAT YOU FACE ME...
...IN THE *TRIPLE CHALLENGE OF THE GODDESSES!*
TRIPLE CHALLENGE... OF THE GODDESSES?
URD! DON'T TELL ME... NOT--
YES, INDEED.
THE ANCIENT TRADITIONAL DUEL, PASSED DOWN AMONG GODDESSES SINCE THE BEGINNING OF ALL THINGS.
BUT HARDLY ANYONE USES IT ANY-MORE...

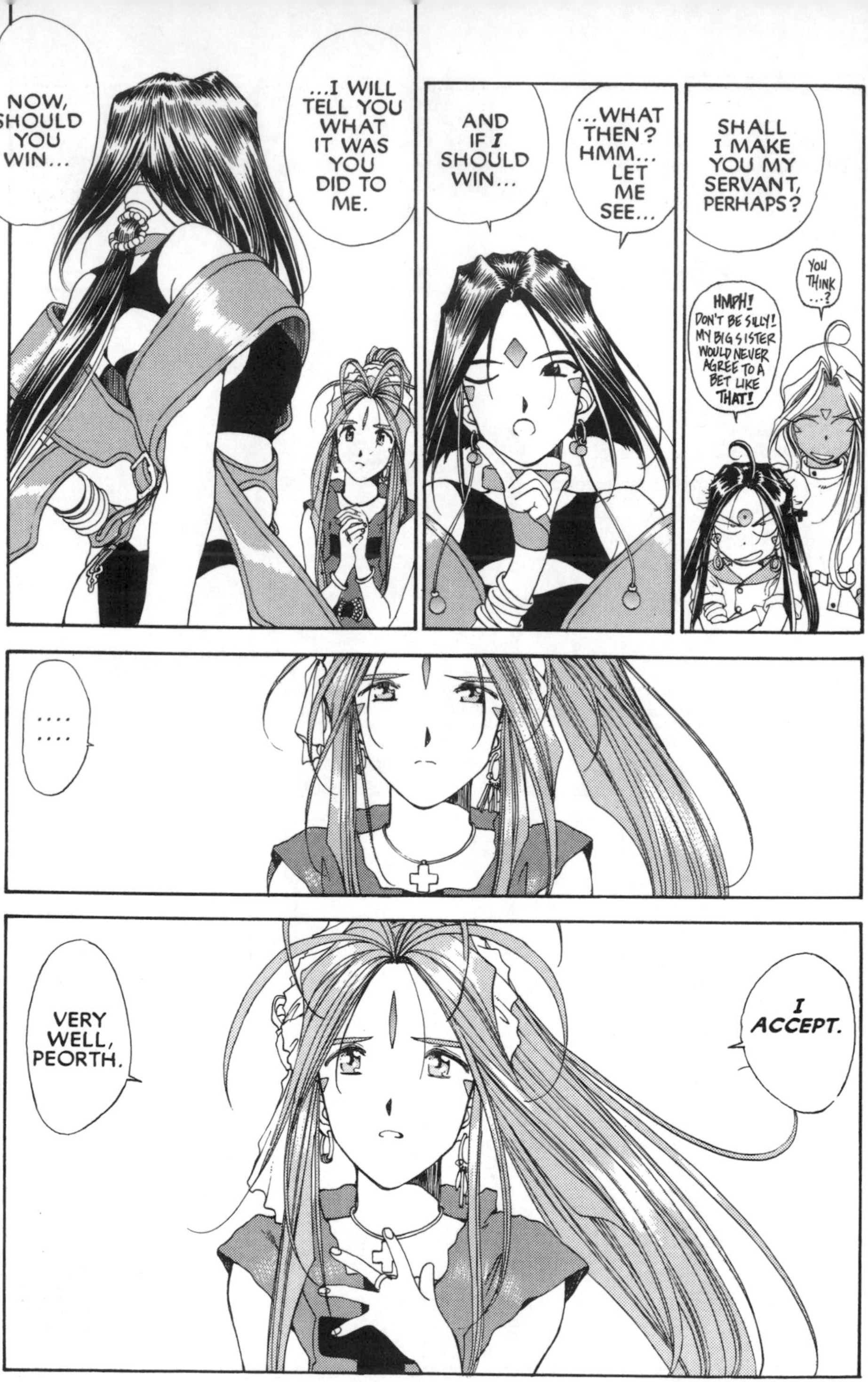
NOW, SHOULD YOU WIN...
...I WILL TELL YOU WHAT IT WAS YOU DID TO ME.
AND IF *I* SHOULD WIN...
...WHAT THEN? HMM... LET ME SEE...
SHALL I MAKE YOU MY SERVANT, PERHAPS?
HMPH! DON'T BE SILLY! MY BIG SISTER WOULD NEVER AGREE TO A BET LIKE **THAT!**
YOU THINK...?
....
VERY WELL, PEORTH.
I **ACCEPT.**

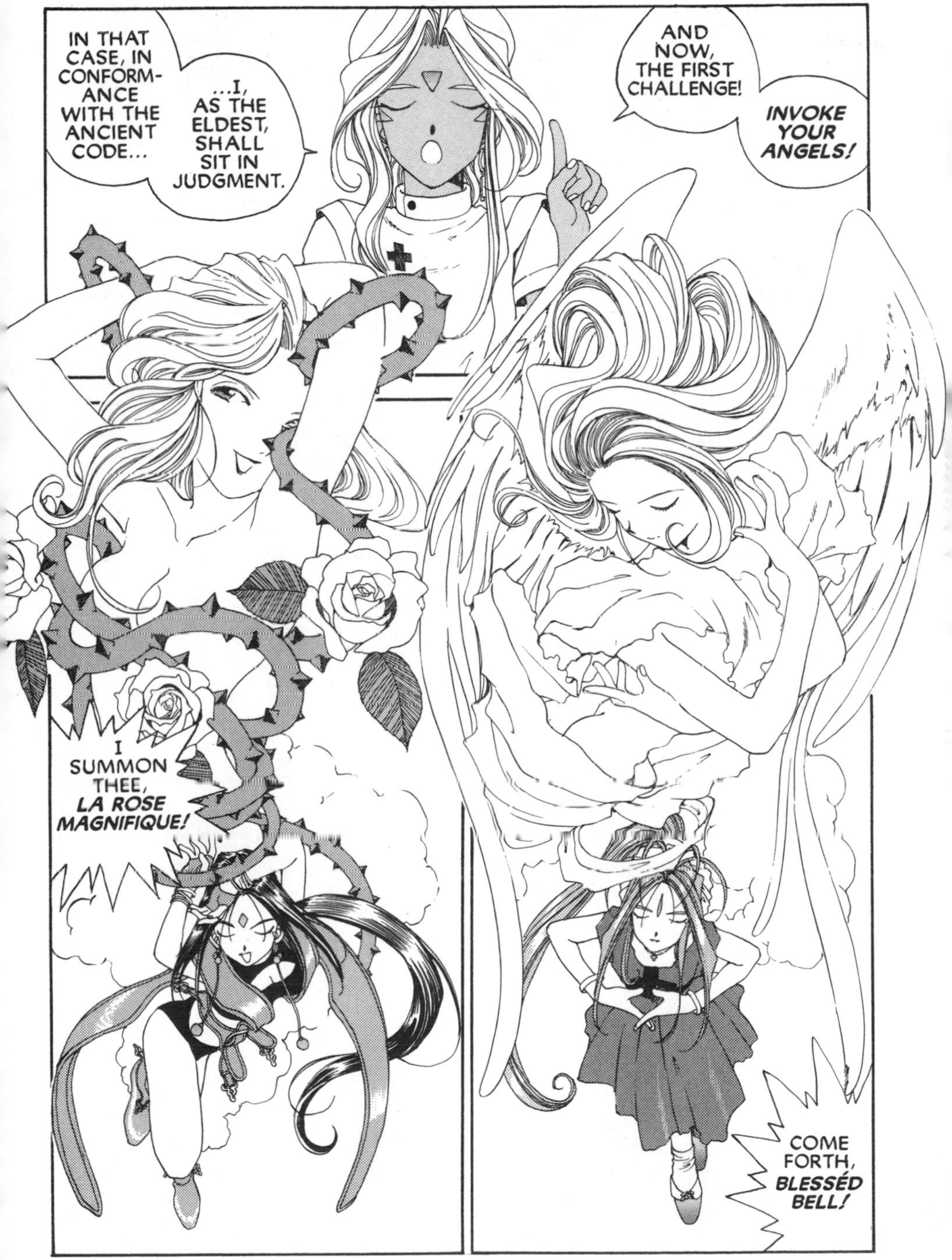
IN THAT CASE, IN CONFORMANCE WITH THE ANCIENT CODE...
...I, AS THE ELDEST, SHALL SIT IN JUDGMENT.
AND NOW, THE FIRST CHALLENGE!
INVOKE YOUR ANGELS!
I SUMMON THEE, LA ROSE MAGNIFIQUE!
COME FORTH, BLESSÉD BELL!

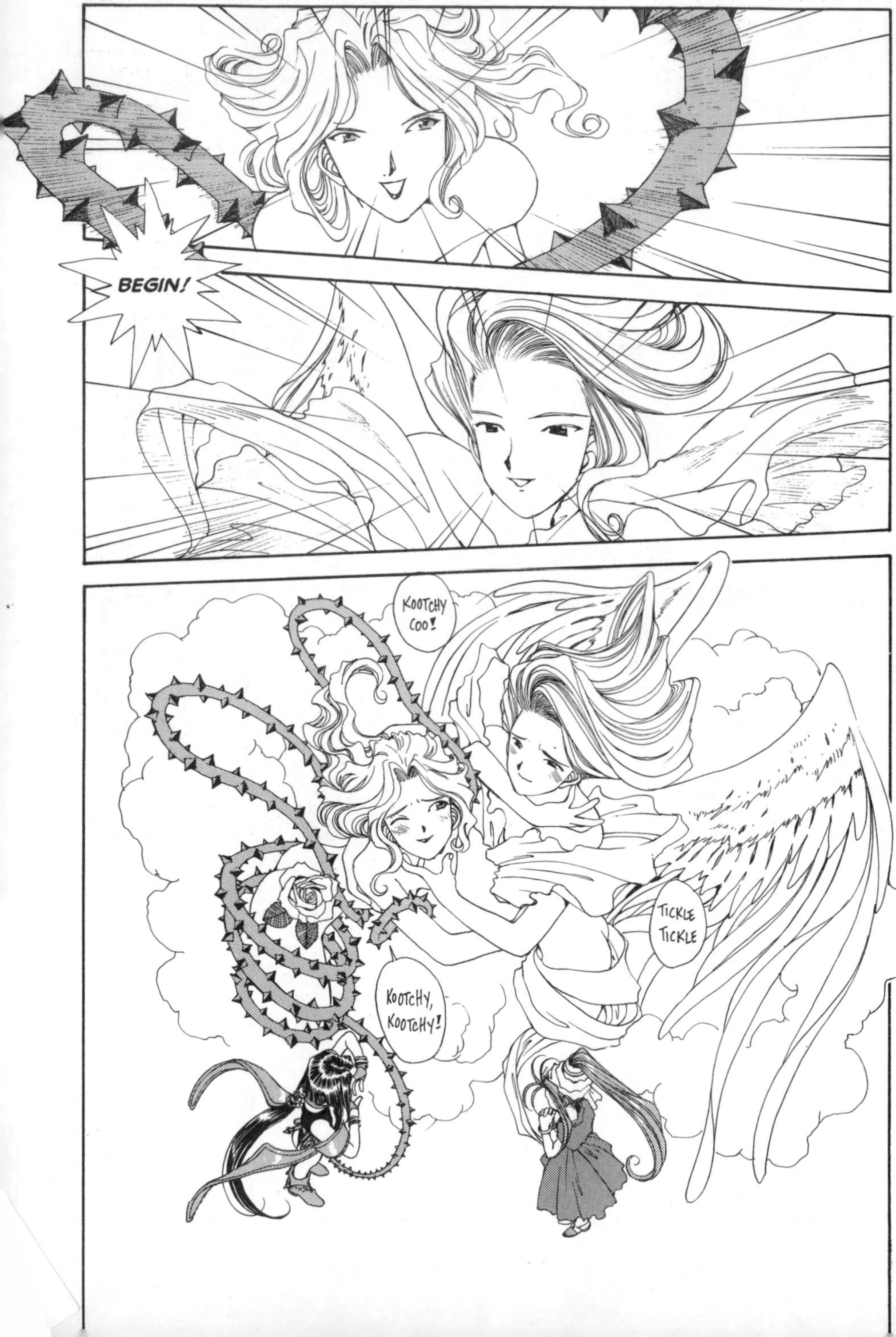
BEGIN!
KOOTCHY COO!
TICKLE TICKLE
KOOTCHY, KOOTCHY!

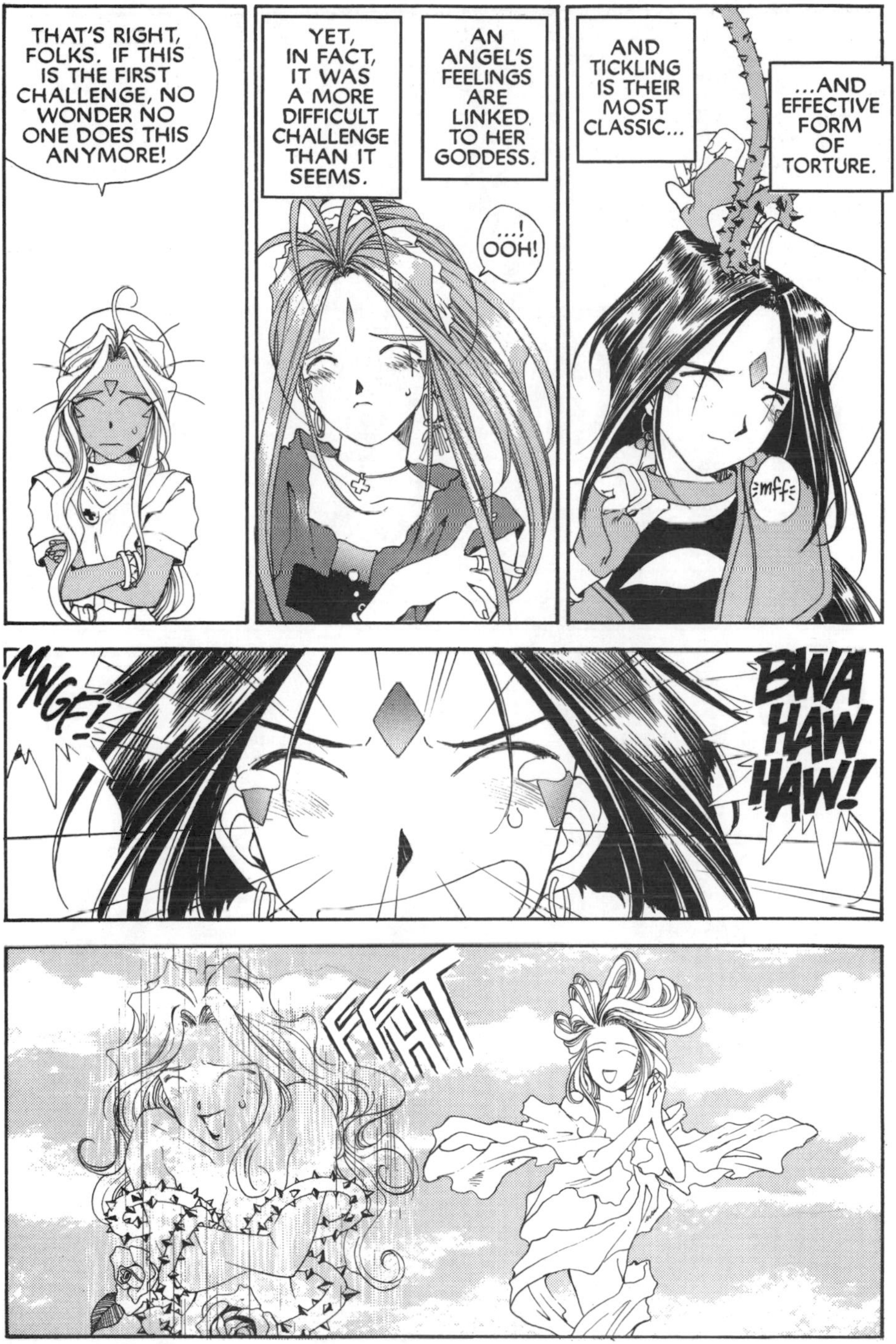
THAT'S RIGHT, FOLKS. IF THIS IS THE FIRST CHALLENGE, NO WONDER NO ONE DOES THIS ANYMORE!
YET, IN FACT, IT WAS A MORE DIFFICULT CHALLENGE THAN IT SEEMS.
AN ANGEL'S FEELINGS ARE LINKED TO HER GODDESS.
...! OOH!
AND TICKLING IS THEIR MOST CLASSIC...
...AND EFFECTIVE FORM OF TORTURE.
mff
MNGF!
BWA HAW HAW!
FFFT

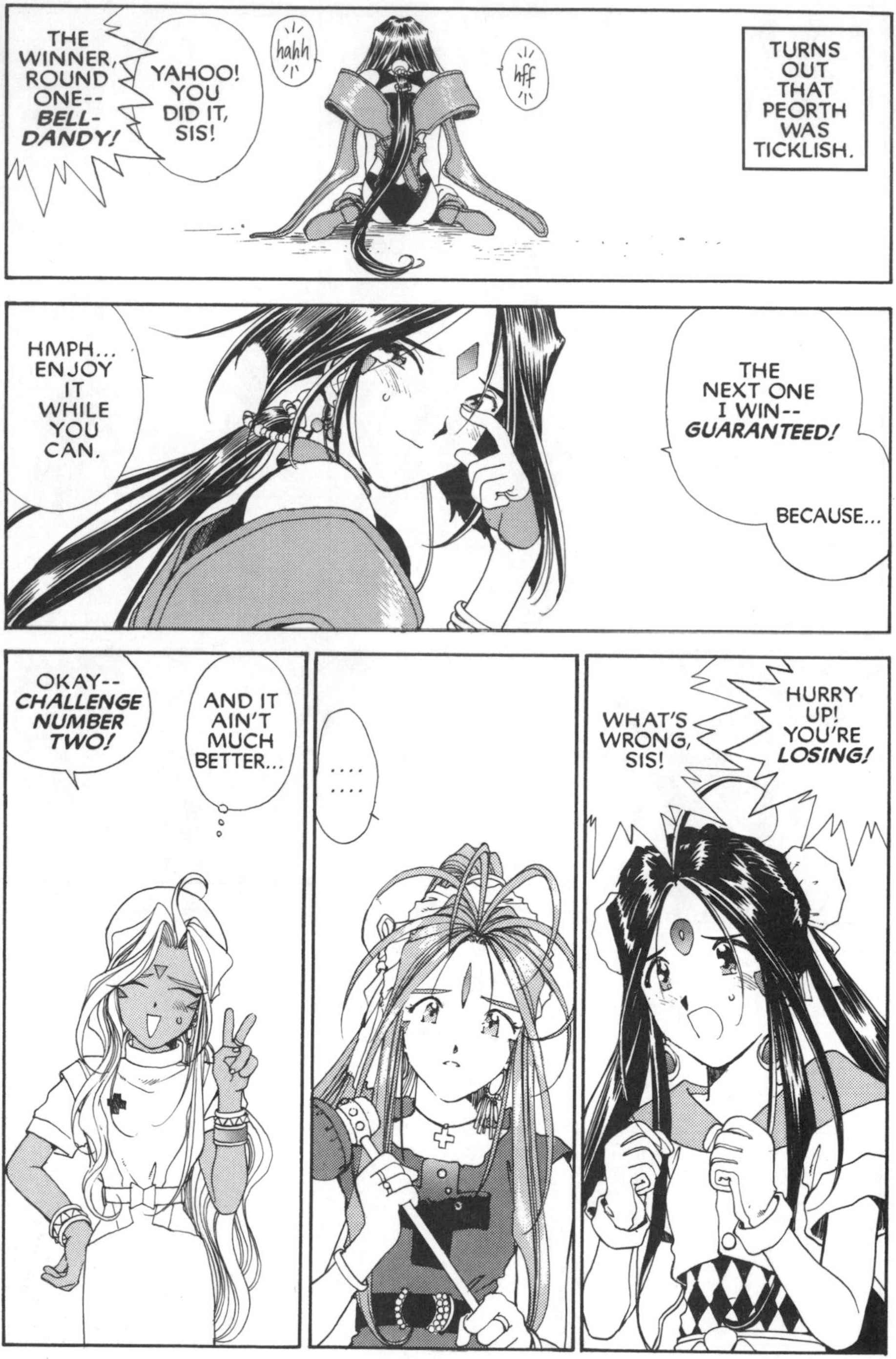
THE WINNER, ROUND ONE-- BELL-DANDY!
YAHOO! YOU DID IT, SIS!
hahh
hff
TURNS OUT THAT PEORTH WAS TICKLISH.
HMPH... ENJOY IT WHILE YOU CAN.
THE NEXT ONE I WIN-- GUARANTEED!
BECAUSE...
OKAY-- CHALLENGE NUMBER TWO!
AND IT AIN'T MUCH BETTER...
....
WHAT'S WRONG, SIS!
HURRY UP! YOU'RE LOSING!

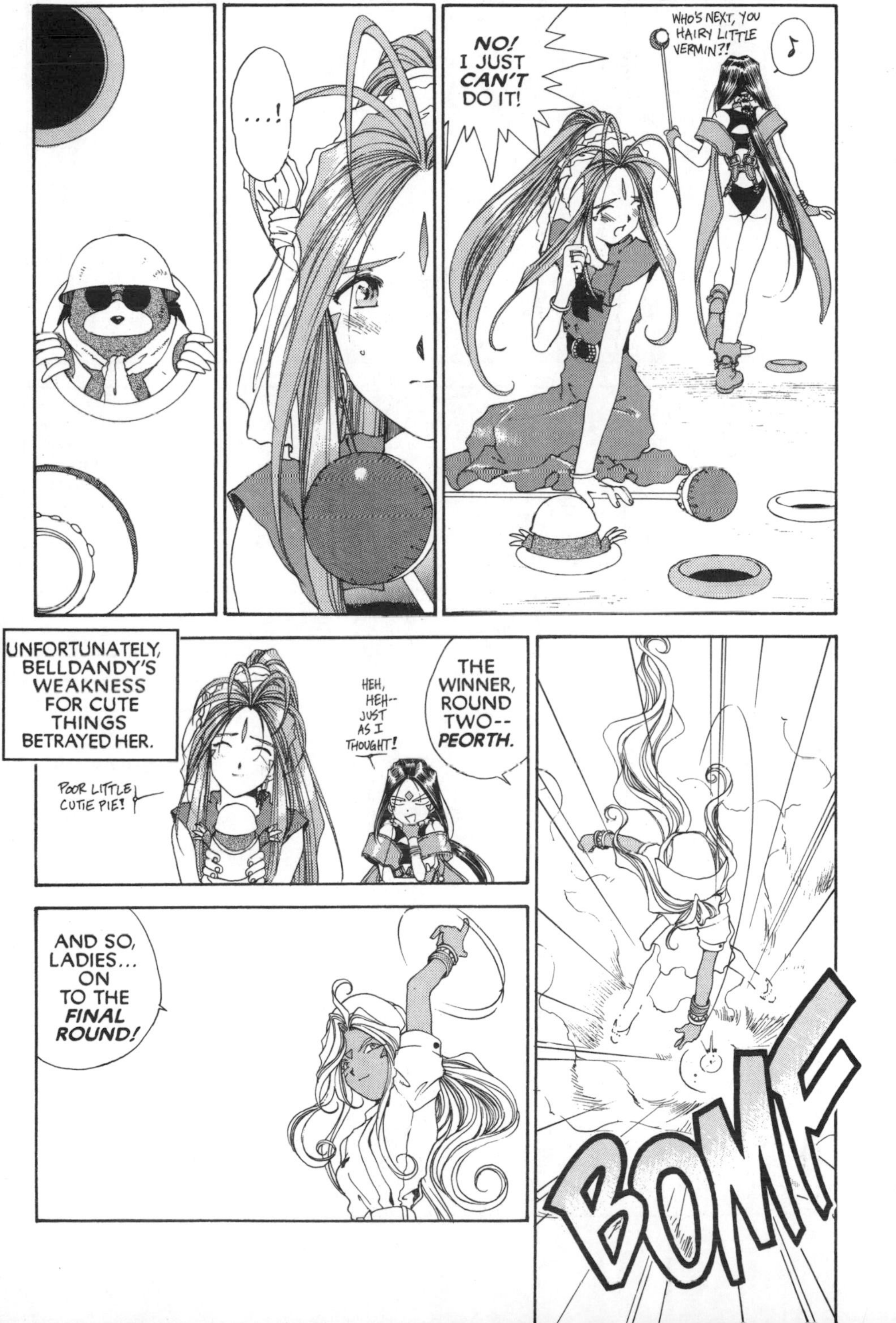
. . . !
NO! I JUST CAN'T DO IT!
WHO'S NEXT, YOU HAIRY LITTLE VERMIN?!
♪
UNFORTUNATELY, BELLDANDY'S WEAKNESS FOR CUTE THINGS BETRAYED HER.
POOR LITTLE CUTIE PIE!
HEH, HEH-- JUST AS I THOUGHT!
THE WINNER, ROUND TWO-- PEORTH.
AND SO, LADIES... ON TO THE FINAL ROUND!
BOMF

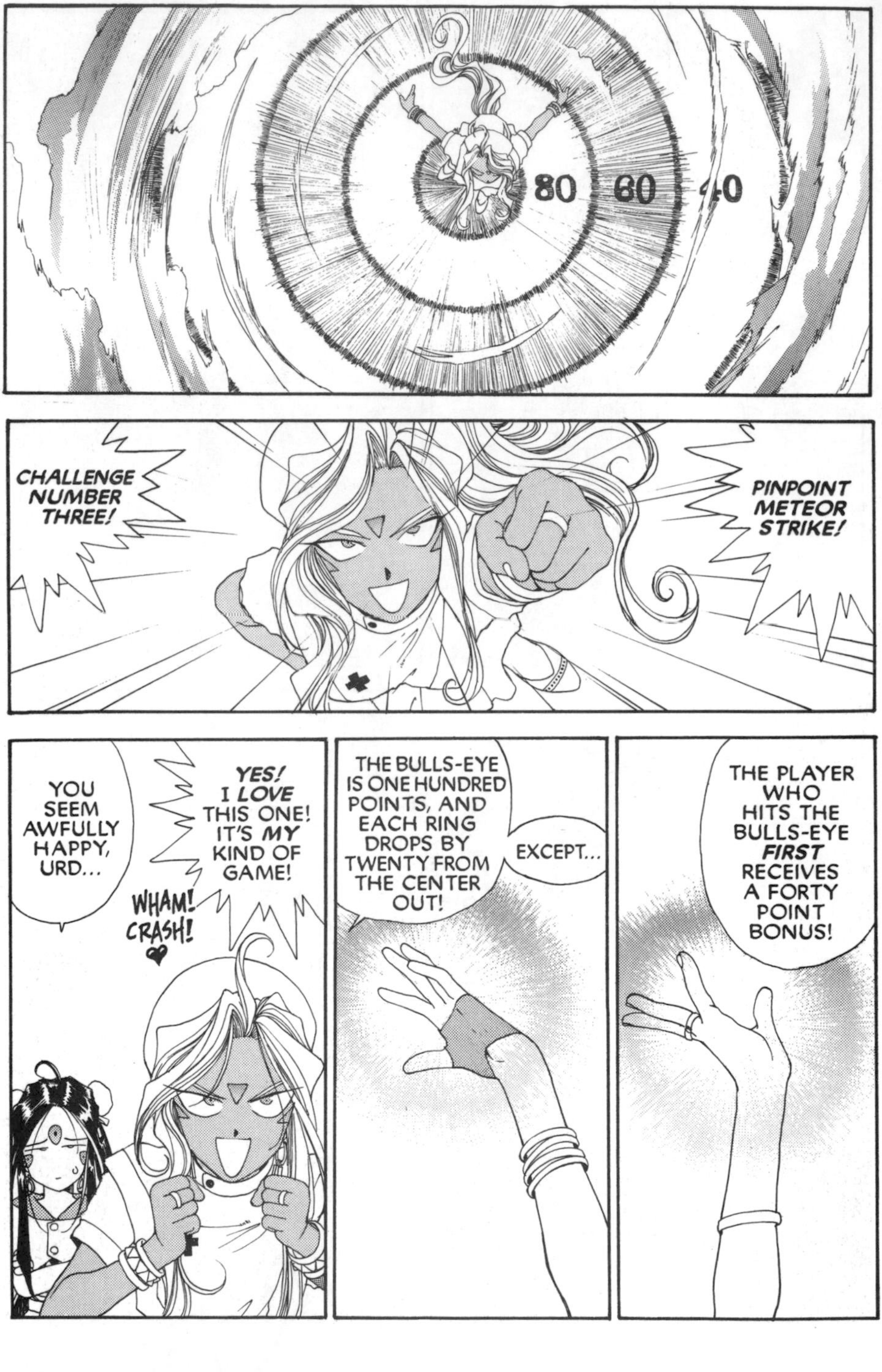
80
60
40
CHALLENGE NUMBER THREE!
PINPOINT METEOR STRIKE!
YOU SEEM AWFULLY HAPPY, URD...
YES! I *LOVE* THIS ONE! IT'S *MY* KIND OF GAME!
WHAM! CRASH!
THE BULLS-EYE IS ONE HUNDRED POINTS, AND EACH RING DROPS BY TWENTY FROM THE CENTER OUT!
EXCEPT...
THE PLAYER WHO HITS THE BULLS-EYE *FIRST* RECEIVES A FORTY POINT BONUS!

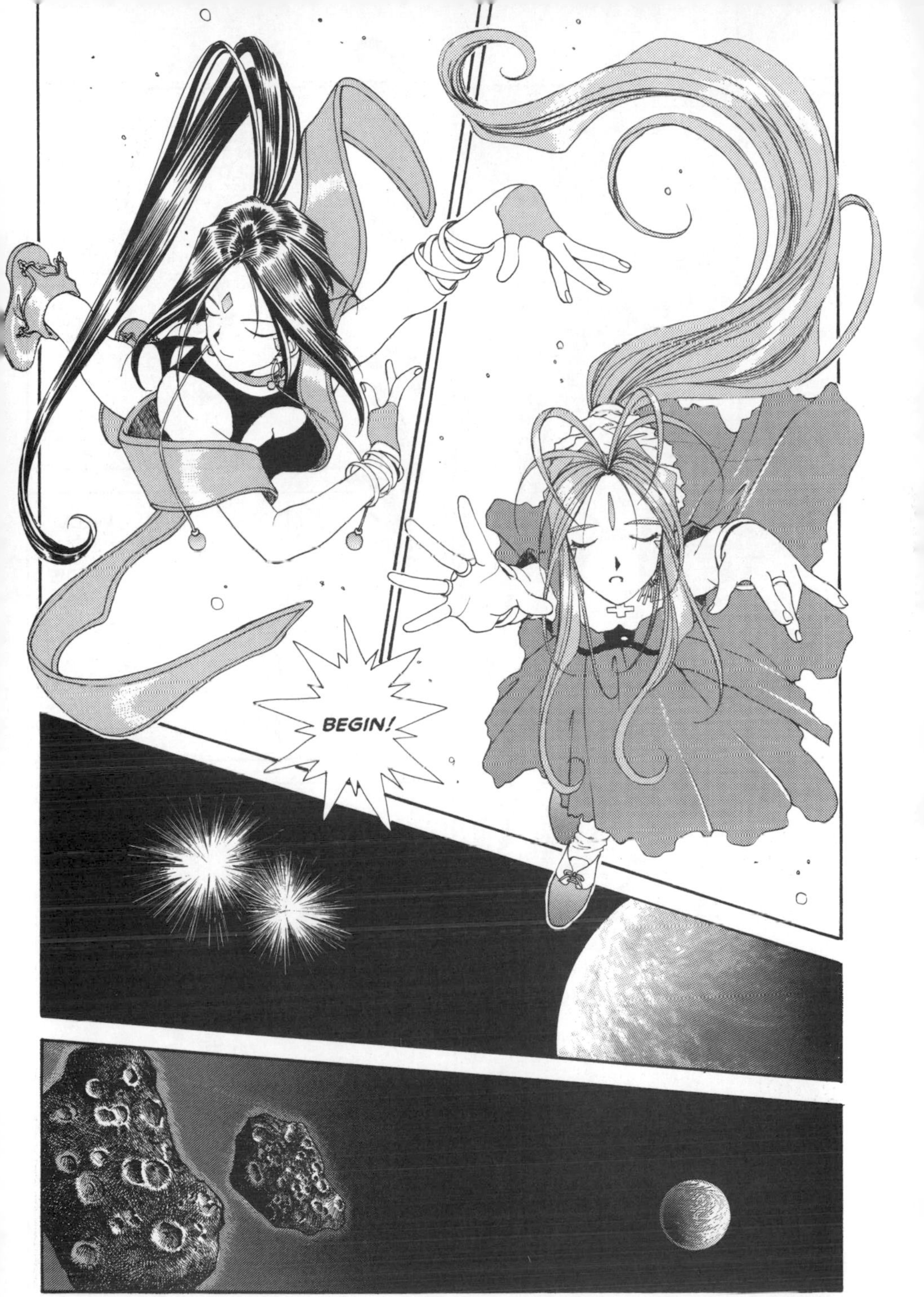
BEGIN!

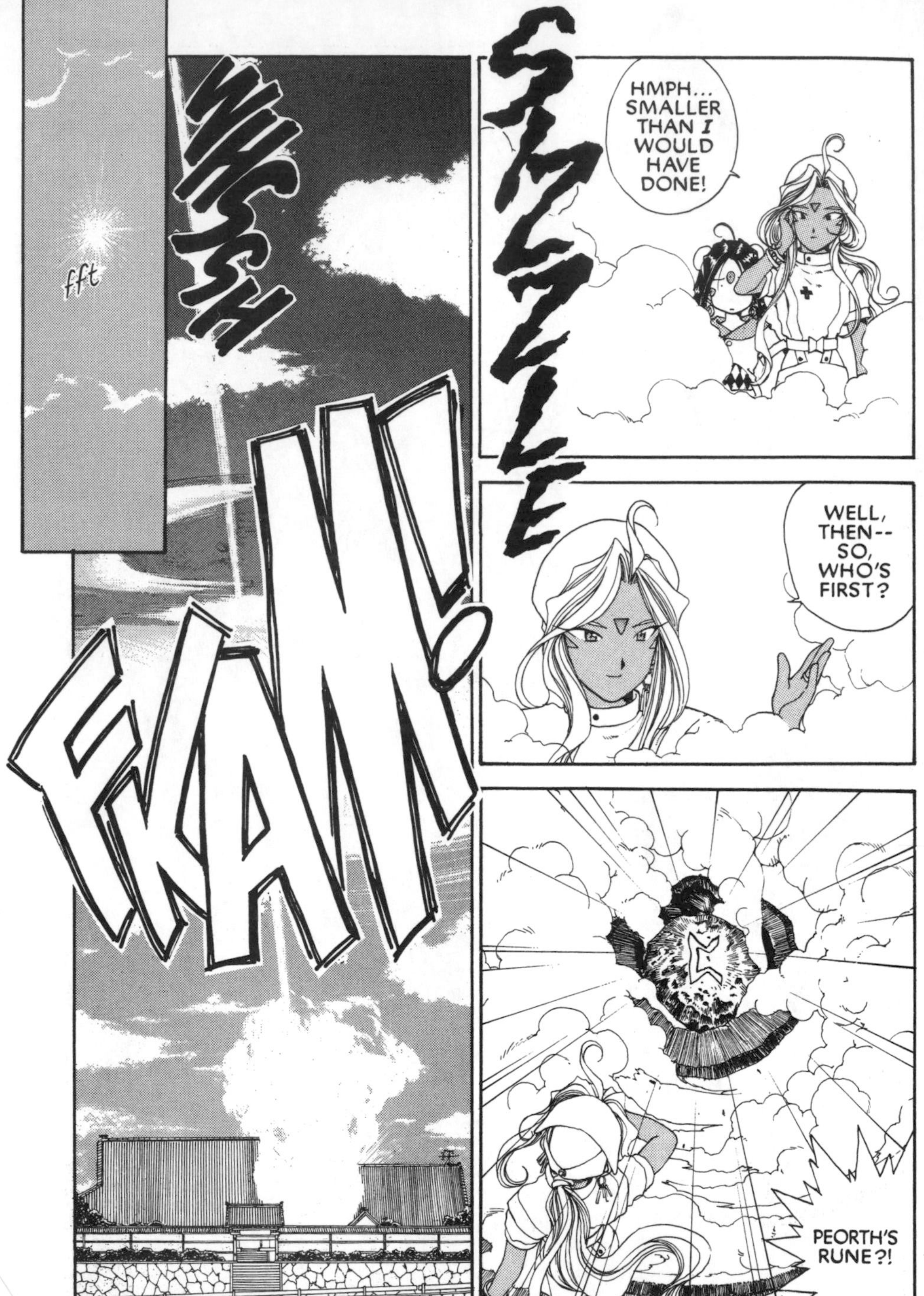
fft
WHSSH
FRAM!
SIZZLE
HMPH... SMALLER THAN I WOULD HAVE DONE!
WELL, THEN-- SO, WHO'S FIRST?
PEORTH'S RUNE?!

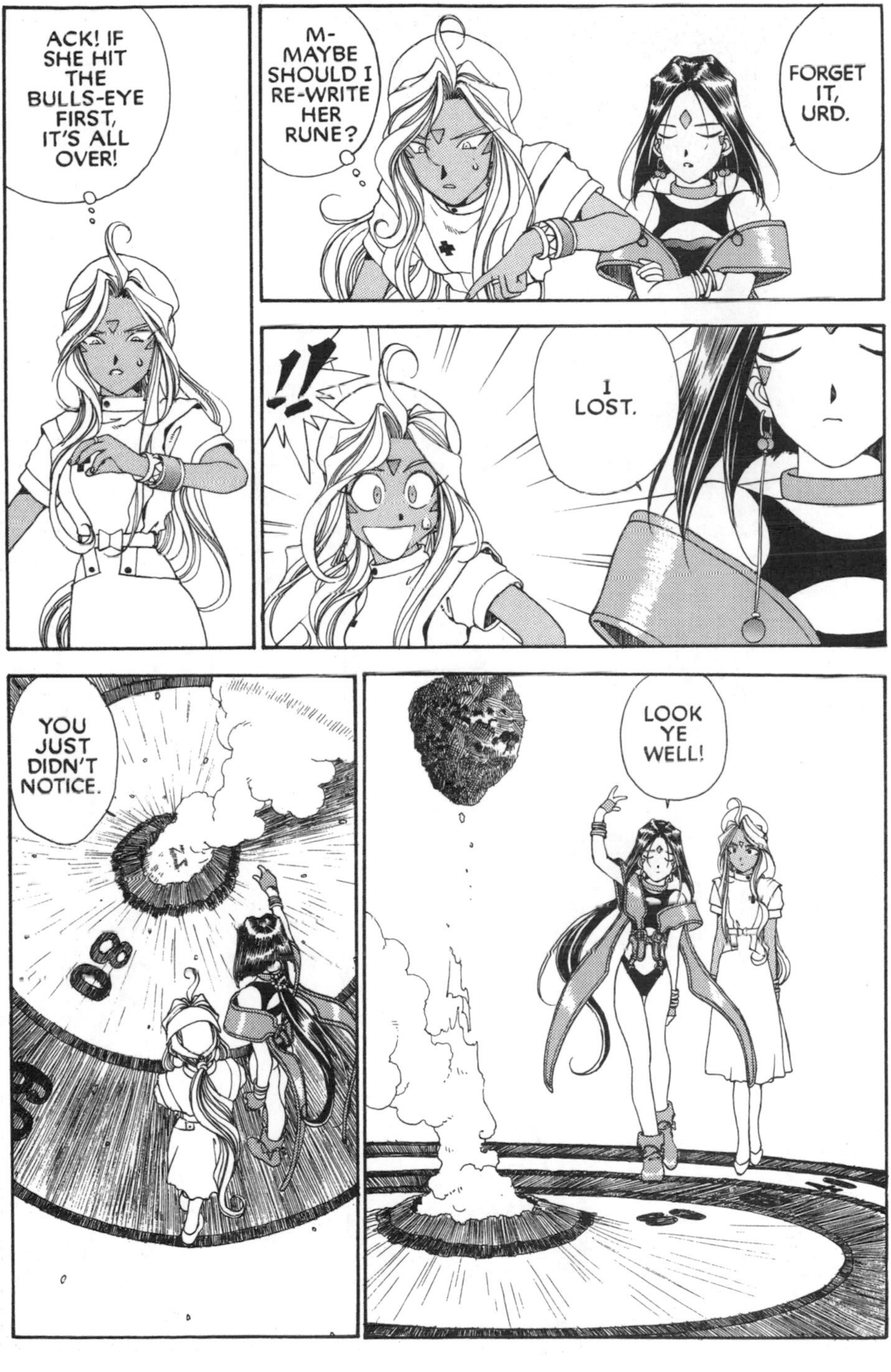
ACK! IF SHE HIT THE BULLS-EYE FIRST, IT'S ALL OVER!
M-MAYBE SHOULD I RE-WRITE HER RUNE?
FORGET IT, URD.
!!
I LOST.
YOU JUST DIDN'T NOTICE.
LOOK YE WELL!

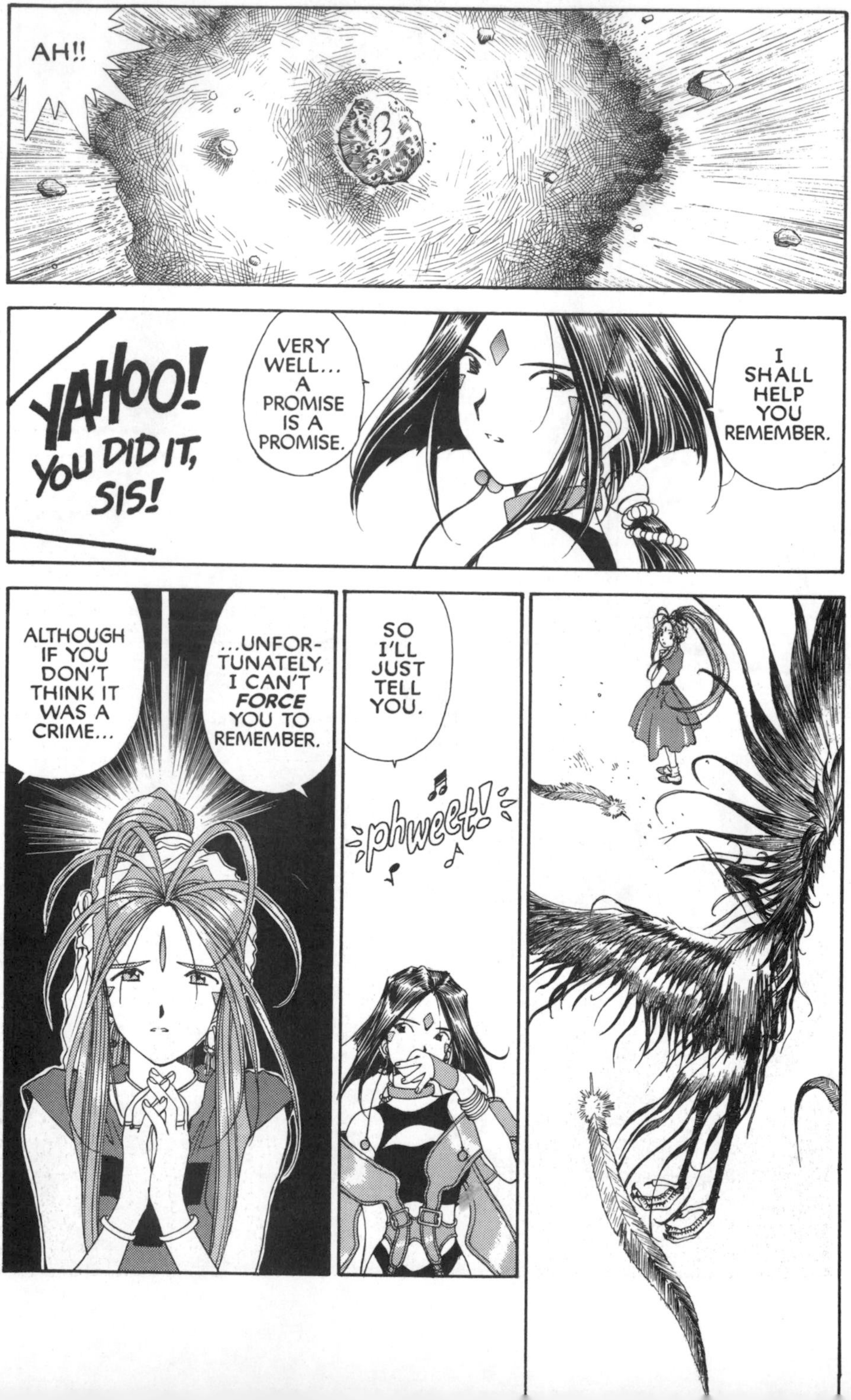
AH!!
YAHOO! YOU DID IT, SIS!
VERY WELL... A PROMISE IS A PROMISE.
I SHALL HELP YOU REMEMBER.
ALTHOUGH IF YOU DON'T THINK IT WAS A CRIME...
...UNFORTUNATELY, I CAN'T *FORCE* YOU TO REMEMBER.
SO I'LL JUST TELL YOU.
phweet!

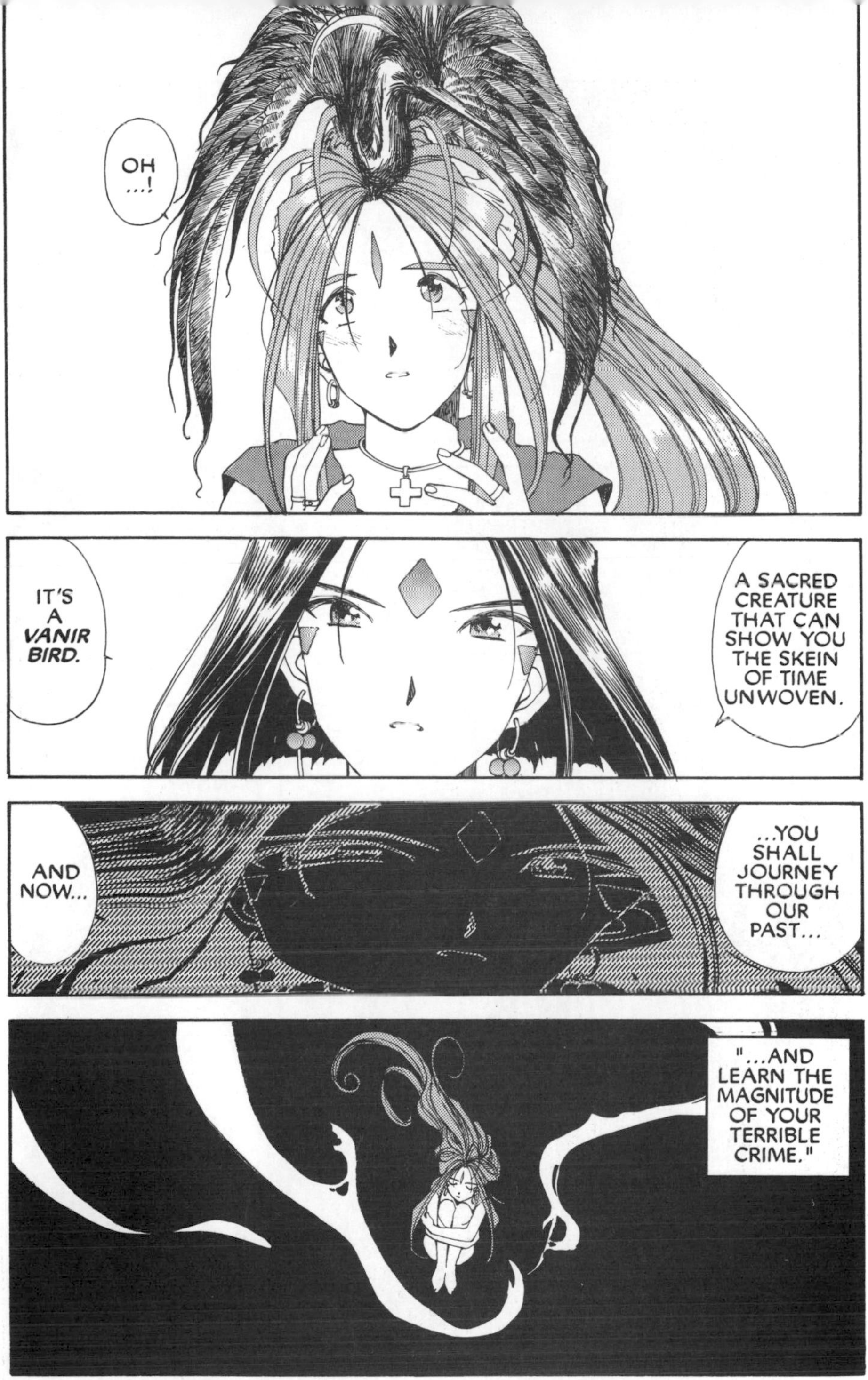
OH ...!
IT'S A *VANIR BIRD*.
A SACRED CREATURE THAT CAN SHOW YOU THE SKEIN OF TIME UNWOVEN.
AND NOW...
...YOU SHALL JOURNEY THROUGH OUR PAST...
"...AND LEARN THE MAGNITUDE OF YOUR TERRIBLE CRIME."

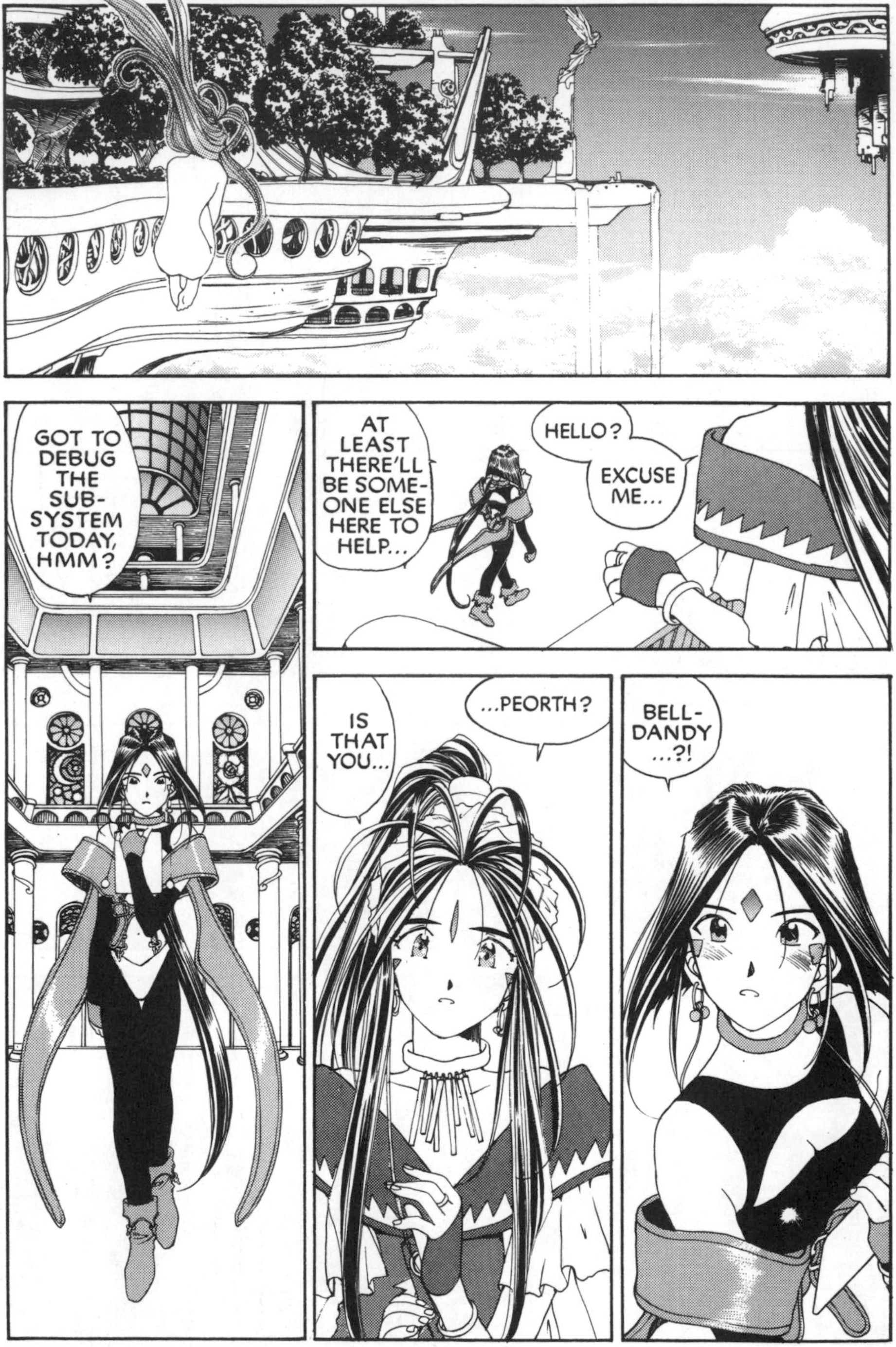
GOT TO DEBUG THE SUB-SYSTEM TODAY, HMM?
AT LEAST THERE'LL BE SOME-ONE ELSE HERE TO HELP...
HELLO?
EXCUSE ME...
IS THAT YOU...
...PEORTH?
BELL-DANDY ...?!

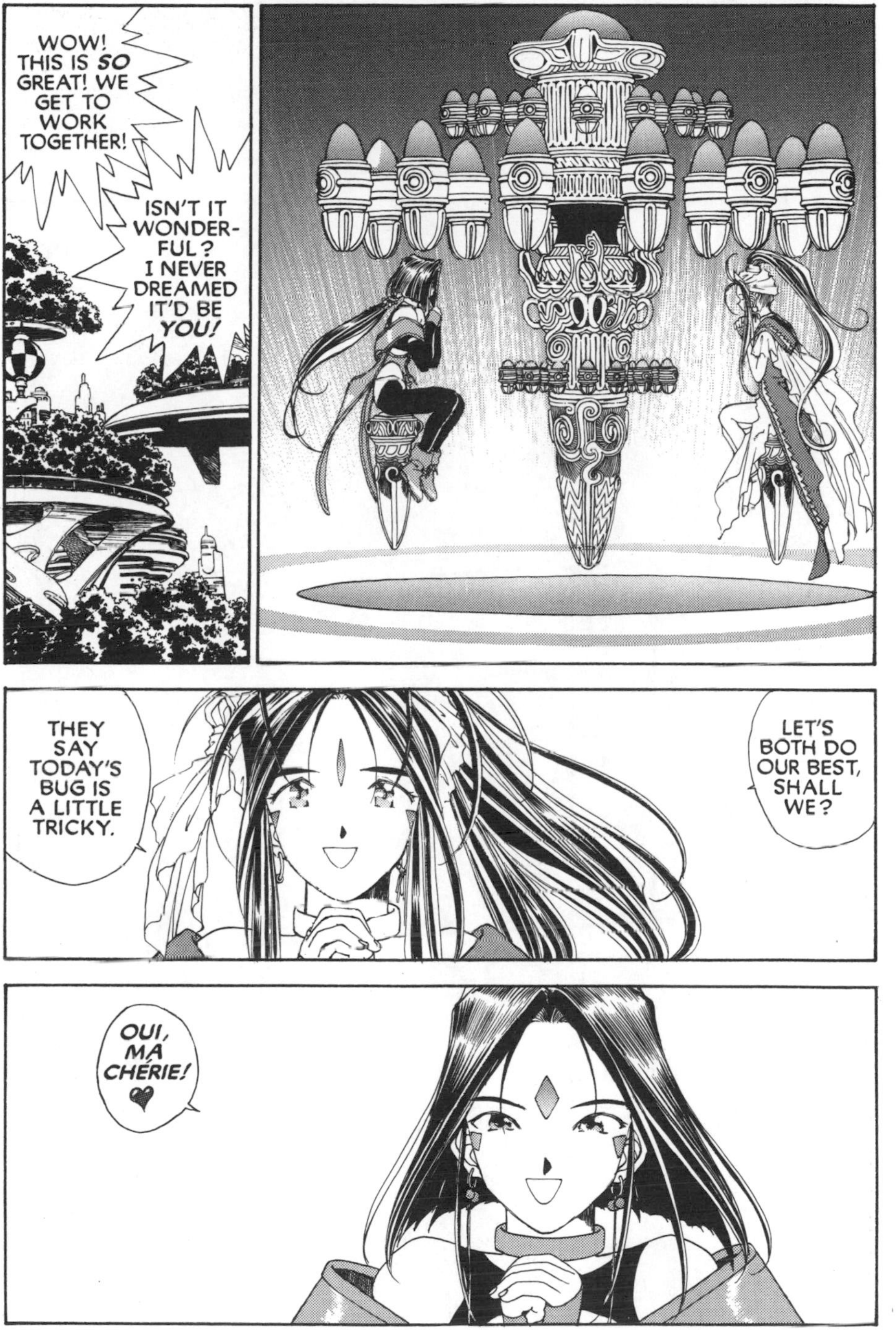
WOW! THIS IS *SO* GREAT! WE GET TO WORK TOGETHER!
ISN'T IT WONDER-FUL? I NEVER DREAMED IT'D BE *YOU!*
THEY SAY TODAY'S BUG IS A LITTLE TRICKY.
LET'S BOTH DO OUR BEST, SHALL WE?
OUI, MA CHÉRIE! ♥

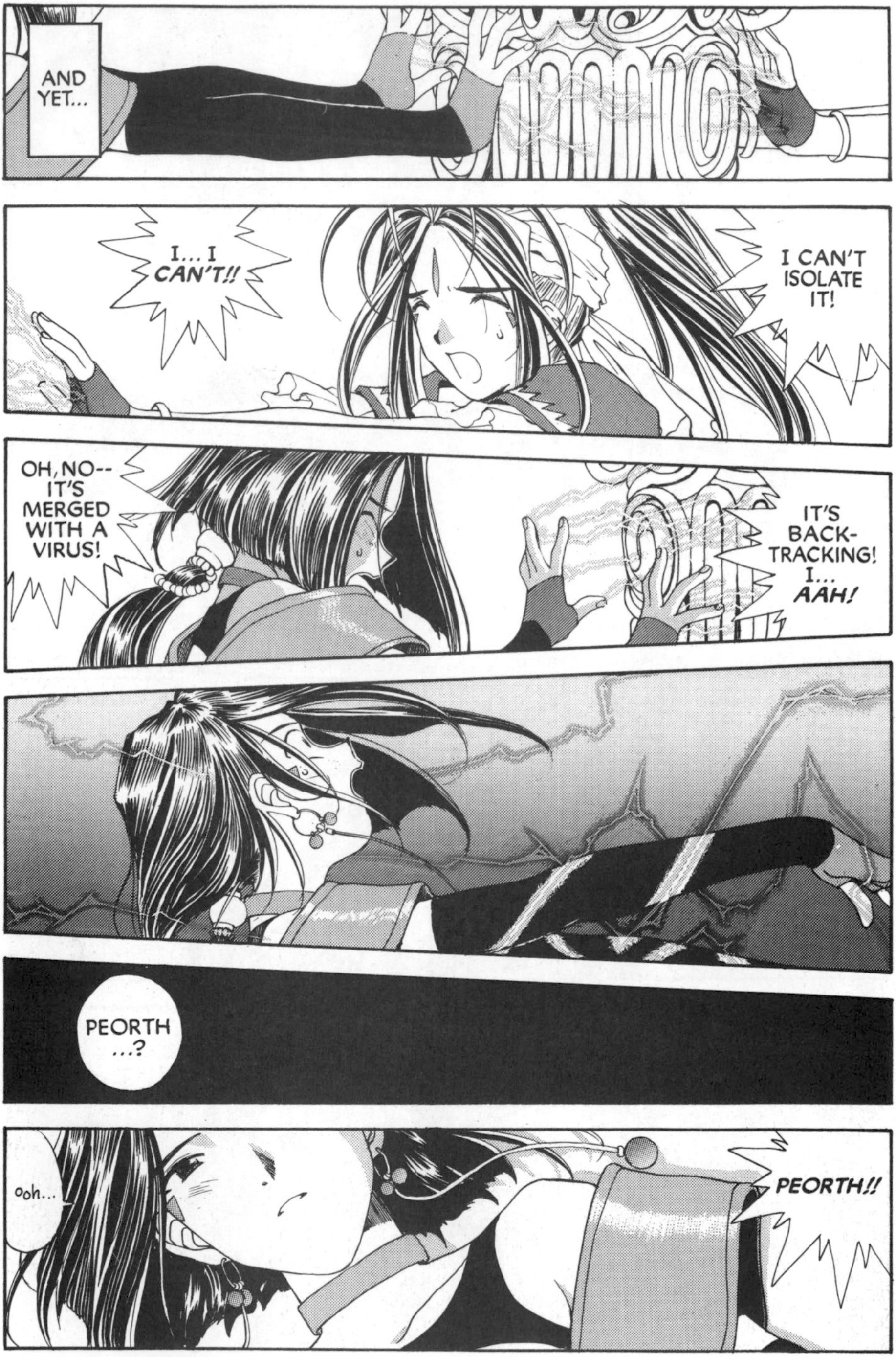
AND YET...
I... I CAN'T!!
I CAN'T ISOLATE IT!
OH, NO-- IT'S MERGED WITH A VIRUS!
IT'S BACK-TRACKING! I... AAH!
PEORTH ...?
ooh...
PEORTH!!

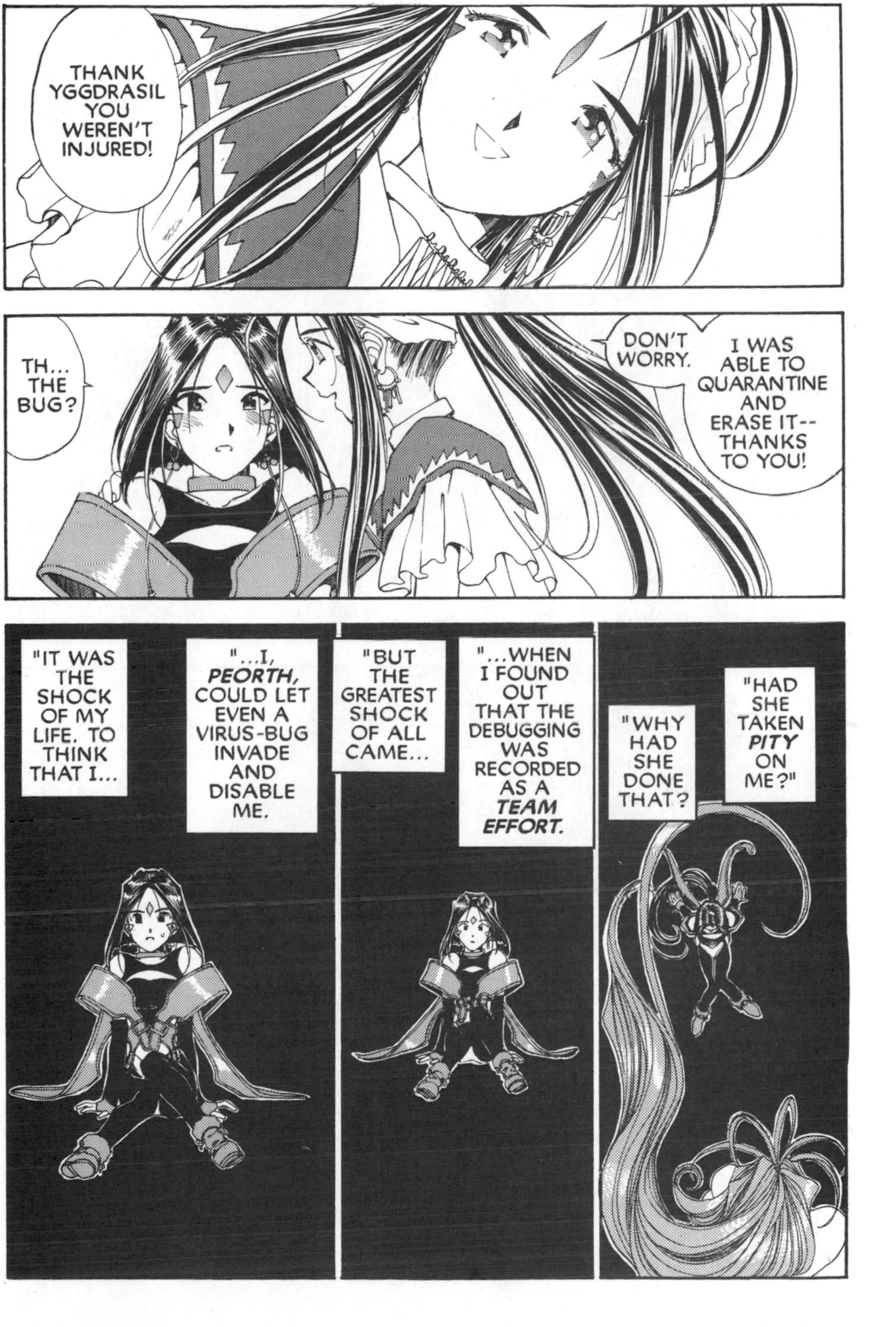
THANK YGGDRASIL YOU WEREN'T INJURED!
TH... THE BUG?
DON'T WORRY.
I WAS ABLE TO QUARANTINE AND ERASE IT-- THANKS TO YOU!
"IT WAS THE SHOCK OF MY LIFE. TO THINK THAT I...
"...I, PEORTH, COULD LET EVEN A VIRUS-BUG INVADE AND DISABLE ME.
"BUT THE GREATEST SHOCK OF ALL CAME...
"...WHEN I FOUND OUT THAT THE DEBUGGING WAS RECORDED AS A TEAM EFFORT.
"WHY HAD SHE DONE THAT?
"HAD SHE TAKEN PITY ON ME?"

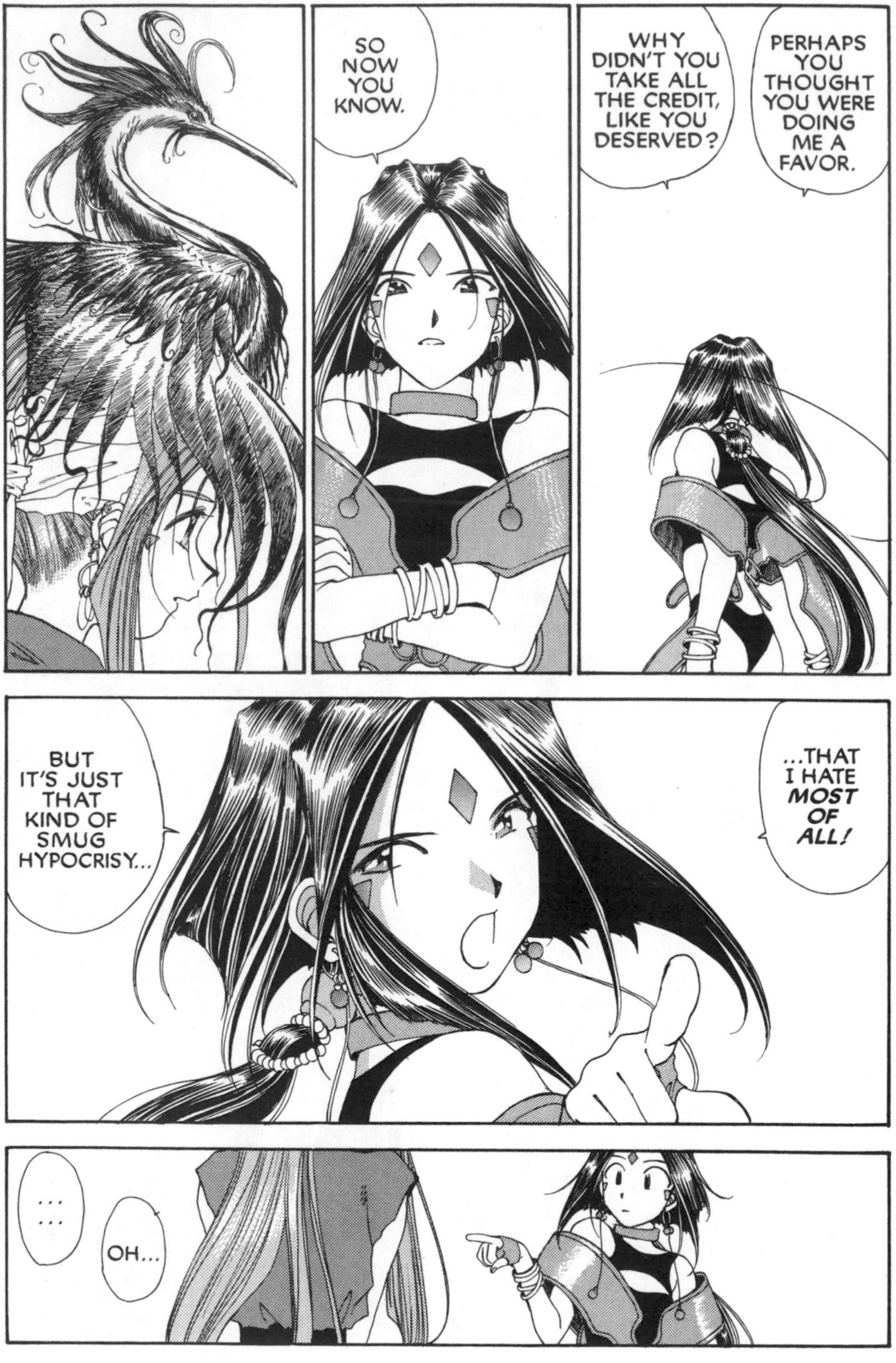
SO NOW YOU KNOW.
WHY DIDN'T YOU TAKE ALL THE CREDIT, LIKE YOU DESERVED?
PERHAPS YOU THOUGHT YOU WERE DOING ME A FAVOR.
BUT IT'S JUST THAT KIND OF SMUG HYPOCRISY...
...THAT I HATE *MOST OF ALL!*
... ...
OH...

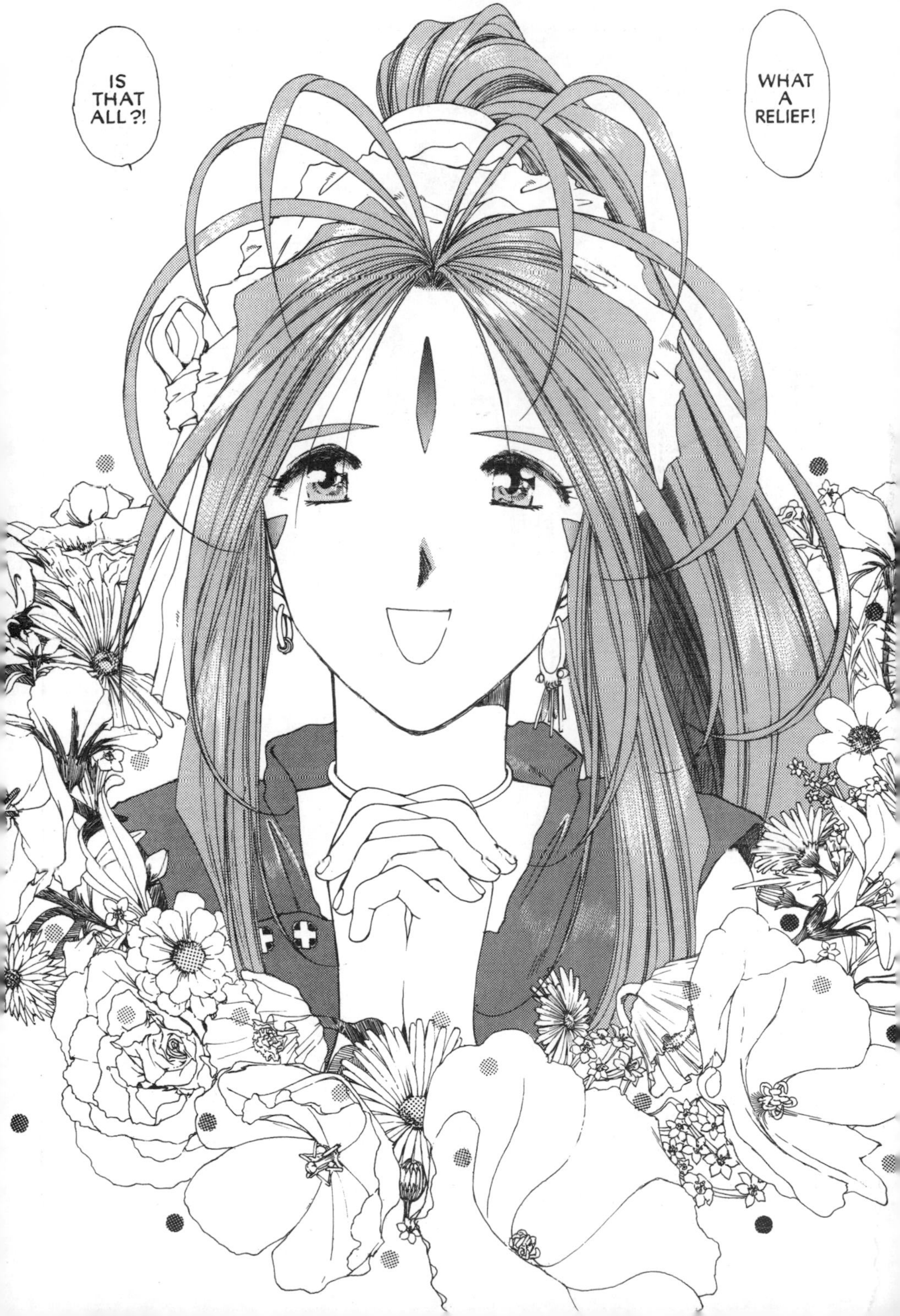
IS THAT ALL?!
WHAT A RELIEF!

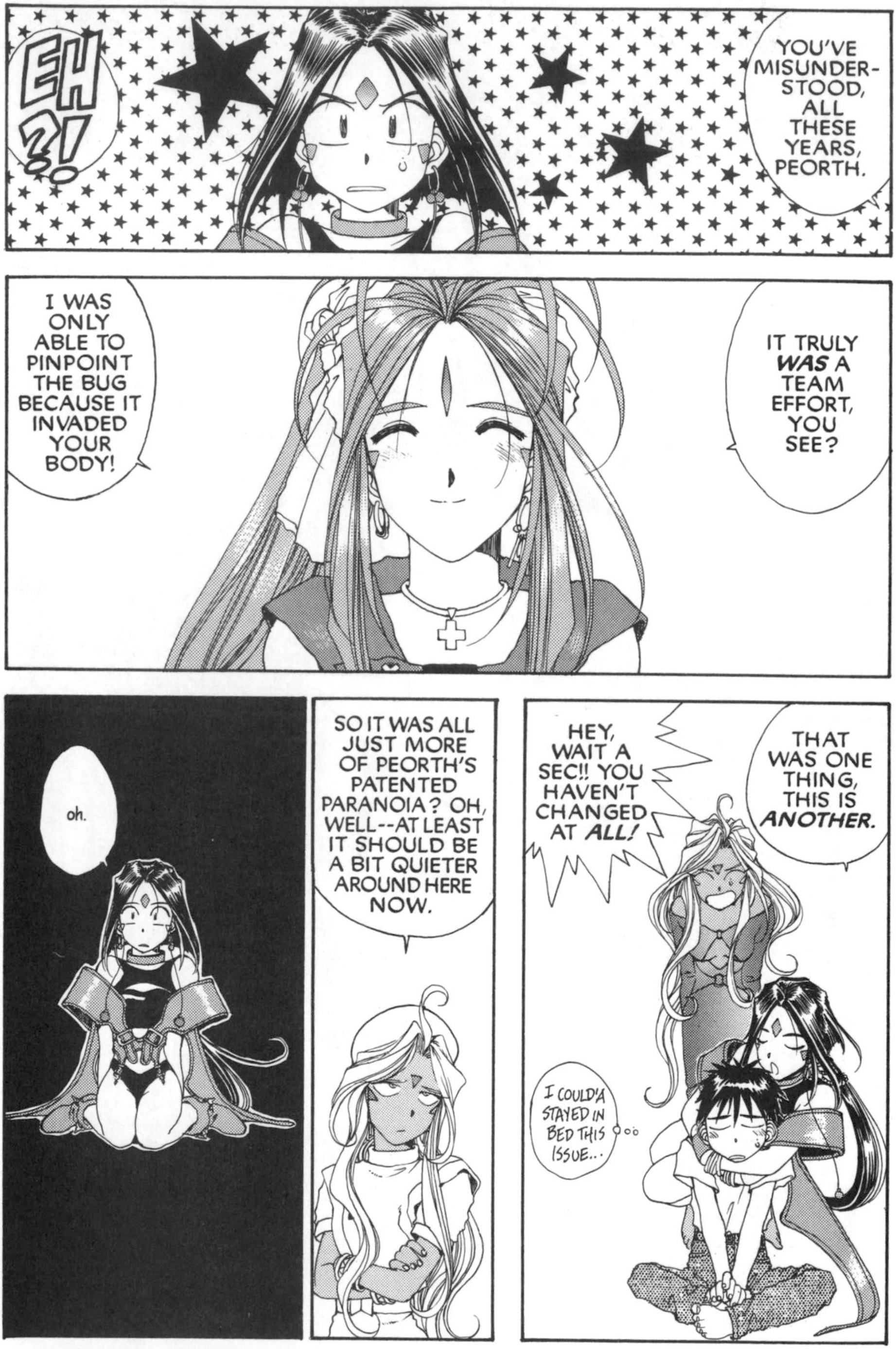
EH?!
YOU'VE MISUNDERSTOOD, ALL THESE YEARS, PEORTH.
I WAS ONLY ABLE TO PINPOINT THE BUG BECAUSE IT INVADED YOUR BODY!
IT TRULY WAS A TEAM EFFORT, YOU SEE?
oh.
SO IT WAS ALL JUST MORE OF PEORTH'S PATENTED PARANOIA? OH, WELL--AT LEAST IT SHOULD BE A BIT QUIETER AROUND HERE NOW.
HEY, WAIT A SEC!! YOU HAVEN'T CHANGED AT ALL!
THAT WAS ONE THING, THIS IS ANOTHER.
I COULD'A STAYED IN BED THIS ISSUE...

Men Are From Earth, Goddesses Are From Yggdrasil

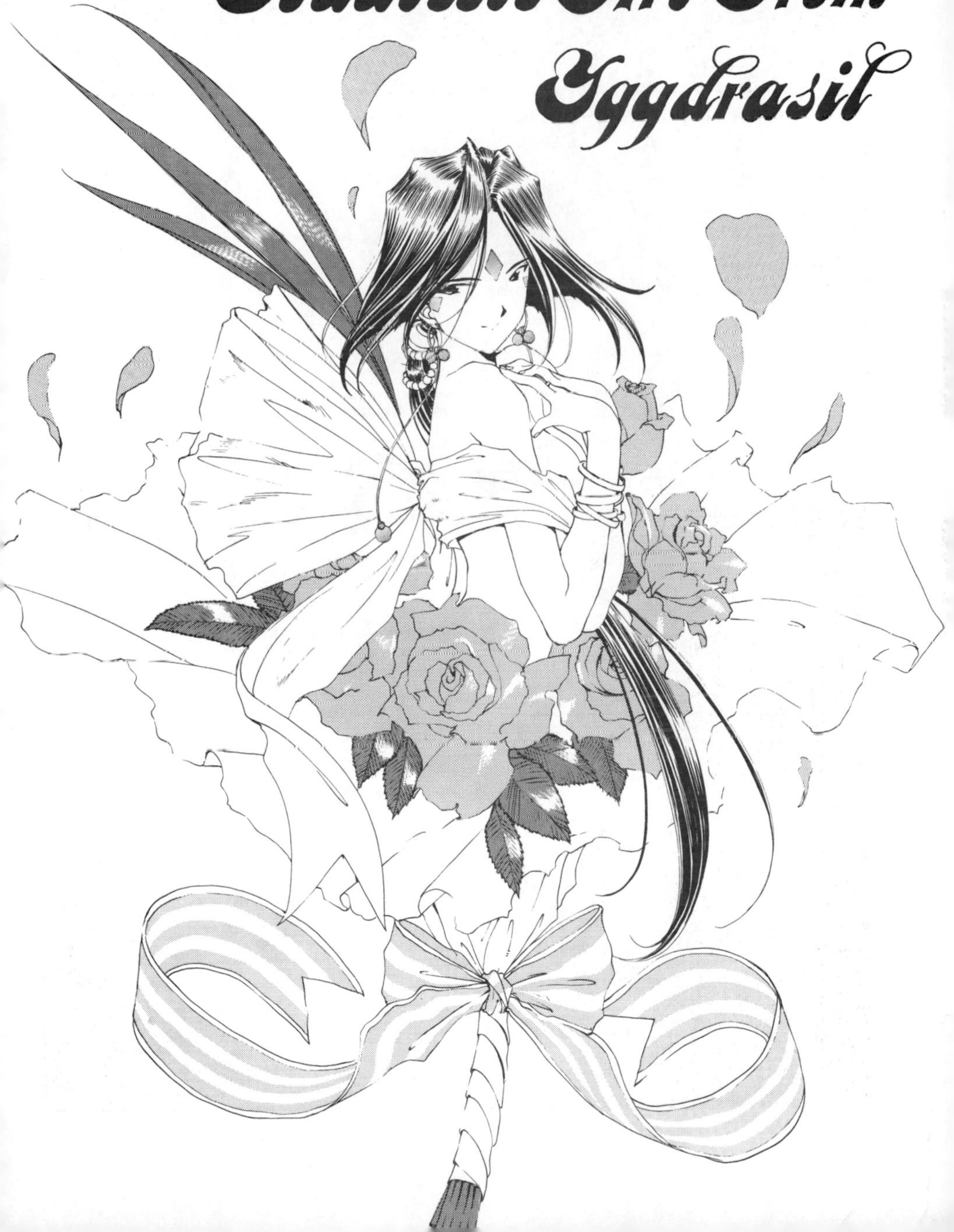

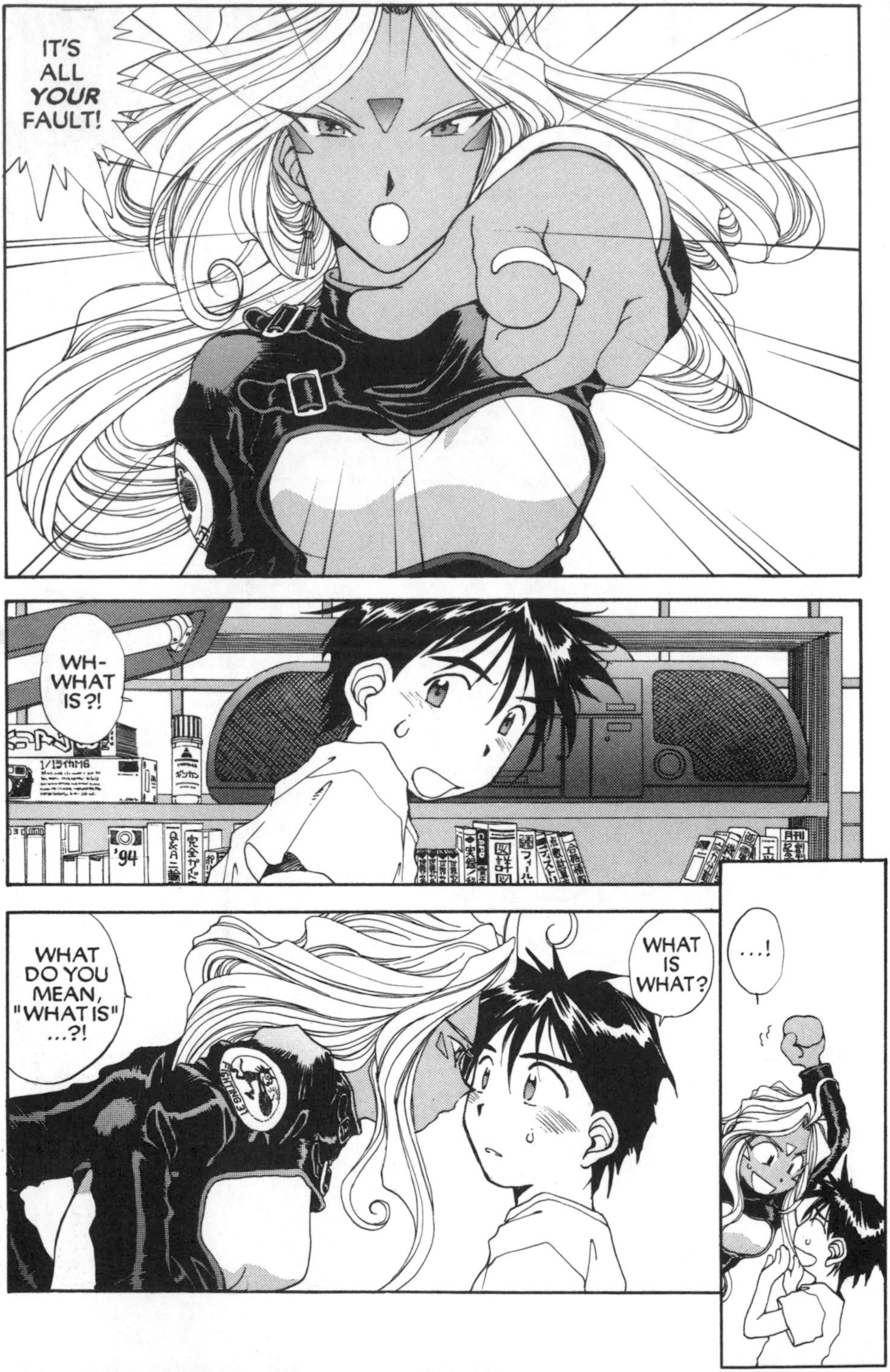
IT'S ALL *YOUR* FAULT!
WH-WHAT IS?!
WHAT DO YOU MEAN, "WHAT IS" ...?!
WHAT IS WHAT?
...!

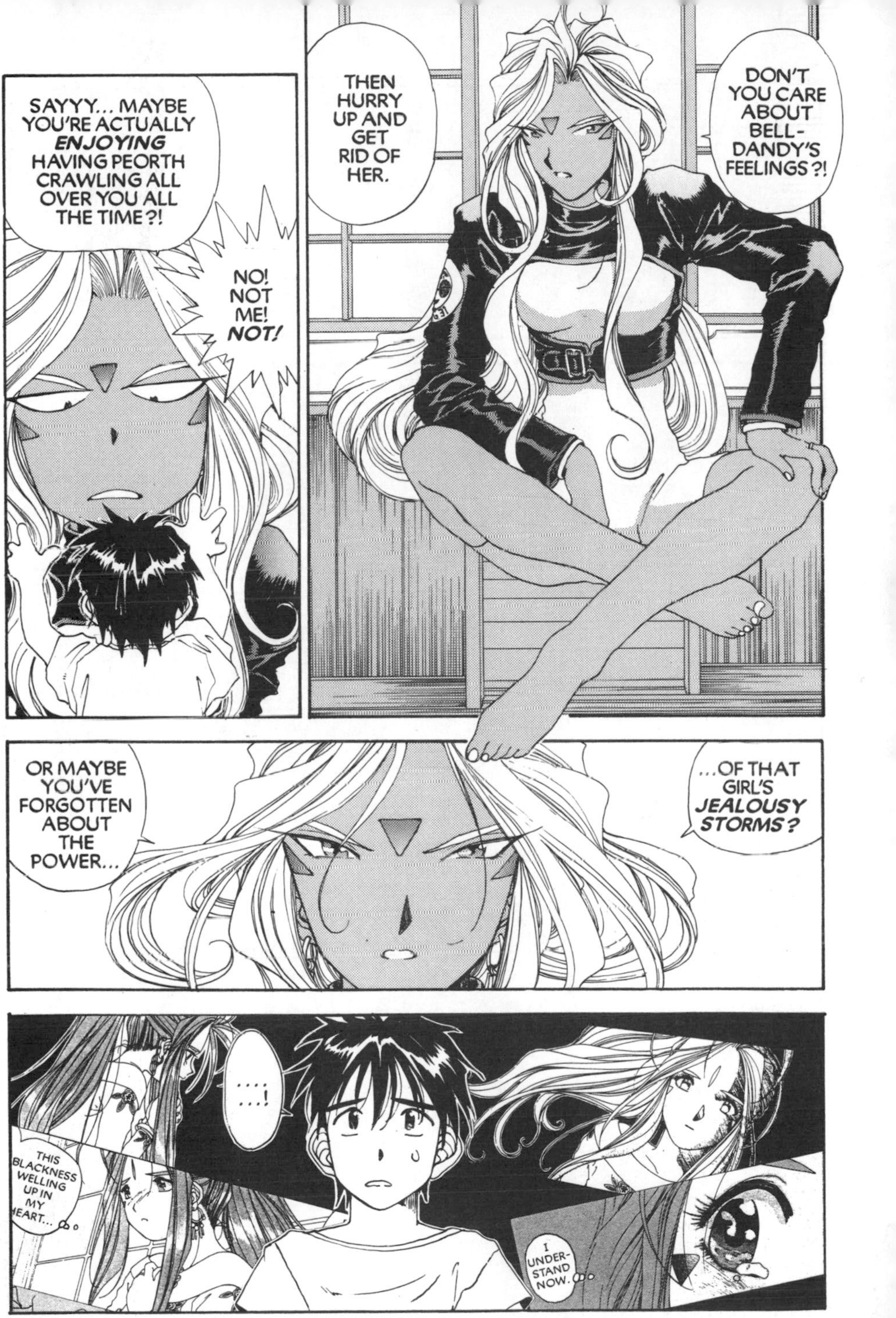
SAYYY... MAYBE YOU'RE ACTUALLY *ENJOYING* HAVING PEORTH CRAWLING ALL OVER YOU ALL THE TIME?!
NO! NOT ME! *NOT!*
THEN HURRY UP AND GET RID OF HER.
DON'T YOU CARE ABOUT BELL-DANDY'S FEELINGS?!
OR MAYBE YOU'VE FORGOTTEN ABOUT THE POWER...
...OF THAT GIRL'S *JEALOUSY STORMS?*
....;
....!
THIS BLACKNESS WELLING UP IN MY HEART...
I UNDERSTAND NOW.

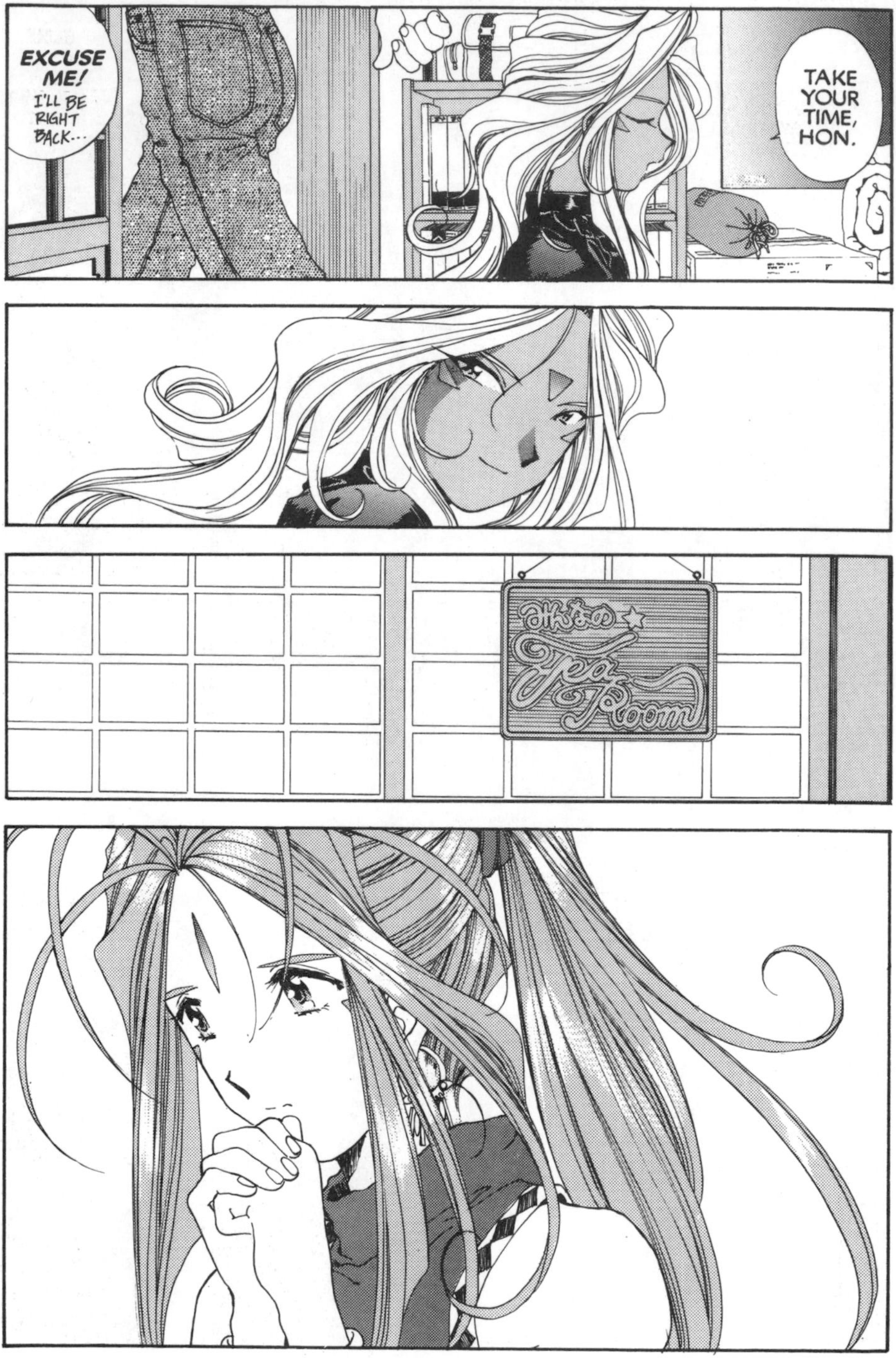
EXCUSE ME! I'LL BE RIGHT BACK...
TAKE YOUR TIME, HON.
Tea Room

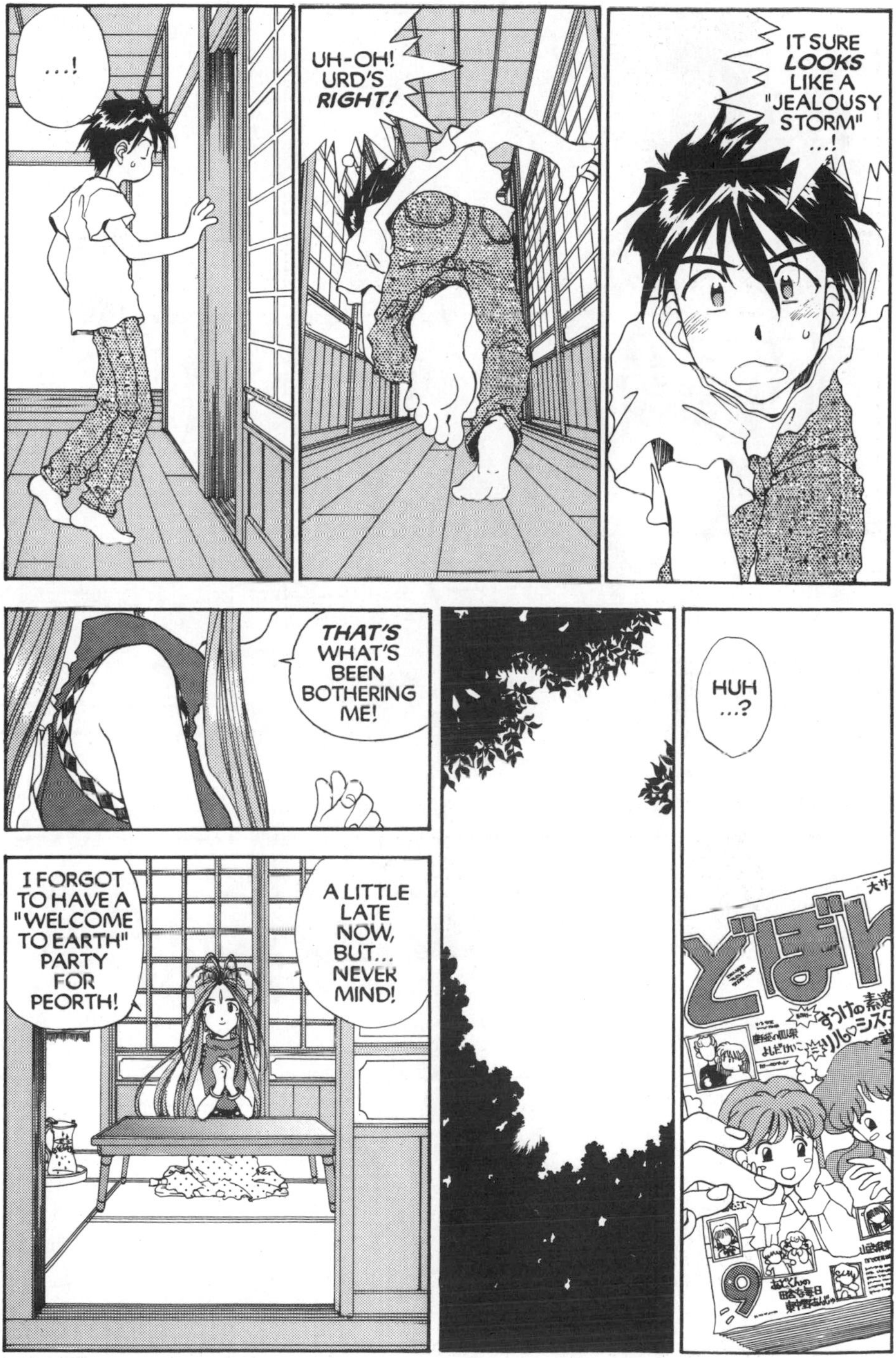
...!
UH-OH! URD'S *RIGHT!*
IT SURE *LOOKS* LIKE A "JEALOUSY STORM" ...!
THAT'S WHAT'S BEEN BOTHERING ME!
I FORGOT TO HAVE A "WELCOME TO EARTH" PARTY FOR PEORTH!
A LITTLE LATE NOW, BUT... NEVER MIND!
HUH ...?

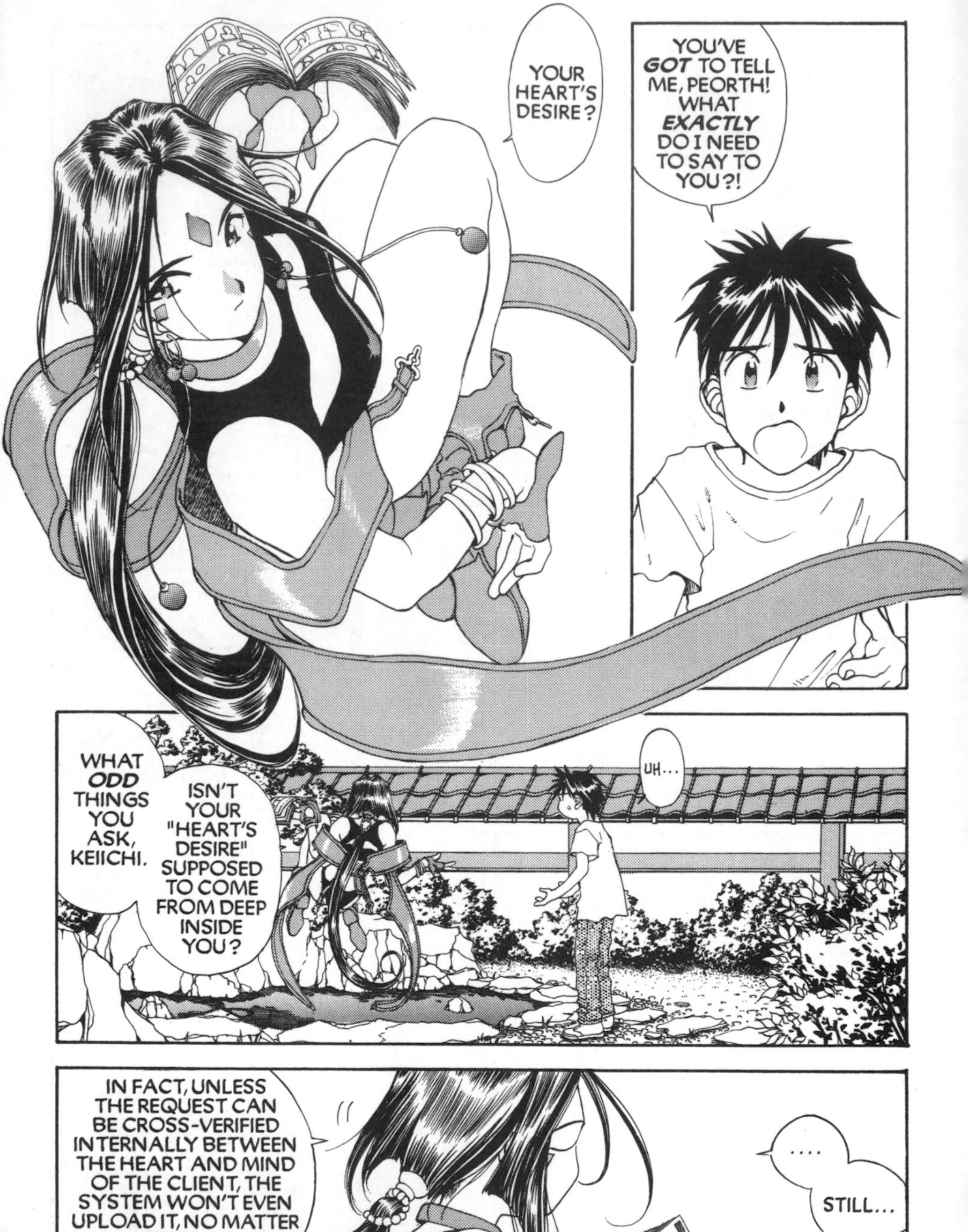
YOUR HEART'S DESIRE?
YOU'VE GOT TO TELL ME, PEORTH! WHAT EXACTLY DO I NEED TO SAY TO YOU?!
WHAT ODD THINGS YOU ASK, KEIICHI.
ISN'T YOUR "HEART'S DESIRE" SUPPOSED TO COME FROM DEEP INSIDE YOU?
UH...
IN FACT, UNLESS THE REQUEST CAN BE CROSS-VERIFIED INTERNALLY BETWEEN THE HEART AND MIND OF THE CLIENT, THE SYSTEM WON'T EVEN UPLOAD IT, NO MATTER WHAT YOU SAY.
....
STILL...

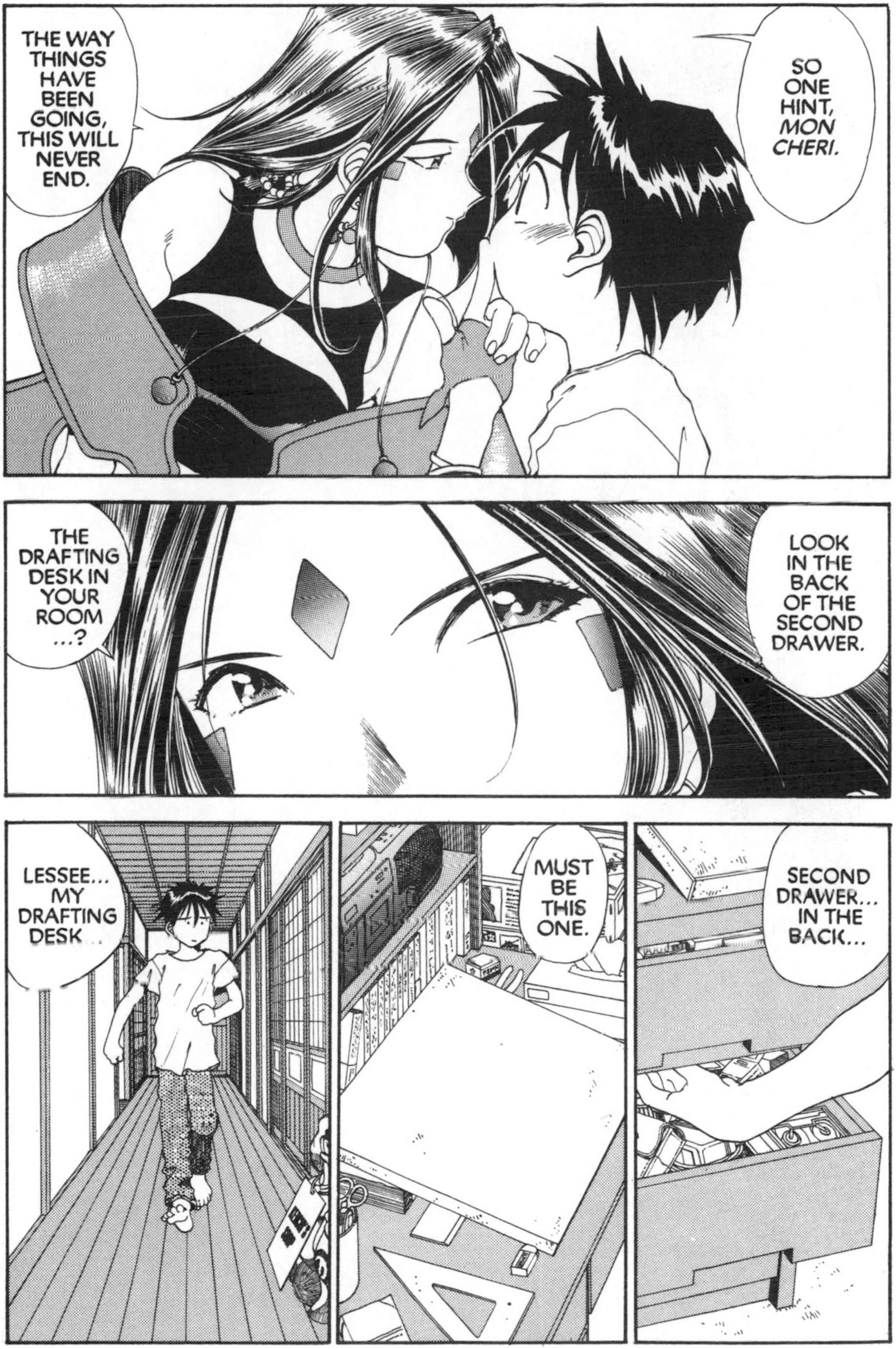
THE WAY THINGS HAVE BEEN GOING, THIS WILL NEVER END.
SO ONE HINT, *MON CHERI.*
THE DRAFTING DESK IN YOUR ROOM ...?
LOOK IN THE BACK OF THE SECOND DRAWER.
LESSEE... MY DRAFTING DESK...
MUST BE THIS ONE.
SECOND DRAWER... IN THE BACK...

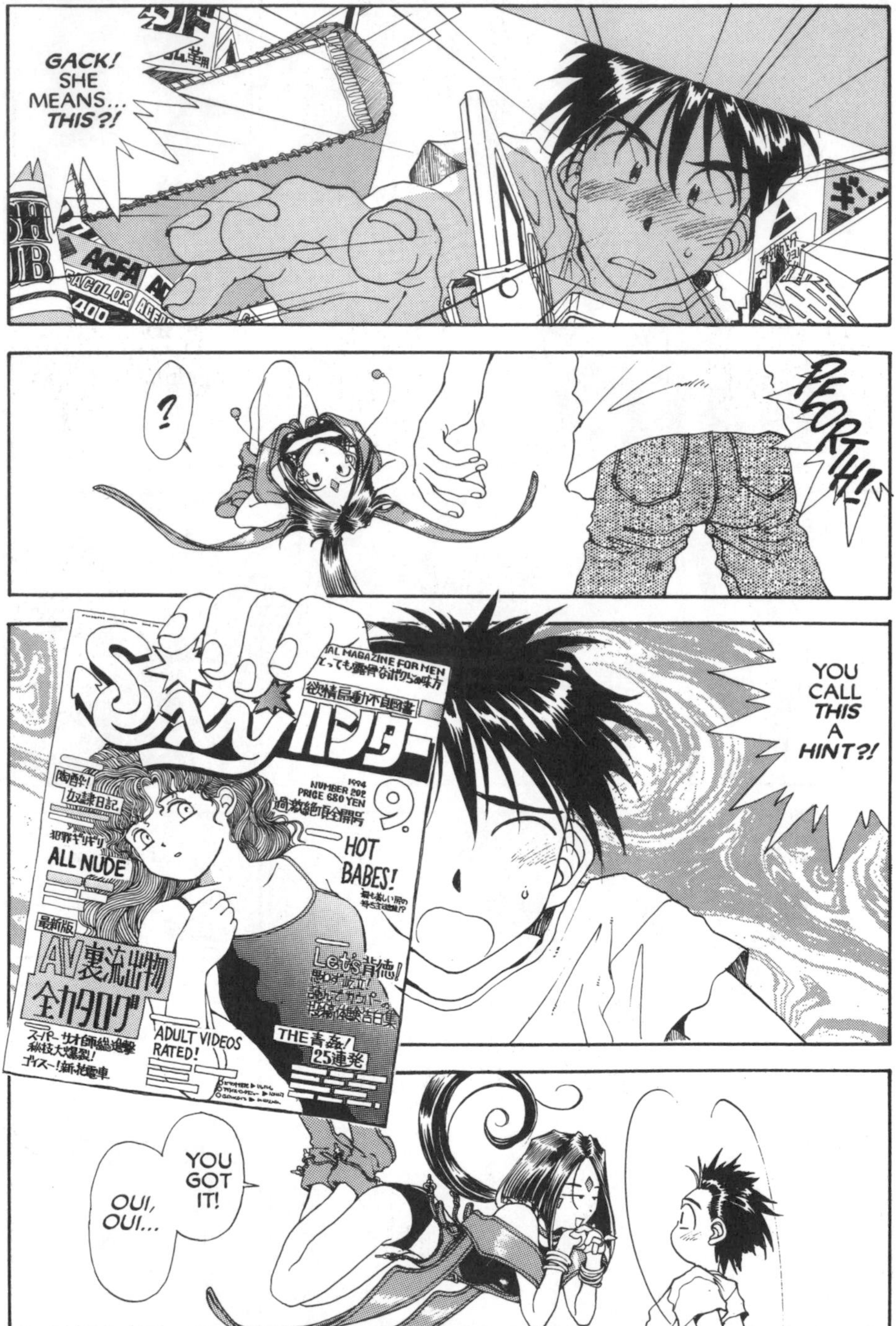
GACK! SHE MEANS... THIS?!
AGFA
?
PEORTH!
IAL MAGAZINE FOR MEN
ハンター
1994
NUMBER 202
PRICE 680 YEN
9.
奴隷日記
ALL NUDE
HOT BABES!
最新版
AV裏流出物
全カタログ
Let's背徳!
ADULT VIDEOS RATED!
THE青姦! 25連発
YOU CALL THIS A HINT?!
YOU GOT IT!
OUI, OUI...

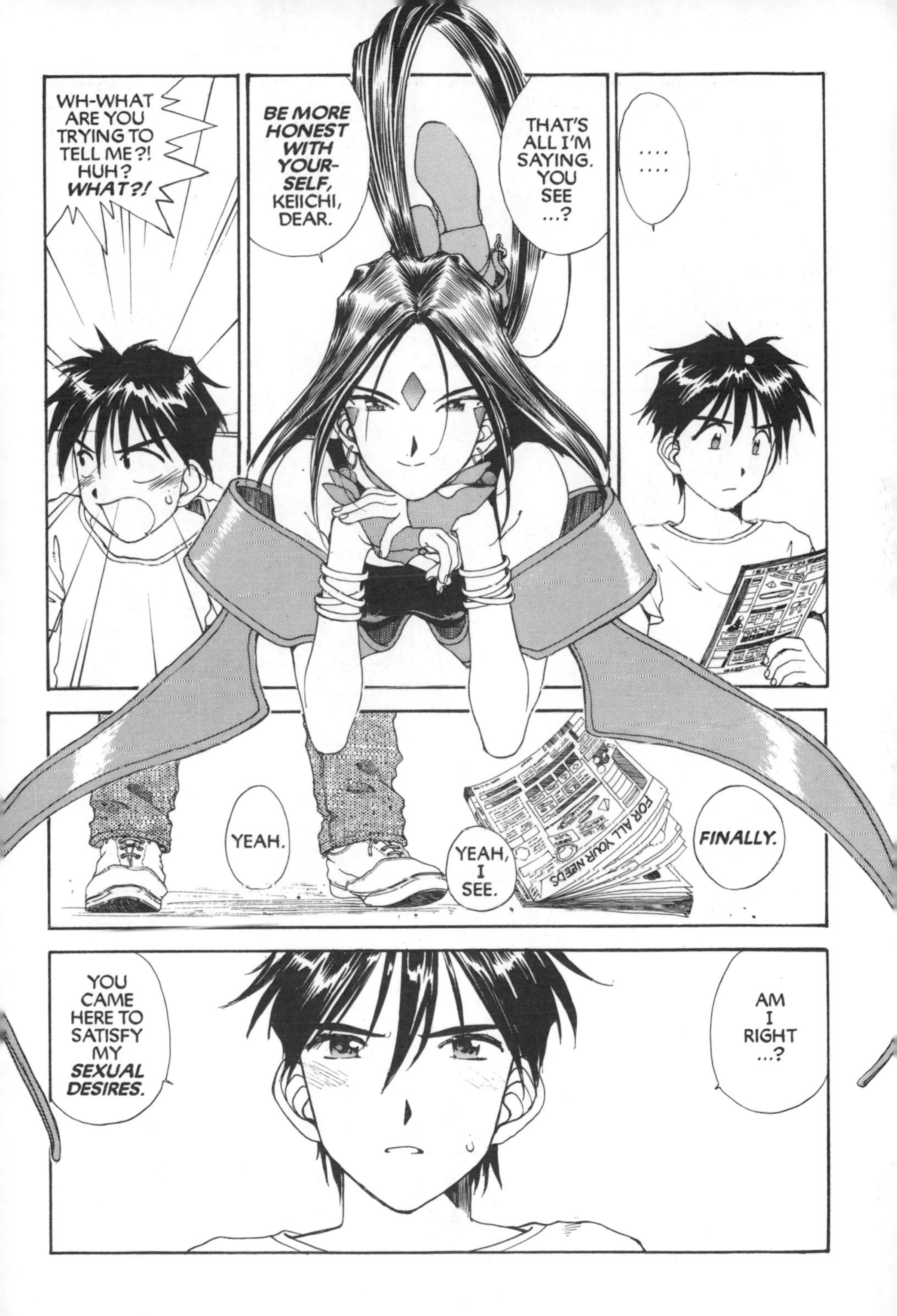

WH-WHAT ARE YOU TRYING TO TELL ME?! HUH? *WHAT?!*
BE MORE HONEST WITH YOURSELF, KEIICHI, DEAR.
THAT'S ALL I'M SAYING. YOU SEE ...?
....
YEAH.
YEAH, I SEE.
FOR ALL YOUR NEEDS
FINALLY.
YOU CAME HERE TO SATISFY MY *SEXUAL DESIRES.*
AM I RIGHT ...?

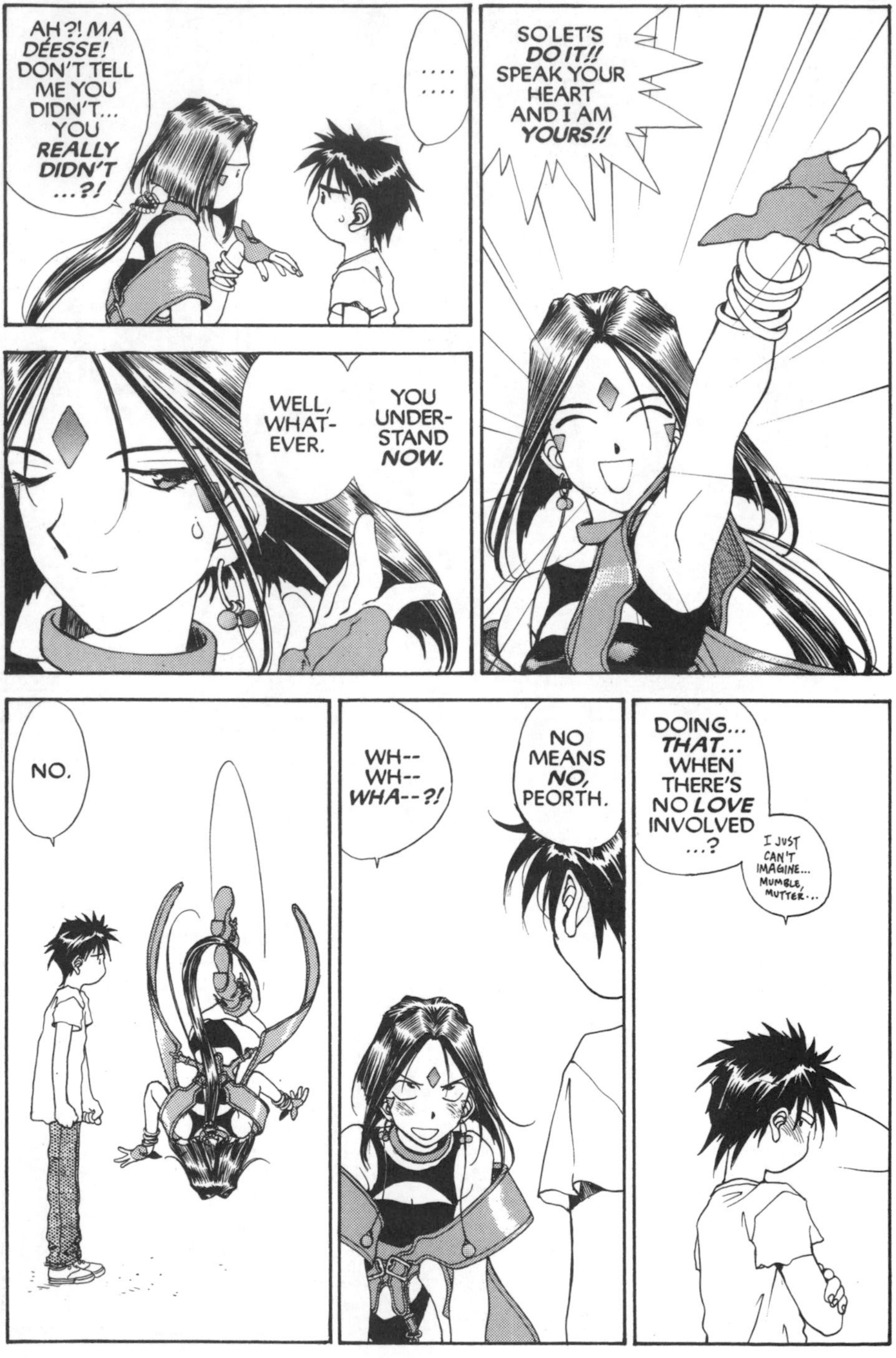
AH?! MA DÉESSE! DON'T TELL ME YOU DIDN'T... YOU REALLY DIDN'T ...?!
....
WELL, WHATEVER.
YOU UNDERSTAND NOW.
SO LET'S DO IT!! SPEAK YOUR HEART AND I AM YOURS!!
NO.
WH-- WH-- WHA--?!
NO MEANS NO, PEORTH.
DOING... THAT... WHEN THERE'S NO LOVE INVOLVED ...?
I JUST CAN'T IMAGINE... MUMBLE, MUTTER...

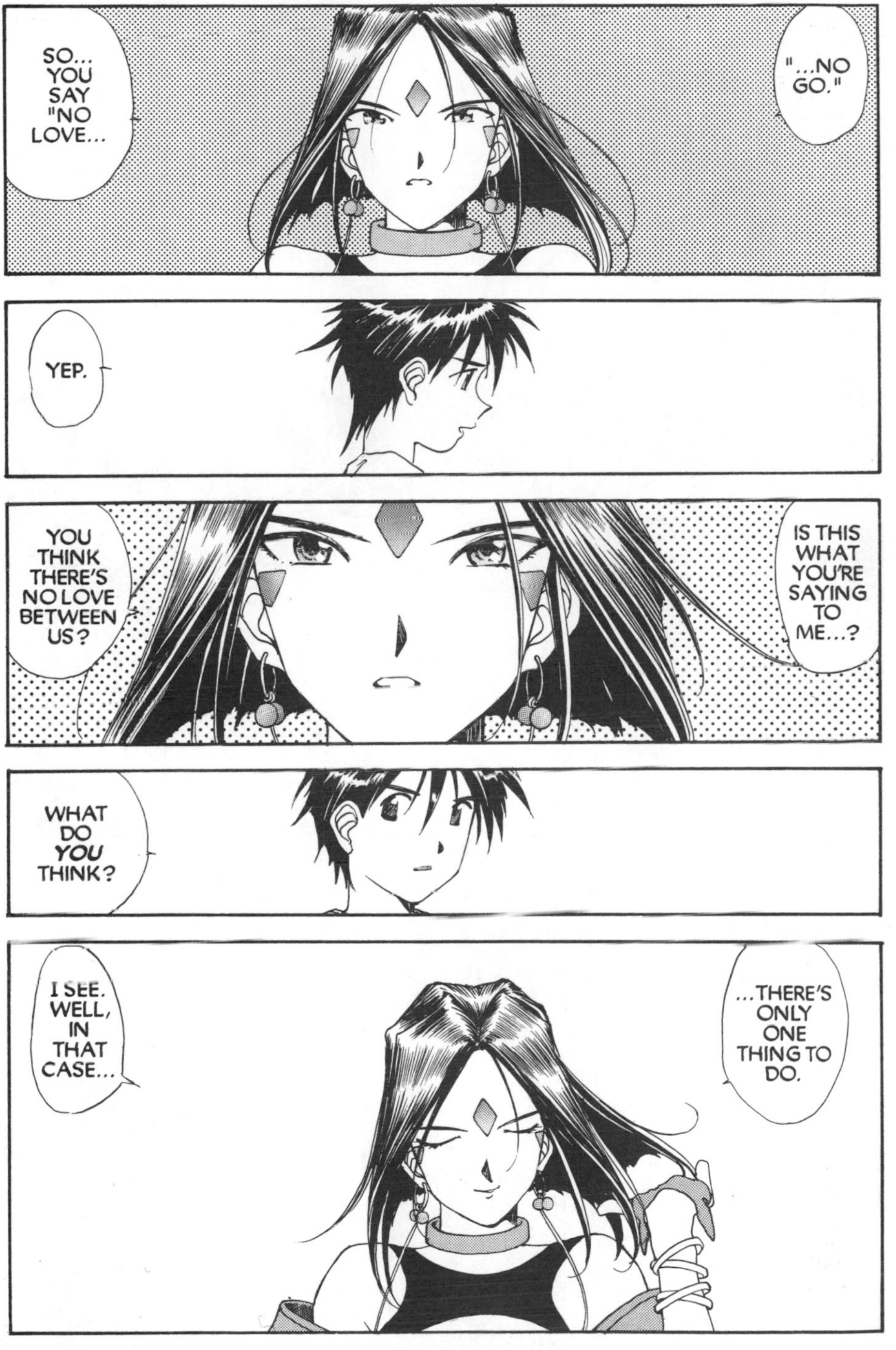
SO... YOU SAY "NO LOVE...
"...NO GO."
YEP.
YOU THINK THERE'S NO LOVE BETWEEN US?
IS THIS WHAT YOU'RE SAYING TO ME...?
WHAT DO *YOU* THINK?
I SEE. WELL, IN THAT CASE...
...THERE'S ONLY ONE THING TO DO.

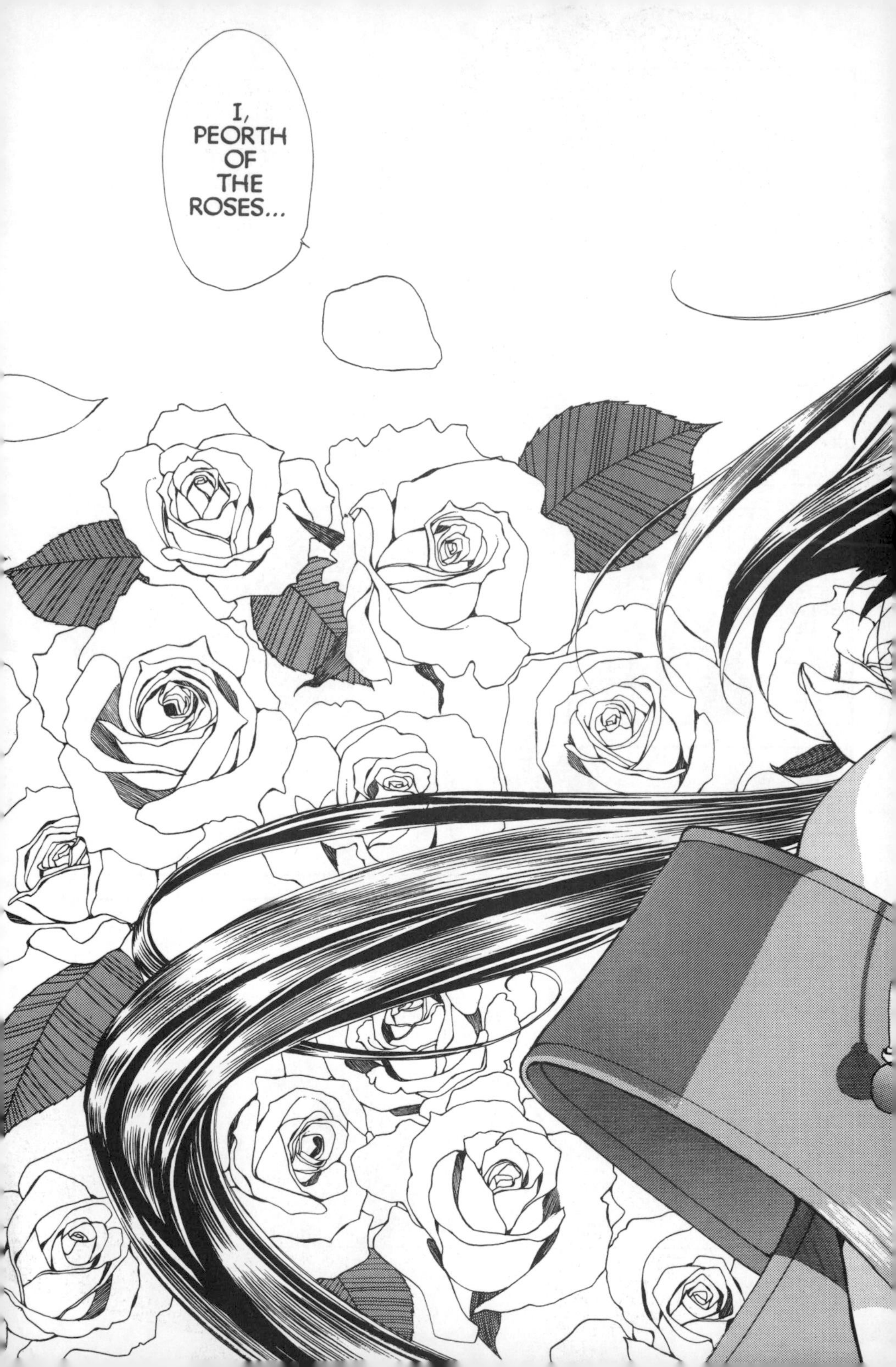
I, PEORTH OF THE ROSES...

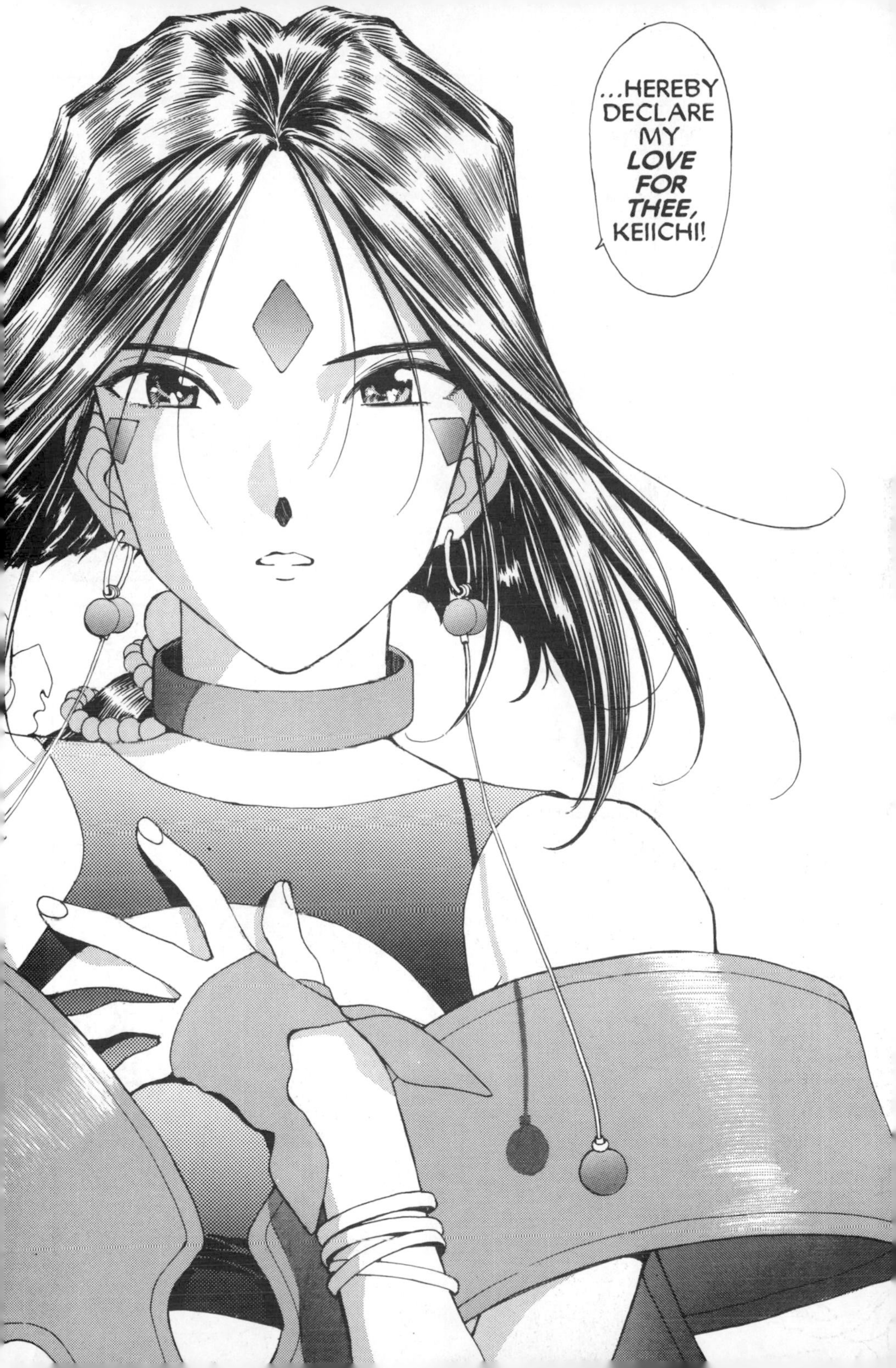
...HEREBY DECLARE MY ***LOVE FOR THEE,*** KEIICHI!

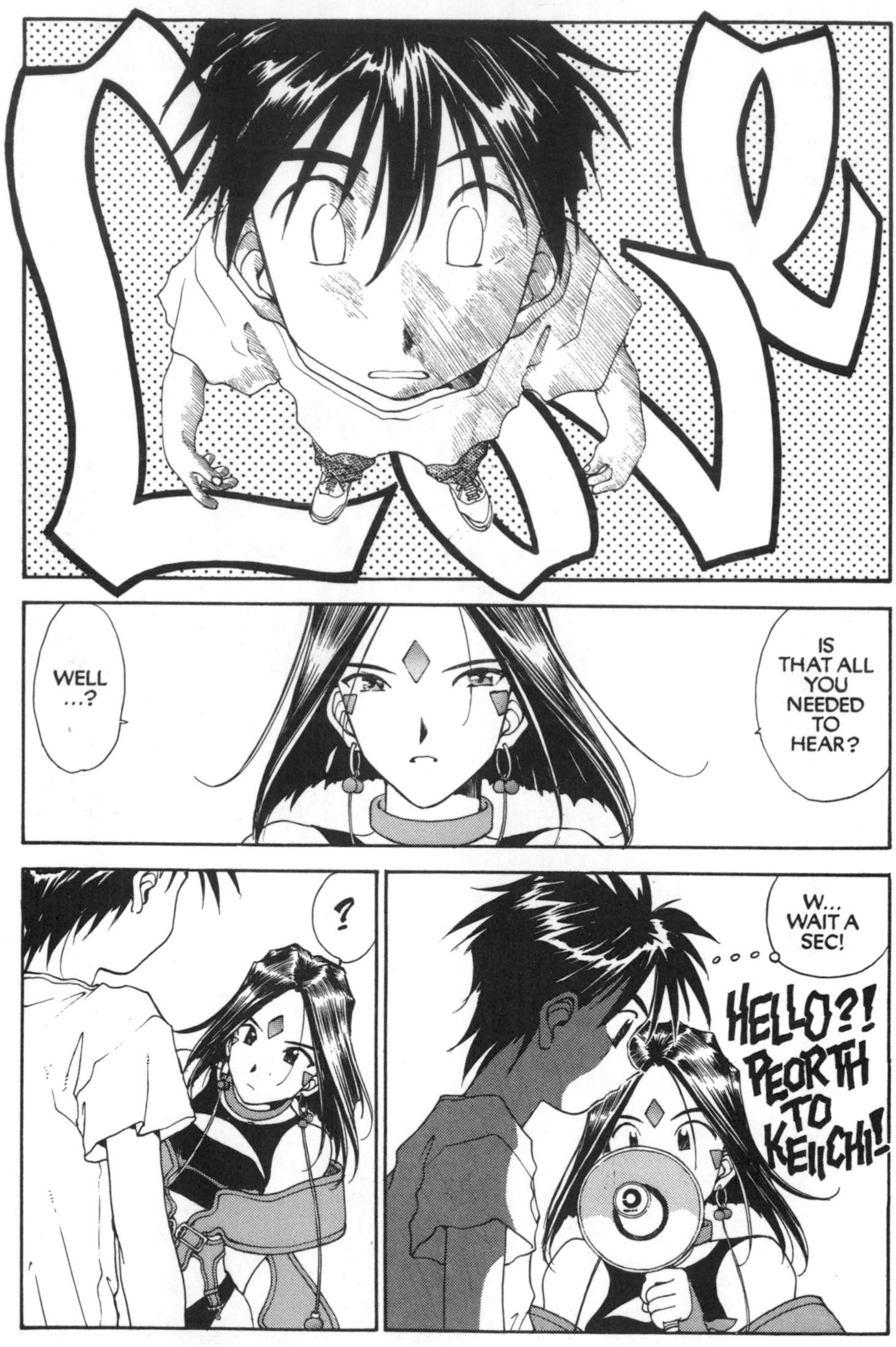
LOVE
WELL ...?
IS THAT ALL YOU NEEDED TO HEAR?
?
W... WAIT A SEC!
HELLO?! PEORTH TO KEIICHI!

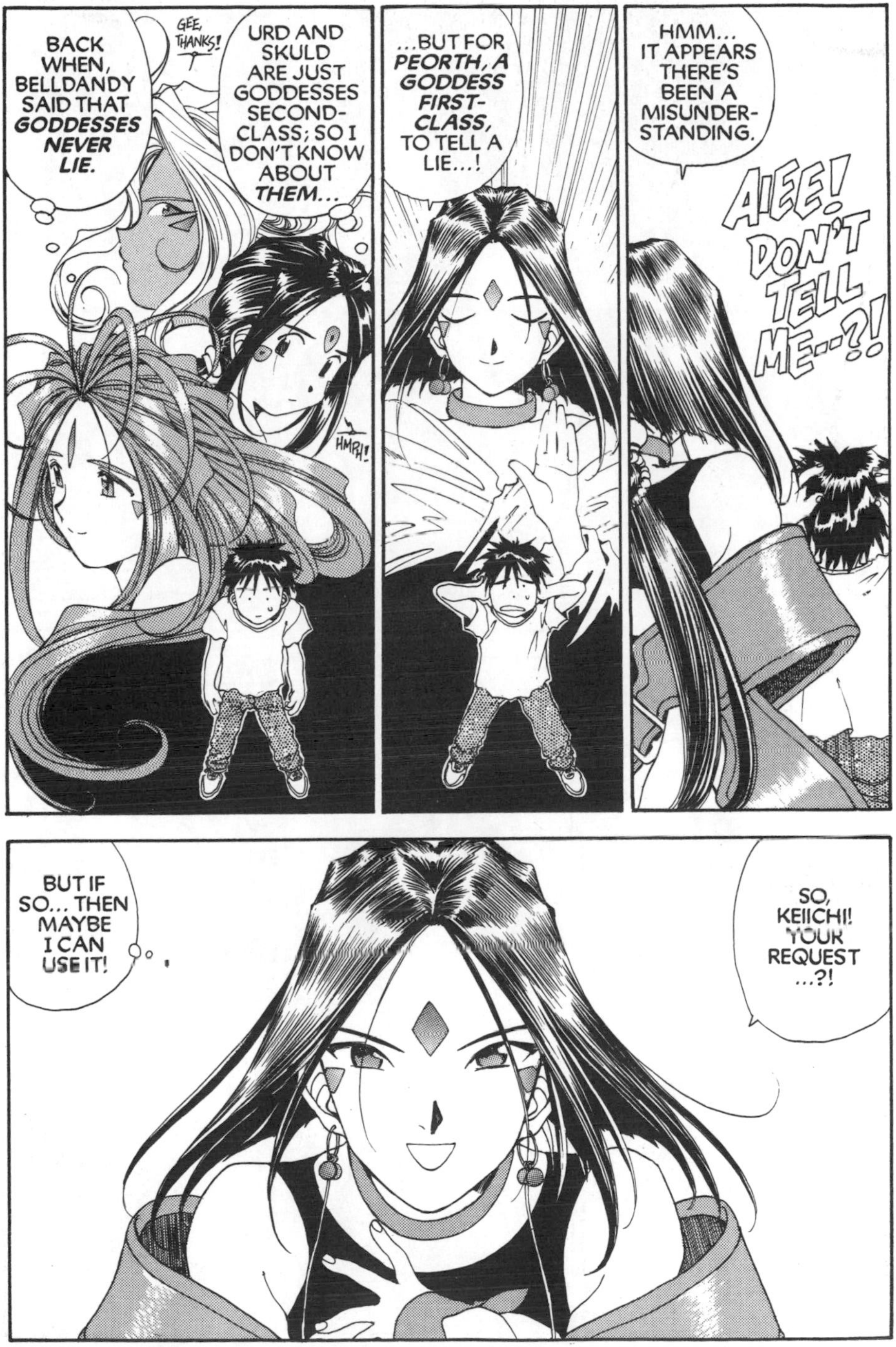

BACK WHEN, BELLDANDY SAID THAT GODDESSES NEVER LIE.
GEE, THANKS!
URD AND SKULD ARE JUST GODDESSES SECOND-CLASS; SO I DON'T KNOW ABOUT THEM...
HMPH!
...BUT FOR PEORTH, A GODDESS FIRST-CLASS, TO TELL A LIE...!
HMM... IT APPEARS THERE'S BEEN A MISUNDER-STANDING.
AIEE! DON'T TELL ME--?!
BUT IF SO... THEN MAYBE I CAN USE IT!
SO, KEIICHI! YOUR REQUEST ...?!

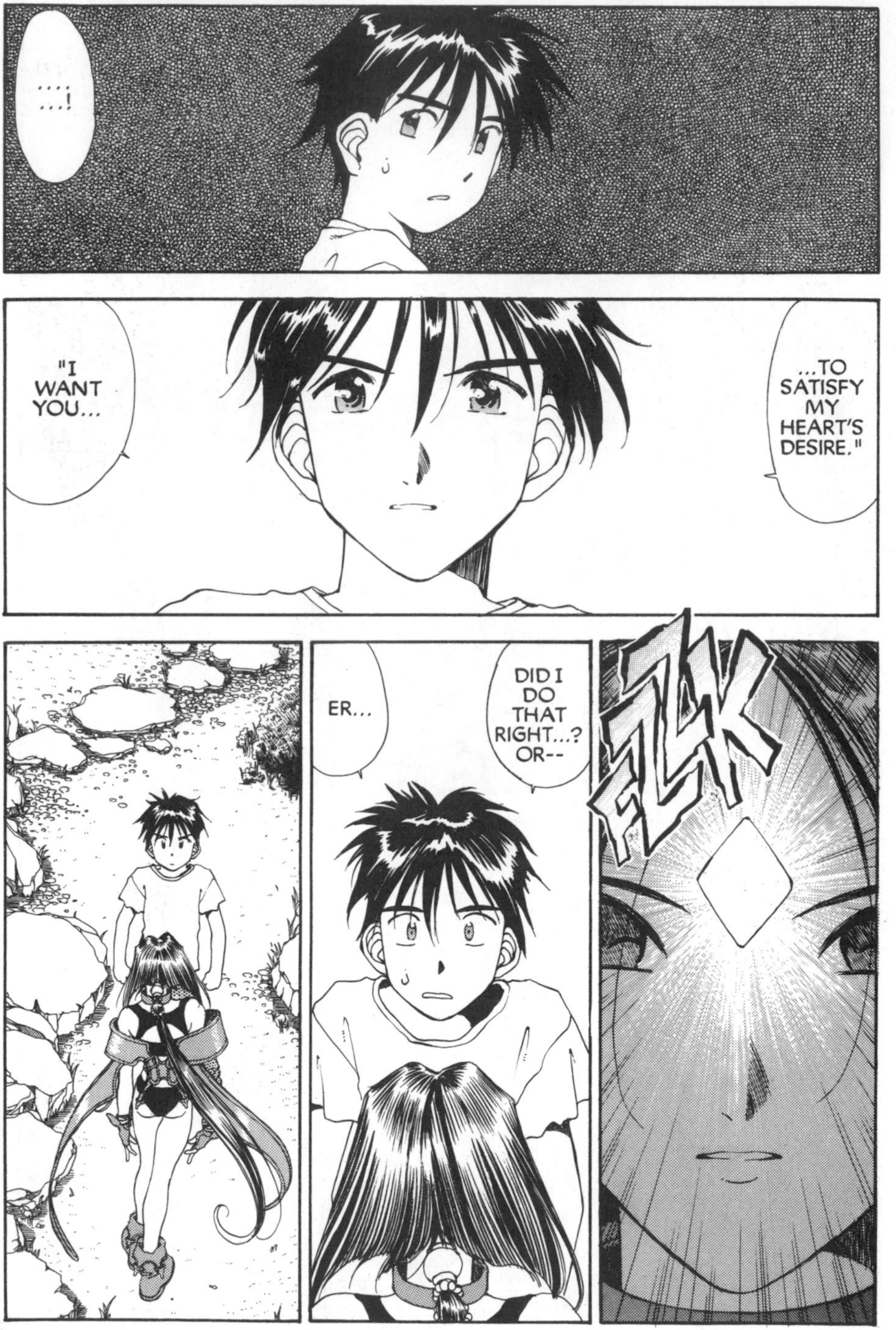

...!
"I WANT YOU...
...TO SATISFY MY HEART'S DESIRE."
ER...
DID I DO THAT RIGHT...? OR--
FLK

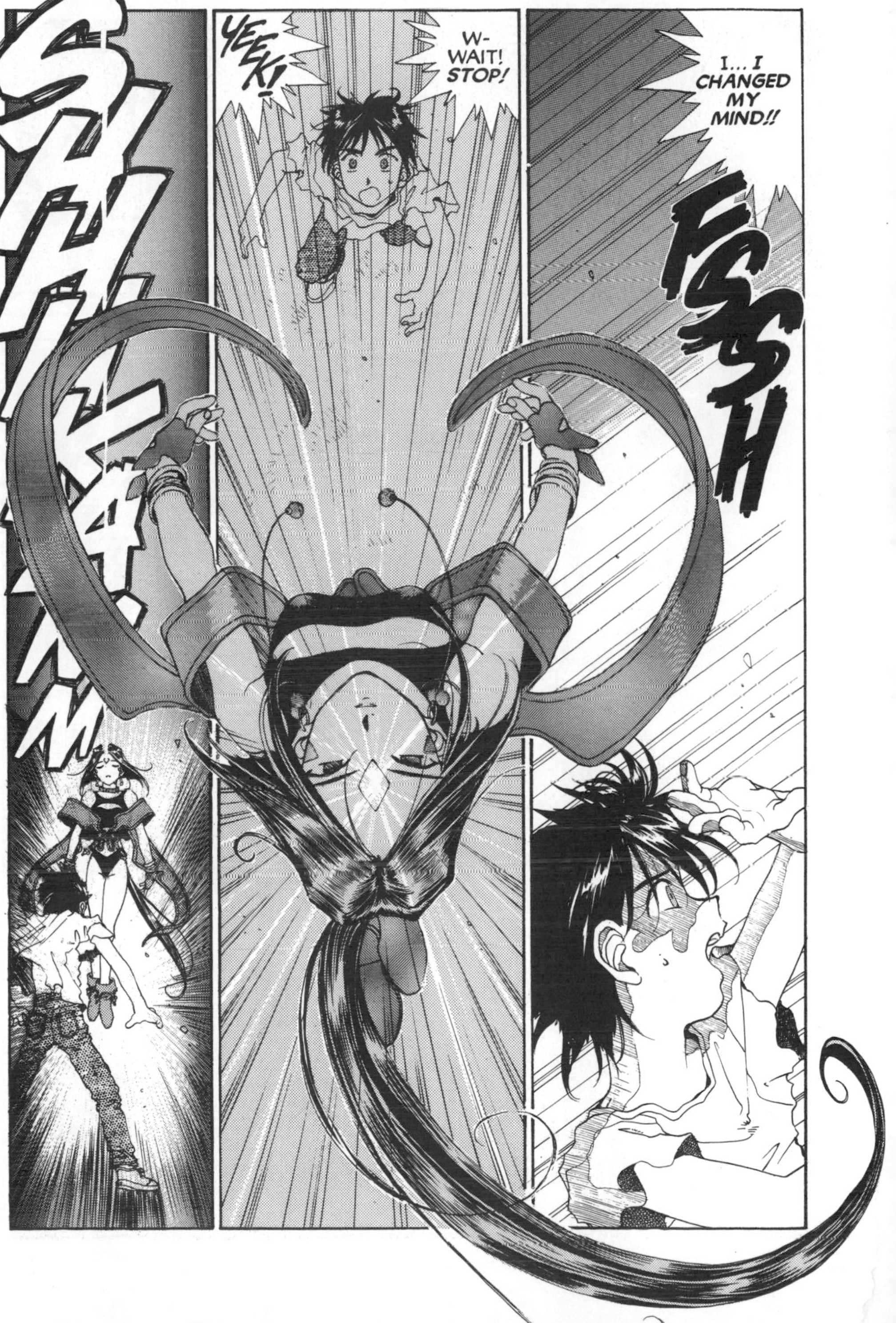
YEEK!
W- WAIT! STOP!
I... I CHANGED MY MIND!!

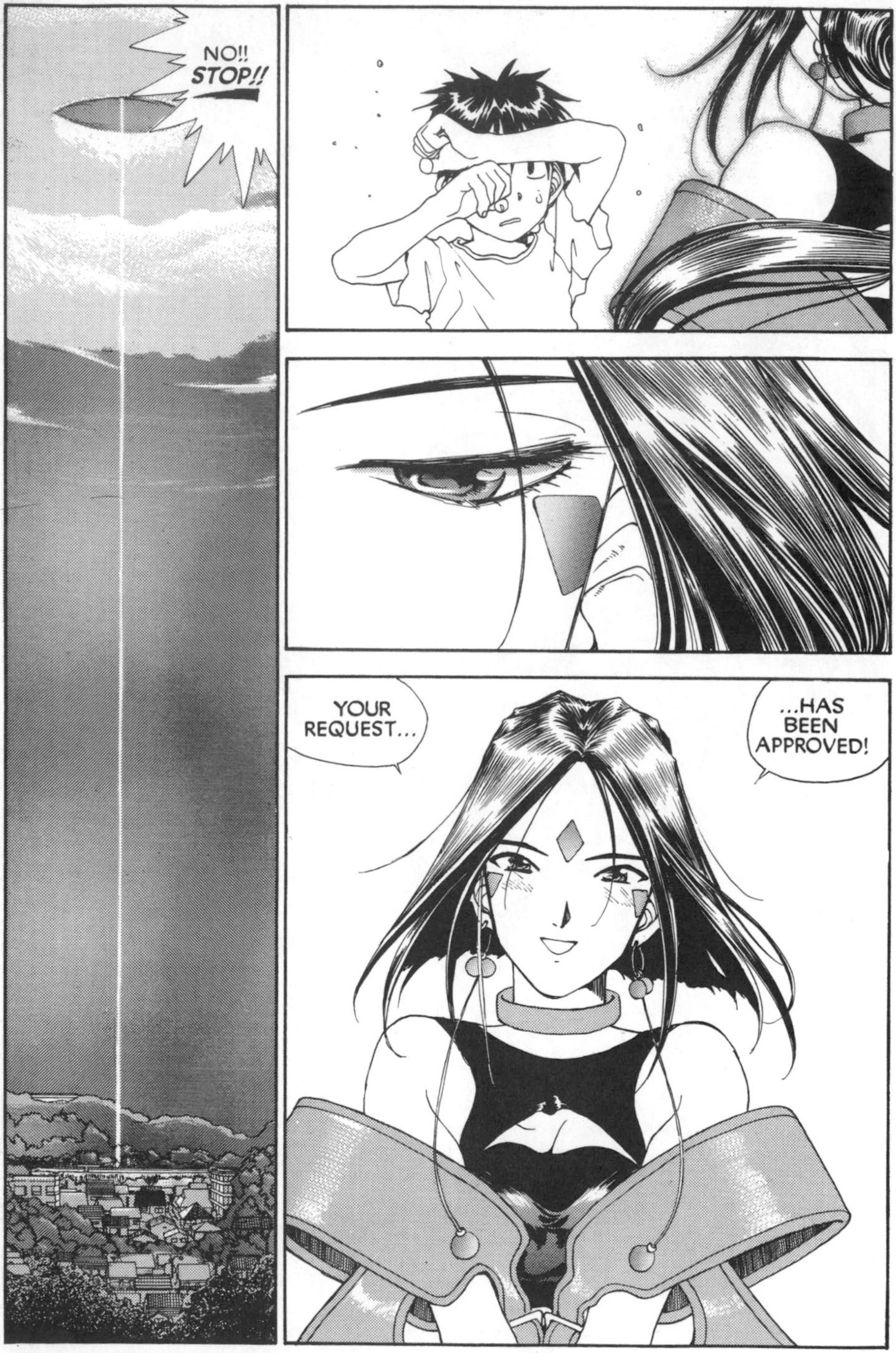
NO!! STOP!!
YOUR REQUEST...
...HAS BEEN APPROVED!

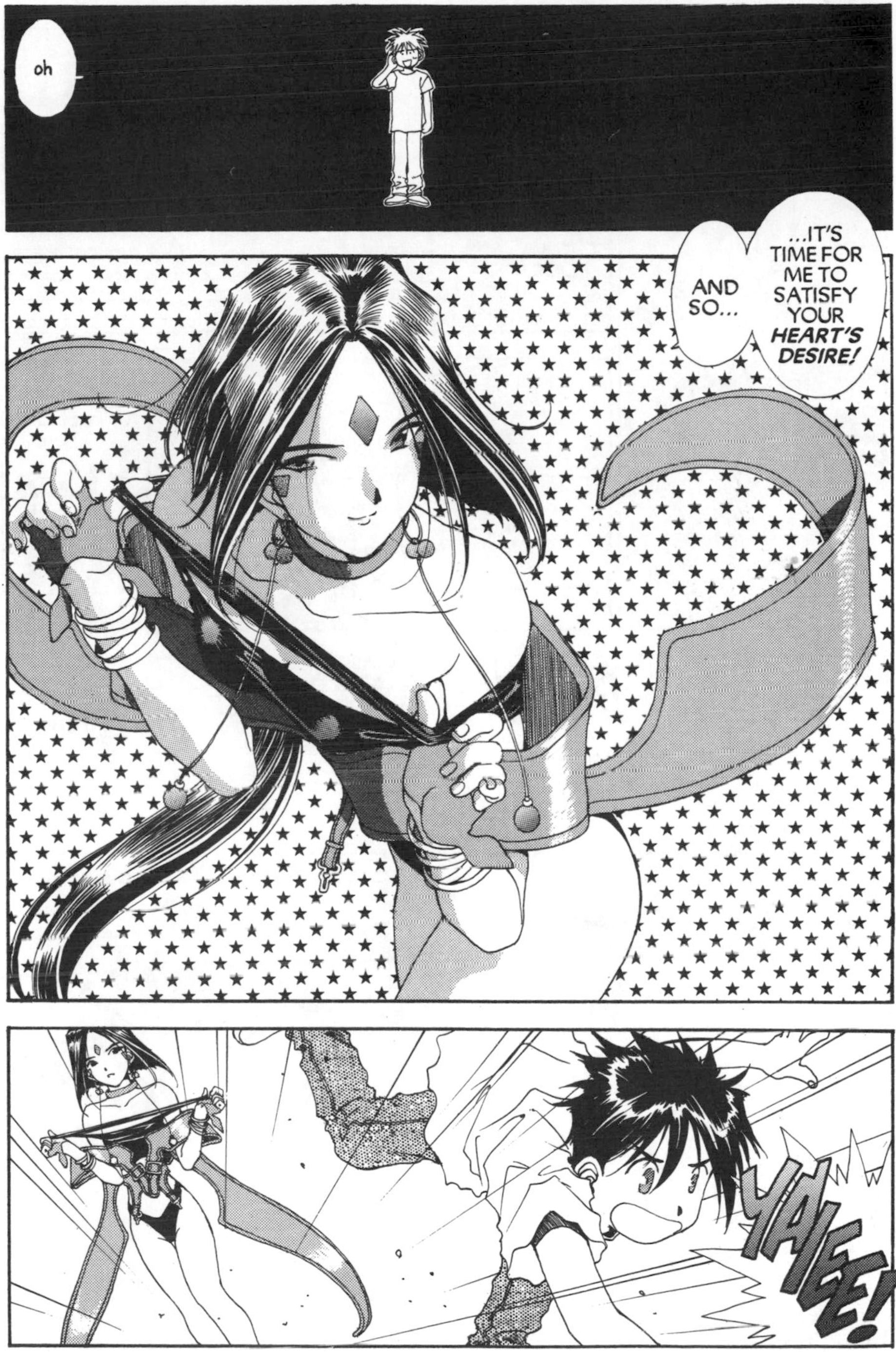
oh
AND SO...
...IT'S TIME FOR ME TO SATISFY YOUR ***HEART'S DESIRE!***
YAIEE!

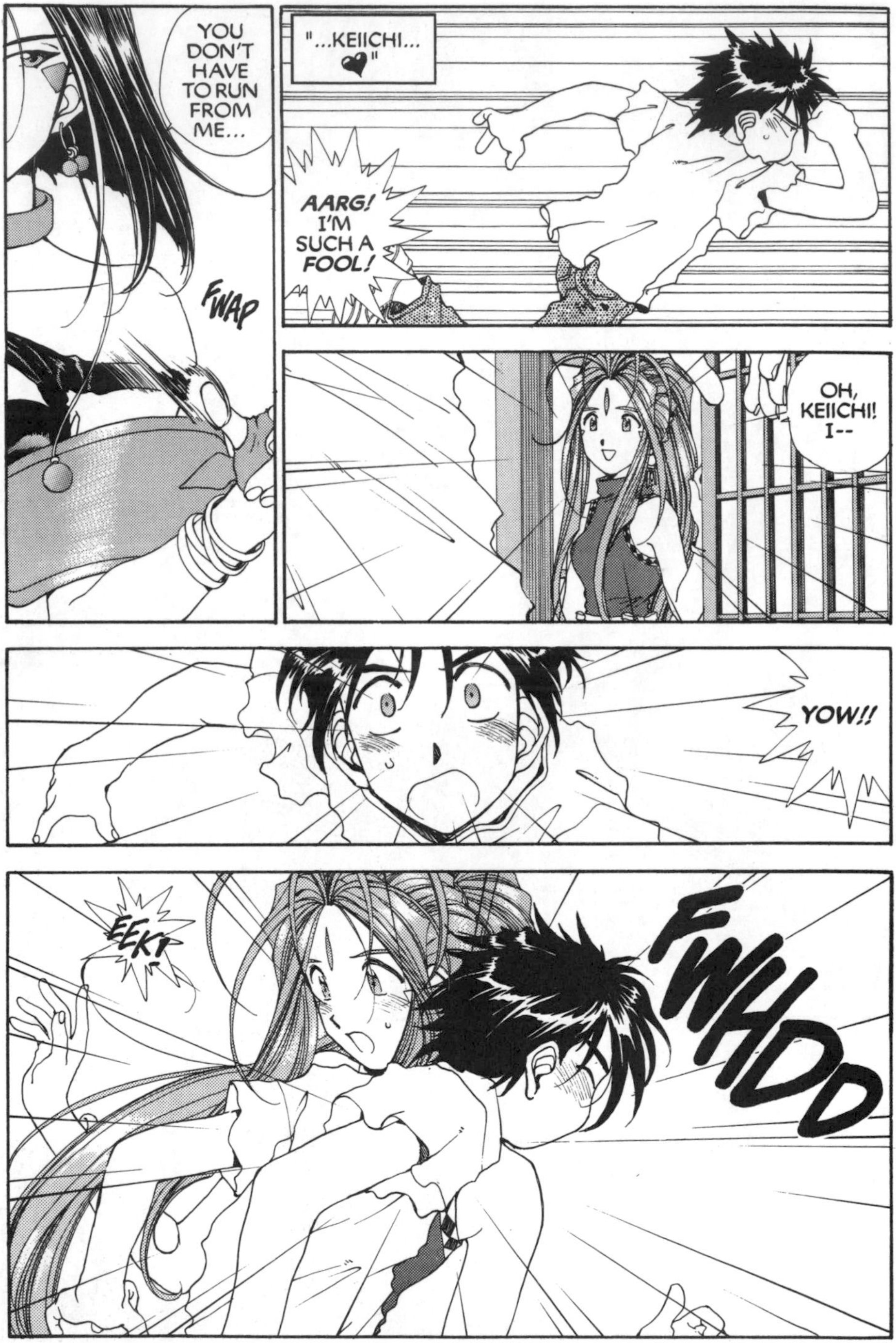
YOU DON'T HAVE TO RUN FROM ME...
FWAP
"...KEIICHI... ❤"
AARG! I'M SUCH A FOOL!
OH, KEIICHI! I--
YOW!!
EEK!
FWHDD

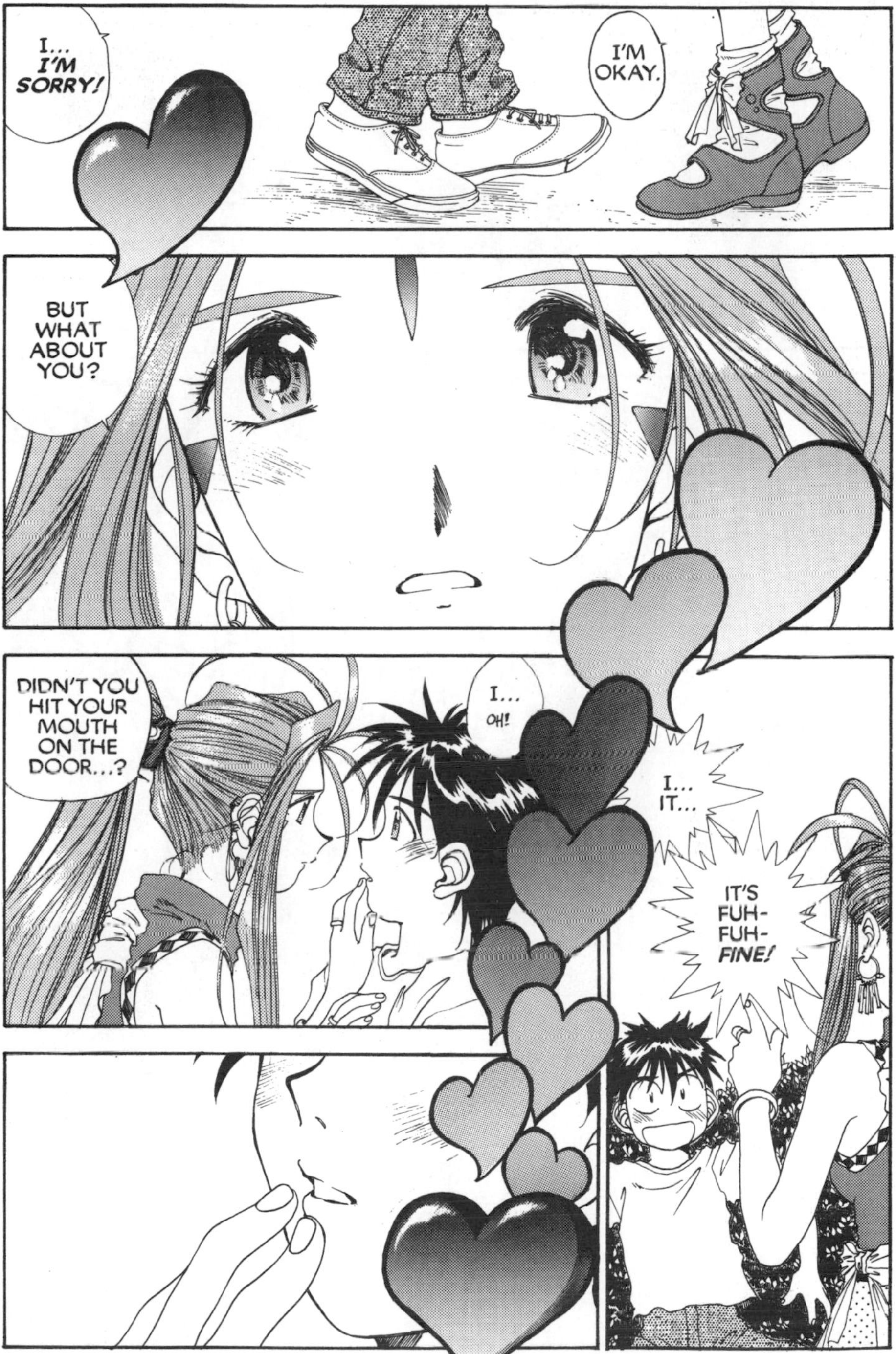
I... *I'M SORRY!*
I'M OKAY.
BUT WHAT ABOUT YOU?
DIDN'T YOU HIT YOUR MOUTH ON THE DOOR...?
I... OH!
I... IT...
IT'S FUH-FUH-*FINE!*

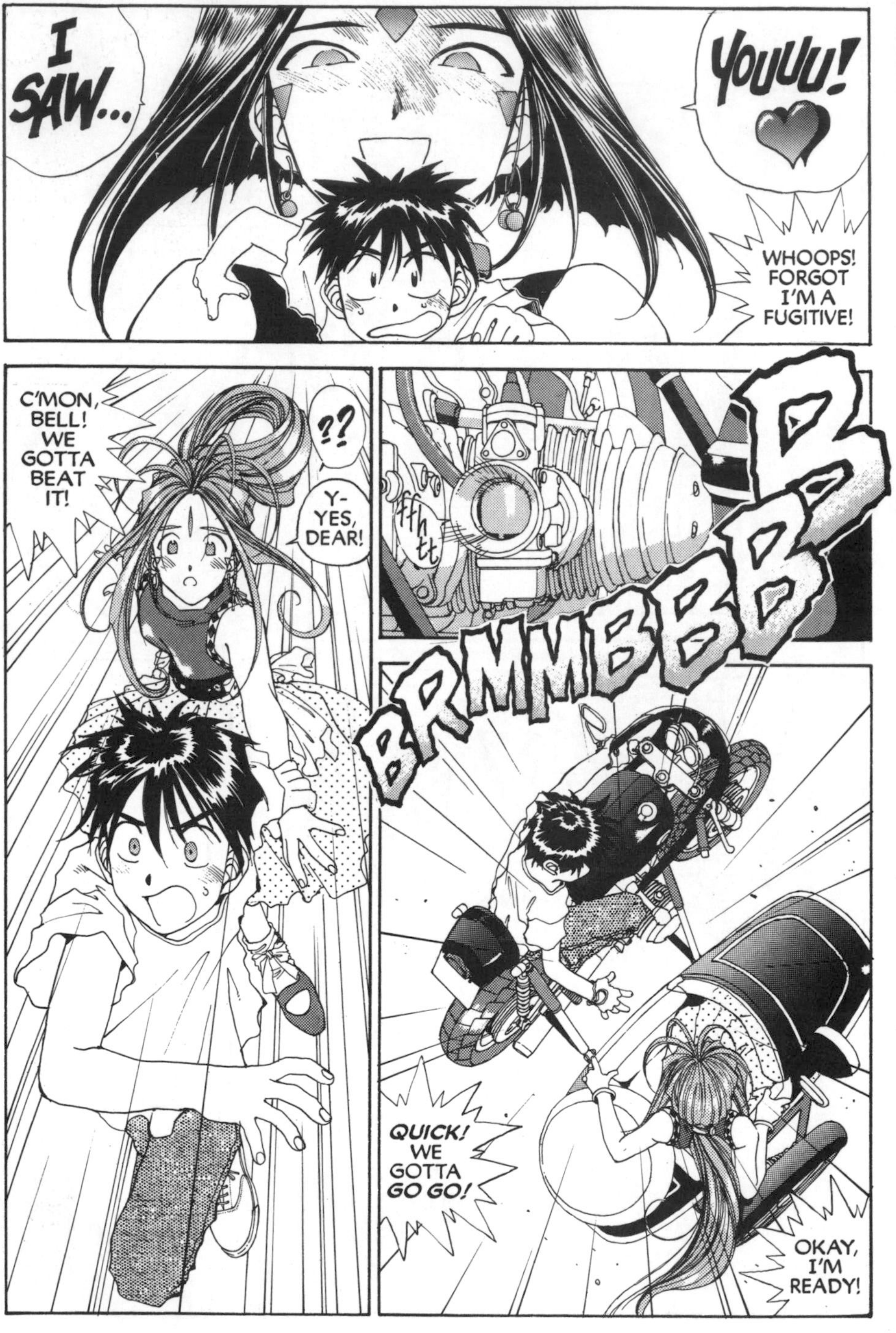
I SAW...
YOUUU! ♥
WHOOPS! FORGOT I'M A FUGITIVE!
C'MON, BELL! WE GOTTA BEAT IT!
??
Y-YES, DEAR!
BRMMBBBB
QUICK! WE GOTTA GO GO!
OKAY, I'M READY!

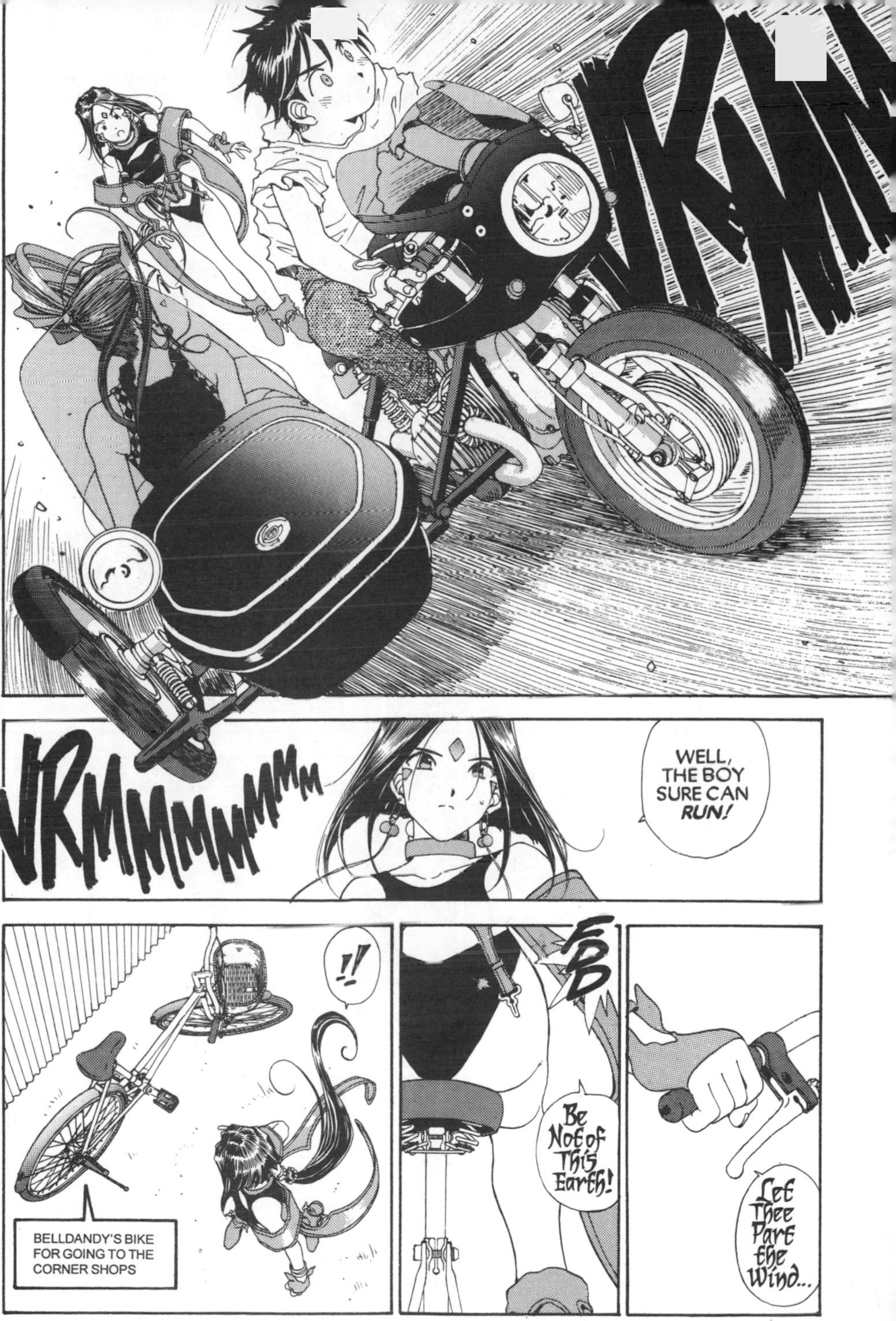
VRMMMMMMMMMM
WELL, THE BOY SURE CAN *RUN!*
!!
BELLDANDY'S BIKE FOR GOING TO THE CORNER SHOPS
FB
Be Not of This Earth!
Let Thee Part the Wind...

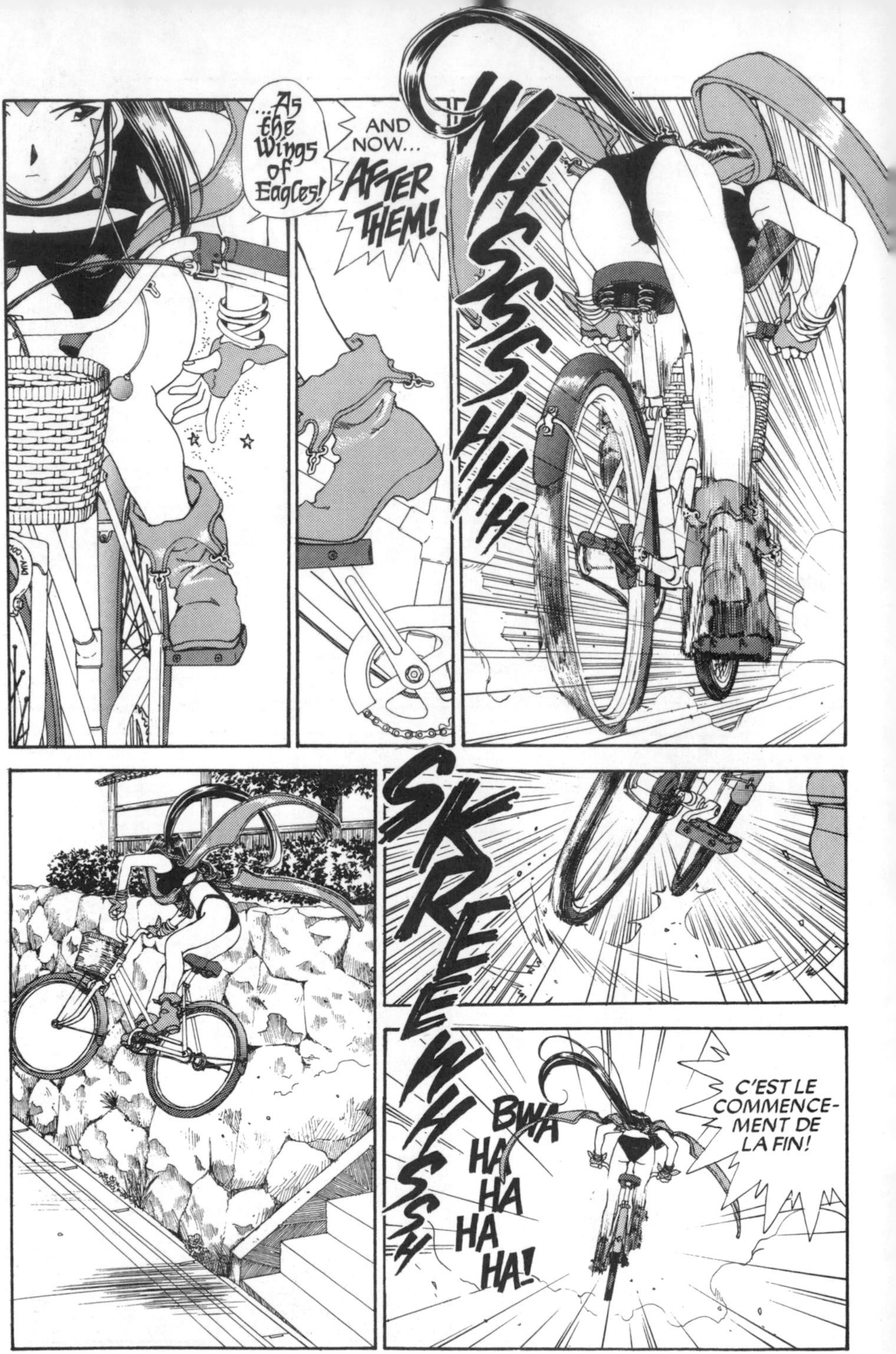
...As the Wings of Eagles!
AND NOW... AFTER THEM!
WHSSSHHHH
SKREEEWHSSSH
BWA HA HA HA HA HA!
C'EST LE COMMENCEMENT DE LA FIN!

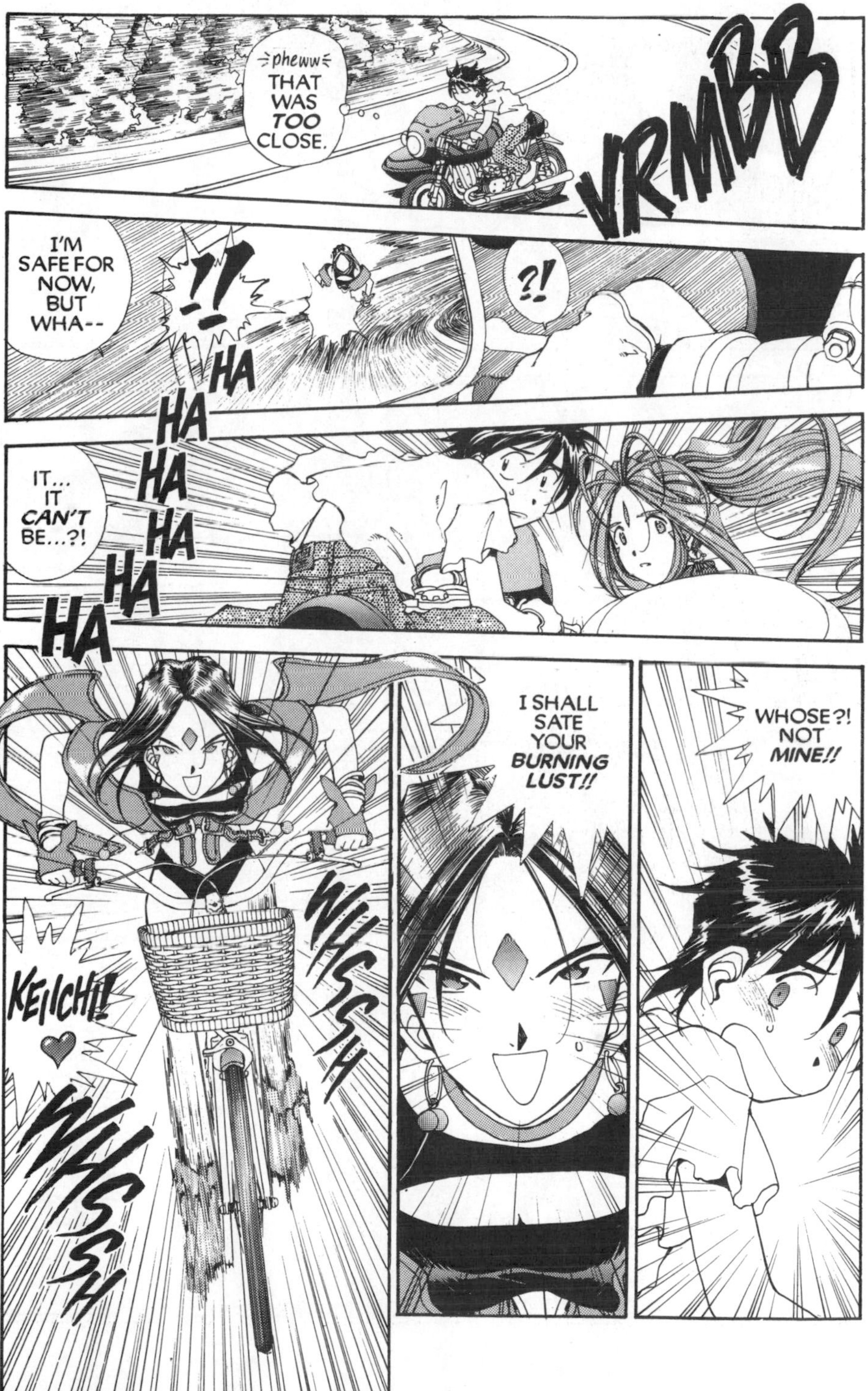

phewww
THAT WAS TOO CLOSE.
VRMBB
I'M SAFE FOR NOW, BUT WHA--
!!
?!
HA HA HA HA HA HA HA
IT... IT CAN'T BE...?!
KEIICHI!! ♥
WHSSH
WHSSH
I SHALL SATE YOUR BURNING LUST!!
WHOSE?! NOT MINE!!

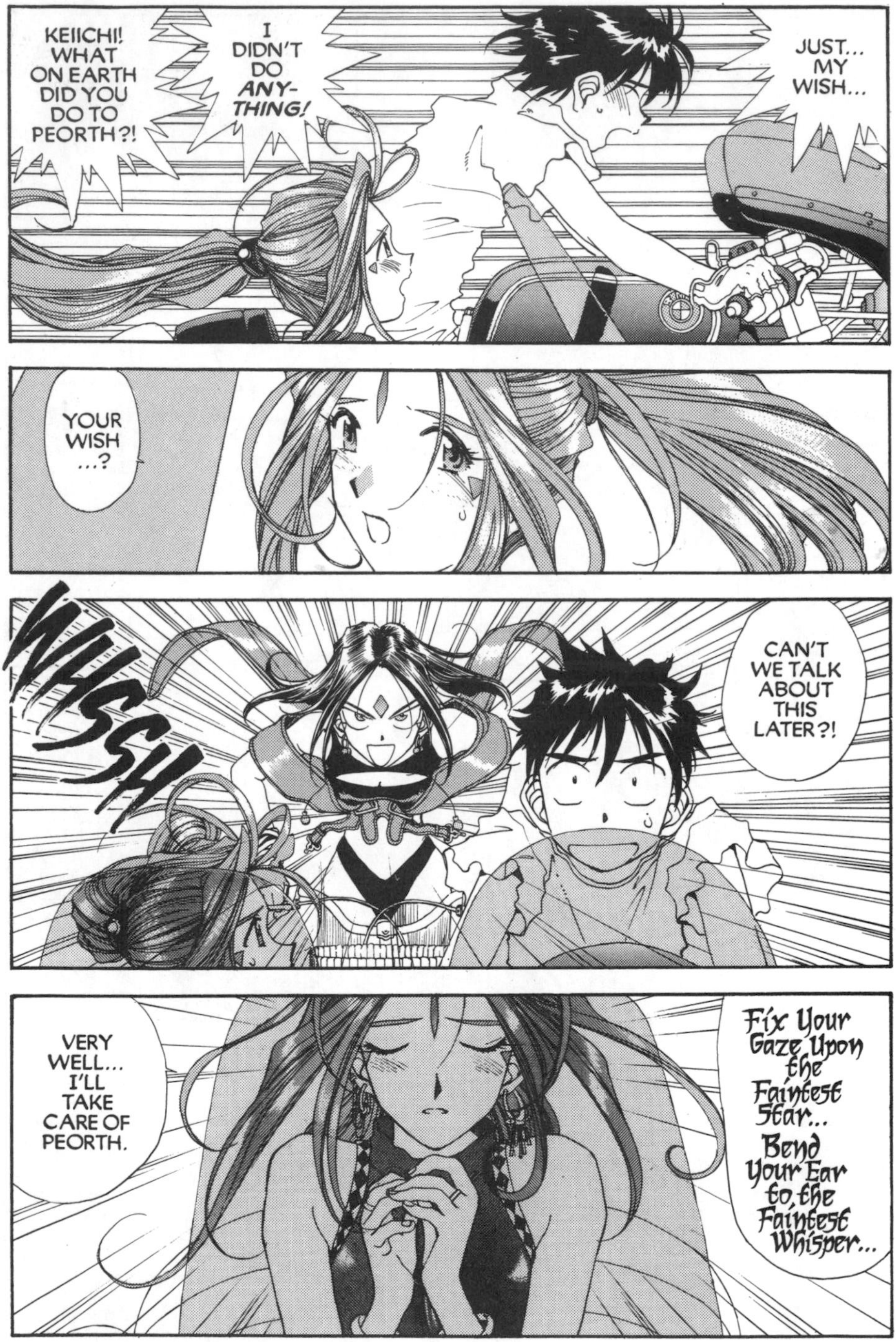
KEIICHI! WHAT ON EARTH DID YOU DO TO PEORTH?!
I DIDN'T DO ANYTHING!
JUST... MY WISH...
YOUR WISH ...?
WHSSH
CAN'T WE TALK ABOUT THIS LATER?!
VERY WELL... I'LL TAKE CARE OF PEORTH.
Fix Your Gaze Upon the Faintest Star... Bend Your Ear to the Faintest Whisper...

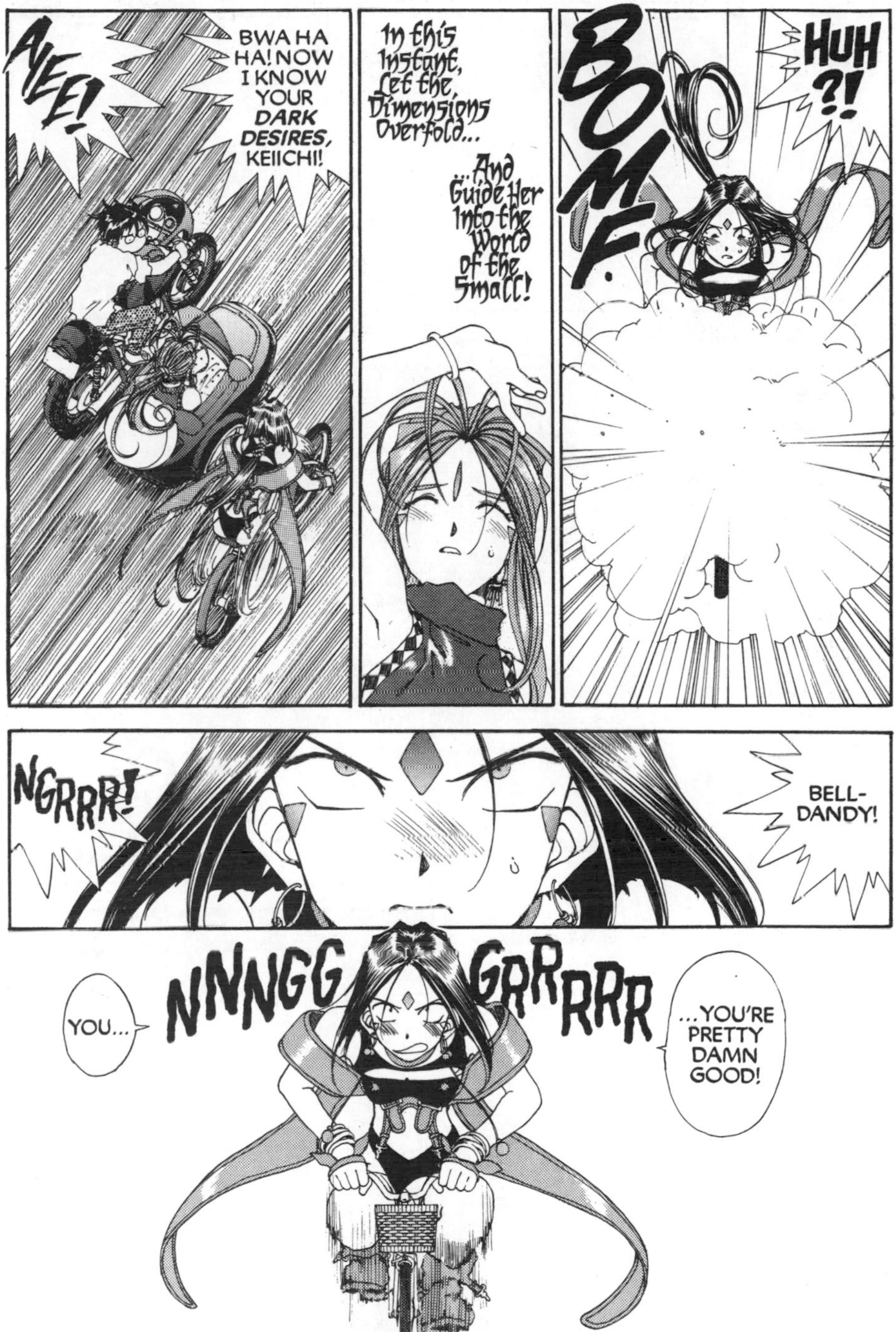
AIEEE!
BWA HA HA! NOW I KNOW YOUR DARK DESIRES, KEIICHI!
In this instant, let the Dimensions Overfold...
...And Guide Her Into the World of the Small!
BOMF.
HUH?!
NGRRR!
BELL-DANDY!
YOU...
NNNGG GRRRRR
...YOU'RE PRETTY DAMN GOOD!

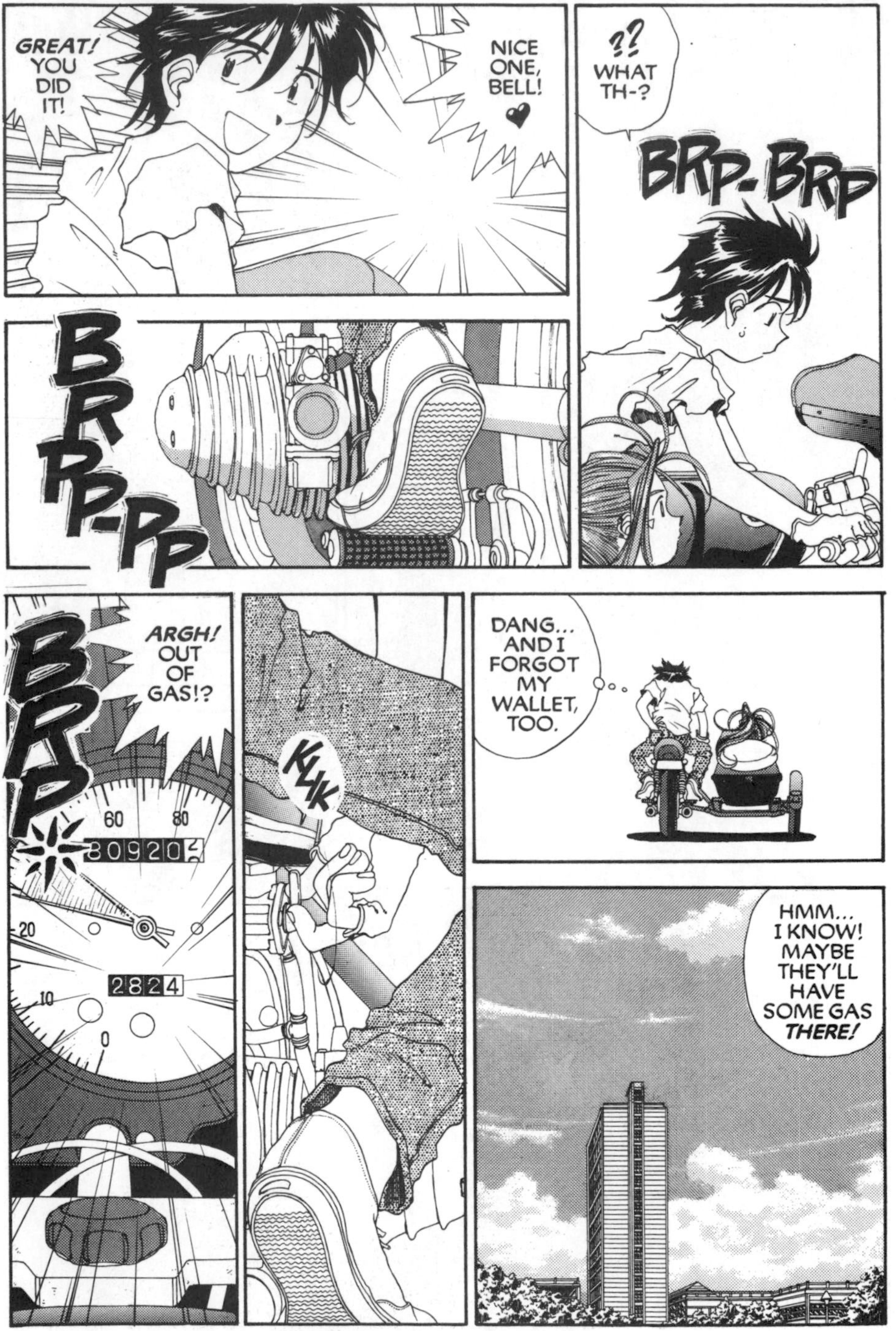
GREAT! YOU DID IT!
NICE ONE, BELL! ♥
BRRPP-PP
?? WHAT TH-?
BRP-BRP
BRRAP
ARGH! OUT OF GAS!?
60
80
80920
20
2824
10
0
KLIK
DANG... AND I FORGOT MY WALLET, TOO.
HMM... I KNOW! MAYBE THEY'LL HAVE SOME GAS THERE!

SWITCHING TO THE ▲
RESERVE TANK.

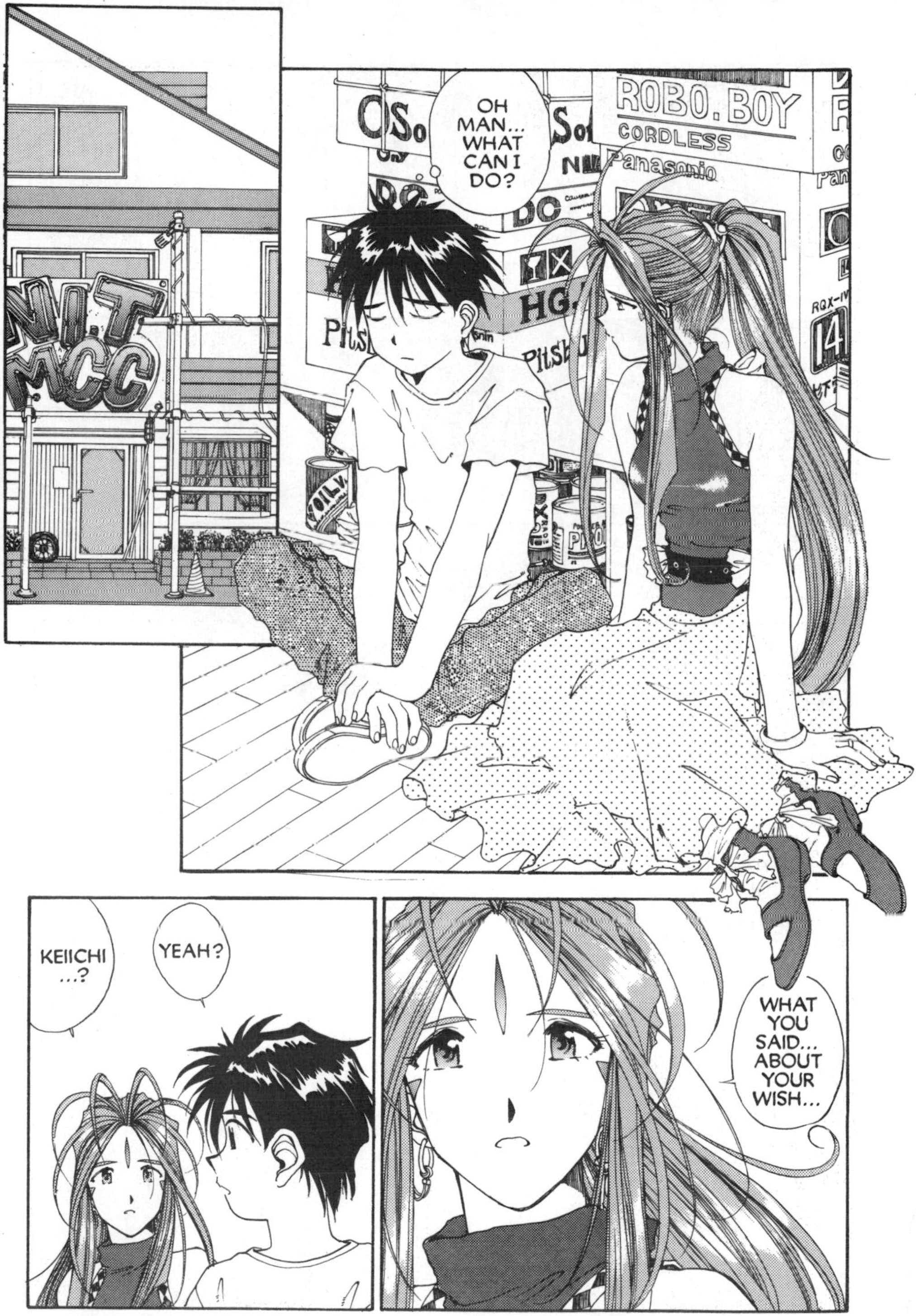
N.I.T
MCC
OH MAN... WHAT CAN I DO?
ROBO.BOY
CORDLESS
Panasonic
KEIICHI ...?
YEAH?
WHAT YOU SAID... ABOUT YOUR WISH...

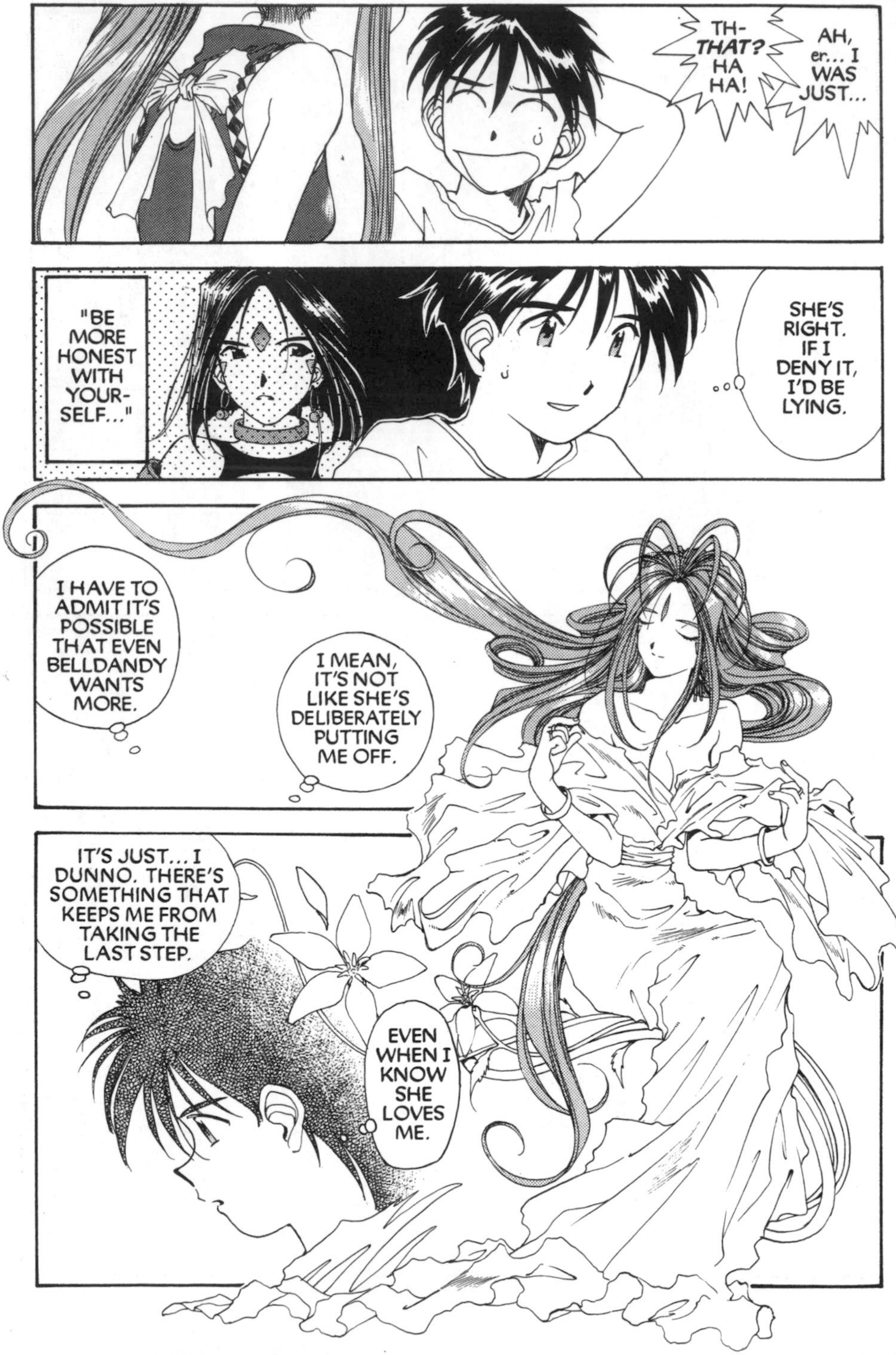
TH-THAT? HA HA!
AH, er... I WAS JUST...
"BE MORE HONEST WITH YOUR-SELF..."
SHE'S RIGHT. IF I DENY IT, I'D BE LYING.
I HAVE TO ADMIT IT'S POSSIBLE THAT EVEN BELLDANDY WANTS MORE.
I MEAN, IT'S NOT LIKE SHE'S DELIBERATELY PUTTING ME OFF.
IT'S JUST... I DUNNO. THERE'S SOMETHING THAT KEEPS ME FROM TAKING THE LAST STEP.
EVEN WHEN I KNOW SHE LOVES ME.

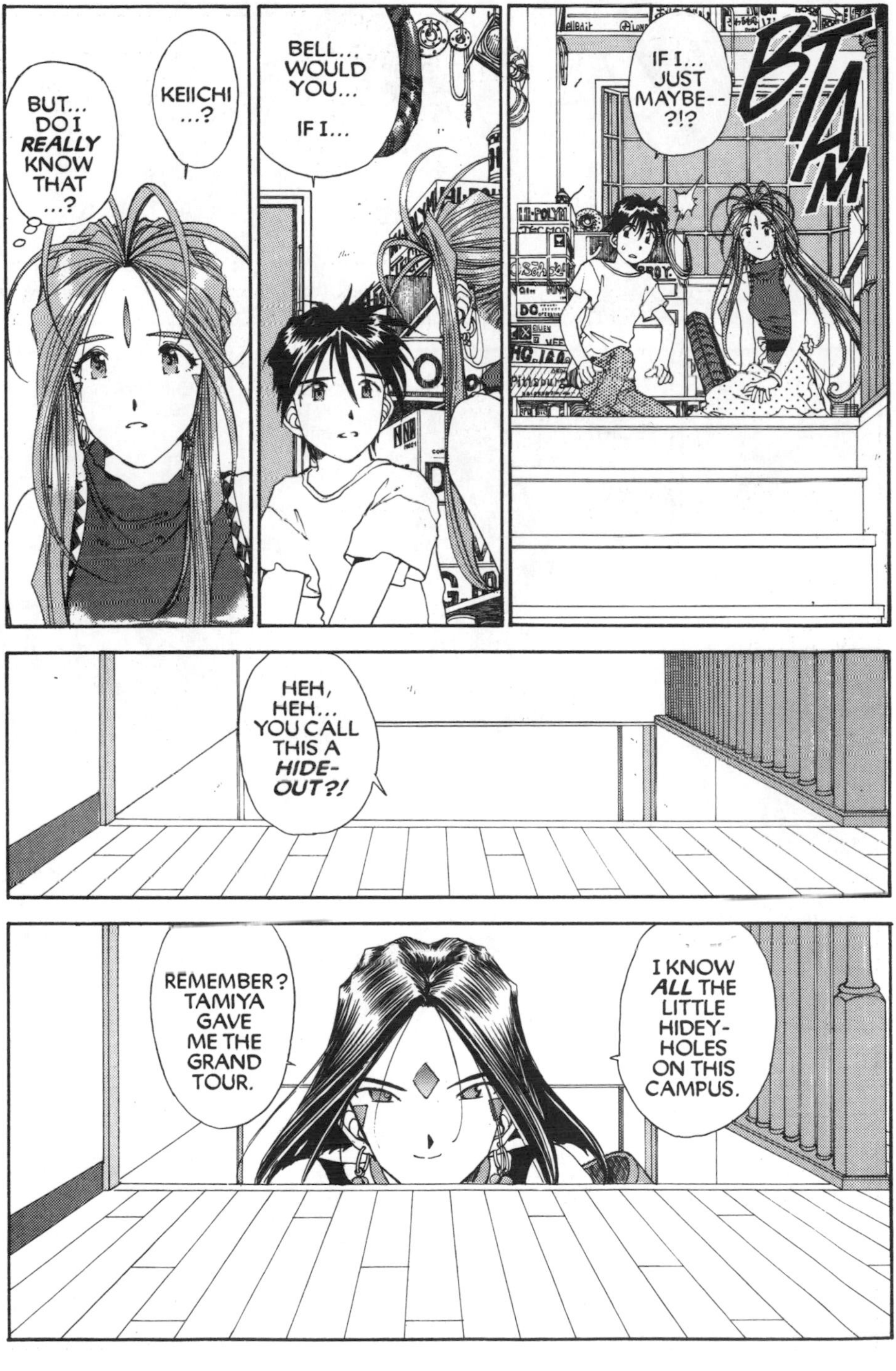
BUT... DO I *REALLY* KNOW THAT ...?
KEIICHI ...?
BELL... WOULD YOU...
IF I...
IF I... JUST MAYBE-- ?!?
BTAM
HEH, HEH... YOU CALL THIS A *HIDE-OUT?!*
REMEMBER? TAMIYA GAVE ME THE GRAND TOUR.
I KNOW *ALL* THE LITTLE HIDEY-HOLES ON THIS CAMPUS.

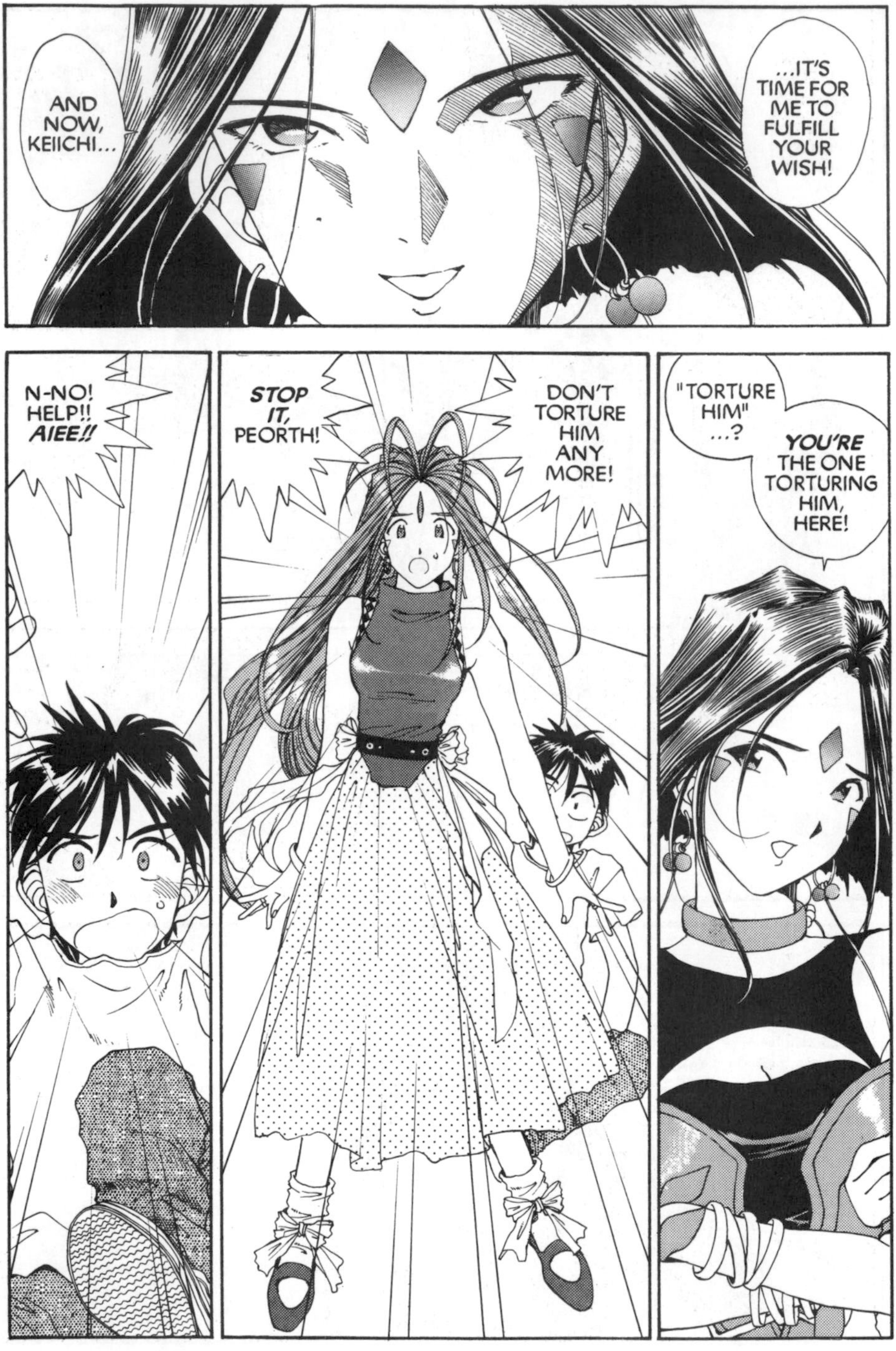
AND NOW, KEIICHI...
...IT'S TIME FOR ME TO FULFILL YOUR WISH!
N-NO! HELP!! *AIEE!!*
STOP IT, PEORTH!
DON'T TORTURE HIM ANY MORE!
"TORTURE HIM" ...?
YOU'RE THE ONE TORTURING HIM, HERE!

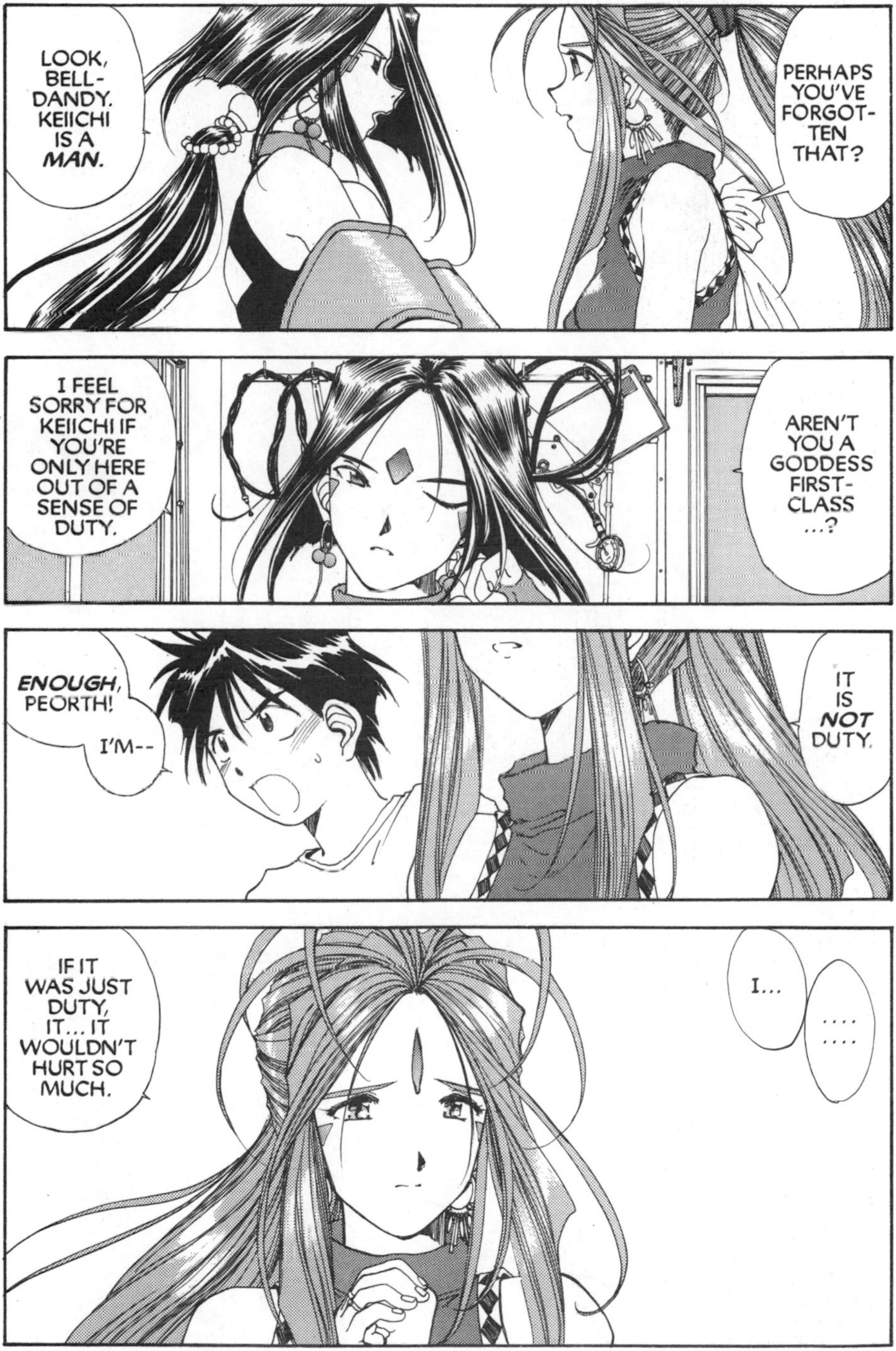
LOOK, BELL-DANDY. KEIICHI IS A *MAN.*
PERHAPS YOU'VE FORGOT-TEN THAT?
I FEEL SORRY FOR KEIICHI IF YOU'RE ONLY HERE OUT OF A SENSE OF DUTY.
AREN'T YOU A GODDESS FIRST-CLASS ...?
ENOUGH, PEORTH!
I'M--
IT IS *NOT* DUTY.
IF IT WAS JUST DUTY, IT... IT WOULDN'T HURT SO MUCH.
I...
....

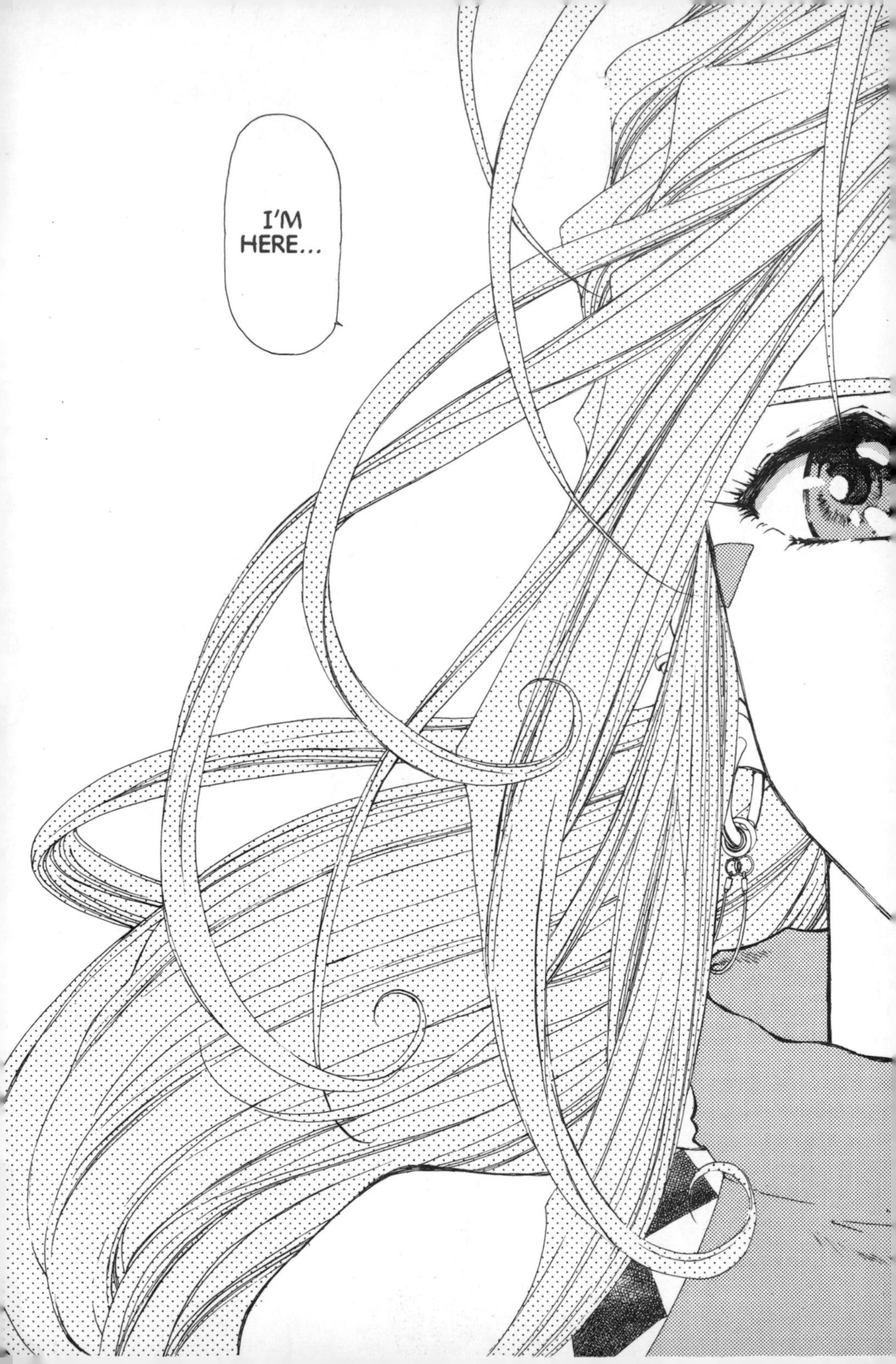
I'M HERE...

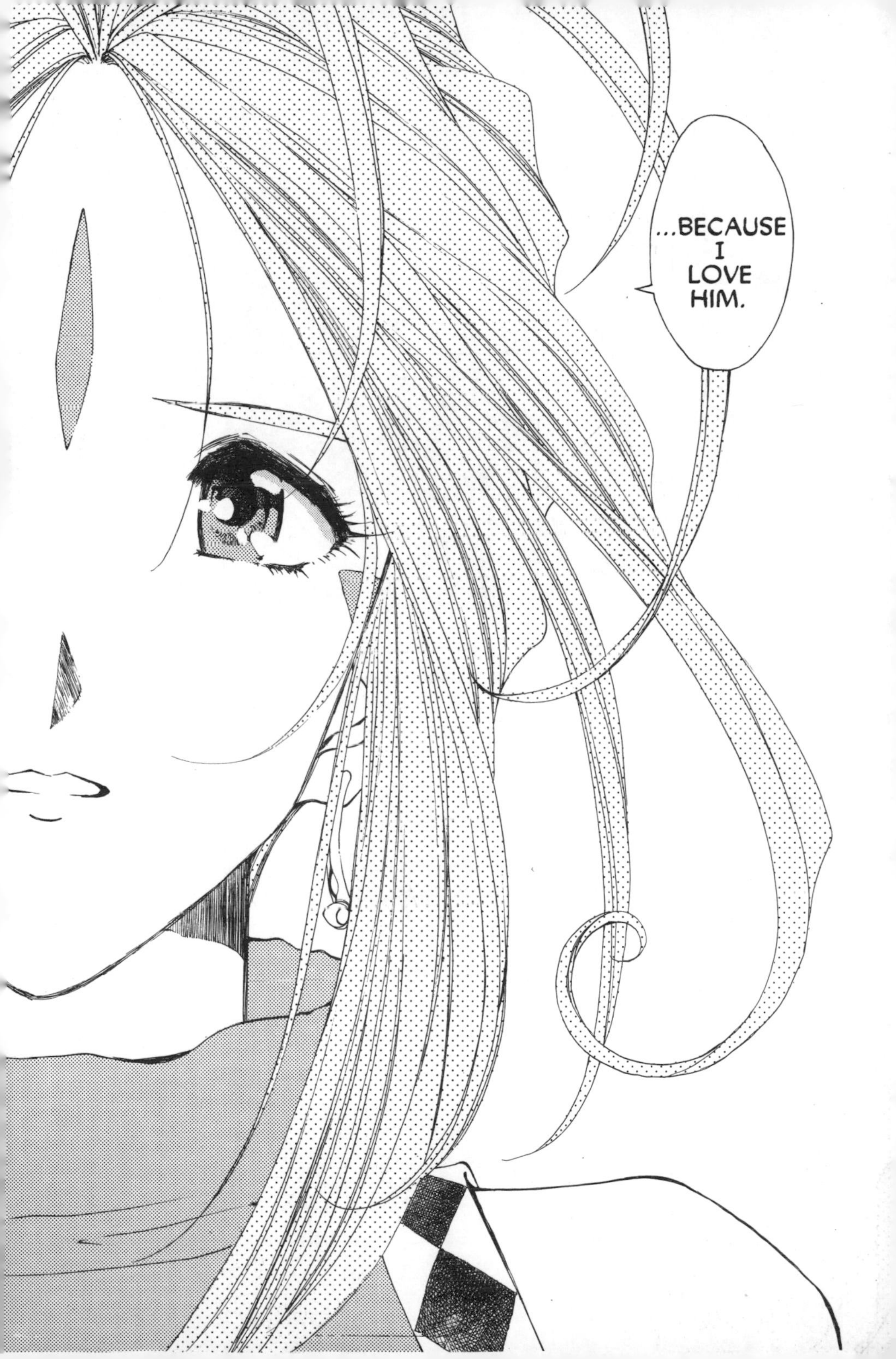
...BECAUSE I LOVE HIM.

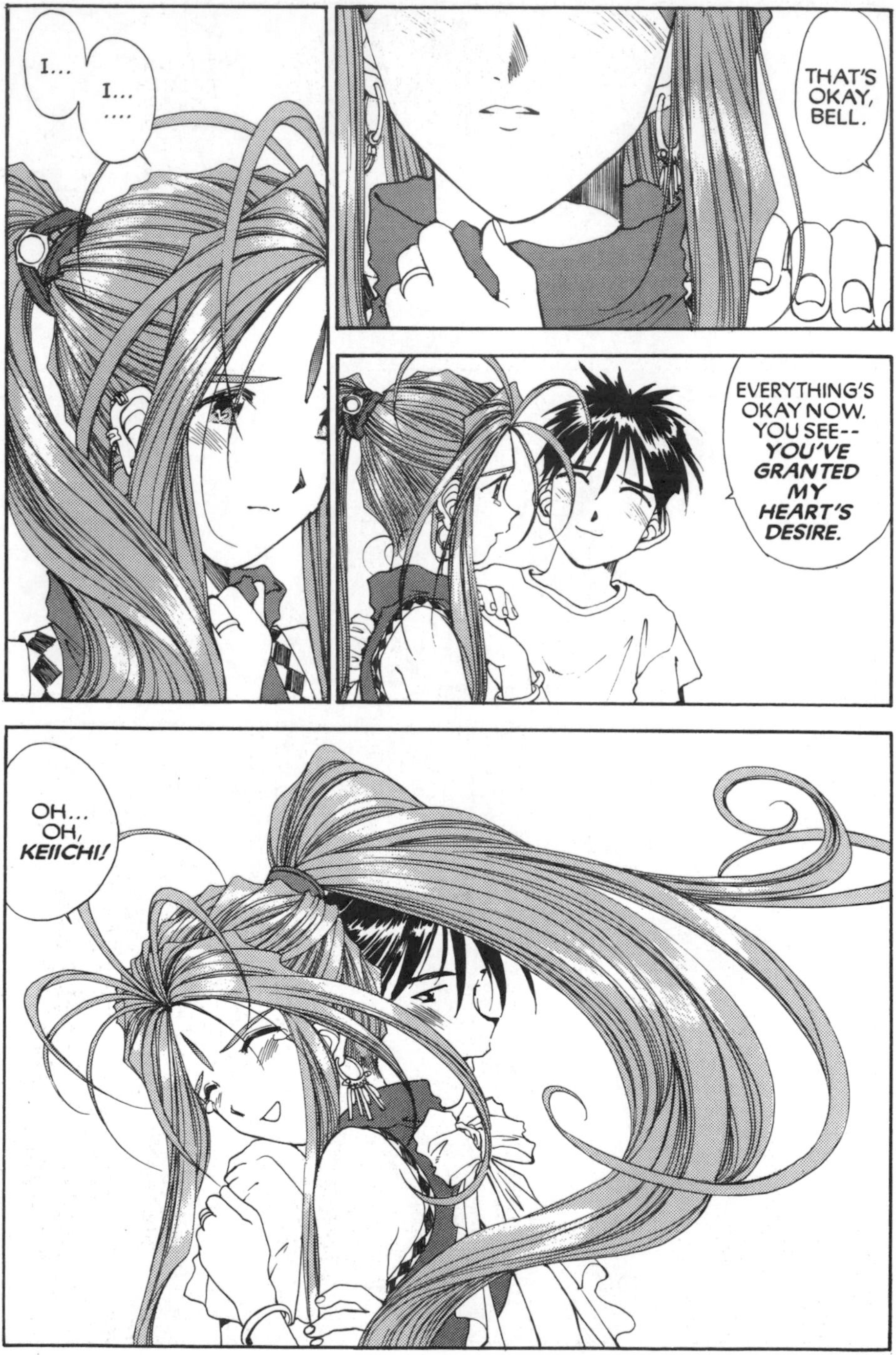
I... I... ....
THAT'S OKAY, BELL.
EVERYTHING'S OKAY NOW. YOU SEE-- *YOU'VE GRANTED MY HEART'S DESIRE.*
OH... OH, *KEIICHI!*

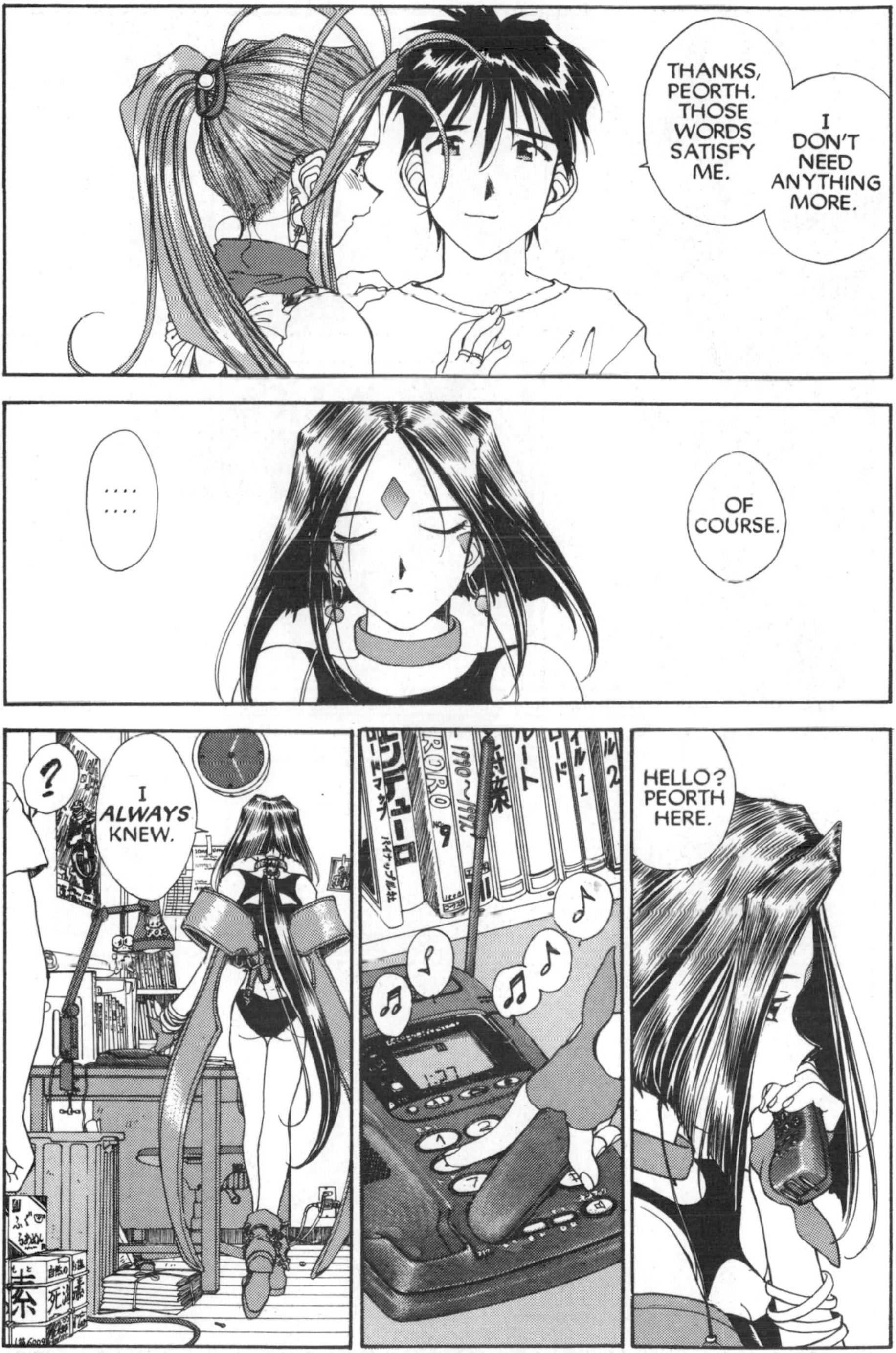
THANKS, PEORTH. THOSE WORDS SATISFY ME.
I DON'T NEED ANYTHING MORE.
....
OF COURSE.
?
I *ALWAYS* KNEW.
HELLO? PEORTH HERE.

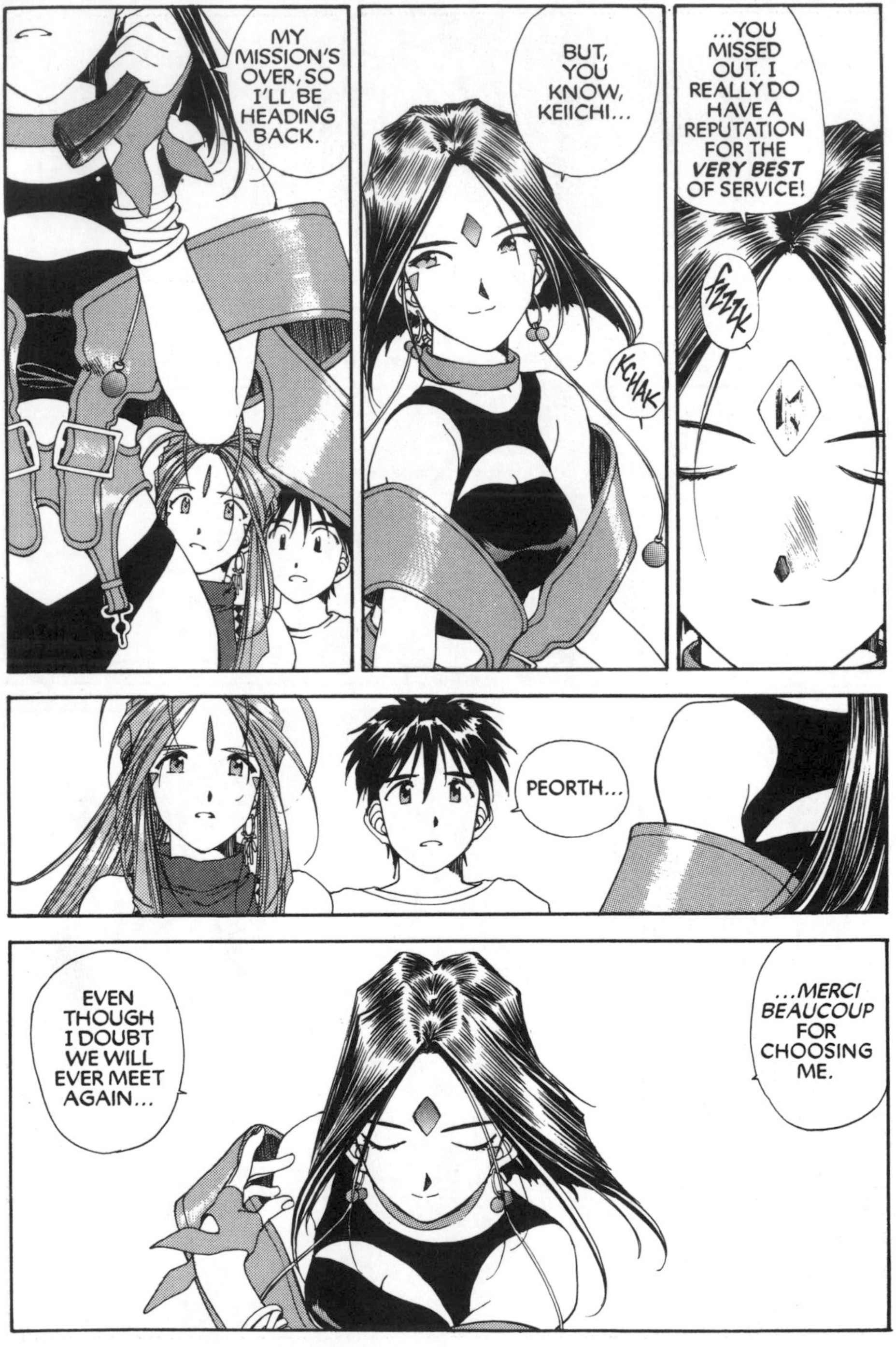
MY MISSION'S OVER, SO I'LL BE HEADING BACK.
BUT, YOU KNOW, KEIICHI...
KCHAK
...YOU MISSED OUT. I REALLY DO HAVE A REPUTATION FOR THE ***VERY BEST*** OF SERVICE!
FZZZZK
PEORTH...
EVEN THOUGH I DOUBT WE WILL EVER MEET AGAIN...
...*MERCI BEAUCOUP* FOR CHOOSING ME.

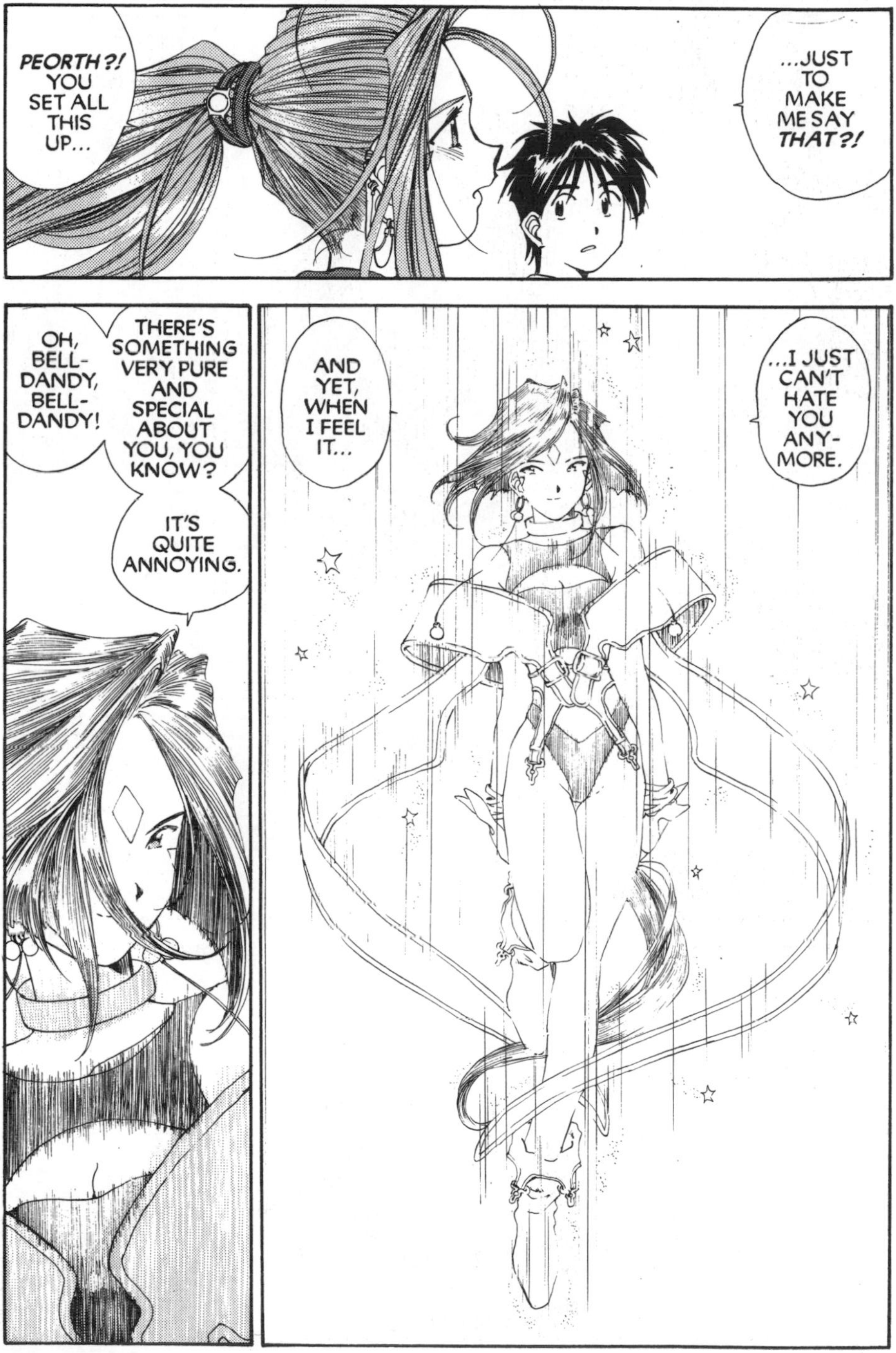
PEORTH?! YOU SET ALL THIS UP...
...JUST TO MAKE ME SAY THAT?!
OH, BELL-DANDY, BELL-DANDY!
THERE'S SOMETHING VERY PURE AND SPECIAL ABOUT YOU, YOU KNOW?
IT'S QUITE ANNOYING.
AND YET, WHEN I FEEL IT...
...I JUST CAN'T HATE YOU ANY-MORE.

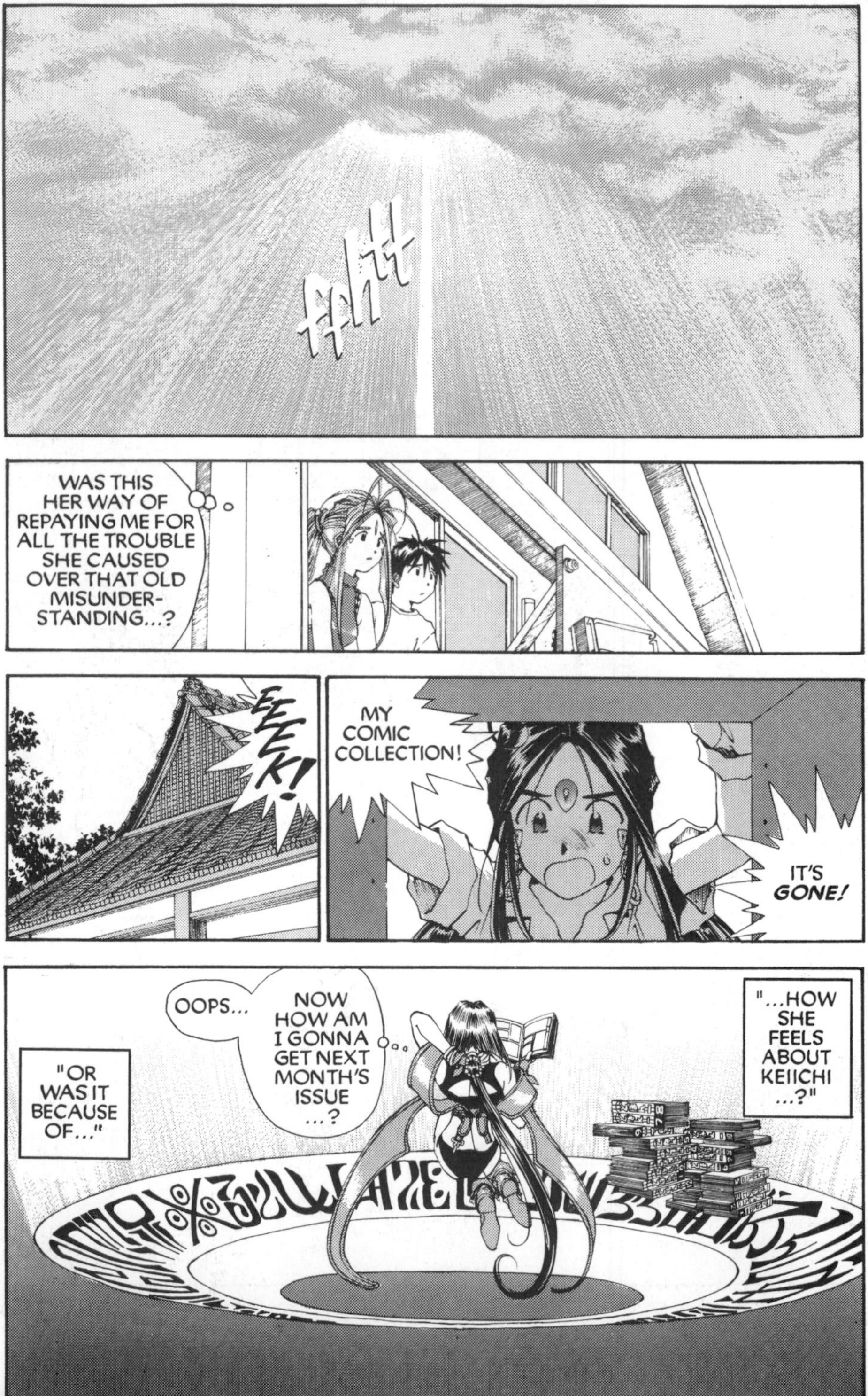
fffftt
WAS THIS HER WAY OF REPAYING ME FOR ALL THE TROUBLE SHE CAUSED OVER THAT OLD MISUNDER-STANDING...?
EEEEK!
MY COMIC COLLECTION!
IT'S *GONE!*
"OR WAS IT BECAUSE OF..."
OOPS...
NOW HOW AM I GONNA GET NEXT MONTH'S ISSUE ...?
"...HOW SHE FEELS ABOUT KEIICHI ...?"

Winner, Parent's Choice Award

KOSUKE FUJISHIMA'S

Oh My Goddess!

Oh My Goddess! has proved to be a favorite with manga fans everywhere and is attracting new readers. The stories, following the misadventures of Keiichi Morisato and the trio of lovely goddesses who live with him, quickly explode into a fantastic romantic comedy with a huge cast of wonderful characters.

1-555-GODDESS
ISBN: 1-56971-207-7
softcover   Ages 8+ $13.95

LOVE POTION NO. 9
ISBN: 1-56971-252-2
softcover   Ages 8+ $14.95

SYMPATHY FOR THE DEVIL
ISBN: 1-56971-329-4
softcover   Ages 8+ $13.95

TERRIBLE MASTER URD
ISBN: 1-56971-369-3
softcover   Ages 8+ $14.95

THE QUEEN OF VENGEANCE
ISBN: 1-56971-431-2
softcover   Ages 8+ $13.95

MARA STRIKES BACK!
ISBN: 1-56971-449-5
softcover   Ages 8+ $14.95

NINJA MASTER
ISBN: 1-56971-474-6
softcover   Ages 8+ $13.95

MISS KEIICHI
ISBN: 1-56971-522-X
softcover   Ages 8+ $16.95

THE DEVIL IN MISS URD
ISBN: 1-56971-540-8
softcover   Ages 8+ $14.95

THE FOURTH GODDESS
ISBN: 1-56971-551-3
softcover   Ages 8+ $18.95

**THE ADVENTURES OF
THE MINI-GODDESSES**
ISBN: 1-56971-421-5
softcover   Ages 8+ $9.95

CHILDHOOD'S END
ISBN: 1-56971-685-4
softcover   Ages 8+ $15.95

AVAILABLE AT YOUR LOCAL COMICS SHOP OR BOOKSTORE
To find a comics shop in your area, call 1-888-266-4226

For more information or to order direct:
• On the web: www.darkhorse.com
• E-mail: mailorder@darkhorse.com
• Phone: 1-800-862-0052 or (503) 652-9701
Mon.-Sat. 9 A.M. to 5 P.M. Pacific Time

FREE MANGA E-MAIL!
Sign up today @ www.mangamail.net!
Powered by Chek - Provided by Tek 21 @
888-862-4465

Oh My Goddess! copyright © 2000, 2002 by Kosuke Fujishima. All rights reserved. New and adapted artwork and text copyright 2000, 2002 Studio Proteus and Dark Horse Comics, Inc. Dark Horse Comics® and the Dark Horse logo are trademarks of Dark Horse Comics, Inc., registered in various categories and countries. All rights reserved.

MANGA! MANGA! MANGA!
DARK HORSE HAS THE BEST IN MANGA COLLECTIONS!

AKIRA
Katsuhiro Otomo
BOOK 1
ISBN: 1-56971-498-3 $24.95
BOOK 2
ISBN: 1-56971-499-1 $24.95
BOOK 3
ISBN: 1-56971-525-4 $24.95
BOOK 4
ISBN: 1-56971-526-2 $27.95

APPLESEED
Masamune Shirow
BOOK ONE
ISBN: 1-56971-070-8 $16.95
BOOK TWO
ISBN: 1-56971-071-6 $16.95
BOOK THREE
ISBN: 1-56971-072-4 $17.95
BOOK FOUR
ISBN: 1-56971-074-0 $17.95

BLACK MAGIC
Masamune Shirow
ISBN: 1-56971-360-X $16.95

BLADE OF THE IMMORTAL
Hiroaki Samura
BLOOD OF A THOUSAND
ISBN: 1-56971-239-5 $14.95
CRY OF THE WORM
ISBN: 1-56971-300-6 $14.95
DREAMSONG
ISBN: 1-56971-357-X $14.95
ON SILENT WINGS
ISBN: 1-56971-412-6 $14.95
ON SILENT WINGS II
ISBN: 1-56971-444-4 $14.95
DARK SHADOWS
ISBN: 1-56971-469-X $14.95
HEART OF DARKNESS
ISBN: 1-56971-531-9 $16.95
THE GATHERING
ISBN: 1-56971-546-7 $15.95

BUBBLEGUM CRISIS
Adam Warren
GRAND MAL
color paperback
ISBN: 1-56971-120-8 $14.95

CARAVAN KIDD
Johji Manabe
VOLUME 2
ISBN: 1-56971-324-3 $19.95
VOLUME 3
ISBN: 1-56971-338-3 $19.95

THE DIRTY PAIR
Adam Warren • Toren Smith
BIOHAZARDS
ISBN: 1-56971-339-1 $12.95
DANGEROUS ACQUAINTANCES
ISBN: 1-56971-227-1 $12.95

A PLAGUE OF ANGELS
ISBN: 1-56971-029-5 $12.95
FATAL BUT NOT SERIOUS
color paperback
ISBN: 1-56971-172-0 $14.95

DOMINION
Masamune Shirow
ISBN: 1-56971-488-6 $16.95

DOMU
Katsuhiro Otomo
A CHILD'S DREAM
ISBN: 1-56971-611-0 $17.95

DRAKUUN
Johji Manabe
RISE OF THE DRAGON PRINCESS
ISBN: 1-56971-302-2 $12.95
THE REVENGE OF GUSTAV
ISBN: 1-56971-368-5 $14.95
SHADOW OF THE WARLOCK
ISBN: 1-46971-406-1 $14.95

GHOST IN THE SHELL
Masamune Shirow
color/B&W paperback
ISBN: 1-56971-081-3 $24.95

GODZILLA
Kazuhisa Iwata
ISBN: 1-56971-063-5 $17.95

GUNSMITH CATS
Kenichi Sonoda
BONNIE AND CLYDE
ISBN: 1-56971-215-8 $13.95
MISFIRE
ISBN: 1-56971-253-0 $14.95
THE RETURN OF GRAY
ISBN: 1-56971-299-9 $17.95
GOLDIE VS. MISTY
ISBN: 1-56971-371-5 $15.95
BAD TRIP
ISBN: 1-56971-442-8 $13.95
BEAN BANDIT
ISBN: 1-56971-453-3 $16.95
KIDNAPPED
ISBN: 1-56971-529-7 $16.95
MISTER V
ISBN: 1-56971-550-5 $18.95

INTRON DEPOT
Masamune Shirow
INTRON DEPOT 1
color paperback
ISBN: 1-56971-085-6 $39.95
INTRON DEPOT 2: BLADES
color paperback
ISBN: 1-56971-382-0 $39.95
INTRON DEPOT 2: BLADES CD-ROM
2 CDs with illustrated mousepad
ISBN: 1-56971-485-1 $79.95

OH MY GODDESS!
Kosuke Fujishima
1-555-GODDESS
ISBN: 1-56971-207-7 $13.95
LOVE POTION NO. 9
ISBN: 1-56971-252-2 $14.95
SYMPATHY FOR THE DEVIL
ISBN: 1-56971-329-4 $13.95
TERRIBLE MASTER URD
ISBN: 1-56971-369-3 $14.95
THE QUEEN OF VENGEANCE
ISBN: 1-56971-431-2 $13.95
MARA STRIKES BACK!
ISBN: 1-56971-449-5 $14.95
NINJA MASTER
ISBN: 1-56971-474-6 $13.95
MISS KEIICHI
ISBN: 1-56971-522-X $16.95
ADVENTURES OF THE MINI-GODDESSES
ISBN: 1-56971-421-5 $9.95
THE DEVIL IN MISS URD
ISBN: 1-56971-540-8 $14.95
THE FOURTH GODDESS
ISBN: 1-56971-551-3 $18.95

ORION
Masamune Shirow
ISBN: 1-56971-572-6 $19.95

OUTLANDERS
Johji Manabe
VOLUME 2
ISBN: 1-56971-162-3 $13.95
VOLUME 3
ISBN: 1-56971-163-1 $13.95
VOLUME 4
ISBN: 1-56971-069-4 $12.95
VOLUME 5
ISBN: 1-56971-275-1 $14.95
VOLUME 6
ISBN: 1-56971-423-1 $14.95
VOLUME 7
ISBN: 1-56971-424-X $14.95
VOLUME 8
ISBN: 1-56971-425-8 $14.95

SHADOW LADY
Masakazu Katsura
DANGEROUS LOVE
ISBN: 1-56971-408-8 $17.95
THE AWAKENING
ISBN: 1-56971-446-0 $15.95
SUDDEN DEATH
ISBN: 1-56971-477-0 $14.95

SHADOW STAR
Mohiro Kitoh
STARFLIGHT
ISBN: 1-56971-548-3 $15.95

SPIRIT OF WONDER
Kenji Tsuruta
ISBN: 1-56971-288-3 $12.95

STAR WARS MANGA
A NEW HOPE
George Lucas • Hisao Tamaki
VOLUME 1
ISBN: 1-56971-362-6 $9.95
VOLUME 2
ISBN: 1-56971-363-4 $9.95
VOLUME 3
ISBN: 1-56971-364-2 $9.95
VOLUME 4
ISBN: 1-56971-365-0 $9.95
THE EMPIRE STRIKES BACK
George Lucas • Toshiki Kudo
VOLUME 1
ISBN: 1-56971-390-1 $9.95
VOLUME 2
ISBN: 1-56971-391-X $9.95
VOLUME 3
ISBN: 1-56971-392-8 $9.95
VOLUME 4
ISBN: 1-56971-393-6 $9.95
RETURN OF THE JEDI
George Lucas • Shin-ichi Hiromoto
VOLUME 1
ISBN: 1-56971-394-4 $9.95
VOLUME 2
ISBN: 1-56971-395-2 $9.95
VOLUME 3
B&W paperback
ISBN: 1-56971-396-0 $9.95
VOLUME 4
ISBN: 1-56971-397-9 $9.95
EPISODE 1—THE PHANTOM MENACE
George Lucas • Kia Asamiya
VOLUME 1
ISBN: 1-56971-483-5 $9.95
VOLUME 2
ISBN: 1-56971-484-3 $9.95

3x3 EYES
Yuzo Takada
HOUSE OF DEMONS
ISBN: 1-56971-059-7 $12.95
CURSE OF THE GESU
ISBN: 1-56971-175-5 $12.95

WHAT'S MICHAEL?
Makoto Kobayashi
OFF THE DEEP END
ISBN: 1-56971-249-2 $5.95
MICHAEL'S MAMBO
ISBN: 1-56971-250-6 $5.95

YOU'RE UNDER ARREST!
Kosuke Fujishima
THE WILD ONES
ISBN: 1-56971-319-7 $12.95
LIGHTS AND SIREN!
ISBN: 1-56971-432-0 $10.95

*All titles are black-and-white paperback unless otherwise noted

Available from your local comics shop or bookstore!

To find a comics shop in your area, call 1-888-266-4226
For more information or to order direct:
• On the web: www.darkhorse.com • E-mail: mailorder@darkhorse.com
• Phone: 1-800-862-0052 or (503) 652-9701 Mon.-Sat. 9 A.M. to 5 P.M. Pacific Time
*Prices and availability subject to change without notice

Dark Horse Comics: Mike Richardson *publisher* • Neil Hankerson *executive vice president* • Andy Karabatsos *vice president of finance* • Randy Stradley *vice president of publishing* • Chris Warner *senior editor* • Michael Martens *vice president of marketing* • Anita Nelson *vice president of sales & licensing* • David Scroggy *vice president of product development* • Mark Cox *art director* • Dale LaFountain *vice president of information technology* • Kim Haines *director of human resources* • Darlene Vogel *director of purchasing* • Ken Lizzi • *general counsel*